OHR YISRAEL

OHR YISRAEL

THE CLASSIC WRITINGS OF
RAV YISRAEL SALANTER

AND HIS DISCIPLE
RAV YITZCHAK BLAZER

Translated and annotated by
RABBI ZVI MILLER
Edited by Rabbi Eli Linas

TARGUM/FELDHEIM

Published by:
TARGUM PRESS, INC.
22700 W. Eleven Mile Rd.
Southfield, MI 48034
E-mail: targum@netvision.net.il
Fax: 888-298-9992
www.targum.com

In conjunction with:
THE SALANT FOUNDATION
1330 N.E. 172 Street
North Miami Beach, FL 33162
305-653-1182
E-mail: miler23@netvision.net.il

Distributed by:
FELDHEIM PUBLISHERS
202 Airport Executive Park
Nanuet, NY 10954

Printing plates: "Frank," Jerusalem
Printed in Israel

The approbations are listed in the order in which they were received.
This book is printed on acid-free paper.

HALACHOS OF MUSSAR STUDY

Rabbi Yisrael Salanter, of blessed memory, dedicated his entire life to awaken the Jewish people to the importance of Mussar (Torah ethics) and the development of good character traits. Hashem blessed his efforts, and the obligation to set aside daily times to study Mussar has become associated with his name.

In order to strengthen and encourage the study of Mussar amongst *am Yisrael*, we are citing the primary sources wherein daily Mussar study is encoded into halachah.

1) "A person must set aside daily periods devoted to Mussar study" (*Shulchan Aruch, Orach Chaim*, ch. 1, note 4 in the *Mishnah Berurah*).

2) "The Arizal wrote that one is obligated to study Mussar throughout the entire year; the Vilna Gaon also wrote in several places that [Mussar must be studied everyday]; and the Rosh also ruled like this" (*Shulchan Aruch, Orach Chaim*, ch. 603, note 2 in the *Mishnah Berurah*).

3) The study of Mussar is an imperative that is incumbent on every soul. No one is exempt: from the rabbinic arbiter who sits in the seat of judgment, to the laborer behind the millstone; both man and woman; Torah scholar and layman; youth and elder; rich and poor; both those who fear Hashem and those who do not — all of them are obligated to fix times to study works on fear and Mussar (*Ohr Yisrael*, "The Gates of Light," first of the Ten Innovations).

May the daily study of Mussar by *klal Yisrael* awaken mercy in Heaven, to bring forth the final redemption.

RABBI MATISIYAHU SOLOMON

Mashgiach, Beis Medrash Gevoha, Lakewood, NJ

עש"ק דברים תשס"א לפ"ק
פה לייקווד יצ"ו

מעת שעלתה נשמתו הטהורה של רבינו ורבן על כל ישראל הגר"י סלנטר זצוקלוי"ה
נשארו כתביו המעטים שנשארו לפליטה כספר חתום לרוב מבני ישראל מחמת
קושי הלשון והמושג על כן נחזיק טובה להאי גברא רבה הר"ר צבי מילר שליט"א
להתעורר לתרגם מכתבו הענקי והיסודי ביסודות העבודה לשפה המדוברת כדי
להנות רבים המצאים לשתות מבאר מים חיים של קדוש ישראל. תרגומו הוא
נאמן לרוחו של הדברים כאשר נמסרו לנו מרבותינו בעלי המוסר - כוחו וחילו
לאורייתא.

ממני הכו"י בברכה

מתתי' חיים סלומון

Rabbi Elchanon Hertzman

Williamsburg

בס״ד

מוצש״ק תצא תשס״א

הנה מונח לפני עיני הספרים הקדושים אור ישראל ואגרת המוסר מרבי ישראל
מסלנט זי״ע ושערי אור ונתיבות אור וכוכבי אור מרבי יצחק בלאזער זי״ע גם
תרגום באנגלית מדויק היטב היטב מאברך יקר יר״ש, עובד מקודם התרגום על
עצמו, כדי שיהא דברים היוצאים מהלב הוא הוא, היקר מהיקרים ר׳ צבי מילר
שליט״א הוא למד הרבה שנים בישיבות התפוצות בהתמדה רבה אשר רוח המוסר
מרחפת בין כותלי בית המדרש ובית המוסר משם, ויש שם ועדים של מוסר לפי
רוח מדור הישן ויכולים לעשות ברכת המאורות שחודר בגנזי נסתרות לקרב
נפשות ישראל תחת כנפי השכינה, לקיים הוי מעמידים תלמידים הרבה לדורי
דורות עם בסיס חזק עם פירות של נצחיות ודורי דורות עד בית גואל צדקינו אמן.
יתקבצו אורות אלו, עם אורות של משיח צדקינו- ואנו רואים היום איזה
פנמיות של קדושה ה׳ בלי ר׳ ישראל מסלנט זי״ע בעולם הישיבות - שהיה גוף בלי
נשמה ובית החולים בלי רופאים היו תולים רק לבושים לבנים על הכותל, החפץ
חיים זי״ע אמר שבתי מסחר בלי רואה חשבונות מוכרח לילך לפשיטת הרגל ובית
מסחר בישיבות זהו וישנו קונה עולמו בשעה אחת או מאבד עולמו בשעה אחת
בודאי צריכים למוסר, שזהו הרואה חשבונות הרוחנים וזהו תמצית של מ״ח
קנינים מ״ח זהו המח של הישיבות ואשרי מי שעוזר לעשות גפרורים רוחנים
להדליק אורות אלו בעולם החושך של הזמן ובחלקם יהא חלקי.
כ״יש היום שנתגלה הקבר של הגריס זי״ע על כל ישראל אמן בכתיבה וחתימה
טובה לכל ישראל בברכת התורה ולומדיה

אלחנן יוסף בן צפורה לרפו״יש

RABBI SHMUEL KAMENETSKY

2018 Upland Way, Philadelphia, Pa 19131
Study: 215-473-1212, Home: 215-473-2798

בס״יד ד אלול תשס״ב

למעייכ הרב הנעלה והנכבד וכו׳ וכו׳

ר׳ צבי מילער שליט״א

אחרי דרך מבוא השלו והדרכה כמשפט.

עבודתו גדולה לתרגם ספר הקדוש אור ישראל שמגלה טפח מגדלותו של אותו גדול הדור רבן של ישראל מרן ר׳ ישראל מסאלאנט זצוק״יל. נתברר מדבריו חידושו בלימוד המוסר בהתפעלות וכל הנהגת כל אדם עפ״יי שו״יע הן בדיני ממנות והן בכל ענייני תורת בין אדם לחברו אנו מכירי טובה לתלמידו הגאון הגדול רבינו יצחק בלאזער זצ״יל, שהוא גילה מעט מזעיר מרבו גאון הדור.

וזכה כב׳ שעל ידו יתקרבו מבקשי השם ויבינו גודל כוחותיו של כל אחד. מפורסם שנשאל אם יש לאדם אפשרות ללמוד חצי שעה במה יתעסק בתורה או במוסר וענה שילמוד חצי שעה מוסר שעל ידי זה יתברר לו שיש לו כמה שעות ברווח ללמוד תורה.

תפלתי שיזכה כב׳ להמנות ממזכי הרבים שצדקתם עומדת לעד.

שמואל קמנצקי

Rabbi Mordecai Goldstein

Dean and Rosh Yeshiva

Diaspora Yeshiva Toras Yisrael Mount Zion, POB 6426, 91063, Jerusalem

E-mail: diaspora@zahav.net.il Website: www.diaspora.org.il

בס"ד
כ"ה אלול תשס"ב

חכמנו הגדישו כמה חשוב זה ללמוד ספרי מוסר, ולקבל הדרכה רוחנית בענין
תיקון המדות. אע"פ שרוב הזמן בישיבות מוקדש ללמוד גמרא ופוסקים, היום
אנחנו מבינים שמוסר זה דבר הכרחי ביותר למוד המוסר מסייע לאדם להגיע
להכרת עצמו ולתקן מדותיו. בכדי להגיע לעבודת ה' צריך גם לעשות הדבר הנכון
וגם שאיפה להיות בן אדם טוב ולקנות יראת שמים. אם האישיות של אחד לא
מתוקן ואז חייב להיות שגם המעשים שלו לא מתוקנים.
בין הגדולים והחכמים שעלו בדרך המוסר, יש אחד מעל כולם גם לעמקות
חכמתו גם השפעתו הניצחים: הרה"ג רבנו ישראל מסאלאנט זצ"ל הוא היה
הראשון בין האחרונים שקרא קריאה בקול ברור על החשיבות של מוסר מתי
שרוב ת"ח לא הרגישו את חשיבתו. הוא נסע בלי הפסק ממקום למקום בשביל
שהמסור יהיה חלק מהעיקר של הישיבה הסבר תורתו וחכמתו חודרת לעמקותו
של תורה ולב האדם.
הפעתו על תלמידיו וכלל ישראל היה מוצלח מאד אבל מכתביו הקדושים לא
הופצו כל כך בעולם. לכן אני מאד שמח שתלמידשיצא מישיבותנו לקח על עצמו
את העבודה לתרגם לאנגלית את הספר של צדיק הקדוש וגאון הזה.
יש לרב מילר שכל ישר ולב טוב, האישיות שלו מלאה באהבה ויראת ה
יתברך. תרגומו מדוקדקת מאד.
אני בטוח שה' הדריך אותו בעבודתו.
תפילת לבי שתורתו של רבנו רב ישראל סלאנטאר זצ"ל יפורסם בעולם. יהי
רצון שהתורה שלו תדריך אותך, קורא יקר, כאשר אתה עולה על דרך התורה
ועבודת ה' יתברך.

מרדכי גולדשטיין

Rabbi Dov Schwartzman

Yeshivath Beth Hatalmud
112 Sanhedria Murchevet, POB 6082, Jerusalem Tel: 581-7804

בס"ד
ט"ו בסיון תשס"ג

הנה הרה"ג ר' צבי מילר שליט"א תרגם את מכתביו של רבן של ישראל מרן
הגרי"ס זצוק"ל לשפת האנגלית. בודאי שדבר גדול עשה שבדרך זו יוכלו רבים
המכירים שפה זו לגשת אל הקודש, להבין משל ומליצה, דברי חכמים וחידותם.
ועוד הגדול לעשות בהערותיו המחכימות אשר מבארים את הטעון ביאור בדברי
הגאון הנ"ל וכן מבאר את יסודות שיטתו בעבודת ה' ולמוד המוסר.
ובודאי שתהיה עבודתו לתועלת, להרבות חכמה ומוסר ודעת את ה'.

בברכה לעמלים
בתורה ובירַאה

דב שווֹרצמן

RABBI CHAIM PINCHAS SCHEINBERG

Rosh Yeshivas Torah Ohr, Morah Hora'ah of Kirat Mattesdorf
2 Panim Meirot Street, Jerusalem

בס״ד

טבת תשס״ד

מכתב ברכה

הובאו לפני גליונות של תרגום מכתבי אור עולם רשכבה״ג מרן הגר״י סלנטר
זצוקלל״ה לשפה המדוברת כאן בארה״ב, שיגע וטרח הרה״ג ר׳ צבי מילר
שליט״א והנה דבר גדול עשה להקל על מבקשי אמת לגשת אל הקודש וכבר
שבחוהו רבנן גדולי תורה ויראה שעשה מלאכתו בנאמנות לרוח הדברים
העמוקים, וגם הוסיף נופך מדיליה בביאורים נחוצים. על כך בואו ונחזיק טובה
להרב המחבר, ונברכהו שיזכה להוסיף לתת פריו לזכות את הרבים בחיבורים
מועילים להגדיל תורה ולאדירה.

הכו״ח לכבוד התורה ולומדיה

חיים פינחס שיינברג

THE SCHEINFELD FAMILY CHARITY FUND
in honor of
our matriarch
Ellen
אסתר מלכה בת לאה ואליעזר צבי

We have nothing more precious than you.

Pesikta deRav Kahana 22:2:4

THE SCHEINFELD FAMILY CHARITY FUND
in celebration of
the life of
Jonathan Joseph (JJ) Greenberg, *z"l*
נתן יוסף בן בלומה והרב יצחק הכהן

ומצדיקי הרבים ככוכבים לעולם ועד.
*Those who lead the many to righteousness
will shine like the stars forever and ever.*
Daniel 12:3

the namesake of our grandson
נתן יוסף אליעזר בן אלישבע ויהושע ברוך

Louis "JJ" Scheinfeld
Chicago, Illinois

The following patrons recognize
that Mussar is the central
pillar of Torah, and have done much
to enable the holy teachings to be
made available to *klal Yisrael*.

An Anonymous Donor

Greg Bernhardt — in honor of Yehudit Sarah Bernhardt

Sol and Rosalyn Borenstein

The Cohen Family — in memory of Harry P. Cohen

Congregation Brothers of Israel, Elberon, New Jersey

Gary and Adina Estersohn

Mark Fisher

Sammy and Laurie Friedland

Ted and Sharon Gelt

Sheldon and Fran Gittleson

Ishaia and Jane Gol

William, *z"l*, and Lilly Goldberg

In memory of Rav Moshe and Rose Goldstein

Hy and Henni Gross — in memory of Raizel Rivka Sal

Michael Hershkowitz

Michael and Linda Jesselson — in memory of J.J. Greenberg

Asher and Cynthia Lazarus

John and Dina Leader

Manfred Leventhal

CONTENTS

FOREWORD

A VIRTUOUS VISIONARY FOR THE AGES

BY RABBI DAVID SCHEINFELD

With every passing century, the greatness of Rabbi Yisrael Lipkin of Salant — better known as Rabbi Yisrael Salanter (1810–1883) — stands out more boldly. Rav Yisrael combined comprehensive, brilliant *lomdus* (learning) with *middos tovos* (good character traits) of the rarest kind. But his extraordinary stature grows even more out of Rav Yisrael's personal union of prophetic vision with a practical, institution-building capability. This combination enabled him to identify and respond to the great challenge of his epoch — the arrival of modernity and its transformation of the condition of the Jewish community.

Growing up in Zagar, Lithuania, the son of Rabbi Zev Wolf, a teacher of Talmud and later the *av beth din* of Goldingen and Telz, Rav Yisrael could have become another of the *iluim* (Talmudic prodigies) who filled Eastern Europe. The teacher of his youth was the esteemed scholar Rabbi Zvi Hirsh Braude of Salant. As a young man, Rav Yisrael came under the influence of Rabbi Yosef Zundel of Salant, a disciple of Rabbi Chaim Volozhin, who stressed *yiras Hashem* and study of classic Mussar literature as the key to personal religiosity. Rav Zundel developed a method of self and *middos* development which he practiced in secret. As Rav Yisrael followed Rav Zundel and explored developing the qualities of modesty and pure, selfless service of Hashem, he weighed the possibility of living a "hidden" life of piety and learning. However, he concluded that achieving such a fulfilled religious life — free of pride but also removed from involvement with the community — would be self-indulgent and wrong. Thereafter, he insisted that true Torah *lishmah* (Torah for its own sake) involved not a private life of learning unburdened by professional obligations, but the opposite: a life of service and communal responsibility. Only such a life put the needs of others and the welfare of Torah first and the individual's "selfish" needs second. For himself, Rav Yisrael set the same high goals of putting aside ego, fame, and self-interest to achieve pure service of God, but these traits would have to be won and lived in the heat of battle of public life and leadership.

From the time Rav Yisrael was called to serve as *rosh yeshivah* in the yeshivah of Rabbi Meile in Vilna in 1840, to the end of his life, he took upon himself the task of guiding the community in a time of extraordinary change. In Western Europe, the conditions for the emergence of modern culture — industrialization, urbanization, the rise of nationalism, liberalism, and democracy — were developing rapidly and becoming dominant. Eastern Europe lagged behind Western Europe by half a century to a century, but the beginnings of the cultural transformation could be seen by a farsighted observer with profound intuition — like Rav Yisrael. He sensed that traditional Jewish life was unprepared for the historic challenge which loomed. The traditional community was marked by conventional observance and conformist ways of living. This way of life would be vulnerable when conditions changed and alternative lifestyles became available. Rav Yisrael felt that the direction of the community must be shifted educationally so that an internalized, meaningful religious identity became the norm. Then if people faced a choice, they would be committed enough to choose the way of Torah and not be dazzled by the rising wealth and social rewards of modernization.

Rav Yisrael feared that the yeshivos needed to innovate new ways to provide the needed mentoring, supervision, and dignified support to attract and hold the brightest and the best. He also felt that the lay people would face more and more temptations as the economy developed and Jews were exposed to non-Jewish ways. He was not convinced that the lay people were properly trained and guided as to the laws between man and man and proper ethics in business matters. Years later, he complained in his famous *Iggeres HaMussar*: "It seems to me that in these districts, praise be to God, the prohibitions of non-kosher and *treife* foods and the like are so rooted in Jewish souls that it takes no special effort to suppress any tendency or desire for them and to distance oneself from them...regrettably, in matters of business it is the opposite situation. Most people do not inquire about possible violation of the prohibitions of theft and exploitation, unless a peer raises the issue; and some, even after the issue is raised, will use shady tactics or brazenly steal. Yet in the Torah all [ritual and ethical] commandments are equal; this is prohibited and this is prohibited...." Rav Yisrael set out to develop ethical teaching and study to strengthen the character and behaviors of lay people as well as of *talmidei chachamim* in the face of growing opportunity and moral risk.

Rav Yisrael's prescription for modernity was internalized religiosity — the development of a religious-ethical self that would choose to remain committed religiously and act properly when facing ethical dilemmas in society and the economy. He tried to strengthen the yeshivos, which were developing religious leadership for the next generation, and he tried to upgrade the leadership of the community wherever he went.

In 1848, the czar's government moved to create a government-sponsored rabbinical seminary which it believed would train rabbis to be modern and, therefore, more forthcoming to the governments' demands that Jews undergo secular education and become more integrated, i.e., assimilated to Russian life. The government felt that it needed a scholar of recognized stature in learning and religious authority to serve as head of the seminary if it was to successfully influence the Orthodox community. Rav Yisrael was identified by the government, and by *Maskilim* ("Enlighteners") who advised it, as the person who had the standing to fill this role. Despite his own commitment to new educational developments, Rav Yisrael felt that such changes in rabbinic education — imposed from outside by a reactionary government which was hostile to Judaism and Jewish survival — would bring destruction rather than renewal to the community. He fled Vilna to escape the government's pressure to teach Gemara in the official seminary. Rav Yisrael's judgment was sound. The seminary turned into a training ground for "puppets" of the government, career time-servers and people of dubious religious commitment and observance. Forced modernization undermined Jewish life, creating a group that idolized secular activity and became corrupted by exposure to modernity. The backlash only strengthened the polarization of European Orthodoxy.

Rav Yisrael went to Kovno, where he actively spread the ideas and practice of the movement for internal renewal — the Mussar movement. Already in Vilna, Rav Yisrael had arranged for the reprinting and dissemination of Mussar books — books teaching character traits, ethics, self-development, and pious spirituality. He also lectured and preached on these topics. In Kovno, he founded circles of lay people who took upon themselves the task of studying such works and developing their ethical sensitivity and discipline to govern both personal and business behavior. Rav Yisrael showed that he saw himself not just as a *rosh yeshivah* teaching scholars, but as a community leader taking responsibility for policies that could renew and anchor Jewish life in the face of gathering change. Under his leadership, special rooms or study places (known as a "*Mussar kloyz*") were established to enable more concentrated study. Rav Yisrael also developed the technique of learning Mussar "*behispailus*" (with emotional fervor, singing, vivid imagery, etc.) and not just intellectually — in order to drive home the lessons and infuse emotional force to change people's character and identity. Thus he hoped to train an elite movement of ethically responsible lay people.

Rav Yisrael had shown his leadership for the entire community, starting in Vilna. In 1848, in perhaps the most famous incident of his life, he responded to the cholera epidemic. He heeded doctors' warnings that this highly contagious killer disease would spread more rapidly if Jews spent all Yom Kippur fasting and praying crowded together. Rav Yisrael called on the public to shorten the prayers, to spend more time outside in the fresh air, and, appropriately, to break the fast and eat in order to avoid becoming weakened and vulnerable. Other rabbis hesitated to give a general direction to eat as necessary lest they be accused of taking the most holy day of Yom Kippur too lightly. Rav Yisrael understood that many lives were at risk. Since the Torah places saving life at the highest level of obedience to Hashem, he stepped forward to assure people that true religiosity involved putting life-saving ahead of fasting. He also showed that honoring Hashem should come ahead of a *posek*'s (halachic decisor's) fear that people will misjudge or demean him. He followed the Torah's instruction to leaders: "[In fearing God and teaching Torah,] you shall not fear any person" (*Devarim* 1:17). Equally striking was his sense of responsibility for the entire community and his willingness to step up and take this action although he was not the official *posek* or community leader of Vilna. In the same way, in his work in Kovno, Rav Yisrael tried to create the ideas, the movement, and the institutions to save the entire community from the encroaching, dissolving force of culture.

From 1857–83, the last twenty-six years of his life, Rav Yisrael gave up his professional career and sources of support to pursue his leadership for the Jewish people at risk. Apparently, he felt that the full force of modernity was being felt to the west of Russia/Poland/Lithuania and that he must face the challenge in the lion's den. In 1857, he left Lithuania and settled in Prussia, living intermittently in Memel, Konigsberg, and Berlin. In 1880, he went to Paris in order to strengthen that community, especially the subcommunity of Russian and Polish immigrants who had moved westward seeking the opportunities — but facing the dissolving effects — of modern life. Throughout this time, he kept in touch with his disciples through letters and visits as he guided them to continue their educational work — to strengthen yeshivos by injecting Mussar and character development into their curriculum and to strengthen lay people ethically and spiritually. There is little question but that the reinforcement supplied by Mussar saved the yeshivos from being undermined by the strong currents of modern ideas, values, and economic opportunities.

Rav Yisrael realized that the battle of ideas was as critical to the survival of Torah as any other front. Therefore, while he lived in Konigsberg, he started a journal which he called *Tevunah* (Wisdom/Understanding) to encourage rabbis to develop their religious thinking and ability to articulate the values and appeal of Torah. Although he found it difficult to get others to write, there was a blessing in this problem. Rav Yisrael was forced to write a number of essays in order for *Tevunah* to have sufficient content. Thus, a scholar

whose communal activity and organizational efforts left him no time for writing was driven to write his most important theoretical work. These essays reveal that in his encounter with Mussar and modernity, Rav Yisrael had come
to some of the most important insights on religion and psychology of any Jewish thinker of that epoch. Rav Yisrael reflects on the power of reason (so elevated by modern culture) and the even greater power of the unconscious in
shaping character and "using" reason for its own purpose. Thus, he showed
the "distortion" and ambiguities in rationalization — anticipating the work
of Freud, later sociologists, and existentialist philosophers in emphasizing
the elements of instinct-driven behavior, choice as the key to the self, and
the powerful, if obscured, effects of group values on the individual's thinking
and life behaviors.

Rav Yisrael recognized the implicit crisis generated by recognition that
the individual can never escape subjectivity because reason itself is shaped
by the forces of the unconscious. This meant that the concept of objective
revelation and *mesorah* (transmission of tradition) was also challenged by the
inescapable subjectivity of the individual. How then can we restore the ob-
jectivity and authority of Torah and tradition? Rav Yisrael's answer (too
complex to be summarized here) is one of the most sophisticated and important intellectual responses by a traditional thinker to the erosion of certainty
and authority in modern and post-modern culture.

Among his other important experiments, Rav Yisrael sought to organize
study circles for Jewish students at universities because they were being
swept away by the assimilating effect of higher education. Despite the fact
that his own yeshivos in Eastern Europe could not and would not follow such
practices, he encouraged Rav Azriel Hilderheimer and the followers of Rabbi
Samson Raphael Hirsch to develop their models of *Torah im derech eretz* education and especially upgraded *chinuch* for women. He sought to enhance the
stature of the Talmud in the eyes of Jewish university students, so that they
would see the Talmud as a text on a par with the great traditions of the world.
In many of these approaches, Rav Yisrael was ahead of his time, and doubly
isolated in that his own primary students were living in a different social reality (Eastern Europe) where they did not understand and could not use these
approaches. Rav Yisrael pressed on, alone, seeking to strengthen Orthodoxy

in Western Europe and in Eastern Europe, each in their own way. Almost alone, he understood the momentous transformation going on and the urgency of finding methods and ideas that would enable Judaism to defend itself — nay, to renew itself — and to flourish in the new civilization sweeping the world.

One of Rav Yisrael's greatest legacies is the most neglected. Some years after Rav Yisrael's death, his disciple, Rabbi Yitzchak Blazer, edited a volume of his letters to students under the title *Ohr Yisrael* (The Light of Israel). He included the classic *Iggeres HaMussar* (Mussar Letter), Rav Yisrael's most widely disseminated piece, and the essays from *Tevunah*, Rav Yisrael's most overlooked writing. The Talmud says that "even a Torah located in the Sanctuary needs *mazel* (luck)," i.e., the scroll needs to be taken out and used. The *Ohr Yisrael* was overlooked and hardly used for study, even in the Mussar yeshivos. The reasons are many. Part of it is due to the compression, complexity, and depth of Rav Yisrael's ideas. As he faced intellectual and sociological challenges that few predecessors did, Rav Yisrael often had to develop his own vocabulary to articulate his ideas. He often used inherited terms in new ways. He wrote under pressure, with little time for editing. There were no chapter heads or editorial directions to guide the reader. Unhappily, until now, there has been no translation into English to make this great work available to English language readers. Thus one of the great classics of traditional Jewish thought in the modern era has languished in obscurity, awaiting its redeemer.

We must all be grateful to Rabbi Zvi Miller. He found this treasure, lifted it up from its neglect, and has presented it to us. He has translated this classic into readable English, edited it for comprehension, and supplied us with chapter titles and sectional headings to make clear the argument. He has lovingly restored the banner of Mussar. In Rabbi Miller's own teaching, he seeks to recreate the *Mussar kloyz*, a place where lay people can go and study and develop their Jewish ethical selves in the spirit of Torah and in the path of Rabbi Yisrael Salanter. This is a work that deserves wide dissemination and study.

In all of my personal philanthropy, I have sought to strengthen text study and Torah wisdom for the masses. Therefore, I was delighted when I was approached by Rabbi Miller to underwrite the publication of this most needed classic. I thank my friend Rabbi Yitzchak Greenberg for calling my attention to this most worthy project.

Due to this book's emphasis on good character and Torah values, I felt immediately that I would like to dedicate this volume to two special individuals. First and foremost, my beloved wife, Ellen, who has been the pillar of my life and my source of goodness and personal inspiration for all the years of our marriage. She has encouraged me to give *tzedakah* and to strengthen our tradition. She has raised our three sons, Moshe, Noah, and Joshua, to walk in the ways of our heritage and to be *mentshen*. Dedicating this book expresses only a little of the great debt and love which I owe her.

I also wish to dedicate the book to the memory of Jonathan Joseph (JJ) Greenberg, *zichrono livrachah*, the son of our lifetime friends Blu and Yitzchak Greenberg. He, too, represents the union of good character, love of fellow human beings, and *avodas Hashem*. Although his life was cut short by a tragic accident, he had already launched important projects to make Judaism available to the Jewish masses (such as Birthright Israel, Partnership for Excellence in Jewish Education, Makor). His life, too, was lived in accordance with the spirit of Rabbi Yisrael Salanter and the *Ohr Yisrael*.

I place this volume before the scholars and the public alike. May it inspire a new generation to live up to the highest ethical values and profoundest religious spirit of our Torah.

PREFACE

In the spring of 5762 (2001) news began to circulate about the discovery of Rav Yisrael Salanter's *kever* (gravesite) in Konigsberg (Kaliningrad), Russia. The investigation had been in progress for some ten years. Then, in the winter of that year, Hashem gave His blessing and the resting place of the *tzaddik* was located. The prestigious committee that conducted the search organized a *hakamas matzeivah* (dedication ceremony) to take place a few days after the ninth of Av.

How I longed to stand at the *kever* of our holy and beloved master. In Hashem's *hashgachah* (Divine providence), at the same time the first draft of the translation of *Ohr Yisrael* was completed, my dream became attainable. With the encouragement of my righteous wife, I made a reservation for the trip. The four-day itinerary included a visit to Minsk, Volozhin, Radin, Vilna, Kovna, Kelm, Slabodka, and then finally to Konigsberg.

And by the grace of Hashem — so it was. On the tenth of Av we flew from Tel Aviv to Minsk. Our group of 250 was comprised of *roshei yeshivos*, *mashgichim*, *rabbanim*, and other distinguished members of *klal Yisrael*. The meaningfulness of our mission charged the atmosphere with a sense of excitement and nobility of purpose.

After three extraordinary days of exploring our roots, the trip came to the climax. We entered Konigsberg early Thursday morning. Perhaps it was more as if Konigsberg entered us — we felt as if Rav Yisrael welcomed us to the city, as if his dignified presence was amongst us.

In the early afternoon we assembled around his *kever*. There we crossed the threshold into new dimensions of spirituality and joy. As *tehillim* were said, tears flowed from our eyes — tears that rose from the depths of our hearts and souls. The uniqueness of our experience may be expressed by the words of Yaakov Avinu, "Surely Hashem is present in this place!" (*Bereishis* 28:16).

It was the most profound moment of my life. We had seen a glimpse of the Light of Israel!

Acknowledgments

This book is dedicated to the memory of my beloved and revered parents, Rav Yochanon Mottel and Mores Esther Leah Miller. It is only through their merit that the privilege of participation in this holy book came to my hand. Their love and respect for Torah inspired them to enable me to learn in *kollel* for over twenty years. May their noble *kiddush Hashem*, which touched all who knew them, and their unprecedented kindness, together with the publication of this book, elevate their souls always higher in Gan Eden.

The following Torah leaders provided invaluable advice and encouragement: Maran HaRav HaGaon Matisiyahu Solomon, Maran HaRav HaGaon Shmuel Kamenetsky, Maran HaRav HaGaon Chaim Pinchas Scheinberg, Maran HaRav HaGaon Dov Schwartzman, Maran HaRav HaGaon Yehoshua Cohen, Maran HaRav HaGaon Elchanon Hertzman, and Maran HaRav HaGaon Mordecai Goldstein (Telz Stone/Ramat Beit Shemesh).

My deepest thanks to Mr. and Mrs. David Scheinfeld, legendary supporters of Torah and Torah causes, for their enthusiastic sponsorship of this project. May they see much *nachas* from their children!

My dear friend and Mussar *chavrusa* Mr. Joel Brauser and his wife Liz are to be commended for their dedication to support this undertaking. Joel's enthusiasm for Mussar is an inspiration to all who know him.

Another cherished friend, who is a man of uncommon sensitivity, wishes to remain anonymous. May Hashem bless him and his family for his humble generosity.

The contribution of editor Rabbi Eli Linas was indispensable. The eloquence of his writing is especially reflected in the intricate and profound letters of Rav Yisrael.

Mrs. Ita Olesker copyedited the entire manuscript. Her meticulous attention to detail, skillful editing, and wise suggestions significantly enhanced the clarity of this book.

In many complex passages of Rav Yisrael's letters I consulted the classic commentary *Ohr Yisrael HaMefurash* for clarification; hence I am indebted to Maran HaGaon HaRav Uri Weissblum, the esteemed author of *Ohr Yisrael HaMefurash*.

Rabbi Moshe Dombey and the Targum staff were always pleasant, accessible, and offered sound advice. My thanks to them for their effort, which was both friendly and professional. A special thanks to Mrs. Diane Liff for the beautiful book design and cover.

My heartfelt thanks to Mr. Moshe Gelbein, who reviewed the entire manuscript. I am also grateful to Rabbi David Sackton for reviewing parts of the manuscript and offering valuable advice. The rest of the editing team included: Rabbi Chaim Tscholkowsky, Mr. Ari Leiberman, Mr. Barry Lynn, Mr. Yehoshua Leventhal, and Rabbi Yehoshuah Mann. My thanks to Mrs. Joyce Litzman and Mr. Steve Fox, who selflessly donated many hours and days to type the manuscript. Mrs. Leah Segal also is to be thanked for typing a section of the manuscript.

Rabbi Yitzchak Greenberg is a caring friend and trusted advisor. Let it suffice to say that he spares no effort to emulate and advance the teaching of Rav Yisrael.

My heartfelt appreciation to the board of directors of the Salant Foundation, whose members include: Mr. David Newman, Mr. Jay Rodin, Mr. Mark Fisher, Mr. Moshe Yehudah Rice, and Rabbi Binyamin Miller (New York); and Mr. Joel Brauser, Mr. Aaron Moses, and Mr. David Goldis (Florida).

Mr. Gary Estersohn is a dear friend who did his utmost to assist in the fulfillment of this project. Rabbi Yisrael Gelbwachs and Rabbi Menachem Shvadron are esteemed colleagues who have made sincere and noble efforts on my behalf. Rabbi Raphael Grossman has offered sound advice and warm friendship.

The completion of this project, which spanned six years, could not have been possible without the generous support of many dear friends. I am grateful to all those who enabled this work, especially to Mr. and Mrs. Ishaia Gol, Mr. and Mrs. Alan Zavodnick, Mr. and Mrs. Sammy Friedland, Mr. and Mrs. Jeff Parker, Mr. (*z"l*) and Mrs. William Goldberg, and Mr. and Mrs. Michael Jesselson.

My brother, Mr. Edward Miller as well as my sister and her husband, Mr. and Mrs. Sheldon Gittleson, have been a fountain of helpfulness and encouragement. My deepest gratitude to my in-laws, Mr. and Mrs. Sol Borenstein, for their continuous support and assistance.

I am eternally thankful to the members of my Mussar *chaborah*: Rabbi Don Channon, Rabbi Yermeyahu Fenster, Rabbi Beryl Glazer, Rabbi Ben Zion Gold, Rabbi Yissacher Granitzky, Rabbi Shabbtai Herman, Rabbi Shmuel Piha, and Rabbi Marcel Rotenberg.

With a profound sense of appreciation, my thanks to Maran HaGaon HaRav Mordecai Goldstein, *rosh yeshivah* of Diaspora Yeshiva, who opened the gates of Torah and Mussar for me, as well as for thousands of others. With untiring devotion he plants the love of Torah and *avodah* into the hearts of his students — and his seedlings have blossomed into fruitful vines. His influence and encouragement in this project was a source of strength.

More than anyone else, the completion of this work could not have taken place without the graciousness of my wife, Zevia — *sheli v'shelchem shelah*. May we merit seeing all of our children and grandchildren follow the path of Torah and *yiras Shamayim*.

I express thanks and praise to Hashem *yisbarach*, Who, in His unbounded mercy, allowed me to render *Ohr Yisrael* into the vernacular. To be associated with the writings and wisdom of Rav Yisrael is a privilege, a gift, and a joyous blessing. Even more, that these exalted teachings should be disseminated in any way by my effort is a merit far beyond what I deserve.

May the pure teachings of Rav Yisrael kindle the flame of *yiras Shamayim* and illuminate the light of goodness in every heart and soul.

Rabbi Zvi Miller
Ramat Beit Shemesh, Israel
Kislev 5764

TRANSLATOR'S INTRODUCTION

THE PURPOSE OF CREATION: HOLINESS AND PURITY

"I found Israel like grapes in the desert, like a ripe fruit on a fig tree in its beginning did I view your fathers."

(Hoshea 9:10)

Six things preceded the creation of the world. Some of them were actually created, while others entered into Hashem's thoughts to be created.... The creation of the forefathers entered into Hashem's thoughts, for it says: "Like a ripe fruit on a fig tree in its beginning did I view your fathers."

(Midrash Bereishis Rabbah 1:4)

THE SPIRITUALITY OF THE AVOS

THE MIDRASH TEACHES the following axiom: The purpose of the world's creation — as conceived by Hashem prior to the creation — is the individual attainment of the level of spiritual excellence attained by the *avos*. Only after Hashem envisioned the *avos* did He create the world — the avenue to bring forth such exceptional people into existence. The pinnacle of spiritual excellence of the *avos* was purity, as seen by the Midrash, which states (*Bereishis Rabbah* 46:3): "Rebbi Yudan said: Just as the fig has no inedible portions save for its stem, and even this defect is neutralized with its removal, so did Hashem say to Avraham, 'There is no impurity within you save the *orlah*; remove it and eliminate your blemish.' " With the exception of the *orlah*, Avraham had purified his entire nature. He was an entity of pure goodness.

Moreover, the Midrash teaches (*Bereishis Rabbah* 11:6), "Everything that came into being during the six days of Creation requires improvement — for example, the mustard seed needs to be sweetened...also man needs rectification." Our world is a world of transformation. When we are improving and refining ourselves, we are in concert with the Divine plan — fulfilling our purpose for existing in this world. Yet the question still remains: What is the goal? How far must we strive?

We read in *Tanna D'Bei Eliyahu* (25): "Therefore, I say that every member of the Jewish people is obligated to say, 'When will my deeds reach the level of those of my forefathers, Avraham, Yitzchak, and Yaakov?' " Every Jew has the potential, and responsibility, to reach a relative equivalency of the level of spirituality of the *avos*.

According to these passages it is clear that the central purpose of the creation is to ascend to the level of the *avos*. Not only is the human being created for this purpose, but he is also given the ability and capacity to attain this supreme goal.

MUSSAR — THE TORAH OF THE HEART

THE MAHARAL M'PRAGUE states that the classical philosophers concluded upon three proofs that the world was created. The first is the multiplicity of every entity that exists, second is the precise detail found in all natural things, and third is the perfection of all things. If the world were random, these three qualities would not be consistently found.

The Maharal asks a penetrating question. If perfection is one of the hallmarks of creation, why then do we find perfection prevalent amongst the animals, plants, and minerals, yet so lacking in man? For instance, animals are perfect in their form and masterful at performing their instinctual life-needed skills. Man, on the other hand, although being distinguished from the animals in his intellectual and emotional prowess, is, however, unperfected in those areas — the feelings of his heart and the thoughts of his mind. Negative traits such as anger, jealously, and conceit often overwhelm us. If the theory of the philosophers is correct, where is the perfection of the human heart and mind?

The Maharal answers that the Creator must have provided man with the wisdom that brings man to perfection — thereby deducing that Torah, i.e., the required wisdom of perfection, must exist. Indeed, the wisdom of character rectification, Mussar, is inherent and pulsates throughout the Torah.

In his introduction to his classic book *Chovos HaLevavos*, Rabbeinu Bachya Paquada cites irrefutable proofs, both from the Written as well as the Oral Law, that the Torah obligates us to rectify our character traits. Thus the study of Mussar, the Torah of the heart, is obligatory — and the purpose of our existence.

RABBI YISRAEL SALANTER — TEACHER OF RIGHTEOUSNESS

RABBI YISRAEL SALANTER — THE VERY NAME is associated with holiness, humility, and righteousness. He was a leader, who earned the universal respect — and love — of his people. A man whose entire being rang true as an example of the authentic Jew. A Torah genius, who devoted his life to teach the all-important, yet terribly neglected, essential lesson of the Torah — righteousness and *yiras Shamayim*.

It is impossible for us to fathom his genius and goodness. Yet if we consider his remarkable accomplishments, we will gain a small measure of understanding of his greatness. Throughout the course of history, there have been very few figures who influenced the core of our observance. Rav Yisrael is a member of this select group. Indeed, he revitalized the very soul of his people.

Already from a young age, he was recognized as a *gaon* (Torah genius). Coupled with this brilliance, Rav Yisrael possessed a heart of tender sensitivity and compassion for his fellowman. As a young man, Rav Yisrael met Rav Yosef Zundel, a student of Rav Chaim Volozhin who was a student of the

Vilna Gaon. Rav Zundel recognized the special qualities of Rav Yisrael, and revealed to him the wisdom of Mussar (Torah ethics).

As Rav Yisrael grew in the wisdom of Mussar, he began to examine the spiritual situation in *klal Yisrael*. He realized that the long and painful exile, as well as the crushing economic conditions, had taken their toll. The moral fabric of *klal Yisrael*, the very essence of the Jewish spirit, was in need of remedy and resuscitation.

After studying the problem, Rav Yisrael concluded that the wisdom of Mussar was the solution. Mussar was a balm that would heal, uplift, and revitalize the weary souls of *am Yisrael*. He refined the concepts of Mussar and developed a methodology which could be practiced successfully and productively by the masses.

We must appreciate that Rav Yisrael single-handedly launched the Mussar movement. He did it with little funds, during a time of extreme persecution, and against intense opposition. He began to train students in Mussar and created a dynamic force that generated practically all the leaders and yeshivos of the next generation. His influence continues today.

THE SPLENDOR OF YISRAEL

THE BOOK CONTAINS the entire collection of writings of Rabbi Yisrael Salanter. His teachings reveal a complete system for spiritual growth and personal excellence. It is a "how to," "hands-on" lucid and detailed guide to understanding and overcoming the lesser traits embedded in oneself. As well, the concepts of Rav Yisrael contain profoundness and innovation, thereby challenging us to think always deeper to fathom their secrets and to strive harder to master ourselves.

There are words and concepts that might concern the reader, such as "the fear of God" and "Divine punishment." We will disassociate the common and incorrect connotations associated with these words, thus allowing us to properly internalize the lessons. These words are terms that represent concepts, and as such must be defined. The reader is advised to read complete sections in order to gain a thorough understanding of the concepts, as Rav Yisrael so eloquently explains them.

REALIZING OUR POTENTIAL

WE SENSE, DEEP within ourselves, goodness and wisdom. Somewhere in the distant recesses of our psyche a precious diamond twinkles like a distant star, light-years away. A mere but steady pinpoint. The purity of character and prophetic words of great Jews, such as Avraham and Moshe, echo across the cavernous centuries and resonate — timelessly — within ours souls.

But how to grasp these priceless gems is perhaps the most elusive secret of human existence, a mystery that resists even the most heroic and persistent advances. Like a "pillar of fire," Rav Yisrael Salanter, of blessed memory, illuminated the sure path to Heavenly fear, good deeds, and character refinement. Indeed, his wisdom teaches us how to change human nature and transform ourselves.

May the "Light of Israel" guide us to ascend the holy mountain — the attainment of the purity of the *avos*, Avraham, Yitzchak, and Yaakov. And may the fear of Heaven fill the hearts of all mankind so that we may merit to see the rebuilding of the Temple soon and within our days.

הקדמה

INTRODUCTION TO THE OHR YISRAEL

Rav Yitzchak Blazer

INTRODUCTION

HEALING OUR SOULS

IN THE THIRD CHAPTER of *Shemonah Perakim* (The Rambam's introduction to *Pirkei Avos*), the Rambam, *zt"l*, writes, "The ancient Sages taught that just as the body can be healthy or ill, so, too, can the soul be sick or well. The sign of a healthy soul is when a person acts virtuously, by continuously performing good deeds and pleasing actions. Illness of the soul is manifested when a person consistently acts in an evil and repulsive fashion. When a person is physically ill, he consults with physicians, who inform him as to which actions he should take and what he must refrain from doing. Similarly, those suffering from spiritual malaise must consult the Sages, who are the healers of the soul. They will cure them through actions which heal the soul's attributes." In the second chapter of *Hilchos De'os*, the Rambam also explains the similitude between physical and spiritual illness.

THE SHIFT OF WELL-BEING

AS WE KNOW, the peace and harmony of the body that provide for its vitality, health, and constitution have generally diminished over the generations. Man's strength has continuously waned until this generation [the late 1800s], where, in the wake of our many sins, our health has deteriorated and we are overwhelmed with frailty. Pain and illness from all types of disorders affect the majority of people. Likewise, peace and harmony of the soul — its very life force — are virtually nonexistent. Each successive generation has become increasingly impoverished spiritually. The soul is afflicted with diseases that increase daily, and its health is constantly diminishing.

FEAR OF HEAVEN HAS FALLEN TO IGNOBLE DEPTHS

HENCE, AS THE GENERATIONS PASS — indeed, in the span of just one generation — there has been a noticeable reduction in the primacy of Torah and the fear of Heaven. Now, due to our many sins in this generation — in the course of but a few years — an impure spirit has succeeded in altering reality, bringing numerous innovations that are patently inferior and a host of substandard modifications in the service of the Creator. In all areas of Divine worship, weakness and fatigue of the spirit are clearly recognizable. The soul's power has continually diminished, until we find ourselves in the most amoral of times, wherein disease of the soul is an almost universal reality, may God have mercy.

Close scrutiny of the general situation of Torah and Heavenly fear reveals that the spiritual degradation of fear of Heaven is much more rampant and destructive than the debasement of Torah study, and the ramifications of this weakness are far more serious. Despite the frailty found in our relationship with the holy Torah — the devaluation of her worth and the desolation of her gates — we have a guarantee from Hashem that the Torah will always be perpetuated, as the verse states, "This song [the Torah]...shall not be forgotten from the mouth of its [the Nation of Israel's] offspring" (*Devarim* 31:21). This guarantee endures and applies even in our generation. The "voice of Yaakov" is heard from the *batei midrashim*, and the Torah's gates remain full of scholars who are proficient in the law. Similarly, there are still pure-hearted people who support the Torah with unflagging devotion.

Unfortunately, however, fear of Heaven has dramatically fallen from the most pristine heights to the most ignoble depths. The precipitous decline has been frightening to behold, with nothing and no one to hinder the descent. The paths of fear are in mourning, the gates of Divine service are desolate, and we are drowning in sin. Immorality rules over us with unassailable strength and impunity, corrupting us and ruining every good portion of God's inheritance. The foundation of fear and Heavenly worship is engulfed in flames. The slanderers have gained power, while those who fear the Almighty's word are derided and despised. Virtue itself is corrupted, and falsehood cloaks itself in a garment of righteousness. Men of violence control the land, and truth is vanquished.

INSEPARABLE TWINS

IT WAS NOT ALWAYS SO in Israel. In earlier times, Torah knowledge and the fear of Heaven perfectly complemented each other, like inseparable twins. Great scholars were adorned with the pearls of fear, and the value of their wisdom was consistent with the value of their reverence. However, due to the multitude of our sins, the previously unseamed tapestry has now become almost completely unraveled. The bonds are broken, and the knot that joined them has been torn asunder. Moreover, the Torah itself is not invulnerable, for without fear, the vitality of Torah will ultimately be debilitated as well, may Hashem have mercy.

As far as physical illness is concerned, medical science has made wondrous advances that keep pace with the increase in infirmity. Researchers labor continuously to expand the horizons of medical knowledge, seeking to understand and fathom the roots of disease. The profound capabilities of wisdom, analysis, and experimentation have led to the discovery of cures and treatments that were previously undreamed of. As many diseases as exist in the world, there are a similar number of physicians and remedies.

However, such is not the case concerning the soul and its afflictions. There is a vast increase in illness, and the diseases are more severe. Weakness has become endemic, and the paths of healing are obstructed. There are no doctors to aid us, no elixirs nor remedies, and neither process nor procedure.

TEACHER OF RIGHTEOUSNESS

IF NOT FOR THE FACT that Hashem is in our midst, all hope would be lost. Let those who fear God praise Him, for He has shown mercy to His people! In His great compassion, He has provided even our impoverished generation with a teacher of righteousness, a faithful shepherd and redeemer to resuscitate our flagging spirits and inject us with new life. This virtuous man has compounded elixirs and remedies for the diseases of our souls and re-stored us to life: the renowned sage, our holy teacher; matchless leader of the exiled ones; saintly and humble light of the world; our master and rabbi, Rav Yisrael of Salant, may his memory be blessed for all eternity. Indeed, the awe-some might of his saintliness, humility, and holiness is known and revered to the ends of the earth.

THE ELIXIR OF HEAVENLY FEAR

HOWEVER, EVEN MORE THAN HIS GENIUS and saintliness, he merited — and brought far-reaching merit to his people — to illuminate the eyes of Israel with his Torah knowledge and his fear of Heaven. All his days, he labored to reconstruct the fallen tabernacle of fear and to restore it to its former glory and preeminence. He courageously endeavored to reconnect the fear of Heaven to the honor of Torah, as it had been in previous times; to heal our spiritual diseases and return our hearts to our Father in Heaven. With his pleasant words, he returned uncounted people to their roots, and with the elixir of Heavenly fear, he brought relief to every afflicted soul.

He raised many students and gave unstintingly of himself to teach them knowledge of Hashem, guiding them in the paths of wisdom and understand-ing. The object of all his efforts was to ingrain the fear of God within their hearts, to implant upright and pleasing character traits in them, and to in-struct them in the ways of Divine service.

WONDROUS COUNSEL

ABOVE EVERYTHING — greater than even his awesome powers and exemplary character — was his counsel: wondrous advice that yielded great salvation and which will provide Israel with a source of merit for generations to come. He bequeathed a sublime healing procedure to cure the diseased souls of his people and to restore them to life. What was this miraculous pre-scription, this wondrous strategy that is guaranteed to bring relief to the soul? It is the in-depth and fervent, verbal expression of Mussar that wells up from the core of one's being [i.e., *hispailus* (see the second of the "Ten Innovations of Rav Yisrael," at the end of "The Gates of Light")]. To arrive at his diagnosis, he listened carefully, then contemplated and investigated the disease. His course of treatment was to teach his people knowledge, wisdom, and Mussar — the general remedy for disease of the soul, which rescues it from the cunning machinations of the evil inclination. To this end, he advised people to set daily, organized times to study works devoted to Mussar and the fear of Heaven. Moreover, he stressed that such study should not be done in a perfunctory manner. Rather, it must be pursued with sincerity of heart, with one's lips aflame. It must be studied in a voice that will arouse regret and remorse, and with an inspired soul. In the wings of this study is salvation and healing, and in its footsteps is the fear of God and humility. It teaches man wisdom and knowledge; righteousness, justice, and uprightness; and every precious and worthwhile character trait.

PILLAR OF FIRE

INDEED, OUR MASTER AND TEACHER, the righteous and pious *gaon*, was sent by Heaven to be a pillar of fire in our midst. His incandescent flame illuminated the eyes of all of Israel with Torah and the fear of God. Through the way of Mussar, he opened the gates of light for us. He dedicated his entire life to establish the paths of this remedy, namely, to study Heavenly fear and Mussar with fiery devotion. He marked a trail not only for the wise and upright of heart, but for the entire nation as well, so that an ever-expanding number of people might avail themselves of it. Thus, he endeavored to bring the many to this path and thereby increase the knowledge and fear of Hashem in Israel. As is well known, Heaven blessed his sacred undertaking with success, and the very foundations of the world shook from his teachings. Heaven privileged him to bring this merit to his people and to render salvation in the midst of the earth, bringing renewal to man's soul. Through the proven healing power of Mussar, countless people grew strong and mighty in the fear of God and virtuous in character. This study proved to be a spring of redemption and a salvation of the soul, and all who undertook it benefited, each man according to his station and ability. Thus, the knowledge of Heavenly fear increased amongst Israel.

We know that the righteous continue to wield influence even after their

passing, and that is the case with Rav Yisrael as well. Just as there is no end to
the achievements he merited during his lifetime, so, too, the beneficial plans
and ideas he intended for his people — to bestow goodness upon them and to
illuminate the understanding of *yiras Hashem* for them — were not lost after
his interment. All that he accomplished to resuscitate the life of the soul remains to give us comfort, thank God. Though he returned his dust to the
earth and his physical eyes no longer remain, his spirit is still alive and seeing.
Truly, the "Light of Israel" has not been extinguished. The luminescence of
his Torah and Heavenly fear, and the path of his Mussar, still influences and
illuminates us today. It enlightens the eyes of the pure and upright ones with
fear of God and His worship.

LIVING WATERS

HIS INFLUENCE HAS BEEN PERPETUATED by his outstanding disci-
ples, who took shelter in the shade of his well and partook of his holy waters.
They merited to stand before him and receive from him the way of Hashem,
strengthening themselves in the path of holiness. They then labored to disseminate their master's teachings and his approach to Mussar, to provide the
masses with merit by encouraging them to study Mussar and works on Heavenly fear. From the wellsprings of their exalted teacher's wisdom and Mussar
in the fear of God, they drew living water for the multitudes to drink. To our
great fortune, many influential yeshivos have established the daily study of
Mussar as a part of their curricula, and numerous groups of Torah scholars
have dedicated an hour each day to studying works devoted to this topic —
all so that they may learn to fear the great and awesome God.

Likewise, the luminous sparks of the "Light of Israel" have illuminated the
Eastern horizon — in Eretz Yisrael and Yerushalayim. In that exalted place
there can also be found a holy remnant who call out to Hashem. Students of
his students, they dwell in the tents of Torah. They have brought the war to
the city gates, and they conduct themselves in the way of holiness — by
studying Heavenly fear and Mussar. They are mighty warriors in Torah and
the pure fear of God, and their paths shine with light.

Behold, our master and our teacher — may his holy memory be for blessing — was a flowing river, a sublime source of wisdom and knowledge about Heavenly fear and Mussar. The ear could never be sated from imbibing his wisdom on Godly worship and the ethical admonishment that poured lovingly from his lips — words sweet like honey that were healing to the soul. To our misfortune, however, we did not merit to have his holy words inscribed on paper. He committed almost nothing to writing, neither his extensive and innovative Torah thoughts, nor his powerful understanding of Heavenly fear and Divine worship. Even concerning the topic most dear to his heart — the study of Mussar and the fear of Hashem — there exists but a paucity of written material. He wrote only the *Iggeres HaMussar*, a small but comprehensive composition on the study of Mussar, and two articles that were printed in *Sefer Tevunah* [a Torah journal that was founded and published by Rav Yisrael]. Brief as they are, these two inspiring articles are filled with the wisdom of fear and the ways of virtue, and they also mention the importance of Heavenly fear and the study of Mussar.

INHERITANCE

BECAUSE OF THIS SITUATION, I resolved many years ago to conduct a thorough search; perhaps I might discover some previously unknown words that he penned concerning the study of *yiras Hashem*. In particular, I hoped to find writings which discussed the study of Mussar. I toiled unceasingly, and with the help of the One Above, I uncovered a hidden treasure: several letters penned by our holy master and teacher. Small in quantity but great in quality, they comprise the correspondence he sent to his students and relatives in order to strengthen their hearts in the fear of God and the study of Mussar. Truly, they are buried treasures that are far more precious than pearls.

THE WORD OF THE LIVING GOD

I, THE AUTHOR OF THESE WORDS, am one of the students who merited to stand before him and "pour water on his hands" — to serve him as a servant attends his master. In turn, he drew me close and I merited to continually hear the word of the living God that emanated from his pure and holy mouth. He taught us the ways of Heavenly fear and how to properly serve the Creator — both on a general level through his own ethical admonishments and on a specific level through teaching about the actual study of Mussar and the fear of Heaven. He addressed the public at large with lectures about righteousness, and spoke to his students on a more intimate level. With the disciples to whom he was especially close — those he knew to be completely dedicated to accepting his influence — he would occasionally confer in private. To these select students he gave his entire being, and spoke with them intimately to guide and teach them in the ways of Hashem. Thus it was that I dedicated my heart to contemplate the ways of our teacher's holy service, which he conducted in righteousness, piety, and with sterling character. He was truly the "Light of Israel," and his holiness illuminated my eyes.

AN ORGANIZED ANTHOLOGY

BECAUSE OF THE SPECIAL RELATIONSHIP I shared with him, I feel obligated to redeem his inheritance by gathering together the widely dispersed letters he wrote, arranging and preserving them, in order to disseminate them throughout the world. Creating such an organized anthology presents several benefits:

1) Since his holy words are beloved to the entire House of Israel, and everyone thirsts to drink them — indeed, his *Iggeres HaMussar* has been reprinted numerous times — I decided to publish the collection of his holy letters. In that way, the public's desire will be sated, and the upright of heart will rejoice and delight as they seek to improve their Divine service and perform the Almighty's will.

2) *Baruch Hashem*, there are many people today with a steadfast commitment to improve their level of Heavenly fear, yet they were not privileged to behold firsthand this wonderful "Light of Israel" and his holiness. Instead, his instructions concerning the obligation to study Mussar only reached them by word of mouth. This collection will serve as "eyes" for these people, for the letters shine with a brilliant light that reflects his opinions and counsel on the study of Heavenly fear. His writings illustrate the resplendent value of Mussar and the wondrous benefits to be accrued by engaging in its study.

Warm and life-giving rays repose beneath the wings of his words, which can bring speedy salvation and heal the diseases of the soul. Indeed, our master explains that the fervent study of Mussar brings eternal salvation. It is the foundation of all that is good, and the obligation to study it is incumbent upon every person, excepting no one. Moreover, every person who merits to awaken himself and to guide others in this exalted area of study is assured of a just reward. The light of his deeds shall be dazzling, and he shall be counted amongst those who inspire the many towards righteousness. He will illuminate the world with the very light of life and will shine forever like the stars in heaven. All the words that I wrote in my exposition "The Gates of Light," which sets down the foundation for the study of Heavenly fear and Mussar, were heard from his holy mouth. The reader will find reference to each of these principles scattered throughout his letters.

3) His letters concerning the ways of Divine worship contain astonishing insights that will inflame the soul to study Mussar — words that penetrate the heart and soul. A master pedagogue, his pen is the pen of an accomplished scribe, his language flowing and eloquent. After imbibing his holy words, the sincere reader's soul will resonate with the fear of Hashem, and his heart will be exalted and uplifted.

4) From the corpus of his letters that remain as a tangible legacy, we learn of and are humbled by the extent to which the Admor ["Admor" is an acronym for the words "adoneinu, moreinu, v'rabbeinu," lit. "Our master, mentor, and rabbi"] gave his soul to bring merit to the masses. Even when he traveled to distant countries, he did not forget the afflicted souls that remained in the land of his birth. He did not hide the light of his countenance, and neither was he lax in composing correspondence and dispatching it to his students and family. Hence, he strengthened their hearts in the fear of the Almighty and in the study of Mussar. Additionally, he roused them to bring merit to others and to strengthen people who are weak in this exalted study, so that everyone might walk in the Almighty's ways all the days of their lives.

5) For various reasons, a man's heart will sometimes turn away from the precious study of Mussar. Indeed, a person might even come to denounce and impugn the reputation of this valuable area of Divinely sanctified study and

bring harsh judgments against it. This idea is mentioned in the work *Divrei Yehoshua*, section 1, chapter 7: "There are seven things that prevent a person from tasting and recognizing the inherent value of Mussar study...the seventh deterrent is jealousy. There are many people who interfere with the study of Mussar by fabricating claims against it. Such false allegations appeal to people who are not sufficiently familiar with Mussar to realize how vital is its study — and especially to those who have never even tasted it nor basked in its radiance. Certainly, their claims do not stem from understanding and wisdom. Rather, they derive from the corrupt wellsprings of jealously, which consume like fiercely burning flames and are as oppressive as Gehinnom. Of course, it must be stressed that if it is properly channeled, there is a place for jealously in the world — for example, when it engenders competition amongst scholars that results in an increase of wisdom. Obviously, however, such jealousy is detrimental if it brings about a decrease in wisdom. Competition amongst scholars is beneficial only if it inculcates Heavenly fear in the heart, and not if it weakens this trait."

We see from the Divrei Yehoshua's words that only one who has personally experienced this sublime area of study can truly comprehend its worth. Only he can realize that it is a cherished treasure built on the foundations of righteousness; a healing tree of life without perversion or crookedness. Such an individual will pay no heed to slanderous allegations, and all the ill winds in the world will not uproot him from his place. On the other hand, a person who has never tasted the study of Mussar and seen its light will be unable to recognize its inestimable value as well as its practical application. Not understanding the benefits of its treasure, he will be perplexed when he hears hostile and defamatory words, and he will not know how to judge the matter. These letters will open such a person's eyes to behold the brilliance of the sun in the zenith of the heavens — to understand the obligation to study Mussar in all its details. It springs from a holy place: from the mighty shepherd, the holy *gaon*, the pious and humble "light of the world" — the holiness of Israel.

MASTER NAVIGATOR

THE WISE MEN VERSED IN KABBALAH and the sages enlightened

in scientific knowledge compare the world to a churning ocean and the body of man to a ship afloat in the midst of the sea. This idea appears in the *Zohar HaKadosh, Parashas Vayakhel*; in the commentary of the Vilna Gaon on *Sefer Yonah*; and in the work *Bechinas Olam*, among others.

We must realize that this is no mere poetic metaphor, but rather a deeply penetrating insight. Let us try and understand: There are entire schools dedicated to teaching navigating skills and the ways of the high seas. Sailors must learn how to best maneuver their great ships over the oceans, even at times of terrifying tempests and overpowering gales. So, too, with the little boat called man, who sails on the open sea of life. He requires extensive knowledge to know how to guide himself on a straight course, so that he will avoid mishap and not lose his way. This is because the ocean of life roars fearfully and unceasingly. The winds of challenge blow constantly, and the evil inclination rips about like a tornado with unimaginable force. The waves of desire and corrupt character traits come crashing down like boulders from a high cliff, and the boat careens between treacherous shoals and dangerous outcroppings. All of life comprises great and endless tests, which can easily capsize the boat and sink it into the murky, nethermost depths.

The accomplished ship's captain is able to navigate a large ship carrying thousands of passengers. He does not come to this knowledge naturally; rather, he has trained for it from his youth. He knows the positions of the stars and their movements, and is intimately familiar with the gale winds and the ocean currents. Only he can make a highway in the sea and a path through the mighty waters. When fearsome winds whip up towering breakers, pitching the ship to and fro and blowing it off course, the passengers turn to the captain, trusting in him to bring them to safe harbor. It would be inconceivable for a man uneducated in the art of sailing — who could not even handle a simple rowboat or raft — to argue with the captain. Imagine if he would try and adjust the masts and sails. If such a person assumed command of the ship, it would set off a frenzied panic in the hearts of the passengers.

THE SMALL BOAT

THUS IT IS WITH THE SMALL BOAT CALLED MAN as he navigates his way through the roaring sea of life. Our master and teacher, the holy *gaon* and *tzaddik*, is like a master captain who studied his craft from earliest youth. He has the knowledge to safely guide the ship between the breakers of the sea — using the sails and masts of Mussar and Heavenly fear. He has toiled in this study all the days of his life. He recognizes the storm winds that whip up the evil inclination, and he can sail the ship amongst them without mishap. Thus, he provides safe passage through the churning sea and saves the boat from being inundated by the mighty waters. Knowledge of Heavenly fear and Mussar will prevent the body from sinking into the miry depths of desire and evil character traits. Is there anyone who can dispute with this giant amongst giants? Should we not raise our eyes to him only, and hearken to his sage advice? We shall make our way using his steady light for guidance, following him on a straight and sure path — the way of Mussar. Then we will learn to fear the great and glorious Name of God and to traverse His paths in righteousness, and it shall be good for us for all eternity.

CONTENTS

ALTHOUGH RICH IN QUALITY, the quantity of these holy letters is quite small and insufficient to form an entire book. Therefore, I have included several opportune supplements. The entire work has one goal: to awaken the heart to fear Hashem and study Mussar. Following is a brief description of the various sections that comprise the book's content:

a) In addition to the actual letters, I have included a few teachings that were heard directly from his holy mouth. Moreover, I have added the two articles that were published in *Sefer Tevunah* and the *Iggeres HaMussar*, so that all his actual writings have been gathered together in one place. I have also included two letters that were composed by Rav Yisrael's own teacher, Rav Yosef Zundel of Salant, *zt"l*.

b) The work also contains some biographical material, so that the reader might be afforded some small sense of our teacher's greatness, righteousness, and Heavenly fear, and have a glimpse of his path of Divine worship. There is also a sampling of his holy words concerning the ways of Hashem and the cultivation of good character traits. Additionally, some biographical information about Rav Yosef Zundel follows at the end of this section.

c) Before the actual letters, there is a lengthy exposition on the study of Mussar and Heavenly fear, written by myself. The purpose of this essay is six-fold: 1) To discuss the general obligation to study Mussar. 2) To demonstrate that the foundations of this study are firmly grounded in our tradition and the teachings of our revered and holy Sages. 3) To explain how it transpired that the way of Mussar should be lost. 4) To point out the activities and innovations of our teacher in this sacred area of study. 5) To bring to light all the ways and details of Mussar that we heard from his holy mouth. 6) To describe how the study of Mussar came to be publicized throughout the world in the name of our master, the holy "Light of Israel."

d) Finally, there are various treatises concerning Heavenly fear and Mussar and the ways of repentance, again prepared by myself. It is my fervent desire that they will be of assistance to those who seek to carry out the Almighty's will.

All of these sections are referred to by an appropriate name. The collection of the letters and the other holy writings of the Admor, zt"l, is entitled "The Light of Israel." The article on his path of Divine worship is called "Paths of Light." The exposition on the study of Mussar is referred to as "The Gates of Light," and the section of essays on Heavenly fear and Mussar is entitled "Stars of Light."

May it be the will of our Father in Heaven that the "Light of Israel" shine eternally, and that the masses utilize his illumination to walk on the upright path. May the fear of God be increased in Israel, and may the day soon come when the world will be full of the knowledge of His great and glorious Name. May we merit to serve Him, all of Israel together, united with one heart.

Written by his student Yitzchak Blazer
former Chief Rabbi of Petersburg, royal capital of the Russian Empire

מאמר שערי אור

THE GATES
OF LIGHT

Rav Yitzchak Blazer

AN EXPOSITION
ON THE STUDY OF
HEAVENLY FEAR AND MUSSAR

1

THE BEGINNING OF WISDOM

CAUSE AND RESULT

IN THE SEVENTH LETTER OF THIS COLLECTION, Rav Yisrael writes, "Every single thing in the world came into existence through a series of causes and results.... In any given process of creation, each cause is the result of a preceding one.... We see, then, that ultimately there exists no result that does not have a preceding cause.... Similarly, there is no cause that is not generated by a preceding one."

THE CAUSE OF DIVINE WORSHIP

It is known to and understood by every man of wisdom and understanding that the value of a desired result determines the necessary causes of its production. The more precious the result, the more and greater are the causes required for it to be produced. With this idea in mind, let us consider worship of the Almighty. Divine service is the most worthy and exalted goal in the entire universe. The world in general — and man especially — was created solely for this purpose. The question therefore arises: What are the causes that generate this most exalted and precious result [of bringing man to Divine service]?

THE FEAR OF HEAVEN IS THE FIRST CAUSE OF DIVINE WORSHIP

When we examine the verses of *Tanach* and the teachings of our Sages, we find that the first cause of the fulfillment of Torah and Divine service is the attainment of Heavenly fear. Fear of God is the linchpin, the focal point around which revolve all of man's endeavors: his deeds, affairs, and strategies, and his conduct vis-à-vis the Almighty and other men. It is the foundation and root of the entire Torah and all of the mitzvos. Thus, David HaMelech informs us: "The beginning [first cause] of wisdom is fear of Hashem" (*Tehillim* 111:10). His son Shlomo echoes his words: "The beginning of wisdom is fear of Hashem" (*Mishlei* 9:10). Similarly, in *Sefer Koheles* he concludes: "The sum of the matter, when all has been considered: Fear God and keep His commandments" (*Koheles* 12:13).

THE ENEMIES OF TALMIDEI CHACHAMIM

We read in the Talmud (*Yoma* 72b): "What is the meaning of the verse: 'Money in the hand of a fool' (*Mishlei* 17:16)? Woe to the enemies of *talmidei chachamim*, who learn Torah and yet do not fear God." It is similarly taught in *Pirkei Avos* (3:11): "Rabbi Chanina Ben Dosa says: Anyone whose fear of sin takes precedence over his wisdom, his wisdom will endure; but anyone whose wisdom takes precedence over his fear of sin, his wisdom will not endure." The Talmud likewise relates (*Berachos* 33b): "Rav Yochanan said in the name of Rav Shimon Bar Yochai, 'The only thing that the Almighty has in His treasury is a reservoir of Heavenly fear.' " Even more dramatically, Chazal inform us (*Shabbos* 31b): "Any person who has acquired a knowledge of Torah, yet does not fear Heaven, is like a treasurer who has been entrusted with the keys to the inner vault, but does not possess the keys to the exterior door. How, then, shall he enter?" Rashi explains this in the following manner: If a person fears Heaven, he will zealously observe and perform the commandments. However, if he has no fear, he will disregard his Torah knowledge. We see from this that fear of Heaven is the outer key [i.e., first cause] that opens the gate which leads to Hashem — the gate of Torah and Divine service.

THE FEAR OF GOD IS COMPRISED OF TWO ASPECTS

Yet a crucial question still remains: What is the essence of this Heavenly fear that unlocks the gates of righteousness — the inner workings of this mechanism that impels us to serve Hashem and fulfill His commandments? It is known that the fear of God is comprised of two aspects. Our Sages refer to them as *yiras ha'onesh*, the dread of punishment, and *yiras haromemus*, the awe of Divine majesty. We find this idea expressed by the *Chovos HaLevavos* (*Sha'ar Ahavas Hashem*, ch. 6): "The fear of Heaven has two aspects: the fear of tribulations and Divine retribution, and the fear of His glory, majesty, and awesome power." Likewise, we read in the *Mesillas Yesharim* (ch. 24): "There is the fear of punishment and there is the fear of majesty. The fear of punishment is self-explanatory, whereby a person fears to transgress the Almighty's word because he realizes he will be punished for his sins. The fear of majesty is when a man refrains from sinning due to the great reverence and respect he bears for the Creator."

THE FEAR OF LOSING THE REWARD

Included in the general category of *yiras ha'onesh* is the fear of losing the reward [Gan Eden] one would receive for performing mitzvos. Just as it is necessary for a person to dread punishment, so, too, must he inculcate within his heart a love of the true reward. Indeed, the love of this reward should be infinitely stronger than the desire for all the pleasures of the world, so that a person longs only to bask in the glory of the Divine presence. This is the true good that no eye has ever beheld, stored away for the righteous in reward for their mitzvos. Can a person honestly not fear the loss of so great a reward, *chas v'shalom?*

THE LOVE OF HASHEM

Like *yiras ha'onesh*, the general category of *yiras haromemus* also has a second aspect: the love of Hashem. Indeed, the fear of Hashem's majesty and love for Him are almost the same. We see this idea mentioned explicitly in the Talmud (*Sotah* 31a), wherein two of Rava's students dreamt of Scriptural verses and turned to him for an interpretation. "The import of your dreams," he told them, "is that both of you are perfectly righteous: one out of love, and the other out of fear." (Nevertheless, it is important to realize that the attribute of love is greater than the attribute of *yiras haromemus*. As is stated in the same passage of Talmud: "Rav Shimon Ben Eliezer taught: 'One who serves the Almighty out of love is greater than one who serves Him out of fear.' ")

ONE MUST FIRST COME TO FEAR HIS PUNISHMENT

We have thus far noted that there are two types of Heavenly fear. However, it must be stressed that the two are not equal. It is clear that the fear of God's majesty is on a more exalted plane than the fear of punishment. Nevertheless, the fear of punishment is also crucial, for it is the beginning of wisdom. In the introduction to his work *Eitz Chaim*, Rav Chaim Vital, *zt"l*, writes: "One who comes to purify himself and to draw close to God must know that the beginning of everything is to fear Him — to comprehend the fear of punishment. This is because *yiras haromemus* is the inner essence of fear, which can only be apprehended with great wisdom." Even more than this, the Sages tell us that it is impossible to attain the exalted virtue of *yiras haromemus* without first acquiring *yiras ha'onesh*. The Malbim, *zt"l*, states this in his commentary to the Torah (*Parashas Yisro*): "The wise of heart have explained that it is impossible to immediately attain the exalted level of *yiras haromemus*. Rather, one must first come to fear His punishment, and only then ascend to the more elevated level of *yiras haromemus*." Likewise, our master and teacher, Rav Yisrael, writes (*Iggeres HaMussar*), "The belief that the Almighty is the True Judge Who recompenses each individual according to his deeds is the first step in the service of Hashem."

The reason for this is quite simple: Experience shows that in every area of life it is impossible to ascend to the highest of heights in one fell swoop — and the acquisition of fear is no different. As with all other things, this exalted quality can only be acquired in increments. First, one must learn to fear Divine retribution, and only afterwards ascend to awe of the Divine majesty.

THREE DIFFERENT TIERS OF FEAR

There is yet another principle that is relevant to our discussion of Heavenly fear. It is mentioned in an early commentary on the Rambam's *Mishneh Torah* (*Yesodei HaTorah*, ch. 1): "We find two verses in the Torah that seem to contradict each other. The first one indicates that Heavenly fear brings a person to the performance of the mitzvos, as it states: 'Now O Israel, what does Hashem, your God, ask of you? Only to fear Hashem, your God...to observe the commandments of Hashem and His decrees' (*Devarim* 10:12–13). On the other hand, the second verse teaches that we were only commanded to perform the mitzvos in order to attain the fear of God, as it is written: 'Hashem commanded us to perform all these decrees, to fear Hashem, our God...' (ibid. 6:24). The resolution of this contradiction lies in the fact that there are three different tiers of fear. The first one is the beginning, which precedes the observance of the mitzvos. This is the fear of the King, which prevents a person from transgressing His directives [*yiras ha'onesh*]. It is concerning this level of fear that we read in *Pirkei Avos*: 'Rabbi Chanina Ben Dosa says: Anyone whose fear of sin takes precedence over his wisdom, his wisdom will endure.' The second tier is the end, and this is the true fear [*yiras haromemus*]. A man cannot attain this level until he first performs all of the mitzvos. After reaching this stage, a person then shifts to the virtue of love, for a person can only love the Almighty after first coming to fear Him."

TWO DIVISIONS OF DIVINE SERVICE

The explanation of this idea is as follows: We know that there are two divisions of Divine service. The first division is deed: the actual fulfillment of the Torah and the mitzvos, in keeping with the verse, "Turn from evil and do good" (*Tehillim* 34:15). The second division is one's attitude and purity of thought, a division that has numerous levels. The basic foundation of Divine service is the actual fulfillment of deed. When a person fulfills the entire Torah, observing all of its mitzvos, he is called a servant of God. On the other hand, purity of thought is only necessary for the perfection of one's service. We find this idea addressed at length in the work *Nefesh HaChaim*.

THE FEAR OF PUNISHMENT IS MANIFEST IN THE ANIMALISTIC SOUL

The fear of punishment is manifest in the animalistic or "natural" soul, for the trait of fear is implanted within every living creature. Accordingly, even when a person follows the whims of his heart and wallows in sin and iniquity, he still retains the capacity to fear punishment. Thus it is that this fear precedes the performance of the mitzvos, for it is the primary deterrent against iniquity and sin. This fear causes one to tremble before the Almighty and to fulfill the Torah and its mitzvos.[1]

YIRAS HAROMEMUS: A PERFECT KNOWLEDGE

Yet as we have stated, the more exalted level of fear is *yiras haromemus*. This level of fear comprises a perfect knowledge and intellectual comprehension of the fact that one must quake in awe over the Almighty's grandeur and majesty. Physical desire, negative character traits, and the filth of iniquity form a barrier between an individual and his Creator. As long as a person continues to commit evil in the eyes of Hashem, to transgress His covenant and rebel against the Divine will, he will be unable to internalize this great fear. Without elevating himself above gross physicality and casting off his putrid garments — the vanities of the world and base desire — there is no hope whatsoever that he will reach this level. Therefore, it is imperative that a person cleanse himself of corrupt character traits and sanctify himself from the body's impurities. This can be achieved solely by observing the Torah and its mitzvos. Only in this manner can one truly come to comprehend His great majesty and tremble in awe over His glorious splendor.[2] Moreover, once a person has achieved this, he can ascend to the loftiest of heights, to love and cleave to Him.

In summary, the exalted level of *yiras haromemus* and love of Hashem results from the performance of the entire Torah and all of its mitzvos; whereas *yiras ha'onesh* causes the actual fulfillment of Torah and mitzvos.

---

1   This pertains to the first verse mentioned in the commentary on *Mishneh Torah*, which teaches us that fear — *yiras ha'onesh* — causes the fulfillment of Torah and mitzvos.

2   This pertains to the second verse, which teaches us that mitzvos lead to fear. In other words, mitzvos purify him, rendering him fit to comprehend *yiras haromemus*.

FEAR OF HASHEM IS ONE OF THE 613 MITZVOS

We must understand that the fear of Hashem is not only the cause to observe and fulfill the Torah's dictates. Rather, it comprises a purpose in and of itself and is universally considered to be one of the 613 commandments, namely, "Hashem, your God, shall you fear" (*Devarim* 6:13). In his *Sefer HaMitzvos*, the Rambam, *zt"l*, writes that this mitzvah refers to the fear of punishment: "This is one of the 613 mitzvos. The Almighty commanded us to believe in His awesomeness and to fear Him. We are not to be like the nonbelievers, who pursue the whims of their hearts and freely follow their desires. Rather, we must constantly live with the fear of His punishment. This is taught in the verse: 'Hashem, your God, shall you fear.' "

THE TERM "FEAR OF HASHEM" INCLUDES BOTH ASPECTS

It is important to note that it does not seem to be the Rambam's intention to eliminate the exalted virtue of *yiras haromemus* from this verse. In the second chapter of *Hilchos Yesodei HaTorah*, he writes, "This glorious and awesome God commanded us to love and fear Him, as it says: 'Hashem, your God, shall you fear.' When a person contemplates His wondrous deeds and creations, he is immediately filled with love for Him. When he meditates on these things, he immediately recoils in fear, realizing that he is an insignificant creation — lowly and dark." Now, we know that this is the way of *yiras haromemus*. It would thus appear that this precept — "Hashem, your God, shall you fear" — includes every aspect of Heavenly fear. This is because logic dictates that one must fear Him with both *yiras ha'onesh* and *yiras haromemus*. When Chazal mention the fear of Hashem, the term includes both aspects, and it must be understood according to its context in any given discussion.

THE OUTER KEYS

Let us now consider the Talmudic passage in which the Sages likened the fear of Heaven to the outer keys of a treasure house. In this discussion, they were relating to Heavenly fear in its role as a causative factor — "So that a person will tremble and fear, and observe the mitzvos" (*Rashi*). The intention of this dictum is unquestionably the fear of Divine punishment. This is the first cause, for it generates the actual fulfillment of the deed. This is what Rashi meant by his statement: "So that a person will tremble and fear, and observe the mitzvos." Our Sages also intended the fear of Divine punishment in the statement: "Anyone whose fear of sin takes precedence over his wisdom, his wisdom will endure."

The comparison of Heavenly fear to a key that opens the gates to Torah and Divine service is a profound teaching. Implicit within it is the following syllogism: Just as it is impossible to open a bolted iron door without the key, so, too, it is impossible to open the gates of mitzvah observance without the key of Heavenly fear. Even if one has acquired some Torah knowledge, his knowledge alone will not insure his fulfillment of the commandments. The first indispensable step is to fortify himself with an adequate supply of Heavenly fear.

THE ESSENCE OF THE YETZER TOV AND THE YETZER HARA

Indeed, in his *Iggeres HaMussar*, our revered teacher [Rabbi Yisrael Salanter] writes: "There is a compromise of both schools of thought concerning the essence of the *yetzer tov* and the *yetzer hara*. [We find that the *ba'alei Mussar* disagree as to what is the exact nature of man's inclinations.] One school of thought holds that the *yetzer hara* is the spirit of impurity in man that leads him to sin, whereas the *yetzer tov* is the force of holiness within him that draws him to the good. The other school of thought views the *yetzer hara* as the power of desire which looks solely to satisfy the needs of the moment. Conversely, the *yetzer tov* is the power of the intellect which considers the consequences that an action will beget.

"In fact, both outlooks are correct and do not contradict each other. The evil inclination encompasses both the power of desire and the spirit of impurity. Likewise, the good inclination is a properly functioning intellect that considers the outcome of an action, as well as the spirit of holiness within man."

DUST FROM THE GROUND

Insofar as man is a physical being — "dust from the ground" (*Bereishis* 2:7) — his heart inclines to the material. Therefore, he desires to "eat, drink, and be merry." He loves wealth and fortune, and longs for honor and dominion. He is full of arrogance and seeks to delight in bodily comforts, running after worldly pleasures and debasing himself with every type of ignoble vice.

A MIGHTY KING

Together with this, the inclination of his heart contemplates only negative thoughts during his every waking moment. This is the evil inclination, rooted in man's spiritual component. Shlomo HaMelech, the wisest of all men, depicted the *yetzer hara* with a compelling image. We read in *Koheles* (9:14–15): "There was a small town with only a few inhabitants; and a mighty king came upon it and surrounded it, and built great siege works over it. Present in the city was a poor, wise man who by his wisdom saved the town." In the Talmud (*Nedarim* 32a), Chazal explain that this verse is a description of man: "A small town," this is the body. "With only a few inhabitants," these are the limbs. "A mighty king came upon it and surrounded it," this is the evil inclination. "Present in the city was a poor, wise man," this is the good inclination.

MAN MUST ALWAYS BE PREPARED

This comparison teaches us that man must always be prepared to defend himself against an organized assault launched by the evil inclination, which seeks to swallow him into the bottomless depths of worldly desire and pleasure. Our enemy is a great and powerful king, who is free of all distractions. The *yetzer hara* has no wife and children and does not have to worry about supporting a family. Neither is he distracted by the vanities of this world. He does naught but fulfill the obligation for which he was created. He executes his tasks with extreme efficiency, with no sign of laziness or weariness.

MAN'S ONLY HOPE IS TO FORTIFY HIMSELF WITH THE FEAR OF THE ALMIGHTY GOD

What of man? He is weak like a worm, overwhelmed with toil and an unending workload. Because of this, his mind is confused and his intellect thick, and he gratefully slumbers in the beckoning arms of laziness. Through the siren call of base desires, he is stricken with blindness and confusion. How can he face his enemy and not fall slain at his feet in the heat of battle? What is the strategy to end the raging war against the evil inclination, and the secret to stop the spirit of desire that roars unendingly like a churning sea? Man's only hope is to fortify himself with the fear of the Almighty God and His punishment. This fear is an impregnable fortress that can deliver him from every enemy and attack. It is mighty enough to bind his desires and prevent the evil intentions of his heart from bursting into a destructive rampage. Only it can serve as a valorous right arm to still the wild tempest of the evil inclination and allow man to emerge victorious in battle. All of this was revealed to us by the wisest of men, Shlomo HaMelech. It was he who taught us that the only effective weapon in the battle against the *yetzer hara* is the fear of Hashem, like arrows in an archer's quiver.

GOD WILL CALL YOU TO ACCOUNT

We read in *Koheles* (11:9): "Rejoice, young man, in your childhood; let your heart cheer you in the days of your youth; follow the path of your heart and the sight of your eyes — but be aware that for all these things God will call you to account." In *Maseches Shabbos* (63b), Chazal explain that the words "Rejoice, young man, in your childhood; let your heart cheer you in the days of your youth; follow the path of your heart and the sight of your eyes" is the *yetzer hara* speaking. Whereas, "...but be aware that for all these things God will call you to account" is the *yetzer tov*.

A CHAOTIC BATTLE THAT RAGES WITH FEROCIOUS INTENSITY

Let us understand the import of these profound words. With this verse, Shlomo HaMelech is explaining the nature and parameters of the war between these two forces — a chaotic battle that rages with ferocious intensity. The *yetzer hara* stands on a cliff edge, entrenched in the fortress of desire and gazing out at all the pleasures and delights of this world. The *yetzer tov* is en-camped opposite it, facing an entirely different direction. It stands atop the mountain of fear, overlooking the exalted heights of trepidation over Heav-enly retribution. The evil inclination casts his net to ensnare a man with his desires, urging him, "Rejoice, young man, in your childhood; let your heart cheer you in the days of your youth; follow the path of your heart and the sight of your eyes." He entices you, telling you to give delights to your soul and sweet honey to your palate, and not to glance behind you. The *yetzer tov,* however, destroys the former's snare with the power of fear. He calls to man in the name of Hashem, the God of Judgment, saying to him, "In the days of your childhood, remember your Creator. To Him is vengeance and retribu-tion, and He will bring judgment to every hidden thing."

A BATTLE BETWEEN DESIRE AND FEAR

Now, we see that even if a man is overflowing and replete with the fear of God, he is still faced with warfare — a battle between desire and fear. The power of fear enables him to fortify himself and repulse his enemies. Yet if a man's heart is empty of the fear of God and His punishment, he will have no hope of victory. He is as one poised for combat, yet lacking any weapon; nei-ther bow and arrow, nor sword, nor spear. Even if the *yetzer tov* shouts and strains its voice from crying out all day long, "Be aware that for all these things God will call you to account," it will not avail him — like a cry in the wilderness with no one to hear it. All this is because the person has not set the fear of Hashem before his eyes; he does not tremble at the prospect of judgment, nor does he fear Divine justice.

2

THE ECLIPSED
AWARENESS

YIRAS SHAMAYIM IS CONCEALED WITHIN THE DEPTHS OF A TENT

WHERE IS THIS KEY OF FEAR OF HASHEM and His punishment to be found? This holy gemstone does not lie exposed in the street, simply to be picked up by any and every passerby. It is not to be obtained by one who casually seeks it. Rather, it is concealed within the depths of a tent, surrounded with reinforced bulwarks and sealed off with iron locks. It is hidden from the sight of the masses, and they do not know of its location.

FEAR OF PHYSICAL DANGER

This quality of fear is unique, different, and distinct from all other types of fear that prevail in the world. For example, it is completely natural to be afraid of dangerous people or threatening situations. Logic and experience dictate that we should fear such things. Hence, by dint of his innate intelligence, a person will experience fear and terror. When confronted with the unknown, fear will instinctually enter his heart and his senses will be heightened. All the chambers of his heart will tremble, and his face will reveal his terror. It is true that man has the power to overcome and dampen his fear: sometimes a person will voluntarily endanger himself, for example, by traveling through an unsafe area. Yet his bones will still convulse in fright, even as they obey the dictates of his will. This is because nobody has the self-control to banish the essence of fear from his soul. There exists no counsel to entirely neutralize it and remove it from one's mind and heart.

YIRAS SHAMAYIM IS NOT FOUND INNATELY WITHIN MAN'S NATURE

However, the fear of Hashem and His punishment is in an entirely different category. This fear is not found innately within man's nature. Neither does belief, knowledge, or intellectual awareness instill it within his heart. It also has no effect on his senses. We see that man has the knowledge, intellectual understanding, and belief that Hashem is aware of all a person's deeds, and that nothing is hidden from His eyes. Likewise, man knows that the Almighty will judge his every action. He will open His ledger and review all the days of a person's life, and recompense each individual according to his conduct and the fruit of his labors. As a man's own hands have done, so shall be done to him. If he walked in the valley of the shadow of death, he will receive great and terrible judgments. If he followed the upright path, he will merit to bask in the light of life, to delight in Hashem with eternal pleasantness and rejoicing. However, his realization of this does not necessarily affect his conduct, and his belief is often at great odds with his behavior. This discrepancy is manifest in both his relationship with the Almighty and with his fellowman.

YIRAS SHAMAYIM RESULTS FROM FAITH AND INTELLECTUAL ENDEAVOR

The reason for this is because this fear — the fear of Heaven — is not a natural component of man's nature. Rather, it results from the power of faith and intellectual endeavor. Because it is not apprehended by the senses, man does not set it before his eyes. He is not afraid of the awesome reckoning that awaits him, and the prospect of judgment does not set him trembling in fright. Neither is he gripped with terror over the horrific punishments he will face. The thought of death does not faze him, and he does not fear the fiery sword. He is not even overcome with trepidation at the very moment he commits a sin. He will transgress with a clear conscience — tranquilly and at ease, with no second thought. This numbness affects the positive aspects of his behavior as well. His heart does not quicken in anticipation of the eternal spiritual bliss and delight that awaits him. His performance of the mitzvos is blasé, and he does not rejoice over the reward awaiting him, like one who found a great treasure. Similarly, he is not bothered by the paucity of good deeds in his possession.

HIS COUNTENANCE WILL THEN RADIATE WITH THE FEAR OF GOD

Nor will he ever grieve over this lacking — unless he sets his heart to seek wisdom, Mussar, and the fear of God. If he does so, his effort will stand him in good stead, enabling him to attain it and implant it within his soul. His countenance will then radiate with the fear of God, and it will spread throughout the chambers of his heart. All the foundations of his body will tremble, and his entire being will be suffused with trepidation and the fear of Heaven. Likewise, he will love and desire spiritual wealth more than physical riches, and fear losing the great reward of *olam haba*. As Chazal tell us in the Talmud (*Berachos* 33b): "Everything is in the hands of Heaven, except for the fear of Heaven." We infer from this that man is capable of obtaining this fear of Hashem, may His Name be blessed.

WHY IS FEAR OF HASHEM NOT NATURALLY ANCHORED IN THE HEART OF MAN?

Thus far, we have described the difference between the fear of Heaven and the fear of earthly things. However, the insight we have arrived at brings a compelling question in its wake: What is the reason for this astonishing phenomenon? Why is fear of Hashem and His punishment not naturally anchored in the heart of the man of faith, without him having to toil in order to obtain it? Why is it so different from all the other fears in the world, which enter his heart unbidden and involuntarily? Is there a greater thing in existence to dread than the fires of Gehinnom? This inextinguishable fire consumes everything, from the soul unto the flesh. What we know as physical fire is only one-sixtieth of this eternal and fundamental spiritual fire, and were all the world to be a burning conflagration, it would still pale in comparison. Why, then, has the portion of fear accorded this great and awesome fire been so diminished in this world?

HOW WILL THE FEAR OF HASHEM ENTER MAN'S HEART?

Let us reflect on this well. The general knowledge of all these things is not concealed from man's eyes. He is aware that Hashem gazes unwaveringly upon all his ways. He also realizes what awaits him after his demise, when he will stand in judgment before the Throne of the Righteous Judge and face His awesome and terrible judgments. Yet despite this awareness, his senses are not stimulated, and the fear of Heaven and the terror of His punishments do not burn in his heart. If so, we may rightfully ask, will his efforts to attain this Heavenly fear be of any avail? This phenomenon has no parallel in worldly affairs and man's response to natural calamity. When the mind considers something as fitting to be afraid of, a person's heart is automatically filled with fear, with no effort on his part whatsoever. On the other hand, if circumstances do not dictate that a person enter into a state of fear and trepidation, then no power or strategy or intellectual exercise can induce him to do so. If so, where is the fear of Hashem to be found? How can it be attained through effort and exertion?

THE CAPACITY TO FEAR IS NOT A TRAIT SHARED EQUALLY BY ALL MEN

It is an amazing fact that the capacity to fear is not a trait shared equally by all men. Rather, it fluctuates according to the natural temperament of each individual. Some people are naturally faint-hearted from the moment of birth. They fear the sound of leaves rustling in the breeze, and the thought of any mishap — remote though it may be — disturbs their peace of mind. Other people are naturally strong-hearted and courageous; even the sound of a lion roaring in the forest does not intimidate them. Such people only experience fear when they understand that they are facing a real and immediate danger. Interestingly, we also find that there is a correlation between fear and intelligence. "The wise man has his eyes in his head" (*Koheles* 2:14). This means that he anticipates danger and thereby avoids it. On the other hand, "A fool walks in darkness" (ibid.). That is to say, he closes his eyes from seeing and his heart from understanding. He does not contemplate harm nor evil — until the net is spread beneath his feet.

FEAR OF HASHEM DOES NOT CORRELATE TO THE MECHANICS OF WORLDLY FEAR

It would be logical to assume that the fear of Hashem and His punishments operates in a similar fashion — despite the fact that it is weak and quite unlike worldly fear. Thus, one's fear of Heaven should be relative to his temperament and depth of wisdom, and we should expect to find various levels of this fear in different types of people. For instance, there should be a marked difference in one's Heavenly fear if he is wise or foolish, cowardly or bold. Astonishingly, we find that even in this area, fear of Hashem does not correlate to the mechanics of worldly fear. It is not bound within man's nature and temperament, and neither is it consistent with his wisdom and intelligence. Thus, in the mechanics of Heavenly fear, the wise man has no advantage over the fool, and the timid person has no primacy over the courageous one. Rather, all men are of the same spirit: "Peace, peace," they cry, and there is no fear (cf. *Yirmeyahu* 6:14). They blithely go about their lives unafraid of the Creator, thinking that their lot will be peaceful.

THE MECHANICS OF HEAVENLY FEAR ARE BEYOND HUMAN COMPREHENSION

I believe that the reason for this is because the mechanics of Heavenly fear are beyond human intelligence and comprehension. In other words, once we see how fear of the physical works, it should follow that spiritual fear operates in a similar manner. As we shall explain, the reason it does not is something that can only be grasped with Divine assistance. In his *Mishneh Torah* (*Hilchos Teshuvah*, ch. 5), the Rambam tells us that the ability to choose is an essential principle of man's makeup. This is the pillar that upholds Torah and mitzvos: man is not dictated to nor forced to choose any course of action. Heaven does not influence him to choose either the path of righteousness or evil. Rather, he himself, from his own knowledge and volition, turns to whatever path he desires. As the Rambam writes (ibid., section 4): "If the Almighty were to decree that a man be either righteous or wicked, or if there was something that inclined him in one direction from the moment of birth… what room would there be for the Torah? On what basis could the *rasha* be punished or the *tzaddik* rewarded?"

THE CONCEPT OF REWARD SEEMS TOTALLY INCONCEIVABLE

At first glance, the concept of reward seems totally inconceivable. We understand that Hashem dispenses justice to those who violate His commandments, each man according to the measure of his transgressions. However, what place is there for mitzvah performance to be rewarded? In the final analysis, the reason a person inclines himself to the goodly path is because he fears Divine retribution. Admittedly, this fear is not within him at the time of his birth. Yet once it materializes and becomes a force that fuels his decisions, he is no longer left with any choice in the matter. Indeed, even before he was born, Heaven arranged a terrifying incentive to spur him on: a deep pit that burns ferociously, waiting to swallow him into its bowels. If so, what greater coercion could there be to go on the upright path, and why is reward given if one chooses good?

FEAR OF HASHEM IS INTENTIONALLY EXCLUDED FROM MAN

With the revelation of a crucial aspect concerning the acquisition of Heavenly fear, this question is easily answered. It is indeed true that this fear is not naturally found in man's heart. Moreover it is even intentionally excluded from him. Dread of the Almighty's punishment does not consume a person, and the fiery pit below does not upset his complacency. The prospect of Divine judgment does not faze him, and the thought of Gehinnom does not frighten him. Rather, a person must toil and exert effort to acquire this fear, and the acquirement thereof enables him to walk on the path of good.

Thus, this Heavenly fear itself is his portion and the fruit of his efforts. This acquisition is his accomplishment, and he justly deserves reward for having attained it.

With this idea in mind, we are now in a position to answer the questions we asked above: What is the reason for the unique property of *yiras Hashem* — that it is not naturally anchored in man's heart — and why has it been deliberately withheld from the perception of human intelligence? Second, what is the source of this fear in the soul that labors to acquire it?

HASHEM DESIRED TO GRANT MAN ETERNAL PLEASURE

As we mentioned above, this entire concept is beyond human comprehension. It is clearly from Hashem, and it is in accordance with His will. We know that the Almighty placed man in this world so that He could shower him with goodness in the World to Come. Hashem desired to grant man an everlasting inheritance and eternal pleasure, namely, to delight in Him and bask in the radiance of the *Shechinah* (the Divine Presence). How does a person merit to attain such sublime reward? Through his efforts in Torah study and his labors in mitzvah observance. [The reader is encouraged to refer to the first chapter of *Mesillas Yesharim*, where this idea is dealt with at length.] It was in order to bestow this eternal reward upon man that Hashem gave him free will, so that his deeds would be in accord solely with his own desire and consent. There is absolutely nothing forcing man or pulling him to follow either an upright path or a wicked one. Hence, through his freely choosing the good path, man will merit to receive his reward.

INNATE YIRAS SHAMAYIM WOULD INFRINGE ON HIS FREE WILL

We can now understand why *yiras Shamayim* is not naturally a part of man's makeup — for if the fear of Hashem and His punishment were implanted in man's heart from the outset, this would be the driving force behind his performance of good deeds. His natural fear of incurring Hashem's wrath would be the reason for his walking on the upright path. This, of course, would infringe on his free will, and his reward would correspondingly be diminished. Hashem, the Source of all that is good, wanted free choice to be entirely in the hands of man, to enlarge the boundaries of human reward as much as possible.

HASHEM REMOVED THE FEAR THAT FORCES A PERSON TO SERVE HIM

The creation of man was effected with astonishing wisdom. The joining of the spiritual with the physical, the construction of the body with its myriad capabilities, is an unrivaled wonder. So, too, one of the marvels of creation, among the multitude of powers that the Creator gathered together within the body, is a natural fear of all things injurious to him. However, in order to increase man's free will and subsequent reward, He minimized the boundary of this fear's power, so that the awe of Him and the dread of His punishment — whether to the body or the soul — would not be a part of man's nature. He also removed the fear of all things that could force a person to serve Him — such as the fear of death. Thus, free choice was given into man's hand.

LOGICALLY, MAN SHOULD GO THROUGH LIFE EMPTY OF YIRAS HASHEM

This entire phenomenon — the removal of Heavenly fear from man's nature — is beyond the power of human intellect to comprehend. We can say only that it is a spiritual matter, a Divine edict that only He in His wisdom could decree and fulfill. It would seem to follow, then, that there should be no way for a person to implant this fear within himself. Logically, man should go through life void and hollow, his heart empty of *yiras Hashem*.

THE FEAR OF HASHEM IS ESSENTIAL FOR MAN

Ultimately, however, the fear of Hashem is essential for man — for *yiras Shamayim* is the beginning of wisdom, and with it, man is empowered to be victorious in battle against the evil inclination. Moreover, the fear of Hashem and His punishment is the key to the exterior gate that opens the path to Hashem — through the observance of the Torah and the fulfillment of the mitzvos. As Rav Chaim Vital, *zt"l*, writes, "When one comes to purify himself and draw close [to the Almighty], the beginning of everything is *yiras Hashem* — to attain the dread of His punishment."

THE ALMIGHTY TRANSFERRED THE AWE OF HEAVEN INTO MAN'S HANDS

For this reason, the Almighty in His wisdom saw fit to transfer the awe of Heaven into man's hands, so that it would be dependent on his knowledge and be within his jurisdiction. Man can thus master it according to his will: whether to quail in terror of Him and His punishment, or to refrain from incorporating this fear into his consciousness. Granted, the acquisition of this fear may seem unattainable from our limited perspective. However, nothing is impossible for the Omnipotent One, and just as He withheld *yiras Shamayim* from man's nature, so, too, He opened a portal of hope and set within man the ability to obtain it — if he so desires. Thus, everything is up to man: if he chooses to be lazy and remain in a slumbering daze all of his life, he will remain naked and empty of this fear. He will go in darkness, and his soul will not shine with the sublime light of Torah and mitzvos. However, if he wants to attain *yiras Shamayim* — to seek it as if it were a buried treasure — then he will find it. Then the dread of Hashem and His judgments will be always before his eyes. He will be sheltered in the shadow of its wings, so that he can fulfill the entire Torah and all of its mitzvos.

THE RESTORATION OF FEAR IS A SPIRITUAL MATTER

We thus see that although *yiras Shamayim* is withheld from man's nature, it is within his power to obtain it. However, when this fear enters the soul of one who seeks it, it is not the result of intellectual endeavor. Rather, it is a spiritual matter, springing forth from the hand of the Almighty and in accord with His will. This concept — that the essential choice of whether to fear or not is within man's province — is a phenomenon that is beyond human comprehension, but nothing is too wondrous for the Almighty.

THE INCREASE OF REWARD

Now, since the choice of whether or not to fear has been given to man, his reward is correspondingly increased — specifically, by a factor of two: On the one hand, there is the aspect of the work involved. Man must toil to acquire this fear, for it is not naturally found in his heart, and he must labor to attain it. It is well known how intensive this labor is, and just as there is no end to his efforts, so, too, there is no end to his reward. On the other hand, there is the aspect of free choice. Even if the fulfillment of the entire Torah is merely the consequence of this fear, stemming directly from its power, the essential *yiras Shamayim* is still the fruit of his own decision. Its acquisition is an absolute free choice that stems solely from man's own volition, and without it there is nothing forcing him to observe the Torah's commandments. Thus, even though the mitzvos performed by a person are the result of compulsion out of fear, they are still considered as falling within the province of free will. His mitzvah observance is the consequence of the first cause; it is the fruit of his absolute, free choice to cultivate the fear of Hashem. Therefore, the reward for his deeds is accorded to him in fairness and justice.

THE ATTRIBUTE OF SHAME

We read in *Chovos HaLevavos* (*Sha'ar HaBechinah*, ch. 5): "Consider the attribute of shame, which is an integral part of man's make up — truly a great and beneficial virtue.... Yet it is astonishing that while shame vis-à-vis one's fellow is naturally implanted within man...shame towards his Creator — Who is constantly aware of his every action — is not! The Almighty did this in order to prevent coercion from being the impetus for one's Divine service, and to weaken one's awareness of the obligation that is incumbent upon him. Rather, we are obligated to feel shame before Him by examining our deeds...and through the realization that He is aware of all our activities — both hidden and revealed."

We thus find that *yiras haromemus*, which is the sense of shame one has before the Creator, should properly be found in man's nature — just as the shame before his fellowman is. However, in His wisdom, the Creator withheld this sense of shame from him. In this way, there is no compulsion to serve Hashem, and man's sense of his incumbent obligation is weakened. Now, if *yiras haromemus* should be a natural component of man's makeup, then *yiras ha'onesh*, which is closer to his perception, should certainly be a part of his nature — just as the fear of every bad thing is. Yet the Almighty decreed that this fear, as well, should be eliminated from man's constitution — the intention being to eliminate all coercion to serve Him. Compulsion would cause a lessening of his free choice and a corresponding reduction of his reward.

MAN HAS THE ABILITY TO ATTAIN YIRAS HAROMEMUS

We see from the above discussion that man has the ability to attain *yiras haromemus* — to stand in fear of His exalted majesty and to feel embarrassed before Him, may His Name be blessed. We derive this from the fact the *Chovos HaLevavos* writes, "We are obligated to feel shame before Him, by examining our deeds...and through the realization that nothing is hidden from His gaze." However, the question arises, how does such an examination help? We already know that the glory of the Holy One fills the entire earth and that nothing is hidden from His gaze — yet we still remain devoid of shame! Furthermore, if what the *Chovos HaLevavos* wrote is correct — that Hashem has withheld from man's nature the sense of feeling embarrassed before Him — then what power does man have to attain it? It would thus seem that the acquisition of *yiras haromemus* is the same as that of *yiras ha'onesh* — it is a spiritual function. True, the Omniscient One withheld from human nature the sense of feeling shame in His presence. However, He also endowed man with the power to attain the awe of His majesty — if he desires to seek it.

3

ABSOLUTE FREEDOM

FREE WILL IS THE CENTRAL PILLAR UPHOLDING THE ENTIRE TORAH

THE CONCEPT OF MAN BEING ABLE to acquire *yiras Shamayim* is in accord with Chazal's statement in *Berachos* (33b): "Rebbi Chanina said: Everything is in the hands of Heaven except for the fear of Heaven, as the verse states, 'Now, O Israel, what does Hashem, your God, ask of you? Only to fear Hashem, your God' (*Devarim* 10:12)." This statement needs elucidation. After all, it is well know that man's free will is one of the basic tenets of our faith; indeed, it is the central pillar upholding the entire Torah. As the Rambam tells us in chapter 5 of *Hilchos Teshuvah*, without free choice, there is no place for punishment or reward. If so, what is Rebbi Chanina telling us that we don't already know? We must say that his intention was as follows: The Torah has unquestionably been given over to man, in accord with his agreement and free will. Thus, regardless of whether or not he fears Heaven, the choice to fulfill the commandments is in his hands. Rebbi Chanina is saying that even the essential fear of Heaven is subject to free choice. This is true even though logic would seem to dictate otherwise, as we discussed above — for thus has the Almighty decreed.

FREE CHOICE MEANS THAT THE CHOICE MUST BE ABSOLUTELY FREE

We are now in a position to more fully understand Chazal's declaration: "The only thing that the Almighty has in His treasury is a reservoir of Heavenly fear." This statement implies that the fear of Heaven is a precious virtue, exalted above all others. Wherein lies its unique value? We can explain it according to that which we have said about free choice. Obviously, free choice means that the choice must be absolutely free — with no trace of coercion whatsoever. Now, granted that someone who already possesses *yiras Shamayim* has no choice but to walk on the good and upright path — for his fear forces him to do so. However, as we have already discussed, the fear of Heaven itself is not within man's nature. Its acquisition is an exercise of free will, and it can only be obtained by one who labors to seek it. But if this is so, what is forcing a person with no *yiras Shamayim* to seek it in the first place? Now we can understand the virtue of Heavenly fear over and above the rest of the Torah. All the Torah and mitzvos are borne on the wings of fear. Yet on which wings is fear itself carried, if there is no coercion to attain it and it is totally dependent upon free choice and man's own volition? This is why its strength is so exalted and *HaKadosh Baruch Hu* has nothing in His treasure house except for it.

IF A PERSON FEARS HEAVEN, HE WILL ZEALOUSLY KEEP THE COMMANDMENTS

With this, the esoteric words of our Sages become clearer. Let us review the passage in *Maseches Shabbos* (31b), together with Rashi's commentary: "Any person who has acquired a knowledge of Torah, yet does not fear Heaven, is like a treasurer who has been entrusted with the keys to the inner vault, but does not possess the keys to the exterior door. How, then, shall he enter?" Comments Rashi: "If a person fears Heaven, he will zealously observe and perform the commandments. However, if he has no fear, he will have no respect for the Torah [that he has learned]." It is striking that the Sages compared man to a treasurer. What is the reason for this? What is true of the treasurer in this parable would seem to apply similarly to every man regarding his house: if he only has the inner keys and not the outer ones, he cannot gain access to the house. This being the case, Chazal could simply have said: "It is like a man who has the inner keys, but who does not have the outer ones. How, then, shall he enter?" What does the parable gain with the inclusion of a "treasurer"?

In their great wisdom, Chazal sought to convey an important lesson by their usage of this imagery. As we shall see, it harbors a profound intention to arouse one concerning the pursuit of Heavenly fear. If a homeowner does not have the outer key to his house, he will not simply stand outside and leave it locked and inaccessible. He will do whatever is necessary to enter, and if he cannot find the key, he will snap the lock or even break the door down. However, such is not the case with a treasurer. His job is to guard other people's money. It doesn't matter if he doesn't have the gate key, because there is nothing pressing him to go inside. It is possible that the gate will remain forever locked, and he will never enter the treasure house.

THERE IS NOTHING WHATSOEVER FORCING US TO SEEK YIRAS SHAMAYIM

Our Sages compared the fear of Heaven to the outer keys which open the gates of Torah and Divine service.[3] A person without the fear of Heaven is like one who does not have the keys to open the outer gate. Despite this, let it not be assumed that he will be forced to obtain the key of Heavenly fear to open the gate to Hashem. He may simply stand outside — because the fear of Heaven is itself the key to open the gate, the cause to fulfill the entire Torah. If someone already holds this key of Heavenly fear, then he can open the gates of Torah and Divine service, for the "key" compels him to scrupulously observe the mitzvos. However, if one does not already fear, then what is forcing him to try and obtain this key in the first place? This is something that is solely within the province of man's free will, which in turn is dependent upon his agreement and volition. If a person does not turn his heart to seek it, it is very likely that the key of Heavenly fear will never be in his hand and the gates of Torah and Divine service will remain firmly bolted. It is for this reason that he was compared to a treasurer who was not given the outer keys;

---

3   The reader may wonder about this characterization of the parable, for Chazal themselves said that the person in question already has Torah, he just lacks fear of Heaven. If so, how could Rav Blazer understand it as saying that the fear of Heaven opens up the gates to Torah? The answer is, true, the person in the parable has Torah — however, it is only on an intellectual level. When the Rav states that Heavenly fear opens up the gate of Torah, he means to say that it is only with this fear that the person's Torah will assume a living reality.

there is nothing whatsoever forcing him to seek the keys or to break the lock.

AND YOU SHALL CHOOSE LIFE

This principle is alluded to in *Parashas Nitzavim*, where we read: "I have given life and death before you, blessing and curse; and you shall choose life!" (*Devarim* 30:19). At first glance, this verse is quite perplexing. We generally understand "choice" to mean that a person chooses something by observing and contemplating a selection that is before him. For example, a person has several similar samples of an item in front of him. He carefully examines each one of them and chooses the best and the most beautiful. Free choice refers to things that are very similar, and that is why they require contemplation and examination — so that he can select the best one of the group. On the other hand, alternatives which require no decision whatsoever — such as the "choice" between gold nuggets or rocks, or between wine and poison — are not subject to choice at all. Therefore, what is the relevance of choice concerning polar opposites such as life and death? Moreover, why does the verse need to say, "...and you shall choose life"? Is there anyone who has to make such a "choice," who won't choose life?

LIFE AND DEATH ARE EQUAL IN MAN'S NATURE

In truth, this verse is revealing one of the deep and wondrous secrets of creation, concerning the ways of Heavenly fear: 1) By nature, man is devoid of *yiras Hashem*. 2) He still has the power to acquire this fear, if he desires to seek it. As we have mentioned above, both of these ideas are contrary to what reason would lead us to think. Life is synonymous with Torah and mitzvos, and death is synonymous with sin and iniquity. It is thus logical to assume that the love and pursuit of life, and fear and revulsion of death, are firmly fixed in man's nature. The verse tells us that this assumption is incorrect. In His great wisdom, the Creator withdrew the awe and dread of Divine punishment from man's heart. Likewise, He withdrew any fear that might force a person to perform the Divine service, such as the fear of death. Thus it is that life and death are equal in man's nature. If his spirit is aroused to pursue his heart's desires, he will follow the path of death, despite all that is good in life.

AN UNIMPORTANT ITEM CANNOT BE CONSIDERED SOMETHING THAT CAN BE GIVEN

This is the meaning of the verse: "I have given life and death before you." Chazal tell us that there is no legal concept of "giving" regarding something that is worth less than a *perutah* (the smallest value of a coin). This is because an item with no importance cannot be considered as something that can be given, and all the more so something with no value whatsoever. This is also true regarding something deadly and dangerous that people are afraid to touch. Since no one is willing to receive it, the idea of giving cannot be applied to it. This being the case, if man had *yiras Shamayim* as an inherent trait — if he naturally feared the Almighty's punishment and shunned the path of death — it would not be appropriate to say, "I have given life and death before you." Death would not be within the boundaries of something that could be given, for man would only desire to receive life — the path of Torah and mitzvos. Death, which is the way of lust and sin, would be something to avoid like the plague, and without acceptance, there is no giving. Yet once Hashem decreed that His fear be withheld from man's nature, Divine judgment and punishment do not disturb his equanimity, and even the day of death does not make him apprehensive. Therefore, the verse states, "I have given life and death before you." Both are valid options in man's eyes, for he will also love sin and lust, even though death and the fearsome pit lie at that path's end.

Still, a person should not think in despair, "If Hashem has promulgated this decree, who can annul it? If I love the path of death, how can I come to hate it?"

HASHEM HAS OPENED A WINDOW OF HOPE

Concerning this, the verse says, "…and you shall choose life" — for in truth, the love of life is in your hands. Hashem has opened a window of hope and enabled man to attain His fear, to love life and spurn death. Wherein does this hope lie? With free choice. When a person wants to choose good and contemplate the virtues of life — both the fleeting existence of this world and the delight of eternal life in the World to Come — as opposed to the bitterness of death and fearsome judgments, he will understand the fear of Hashem. He will choose life — to love and embrace it.

"I HAVE GIVEN LIFE AND DEATH BEFORE YOU"

With this idea, we can understand a statement made by Chazal in the *Sifri*: "The verse states: 'I have given life and death before you; blessing and curse.' Perhaps Israel will say, 'Since the Almighty has set two paths before us, we will walk on whichever one we desire.' Therefore, the verse concludes: '...and you shall choose life.' " Incredible! Could anyone seriously think that a person has permission to go on whichever path he wants? What about the Torah that the Jewish people received on Har Sinai? Moreover, exactly how is this claim derived from the fact that Hashem set two paths before them?

The answer is that this midrash parallels the concept we have set forth above. The path of Torah and mitzvos is the course that uplifts people to all that is good in life, whereas the wicked path of iniquity and sin is the way of death. If so, logic dictates that man's natural inclination would be to love the former and fear the latter. If that were the case, everyone would direct his steps to the path of Torah and mitzvos — the way of life. However, since the Almighty withheld *yiras Shamayim* from man's nature, the way of death also seems sweet and alluring. Hence, the verse states: "I have given life and death before you." In other words, death is also a valid option in man's eyes. If so, what power does man have to reject it? As the *Sifri* says: "Perhaps Israel will say, 'Since the Almighty had set two paths before us, we will walk on whichever one we desire.' " Both paths are defined as being "given" before us, for man has been granted the ability to view the path of death as a viable alternative — one that he can love and willingly accept. If so, perhaps we will walk on whichever path our hearts lead us, and if a person desires the path of death, he will not have the power to conquer this desire and incline himself to life. In order to refute this notion, the verse tells us, "...and you shall choose life." Despite all this, the love of life and the hatred of death are in your hands. If you employ your free will to contemplate these two paths, then you will surely understand the difference between them — and you will choose life!

4

CONTEMPLATION AND REFLECTION

THE PROGRAM TO OBTAIN YIRAS SHAMAYIM

WE HAVE THUS FAR ESTABLISHED that Hashem withheld the fear of Heaven from man's nature, and that it can only be acquired if one labors to seek it. If so, a crucial question arises: What is the program that a person must pursue in order to unearth this precious treasure and obtain the key of *yiras Shamayim?*

THE ACQUISITION OF HEAVENLY FEAR

Scrutinizing the words of Chazal, we find that the acquisition of Heavenly fear is facilitated by meditating on all matters which lead to wisdom and Mussar — for example, by contemplating the concept of reward and punishment, by considering His influence over our affairs, and by pondering over the munificence that He showers upon all His creations. It is important to realize that simple knowledge of, and faith in, these concepts will not make a deep and lasting mark on the soul. However, profound contemplation of them has the power to move worlds, to impress the spirit of Heavenly fear on all the powers of the soul. When one engages in such reflection, *yiras Shamayim* will pour into him like water and flow through his bones like oil. The fear of the Almighty will be always before him, and all his senses will be inundated with *yiras Hashem.*

IT IS UNIVERSALLY KNOWN THAT HASHEM WILL JUDGE A PERSON FOR ALL HIS ACTIONS

Chazal teach in *Pirkei Avos* (2:1): "Rabbi says: ...Calculate the loss of a mitzvah against its reward, and the reward of a sin against its loss." Similarly, we learned in the third chapter (*mishnah* 1): "Akavia ben Mahalalel says: Consider three things and you will not come into the grip of sin: ...'Whence you came?' — from a putrid drop; 'whither you go?' — to a place of dust, worms, and maggots; 'and before Whom you will give justification and reckoning?' — before the King Who reigns over kings, the Holy One, Blessed is He." At first glance, this idea is incomprehensible! How will engaging in this calculation and contemplation prevent a person from sinning? Is there a person alive who does not understand the concept of reward and punishment? Does anyone not know that man is made of dust, and that in the end he will return to the earth and to the maggots and worms? Is it not universally known that Hashem will judge a person for all his actions — even those that are hidden from the sight of other men? Yet we see that these awesome realities make no impression on man's soul, and they neither cause him to fear Hashem nor to walk in His ways and abandon evil! Indeed, man is immersed in evil and wallows in transgression.

INTENSE CONTEMPLATION

The key to understanding Chazal's advice lies in a careful examination of their phraseology. It may be true that man is aware of the reality of [our temporal] existence, but this knowledge alone does not bring a person to fear the Almighty. However, there is a more profound level of knowledge that can engender this fear. What is needed is intense contemplation of the three ideas mentioned above, with the depths of one's intellect, sincerity of heart, and vivid use of the imagination. In keeping with this notion, let us consider a statement made by the Vilna Gaon in his commentary on the *Shulchan Aruch*. We read (*Shulchan Aruch, Orach Chaim* 229), "One who sees a rainbow should recite [the following blessing].... However, it is forbidden to look at it excessively." Writes the Gra: "The Tur and the Rida ask how it can be forbidden to look excessively, being that it is necessary to look at it in order to recite the blessing? The answer is, the prohibition is not against looking at it at all, but against staring at it intently." So, too, with the Tanna's statement: "Consider [lit. "look at"] three things and you will not come into the grip of sin...." The "looking" here refers to intensive contemplation and in-depth study, extending over a lengthy period of time. Moreover, it is important to stress that engaging in such contemplation for only one or two times will not make an impression on the soul. This is particularly true concerning one whose heart is as if made of stone. Yet to the degree that a person contemplates the three aforementioned things on a daily basis — each man according to his temperament, affairs, and character traits — there will most assuredly be an impact.

Perhaps the reader is surprised that the focus of this accounting concerns such obvious concepts as the beginning and end of existence and the judgment of one's actions. True, man's familiarity with these things does not bring him disconcertment or cause his heart to soften and allow the fear of Heaven to enter. If so, one may ask, of what benefit and advantage is such contemplation, when even without it he is already aware of these ideas?

HASHEM ENDOWED MAN WITH THE POWER TO RESTORE THIS FEAR

As we have already stated previously, all of this is beyond human comprehension. In His wisdom and omnipotence, the Creator limited the power of *yirah* within man, withholding the fear and dread of punishment from his nature. Likewise, Hashem endowed man with the power to restore this fear to his soul. If man desires to toil and seek it out, he will find the fear of Hashem, wisdom, and Mussar.

CONSIDER THE ACCOUNT OF THE WORLD

This idea of profound contemplation is seen in a statement by Chazal, which exegetically explains the following verse (*Bamidbar* 21:27): "Regarding this the *moshlim* [lit. "the poets," but also able to mean "rulers"] would say, 'Come to Cheshbon' [in the simple meaning, the name of a place, but also able to mean "account"]." Comment the Sages (*Bava Basra* 78b): " 'Regarding this the *moshlim'* — i.e., those who rule over their evil inclination — 'would say, "Come to Cheshbon" ' — i.e., let us consider the *cheshbon* [account] of the world: the loss incurred through the performance of a mitzvah, as opposed to the reward secured thereby, and the benefit received from a transgression, as opposed to the loss it entails." It would seem from this passage that only those who rule over their evil inclination — in other words, those who have been victorious in the battle against the evil inclination — can offer this trustworthy advice to "consider the account of the world." The *Mesillas Yesharim* writes similarly (ch. 3): "This reliable advice could not be given nor truly perceived except by those who have already escaped the clutches of the evil inclination and rule over it." At first glance, this concept is bewildering: What is so wise and profound about this counsel? On the contrary, the soundness of such a strategy to enable one to depart from evil and turn to good seems simple and obvious!

The answer is as follows: It is true that these ideas are revealed and known to all, even before one makes such an accounting — however, they do not make an impression on the heart. Nevertheless, one should not think in despair, "I know all this and believe in it. I understand that mitzvos are rewarded and transgressions punished — yet the fear of Hashem still remains a distant concept to me. Of what benefit, then, are all these accountings?"

THESE WARRIORS KNOW THAT SUCCESS IS POSSIBLE

Instead, let such a person turn to those who rule over the evil inclination, those who have already successfully engaged the enemy in the battle against the *yetzer hara*. Through first-hand experience, these warriors know that success is possible. They recognize that faith and knowledge alone — lacking conviction and without reckoning or cognizance — will not bear any fruit. However, when a person has the will to seek wisdom and Mussar, reckoning and knowledge (and there is no reckoning without contemplation of "the account of the world"), then he will be empowered to win the battle and rule his *yetzer hara*. Therefore, only the rulers of their evil inclination — those who have already conquered the enemy — can give advice and impart their wisdom: "Let us consider the account of the world."

REPEATEDLY VERBALIZING THE STATEMENTS OF CHAZAL

Man has no control over his spirit to stop the profusion of disturbing thoughts that fill his heart, profaning him with the futilities of the world and the troubles of life. He is also incapable of purifying his thoughts from the material vanities of the world so that he can sit silently, in solitary contemplation of "the account of the world." Moreover, the fear of Hashem involves many calculations, and man does not know how to go about the task: how to seek the knowledge he needs, and what to think about and meditate on. Therefore, we must say that the contemplation of the aforementioned reckonings can only be undertaken by reading and reflecting on the contents of a Mussar *sefer* — in particular, by repeatedly verbalizing the statements of Chazal in the Talmud, Midrash, and the *Zohar HaKodosh* that discuss these matters. When a person reflects on our Sages' words in this area, his heart will ignite and his soul will catch fire. He will be garbed in fear and trepidation, and be humbled and abashed before the Creator. It was this idea that Chazal were referring to by their statement in the *Talmud Yerushalmi*: "Anyone who has never 'tasted' *aggadah* [the homiletic teachings of the Sages], has never tasted the fear of sin."

The pious luminaries who lived in the generations after the Talmudic Sages furnished wondrous advice through which one can increase and strengthen his knowledge of Heavenly fear and Mussar, and composed works dedicated to this body of wisdom. They gathered together all the statements made by Chazal in the Talmud, Midrash, and the *Zohar HaKadosh*, as well as the words of the sages versed in Kabbalah, concerning the fear of Hashem in general, and each character trait in particular. They also recorded incidents that took place in the lives of righteous people, which concern the ways of their holy service and the miracles that they experienced — for Hashem performs the will of those who fear Him. Furthermore, these works discuss all aspects of *yiras Shamayim*, personal introspection, and self-reckoning. From them, we may learn wisdom and Mussar, to fear Hashem and walk on His path.

These works include: *Chovos HaLevavos*; *Sefer Chassidim*; *Sefer Goren*

Nachon, by Rav Shlomo Gavriel; *Sefer HaYashar*, by Rabbeinu Tam; *Sha'arei Teshuvah* and *Sefer HaYirah*, by Rabbeinu Yonah; *Orchos Chaim*, by the Rosh; *Orchos Tzaddikim; Menoras HaMe'or; Maggid Mesharim*, by Rav Yosef Karo; *Tomer Devorah*, by the Ramak; *Reishis Chochmah; Sefer Chareidim*, by Rav Azkari; the writings of the Maharal; *Sha'ar HaKedushah*, by Rav Chaim Vital; the *Shlah HaKadosh; Ohr Tzaddikim*, by Rav Papirash; *Yesod Yosef*, by the Mahari M'Dubna; *Mesillas Yesharim*, by Rav Moshe Chaim Luzzato; *Nefesh HaChaim*, by Rav Chaim Volozhiner; *Yesod V'Shoresh Ha'Avodah*, by the Mahara Ziskind MeHaradno; as well as many others works devoted to the topic of Mussar.

In a certain sense, these books may be compared to the great pharmaco-poeias, which contain information relating to all the various herbs and medications that treat physical disease. Likewise, our pious sages have compiled works pertaining to Heavenly fear and Mussar, which discuss all the "herbs" and remedies to treat illness of the soul.

SIMILARITY IN THE TREATMENT OF PHYSICAL DISEASE AND ILLNESS OF THE SOUL

There is yet another similarity between the treatment of physical disease and that for illness of the soul. If a sick person is not interested in pursuing treatment, then none of the medications and remedies in the world will avail him. The same holds true concerning ailments of the soul. If a person is not concerned about *yiras Shamayim* and Mussar, then all the books in the world on this topic will not help him.

THE OBLIGATION TO STUDY MUSSAR

The pious sages who composed books on Heavenly fear and Mussar did not include a discussion on the obligation to study this topic. They understood that such study is essential in order to acquire the knowledge, wisdom, and Mussar. It was self-evident that this study brings relief to every disease and weakness of the soul. Therefore, it was obvious that every person has a sacred obligation to engage in the study of Mussar, to set organized times to study the works devoted to this topic, and to meditate deeply on their contents.

Indeed, their actions testify to their thoughts about this obligation, for why else did they labor to compose their holy works? It is thus manifest that they intended for their books to be studied and contemplated, so that one might learn to fear the great and glorious God: to walk in His path, to love Him, and to cleave unto Him.

In truth, however, no proof is required to show the necessity of this study, which revives and restores the soul and heals its malady. It is known that the greatest love in the world is that of man for himself. All a person's labor, for all the days of his life, is for himself. All of his yearning, during his entire time on the earth, is solely to gratify his body's desires. There is no end to his toil, for his soul is not satisfied with any amount of goodness. Moreover, he would give all of his wealth just to be free of any pain and affliction that might grip him. His greatest concern is to provide security for his old age — for the day fades quickly into night, and all too soon his strength will wane. Despite the fact that a man would rather not think about this time, he still wants to insure that his final days will be spent in pleasantness and tranquility.

WHEN HIS SOUL HAS SEPARATED FROM HIS BODY

Is it then possible that a person will only worry about his well-being at the time of transition — during his final moments in this world? Will he be confident about what will happen to him immediately afterwards — when his soul has separated from his body — and leave everything to chance? Every man of sound faith knows and believes that although the vessel may shatter, there is still no escape! There is no difference between the last second and the next one, except for the shedding of physicality. A person's essence remains alive, but merely assumes a different form. Our master and teacher spoke about this in one of his letters: "For the body of man is only a garment. However, his ability to feel pleasure and pain lives on, even after the covering has been stripped off."

A CRIPPLE AND A BLIND MAN

We also know that through Divine inspiration, Chazal conceived a vision that divulges the secret of the soul and uncovers the mystery of its judgment together with the body. They explain with the following parable: There was once a cripple and a blind man. They could only travel by cooperating together, with the cripple sitting on the blind man's shoulders and "steering" him in the right direction. Once, these two men decided to rob an orchard, with the cripple directing the blind man to the trees, and he himself able to reach the fruit only while on his companion's back. When the owner saw them afterwards sitting by the orchard, he accused them. They, however, both proclaimed their innocence — for how could either one of them have propagated such a crime? The owner, however, understood that they had worked together as a team, and punished them accordingly. Likewise, after the vessel of the body shatters and returns to the dust, it may be clear that it and the soul are distinct entities — and how could either one commit a sin on its own? Despite this, when the person was alive, his body and soul were bound to one another — and together, they transgressed. Thus, even in death they will not be dealt with as separate parts, each incapable of sinning on its own. Rather, just as they pursued worldly desires and delighted in physical pleasures together, so, too, will they be called to judgment together. As one, they will receive payment for their joint transgressions.

Chazal tell us that one hour of punishment in the World to Come is more bitter than all the sufferings of this world combined. Likewise, one hour of bliss in the Next World surpasses all the delights and pleasures of whatever this world has to offer. As we have already stated, man's only desire is to pursue self-gratification. Is it then possible that he will not be concerned over his fate in the afterlife — the time when his soul will be separated from his body and he will no longer be capable of performing any action or deed?

Therefore, it is self-evident that when a man diligently studies Mussar and Heavenly fear — which remind him of "the account of the world" — he will have no peace until he prepares a refuge for his soul and body. Moreover, it is known that this very study is an effective cure for the soul's disease. Now, is it conceivable that a physically ill person would not energetically follow a proven and free course treatment for his disease? Likewise, it is beyond belief that one afflicted with illness of the soul would abandon himself to the pit and not endeavor to seek a remedy for his disease — through studying works of Mussar and Heavenly fear, which are the keys to redemption and healing.

5

UNIVERSAL TASK

IT IS INCUMBENT ON EVERY PERSON TO SET A TIME FOR MUSSAR

DESPITE THE FACT THAT EARLIER SAGES did not feel it necessary to discuss the obligatory nature of Mussar study, we see that men of piety in subsequent generations did feel it was important to do so. Their works are full of unambiguous exhortations concerning the sacred obligation to engage in this study. In addition, they emphasize that it is incumbent on every person to set a time for it in his daily schedule.

EVERYONE MUST STUDY ONE PAGE FROM A MUSSAR SEFER ON A DAILY BASIS

In his work *Ya'aros D'vash*, Rav Yehonasan Eybeshitz, author of the *Urim V'Tumim*, writes (section 1, exposition 5): "The main thing is that everyone — Torah scholar and layman alike, both men and women — must study one page from a Mussar *sefer* on a daily basis. Each person should choose a work that is appropriate for his station and level, whether it be the *Shlah HaKadosh* or any other book on this topic. Indeed, there are even several books translated into languages other than Hebrew that contain profound thoughts on Mussar. Fortunate is the one who delves into these works. This study will fortify his spiritual defenses and provide him with numerous strategies, so that that he will not be easily caught in the evil inclination's web."

In his *"Drush Hesped"* (year 5507 [1747]), he states similarly, "Anyone who is designated by the name 'Yisrael' is obligated to study each day, morning and evening, a few pages from a Mussar *sefer. Baruch Hashem*, there are many that have been published. Viewing this as an obligation will help one to learn it with diligence. At this time, I am personally taking it upon myself, *bli neder*, to study Mussar with both my students and the laymen in the community. Before starting a class in Gemara or Chumash, I will review with them a page of the *Shlah HaKadosh*, from his lessons in reproof and rebuke. This way, the students will neither be devoid of fear, nor gravitate towards worldly desires. One who learns from these books each day will comprehend the serious sins he has committed, and the evil deeds he has perpetrated. The word of Hashem will make him shake and quiver, so that he will 'Turn from evil and do good' (*Tehillim* 34:15)." He writes further: "Let the one who needs life for his soul constantly fortify himself to study works on Mussar. If one does this, I am confident that the essence of *yiras Shamayim* will be implanted in his heart. He will then fear the awesome presence of Hashem and be repulsed at the very thought of sin."

THE ONLY APPROPRIATE METHOD IS STUDYING WORKS ON FEAR AND MUSSAR

In his work *Mesillas Yesharim*, Rav Moshe Chaim Luzzato, *zt"l*, the Ramchal, delineates the ways of attaining the virtues that were taught by the Talmudic Sage, Rebbi Pinchas Ben Ya'ir. In order to be acquired, each virtue requires intense study and deep reflection. As we previously noted, the only appropriate method of contemplation is through studying works on fear and Mussar. Indeed, without such study, it would be impossible for a man to stop the flood of disturbing thoughts that fills his mind with the vanities of the world — for there is no man who, of his own accord, turns his heart to an accounting of the soul. The Ramchal himself explicitly expresses this idea in a few places, such as in chapter 4, "The Way of Acquiring Watchfulness": "In particular, that which brings a person to watchfulness is the contemplation of the seriousness attached to Divine service, and the depth of judgment upon it. This awareness is developed through scrutinizing the deeds of the righteous that are recorded in rabbinical writings, and study of the statements made by our Sages on this topic." In chapter 12, "The Ways of Acquiring

Cleanliness," the Ramchal writes further: "The true means to acquire cleanliness is by constantly reading the words of our Sages, whether in matters of
halachah or of Mussar. Likewise, concerning the acquisition of good virtues,
one must read the Mussar treatises of the ancient or latter-day sages." He
writes similarly in the introduction: "The benefit from this book will not be
derived by reading it one time; rather, it must be constantly studied and reviewed in order for it to yield its goodness."

In the same vein, Rav Luzzato writes that one should engage in the contemplation of fear and Mussar for at least one hour per day. In *Derech Etz
Chaim* he states, "A person does not hesitate to make calculations regarding
temporal affairs. Why, then, does he not turn his heart, even for one moment, to life's most essential questions: who is he, why did he come to the
world, what does the King Who rules over kings require of him, and what will
be his end? Engaging in such reflection is the most potent weapon with
which to defeat the evil inclination. It is easy, powerfully effective, and will
bear abundant fruit. A person should set aside at least one hour a day to free
his mind of all other considerations and contemplate solely the purpose of
creation in general, and his purpose in particular. Moreover, he should search
his heart and ask himself, 'What did the patriarchs do that caused the Almighty to love them so much? What did Moshe Rabbeinu do, may peace be
on him? What did David HaMelech, the anointed of Hashem, do?' The
power of his intellect will tell him what is good for a man all the days of his
life. He shall then act upon it, and it will be good for him."

In the book *Ma'aseh Rav*, the author writes in the name of the Vilna
Gaon that one should study works of Mussar a few times each day. In *Alim
L'Trufah*, the famous letter the Gaon wrote to his family during his attempted
journey to the Holy Land, the pious sage himself writes, "Amongst the books
in my library is *Sefer Mishlei*, with a translation into the vernacular — for the
sake of the Almighty, one should read it every day.... You should also read
Sefer Koheles, for it exposes the trivialities of this world's affairs. There are
other Mussar books as well.... I also include my son-in-law in this exhortation.... It is important to learn *Pirkei Avos*, and in particular *Avos D'Rebbe
Nosson*, as well as *Maseches Derech Eretz*, for our Sages tell us that *derech eretz*
[proper conduct] precedes the Torah."

THE REMEDY FOR THE EVIL INCLINATION LIES IN MUSSAR

The Chida, Rav Chaim David Azulai, *zt"l*, writes in his work *Birkei Yosef* (section 1): "It is proper to set a fixed a time for Mussar study… for the greater the man, the greater the evil inclination.… I have a tradition that the remedy for the evil inclination lies in the Mussar admonishments that are contained in the statements of our Sages."

The pious sage Rav Yaakov of Lisa, *zt"l*, the author of *Chavas Da'as*, writes in his ethical will, "I adjure you to set a fixed time every day for Mussar study, for in the multitude of our sins, our hearts have become as stone — and through Mussar study, the heart is softened."

BEFORE ENGAGING IN TORAH STUDY LET ONE PONDER HIS CREATOR

In his work *Nefesh HaChaim*, Rav Chaim Volozhiner, *zt"l*, writes (*sha'ar* 4), "Before engaging in Torah study, it is fitting for every person to ready himself in the proper fashion. With a pure heart and fear of Heaven, let him ponder his Creator for a moment. By doing so, he will be moved to repent for his transgressions and become purified. Moreover, a person may even briefly interrupt his Torah studies for this purpose — so that the fear of God he accepted at the outset of his study session will not be extinguished from his heart. In that interlude, let him contemplate anew the fear of Heaven.… However, it should be clear that during this 'break,' one is permitted only to engage in the contemplation and acquisition of Heavenly fear. Moreover, this undertaking should be taken according to the dictates of common sense — each person in keeping with his nature and situation. One should make a precise calculation and insure that the time taken is truly essential for him to engage in the acquisition of fear and Mussar." We see from this that each person can make his own estimation of how much time is necessary for him to commune with His Creator.

THE INSPIRATION GENERATED BY MUSSAR AND HEAVENLY FEAR IS WELL KNOWN

Rav Alexander Ziskind, *zt"l*, in his work *Yesod VeShoresh HaAvodah*, writes (*Sha'ar HaNitzotz*), "The inspiration generated by books on Mussar and Heavenly fear is well known. Studying Mussar on a continual basis will help to implant the wondrous pleasures of Heavenly fear within a person's heart, and the fear of Hashem will thereby be increased.... This concept needs no proof, for it is obvious that the contemplation of works on this topic will lead to dedicated immersion in Torah study. As the *Zohar Chadash* states: 'Man must know...from whence he comes, and to where he is going...and that he will ultimately be summoned for judgment before the King.' Hence, it is clear that man has an obligation to investigate and comprehend the judgment and punishment of the Upper World — and all of this is found in the works on fear and Mussar. Moreover, by studying these works, man will be led to piety in all aspects of Divine service, and his character traits and behavior will become upright. All of this is contained in the books of fear. There is thus a great obligation on man to study works on this topic, daily and in a fixed measure. Indeed, the Arizal strongly adjured every person to study books of fear and Mussar on a daily basis, and stressed that one should not skip this study for even a single day."

"IF A DAY PASSES WITHOUT MUSSAR, I FEEL A COOLING OFF OF HEAVENLY FEAR"

The book *Chut HaMeshulash* is a biography of the Chasam Sofer, *zt"l*. Written by the sage's pious grandson, the work includes several passages concerning the Chasam Sofer's sanctified conduct. Says the author: "We read in Scripture: 'The beginning of wisdom is fear of Hashem' (*Tehillim* 111:10). In keeping with this verse, he [the Chasam Sofer] would begin each class he taught by teaching a few passages from the *Chovos HaLevavos*, in order to set his students' hearts aflame with the fear of Hashem. The words of this holy book were the basis for almost all of his Mussar exhortations, and they served as the inspiration for his own personal conduct as well. He greatly desired for his students to study it in their youth, so that they would have a path in Divine worship for the rest of their lives. Additionally, he encouraged his disciples to delve into the book *Menoras HaMe'or*, which contains an excellent collection of our Sages' aggadic statements. He was often heard to say to the yeshivah students, 'Believe me when I tell you that if a day passes without my studying works of Mussar, I feel within myself a cooling off of Heavenly fear.' "

EACH PERSON HAS AN OBLIGATION TO DAILY STUDY WORKS ON HEAVENLY FEAR

Rav Avraham Danzig, *zt"l*, author of the halachic compendium *Chayei Adam*, writes in the section pertaining to the laws of Yom Kippur, "And it is elementary that each and every person has an absolute obligation to daily study works on Heavenly fear, whether a little or a lot. Indeed, this imperative is greater than all other obligations to study Torah. Even if such a daily session will take time from other areas of study, and cause him to forgo studying a chapter of *mishnayos* and the like, it is still the correct course of behavior — for what does Hashem your God ask of you? — only to fear Him. As it says in *Pirkei Avos* (3:21), 'If there is no fear, there is no Torah.' "

IN NO WAY WILL ONE'S TORAH STUDY BE HARMED THROUGH STUDYING MUSSAR

The point of the aforementioned sage is well taken. A person's heart should not trouble him with worries that his Mussar session will cause him to neglect the study of a chapter of *mishnayos* or any other topic. In no way whatsoever will his Torah study be harmed through his studying Mussar — for when a man's heart is inspired to fear the Almighty, his determination to increase the amount of his Torah study grows. As a result, he will find many opportunities to study Torah and to utilize hours that might otherwise be wasted.

AN ANGEL ADJURED RAV YOSEF KARO TO STUDY MUSSAR EVERY DAY

Indeed, Mussar study is greatly honored! In the book *Maggid Mesharim*, written by the Beis Yosef [Rav Yosef Karo, author of the *Shulchan Aruch*. He is referred to here as the Beis Yosef, the title of his commentary on the *Tur*], we find that Rav Karo's heavenly study partner adjured him (end of *Parashas Behar*): "Read *Marganisa D'Bei Rav* every day. Also read one selection from the *Chovos HaLevavos*, which humbles the evil inclination and saps its strength." The work *Marganisa D'Bei Rav* is mentioned in the book *Reishis Chochmah* (*Sha'ar HaYirah*, ch. 12), where it states, "I found additional concepts concerning death and spiritual accounting in a manuscript entitled *Marganisa D'Rebbe Meir....* And what pleasure does man have, when ultimately he will pass from world to world.... And this is what is written in the book *Maggid Mesharim*, where the angel said to our master, the Beis Yosef: 'Remember what the Rav said in his *Marganisa*: "What pleasure does man have...." ' " The reader is encouraged to look in the work *Reishis Chochmah* in order to peruse the writings of the *Marganisa* at length, for they are straightforward words of Mussar, dealing with death and spiritual accounting.

CAN ANY MAN PURIFY HIS PATH BY SITTING COMPLACENTLY?

Now anyone who reads the angel's exhortation to our teacher, the holy Beis Yosef, should be gripped with trembling and fear. Consider the exalted spiritual stature of this "Cedar of Lebanon" — our righteous master, Rav Yosef Karo. His great piety is proverbial. He was a man who did not cease from thinking Torah thoughts for even a single moment (as is related in *Maggid Mesharim* in several places); one who attained such great spiritual heights that an angel of the Almighty communicated with him. Yet, with all this, the angel commanded him to study the *Marganisa D'Bei Rav* on a daily basis, a work that contains fundamental words of Mussar about death and spiritual accounting. Additionally, the Heavenly emissary directed him to read from the *Chovos HaLevavos* every day, in order to humble the evil inclination and ward off its attack. What will those who abandoned their task answer? Once he becomes aware of this, can any man purify his path by sitting complacently and exempting himself from the punctilious study of Mussar on a daily basis?

In his work *Ohr Tzaddikim*, the pious kabbalist Rav Papirash, *zt"l*, writes: "Each day, a person should read a passage from the *Chovos HaLevavos*, which the *maggid* said is good to study. It seems to me that at the time, the book *Reishis Chochmah* had not yet been written. However, now that we have it, one should not depart from it."

THE SAGES OF THE TALMUD UTILIZED THIS REMEDY OF REVIEWING MUSSAR PASSAGES

The Admor notes that we even find the Sages of the Talmud utilizing this remedy of reviewing Mussar passages, by repeating verses concerning Heavenly fear and the vanities of this world. For example, in *Maseches Sanhedrin* (7b) we find the following: "Whenever [Rav] noticed a crowd [of students and admirers] following behind him he would say, 'Though his majesty rises up to the Heavens and his head touches the clouds, he will perish forever like his own dung' (*Iyov* 20:6–7). When the people lifted Mar Zutra Chasida onto their shoulders during festival Shabboses, he would quote the verse: 'For strength endures not forever. Does the crown [of wealth] last from generation to generation?' (*Mishlei* 27:24)." Comments Rashi: "Rav uttered the verse, 'Though his majesty rises up to the Heavens...' to guard himself against arrogance." Indeed, this idea is the foundation of Mussar study: to verbally repeat Scriptural verses or statements of Chazal that teach about Heavenly fear and Mussar. If one wonders which Mussar texts the Sages themselves used, let us note that because of their exalted spiritual level they merely needed to mention an appropriate verse a single time. For example, recalling a verse that portrayed the emptiness of worldly affairs would immediately help them to maintain a perspective on the proper priorities in life. We, however, must constantly repeat these verses — as well as the inspiring statements of our Sages — just to make a minimal impression on our hearts. This is so concerning even the smallest detail that relates to the trait of arrogance, so that one will be able to keep a balanced outlook.

THE DISGRACE INHERENT IN SIN

Let us end this section with a quote from the third section of Rabbeinu

Yonah's *Sha'arei Teshuvah*, which discusses the verse: "To know wisdom and Mussar" (*Mishlei* 1:2). Comments Rabbeinu Yonah, "Performing proper actions and departing from sin is called wisdom, as the verse says: 'For it is your wisdom and discernment' (*Devarim* 4:6). After a person learns and understands what is a mitzvah and what is a transgression, he must then learn the disgrace inherent in sin and the loss that transgression entails. He will thereby distance his soul from it, and admonish himself — as well as those around him — by recalling the punishments that are the consequences of sin. This knowledge is called Mussar, and it is pleasant for those who give admonishment to learn it."

6

NEGLECT OF MUSSAR STUDY

A DAILY OBLIGATION ON EVERY INDIVIDUAL

IN THE PREVIOUS CHAPTER, we presented a series of quotes from various sages and kabbalists who explicitly discuss the importance of Mussar study. It is thus clear that there is a sacred obligation on every individual to fix a daily time period dedicated to this study. Indeed, some sages, such as the Vilna Gaon, even assert that works on Mussar and fear should be studied twice a day, in the evening and morning, as we mentioned above. There are some sages and pious men, *roshei yeshivah*, who have even taken the step of establishing Mussar study sessions in their institutions. Over and above all this, the fact that numerous scholars have labored to compose books on this subject testifies to their belief and viewpoint regarding Mussar study. Their whole intention was for these works to be studied and contemplated, so that one might come to fear Hashem, love Him, and cleave unto Him.

A GENERATION THAT WAS FULL OF DIVINE KNOWLEDGE

It is incumbent upon us to understand that all of the aforementioned sages were from an earlier period in our history. They lived in a generation that was full of the knowledge of Hashem, through both Torah study and the fear of Heaven. It was a time when the people's spirits believed in Hashem, when almost the entire nation — from the greatest person to the least — was whole in the faith of Israel. In those days, the sciences did not hold as great an attraction as they do now. Scientists were not held in as great esteem, and Jewish ones were few and far between. Consequently, all of Israel's intellectual faculties were focused exclusively on the apprehension and knowledge of Hashem, and the ideals of Torah study and Divine service reigned supreme. It was Torah sages and those who feared Hashem who were the recipients of honor, glory, and praise. In that era there was jealously of neither decadent people nor transgressors. The uppermost goal to which people strove was to fear the Almighty for every minute of their lives. The modern outlook that is referred to as "the spirit of the times" had not yet appeared on the face of the earth. The only spirit that existed was that of knowledge and the fear of Hashem. Yet despite all this, the sages and the men of piety in those times found it necessary to stress the importance of Mussar study, so that a person could build the foundation for eternal life.

TORAH AND DIVINE SERVICE HAVE BEEN UPROOTED FROM THEIR PLACES

However, much time has passed since those days. The picture has changed, and there are new ideas circulating in the world. Here there is disturbance, there uproar. A mighty wind blows — a tempest with powerful gales — and it has penetrated into the house of Hashem and the tents of Yaakov. Torah and Divine service have been violently uprooted from their rightful places. Their foundations have begun to crumble and their pillars are trembling. The glory of Torah has been desecrated, and the adornments of fear have been diminished. The "righteous man has been forsaken" (*Tehillim* 37:25), and people no longer turn from evil (cf. *Tehillim* 34:15). Those who fear Hashem hide in "rock clefts" (cf. *Shemos* 33:22), and they grow fewer from day to day. The primacy of Torah and Divine service deteriorates on a daily basis, as if they were old garments being exchanged for new ones. The Torah's honor is on a constant downward spiral, with a multitude of substitutions and a host of alternatives arising to take its place. In light of these grim facts, it is clear that there is an awesome obligation to study Mussar and awaken the fear of Hashem in man's heart. When a person fortifies his spirit with such study, then all the winds in the world will not be able to move him from his place.

THE ONLY REMEDY IS FOR TORAH AND FEAR TO BE UNITED WITHIN A PERSON

The outstanding scholar, Rav Yehonasan Eybeshitz, *zt"l*, author of the work *Urim V'Tumim*, states that he was accustomed to study Mussar texts with the students in his yeshivah. He did this, he said, "So that in the multitude of our sins, there will not be youths devoid of Heavenly fear who will follow after the ways of the world." Indeed, how honorable and true is this idea: to guide our youth in the study of Mussar, so that from their earliest youth until old age, the fear of Heaven will be instilled within them. The aforementioned sage wrote his words 150 years ago[4] during an era in which Torah and fear of Hashem enjoyed a truly exalted status. Nevertheless, even then he recognized that young people are easily influenced to go in whatever direction their spirit moves them, like trees swaying in the wind. Therefore, he gave sound advice to direct them on the upright path, so that they would not be devoid of fear and chase after the vanities of the world. The only remedy is for Torah and Heavenly fear to be wholly united within a person. As we mentioned previously, the pious sage Rav Moshe Sofer, *zt"l* [the Chasam Sofer], followed in Rav Yehonasan's footsteps and taught Mussar in his yeshivah.

As for us, "what can we say, what can we reply?" (cf. Selichos service). When we take an earnest look at the spirituality of earlier generations as compared to ours, it becomes clear that we have a vital obligation to establish a fixed program for Mussar study in all yeshivos. Such a program will insure that our youths are well grounded in the fear of Heaven and in every other praiseworthy virtue as well. It is crucial that people embark on this study when they are yet young and their branches are fresh and pliant. When they do so, they will be like a "fruitful vine" (*Tehillim* 128:3) in Torah and Heavenly fear, and be endowed with upright character traits.

We read in Scripture: "The wise will shine like the radiance of the firmament" (*Daniel* 12:3). Chazal tell us (*Bava Basra* 8b) that this refers to a judge

---

4   Now 250 years ago.

who gives just ruling based on factual evidence. The verse continues, "And those who teach righteousness to the multitudes [will shine] like the stars forever and ever," on which the Sages comment, "This applies to teachers of young children." Rashi adds to this explanation, saying, "The teachers of children turn many to righteousness, because they train them to go in the way of good."

THIS INVALUABLE BODY OF STUDY IS NEGLECTED

In spite of this, we are witness to an almost unimaginable phenomenon in these times. Our pious sages have prepared a wealth of precious material on the topics of Mussar and Heavenly fear, and we know that study of these matters provides a remedy for every illness of the soul. Their works are founded on both the "holy mountains" of our Sages' words and on the dictates of common sense. Moreover, the righteous in our midst have solemnly adjured us to engage in this area of study, as we have noted above. Nevertheless, this invaluable body of study goes neglected and unrecalled — just as the memory of a dead person is forgotten from the heart. Indeed, it is hidden behind a thick cloud and obscured by a dense fog. Its fate is like that of the poor, wise man who, with the power of his wisdom, escapes from the small city that is besieged by the mighty king, and about whom Shlomo HaMelech wrote: "Yet no one remembered that poor man" (*Koheles* 9:15).

This has been the ignoble lot of this precious area of study. Eternal deliverance and healing are found beneath its wings, and it carries the power to save man's soul from the grip of the netherworld — yet man still does not set his heart to remember it. There is no difference between businessmen, who are preoccupied with their myriad concerns, and those who dwell in the tents of Torah — none of them worry about the state of their souls. Though study of these works is exactly the same as Torah study, still, there is no one who dedicates a brief daily session to engage in it.

THE STUDY OF FEAR IS TERRIBLY NEGLECTED

Let us consider the worthy thoughts and noble intentions of those pious sages who toiled to compose works on Heavenly fear, thereby gracing the public with merit. By promoting the need to study Mussar and wisdom, they endeavored to clear the path and straighten the trail to Divine service. This study brings in its wake upright guidance and deliverance, Heavenly fear and true humility, as well as every worthy trait. Nevertheless, it would seem that their efforts are almost for naught, for their holy writings rest in a dusty and neglected corner. There is neither seeker nor searcher, except for a miniscule few to whom Hashem beckons. Only a tiny fraction of Mussar works have been rendered into the common language — something that makes them accessible to the general public. On the other hand, uncountable works on secular topics have been translated into the vernacular. We see from all this that works on Mussar have almost ceased to be a guide for the general populace. As a result, the study of fear is terribly neglected and practically severed from its crucial association with the Almighty's Name.

WHY DOES MUSSAR LIE SO NEGLECTED AND ABANDONED?

Who is to blame for this evil? The precious study of Mussar teaches man wisdom, the knowledge of Heavenly fear, righteousness, uprightness, and every precious and noble virtue. If so, why does it lie so neglected and abandoned? Why are there almost none amongst the living who follow it? Earlier, we quoted the Divrei Yehoshua, who lists seven reasons for this occurrence. However, in addition to these constraining factors, there are other causes that have blocked the path with an impenetrable wall of stone. These impediments stem from basic principles in both the physical and spiritual realms.

THE PHYSICAL CAUSE

The physical cause [of why Mussar is left unstudied] lies in the fact that although Mussar study provides a cure for the soul's disease, it is first necessary for man's heart to recognize that his soul is, in fact, seriously ill — for only then will he avidly seek out a remedy for his ailment. The remedy is the quest to know Hashem's will and the desire to draw close to His service. This itself requires an extensive accounting on the part of the soul — and without

Mussar, there is no accounting or knowledge. Moreover, there is nothing within him to spark this initial recognition and awakening. Without the study of Mussar and with no arousal or awakening, his soul will be shrouded in darkness.

RECKONING AND INTROSPECTION

Moreover, the treasure of Heavenly fear includes much reckoning and introspection. Indeed, it is known that the foundation of Mussar study is the contemplation of *yiras ha'onesh* — the contemplation of the world's accounting. Man must consider that he has been allotted a certain amount of time on the earth, and that he will depart in the same manner he arrived — just as he came naked from the womb, so, too, will he return to the earth. Similarly, he should recall the long days of darkness he will face in the future, and the fact that Hashem will execute judgment on every hidden thing. As Chazal teach in *Pirkei Avos* (3:1): "Consider three things and you will not come into the grip of sin...." Now, without proper consideration, people generally think that the study and contemplation of these matters brings one to melancholy and sadness. Man, whose sole desire is to be happy and cheerful, to remove worry from his heart and grief from his flesh, naturally shies away from such endeavors. Therefore, he does not wish to have even the most remote and tenuous connection to Mussar study, so that he can keep his heart from being saddened and his spirit from being embittered.

AN UNFORTUNATE MISCONCEPTION

In truth, however, this is nothing but an unfortunate misconception, for while it is true that this spiritual pill is bitter to swallow at the outset of the treatment, it is as sweet as honey upon its completion. This is so for a very simple reason: when a man accustoms himself to study works on Mussar and Heavenly fear, his eyes will see and his heart will understand that ultimately, there is no benefit to be derived from mirth. He will similarly realize that it is futile to close his eyes to the evil that will befall him at his life's end. Is it possible for a person to blunder through life like a blind man in darkness, when in the end he will not be able to escape his destined fate? As our Sages teach in *Pirkei Avos* (4:29): "Against your will you die; and against your will you are destined to give an account before the King Who rules over kings, the Holy One, Blessed is He." On the other hand, one who studies Mussar will be happy with his portion and rejoice with trembling (cf. *Tehillim* 2:11), for his eyes will be opened to the knowledge of good and evil. He will thereby be motivated to "contemplate the future" (*Avos* 2:13) and to prepare himself to meet the evil day.

THE SPIRITUAL CAUSE

Let us now turn to the spiritual cause for the abandonment of Mussar study, which is actually quite simple: it is nothing more than the advice of the evil inclination — the mighty king who besieges the small city. In this parable, the city alludes to the body and its multitude of powers. The king built siege engines and ramps around the city walls in order to capture and conquer it. The shadow of his might spreads over all the inhabitants. However, the fear of Hashem is like an arrow in the hand of an accomplished combatant. Thus equipped, a warrior can confidently engage the king in battle and stand against him in a disciplined formation. Mussar study endows one with the fear of Hashem. Therefore, the evil inclination does everything in its power to sabotage a person's attempt to engage in it, so that he will walk in utter darkness and not have a shred of light to guide him. Hence, in the profusion of his transgressions he goes astray, barren of wisdom and Mussar, and bereft of reckoning and cognition of what was and what will be. When a person is left in such a defenseless state, it is easy for the evil inclination to trap him in its net — like fish that are caught by a fisherman, and eggs that are gathered by a farmer — and man is left without a rescuer or redeemer.

LIKE A BIRD CAUGHT IN A SNARE

Moreover, the evil inclination is crafty and cunning in its work. It is not enough for it to overpower a man — to chain him in manacles, diverting him from the path of good to one of corruption and chaos, and to rule over him with a strong hand. Even if many years have thus gone by, the evil inclination is still in a state of continual fear and dismay. It is never confident of its complete victory — and for good reason. There exists a spirit in man that is never extinguished, and free choice is always in his hand. Therefore, the evil inclination is constantly fearful that the person's intellect will awaken and he will want to escape his captor — one day, perhaps, he might repent and regret his evil, and flee for his life. If this were to happen, then all of the evil inclination's labors will have been for naught. Because of this threat, it watches over its victim with "seven eyes," and appoints sentries to oversee him. They prevent him from coming across the pathway to the tree of life [Mussar], stalking his movements and counting his footsteps, so that he will not flee and escape from his master's clutches — like a bird caught in a snare.

THE INSIDIOUS COUNSEL OF THE EVIL INCLINATION

From whence springs this great force that stifles man's spirit? What is the source of this power that does not let him free himself from his earthly bonds and that thwarts him from awakening and arising from the hideous depths to the gate of hope? We find an answer for this question in the *Mesillas Yesharim* (ch. 2): "This is one of the cunning strategies of the evil inclination. It continuously piles travail upon man's heart, so that he is not left with even a moment to contemplate and reflect on which path he is proceeding. This is because it knows that if man were to set his heart for even a second on the path he was following, he would certainly and immediately regret his ways.... Indeed, this was the very strategy followed by Pharaoh, who said: 'Increase the workload....' By means of relentless and uninterrupted labor, he endeavored to trouble the Jewish people's hearts and distract them from all contemplation. So, too, is the insidious counsel of the evil inclination against man."

CARES AND LABORS CONNECTED TO WORLDLY AFFAIRS

Aside from answering the fundamental question that we raised, the Ramchal does not elaborate on the subject. What, then, is the actual nature of this work that overburdens man's heart? It appears that it can be divided into two categories. The first is the cares and labors connected to worldly affairs, the necessity of providing for his family and the desire for luxuries. Man is immersed in this pursuit with all his heart and soul — to gather and collect, to further his acquisitions and increase his property. There is no end to all his labor, for there is no limit to this longing. As Chazal state (*Koheles Rabbah* 1:32): "A man does not die with half of his desires fulfilled — if he has one hundred, he wants two hundred."

MAN'S CONTINUAL STRUGGLE WITH THE EVIL INCLINATION

The second factor is man's continual struggle and preoccupation with the evil inclination.[5] As Chazal state (*Yoma* 35b): "[When a wicked person is called up for an accounting before the Heavenly court, he will attempt to defend himself by claiming,] 'I was attractive, and [therefore] engrossed with [satisfying] my evil inclination.' " There is nothing that bothers man and confuses his thoughts like the distraction of the evil inclination. It constantly urges him to chase after worldly pursuits, to follow the path of his heart and the sight of his eyes, to satisfy his every craving and fancy, and to stoke his every bad character trait, even though it will lead him to devastation and destruction. From these two elements — the pursuit of worldly affairs and the preoccupation with the evil inclination — man is stricken with blindness and an unfeeling heart. He is flung about like a stone shot from a slingshot: his head spinning and his heart pounding, his eyes plastered shut and his intellect dulled. This is

---

5   The reader may wonder at this second factor, for above, Rav Yitzchak Blazer said that we are discussing a person who is completely in the grips of his evil inclination. If so, how can he now state that such a person is involved in a constant battle against it? In other words, if he is completely subjugated to the evil inclination's bidding, what struggle does he face? The opposite would seem to be true: he is so dominated that he is not even aware he is being controlled! The answer is that there are two tiers of control involved here. The evil inclination's main attack is focused on stopping a person from studying Mussar. However, this does not mean that he has totally abandoned Torah and mitzvos. Instead, he has been deprived of the main weapon that will offer him the chance to make a successful counterattack. Therefore, he will never be able to defeat the evil inclination, and instead, in every action, he will be involved in a debilitating struggle to perform the Almighty's will. It is this "secondary" struggle that the Rav is discussing here. For further elucidation of this idea, please refer to Rav Yisrael's first letter in the section entitled "The Light of Israel."

the overburdening travail on man's heart that the Ramchal discussed.

THE EVIL INCLINATION MARSHALS ALL OF ITS ENERGIES TO FIGHT AGAINST MUSSAR STUDY

This is the entire purpose of the evil inclination's machinations. All of its considerable efforts are directed towards casting a deep slumber on man, and thereafter insuring that he will not awaken to know good and evil and extricate his soul from its bonds. Therefore, it overburdens man's heart with constant, arduous labor, so that he will not have a moment to contemplate and reflect on the path he is taking, as is written in the *Mesillas Yesharim*. It is self-evident that Mussar study is a painful thorn in the eyes of the evil inclination, for through it, all his counsel and wisdom are uprooted. Indeed, the fruits of Mussar study are the consideration of the world's account and the contemplation of Heavenly fear. Moreover, if a person resolves to set a fixed, daily time for Mussar study, then all the evil inclination's efforts to keep him from finding the way to the tree of life will be in vain — for when man's soul is impassioned with the fear of Hashem and he contemplates his path, the fortress of the evil inclination will be destroyed and its bonds will be torn asunder. Then the road will be open before him to flee and escape for his life — to be saved like a deer from the hunter, to regret his evil and return to Hashem. It is thus self-evident that the evil inclination marshals all of its energies to fight against Mussar study. It does not hesitate from utilizing all available means to turn man's heart away from this study — whether with empty but enticing arguments, or with any other effective tactic. It does everything within its power to block his way and strew his trail with hewn stones, so that his feet cannot traverse the upright path.

THERE IS NOTHING THAT WISDOM CANNOT CONQUER

However, a person should not despair, for there is nothing that wisdom cannot conquer. Man, in his wisdom, will enrage the lion — entangling and trapping him in a cage; also the great serpents he can capture with a hook. He can also "capture" a heart of flesh — drawing it up with the cables of fear and Mussar, so that it will be good for him all of his days. Therefore, if only there were supports at his right side — the study of Mussar and fear — to guide him with wisdom and good instruction, the evil inclination would be unable to wreak so much havoc and destruction. In the physical world, it is an accepted principle that all good and worthy things are maintained solely through counsel and strategy. For example, every accomplished building contractor employs set standards, certification, support systems, and maintenance. In the spiritual realm, however, people tend to ignore this. Thus it is that the exalted matter of Mussar study resides in silence, quietude, and total stillness. No one arises nor awakens, and none embrace it. No one stands in its support — neither in speech nor in deed. There is no unifying vision nor admonisher in the gate; no one to proclaim righteousness unto the masses, saying, "This is the path — traverse it! Partake of the fruits that Mussar has to offer. Illuminate your eyes and restore your soul to life — so that you may be spared from Gehinnom and be sated with pleasure, riches, and eternal delight."

7

THE ILLUMINATION

RAV YISRAEL LIPKIN OF SALANT, ZT"L

SHLOMO HAMELECH TEACHES US that "Everything has its season, and there is a time for everything under the heaven" (*Koheles* 3:1). Thus it is that the time to reclaim this precious treasure from the dust heap has come about, so that once again, it might serve as a fount of salvation and resuscitate the spiritual life of the multitudes. In Hashem's great mercy for His people, He caused the morning sun to burst forth — the holy light of Israel, His chariot and horseman, the pious and illustrious sage, Rav Yisrael Lipkin of Salant, *zt"l*. However, let the reader not think that our great master and teacher sprung forth from a vacuum — far from it! In the days of his youth, he merited to draw from the wellsprings of a holy and awesome man: the incomparable sage, light of the world, our righteous and honorable master, Rav Yosef Zundel Salanter, *zt"l*. Rav Zundel himself was a primary disciple of the outstanding scholar and leader of all the exile — our holy and exalted teacher, Rav Chaim Volozhiner, *zt"l*.

RAV YOSEF ZUNDEL SALANTER, ZT"L

Rav Yisrael was privileged to serve his holy master and receive his guidance in the ways of Mussar and Divine service. He sat at Rav Zundel's feet for many years, until the sage departed for the holy city of Yerushalayim to live out his final years in honor and glory.

It would be impossible to fully recount here the brilliant eminence of our master, Rav Yosef Zundel, *zt"l*. The awesome power of his piety, humility, and holiness, as related to us by Rav Yisrael, *zt"l* — who frequently extolled the wondrous qualities of his teacher — is beyond our ability to express. Herein, let it suffice for us to note the comments written by Rav Yisrael in the introduction to his work *Sefer Tevunah*: "I 'poured water' for my teacher [i.e., served him and sat at his feet], our master, Rav Yosef Zundel, who currently resides in Yerushalayim, may it be quickly rebuilt in our days. In comparison to his great spirituality, I do not even reach his ankles. This exalted man is one of the lights of the world, and I have taken this opportunity to elaborate on his great and lofty virtues." In one of his holy letters, Rav Yisrael writes further: "I served the righteous sage, Rav Yosef Zundel, for many years. Thus, I fully knew that the majesty of his righteousness was greatly exalted; I found him truly wondrous...and in my estimation, there is not to be found in our midst another servant of Hashem who is equal to our teacher."

HE WOULD CONSTANTLY REPEAT VERSES PERTAINING TO YIRAH AND AHAVAH

Indeed, the pious scholar, Rav Yosef Zundel, our holy teacher's master, followed the sacred practice of engaging in daily in-depth Mussar study. Likewise, he would constantly repeat verses pertaining to *yirah* and *ahavah*, and statements of Chazal that inflame the heart with *yirah* and Mussar. Often, he would seek the quiet solitude of the fields and forests surrounding Salant, so that he could study and contemplate matters of *yirah* and Mussar. Similarly, on the long winter Shabbos nights, when the sage was scrupulously careful to avoid studying by candlelight and would instead review his studies by heart, he would also repeat teachings on *yirah* and Mussar. He would thereby fortify himself for the upcoming week, regarding both his character traits and any issues that occupied his attention. In a letter the *gaon* wrote to his son, which I was privileged to read, he writes, "You should continuously repeat verses that relate to the concepts of *hashgachah*, faith, and salvation. For example: 'Hope to Hashem; strengthen yourself and He will give you courage, and hope to Hashem' (*Tehillim* 27:14); 'My eyes are constantly towards Hashem, for He will remove my feet from the snare' (ibid. 25:15), etc. By doing so, you will walk in security — and, 'The salvation of Hashem will come as the blink of an eye.' " There can be no doubt that Rav Zundel received guidance in the path of Mussar from his rebbi, the pious *gaon*, Rav Chaim Volozhiner, *zt"l*.

Rav Yisrael, our holy master and teacher, was an outstanding genius. Even while a youth, his intellect had stretched out to touch the heavens. The radiance of his wisdom shone brilliantly. In his early years, he was already renowned as a mighty scholar who brought splendor to Israel. When he drew near to his holy teacher, the pious *gaon*, Rav Yosef Zundel, he was privileged to be treated by the Rav like a member of his family. He carefully observed his teacher's every action, and contemplated deeply his holy ways. Indeed, it is no exaggeration to say that he literally counted each step that Rav Zundel took. When his master would walk to the outskirts of the town to meditate on *yirah*, young Yisrael would covertly follow behind him, to listen and absorb the delightful pearls of Mussar that flowed from his lips. In turn, the pious *gaon* realized that this "tender sapling" would grow to be a mighty cedar of Lebanon (cf. *Tehillim* 92:13), and that one day, "the light of Yisrael" would shine forth upon the four corners of the earth. Thus it was that Rav Zundel harbored a profound love for his disciple and imbued him with the splendor of his righteousness and his holy path.

"YISRAEL, STUDY MUSSAR, AND YOU WILL BECOME A YIREI SHAMAYIM"

Upon taking him under his wings, Rav Zundel's first step in his student's education was to instruct him to study Mussar. Rav Yisrael once confided in me that Rav Zundel told him the following: "Yisrael, study Mussar, and you will become a *yirei Shamayim*." Like an arrow shot from a bow, these words were true to their mark, and penetrated deeply into the inner chambers of his heart. Following the path of his pious teacher, he began regularly studying books of *yirah* and Mussar. Within a short time, his soul was deeply infused with a pure spirit of Heavenly fear, and a feeling of holiness stirred in his heart. He was raised above the vanities of this passing existence, and inspired to seek the Divine will. Together with this, his Torah knowledge continually increased, and he grew strong in both Torah and *yirah*. With his brilliant mind, he delved deeply and expansively into the wisdom of *yirah* and Mussar.

He labored and toiled to understand all the paths of Divine service and the rectification of every character trait. He surged like a "spring flowing stronger and stronger" (*Avos* 2:11), and ascended to exalted levels of Torah, piety, humility, and fear of sin.

Even when he was yet a young man, many people turned to him and submitted themselves to his guidance, thirstily drinking in his profound words concerning *yirah* and Divine worship. So it was that his lifetime pursuit in public service commenced at a very early age. He continually progressed in his Torah knowledge and character development, until "he was very great" (*Bereishis* 26:13). With his bountiful Torah and Heavenly fear, he nurtured his entire generation — and especially the students who attached themselves to him. Indeed, he dedicated his soul to guiding his disciples on the path of Hashem. He implanted within them the precious seeds of *yiras Hashem* and good character traits. He brought merit to his people and purified them, and uplifted the pride of Torah and *yiras Hashem* in the world. He became a sign (cf. *Bamidbar* 26:10) for the exalted life of the Torah, and his fame spread to the ends of the earth. A figure of towering scholarship and piety, he was truly the leader of the entire exile, and in his righteousness, humility, and genius, he was literally one of the foundations of the world.

8

THE TEN INNOVATIONS OF RAV YISRAEL

R AV YISRAEL'S PROFOUND CONTEMPLATION of Mussar led him to realize that its "light was good" (*Bereishis* 1:4) and that it was an excellent means to strengthen Torah observance amongst the general public. Thus, with the Godly wisdom that permeated his being, he investigated, considered, and refined this body of study. His goal was to prepare and streamline a method that would make it easily accessible to the masses, as well as to raise the banner of its glory. He developed and nurtured it with righteousness and nobility, in order to set it as a path amidst the people and a trail amongst the living.

At this point, let us review the innovations that he engendered and taught concerning the foundations of this body of wisdom:

1) THE ESSENTIAL OBLIGATION TO STUDY MUSSAR AND HEAVENLY FEAR

Rav Yisrael took careful note of the deplorable spiritual conditions that prevailed in his generation. In his time, Heavenly fear had plunged to the depths, Divine service had diminished, and virtuous character traits were disregarded. The cause for all this was the everyday cares and concerns of life, which increase from day to day. Man is caught in a great thicket of troubles and worries, and new trials spring up to face him each morning. The unrelenting assault of the *yetzer hara* weighs heavier and heavier upon him, as the hand of evil brazenly wages its war against him on all fronts. It was clear and obvious to the Rav that the abundant goodness hidden within Mussar study would be an effective means to combat the situation. Even under such grievous circumstances, Mussar retains within it a spirit that effects salvation upon the earth (cf. *Tehillim* 74:12). Redemption and healing lie under its wings; it hastens deliverance and restores afflicted souls to life with a healing balm. Yet, despite its wondrous powers, there was no one to strengthen its hand or champion its fate, and its remembrance was almost forgotten.

Therefore, our master and teacher arose like a lion to perform mighty deeds. He raised his voice like a shofar, to call out before the noisy throngs (cf. *Mishlei* 1:21), to expound before the masses, and to publicly make known the obligation to study Mussar. He heightened the awareness that, beyond this study, there is no way for man to elude the ever-present net of the evil inclination that waits to entrap him. Also, for the person who is already ensnared and imprisoned, there is no hope to switch from the evil path to that of the good save through Mussar study. Rav Yisrael also publicized the nature and essence of this study — its inestimable value and its graceful effectiveness. Indeed, it is like the dew of revival, for it has the potency to impart life to dried-out bones that are empty of Torah and mitzvos and overlay them with the sinew and skin of Heavenly fear. With its power, it can transform a heart of stone to one of flesh, and revitalize a troubled spirit.

Verily, the omnipresent shadow of the evil inclination is spread over every intelligent being. Therefore, the study of Mussar is an imperative that is incumbent on every soul. No one is exempt; from the rabbinic arbiter who sits in the seat of judgment, to the laborer behind the millstone; both man and woman; Torah scholar and layman; youth and elder; magnate and pauper; commoner and aristocrat alike; both those who fear Hashem and those who do not — all of them are obligated to fix times to study works on fear and Mussar.

Thus it was that our teacher went out and raised a great hue and cry in the name of Mussar — for from it flows the stream of life, the fear of Hashem, and the beginning of wisdom. He was like a crier for the House of Israel, awakening and inspiring people to their duty. Moreover, in addition to his public exhortations, he taught this body of wisdom to his students. In doing so, he trained a cadre of dedicated assistants to help foster the awareness of this study and establish it as a widespread custom amongst the masses. He performed his sacred task valiantly and indefatigably. His untiring efforts bore fruit, and knowledge and the fear of Hashem were increased amongst Israel — and the earth shook to its very foundations, as is well known. Because of his work, the obligation to study Mussar was proclaimed throughout the world and became inextricably linked with his name. From the tender years of his youth, when he first assumed his holy task, until his very last day, he did not desist from this work.

2) HISPAILUS: IN ORDER TO BE EFFECTIVE, MUSSAR MUST BE STUDIED WITH FERVOR

In his great wisdom, Rav Yisrael changed the entire face of Mussar study and garbed it in a new and different form. In previous times, when a person happened to peruse a work on Mussar, he would either adapt the singsong style of Gemara study, or simply read the text in silent and intense concentration. The Rav, however, realized that neither of these two methods were fully effective. This is because the benefit of Mussar study is manifest in two ways: First, there is the knowledge and apprehension of the wisdom of fear — to know the path to Hashem and to comprehend the ways of Divine service. This is a profound and singular level of wisdom, as is alluded in the verse, "Behold, the fear of the Lord is wisdom" (*Iyov* 28:28). Chazal expound (*Shabbos* 31b): "Rabbi Eliezer said, 'The Almighty wants nothing else in the world except for us to fear Him, as it says: "Now O Israel, what does Hashem, your God, ask of you? Only to fear Hashem, your God." It states elsewhere (*Iyov* 28:28): "And He said to man, '*Hayn* [usually translated as 'behold,' but here having an exegetical meaning as well, as will become apparent] the fear of the Lord is wisdom' " — and in Greek, the word for "one" is *hayn*.' " The Ramchal comments in the introduction to his *Mesillas Yesharim*: "We see, therefore, that fear, and only fear, is ascribed as wisdom [see there for a more lengthy elucidation]." Second, there is the arousal that is generated by the study of Mussar books. This inspiration enflames the heart by awakening the soul and humbling the spirit, arousing within a person the fear of Hashem.

Regarding the perfection of knowledge, the manner in which one learns makes no difference, and even studying by oneself is sufficient. However, for the purpose of acquiring fear — to be aroused through learning to fear Hashem — the above-mentioned style of learning is quite ineffective in making an impression on the heart. This is because knowledge alone will not fill a person's soul with disquiet and foreboding. Indeed, even before studying, man has a general knowledge of *yiras Hashem* and the fear of Divine punishment; nevertheless, the fear of Heaven is still far from his being. As Chazal tell us (*Shabbos* 31b), "What is meant by the verse, 'This is their way: folly (*keisel*) is theirs...' (*Tehillim* 49:14)? The wicked know that their path leads to death, but they have fat on their kidneys (*kislam*). Lest you think that this [fat] causes [their kidneys] forgetfulness, it is therefore stated, '...yet their mouths speak soothingly' (ibid.)."

Chazal tell us that the kidneys are the seat of understanding. Thus, wicked people having "fat on their kidneys" indicates that their understanding is compromised.

Therefore, in order to attain the goal of acquiring fear, it is necessary for Mussar to be studied in a passionate manner that will stir the soul: with a sincere heart, a mournful voice, and lips aflame [i.e., it must be expressed verbally]. Additionally, one should flesh out any given concept by utilizing the power of his imagination. This is a great aid to Mussar study, for it viscerally arouses the soul, inculcating within it the knowledge of the punishments awaiting the body and the soul, knowledge that was previously confined to the intellect alone. This *hispailus* is similar to the power that musical instruments and singing have to inspire man and awaken his spirit — either to happiness or sadness. When a person reads the statements of Chazal and works on Mussar with solemn fervor — which ignite the heart with Heavenly fear — then his heart will warm up and his spirit will become stormy and agitated. His senses will become electrified, and the words he reads will strike roots in his inner heart and implant the fear of Hashem within his soul. Sometimes, too, this passionate study will arouse him to weep; torrents of water will stream down his face, as he exudes tears like the dew of Mt. Hermon (cf. *Tehillim* 133:3). He will then find that a new spirit has entered him, and the fear of Hashem will flow like water into his innards and like oil into his bones (cf. *Tehillim* 109:18).

3) REPETITION IS AN INVALUABLE AID

Because the goal of Mussar study is to internalize its message, constant repetition of an idea is an extremely effective and beneficial tool. This is especially true concerning a particular dictum of Chazal or a Mussar thought that resonates in one's soul and penetrates into the inner chambers of one's heart. A person should repeat such a statement over and over again, until it becomes engraved on the tablet of his heart (cf. *Shemos* 32:16) and as ornaments between his eyes (cf. *Devarim* 6:8). This exercise can be conducted at any time he finds his mind free — when he walks on the way, or when he retires at night (ibid. 6:7). Then, the statement will ring in his ears like a bell and will not depart from his memory.

Rav Yisrael himself would study Mussar books with an overpowering passion, in a beautiful voice that stirred feelings of sadness and sorrow. Occasionally, he would stop his studies and focus on a certain statement, repeating it time after time. His sweet and fervent voice melted the heart of anyone who heard it. He maintained this practice even into his old age, when he was at the height of his mental abilities and his holiness and awesomeness were astonishing to behold. In those later years, when his frail body could hardly contain the intense sanctity of his soul, he still did not cease from devotedly studying and pondering works on Mussar, sometimes bursting into copious tears.

4) FOCUS ON THE ESSENTIALS

The pious authors of the works on Mussar gathered all the statements concerning this topic in general, and the specific teachings regarding each character trait in particular. Therefore, a person should focus his attention on a given trait that he feels to be the most corrupt within himself and set his heart to rectify it. He can accomplish this by fervently repeating the statements of fear and Mussar that pertain to this trait, until it is mended and healed. The same is true concerning favorable traits: if a person is confronted with a trial wherein he must overcome his evil inclination, let him hasten to flee from the storm of evil — by studying Mussar thoughts that relate to the particular trait under attack, until the battle is won. We thus see that the approach to rectifying or strengthening an individual trait is to repeat the teachings that concern it, until the task has been completed. At that point, the Mussar is no longer necessary. However, the study of Mussar regarding the general acquisition of *yiras Shamayim* — by making an "accounting of the world" — is of a different nature entirely. The statements relating to this area must be repeated and reviewed on a constant and continual basis.

5) THE IMPERATIVE TO STUDY MUSSAR WITHOUT INTERRUPTION

Man's obligation to study Mussar consists of fixing set times to study it — with earnestness and enthusiasm, and without long interruptions between sessions. Indeed, lengthy interruptions that do not contain even the slightest amount of inspiration are a major reason for the occasional failure of Mussar to effect change in a person. In addition, there is a spiritual cause as well: the transgressions that numb the heart and turn it to stone, *chalilah*. The essential remedy for this is Torah study and praying with a spirit of humility and submission. Engaging in these will soften a person's heart, allowing him to be aroused by words of admonishment and Mussar.

A man consumed with business interests imagines that he has precious little spare time to indulge in the "luxury" of Torah study. In fact, however, it is generally in just such a person that spiritual malaise runs deepest. The first step in his "program of treatment" is for him to set fixed sessions for Torah study. At the very least, he should take some time on Shabbos to engage in fervent study of a Mussar text. In addition, he should set aside a brief period of time on weekdays to review what he has learned — even if it is only for a few minutes. By doing so, he will insure that the impressions that were generated in his soul are not lost during the span of time from one Shabbos to the next.

6) THE PRIMACY OF YIRAS HA'ONESH

Rav Yisrael's approach to Mussar study was simple and focused. He did not concentrate on such lofty concepts as *yiras haromemus* and *ahavas Hashem*. Rather, he directed his efforts in a single direction, and most of his

Mussar teachings relate exclusively to the fear of Divine punishment. It is this fear that is the beginning of knowledge, and it comprises the first step in Divine service — to "turn from evil and do good" (*Tehillim* 34:15). He writes of this in his *Iggeres HaMussar*, as we shall see later on. He based his method on the words of our holy Sages. In *Pirkei Avos* (3:1) they teach: "Consider three things and you will not come into the grip of sin: Know whence you came, whither you go, and before Whom you will give justification and reckoning." This contemplation — the study of *yiras ha'onesh* — benefits the soul more than all the proverbial balms of Gilad (cf. *Yirmeyahu* 46:11).

We have mentioned previously that one of major causes blocking man from the path of Mussar study is based on its foundation — the fear of Divine punishment. This includes making an accounting of the final day, when one's every action will be judged and the pit of the netherworld looms large. At first glance, it seems that contemplation of these matters leads to sorrow and grief — whereas man's whole desire is to remove sadness from his heart and live in contentment and happiness. He wishes not to recall his end, so that fear will not trouble him and his tranquility might remain undisturbed. He therefore steers himself away from the path of this study so that his heart will not be saddened.

In truth, it is astonishing that man does not set his heart to the labor of acquiring this fear. More astounding is the fact that the numerous catastrophes which storm into the world — that shake every soul to its core and should logically fill one's heart with dread — actually fail to make an impression on the soul. This is because man prefers to distract himself and forget everything that might bring him to sadness.

Indeed, man's nature is such that, whenever something unexpected and untoward happens to him, *chas v'shalom*, he thoroughly investigates the matter to determine its cause, seeking to ascribe it to some natural reason. Even if he finds the most farfetched and dubious possibility, his will is satisfied. Thus, he covers his eyes and puts his spirit at ease.

This is the way of man — yet it is foolish and hollow. Rav Yisrael illustrates this by way of a parable about a person who fears thunder and lightning. When he hears the awesome roar of thunder in the skies, his response is to hide under his pillow and blankets and stick his fingers in his ears —

thinking that he will thereby be safe. So it is with anyone who indulges in the above-mentioned behavior. What profit is there in closing one's eyes from seeing and one's heart from understanding the evil that will befall him at the end of his days, when he reaps the fruits of his actions? No refuge exists to save him! Where can he flee to escape from Hashem? Where can he go to hide from His countenance? As Chazal tell us in the fourth chapter of *Pirkei Avos* (*mishnah* 29): "Against your will you die; and against your will you are destined to give an accounting before the King Who rules over kings, the Holy One, Blessed is He."

In truth, this idea, which causes man to wash his hands of Mussar study lest it bring him to sadness, is nothing more than a false illusion. Moreover, the very agent of this fantasy is the absence of regular Mussar study. When a person accustoms himself to study works on this topic, he will understand that his anxiety is unfounded. As we will now explain, there are several reasons why such concern is unwarranted:

a) Dullness of the heart: Mussar study does not immediately awaken the heart and cause the soul to tremble in terror from *yiras Hashem* and the dread of Divine punishment, nor will it cause one to collapse in a paroxysm of fear. The reason is because transgression has dulled man's heart and made it hard like "a rock of flint" (*Devarim* 8:15). Thus, even the study of Mussar works and Chazal's awesome statements concerning *yiras ha'onesh* will only affect him minimally. The spirit of *yiras Shamayim* will only breathe within him after lengthy study over the course of time. Only then will his brazen heart be humbled and his soul awakened to flee from the valley of grief into a portal of hope (cf. *Hoshea* 2:17).

b) Preoccupation with the task at hand: Once Mussar study makes an impression on the soul, and a person is filled with *yiras Hashem* and the dread of His punishment, sadness still does not accompany the awe. Rav Yisrael explains why this is so by noting the attitude of a soldier who toils to fulfill his onerous duties. If he makes a mistake or violates army regulations, his superiors will mete out a punishment in accord with the severity of his infraction. Perhaps he will be subject to bodily punishment, or to perform some other equally difficult task. Nevertheless, we do not subsequently see him moping

around, depressed and despondent. Instead, immediately after the punishment has concluded, he puts it behind him and continues on with his duties
— all the while, his face shining with joy. The reason for his swift recovery is
because the constant and overbearing obligation of his duties absorbs all of
his energies. He does not have a spare moment to distract himself with un-
constructive considerations. His only thought is to strengthen and improve
his performance, particularly in the area of his failing.

The same is true with our service of the Almighty. When a person studies books on fear and Mussar, his heart is awakened with *yiras Hashem*. He
understands the great and noble service that he has been charged with — to
fulfill all the words of the Torah and its mitzvos, and to walk in the path of the
Almighty. The Heavenly fear that he acquires will banish all counterproductive thoughts from his mind, and inspire him to serve the Creator without
doubt or hesitation.

c) The joy of knowledge: When a person accustoms himself to study works
on Mussar, his eyes will also be opened to see the immense reward reserved
for those who perform Hashem's will, and the goodness that is hidden away
for the righteous — which not even the greatest prophet could truly comprehend (cf. *Berachos* 32b). Therefore, when he has internalized the fear of
Hashem, his soul will perforce be stirred to pursue the path of goodness —
whatever the degree. When this happens, not only will he not be saddened,
but the opposite will occur — he will delight in his portion and "rejoice with
trembling" (cf. *Tehillim* 2:11) — for his eyes will have been opened to know
good and bad (cf. *Bereishis* 3:4) and to foresee the outcome of a deed (cf. *Avos*
2:13). The fear will give him strength and power. The great reward will nurture him and grant him the encouragement to improve his path even more:
to save his soul from the shadowy depths of Gehinnom and to be illuminated
by the precious light of life and eternal delight. His soul will be transformed,
and an upright spirit will be renewed within him (cf. *Tehillim* 51:12).

Nevertheless, one who is faint of heart and does not wish to initially
delve into works dealing with *yiras ha'onesh* has many other options before
him. There is a wide selection of Mussar books on other topics through
which he can grasp hold of the tree of life, for example, works that focus on

the reward of mitzvos in the eternal life of the World to Come. Similarly, there are books that adjure one to observe the ways of Hashem in the world, such as the workings of Divine Providence and how He showers us with His bountiful goodness, kindness, and mercy. In the work *Chovos HaLevavos*, the pious author arranged two sections for this purpose: *Sha'ar HaBechinah* (the Gate of Examination), and *Sha'ar Avodas Elokim* (the Gate of Divine Service). All of this will suffice to enlighten the eyes of man so that he might understand how to draw close to the service of Hashem.

7) ONE MUST NOT DESPAIR, FOR THE EFFECT OF MUSSAR IS CUMULATIVE

In one of his letters, Rav Yisrael writes, "If one undertakes to study Mussar and feels unaffected and that a notion to change has not been imprinted on his soul, still, let his heart not blacken within him. Know that even if the impression is not revealed to the physical senses, it is, nonetheless, perceived by the mind's eye. With much study, the hidden impressions accumulate over time, and one is transformed into a different person. Desires are restrained and cannot burst out in excess, and some are even nullified entirely. Experience and minimal observation testify to the sure effects of Mussar study. In his thoughts and in his conduct, the Mussar student will be more refined and elevated than his peers."

8) THE IMPORTANCE OF SETTING FIXED TIMES FOR STUDY

It is crucial to understand that this topic [Mussar] is extremely voluminous, and profuse study alone is not enough to grasp it — particularly when it is undisciplined. In extolling the wisdom inherent in the study of *yiras ha'onesh* and, specifically, the topic of spiritual punishment, Rav Yisrael would point out its exceeding awesomeness, which is beyond human comprehension. Employing an example from the physical world, he would point to the stars. When we gaze up in the heavens, the stars appear to us as tiny points of light. Looking through a telescope, which magnifies objects thousands of times, we see that they are actually quite large. Yet, in truth, there is no measure to their vastness; in reality, each star is many times larger than our entire planet. So it is with the fundamental concept of spiritual punishment: even if one employs all the powers of his imagination to fathom the prodigious bitterness of punishment, he will not attain a complete understanding of its true magnitude.

Therefore, Rav Yisrael advised that one should regard Mussar study in the context that he views a sensible business practice, and for his entire life he should set a fixed, daily time to engage in it. The Rav stressed that this study is akin to the pursuit of any other sphere of Torah knowledge, and is equal to other essential areas of study — it is an integral part of the body of the Torah (cf. Avos 3:23). Even if the only fruit it bears is to keep a person from committing a single transgression — for example, causing him to refrain from speaking one word of *lashon hara*, or to overcome the temptation to neglect Torah study for even a single moment — it is well worth it. We see from the words of the Vilna Gaon just how severe the sin of evil speech is — and, by extension, the priceless value of refraining from it on even one occasion. In his work *Alim L'Trufah*, he writes, "For every word of emptiness, a person should be flung from one end of the earth to the other. Yet this refers only to unnecessary speech. Concerning forbidden talk, such as slander and scoffery...he must descend to the very bowels of Gehinnom. It is impossible to gauge the magnitude of pain and affliction he will bear for even one word." Thus, if a person saves himself from even one hour of punishment in the spiritual realm, it is an achievement which is unparalleled in this world. It is, therefore, well worth his while to fix a daily time for Mussar study throughout his entire life, even if it prevents only one transgression. In truth, however, it will bring him immeasurably greater benefit, for such study will assuredly prevent many words of slander from being spoken, not to mention much foolish and unnecessary talk. In its place, there will be several hours of Torah study and mitzvah performance.

9) THE BEIS HAMUSSAR: THE IMPERATIVE TO HAVE A SPECIAL LOCATION FOR MUSSAR STUDY

Rav Yisrael felt very strongly that in order to maximize the benefit of Mussar study, it is crucial to have a special location to engage in it. This place must be devoted exclusively to the study of Mussar and should be well stocked with an abundance of Mussar books. Its doors should be always open, and both scholar and layman should gather there — anyone whose soul inspires him to study works of Mussar. According to the degree of one's "illness" regarding Divine service, he should ardently give his heart to study books on fear — each person according to the affliction of his heart and his pain. The Rav made sure to follow his own advice. With the assistance of generous benefactors, he endeavored to erect a facility for Mussar study, which [at the time this work was composed] stands to this very day. He would regularly go there to study Mussar with intense fervor, as was his holy way. Sometimes, he would go when the public was accustomed to meet there, after the Minchah service; other times, he would go when no one else was there, and study in solitude.

Some people question the need to have a special facility for Mussar study, wondering why one can't just study in his house or go to the *beis hamidrash*. Let me now offer the correct answer and reveal what the crucial need is, for it is a profound idea that emanated from our master's heart, and it is a cornerstone and foundation of Mussar that strengthens the entire edifice.

Every person enlightened with the fear of Hashem must acknowledge that Mussar study is essential to man and the life of the soul. Indeed, we have previously noted the exhortations of our pious sages concerning this matter. Nevertheless, we see with our eyes that this study has almost vanished from the face of the earth. No man turns his heart to set fixed times for Mussar study, and very few strive to grow wise and understand its incalculable benefit and vital import. Moreover, one who never studies Mussar will not even find any lack in his soul in the first place. It was only such a unique individual as Rav Yisrael who was able to restore the crown to its former glory (cf. *Yoma* 69b) and to proclaim to all the obligation to study Mussar. It is, therefore, self-evident that much cleverness is needed to draw man's heart to this study. So, too, great wisdom is required to clear a path for those who desire to study fear and Mussar — to straighten it and remove all hindrances and obstacles. It is for this reason that the Rav stressed the importance of having a special place for Mussar study. This idea connotes a masterful strategy for drawing souls to this study. It represents the straight and upright path, vitally important, for the following reasons:

a) An appropriate atmosphere: Even if a person has purified his heart and inclined himself to study Mussar, he still needs an appropriate place where he can do so. This is especially true when considering that the main benefit of Mussar is achieved when it is learned with ardor and passion. Can it be that he will study in his house, surrounded by his family? Likewise, will he go to the *beis hamidrash*, where his fervor will disturb others' Talmudic study — and their study will disturb his as well? Moreover, sometimes he may be aroused to tears, and his eyes will flow with streams of water. Won't he, then, be too embarrassed and ashamed to study? Finally, it might very well be that a person does not always have access to all the Mussar works he needs. However, if he has a special location to go to, where fervent Mussar study is the accustomed practice, then none of the above mentioned deterrents or distractions will be there to disturb him. So, too, several books will be ready and waiting for him there. In such a place, every person can study Mussar with great fervor, as much as his heart desires. He can cry out from all the pain in his soul, with no impediments or hindrances. There, he might be aroused to mourn and lament like the jackal and the ostrich (cf. *Eichah* 2:5; *Yeshayahu* 43:20), and to let his tears gush forth, unchecked.

b) Inspiration to others: Since most people are devoid of this knowledge, and the ways of its study are foreign to them, how then will they be aroused and guided to follow the proper path? It is thus self-evident that a special facility is required for proper Mussar study to become widespread and popularized. In such a place, both novice and master can gather at a specific time to study Mussar. Anyone going to such a place will hear pious scholars mournfully repeating Chazal's awesome statements concerning Mussar and *yiras Hashem* in a manner that shakes the soul, melts the heart, and subdues the spirit. The listener will thereby be inspired to emulate the ways of those whose voices he hears and to study the same concepts as they do. As the Rambam, *zt"l*, writes (*Hilchos De'os*, ch. 6), "It is human nature for a person to be drawn after the views and actions of his friends and associates. Therefore, a person should associate with sages and scholars, so that he may learn from them."

c) Encouragement and reinforcement: The obligation of the mitzvah to learn Torah is well known. Indeed, we are taught in the Talmud (*Shabbos* 31a): "When a man is led in for judgment [in the Next World] he is asked…'Did you fix [daily] times for Torah study?'" Therefore, every God-fearing person should endeavor to strengthen himself in this area, thereby ensuring that he will not be interrupted by any incident or problem, or be distracted by cares or laziness. Accordingly, even if a person can study in his house, he should, nonetheless, choose a place for himself in the "Abode of God" (*Bereishis* 28:17), and go to study in the *beis hamidrash*. In this way, his conduct will be governed by the force of habit. Furthermore, the man of understanding will employ strategies to fortify himself in this area, such as joining together with others who have similarly established set times for Torah study. This is particularly true concerning the neglected subject of Mussar, a topic wherein the obligation to study is hidden from the eye, and which many consider to be unnecessary. Even a person who has already resolved to set fixed times for this study is easily derailed — a light breeze can carry away all his resolution and cover over its every trace. Hence, this matter is quite serious, and it is critical that one deeply embed and strengthen his commitment — by the means of a special facility and a clearly scheduled time for the public to gather and engage in Mussar study. Once a person accustoms himself to go to the "house of Mussar," his habit will direct him and the fear will sustain him. His set time will become an unchanging decree (cf. *Tehillim* 148:6), like a firmly planted stake that does not move (cf. *Yeshayahu* 22:23).

d) Promoting public awareness: This facility will be marked with the unambiguous title of *beis hamussar* — the house of Mussar (cf. *Yechezkel* 9:4). This itself will publicize to the masses the obligation to study Mussar. At the head of noisy throngs it will cry out, and in the streets it will give forth voice and speak its words, exclaiming, "Who is the person who desires life — a life of good sense, so as not to drown in the depths of desire? Who is the person afflicted with spiritual ills, and desires a remedy for his disease? Let him turn to my tent — all the balm of Gilad is found within my walls. Seek me out — and live" (cf. *Mishlei* 1:20–21, *Tehillim* 34:13, *Yirmeyahu* 46:11). Additionally, every passerby will be reminded that this place is devoted to the path of life — the admonishment of Mussar. Likewise, such a special facility will remind those who, for various reasons, do not attend the *beis hamussar* that in any event, they should endeavor to study Mussar.

10) BRINGING MERIT TO THE PUBLIC THROUGH MUSSAR STUDY

Rav Yisrael strove to confer merit upon the Jewish people by encouraging the study of Mussar. Indeed, this study is a tree of life (cf. *Mishlei* 3:18), bringing healing to the soul and teaching understanding of Heavenly fear and pious humility. It girds man with good counsel and resourcefulness, giving him strength and valor to battle the *yetzer hara*. This is the only way to restore the fear of Hashem — and through it, the Jewish people will achieve salvation of the soul. Consider, then, the reward for the mitzvah of drawing hearts close to Mussar study. It is eternal and inconceivably exalted. For this reason, the Rav aroused his students and those close to him to set their hearts to understand and to bring merit to the public, by awakening their souls to the study of fear and Mussar.

In his *Iggeres HaMussar*, Rav Yisrael extolled the sublime preciousness of the mitzvah of bringing merit to the public through Mussar study, as well as its great reward. The following is an excerpt of his holy words: "To this a person should give his heart: to confer merit upon the public by awakening them to contemplate fear and Mussar.... Likewise, he should endeavor with all of his being to strengthen the study of Mussar, so that the masses will endeavor to study Mussar, thereby increasing the fear of Hashem. When he does so, the public merit will be ascribed to his efforts. How lofty should this mitzvah be in man's eyes — to give his heart and soul to guide people in Mussar study and to save their souls from Gehinnom. As it says in *Maseches Shabbos* (151b), 'Anyone who has mercy on God's creatures will himself be extended mercy from Heaven.' There is no greater mercy than to call notice to the fear of Hashem and to arouse people to study it. One who does so will have a goodly portion in everything that is generated from it — to delight in the eternal pleasure that no eye has ever beheld. It is beyond human ability to comprehend the quantity and quality of the mitzvah of bringing merit to the public that will result from this simple task. The labor is minimal and the reward is abundant — priceless and immeasurable. Therefore, every spiritually sensitive person should direct his eye and the power of his intellect to this lofty undertaking."

Likewise, in the letters the Rav wrote to his students and relatives in order to strengthen their hearts in *yiras Hashem* and Mussar study, he would also encourage them to bring merit to the public — to focus all of their energies on strengthening the study of Mussar. Here is a quote of his pure and holy words: "Open rebuke is better than hidden love. My intent herein is to admonish you and to stir your sense of noble purpose. You must fortify yourselves with all of your ability — each man according to his intelligence and situation — to enthusiastically strengthen and encourage the study of Mussar.... Do not let the matter of bringing merit to the public appear light in your eyes. Awaken the masses to engage in fierce and unrelenting battle against the evil inclination, with the only weapon that can bring victory — proper Mussar study."

In another letter, he writes: "To this end, the beginning of our task is to strengthen weak hands — to employ wisdom and knowledge and guide people to the *beis hamussar*. This is an easy and effective remedy that bears abundant fruits. 'Who is the man who desires life' (*Tehillim* 34:13), to be counted amongst those who bring merit to the public — those who shine like the stars and whose righteousness will never dim (cf. *Daniel* 12:3)? Let him grab this mitzvah now, when the time is ripe, for who knows what the morrow will bring — 'and if not now, when' (*Avos* 1:14)? Moreover, we shall also be built through this, and our minds will be sharpened to conquer the evil inclination and its desires — for one who comes to teach will ultimately learn."

Sublime and exalted were our teacher's ways, and profound were his thoughts, for he set his mind to bring benefit to his people by enlightening them with the fear of Hashem. How accurate were his words — for we know how our Sages extolled the virtue of conferring merit upon the public. But the question we must ask is, how can a person attain this level of being able to positively influence others? Simple admonishment and rebuke are limited in their ability to extract a precious thing from the dross surrounding it. Moreover, in light of the principle that in order to turn others from iniquity one must first perfect himself (see *Bava Basra* 60b), this is an extremely difficult task to undertake. Yet even if this were not a deterrent, and even if the one giving admonishment were to increase his words like grains of sand, no one would heed him — for who will incline his ear to words of rebuke to change his ways? However, awakening and arousing man's heart to study Mussar provides fertile ground to bring merit to the public (cf. *Yeshayahu* 30:23), with minimal effort. It is easy to draw the heart to this study, for it is self-evident that it is essential for the life of the soul.

This "back door" approach applies to many areas of mitzvah observance. Consider the performance of good deeds and the dispensation of charity to the poor — being compassionate and merciful to the indigent. It is very hard on a benefactor to constantly give small amounts. It is also difficult for the recipient, who never receives as much as he really needs — for who can provide a man with everything that he lacks? However, one who contemplates the plight of a poor person will come to the realization that there is one effective way to support him: by providing him with the means to make a living, so that he can eat and be satisfied from the fruit of his own labors. Indeed, such an act of kindness is considered to be a source of everlasting righteousness for the benefactor. The same is true with the life of the soul — it is beyond human ability to constantly give or receive admonishment and rebuke. However, one who contemplates the fear of Hashem will understand that the most effective way to reach people is to incline their hearts to study Mussar — for then, they will begin to admonish themselves. From the toil of their souls, they will be sated with the goodness of Heavenly fear — to fulfill the Torah and the mitzvos. Moreover, blessing will envelop the teacher who showed them the path. He will have a portion and an inheritance in all of their skillful enterprise (cf. *Koheles* 4:4), and he will enjoy the fruits of their deeds together with them.

Nevertheless, not just anyone can influence others in this area. It requires great wisdom to draw souls to the study of Mussar and much intelligence to instill knowledge and understanding within people so that they can utilize this precious treasure to make upright judgments. This study is a fair jewel (*Mishlei* 17:8), a desirable treasure in the abode of righteousness (cf. *Mishlei* 21:21, *Yirmeyahu* 31:22) that contains no corruption or perversion (cf. *Mishlei* 8:8). Moreover, the potential teacher must first perfect his own character traits — and particularly the virtue of patience. Then he will understand, and Hashem will grant success to his efforts. Concerning this, Rav Yisrael writes in one of his letters, "This topic — to draw hearts close to the study of Mussar — must be firmly grounded in Mussar. It will be strengthened with patience, and with wisdom it will blossom and give forth its flower." He similarly addressed this subject in many other letters, teaching the knowledge of how to draw souls to the study of fear and Mussar, and how to incline them to true perfection.

In his *Iggeres HaMussar*, the Rav writes, "How exalted should this mitzvah be in man's eyes — to give one's heart and soul to guide others to study Mussar.... The person who is inspired to do this will have a fitting portion in all that his efforts generate, to delight in the eternal pleasure that no eye has ever beheld." In another letter he writes, "Who is the man who desires life" (*Tehillim* 34:13), to be counted amongst those who bring merit to the public — those who shine like the stars and whose righteousness will never dim (cf. *Daniel* 12:3)? Let him grab this mitzvah now, when the time is ripe."

With this, we are in a position to comprehend how mighty and powerful is this "tree" — our master, the pious sage, the "holy one of Israel" — and how great and awesome is his merit. Consider the following: In addition to his great righteousness and piety, is there anyone who conferred more merit upon the public than him? He was the first to rally to the task of guiding people to study Mussar. From his earliest youth, he enthusiastically began to advocate the study of this holy topic, from whence emanates the life of the soul. Until this day, we walk in his light. He has a portion and an inheritance in all the perfection of deeds that has been generated from the study of Mussar — until this day, and forevermore.

Once, when Rav Yisrael spoke to his students about how Mussar study has spread throughout the world, he told them that Heaven left him an area in which he could shine and make his mark. As the Gemara (*Chullin* 6b) expounds on the verse: "And he [Chizkiyahu] ground up the copper serpent that Moshe had made — for until those days the Children of Israel used to burn incense before it; he called it [derogatorily] 'Nechushtan' " (*Melachim II* 18:4). Asks the Gemara, "How is it possible that [the righteous] Assa did not destroy it in his time? How is it possible that [the righteous] Yehoshafat did not destroy it in his time? Didn't Assa and Yehoshafat destroy all the idols in the land? Rather, we must say that his forefathers left him room in which to shine."

May it be the will of our Father in Heaven, that the well which springs from a holy place — the "holy one of Israel" — does not cease. May his waters not become falsified, and may they be as a river overflowing with Heavenly fear, diverging into numerous mighty streams.

Herein concludes my essay, crowned with the title "The Gates of Light." This is the gateway to Hashem. Let the upright of heart enter within and proceed forward, and their eyes will be illuminated by the "Light of Israel" and his holiness.

These are the words of his student,

Yitzchak Blazer

אור ישראל

THE LIGHT
OF ISRAEL

Rav Yisrael Salanter

The first five letters were written by Rav Yisrael, *zt"l*, when he first moved from Vilna to Kovno in 5609 (1849). These letters were addressed to his students and relatives in Vilna.

LETTER ONE

THE BRILLIANT LIGHT

[Just at the moment when all seems dark] we behold a brilliant, sparkling light — to confer merit upon the public, to strengthen the masses through Mussar study, and to give advice and provide strategies for it to become an accepted habit.

LACK OF HABIT IN YIRAS SHAMAYIM

MY BELOVED FRIENDS, I will begin to speak:

My primary aspiration that I desire [for you to accomplish] is a matter which I have consistently presented before you. [I expected that you would] set your hearts upon them [i.e., my instructions] and deeply contemplate them. In truth, have I uttered any words (cf. *Mishlei* 8:7)?[1] Almost the second my words would enter your ears — in the next moment — they became nonexistent. My words entered one ear and exited the other. The cause of this is the customary [i.e., prevalent in the world] deficiency of not pondering matters relating to Heavenly fear and Mussar. Rather, [it is the norm for people] to conduct themselves in these matters by following after the dictates of desire — according to the whims of the [natural] will — like the behavior of an animal.[2]

---

1   That is, it appears that what I have taught you in the past has not made the impression that I had hoped. When Rav Yisrael resided in Vilna, he instructed his students to follow a course of strengthening Mussar that he had outlined for them. Subsequently, he moved to Kovno. It was from there, in Kovno, that he expressed to his students his concern.

2   His intention is not that the students are following the whims of desire to pursue earthly pleasures like an animal, but that they do not sufficiently contemplate concepts of Heavenly fear and Mussar. Rather, their pursuit of Heavenly fear is constricted to the bidding of their nature — just like an animal who is controlled by natural forces of arousal. Rav

ANALYSIS OF WORLDLY MATTERS

Don't you see that the known, routine practice in the world is for people to invest all of their intellectual and analytical energies in all material matters [that interest and concern them]?[3] Consider, for example, a merchant and his wares: before executing a deal, he examines it from every angle to decide whether or not he should risk it. He thinks it through by himself and seeks the counsel of trustworthy friends, reviewing the details and looking at every possible miscalculation. [He explores all the issues,] until he reaches [what he hopes is the right] decision, according to the best of his ability.

ANALYSIS OF TORAH

The same is true of a scholar devoted to study of the holy Torah. Each person, according to his ability, will engage in in-depth study and contemplation of a topic to reveal all its subtle aspects, discover new understandings, and answer any questions that may arise. [It is manifestly clear that the serious student] does not jump to hasty conclusions in the blink of an eye.[4]

MUSSAR STUDY

However, such is not the case with Mussar study.[5] Mussar is the contemplation and exploration of all the paths and actions of man. [Through it] one

---

Yisrael does not attribute their lack of mastery of Mussar to neglect of Mussar study, but rather to a level of devotion that is somewhat less than total. The goal of Mussar is the purification of one's emotions and motivations. Indeed, it is nothing short of changing human nature. Yet this transformation is created only through total immersion in Mussar: something that requires total mastery of one's nature. Since this level of discipline is quite challenging, Rav Yisrael reminds his students of an effective plan he designed to facilitate their success.

3 Rav Yisrael now points out that the unsystematic approach to Mussar is very common, and in sharp contrast to our approach to other areas of life.

4 We thus see that people invest much thought in a matter before coming to a conclusion and taking a course of action — be it in physical or spiritual endeavors.

5 In other areas, man understands that he needs a well thought-out strategy in order to succeed; in Mussar study, however, we assign no importance whatsoever to strategic planning. Yet we cannot successfully instill Mussar in our hearts unless we design and implement a course of action.

is protected from the inclinations of desire and the *yetzer hara*, which disturbs and prevents every good and praiseworthy thing. [This study is] a critical and obligatory component in the attainment of *yiras Shamayim*. Yet the Mussar one imbibes and the resultant positive conduct will not be realized in a person unless he employs sophisticated strategies. One's intellectual faculties must be closely bound to the concepts he learns, until a strong impression has been made in his heart. [The intensity of this impression] will strengthen and fortify his external limbs.[6] [And ultimately he will] put into practice the lofty concepts [of Mussar], without interference from worthless physical cravings and base traits such as jealousy and the desire for honor. Unfortunately, man is very lazy in this entire matter.[7] He considers it a burden, and even if he allots a negligible amount of time for its pursuit, he considers it to be a waste of time.

THE BATTLE IS RAGING

What, then, is there for us to do? The battle is raging. The *yetzer hara* waits in ambush; desire is unrestrained and negative character traits overwhelm us. We have no weapon [with which to fight the *yetzer hara*]. Can an instrument be formed without an expert craftsman?[8] So, too, there is no hope to be saved from the snare of death unless we grasp the weapon — the ideals of *yiras Shamayim* and Mussar study.

THE SOLUTION

I have one message to tell you: do as I instruct you and it will be well for you. Consider a person beset with business woes, who finds unfavorable circumstances in whichever direction he turns. As his affairs become increasingly darker, his mind is befuddled and shackled in the bonds of worry and confusion, which sap all of his strength. Now, consider if someone were to approach him and say, "I will show you the light [i.e., the solution to all of your problems]! If you do as I say, according to the proper estimation, you will re-

---

6   Facilitate the control of his external behavior.
7   In contemplating and utilizing strategies to instill and establish Mussar and *yiras Shamayim* within his nature.
8   Mussar is the weapon to fight the *yetzer hara*. If we don't study Mussar — it is as if we are not "making" for ourselves a weapon.

alize an enormous profit. Moreover, it will not overly distract you from your other dealings, and it will not take up too much of your time." There is no doubt that he would focus all of his attention on what his advisor had to say. He would dedicate all his energies to fully understand the plan that was being proposed to him, until it was firmly rooted in his heart. He would certainly set aside a small amount of time in order to contemplate what was said to him so that he could achieve a proper understanding. Moreover, he would not hesitate to seek out trustworthy friends who could assist him in the endeavor, and disregard any minimal loss of honor or demands on his patience that the proposal might entail.

STRENGTHEN THE MASSES IN MUSSAR

So it is with us today. We suffer from unrelenting afflictions of the soul. Our transgressions are amassed over our heads, each person according to his level. We stand far, far distant from the central purpose of our creation and from the goal for which we came into this physical world — to prepare for the Hereafter. And now, [just at the moment when all seems dark,] we behold a brilliant, sparkling light — to confer merit upon the public, to strengthen hands that are weak in the study of Mussar,[9] and to give advice and provide strategies for it to become an accepted habit — to the point where it is a source of pride in people's eyes, and they praise one who studies it, saying, "See this person who is so strong in the wisdom of fear and Mussar!" Eventually, pure intentions will arise from impure ones. One cannot even imagine how much [our efforts to spread Mussar to the community] will generate an increase in the value of Mussar, if Hashem will grant success to our paths. We will also be built up through this [i.e., our efforts to spread Mussar to the community], and we will eat of the fruits of our endeavors, whether in great quantity or small.[10]

---

9 To influence the masses, who generally do not study Mussar, to study Mussar. This is the counsel that Rav Yisrael had instructed his students to accomplish, referred to in the opening paragraph of this letter. He admonished them for not heeding his instructions. He points out to them that just as it would be foolish for a man beset by financial woes to ignore wise counsel, so, too, it is irresponsible of his students to dismiss his expert counsel

10 Rav Yisrael innovated an ingenious counsel to internalize Mussar. He reasoned that since the *yetzer hara* subverts us from properly engaging in Mussar, an alternative motivation needed to be created. His solution was for his students to encourage others to study

DISCUSS HOW TO SPREAD MUSSAR

To this end, [I adjure you all to] designate a fixed time on *Shabbos Kodesh*, to gather together at an appointed time, and contemplate how you might influence the prominent members of the community to study Mussar, so that the masses will follow their example and go in their footsteps.[11] Speak in a pleasant and relaxed manner, without laughter and levity. Evaluate the virtues and deficiencies of the person [under discussion], and determine the best approach to admonish him and to bind him[12] [to study Mussar]. Do not decide the matter too hastily. Divide the work amongst all of you, so that it will only be necessary for each of you to devote a minimal amount of time and effort to the task

---

Mussar. This has the double advantage of influencing others, as well as strengthening themselves in Mussar. Rav Yisrael elaborates on this in *Iggeres HaMussar*, which follows Letter Thirty-one. Here is an abridged quote (see the text in full): "The enemy that ambushes man is the evil inclination. It works on him to turn his heart to stone. Man is rendered so blind that he does not sense his awful transgressions, nor his shortcomings. Hence, he does not endeavor to save himself. He does not contemplate the fear of God, to seek an effective remedy.... In order to heal himself, then, a man should direct his heart to bring merit to the public by arousing them to contemplate the fear of God and Mussar. It is human nature to observe other people's shortcomings and recognize that they need much Mussar. Thus, he should strengthen himself with all of his power to inspire the public study of Mussar. When many people will be helped and the fear of God will be increased, then the merit of many will be dependent on him. Consequently, ever so slowly, the study of Mussar will guide him on the path of righteousness.... How exceedingly great should this mitzvah be in the eyes of man! He should dedicate his heart and soul to guide people to study Mussar.... There is no greater mercy than to remind and inspire people to study the fear of God. Then, with their eyes they will see and with their ears they will hear, and their heart will understand the great stumbling block before them. They will sigh about the time of judgment. Then they will return to God, may He be blessed, so that they will depart from evil and do good. The man that is so inspired to do this will share a goodly portion in everything that is generated from his efforts. He will delight in the eternal delights — that no physical eye has ever seen. It is beyond human understanding to fathom and perceive the quantity and quality of the reward of this mitzvah."

11 Rav Yisrael devised a program for his students to promulgate Mussar study in their community of Vilna. One phase of the plan called for the students to meet on Shabbos and discuss the most effective approach to enlist the participation of the prominent members of the community. Once these leaders would engage in Mussar study, the general populace would follow their influence.

12 See Letter Four, where Rav Yisrael explains the technique of drawing a person into *avodas Hashem* through his own weaknesses.

— as the verse states, "That gathered by hand [i.e., gradually and diligently] will increase" (*Mishlei* 13:11). Proceed with peace of mind, calmness, understanding, and sincerity. Each man should strengthen his friend, for by doing so the foolishness of his heart will thereby weaken and the laziness of his habit will diminish. Act with courtesy and pleasantness, and take care to respect the honor of one another. Conduct yourselves with pleasantness and patience. Follow the majority opinion, without obstinacy and disagreement. In this way the Mussar will be properly established in your souls, as you so desire.

TRANSLATOR'S SUMMARY OF LETTER ONE

1. Mussar is the exploration of all the paths and actions of man, and awakens *yiras Shamayim*.

2. Through Mussar study, one is protected from the influence of the *yetzer hara*.

3. Mussar cannot be internalized without sophisticated strategies.

4. The primary counsel of Rav Yisrael to inculcate Mussar values is for the pursuers of Mussar to influence others to study Mussar.

LETTER TWO

SECRETS OF GROWTH

Where can we flee for help, and to whom shall we turn? All that we have is the study of Mussar, which impels man to remember the Hereafter — for life in this lowly world is not forever.

DRAW CLOSE TO THE LIGHT

MY BROTHERS AND FRIENDS, I previously related an analogy concerning a man afflicted and crushed by the vanities of this world.[1] [The burden of providing a] livelihood for himself forces onerous labor upon him, and he has no peace of mind in all his affairs. When he becomes aware of a correct path stretched before him — [a path] which offers great hope that a place will be found for him to calm his turbulent spirit — he will surely not rest nor be silent until he implements the plans of his heart. [He will set up his plan securely] as a sturdy peg, fixed firmly in its place. Is there any fool who would walk in darkness when a brilliant light shines before him? Who would not reflect upon his actions in order to draw himself close to it [i.e., the light]?

PREPARE FOR THE HEREAFTER

So it is with us today concerning the proceedings of our spiritual endeavors, to prepare provisions for our [life in the] Hereafter, to turn away from the dismal pit and from everlasting anguish and shame in the Eternal World. We are afflicted with the illusionary desires. The [pursuit of] honor — which removes a man from the world (cf. *Pirkei Avos* 4:21) — subverts our

---

1   See Letter One.

spirits, and we [blindly] follow it, and in its footsteps we are removed [from the world]. Our minds are in turmoil and our energies drained [by our effort] to prepare a sufficient supply [of honor for ourselves].[2] [In turn,] this causes us to neglect Torah study, which is "our life and the length of our days" (Siddur, Ma'ariv Prayer) — both in this world and the Next. Moreover, it hinders our mitzvah performance and all of our positive character traits, and leads us to iniquity and transgression that reaches up to the very Heavens.[3]

ONLY MUSSAR CAN SAVE US

Where can we flee for help, and to whom shall we turn, if not to the study of Mussar? It admonishes man to remember the Hereafter — for life in this lowly world is not forever. Rather, we are but sojourners during this phase of our existence, [put here] to perform our Divine service with which we have been charged, so that we may receive our reward in the place where we truly belong. Now, what honor will we inherit in this foreign world, which passes like a shadow and is no longer seen (cf. *Tehillim* 144:4)?[4]

SET FIXED TIMES FOR MUSSAR STUDY

What we have thus far mentioned is a mere glimpse of the awesome power of Mussar. It is a shining light — whereas we walk in darkness, following after our lowly and disgraceful bodily desires. How can we not worry about [correcting] our deeds, [which is accomplished] by drawing close to this study? How can we build sturdy, fixed foundations so that no adverse incident will befall us, *chas v'chalilah*, and interrupt this exalted study? It is therefore eminently correct to firmly secure it with "well-placed nails" — to

---

2   We are trapped in the inexhaustible demand for honor.

3   Thus, without Mussar study man is vulnerable to a multi-level attack of the *yetzer hara*: 1) When man is devoid of Mussar, he follows the whims of the body. 2) Consequently, he is stricken with spiritual blindness, turmoil, and fatigue. 3) In turn, he neglects Torah study, mitzvos, and the pursuit of a virtuous character. 4) Then he falls to transgressions. 5) Finally, he is subject to Gehinnom.

4   The study of Mussar saves man from the subversion of the *yetzer hara* in the following way: By studying Mussar he instills within his heart the awareness of Divine reward and punishment. He therefore avoids transgression; he studies Torah, performs mitzvos, and pursues virtue of character. Ultimately, he merits a share in the World to Come.

set a daily, fixed study time between Minchah and Ma'ariv [to study Mussar]. Each person should strengthen his friend [in this matter], and be quick to plan strategies to insure that this period is properly [devoted to Mussar study], without missing even one day. If he misses a session, or perhaps something interferes with his Mussar session, *chas v'shalom*, then it is proper to investigate the matter. One should seek out counsel and strategy on how to cast aside his foolishness, and how to draw his heart back to Mussar with gentle words[5] — each person according to his temperament and intelligence. In this way, the Mussar study will be anchored with a solid stake (cf. *Yeshayahu* 22:23).

HISPAILUS

[The key to success in Mussar is] to accustom [ourselves and others] in this wisdom. This is achieved by employing two methods. The first is to kindle the soul with purity of thought, by studying exalted [Mussar] concepts. This study should be pursued with lips aflame, an appropriate frame of mind, and broad visualization to enrich each idea and bring it close to one's heart with fitting analogies.[6] Continue in

5   Rav Yisrael reiterates here one of his most important themes — the gentle approach. We would have assumed that if one missed or neglected his daily Mussar session, then it would be appropriate to sharply castigate oneself, "How could I be so careless as to miss a Mussar session? Am I completely devoid of *yiras Shamayim?*" Yet Rav Yisrael instructs us not to be harsh with ourselves. An abrasive rebuke will prove to be counterproductive. It could cause one to swiftly abandon the path of Mussar. We must use a gentle approach with ourselves, and all the more so with others, as will be discussed later on in this letter. For a gentle approach is the most effective and sensitive way to speak to the heart. Gentle words will find an open and receptive heart and therefore will have a positive and lasting influence.

6   The study of Mussar with vocalization and fervor is called "*hispailus.*" In the second innovation of The Ten Innovations (found at the end of "The Gates of Light"), *hispailus* is defined as follows: "Therefore, in order to attain the goal of acquiring fear, it is necessary for Mussar to be studied in a passionate manner that will stir the soul: with a sincere heart, a mournful voice, and lips aflame.... This is a great aid to Mussar study, for it viscerally arouses the soul, inculcating within it the knowledge of the punishments awaiting the body and the soul, knowledge that was previously confined to the intellect alone. This is similar to the power that musical instruments and singing have to inspire man and awaken his spirit — either to happiness or sadness. When a person reads the statements of Chazal and works on Mussar with solemn fervor — which ignite the heart with Heavenly fear — then his heart will warm up and his spirit will become stormy and agitated.

this way until the heart will ignite with flames, whether a little or a lot. Then one will be endowed with the power to prepare his limbs to perform every good deed with pure intentions — whether with the body's consent or against its will.

WORLDLY WISDOM

The second method is to employ worldly wisdom — to anticipate the ramifications [of one's deeds] so that he oversees [his conduct] from the outset, before the evil days arrive.[7] This includes the preparation of counsel and strategy on how to guide both oneself and others, and how to minimize the matter and ease the test, until the fear of Hashem is greater than the bodily desires. This is the sum of man's duty (cf. *Koheles* 12:13), to strengthen fear and weaken desire through the study of Mussar and [worldly] wisdom.[8]

THE FOCAL POINT

To this end, how remarkable would it be to discover the focal point around which revolve the study and proper discipline in Mussar and [reflection on the strategies of worldly] wisdom! Indeed, the focal point is to draw people's hearts close to the study of Mussar.[9] Mussar [with *hispailus*] will build strong foundations,[10] unwavering patience[11] will strengthen

---

His senses will become electrified, and the words he reads will strike roots in his inner heart and implant the fear of Hashem within his soul."

7   "Worldly wisdom" is the term that Rav Yisrael uses to describe the study of human conduct and motive. It does not connote, nor advocate, a secular education. Rather, it means knowledge gained through the observation and study of human personality (i.e., worldly wisdom), as distinguished from the knowledge gained from the considered study of Mussar. The subject of such a study is either oneself or another person. In general, it is the observation and assessment of one's character flaws — and strategic planning to confront future tests in those areas. "The evil days" refers to the actualization of the challenge that he anticipated and prepared for in advance. The importance that Rav Yisrael places on worldly wisdom is expressed in the last paragraph of this letter: "The comprehension of this concept — employing worldly wisdom to lighten the task and minimize the test until the fear is reinforced — needs extensive explanation, along with appropriate analogies. These matters are not discussed in the classic Mussar works. Rather, each person must draw it from his own understanding, by contemplating his own life experience." See Letter Four for an elaboration of worldly wisdom, as well as Letters Nineteen and Twenty, where Rav Yisrael explains that this knowledge of

[others], and with worldly wisdom it will blossom and give flower.[12]

PATIENCE AND HUMILITY

Along with this, if we shall be men of valor, at all costs, one must not become angry at his companion and exclaim, "Why is his heart closed to understanding this study's importance!" Rather, we must remind ourselves that foolishness prevails in many areas of our own lives as well. It is crucial that we conduct ourselves with patience and humility, and engrave these virtues upon our hearts. We must never think of ourselves as better than others.

We must contemplate deeply to prepare counsel and strategy for how to admonish others with compelling words, and draw them close to our Father in Heaven. Doing so strengthens us as well, for it will spur us on to awaken and admonish ourselves in many areas. As a result, our souls will be drawn to perform the Divine service, which [is the reason that] we were created — for our benefit.

FOCUS ON THE AREA IN WHICH ONE IS GIFTED

Moreover, when we convey our task to others [i.e., convince others to follow the path of Mussar], each person should focus on the area in which he is gifted. When approaching an individual, the one of you[13] [who is intellectual] should admonish him in a scholarly fashion. The one [who is friendly] should draw him close with an amiable countenance. The one [who is intense and fervent] should encourage him with the passion of his pure heart, and the one [who is clever] should convince him through sound strategies and the requisite wisdom. This practice [of utilizing every person's unique talents] is an extraordinarily effective method [to convince others] to establish the practice of Mussar study and to pursue virtue of character. Further-

---

human behavior is classified as practical wisdom and not theoretical.

8   By engaging in both Mussar study with *hispailus*, as well as worldly wisdom.

9   As discussed in Letter One.

10 Of *yiras Shamayim* and virtue of character.

11 To draw other people close to Mussar study.

12 The *yiras Shamayim* will reach fruition.

13 As noted, these first five letters were written to his students. Rav Yisrael had assigned them the task to strengthen Mussar study in their community.

more, it will preclude many tests that might confront a man.[14] This is a matter of saving a life, [for the wrong approach] is capable of suddenly corrupting him, terribly and irreversibly, *chas v'chalilah*. If we accustom ourselves to pursue our goal with joint participation — each person utilizing his particular path and affairs — then each objective will be achieved easily, with minimal effort and exertion. This will give life to numerous souls, and contribute to the sustaining of the entire world.

The comprehension of this concept — employing worldly wisdom to lighten the task and minimize the test until the fear is reinforced — needs extensive explanation, along with appropriate analogies. These matters are not discussed in the classic Mussar works. Rather, each person must draw it from his own understanding, by contemplating his own life experience. *Bli neder*, we will speak more about this later, with Hashem's help.

TRANSLATOR'S SUMMARY OF LETTER TWO

1. It is imperative to reserve daily times for Mussar study.

2. Mussar growth encompasses two methods:
   a) *hispailus* (emotional arousal)
   b) worldly wisdom (learning from one's mistakes)

3. The focal point of Mussar study and its two methods is to draw people's hearts to Mussar.

4. When enlightening others about Mussar, each person should express himself in the area in which he is gifted.

---

14 An unfavorable reaction to reject Mussar that the subject might feel had he not been approached in this group method.

LETTER THREE

THE HIDING PLACE OF THE YETZER HARA

*Our wish to fulfill our earthly desires stems directly from our primal
desire for life itself — for the basic will to live implants within us a
feeling of want and desire that does not discriminate between valid
and illegitimate need.*

MUSSAR STUDY IS INCUMBENT ON ALL PEOPLE

MY BELOVED FRIENDS! I thought for certain that the words of my
first letter would suffice to awaken your hearts to strengthen the
study of Mussar. This body of wisdom is unlike any other, for there is no other
study that is incumbent on all people. Women, of course, are exempt from
Torah study — the challenges of daily existence and the distractions caused
by life's difficulties, *chas v'shalom*, provide ample ground for their exemption.
Likewise, many men, according to their individual situations and need for
livelihood, are relieved from their obligation to study.[1] Conversely, the more
opportunity a man has to study, the greater is his obligation to do so.

---

1   Apparently, Rav Yisrael's intention is that the need for livelihood releases one from the
    obligation to be continuously engaged in Torah study, in keeping with the verse, "And
    you shall contemplate them [words of Torah] day and night" (*Yehoshua* 1:8). The
    Rambam (*Hilchos Talmud Torah* 1:8) rules, "Every Jewish man is obligated to study Torah
    whether he is poor or rich, healthy or ill, whether young or old...even a poor man who is
    supported from charity and collects money by going door to door, and even a married man
    with a family, is obligated to set fixed times for Torah study both day and night."

WHAT WILL WE DO ON THE DAY OF RECKONING?

Such is not the case with Mussar. The obligation of this study encompasses all souls, without exception — for the war engages every being who is endowed with the power of speech. It is the war of the *yetzer hara* and its strategies: the desires of man and his crooked ways that trap him in their web and leave him no chance to escape, *chas v'chalilah*. In the briefest of instants, a person can come to sin profusely, with nothing to impede his spirit. He will indulge in every form of corrupt behavior and become an abomination in the sight of all (cf. *Shmuel II* 12:11) — woe to us! What will we do on the day of reckoning, when the Almighty sits in judgment over every living being [and will pass sentence] on our deeds and motives? How can man gird himself with the strength and fortitude to prevail in this fierce war — if not with the study of Mussar? This study will help us to partially purify our thoughts, to slightly inflame our hearts, and to contemplate on our fates in the Hereafter. It will provide us with a guiding light, so that our external limbs [i.e., our conduct] will walk by this illumination. Thus strengthened they will fight their war [against the *yetzer hara*] for truth and righteousness. This is a major focus of all our aspirations: namely, that we guard at least our external limbs [i.e., external conduct] from all evil disease and illness of the spirit[2] regarding both our character traits and mitzvah performance — something that cannot be accomplished save through self-discipline and with much habit.

MUSSAR SPURS US TO PERFORM GOOD DEEDS

Yet who will restrain and conquer them [i.e., the external limbs]? What will spur them on to perform every good and beneficial thing, if not the study of Mussar? This study shatters the heart and somewhat cleanses it of impurity. It helps to arouse and inform one of the proper method to fight this battle — namely, the battle to soundly conquer the limbs of the body and to guard against every evil disease and illness of the spirit. Thus, to the degree that the *yetzer hara* continues to intensify its battle against a person,

---

2   See Letter Thirty where Rav Yisrael distinguishes between *kivush hamiddos*, subduing the *yetzer hara* by controlling one's external conduct, and *tikun hamiddos*, the rectification of the *yetzer hara* through purifying one's heart and spirit.

so does his obligation to study Mussar grow. This is especially true in these times, when things are not good and the war [of the *yetzer hara*] rages fiercely amongst us; thus, our obligation to study Mussar increases [exponentially].

My sense is that you are quite weak in this area. To this I say that the wisdom of Mussar is nothing more than the elaboration of things that are simple and obvious. Hence, it is only proper to expand on the matters we mentioned in the first letter.

WE ARE FAR REMOVED FROM THE CENTRAL PURPOSE

When we contemplate the substance of our wants and longings, we discover that the desire for the illusory life of this world supercedes all others. This will to live is anchored deep in our hearts, like a stake set firmly in the earth. [Indeed, there is no doubt that] we would be willing to exchange everything that we possess for the sake of our survival. We live in doubt, not knowing the time of our demise. [In actuality, for this] we must rely solely on our Father in Heaven, Who desires to grant us life so that we may serve Him in truth and faithfulness.[3] However, if we do not find grace in His eyes, then He will only reward us in this worthless world.[4] Now, an honest evaluation of our standing reveals that we are far, far removed from the central purpose of life. Our service is not for Hashem. More often than not, we walk in darkness, our goal being to fill our stomachs and satisfy our every base and ignoble desire. In addition to this the sins and transgressions are heaped upon our heads. The paltry amounts of good deeds that we have performed are broken like the fragments of shattered pottery. We neither see nor know the proper and upright path.

PERHAPS OUR TRANSGRESSIONS OUTWEIGH OUR RIGHTEOUSNESS

Thus, Hashem derives no pleasure from our lives because He looks to

---

3   If we do so, then we will receive bounteous reward in the World to Come.
4   We will be rewarded only in this world for any good that we do, but we will receive no share in the World to Come.

the overall picture of our deeds.[5] [And concerning the question:] If [we are living] to receive reward for the minimal righteousness that we do possess — something which provokes disgrace and wrath (cf. *Esther* 1:18)[6] — we don't really know what our status is. Perhaps our transgressions outweigh our righteousness.[7] For our sense of lacking [i.e., our craving] for the illusionary corporal desires — this very sense of lacking stems only from our sense of the desire of our will.[8] Indeed, if we fall a few levels lower than our present status, who is to say that all the righteousness we possess is not far outweighed by our corruption? [At such a stage,] our very lives are dependent on Heavenly mercy. This occurs [i.e., we remain alive] by virtue of a miracle — and perhaps we cannot necessarily expect such a miracle to be performed for us on a daily basis.

GIVING OURSELVES TO THE COMMUNITY

Hence, let us deeply consider and contemplate the following: It states in *Pirkei Avos* (1:13): "He who does not learn [Torah] is liable for death." We see from this that there is never a time when death is not standing over a person, *chas v'chalilah*. Where, then, will we find a remedy for our desires — [which are as strong as] the very desire for life itself, which burns within us like a burning fire — so that Heaven's mercy will be aroused [upon us]?[9] Our

---

5 And He sees that our main occupation is material desire and transgression.

6 The Divine will grants man life so that man will serve Hashem. If man lives mainly to pursue his material desires, he is in opposition to the Divine will. Moreover, by choosing to pursue his desires he effectively neglects the Divine service. Thus, he has disgraced himself in the eyes of Hashem because he has abused the gift of life by using it for material gratification. Therefore, if he is still granted life, it is only a compensation for his minimal righteousness.

7 For we are so unaware of the corruption that is bred by our unchecked pursuit of the material desires.

8 Our material desires are blended together with the very desire for life itself. Therefore, our sense of desire does not discriminate between valid and illegitimate need. We falsely imagine that everything that we desire is a necessity of life. Rav Yisrael alludes to this in the opening passage of the *Iggeres HaMussar*: "Man is free in his imagination...his imagination draws him mischievously in the way of his heart's desire."

9 Rav Yisrael has demonstrated that it is more than likely that we are not deserving of the privilege of life. For we pervert our life's purpose by abandoning the Divine service. Instead of spirituality, we pursue material gratification. Therefore, in order to merit life, we must do something to find mercy in the eyes of Hashem.

only hope lies in giving of ourselves to the community, to whatever degree we are able.[10] If we do so, then "the Almighty does not despise us" (cf. *Iyov* 36:5). We will take shelter under the protective shadow of our community, and in its merit we shall live for lengthy days.

ENCOURAGE OTHERS TO STUDY MUSSAR

What can we — who are desperately impoverished — do? We have no funds to help strengthen the Torah and those who study it. Our only recourse is to utilize the power of words to encourage those weaker than us; to employ knowledge and understanding and arouse them to study Mussar, wherein lies the cure for every spiritual ill. We must exhort others to "learn, teach, safeguard, and perform" (*Birkas Krias Shema*) according to the dictates of this wisdom. Only through this can we have good hope for the Hereafter, for everyone who is attached to life has faith. If we follow the path of Mussar by working to transform evil to good and extracting the precious metal from the dross, then the Beneficent One will strengthen our hearts. Our sole hope lies in being counted amongst those who confer merit upon the public, for they, as *Pirkei Avos* (5:18) relates, "Shall not be the cause of sin."

MUSSAR IS INDISPENSABLE

Now, let us examine this point with a discerning eye: Can a man walk if he does not have legs? Can he see if he does not have eyes? Likewise, without Mussar study, Torah and Divine service cannot be established within a man who is stricken with the disease of the *yetzer hara*.

MUSSAR IS THE SOLE WEAPON

Let us, then, consider the path we are on. Illness of the spirit attacks us from all sides. Desire and the longing for honor form a barrier around us, and thievery and wickedness surround us. Conceit, anger, jealousy, and selfishness are our most prominent traits, and the tongue rules over us with nothing to stop it. Why do we not run to the hospital[11] — perhaps a remedy exists for our affliction? Who but a fool, lacking an understanding heart, does not seek

10 See Letter One.
11 The study of Mussar, preferably in the *beis hamussar*.

a cure for his sickness? This is nothing but the counsel of the *yetzer hara*, who is trained in the art of warfare. He has prepared for his vocation from the earliest of days, and the vagaries of time and the troubles of old age do not confound him as they do us. His only aspiration is to relieve us of the sole weapon at our disposal — the study of Mussar. In this way he shackles us, leaving us with no hope of deliverance.

THE NOBILITY OF MUSSAR STUDY

Therefore, it is imperative that we should learn [i.e., take our cue] from him and adapt his methods as our model — to strengthen ourselves in Mussar and not weaken in it. We must make it great and glorious, and clothe it in the garments of illusionary desire, so that our impure intention will rule over it and pave the way for pure intention to develop. The nobility of Mussar study is an indication that it is not an empty thing; rather, it is capable of imparting life within us, as clear as this day (cf. *Bereishis* 50:20). Therefore, we should pursue it, so that we can teach ourselves to conquer our desires. So, too, since we love our friends, we should work to incline them to the paths of Hashem and His Torah, in righteousness, justice, uprightness, and every precious virtue. In this way, we will find grace and goodly understanding in the eyes of God and man (cf. *Birkas HaMazon*).

You, my dear friends, grant me, please, the following favor: inform me of who is proceeding wholeheartedly and who is weak.

Your beloved companion, who seeks your peace

Translator's Summary of Letter Three

1. The negative impulse battles against every human being; therefore, every soul, with the exception of none, is obligated to study Mussar.

2. The greatest desire of man is the desire to be alive.

3. Man falsely perceives that the pursuit of material desires is necessary for life itself.

4. Our only hope to find favor in the eyes of Hashem is to encourage others to study Mussar.

LETTER FOUR

WORLDLY WISDOM

Left to his own devices, man has an inescapable tendency to trap him-
self in a web of self-deception — each person according to his way.

AS HE SOWED, SO SHALL HE REAP

MY BELOVED FRIENDS! My purpose in this letter is to fulfill that which I previously promised (in Letter Two): to elaborate on the idea of employing worldly wisdom — the ways of the world[1] — which is needed [to complement the] wisdom of Mussar. Without this understanding, the task [of acquiring *yiras Shamayim*] is difficult and elusive. For the diseases of the soul — desire and misjudgment — pollute it. Lustful craving burns [incessantly], and tendencies are inflamed, urging one to declare the impure pure.[2] [Whereas, in truth] it will be declared, "Impure! Impure!" (cf. *Vayikra* 13:45) at the time he will be called to judgment and accountability for the fruits of his deeds, and he will be recompensed accordingly. As he sowed, so shall he reap. Thus, even though the Torah has been entrusted to man so that he may decide on matters according to his intellectual ability, nevertheless, one is not free to manipulate the Torah in order to follow after the whims of his volition and desire. [Such a course] is completely unacceptable. It is incumbent upon us to give just and honest answers to our questions and to make upright decisions.

---

1   The Vilna Gaon, in his commentary to *Mishlei*, uses the term "the ways of the world" in reference to the knowledge of human behavior and diverse personality flaws that a judge is required to know. For instance, in order for a judge to render a just ruling, he must be able to recognize the various manifestations of deception and fraud found within people.

2   This refers to misjudgments generated by subconscious tendencies.

YIRAS SHAMAYIM COMBATS THE YETZER HARA

In light of this, [it behooves us to recognize] how foolish we have been in all of our ways! Who will instruct us concerning the upright path? Desire, the pursuit of honor, envy, and the competitive drive — [traits such as these] cast their influence over all our intellectual faculties and permeate the very foundations of our minds. Nevertheless, Heavenly fear rules over everything. Heavenly fear binds desire with its power, so that desire cannot overstep its boundary; it thus allows only those needs that are necessary and permissible. *Yiras Shamayim* shoots its arrows towards man's tendencies [i.e., subconscious proclivities], frightening him to examine his ways, to scrutinize every intention of his heart, until the chaff [i.e., improper drives] is separated and driven away by the wind. Yet, do we focus on this fear, making it a fortress and a steadfast foundation for all of our deeds so that the *yetzer hara* will be powerless to cling to us?[3] Do we not find that our Divine service stands at a far distance [from truthful Divine service]? For although "we may not have heard, we have seen" — and experience shows how arduous it is for man to firmly inculcate Heavenly fear within his heart so that it is spread over his "stiff neck." However, if he toils mightily in the fear of Hashem, then his thoughts will not turn even one degree towards desire, which constantly grows ever stronger.[4] What can give the strength to begin fighting this battle against the tendencies which confuse us and dance within us, fulfilling their schemes with diabolical ease?[5]

EXPOSE OUR ULTERIOR MOTIVES

We must endeavor to set the truth before our eyes and purity as a lamp for our steps. It is incumbent upon us to profoundly contemplate the truth, and not allow confusion to distort our thoughts and distract us from

---

3   The only antidote for the *yetzer hara* is *yiras Shamayim*, and the only way to acquire *yiras Shamayim* is through the study of Mussar. See "The Gates of Light," chapter 2.

4   Since, the Heavenly fear does not penetrate our hearts, our desires remain unchecked. Therefore, since we are subject to the whims of desire, then surely we are dominated by subconscious tendencies, which are hidden from our awareness. The question, therefore, remains.

5   Since we are deficient in Heavenly fear, we need an additional force to augment the *yirah*.

constantly scrutinizing our deeds. We should proceed in this way until we expose the ulterior motives of our hearts (cf. *Iyov* 17:11). Then, we will be ashamed to substitute falsehood for truth, and to disguise the foundations of iniquity with a patina of righteousness. No longer will we blunder about in the darkness, like a blind man who does not even know what he is stumbling over.[6]

MAN TRAPS HIMSELF IN SELF-DECEPTION

In addition to this, it is correct for us to deepen our understanding of the ways of the world, which are rooted in deceit.[7] It is human nature to endeavor to trap others in a web [of deception] — each person according to his way.[8] The fool will give gold in exchange for pursuing the sirens of folly. The person who is consumed by desire for food and drink will be trapped in the net of his cravings, the *yetzer hara* glibly urging him to indulge in every sweet delight (cf. *Tehillim* 35:16). The one who desires illusory honor — his very desire is his net. Flattery will trap one who is so predisposed into granting people whatever they desire, according to his ability to so do.[9] Likewise, each

6   This method of soul searching is an application of worldly wisdom, as explained in Letter Two.

7   One aspect of worldly wisdom is the ability to discern the foolishness of others.

8   Left to his own devices, man has an inescapable tendency to trap himself in a web of self-deception. Therefore, it is relatively easy for the deceivers to find character weaknesses in their victims and manipulate them to their own advantage, as Rav Yisrael will now explain. Moreover, these character flaws generate mistakes and misjudgments of great magnitude even without the schemes of an outside deceiver.

     For instance, one may observe the path of a colleague who truly values Torah study, yet ultimately his desire for money subverts him to abandon his Torah study. After viewing such absurd conduct in others, one then looks to oneself to see if he has fallen to similar misjudgments. The tragic blunder that has ruined his friend will serve as a warning and a motivation to prepare himself for any future assault of the *yetzer hara* in this area. Moreover, now that he understands the mistakes of his friends, he is in a better position to encourage them to study Mussar.

9   For instance, the Talmud (*Sanhedrin* 52a) reveals that the 250 *talmidei chachamim* that were recruited by Korach in his futile rebellion against Moshe surrendered to desire and flattery: "Reish Lakish taught: 'What is the meaning of the verse "With flattery and mockery, for the sake of a loaf, he gnashes his teeth at me" (*Tehillim* 35:16)? On account of the flattery with which they flattered Korach, due to matters of feasting, the chief of Gehinnom gnashed his teeth at them.'" In other words, the 250 *talmidei*

person is trapped by his own proclivity. The deceivers look to the character weaknesses [of their victim] to know how to shackle him with the sufficient fulfillment of his [i.e., the deceiver's] desires. This is but a brief glimpse into the [deceptive] ways of man. The topic is too extensive to be completely covered in a single letter.[10]

THE WISDOM TO LEARN FROM MISTAKES

Man also utilizes wordly wisdom to grow wise by contemplating the results of his actions in all of his affairs. He can thereby endeavor to rectify things before calamity occurs — each person according his ability. The dealings of the business world will teach him concerning its proceedings and ways.[11] Each person, according to his individual nature, will establish its wisdom [i.e., a business sense] in his heart. Man has the wisdom to learn from his mistakes. According to the degree that he refuses to embrace foolishness, so will his wisdom increase. Routine and experience are the keys to control in every matter.

Therefore, if one's integrity remains strong,[12] these concepts [of worldly

---

chachamim accepted an invitation to feast with Korach. Once they benefited from his food, they felt compelled to join his sedition.

10 The Alter M'Kelm (Ohr Rashaz, p. 198) explains that in the confrontation between Yaakov and Eisav, in Parashas Vayishlach, Yaakov fears Eisav because Eisav has the merit of two mitzvos — honoring his parents and living in the land of Israel. This implies that Eisav was an intelligent person, for his mitzvos had merit. Furthermore, for over thirty years Eisav was planning to take revenge by killing Yaakov for taking the blessing. Now, when Yaakov is finally in sight and the opportunity arises for Eisav to unleash his wrath on Yaakov, he suddenly switches track and showers great affection upon Yaakov. What caused his sudden change of heart? It was the gifts that Yaakov sent to Eisav before they met. For a few material gifts, all the fire of seething hatred was extinguished from the heart of Eisav. All of his planning and strategy was forgotten. For a few kind words or gifts, man will literally sell his soul.

11 We might ask: perhaps man does not possess the ability to fathom the inner motives and inherent self-deceptive devices within the human personality? Yet we see through man's finesse in his business endeavors that this incisive ability to deeply and accurately analyze human character is an inherent human power. Moreover, he can use it to gain profound insights into his own personality. Life experience, in and of itself, teaches man much about himself and others. We see uneducated people who possess sharp insight into the personalities of their fellowmen. Since they had no formal training, we must attribute their wisdom to their observations gleaned through human interaction.

12 Since one aspect of worldly wisdom involves contemplating the foolish path of others, as

wisdom] will be a positive force in following in the ways of Hashem. We will grow wise in the knowledge of the nature of our souls — understanding how we can be "captured" to incline our hearts to the Divine service and to minimize all tests.[13] The fear of Hashem will provide us with strength and power, and each person will encourage his companion. Worldly wisdom will lighten the burden, and Heavenly fear will strengthen us. We will fear and tremble at the thought of committing every wicked act and transgression, and we will flee far from the evil snare.

SINCERITY OF HEART

My pen does not suffice to express my thought, yet we can apply to this the verse, "Give to the wise man and he will become even wiser" (*Mishlei* 9:9). The very involvement in the ways of Divine service will teach a man its paths. Moreover, each person should instruct his friend — and he shall guide

---

well as his own, the purity of our motives must be constantly monitored. We must be sure not to use our insights of people's flaws to take advantage of them. Moreover, if this analysis of others results in a critical eye, always finding fault in our fellow, then we have defeated our purpose. We may only view the mistakes of others as a lesson to ourselves, but not as a personal disqualification in the least. Although this might seem an impossible task, it is in compliance with Torah thought. For instance, the Torah (*Bamidbar* 11:1) reveals the sin of Miriam when she spoke improperly about Moshe. Although we learn from this incident aspects of the laws of forbidden speech, nevertheless, our image of Miriam the Prophetess does not change whatsoever. The Ohr HaChaim teaches us that even though the Cloud of Glory had lifted, indicating that *klal Yisrael* could continue on their journey, the people did not travel while Miriam was in quarantine. Rather, the nation decided to honor Miriam by waiting for her to return.

13 For instance, the Talmud (*Bava Metzia* 84a) explains that Resh Lakish, the famous Talmudic sage, started out in life as a notorious criminal. Upon seeing that Resh Lakish was attracted by beautiful women, Rebbe Yochanan devised an appropriate plan to convince Resh Lakish to repent. Rebbe Yochanan promised Resh Lakish that if he would repent from his evil ways and come to learn Torah in the yeshivah, then Rebbe Yochanan would arrange for Resh Lakish to marry his sister — who was exceptionally beautiful. This strategy brought about the meteoric rise of Resh Lakish, who became one of the most illustrious *Amoraim*. Similarly, the Talmud (*Bava Basra* 110a) relates the story of Yonatan, a descendant of Moshe. Yonatan hired himself out to serve as an idolatrous priest. When King David saw that Yonatan had a penchant for money, he put him in charge of the treasuries. This brilliant plan of King David effectively engendered the complete repentance of Yonatan.

his friend to purity and capture him in the trap [of his nature].[14] However, [let it be clear] that this is not for the sake of honor, but for truth and uprightness. [By setting our focus] to discern the proclivities of the man, we must subtly influence him, in order to incline his heart to Heavenly fear and Torah study. Let any errors provide a guiding light so that the truth can stand firm. Then our righteousness will shine like the light of dawn. If we will observe the ways of the world in order to understand the paths of man and his falseness, so that his deceptive flaws stand clearly revealed before us — and our approach be refined of all dross until it is absolutely pure[15] — then this study [of worldly wisdom] coupled with the help of the fear of Heaven has the power to purge all irregular behavior and improper thoughts.[16] This is ultimately accomplished through strengthening the paths of Mussar [for others], and by in-depth study and understanding how to utilize worldly wisdom to strengthen Mussar — and not to destroy it [if worldly wisdom is used improperly], *chas v'chalilah*. Without strategies, there can be no [worldly] wisdom[17] — and there can be no [worldly] wisdom without study. Therefore, we must keep in mind that the purpose of studying [worldly wisdom] is so that we may draw people close to Mussar, and we must use worldly wisdom to instill Heavenly fear and the power of purity within them.

---

14 In the previous paragraph Rav Yisrael explained how worldly wisdom may be applied to draw people to Mussar by appealing to the base side of their nature. For instance, by making Mussar something to be proud of, it will appeal to our sense of pride, as explained at the end of Letter One. However, here he is advocating an alternative approach: we can also influence others by appealing to their spiritual side — "and he shall guide his friend to purity." Since souls long for purity, we can inspire them to pursue Mussar and Torah — which will lead them to the holiness that they desire.

15 Our intention must be wholly sincere to lead our subject to righteousness.

16 Observing and detecting the foolishness in others, coupled with *yiras shamayim*, creates a dynamic force to heal our own foolishness.

17 Since worldly wisdom involves focusing on the flaws of other people, it could lead to conceit and condemnation. Therefore, a strategy is required to insure that this study does not taint us with negativity. Rav Yisrael thus advises that the study of worldly wisdom be approached with the intention to understand ourselves and others — in order to draw people to Mussar. It is interesting to note that even though the pursuit of worldly wisdom could potentially be counterproductive, nevertheless, Rav Yisrael realized that it is so essential to *middos* growth that it cannot be forsaken. Since wisdom cannot be acquired "without study," it behooves us to study it, albeit with the strategy to apply it for strengthening others in Mussar.

TRANSLATOR'S SUMMARY OF LETTER FOUR

1. Worldly wisdom (learning from our mistakes) is an indispensable aid to Mussar growth.

2. We must set the truth of our ulterior motives before our eyes.

3. Man has an inescapable tendency to trap himself in self-deception.

4. Observe other people and learn from their mistakes.

LETTER FIVE

THE REMEDY

Mussar enables one to wage the war with his own hand and his free will
so that he may emerge victorious and incline his limbs to true perfection.

EMULATE THE GOODNESS OF HASHEM

WE, THE CREATIONS OF HASHEM, may He be blessed, hope for His kindness and await His mercy. What will grant us merit in the eyes of our Master, and how shall we find grace before Him? The answer is that we must strive to emulate His ways, in as much as we are able. [This is especially so] concerning His trait of goodness, which is spread out over the entire creation. His goodness is bestowed without any reason; it is naught but pure mercy that is extended without motive. Similarly, "we must arm ourselves swiftly" (*Bamidbar* 32:17) to help the weak — without request and with no precipitating cause.[1]

WE MUST EMPLOY INTELLIGENCE

Yet, what power do we have? Our strength is likened to an insubstantial vapor. Evil bursts forth, and wickedness prevails.[2] There is neither escape nor refuge, unless we act cunningly to annul immoral counsel. We must employ intelligence to achieve our aspiration of conquering this wickedness — using bonds of righteousness, shackles of virtue, and abstention

---

1   We must give of ourselves to influence others — who are unacquainted with Mussar — to engage in Mussar study (see Letter One).
2   To promote Mussar to people who do not recognize its value — especially to those who are scorners — seems to be a daunting task.

from desire.[3] This strategy is the foundation upon which the dike is built. Yet, who will prepare the mortar and bricks? Who will perform this task? The virtue of uprightness does not exist in man; he also lacks knowledge and understanding. It is these [deficiencies] that have caused us to regress so astonishingly. Are there none amongst Israel who fear Hashem? Why are remedy and healing so distant from us? Those who fear Heaven must garb themselves in strength to trap the wicked one in the net of his desires.[4] But what can stop [the wicked]? They are prepared to pursue their every desire and to bring all their schemes to fruition! How can any physical being stop them? Yet, if we allow shame and disgrace to confound us,[5] can we truly be called "fearers of Hashem"? Is this the way of Torah? The first principle of the Torah is to be unembarrassed in the face of scorners, and to cast away vain desire! In this, intelligence[6] and emotion[7] are in conflict with each other.

THE SOURCE OF HEAVENLY FEAR

In *Sefer Tehillim*, David HaMelech adjures us, "Seek peace and pursue it" (34:15).[8] The starting point is to discover the source of Heavenly fear, the spring from whence it flows — whether from the daily habit [of Torah study and mitzvah observance], or from knowledge and scholarly study [of Mussar]. Our inner feeling[9] testifies that knowledge and understanding have

---

3   Only through cunningness and intelligence will we be effective in influencing others to better their conduct and character through the study of Mussar.

4   See Letter Four, where Rav Yisrael discusses the concept of manipulating the negative forces of others as a means to direct them to walk on the path of good.

5   That is, if we are embarrassed before the scorners who ridicule our efforts to spread Mussar.

6   Our awareness of the importance of influencing others to engage in Mussar study.

7   Our embarrassment before the scorners who ridicule us, which stifles our efforts to promote Mussar.

8   Let us, then, find the way to reconcile our intellect (we understand the importance of influencing others to engage in Mussar study) with our emotions (we are embarrassed to promote Mussar to others).

9   "Our inner feeling" refers to the embarrassment that holds us back from promoting Mussar to others. *Yiras Shamayim* is wisdom and therefore requires deep study. Since the students' *yiras Shamayim* was not sufficiently based on the wisdom gleaned from study, they were embarrassed when instructed to influence others to study Mussar.

neither resting place nor portion in *yiras Hashem*, and lack even a superficial connection to it.[10] Indeed, this feeling [of embarrassment] is indisputably real. Of what value are thoughts and understanding[11] if they wield no power in the foundation of *yiras Shamayim*? Yet, who does not recognize that feelings are but malleable vessels that are prepared to accept all forms, and with the change of the form, the feeling is changed as well.[12] If we employ strategies[13] to join understanding to Heavenly fear, then the feelings will automatically change.

---

10 Rav Yisrael is addressing the question: If his students understand intellectually the value of Mussar, why do they feel a sense of embarrassment to promote Mussar study to others? He answers: "Knowledge and understanding have neither resting place nor portion in *yiras Hashem*." On one hand, Rav Yisrael says that they understand the value of Mussar, and it is only their emotions that are not in concert with what they know to be true; and on the other hand, he says that they have no understanding of it whatsoever. This human phenomenon of "knowing and not knowing" is explained in the opening paragraph of the *Iggeres HaMussar*. As Rav Yisrael explains there: Man is free in his imagination — meaning that he imagines that there is no judgment and punishment that takes place at the end of his life. Therefore he imagines that he can follow his heart's desire with no accountability. Moreover, even if he is taught the truth, so that his intellect clearly recognizes the truth of the ultimate, awesome judgment — nevertheless, the power of his imagination will eradicate all remembrance of judgment from his intellect. Only through the study of Mussar is man protected from the imagination, so that the truth of judgment is remembered by the intellect and inculcated in his heart. (See *Iggeres HaMussar*.) Likewise, Rav Yisrael is explaining here, in Letter Five, that although the students know the value of *yiras Shamayim*, it is a superficial knowledge. As the Ramchal points out in his introduction to *Mesillas Yesharim*: *Yiras Shamayim* is wisdom and, as such, can only be acquired through study (of Mussar). As long as there is a deficiency in their wisdom of *yiras Shamayim*, their emotions, which are subverted by the false images of the imagination, will continue to vacillate.

11 That is, a superficial understanding of *yirah* and Mussar.

12 Once the wisdom of *yiras Shamayim* is understood, then we will no longer be stifled by embarrassment, and we will have confidence to promote the study of Mussar to others.

13   As Rav Yisrael points out in Letter One, only through strategies can we succeed in binding and perfecting ourselves with Mussar. In the *Iggeres HaMussar*, as well as most of the letters, Rav Yisrael reveals his primary strategy: by reaching out and devising plans to influence others to engage in Mussar, his *talmidim* themselves will be strengthened in Mussar and *yirah*. In the next paragraph he instructs them on a specific course of action in this regard.

TAKE PART IN THIS MISSION

In light of this, the first thing that we must do is to strengthen those who are weak, by guiding them to the *beis hamussar*. There, Mussar must be studied with insight and intelligence, with sincerity of heart, and with lips aflame. Its study should be effected by the continuous repetition of our Sage's fiery statements in this area — each person according to his deficiencies. Hopefully, the Almighty will be with us, and we will be able to successfully accomplish our task. Therefore, it befits every person who desires closeness to Hashem to diligently take part in this mission. Through proper and effective strategies, let each person remove and nullify all the obstacles and hindrances that lie before him.

MUSSAR CURES EVERY AFFLICTION

There is one thing that cures every affliction and illness, both in one's actions and in his character traits [and that is the study of Mussar]. Even in situations where positive routine enhances *yiras Shamayim* and Torah study, without Mussar study the desired goal remains elusive. [Without this study] character traits continue to be corrupted, and there is no possibility of victory in the war with the *yetzer hara* — the very reason for our coming into this world. Instead, we focus all of our energies on following our desires. What can we say now, when our routine conflicts with the fear of Hashem? If we do not turn to the all-encompassing remedy of Mussar, there is no place for Divine worship, and the situation is essentially one of utter despair.

"IF NOT NOW, WHEN?"

Despite this, there is an easy remedy that yields abundant fruits. "Who is the one who desires life" (*Tehillim* 34:13) and is numbered amongst those who bestow merit upon the public?[14] Such individuals will shine like the stars, and their righteousness will never diminish. Let those who desire to be illuminated with the light of life embrace this mitzvah, which is so auspicious in these times. Who knows what the dawn will bring forth, and as Hillel teaches: "If not now, when?" (*Avos* 1:14). In addition, we ourselves will be

---

14 That is, who influence others to engage in Mussar study. See Letter One and Two.

built up through this, by sharpening our understanding of how to conquer the evil inclination and its desires. As Chazal teach us: "That which comes to shed light is itself illuminated" (*Sanhedrin* 73a).

MUSSAR STUDY PROVIDES A FOUNDATION

The first step in this process is to recognize a person's individual makeup. What constitutes his aspirations, desires, and will; in brief, who is he? Furthermore, we must grasp how distant he is from the true purpose of his creation. How can he bind his desire and how shall he guide it to the most excellent aspect of Divine Service — the pursuit of Mussar study — which provides a foundation on which to base the mandatory war against the *yetzer hara*.[15] [This is achieved in a number of ways, all of which must be utilized. First] by forcing the body to overpower its will; and also by sharpening one's understanding of the concept involved, thereby subduing the heart to at least some extent; and by constant and in-depth review of Chazal's statements; and by deep contemplation in order to broaden one's understanding of the issues involved. [The important thing is for each person to proceed] according to the inclination of his nature and temperament. How exalted are these matters! Their obligation is incumbent upon everyone with the breath of life in his nostrils. It enables one to wage the war with his own hand and free will so that he may emerge victorious and incline his limbs to true perfection.

---

15 One of Rav Yisrael's most brilliant insights is that Mussar is multifaceted. Hence, control of the *yetzer hara* and the acquisition of *yiras Shamayim* requires more than just reading concepts from a Mussar book. Here, Rav Yisrael explains four different "techniques" that are all essential components needed to master oneself through Mussar. The first is for a person to exercise self-restraint from the bodily desires, second is sharpening one's understanding of why a particular trait is unworthy, third is *hispailus*, and last is the deep contemplation of the concept until it makes an impression in one's heart.

TRANSLATOR'S SUMMARY OF LETTER FIVE

1. Just as Hashem bestows life without reason, we should emulate Hashem and influence others to study Mussar — which imparts spiritual life.

2. Our commitment to Mussar must rest on strong logical foundations.

3. Influencing others to study Mussar will foster a sturdy intellectual understanding of Mussar values within ourselves.

4. Mussar must be offered to people in a way which is harmonious with their personality, intellect, and outlook.

LETTER SIX

ACTIVATING THE SUBCONSCIOUS

Mussar study is a function of the conscious mind in conjuction with emotional arousal — which makes an impression on the subconscious forces of man's soul.

YOM KIPPUR

IN THE INTRODUCTION to his work *Mesillas Yesharim*, the Ramchal states that he wrote only about concepts that are basic and well known. Similarly, I, too, will write only about a concept that we have discussed and reviewed many times. Specifically, I wish to discuss Yom Kippur. We know that the observance of this day is a positive commandment, and if one transgresses its strictures, he is punished with spiritual excision. However, aside from the benefit accrued by observing its commandments, the day itself affords immense benefit to man, saving him from uncountable and perilous calamities.[1]

HIS INNER SELF REMAINS ALIVE

The essence of a man can only be referred to as the "self." This self is the inner spirit of him that speaks, thinks, desires, and toils to fulfill his desires.[2] [The true self] is concealed in the corporal substance of the body. When a

---

1 Not only does the observance of Yom Kippur save man from spiritual excision, even more, the preparation for Yom Kippur is fertile ground for spiritual growth.

2 The essence of man lies not in his physical appearance and being, but in his spirit.

person's bodily powers are terminated upon dying, this self still remains alive and endowed with its capabilities. [At that time, the self] is separated from the physical world — that phase of existence wherein the soul is linked with the materialistic substance of the body. [It is important to understand that] the perception of pain and pleasure is not limited to the physical; the self has an innate capacity to perceive pain and pleasure. This inherent sensitivity serves to either benefit or afflict him [Gan Eden or Gehinnom]: the pain is frightening and terrible, while the pleasure is wondrous and supreme. [The pain and pleasure of the Next World] far exceeds that which one is capable of feeling in this world, while he is still connected to his body. This future pain and pleasure is dependent on a person's actions — how the self conducts itself in this world. By observing and fulfilling the Almighty's commandments, man — the self — will attain sublime delight. Conversely, if he transgresses the commandments, he will be subjected to terrible pain and suffering.

THE GRADATION OF DIVINE JUDGMENT

Each category of transgression is distinctly different in the severity of punishment, depending on Heaven's judgment. Moreover, each person is judged differently than anyone else for each detail of the transgression; each person receives his punishment according to his own unique temperament and circumstances in this world, whether he is wealthy or poor, wise or foolish, zealous or lazy by nature, and countless other aspects. Even concerning each man, the individual self, distinctions are made in the punishments rendered for the particular transgression according to variations in the nature of his situation. For example, whether the sin was committed in a time of tranquility or turmoil, and how he reacts to stress and pressure; whether his mood was calm or excitable; whether he is lucid of thought or confused; and many other fluctuating factors. The easier it is for a person to refrain from desecrating the Divine will, the more his punishment will be increased if he does so. This axiom holds true concerning both the level of difficulty involved in refraining from a transgression, as well as that of neglecting the performance of a mitzvah. Hence, punishment takes into account the gradation of difficulty or ease involved in committing a sin or in not performing a mitzvah. Great pain corresponds to a more easily avoided transgression, while minimal pain corresponds to a transgression which is more difficult to avoid.

THE PUNISHMENT IS MORE SEVERE

When man deeply contemplates with his own intellect, or [is enlightened] through seeking instruction from a man of greater knowledge, as to what [is the maximum] extent of difficulty the Torah obligates him [to endure] in order not to violate a particular transgression, [he will perceive a great truth.] This realization of the [maximum] level of adversity [that man must endure, under which the Torah still obligates him to avoid a transgression,] pertains both to the [effort required] to refrain from committing a sin, as well as [the effort required] to not neglect a mitzvah.[3] [Among other important factors to consider is] whether a given injunction is biblical or rabbinic in nature. [When one reflects on the maximum effort that man is obligated to make in order not to violate the Torah, in contrast to the punishment meted out for a transgression] it is obvious that the punishment meted out for a transgression is far more difficult to bear than the adversity involved in not committing it.[4] Moreover, let him consider that common sense also tells us there are many different categories of difficult circumstances that are even more difficult than his — and [those suffering such difficulties] are still obligated to observe [Torah precepts]. These categories of difficulty range from easy to severe, and each category has many subdivisions. Accordingly, punishment increases in keeping with the ease involved [in doing a mitzvah or refraining from

---

3　Meaning that the neglect of mitzvah is also a transgression.

4　This sharp contrast is even more pronounced when taking into consideration that man is not obligated to go beyond the maximum effort prescribed by the Torah. For instance, in most cases, if the performance of the mitzvah will endanger his life, then he is exempt from his obligation to perform that mitzvah. Hence, there is a limit to the adversity that the Torah requires him to endure in order to fulfill a precept. However, the terrible pain that he experiences in Gehinnom is not grounds for exemption from punishment, whatsoever. In fact, just the opposite is so. The awesome magnitude of suffering, regardless of the subject's ability to tolerate it, is needed in order for the sinner to rectify his transgression.

aveirah].[5] [This reflection is a great tool to] send the fear of Heaven into the heart of a good-hearted man — even without deliberation and in-depth study of Mussar.

This concept is alluded to in a verse from *Tehillim* (94:12): "Fortunate is the man who God disciplines, and to whom You teach from Your Torah." As we mentioned above, this means that a person is saved from severe and bitter punishments in the Next World by being subjected to adversity in this one. From where does man know — at least, in a general sense — that he will face awesome and terrible punishment? As the above verse states, "...from Your Torah." Although few in quantity, these words are great in quality, providing much food for contemplation.[6]

TWO FACTORS IN THIS WORLD

[I am writing] these words during the Ten Days of Repentance — a time of action when we must strive to improve our ways so that we might have peace during the upcoming year. As Chazal tell us (*Rosh HaShanah* 16a): "[The judgment of] those of indeterminate status is suspended from the beginning of the year until Yom Kippur."[7] During a man's sojourn in this world, there are two factors confronting him. One of them is beyond his control — namely, the desire to have all of his worldly needs filled in their entirety. In contrast, the second aspect — the fulfillment of his needs according to the

5   Level of adversity   1 . _._._._._._._._._._._._._._._._._._._. 100
     Level of punishment 100._._._._._._._._._._._._._._. _._._. 1
     Observe these two parallel lines, the first marked with gradations numbered from 1 to 100, and the second marked with gradations from 100 to 1. The first line indicates the level of adversity he must endure in order not to commit a particular transgression — with 1 being the easiest and 100 being the most difficult. The second line indicates the level of severity of punishment — with 100 being the most severe and 1 being the least severe. This diagram shows us that an easily avoidable transgression (1) is subject to the most severe punishment (100), whereas, a transgression committed under difficult conditions (100) receives a relatively lighter punishment (1).

6   Why does the Torah consider the recipient of discipline (punishment) "fortunate"? Rav Yisrael answers, if discipline is advantageous, then there must be two dimensions of punishment: one in this world and the second in Gehinnom. Since the suffering in Gehinnom is infinitely greater than the discipline of this world, it is advantageous to receive the punishment in this world, deducting punishment from the Next.

7   His fate is in question and is dependent on repentance.

constraints of his circumstances — is completely within his charge. It is axiomatic that the more difficult his physical situation, the greater effort he will have to invest in order to attain his desires. A pauper, who must go from door to door begging for his bread, works harder than anyone. Nevertheless, he does not consider his struggle to collect a few coins or a little food to be difficult or unusual. Similarly, a poor man must work harder than one of average wealth, and a person of average wealth must work harder than a rich man — and none of them considers the efforts they must invest to be unseemly or below their dignity.[8] Why is this? The reason is as follows: [Take the pauper for example.] Aside from the fact that the very necessity for survival leaves him no choice, the indignity and hardship involved is easier to bear than the pain of a hungry stomach. Likewise, according to the pain that the poor man experiences from his particular lacking, he will subject himself to more difficulty than the householder, etc.

TWO FACTORS OF DIVINE SERVICE

[Just as there are two factors confronting man in the physical world] so, too, there are two factors relative to his obligation of Divine service. [In contrast to the physical realm] both factors in this area are under his control. The first one is that at all times, every person has the free will to be completely devoted to Hashem's service. Also, during the Ten Days of Repentance, a person has the opportunity to entirely transform himself — to be a *tzaddik*, a man of peace in the upcoming year. The second factor concerns [improving] the standing of one's Divine service — at all times, but particularly during the Ten Days of Repentance. Regarding this, the essential principle is to reflect on and contemplate one's ways. Then, he should see to it that he at least observes the easier part [of a precept] — each person according to his situation and fear of Heaven. By following this [procedure] he will be delivered from [trans-

---

8   Even though both the rich and the poor work, the degradation and physical exertion of the poor man's work is greater than the rich man's. A wealthy man could not tolerate the indignities that a poor man suffers in order to win his daily bread. However, the poor man's instinct for survival shifts his focus from the difficulty of the task to the result of procuring his basic needs.

gressing] the graver aspects of that particular sin, as we mentioned above.[9]

A VERY EASY MATTER

This concept can be clarified by an analogy relating to the study of Mussar. Now, this study is incumbent upon every person, and therefore a person should go to a *beis hamussar* at least on an occasional basis — something that is relatively easy to do. Perhaps this idea is analogous to other matters related to Divine service.[10] The walk to the *beis hamussar* is a very easy matter, especially on Shabbos — and this is true even for one who is immersed in worldly affairs. However, we know that the study of Talmud or halachah is a greater obligation on Shabbos [than is Mussar study], and especially for one who is preoccupied with other concerns during the week. Therefore, it is preferable that the *beis hamussar* be set up in close proximity to the *beis hamidrash*, or in an adjacent room, so that he will not have any opposition to learning Mussar on the grounds that the place is far from the *beis hamidrash*. In that way, he will be able to engage in the day's essential obligation — Talmudic study — and as a consequence, also be able to undertake the task of "secondary" importance — Mussar study — with minimal effort.[11]

---

9   In summation, there are two physical aspects that pertain to man: one is not under his control (his desire to have all of his material needs), yet one is under his control (the fulfillment of his basic needs). Parallel to this, there are two spiritual aspects that pertain to man. However, they are both under his control. The first is the free choice to totally devote himself to Divine service. The second spiritual aspect, also under his control, is his ability to save himself from Divine punishment by eliminating his transgressions. The comparison to the physical realm is as follows: just as a person will do whatever is required to save himself from starving, so, too, man will abandon sin to save himself from the suffering of punishment. Rav Yisrael advises that the process of departing from sin should initially be focused on the sins that are easy to avoid because they impose the worse punishment. (See Letter Eight.)

10 Just as one goes to the *beis hamussar*, a relatively easy thing to do, so one should contemplate the mitzvos and *aveiros* and identify those which he can easily fulfill, and make sure to at least fulfill these easy aspects.

11 Study in the *beis hamussar* is relatively easy and profoundly effective for improving Divine service. Therefore, he should embrace the mitzvah of going to the *beis hamussar*. This mitzvah facilitates both the fulfillment of Divine service, as well as repentance from sin.

COMPREHENSION BEGINS WITH CLARIFICATION

The study of Mussar is obligatory for man — and especially for a person who is preoccupied with his affairs, whose Divine service is hampered by spiritual illness. This is so, even though it is no easy matter to apply Mussar study to treat a grave illness in need of powerful ministrations.

[Let us try and understand this.] Turning our attention to man's intellectual powers, we find that the process of comprehending something begins with an attempt to achieve clarification. This course proceeds with great difficulty. For example, consider a child who begins to study Hebrew. His first task is to learn the proper pronunciation of the words. At this stage, his teacher must exert great effort in order to teach him the individual letters and help him string together a complete word. The child must work mightily to be able to learn how to read letters and words. However, once he acquires the necessary skills — each child according to his natural ability — he reads easily, with no deliberation. The psychologists call this [process of learning a function of] the inner powers of man. [During the initial phase, when the child is learning to read, he must employ] the power of clarification, i.e., the "conscious mind." [Afterwards, reading is] a function of the "subconscious mind."

We can apply this model to the realm of emotions as well, as there are both conscious factors and subconscious ones. The subconscious forces are stronger and produce powerful results with minimal stimulation. For example, the love of a father for his children is a function of the subconscious mind. In general, this love is almost imperceptible to the man himself. However, it ignites to a roaring fire with even the slightest stimulation. Likewise, man's earthly desires are manifest in the subconscious. When there is no stimulation, their existence is almost imperceptible. Because of this, they wield tremendous power over man.

MUSSAR AFFECTS THE SUBCONSCIOUS

Mussar study is founded upon and begins as an aspect of clarification in relation to emotional arousal. Now in most cases, man does not have the innate strength to master his desires, which are based in the subconscious and are naturally very powerful.[12] But just as in the realm of intellectual endeavor, each session of "clarification learning" makes an impression on the subconscious, [so, too, the fervor aroused in the soul through Mussar study makes an impression on the subconscious]. It is important to point out that the only way a learned skill can be made second nature is through initial conscious effort — for if this weren't true, it would be unnecessary to employ conscious study in order to generate "reflex" knowledge in the subconscious. [Moreover, this educational process] will only succeed if there is not an extended interval between study sessions, so that the impressions on the subconscious will not be diminished and nullified with the passage of time, and one will not have to begin anew each time, in a process that would repeat itself ad infinitum.[13]

The same process of learning applies to emotional arousal. Every emotional arousal that a person engages in makes an impression on the subconscious. Eventually, the impressions engendered by each study session regarding a particular area will join together, and subconscious powers capable of producing potent results will be generated — just as any learned skill eventually takes root and becomes automatic. As we noted, of course, this is contingent upon the sessions not being unduly interrupted. Additionally, the subject of study must be reinforced between sessions by periodic stimulation through Torah study.

The inculcation of Mussar is based on the same process. If a person fervently devotes himself — each according to the condition of his "disease" in relation to Divine service — to fervent Mussar study — without extended interruption between study sessions, and with periodic stimulation — then subconscious powers will be engendered to aid him in the battle against rampant desire. Granted, this is no easy task for one who is burdened by his worldly affairs, whose disease is overwhelming, and whose time is limited. Moreover, there is another task that overrides everything else — the imperative to study Torah, which is the first thing for which a person is judged in the World of Truth.

---

12 However, this is not to say that there is no hope; rather, it is all a matter of investing the proper effort.

13 With undue interruption, everything learned in the previous session will effectively be forgotten.

THE PROGRAM IS EASY

Nevertheless, a person is certainly capable of going to the *beis hamussar* on Shabbos Kodesh, where he can engage in ardent Mussar study (of course, devoting the majority of his time to Talmud study, which is the main focus, as we mentioned above). Likewise, he can go there several times a week, even if only for a few minutes. He will thereby reinforce what he learned previously, so that the impression on his subconscious will not nullified during the interval between Shabboses. Such a program is easy to undertake and yields abundant fruit, aiding one to acquire the subconscious power to overcome his desires. At the very least, it will grant him the self-control to "turn from evil and do good" (*Tehillim* 34:15), especially concerning transgressions which are relatively easy to avoid — things for which man, the "self," will be held particularly accountable for in the eternal World of Truth.

GO TO THE BEIS HAMUSSAR

Hopefully, one will realize that it is easy to go to the *beis hamussar* at any time of the day, with no disturbance or trouble, whenever it enters his heart — even if only for a few minutes. He should not let anything prevent him from going to the *beis hamussar*, for undue interruptions, without brief and periodic stimulations between sessions, serve to render Mussar study ineffective. Likewise, transgression is a spiritual precipitant that prevents Mussar from rendering the desired effect, for it dulls man's heart, and makes it as hard as stone, *chas v'shalom*. The essential remedy is Torah study, as well as to pray with feelings of subjugating oneself to Hashem. Preferably, one should gather together ten like-minded people. First, they should study some Mussar, and afterwards pray together to be saved from the evil inclination.[14]

TORAH PURELY LISHMAH

Man's primary obligation is to study Torah purely *lishmah* — for the sake of Heaven. However, even if one has not yet attained this level, his study should at least be comprised of the same content as is found in studying

14 See the end of Letter Fourteen.

lishmah.[15] This is similar to a mitzvah that is not performed purely *lishmah*; it may be performed only if it is comprised of the same content as when the mitzvah is done for the sake of Heaven. It is true that most of the Torah studied today is not that which is deliberated on when one studies purely *lishmah* — the central focus of which is to know the required laws in *Orach Chaim*.[16] This is the primary obligation for both beginning and advanced students. The reason it is not emphasized is because the student must first build a foundation and develop his learning skills before he can accurately study it. The prevalent custom of theoretical study enhances the development of learning skills. I will not discuss this now at length; rather, I am merely alluding to it, so as not to overly distract the reader.

THE GIFT OF THE SEA OF REEDS

What we call "Torah study" is characterized by sharp analysis, with a student passionately defending his own line of reasoning. [After this initial stage is completed, then the concluding phase,] "Torah *lishmah*," is activated. This is characterized by an unruffled and calm spirit, when a person accepts the validity of a conclusion regardless of whether he or his colleague was correct. These two stages are on opposite ends of the spectrum. Chazal allude to them in their instruction on how one should conduct himself in the realm of "Torah study" (*Kiddushin* 30a): "Even a father and son, or a teacher and student, who study Torah together in the same place [lit. "in the same gate"] initially become enemies of one another; yet they do not move from there until they come to love one another, as it is written (*Bamidbar* 21:14): 'Therefore it is said in *Sefer Milchamos Hashem*: "The gift of [the Sea of] Reeds" ' [*V'es vahav b'sufah* in Hebrew, which can also be read as "and love at the end"]. The initial animosity is the aspect of learning with sharp analysis. The love at the end is the aspect of *lishmah*. At that stage, each person nullifies his own opinion in order to follow the majority or the most outstanding Sage; or each one holds to his own opinion, as with the schools of Beis Shammai and Beis Hillel (*Yevamos* 14a) — all in accord with the guidelines which are clarified in the

---

15 See Letter Twenty-nine.
16 Since *Orach Chaim* teaches the most commonly needed halachos, such as the laws of prayer and Shabbos, it is the most *lishmah*.

Talmud and the halachic authorities. Of course, this latter way is carried out within the framework of endearment and friendship — with the aspect of *lishmah*. The imperative to establish the truth relates to the aspect of scholarship, where each scholar states and embraces the line of reasoning which seems correct in his eyes. The peace — the mutual respect and love they ultimately display towards one another — is the aspect of *lishmah*.

TO KNOW THE ALMIGHTY'S WILL

The same is true when approaching any contemplation that relates to Divine service. Take, for example, the supervision of Torah education for the children of impoverished families; this is also an aspect of Torah.[17] For what is Torah but to know the Almighty's will. Indeed, determining the the Divine will as regards any given mitzvah is to be considered a branch of Torah study. Hence, such inquiries must also begin with sharp intellectual analysis and conclude with *lishmah*, with each person nullifying his viewpoint in peace and friendship, in deference to the majority view. Regarding the analysis of how best to approach matters dealing with Divine service — the *lishmah* aspect is easier to fulfill. The main thing is that a person must accustom himself to strive to attain the level of *lishmah*. Regarding Torah study, experience shows that a deficiency in the aspect of intellectual analysis is worse than if the aspect of *lishmah* is lacking. Thus, the student must invest more effort towards such analysis. On the other hand, in other areas of Divine service, deficiency in the aspect of *lishmah* is more serious, and one must therefore incline oneself more towards this aspect.

Thus, in matters relating to Divine service, man should devote his heart and soul to attain the level of *lishmah*, which is relatively easy to attain. On the other hand, a flaw in this aspect is a great transgression, for it can cause, *chas v'chalilah*, a crooked manner of conduct that is in opposition to the Divine will.

THE REWARD IS IN PROPORTION TO THE EXERTION

The most difficult aspect of Divine service is to be scrupulously honest

---

17 That is, how to best provide this educational service.

in one's business transactions, and this is the first thing for which a person is judged when he faces the Heavenly court (*Shabbos* 31a). Logic dictates that if one commits a kind of transgression that is in the category [of transgressions which are] easy to avoid, then his punishment for transgressing it will be more severe than the punishment for a transgression in the difficult category [i.e., transgressions which are difficult to avoid].[18] Moreover, even if he committed this same transgression when it was in the difficult category, it falls somewhat within the category of a transgression that is easy to avoid, since he would have transgressed even if it had been easy.[19] This concept also applies to positive actions. The more difficult it is for one to perform a good deed, the more reward he will receive for doing so, as Chazal state, "The reward is in proportion to the exertion" (*Avos* 5:26). Therefore, when he performs the very same mitzvah [that previously was difficult for him to perform] which is [now] in the easy category, it will fall within the category of the difficult mitzvos, because he would have performed it even if it had been difficult.[20]

It is possible that Chazal were alluding to this idea in the following Talmudic passage (*Sukkah* 52a): "In the future, *HaKadosh Baruch Hu* will bring the evil impulse…to the righteous, it will appear as a towering mountain; and to the wicked, it will appear as a strand of hair." The righteous fulfill even the difficult aspects of Divine service. Thus, it will appear to them that even

---

18 This is not referring to a particular sin that is easily avoidable and one time violated. Rather this case is where he intentionally downgraded the severity of the sin. Meaning, initially he realized the severity, then chose to deliberately dismiss this awareness from his heart. If he had not downgraded the severity, he could have easily avoided the sin. Now that he removed the fear from his heart, he effectively permitted himself to commit the sin. Therefore, his punishment will be worse than the punishment for a sin that he regarded as severe, but nevertheless commits. In this second case, the sin was committed not because he rationalized that it is not so serious, rather, he maintains that it is severe, but he could not control the *yetzer hara*.

19 That is, he previously committed the sin when it was in the "easy-to-avoid" category and chose to dismiss its severity. Subsequently if he is in a situation where it is difficult for him to refrain from committing the very same sin, he will be punished as if it were easy to refrain. For even if it had been easy to avoid, he still would have committed it because he would have dismissed its severity.

20 Even though it was easy for him to perform this same good deed, he is rewarded as if it were difficult for him to do so.

the easy aspects were actually difficult. The wicked, on the other hand, transgress even the easy aspects of Divine service. Thus, their perception will be that even the difficult aspects fall somewhat within the easy aspects. Therefore, we should strive to be honest in our business transactions — at least as regards relatively easy aspects.

ORGANIZE LESSONS IN CHOSHEN MISHPAT

We read in *Pirkei Avos* (4:16): "Rabbi Yehudah said, 'Be meticulous in study, for a careless misinterpretation is considered tantamount to willful transgression.' "[21] [Therefore,] we should organize lessons in *Choshen Mishpat*, the section of the *Shulchan Aruch* that deals with these laws. Along these lines, we should invite businessmen and merchants to participate in these lessons. This area of study is relatively easy to undertake, with each section comprising an independent unit. And these businessmen will understand that the nature of business transactions has changed over time, and the study must be directed to understand how the laws are applicable today. Indeed, the initial study in *Choshen Mishpat* consists primarily of knowing how these rulings are relevant to contemporary business practices. Involving businessmen in such a framework will enable them to consult with Torah scholars, and they will learn to conduct at least the easy aspects of their dealings according to halachah.

CONDUCIVE TO SPIRITUAL GROWTH

Concerning all we have discussed until now, we have to realize that the atonement facilitated by Yom Kippur is dependent on repentance. The essential component of repentance — resolving to never repeat the transgression — is difficult to attain. However, a person should not be lax in preparing for the Day of Atonement — at the very least, as regards the relatively easy aspects of repentance. This is particularly true concerning the Ten Days of Repentance, which are especially conducive to spiritual growth. Let him go to the *beis hamussar* at night, when he is free from his business involvements.

---

21 We see from this, that one must be extremely careful in all aspects of mitzvah observance
— including financial matters.

This is something that can be accomplished with relative ease. Let him learn Mussar with passion and fervor. Such study will stimulate his subconscious and help him to make a commitment to Mussar study in general. It will motivate him during the upcoming year to run to the *beis hamussar* on Shabbos, as well as for a few brief sessions during the week. This will insure that the impressions on his subconscious will not diminish. It will also help accustom him to reflect on his ways so that he can distinguish between the easy and difficult [categories of mitzvos]. Minimally, Mussar study will assist him in observing the easy aspects of Torah and mitzvos. Then, through his resolution to abandon at least the easy aspects of his transgressions, he will attain the level of a sincere penitent, at least in these easy aspects that he has abandoned on Yom Kippur. In turn, this will bring upon him the following blessing: "One who strives to purify himself is granted Divine assistance." He then will ascend from level to level in fulfillment of Torah and mitzvos — even in the difficult aspects, which will benefit him — the "self" — in the World to Come.[22]

TRANSLATOR'S SUMMARY OF LETTER SIX

1. The essence of man — his spirit, the "self" — exists after his demise, and experiences either pain or pleasure in the World to Come.

2. The easier it is for a person to avoid a transgression or perform a mitzvah, the greater the punishment for its violation.

3. During the Ten Days of Repentance one should correct the easier aspects of mitzvah observance.

4. One of the "easiest" ways to initiate *teshuvah* is to go to the *beis hamussar*.

---

22 Since he actively rectified the easy aspects, which are "in his control," Divine assistance will then be awakened to help him master the difficult aspects, which are seemingly "not in his control." Thus, we see that even if he merits Divine assistance to fulfill injunctions that are difficult for him, nevertheless, this is classified as "in his control." Hence, as Rav Yisrael postulated, spiritually, both aspects are in his control.

Letter Seven

THE NEW SHOFAR

Even the smallest amount of preparation to help enhance one's Yom Kippur experience is invaluable, bringing boundless blessings of success to his soul.

THERE IS NO EFFECT WITHOUT A CAUSE

EVERYTHING IN THE WORLD [that is achieved by man] is brought into existence through the process of cause and effect. The harvest of produce is the result of many preceding causes, such as planting seeds and plowing. The acquisition of money results from causes such as commercial transaction and leasing. Each cause is the effect of a preceding one. For example, seeding a field is the initial cause of grain sprouting. The seeding itself is the result of the person who plants the seed, and the planting of the seeds is the result of his desire — either to utilize the grain or to earn money through his labor. In the final analysis, there is no effect without a preceding cause that generates it. Likewise, there is no cause that is not generated by a preceding one. Ultimately, this chain of cause and effect traces back to the first, essential Cause — the Almighty.

THE CAUSE OF MAN'S NEEDS

Let us consider man in terms of his earthly needs and drives: the pursuit of money, honor, and the like. The initial cause of these matters (meaning, from the human perspective, not from the perspective of the intellect — for as we said above, ultimately, everything is dictated by the first, true Cause) is the desire of his will, which proceeds from and is generated by him. The effects blossom from this first cause, which in turn are causes of further effects — until his desire is actualized. Additionally, his initial motivation may stem from an external source, such as coercion or persuasion by another individual to arouse his will and volition. In this case, the first cause (from the human perspective) is generated and effected by another person. This other person himself has reasons that motivate him to become the first cause for his fellow.

STUDY MUSSAR IN ELUL

Now let us reflect: What will be the first cause to arouse man to examine his deeds and study Mussar in the month of Elul (and the rest of the year as well, improving everything related to the service of Hashem)? In contrast to materialistic things, there is no natural desire for this.[1] The Sages of earlier times literally shook in trepidation at the approach of Elul. Relying on the teaching from *Pirkei D'Rebbe Eliezer* (ch. 46), they enacted a decree to blow the shofar in Elul. This was the first cause to awaken man from his sleep and from his vain pursuits in order to examine his deeds. This is alluded to in the verse, "Is the shofar ever sounded in a city and the people do not tremble?" (*Amos* 3:6).

Yet, we know that an effect will not be generated unless the cause is commensurate. Thus, a momentous effect will not be produced from an insignificant cause.

---

1 One might ask: If Hashem furnishes man with a natural instinct that stirs him to provide for his physical, temporal needs — why does Hashem not furnish man with a natural instinct to awaken him to prepare his spiritual, eternal needs? Moreover, even if we could explain such a phenomenon as pertaining to our lowly generation, how could we possibly understand this lack of instinct in the earlier generations? Did they not see prophets, and worship at the Holy Temple, in all of its glory? The answer is: The purpose of creation is for man to earn a share in the World to Come through exercising his free choice to fulfill the Divine will. Therefore, free choice is crucial for man. If Hashem would have implanted *yiras Hashem* within man's heart as a natural instinct, it would have diminished man's free choice. Therefore, in order to preserve free choice, Hashem deliberately withheld the instinctual sense of *yiras Shamayim* from the hearts of men. The study of Mussar inculcates and awakens the heart with *yiras Shamayim*. See "The Gates of Light," chapters 2, 3, and 4.

OUR HEARTS ARE UNFEELING

According to this concept, the blowing of the shofar is the first cause for the type of individual who is totally immersed in the service of Hashem. It only requires a minor cause to awaken him to a thorough self-examination. However, "what can we reply, and what can we do" (*Selichos* service) now that we are completely immersed in the vanities of this world? Our hearts are unfeeling and hard as stone. Will a minor arousal make an impression in the hard stone?[2]

A MIGHTY CAUSE

Yet if we will not be drawn after the deceptions of the negative impulse, which induces us to unwittingly transform light into darkness by asserting that the easy is difficult, then there is hope. It is clear that going occasionally to the *beis hamussar* in Elul is a very easy matter. Despite all of life's burdens, there is ample time for this — with minimal effort, either by day or night. The blowing of the shofar will sufficiently serve as a cause to awaken us [to go to the *beis hamussar*]. Then, when a person goes to the *beis hamussar*, it serves as a mighty cause that has the capacity to yield significant and vital results.[3]

THE GENERAL AND PARTICULAR HEALING POWERS OF TORAH

This idea is taught in a statement by Chazal (*Kiddushin* 30b): "If this disgusting creature [the *yetzer hara*] assails you, drag it to the *beis hamidrash*." There are many different types of *battei midrash* [i.e., areas of Torah study]. For example, there is study relevant to proper business practices, study relevant to kashrus, and so forth. Now, the Torah's power to heal the disease of the negative impulse is both general and particular in nature. In general, "Torah study serves to shield and deliver a person" (*Sotah* 21a). In particular, the beginning and nearly the principal remedy is [to study the particular area that needs to be corrected]. For example, to correct the trait of honesty in business dealings, one should study the laws germane to business; to correct

---

2   We fool ourselves, thinking that the shofar awakens us.
3   To examine his ways and make improvements.

one's speech, study the laws germane to speech; and so forth. In every area that the "disgusting creature" assails a person, he should turn to the relevant "*beis hamidrash*" [i.e., area of Torah study].

THE PHYSICAL BENEFITS OF STUDYING MUSSAR IN ELUL

In light of this, it is imperative to study Mussar in the month of Elul. This study yields two distinct benefits — physical[4] and spiritual.[5] Concerning the physical, each person is in great danger during this period, for Rosh HaShanah is the time of judgment. When the shofar is sounded on Rosh HaShanah, a person is remembered and judged for his deeds. At that moment, his situation is comparable to the *kohen gadol* when he enters the *Kodesh HaKodashim*, as Chazal state (*Rosh HaShanah* 26a): "Since the shofar on Rosh HaShanah awakens remembrance, it is equivalent to entering the *Kodesh HaKodashim*."[6]

How the heart should tremble! Man, who loves himself and those dependent upon him, should strive to improve himself. (Do we see people excel in righteousness without preparation and exhortations of *yiras Shamayim* and Mussar?) Or at the very least, man should humble his spirit through the breaking of his heart, which provides the primary shield against the awesome danger that hovers over him. As Chazal teach (*Rosh HaShanah* 16b): "Every year which is poor[7] becomes rich before it ends." This teaching refers to the breaking of the heart, as Chazal state further (ibid.): "The more a person humbles himself on Rosh HaShanah, the more effective is his prayer."

INDIVIDUAL JUDGMENT

Shlomo HaMelech teaches us, "There is a time for everything" (*Koheles* 3:1) and yet, man does not know when his end is, as it states, "When it [the

---

4   The judgment determines whether he should be granted another year of life in this physical world.

5   He will be saved from punishment in the World to Come.

6   If the *kohen gadol* were not worthy, he would expire when he entered the domain of the *Kodesh HaKodashim*.

7   Meaning, when Israel humble themselves and make themselves lowly.

moment of disaster] falls upon him suddenly" (ibid. 9:12). Then, he will be insufficiently prepared [for judgment]. Nor will he be equipped with shield and armor to protect himself from the snare — the awesome day of judgment. Indeed, we see with our own eyes that on virtually every Rosh HaShanah there are young men who are sentenced to die, may Hashem have mercy. It is true that the majority of youths are spared; however, this is only because the Almighty demonstrates forbearance until a person's appointed time has arrived. Therefore, one must not look at others who remain alive without having prepared [for Rosh HaShanah], for Hashem deals with each person on a completely individual basis.

THE POWER OF THE IMAGINATION

Since the power of the imagination enhances Mussar study, let a person consider himself as if he were the High Priest entering the *Kodesh HaKodashim* on the Day of Atonement. Under those circumstances, he would surely tremble for fear of his life, lest he die, Heaven forbid. Likewise, let him [tremble for fear of his life on Rosh HaShanah and] strengthen his faith in the words of our Sages. They ruled that a shofar made from the horn of a cow is invalid because "An accuser cannot become an advocate."[8] However, while it is permissible to enter a synagogue with gold apparel, it is not permissible to use the shofar from a cow because it awakens remembrance. Therefore, when the shofar [is sounded on Rosh HaShanah,] each man is remembered and judged for all of his deeds. [Therefore, each Jew who hears the shofar on Rosh HaShanah] can be likened to the High Priest entering the *Kodesh HaKodashim*! How intensely should the heart tremble upon contemplating this awesome matter.

THE SPIRITUAL BENEFITS OF STUDYING MUSSAR IN ELUL

Let us now turn to the spiritual benefits of studying Mussar in Elul. We know that "Hashem waits compassionately [for a person to repent, but if he

---

8   The Jews stumbled in the episode of the Golden Calf. Therefore, a cow cannot come to their defense as an advocate.

does not seek atonement] then Hashem will eventually collect His due" (*Bereishis Rabbah* 67:4). The very man who violates a Torah principle has contravened the Divine will, and will unquestionably be subject to retribution. The physical body is only a shell [that disintegrates upon death]. However, the actual life force — that which experiences pleasure and pain — endures even after the body expires, and retains the capacity to receive pleasure and pain [for all eternity]. If man studies Torah and fulfills the mitzvos, then he will experience vast and wondrous delights after his death. However, if he transgresses, or neglects Torah study and mitzvah performance, he will be disciplined with awesome and fearful suffering. His entire existence will be one of sorrow and groaning. There will be no hope of escape — unless he prepared a refuge for himself when the spiritual forces were still joined to the corporal body.

THE VALUE OF YOM KIPPUR

Yom Kippur is good in its entirety, a day of forgiveness and atonement. As our Sages state (*Ta'anis* 26b): "There are no days good for Israel like Yom Kippur." If we make the proper preparations to rectify our ways, then we have nothing better than the Day of Atonement, for it effects atonement when accompanied by repentance—which [essentially] is the repudiation of our iniquities. Indeed, even a minor amount of preparation is highly beneficial, with nothing in the physical realm to compare with it! On the Day of Atonement, we should endeavor to at least make some minimal resolution for the future. There is no enterprise that yields profit like preparation for the Day of Atonement through studying Mussar and reflecting on how to improve one's ways, until he is inspired to make a resolution for the future on Yom Kippur itself. Even the smallest, most minute aspect of preparation to help enhance one's Yom Kippur experience is invaluable, bringing boundless blessings of success to his soul. It saves one from many troubles [punishments] — and there is no greater profit than this.[9]

---

9   One might wonder, what is the benefit and significance of a minimal resolution as compared to full repentance? See "The Gates of Light" (number eight of the Ten Innovations), where Rav Yisrael explains that there is no greater success for a human being than if, through the study of Mussar, he saves himself from committing one transgression. For

FEAR OF JUDGMENT

Man should devote his heart and soul to integrate the two above mentioned aspects[10] and weave this understanding within the joining of the spiritual and physical. At the outset, let his heart shatter in fear over the judgment on his body. This is an awesome matter, for his life, the life of his family,
as well as his and their provision for the upcoming year are dependent on the
outcome of this judgment. Such contemplation will motivate him to rectify
his ways and enhance the benefit of Yom Kippur. If you encounter an impediment, the negative impulse — drag him to the appropriate *beis hamidrash*,
the *beis hamussar*. If [the adversary assails man by hardening his heart as]
stone — then through the study of Mussar (this is the appropriate study for a
non-feeling heart) his heart will melt.

THE AROUSAL OF YIRAS SHAMAYIM

[Up to this point, we have discussed the reflections that will awaken
man during the month of Elul. Now we will touch on the reflections that will
awaken man] during the rest of the year. The first cause of arousal is *yiras
Shamayim*. [In general] a person has Heavenly fear planted within his heart,
and he knows and believes that the consequence of abandoning the Torah
and mitzvos of Hashem will be terrible and bitter. However, the desire for
earthly pleasure subverts his spiritual objectives. The solution to this is to
study practical halachah[11] (of course, this does not mean at the expense of
his other studies, as the Talmud states [*Bava Basra* 3b]: "One should not destroy a *beis kenesses* until a new *beis kenesses* is built").[12] If he comes across a
ruling in an area wherein he needs strengthening, he should study it from the

---

the pain of Gehinnom is infinitely greater than any suffering in this world. Likewise, if all
his preparation for Elul, Rosh HaShanah, and the Ten Days of Repentance, through
Mussar study, results in him making a minimal resolution on Yom Kippur to improve his
Divine service — there is no greater profit. For it saves him from that untold suffering in
the Next World.

10 The redemption of body and soul.

11 See the *Iggeres HaMussar* for an elaboration of this concept.

12 One should not give up his established times of Talmudic study in order to study practical
halachah. For perhaps he will not succeed in replacing it with an equivalent measure of
practical halachah.

source and in great depth, each person according to his intellectual ability. The material he thereby learns will make a lasting impact on his soul to observe this precept — almost more than contemplation of *yiras Shamayim*. Nevertheless, one should not desist from contemplation of *yiras Shamayim*, for "If there is no wisdom, there is no fear of God; and if there is no fear of God, there is no wisdom" (*Avos* 3:21).

TRANSGRESSIONS HAVE DIFFERENT ASPECTS

Let us now address those who, upon seeing the great power that desire wields over them, are afflicted by despair. There is no affliction as severe as despair. Therefore, it is important for people to understand that every transgression has several different aspects. Some transgressions are more difficult to refrain from than other transgressions. In various situations or times, it will be difficult for one to refrain from a transgression, and in other situations, it will be easy for him to refrain from the same transgression. For example, let us consider the transgression of neglecting Torah study. The aspect of difficulty of not doing so varies from Shabbos to weekday, from a time when he is preoccupied with his affairs to when he is not so encumbered, and from a situation when he is distressed to when he is tranquil. Thus, any given transgression is divided into numerous aspects according to a person's circumstances. Neither all times nor all circumstances are equal. The easier it is for man to refrain from a transgression, the more he will be punished if he commits it, as Chazal teach (*Menachos* 43b): "Rebbi Meir said: [Regarding the mitzvah of tzitzis] the punishment for not wearing white threads is greater than [the punishment for] not wearing blue ones."[13]

With this in mind, a person should accustom himself to fulfill the verse, "If you seek it as [if it were] silver, and search for it as [if it were] hidden treasures — then you will understand the fear of Hashem" (*Mishlei* 2:4). Therefore, let us contemplate man's course in fulfilling his physical needs and apply the lesson to our spiritual endeavors. We see that a person labors terribly to procure his bodily needs even when the return for his efforts is minimal.

---

13 This is due to the fact that the white threads are readily available, whereas the blue ones are made from a rare dye.

Amazingly, we find that it is not overwhelming for a man to try and relieve his physical plight, even though he is concurrently enduring a distracting misfortune!

PERFORM THE EASY MITZVOS

It is incumbent upon us to follow the same course concerning our spiritual needs.[14] Let us endeavor to at least perform the mitzvos that are easy for us to fulfill, and avoid the transgressions that are easy for us to avoid. Adherence to this principle will save us from terrible and bitter discomfort. Thus, despair is absolutely inappropriate for man! Rather, let him follow the same course in the pursuit of his spiritual needs that he employs to fulfill his physical ones. Of course, he should not desist from aspiring to perform all the mitzvos, to study the Torah in a perfect fashion, and to refrain totally from transgression.

In Elul, specifically, even though the time is short, one should endeavor to study a short book, such as Rabbeinu Yonah's *Sha'arei Teshuvah*, which basically touches on the roots of all the mitzvos and transgressions. When he comes across a passage that is relevant to his own particular shortcoming, he should contemplate it deeply, according to the power of his understanding and the constraints of time. He should also categorize the various aspects of the injunction's difficulty, in accord with what we mentioned above. The rectification of any aspect of this transgression will generate hope that the Day of Atonement will see him as a complete penitent in these easy aspects. His sincere resolution to abandon the transgression when it is easy for him is valued by Hashem with incomparable worth. This will bequeath much merit to him, both in this world and the Next.

We see with our own eyes that it is easy for man to fulfill that which he observes because of his internal nature and inclination, even if the effort is difficult due to external factors. Each location in the world varies in this regard. For example, in our country it is easy for one to observe Shabbos and even to endure trials on its behalf. In Germany, on the other hand, Shabbos

---

14 Just as a man who is enduring discomfort still perseveres to provide for his material needs, so, too, a man who is overwhelmed with passion should persevere to perform the mitzvos that are easy for him.

observance is more difficult than all other areas of Divine worship. The remedy for this is to study the laws of Shabbos in great depth, until it makes a lasting impact on one's soul. Consequently, its observance will become as second nature to him. This may even be accomplished without the aid of Mussar. An appropriate amount of in-depth Torah study alone will endow one with the fortitude to withstand trials on behalf of Shabbos.

TRANSLATOR'S SUMMARY OF LETTER SEVEN

1. Unlike the innate drive to pursue material needs, there is no natural desire to do *teshuvah* before Rosh HaShanah — the Day of Judgment — when our life is at stake.

2. Our Sages enacted the blowing of the shofar to awaken us to do *teshuvah* before Rosh HaShanah.

3. An honest evaluation reveals that in our latter generation, our hearts do not respond and are not aroused by the sound of the shofar.

4. For us, the sounding of the shofar reminds us to go to the *beis hamussar*, which will help us do *teshuvah* on the aspects of our observance that are easy to correct.

LETTER EIGHT

THE FACTOR OF REDEMPTION

In Egypt, where the burden of servitude was overwhelmingly heavy, the reward for any mitzvah the Jews were able to perform was very great. This is why they merited not only to be redeemed, but to be redeemed in so miraculous a fashion.

OLD ONES AND NEW ONES

COMMENTING ON THE VERSE, "Both new and old ones have I hidden for you, O beloved" (*Shir HaShirim* 7:14), the Midrash (*Vayikra Rabbah* 2:11) states: "The 'old ones' refer to Avraham, Yitzchak, and Yaakov, while the 'new ones' are Amram son of Kehas and all the worthy men who were in Egypt.... The 'old ones' refer to the fellowships of Moshe, Yehoshua, David, and Chizkiyahu, while the 'new ones' refer to those of Ezra, Hillel, Rebbi Yochanan ben Zakkai, and Rebbi Meir. Concerning all these, the verse states: 'Both new and old ones...' "

PESACH, MATZO, AND MAROR

We read in the Talmud (*Pesachim* 116a): "Rabban Gamliel used to say: Whoever does not mention these three things on Passover has not fulfilled his duty, namely: *pesach*, matzo, and *maror*." The Rashbam explains this to mean: "If they did not explain the significance of these three things." We see, therefore, that the Torah permits us to investigate and examine the meaning of these three mitzvos. If so, let us inquire, why did Rabban Gamliel place the mention of *maror* after that of the matzo? We know that *maror* represents our servitude under the Egyptians, while matzo represents the redemption. If so, it would seem that the *maror* should precede the matzo, just as the servitude preceded the redemption!

HALF CULPABLE AND HALF MERITORIOUS

To answer this question, let us consider a different teaching of Chazal. The Talmud states (*Kiddushin* 40a), "A person should always regard himself as if he is half culpable and half meritorious." We may ask, how can the Sages give such blanket instruction? Doesn't a man sometimes see clearly that he is inclined to one side more than the other? To understand this, let us turn to the Rambam, *zt"l*, who writes the following (*Hilchos Teshuvah*, ch. 3): "Each person has both merits and sins. One who has more merits than sins is righteous, whereas one who has more sins than merits is wicked…. This calculation is not based on the quantity of merits and transgressions; rather, it is based on their respective quality. There are some merits that offset many sins, and some sins that offset many merits.[1] Only Hashem, the source of all knowledge, can make this computation. He alone has the wisdom to assess the quality of one's merits against the quality of his sins."

THE LEVEL OF DIFFICULTY WILL FLUCTUATE

It is clear that there are many factors that increase the magnitude of either one's merits or sins. Let us examine one of them. We know that mitzvos are valued according to the level of difficulty required to perform them, as

---

1   The Rambam is not asserting that mitzvos cancel out sins and vice versa, for there is a clear axiom of Torah that each and every mitzvah and transgression will be judged and the appropriate reward and/or punishment will be administered. Rather, the Rambam is teaching that in judging the status of man — whether he is righteous or wicked — the determinant is not the quantity of mitzvos and sins, but rather the quality. A great mitzvah or transgression counts as a greater merit or detriment than a lesser mitzvah or transgression. For instance, amongst a person's deeds he has performed the mitzvah of saving a life, and on the other hand he committed the sin of inadvertent Shabbos desecration. When Hashem classifies his status, the weight for that particular mitzvah will far outweigh the weight for that transgression.

Chazal teach (Avos 5:26): "The reward is in proportion to the exertion [required to perform the mitzvah]." Thus, a person can perform the exact same mitzvah on two different occasions, and the level of difficulty will fluctuate drastically. Indeed, there are countless gradations, with each situation divided into many infinitesimal portions, and the difficulty varies proportionally to the context under which the mitzvah is performed.

For example, let us consider a person who studied on one occasion for an hour, with his mind clear. Under the circumstances, his nature did not resist the study, and he did not feel distressed — or if he did, only very minimally. Conversely, on a different occasion things were quite different. [He was preoccupied with other matters, and] the effort to study was as burdensome to him as if he were carrying sandbags on his back. In this case, the strain was intense. It is true that the content of the mitzvah — the study of Torah for one hour — was the same on both occasions. However, the context of the study was dramatically different! This holds true for everything in life — contextually, there are no two moments alike. Even if the contents of a mitzvah and the way it is fulfilled are identical, there is still a remarkable variance between different contexts under which it is performed!

The same is true concerning transgressions. We find that punishment varies from sin to sin according to the level of difficulty required to refrain from each one. This concept is expounded on in the Talmud (Menachos 43b): "Rebbi Meir said: '[In the mitzvah of tzitzis] the punishment for not wearing white threads is greater than for not wearing blue ones.' "[2] Similarly, the punishment for any given transgression — whether in this world or the Next — will fluctuate according to the context in which it was committed. For a time when a person could have easily restrained himself, the punishment will be correspondingly greater, and vice versa. We thus see that the exact same transgression can be committed under different circumstances, and the severity of the punishment will be different. It is dependent upon thousands of considerations, and is proportional to the gradations of difficulty required for one to refrain from the transgression.

---

2   This is due to the fact that the white threads are readily available, whereas the blue threads are made from a rare blue dye.

CONTRASTING LEVELS OF DIFFICULTY

A person should reflect deeply upon the magnitude of punishments that are meted out for Torah transgressions. This includes both violating negative injunctions (*lo sa'aseh*), as well as refraining from performing positive precepts (*aseh*). He should look into the Torah and see how far the Talmud and halachah obligates him to uphold the Torah's laws — whether in performing positive commandments or refraining from negative ones. He must calculate how far his obligation to uphold an *aseh* or *lo sa'asah* extends in contrast to the level of difficulty generated by observing it. Then, let him consider that if he were to transgress it, the resulting punishment would far exceed the level of difficulty generated by fulfilling it. This method of contrasting the levels of difficulty entailed by fulfillment with the punishment engendered by transgression, serves to caution him against violating the Torah. Failure to comply with the Divine commandments will result in far more suffering than is required to observe them.

After this reckoning, he should envision the most extreme difficult circumstances under which he would still be required to uphold the commandment's observance. Contrasting that theoretical situation to the one actually facing him, he will find that there are thousands of stages of difference between them. He should then realize that if he were to refrain from fulfilling the Divine commandment, his punishment would be hundreds of thousands of times greater.[3]

If he will devote himself to in-depth study of the mitzvos, and learn to what extent he is obligated to fortify himself and fulfill them in the face of opposing difficulty, it will have a profound impact on him. This is especially true

---

3   In summation, the first contemplation contrasts the maximum level of difficulty endured to fulfill the injunction and still be obligated by the Torah, and the punishment for violating the injunction. As difficult as this fulfillment would be while enduring the maximum level of difficulty, this pain is insignificant in contrast to Divine retribution for violating the injunction. Second, consider not the maximum level but rather your actual level of difficulty. Then you will see that there are thousands of gradations of difficulty — which span from the actual to the theoretical. Then consider that the punishment meted out to one whose situation was at the most severe level of difficulty is far worse than the difficulty endured to observe the injunction. Then surely since your actual level of difficulty is many times easier than the theoretical level of difficulty — your punishment will be far more severe.

concerning areas that are relevant to him personally. Almost every person is responsible for fulfilling more Torah obligations than he presently upholds, each according to his unique character and situation. For example, some need to delve more deeply into the laws concerning Torah study; others must study the laws pertinent to business transactions, such as the prohibitions against taking interest and overcharging; and so on.

AVOID THE EASY TRANSGRESSIONS

The Jewish people have always utilized the Ten Days of Repentance to forge the path that leads to the abandonment of sin. This pursuit is the fundamental pillar and cornerstone underlying repentance. Yet, it is difficult to discover the way that leads to the rectification of our habitual sins. However, when we reflect on our lives and the transgressions that we find easy or difficult to avoid, we come to a vital realization: It is a relatively simple matter to uphold a resolution to not trespass the easy ones. Indeed, these transgressions are in a category by themselves. If one resolves to separate himself from them, he will succeed in avoiding a substantial amount of culpability. This is because, as we have said, accountability is far more severe for transgressions that are easy to avoid than for those that are considered difficult to resist.

Thus, in general, we may divide the mitzvos and transgressions into two categories — easy and difficult. Of course, as we have mentioned, there are multiple gradations between these two spectrums. Sometimes, man errs in his calculation of which is which. He may consider a particular mitzvah difficult for him to uphold, and believe that he will receive abundant reward for it; or think that a certain injunction is hard for him to refrain from, and imagine that he will receive minimal punishment for it. However, his perception may be distorted in this, for at times the difficulty in observing the commandment is not due to one's inherent nature. Rather, it is because of his submission to the *yetzer hara*, or because the *yetzer hara* has attacked a different area that resulted in a weakening of this one as well, for the forces within man are interrelated and interdependent. In these cases, Hashem considers the person to be confronted only by easy impediments, for it was his choice not to neutralize the negative impulse.

The reverse is also true. Sometimes, it is easy for man to perform a mitzvah not because of his inherent nature, but because he achieved mastery of it through Heavenly fear and habit. Or perhaps he achieved mastery in a different area that helps him in this one. In this case, even though it may be easy for him to observe the mitzvah, Hashem attributes it as being difficult, and as a result his reward is abundant.

TWO DIFFERENT PERSPECTIVES

We see from all this that the qualities of mitzvos and transgressions — whether they are classified as difficult or easy — and all the configurations of various situations cannot be accurately fathomed by man. How true are the words of the Rambam: "Hashem alone has the wisdom to assess the quality of one's merits against the quality of his sins."

This idea is alluded to in the Talmud (*Sukkah* 52a): "Rebbi Yehudah expounded: 'In the future, the Almighty will bring the evil impulse and slay it in the presence of the righteous and the wicked. To the righteous, it will appear as a towering mountain; and to the wicked, it will appear as a strand of hair.' " This concept is amazing! How can the same thing appear to be so dramatically disparate from two different perspectives? Perhaps the explanation is found in the concept we presented above. The wicked willfully subject themselves to the control of the *yetzer hara*. Consequently, it is, indeed, quite difficult for them to conquer it. Therefore, although they acknowledge that they will pay the price, they assume that the magnitude of punishment will be configured as if their sins were in the "difficult to avoid" category. However, this is a grave misjudgment on their part. Since it was their choice to engage the *yetzer hara* in the first place, it was they who brought the difficulty upon themselves. In order to disprove their false assumptions, the *yetzer hara* appears to them as a strand of hair. This indicates that when Hashem judges them, He calculates their transgressions as if they could have easily avoided them.

THE EASY IS DIFFICULT

On the other hand, the righteous have trained themselves in Divine service, and reached a point where they consider it to be a genuine pleasure and something easy to do. Therefore, they assume that their reward will be correspondingly lessened, for why should there be great reward for something that one does eagerly and easily? In reality, however, this is a mistaken calculation on their part. Since it was their choice and impetus, Hashem considers the "easy" to be "difficult," and their reward is abundant. Therefore, the *yetzer hara* appears as a towering mountain to them — something that is only overcome with great difficulty.

How man's heart should tremble when he contemplates his situation and character! Who knows how many thousands of transgressions will be considered easy even though he experiences them as being difficult? Since the difficulty he encounters is due to his continuing choice to be so encumbered, the punishment he faces will be far more severe then he may imagine.

JUDGMENT AND ACCOUNTING

We can now understand the *mishnah* in *Pirkei Avos* (4:29): "Against your will you are destined for judgment and to give an account before the King who rules over kings." The "judgment" here corresponds to the actual experience of his situation; in other words, the fact that he committed a transgression and will be punished for it. On the other hand, the "account" refers to the leniency or severity of the actual punishment that he will receive; in other words, this takes into account what his situation would have been had he not allowed the *yetzer hara* to influence him, which would have made his Divine service significantly easier.

THE BURDEN OF SERVITUDE

At this point, let us summarize: We have seen that the reward for mitzvos is given in proportion to the difficulty of their performance. Similarly, the punishment for transgressions is diminished according to the difficulty involved in refraining from them. Moreover, we have seen that one mitzvah can offset many transgressions. Therefore, in Egypt, where the burden of servitude was overwhelmingly heavy, the reward for any mitzvah the Jews were able to perform was very great. This is why they merited not only to be redeemed, but to be redeemed in so miraculous a fashion. We see this in the following verse: "And the children of Israel groaned because of the work and they cried out. Their outcry because of the work went up to God. God heard their moaning and God remembered His covenant with Avraham, Yitzchak, and Yaakov. God saw the children of Israel; and God knew" (*Shemos* 2:23–25). Why was their prayer on such an exalted level? Because it was engendered from both the bondage they endured and the transgressions they committed, which were difficult to avoid committing.[4] Therefore, their mitzvos [in this case, prayer] were qualitatively greater than their transgressions, even though they were few in number.[5]

BITTERNESS CAUSED THE REDEMPTION

With this idea in mind, we are now in a position to understand why Rabban Gamliel placed mention of the *maror* after that of the matzo. The redemption and the servitude are not merely two things that are juxtaposed, with no intrinsic connection other than the fact that one happened to precede the other chronologically. If that had been the case, then *maror* should, indeed, have been mentioned before matzo. Rather, they were a cause and an effect: the bitter and difficult slavery was itself the cause for the redemption and its exalted nature! If it had not been for their having fulfilled mitzvos under the most trying of circumstances, they never would have been redeemed. It is thus understood that even though the cause precedes the effect, when recounting an event, the effect is mentioned first. It is for this reason that matzo is mentioned before *maror*.[6]

Let us return to what I wrote at the beginning of this letter. According to the midrash, "old" refers to something that is easy, and "new" refers to

---

4   It was difficult to refrain from sin because of the pervasive decadence of the Egyptian idol worshippers, as well as the slavery. In Letter Twenty-three the difficulty of fulfilling the Torah under the oppression of captivity is explained.

5   The Seforno comments that the righteous Jews of the generation prayed to Hashem, and Hashem heard their prayer and initiated the redemption.

6   In the wisdom of rhetoric, the most effective way to portray the cause of a cataclysmic event is to first focus on the dramatic outcome. Therefore, we focus first on the miraculous redemption. The listener is filled with astonishment: What caused this phenomenon? His heart is awakened to fathom the mystery. Then, when the factor is revealed — the significance of serving Hashem despite trying circumstances — it penetrates with full impact.

something that is difficult. The patriarchs, who were free and had direct communication with the Almighty, lead relatively easy lives compared to Amram and the people of his generation, who lived under oppressive conditions during a time of *hester panim*.[7] Therefore, the latter are classified as having a "new" and exalted status. This is the meaning of the verse: "Both new and old ones have I hidden for you, O beloved..."

We can apply this idea to Mussar study as well. Mussar is something that is easy [i.e., old] in and of itself. Namely, to learn Mussar at organized time periods, with deep feeling. Yet, it is also difficult [i.e., new].[8] Let us, then, embrace Mussar and not weaken our devotion to its study, and our reward will be great. Let me know if my letter arrived. May Hashem bless you with a good year, as befits you and as your beloved friend desires for you.

Seeking your peace,

Yisrael

Rosh HaShanah Eve 5620

TRANSLATOR'S SUMMARY OF LETTER EIGHT

1. The reward for a mitzvah is proportional to the level of difficulty required for its performance.

2. The punishment for a transgression is proportional to the level of difficulty required to abstain from the transgression.

3. The ease or difficulty of mitzvos or transgressions is not based on subjective experience, but rather on Divine determination.

4. The violation of a sin which seems very hard to avoid could be categorized by Hashem as very easy to avoid — and, therefore, subject to the worst punishment.

---

7   The same was true of those who lived during the times of the first Beis HaMikdash as compared to those who lived during the period of the second one.

8   How can we explain this? When one first undertakes this study, it is "new," and very difficult. However, with both time and the discipline of set and organized study, it becomes easy. This "ease" is due to habit, similar to what we discussed above. Therefore, its reward is, and always remains, abundant.

LETTER NINE

YIRAS SHAMAYIM

The fear of Hashem has the power to shackle the forces of desire, so that neither iniquity nor culpability can burst forth.

THE FEAR OF HASHEM

CHAZAL STATE: "Everything is in the hands of Heaven, except for the fear of Heaven." We thus see that the acquisition of Heavenly fear is dependent upon the knowledge and decision of man. As the verse states, "Now, O Israel, what does Hashem, your God, ask of you? Only to fear Hashem, your God" (*Devarim* 10:12). The fear of Hashem has the power to shackle the forces of desire, so that neither iniquity nor culpability can burst forth (cf. *Vayikra* 5:23). How frightful is man's obligation — for Hashem will judge everything that he has done. As Shlomo HaMelech tells us: "When all has been considered" (*Koheles* 12:13) — in other words, not one of a person's acts escapes judgment and accounting. Severe and bitter punishments will be administered to him according to all that he has done. How good it is, then, for his heart to be stirred to remember his end while he is yet alive.

The question arises, what exactly is the fear of Hashem, and how is it acquired? In brief, it is embodied in one idea, the expanding of a concept that is universally known: namely, fear of the punishment to which the body and soul will be subjected at the time of ultimate judgment.[1] These punishments far transcend all worldly suffering. Yet, a person will not restrain himself from sinning through mere knowledge. We see this from a passage in the Talmud

---

1   See "The Gates of Light" (ch. 4), where a parable about a blind man and a cripple illustrates the judgment and punishment of both body and soul in the Next World.

(*Shabbos* 31b): "The wicked know that their path leads to death.... If you think that perhaps they have forgotten death, therefore Scripture states, 'Yet of their destiny their mouths speak soothingly' (*Tehillim* 49:14)." Only by arousing the soul will this concept be firmly implanted in one's consciousness; only by expanding on it through vivid conceptualizations and fervent expression will awareness of its true import be engendered. By such exercises, it will be set firmly within the heart. A person must realize with absolute certainty that the punishments of the body and soul will not be administered to a "stranger"; rather, they will be executed against he himself — the one who committed the transgression. He, and no one else, will be subjected to a bitter and comfortless punishment.

MUSSAR CLEARS THE HEART

Let us appreciate our great sages, the "eyes of the community" (cf. *Bamidbar* 15:24), who expound upon Mussar concepts in order to clear the stony field of the heart. As for us, what is our task? To study and to contemplate their teachings; to increase learning and discerning (cf. *Mishlei* 1:5). Particularly, one must employ visualizations and personal conceptions that are uniquely relevant to him. This exercise should be undertaken in the *beis hamussar*, where one can study without interruption or distraction. Furthermore, involving the whole body in these imaginative exercises, by dramatically moving one's limbs — shaking one's arms and gesticulating with one's hands — is an integral factor of this in-depth study.

TRANSLATOR'S SUMMARY OF LETTER NINE

1. Acquiring *yiras Shamayim* is dependent on the decisions of man.

2. *Yiras Shamayim* empowers one with strength to master the *yetzer hara*.

3. Therefore, if a person acquires *yiras Shamayim*, he will be spared bitter consequences in the World to Come.

4. *Yiras Shamayim* is acquired through learning Mussar with *hispailus*, visualizations, visiting the *beis hamussar*, and dramatically gesticulating with his hands.

LETTER TEN

IMPERCEPTIBLE
IMPRESSIONS

The sweet waters of Torah will penetrate into his heart; they will guard him from all evil and transform his ways to good.

MY HEART REJOICED

I READ YOUR LETTER, my esteemed students, and my heart rejoiced when I saw that you are pursuers of righteousness who desire the nearness of God (cf. *Yeshayahu* 58:2). My soul was bedecked with joy, unencumbered by any personal desires. How blinded is my mind! Who can assure that our own hearts, for ourselves, will rejoice in the fear of Heaven (cf. *Devarim* 5:26), with no corruption of [personal] desire?[1]

TREE OF LIFE

Do not fear the voice of tumult (cf. *Yirmeyahu* 11:16) [that opposes Mussar study], neither be unnerved (ibid. 23:4). Grasp the "tree of life" (*Mishlei* 3:18) — the study of Mussar. It revitalizes the intellect, protecting it from drowning in the forces of the habitual desires.

---

1   Although he experienced joy for the spiritual achievements of his students, he questioned whether the happiness he felt for his own attainment of *yiras Shamayim* emanated from a pure place — or perhaps was tainted by some personal "self-satisfaction." This introspection reflects his profound humility and his quest for the truth.

A BLESSING

The study of Mussar calls out, "Life!" and within its sphere, every person is moved in his heart to know his deficiencies and yearn to rectify them.[2] Do not fall into the net of the *yetzer hara*, who ridicules *yiras Shamayim*. [One engaging in such unprovoked mockery] is like a thief who uproots souls from Divine service. [He commits this evil deed] even though no personal desire is found [to motivate such behavior. Through the lens of Mussar], the eye sees [i.e., one truly realizes] that transgression ascends to the Heavens, and the heart desires to strengthen itself in Mussar, so that it might be saved from the netherworld. As for those who draw others close to *yiras Shamayim*, a blessing is invoked — something that is not the case for those [that ridicule it]. The effort required [in this sacred endeavor] is small, and the reward is abundant. As it states in Tanach: "Those who teach righteousness to the multitudes [will shine] like the stars, forever and ever" (*Daniel* 12:3).

MUSSAR ELEVATES A PERSON

Let a person's heart not despair if he studies Mussar and is not awakened, or if he feels no impression on his soul motivating him to change his path. It is known with certainty that even if the physical eye does not perceive the impression, the eyes of the intellect nevertheless perceive it. Through an abundance of [Mussar] study over an extended period of time, the hidden impressions will accumulate, and he will be transformed into a different person. His desires will be reigned in, without excessive indulgence, and some [desires] will even be completely neutralized. Experience testifies [even] through a cursory observation, that Mussar study — whether a lot or a little — elevates a person above his peers, both in thought and conduct.

---

2   Only one who recognizes his sins and deficiencies is considered alive, because he is close to repentance. However, one who sees himself without flaw is not considered to be alive, because he is distant from repentance. And it is the study of Mussar that awakens one with *yiras Shamayim* and the insight to see his flaws, and thus be considered truly alive. See Letter Thirty, section 5.

REBBI AKIVA

Chazal allude to this concept in *Avos D'Rebbi Nosson*, where we read (ch. 6): "What was the beginning of Rebbi Akiva? It is told that at the age of forty, he had learned no Torah whatsoever. Once, while standing next to a well, he queried, 'Who chiseled this stone?' They responded to him, 'The water that continuously falls on it every day.' They said to him [further], 'Akiva, aren't you aware of the verse, "Stones are worn away by water" (*Iyov* 14:19)?' Immediately, Rebbi Akiva applied a *kal v'chomer*[3] to himself: 'If that which is soft carves into that which is hard, then all the more so, the words of Torah, which are as hard as iron, will penetrate into my heart, which is flesh and blood!' Immediately, he returned to study Torah...."

THE CONSTANT FLOW OF WATER

[We see from the fact that Chazal state that Rebbi Akiva "returned" to study that] Rebbi Akiva [experienced a problem] when he began to study. When he found [his Torah studies left] no impression on him, he was convinced that it was hopeless [for him to continue]. They showed him a contradiction to his way of thinking through the flow of water on the stone. The changing of the stone is not discernable to the senses, whatsoever. In reference to this, the natural scientists decreed that an impression is made that is imperceptible to man. Thus, the groove in the stone is caused by the abundant [flow of] water over an extended period of time, [that continuously renders a series of] cumulative, impalpable impressions.

TRANSFORM HIS WAYS TO GOOD

Let us, then, consider a person who is not naturally endowed with the power to numb the sensation of his desires. His intellect lives to seek eternal comfort for his soul, but his heart is as hard as stone. Let such a person pour abundant water upon his soul by engaging in Mussar study. [Slowly and] imperceptibly, impressions will be generated within his heart that will guide him to the path of life — the study of Torah. As Chazal

---

3   An exegetical method whereby a conclusion is inferred from a lenient situation to a stringent one.

teach (Yerushalmi, *Pe'ah* 1), "The entire world and all of the mitzvos are not equal to the mitzvah of Torah study." Moreover, Torah study itself is likened to water. These sweet waters will penetrate into his heart; they will guard him from all evil and transform his ways to good.

TRANSLATOR'S SUMMARY OF LETTER TEN

1. A person should not despair if he studies Mussar and does not sense any impression in his soul.

2. Even if he does not sense the impact of Mussar, it is nevertheless perceived in his subconscious.

3. Through consistent study of Mussar over an extended period of time, hidden impressions will accumulate and render a dramatic transformation.

4. Mussar study elevates a person above his peers, both in thought and conduct.

LETTER ELEVEN

STRENGTHEN OTHERS IN MUSSAR

The only course to follow, the only way to repair the breach in Heavenly fear, is to engage in the proper study of Mussar, which purifies all diseases of the soul.

THIS LETTER IS DEDICATED TO the honor of my friends and companions — may your light shine. May each one be praised according to his special quality, and may you receive blessings from Hashem, commensurate with the good that your souls desire.

THE SUPPORT OF THE GEDOLEI HA'AM

Shlomo HaMelech teaches us, "Open rebuke is good if it stems from hidden love" (*Mishlei* 27:5). My purpose with this letter, therefore, is to admonish and encourage you. Let every one of you — each according to his intelligence and situation — thoroughly commit yourselves to strengthen others in the study of Mussar. Pursue this mission with the utmost commitment and enthusiasm. I wish to stress that your central undertaking should be to seek the support of the *gedolei ha'am* [the leading sages and scholars of the generation], for the masses look up to them and comply with their rulings. Convince them to endorse your efforts to the best of their abilities. If you put your hearts to it, it is relatively easy to obtain letters of approbation from them, providing that you proceed with intelligence and devotion to truth.

FOSTER AN AWARENESS

Let not the task of conferring merit upon the community — particularly, by fostering an awareness of the blazing war being waged by the *yetzer hara* — be inconsequential in your eyes. Man cannot triumph in this conflict without proper Mussar study. When devoid of *yiras Shamayim*, all Torah study and Divine service is a mere mechanical performance of mitzvos, with virtually no spiritual component. A person going through life in this manner can be blown off course by the slightest breeze, as stated by Chazal (*Avos* 3:11): "Rabbi Chanina ben Dosa says: Anyone whose fear of sin takes precedence over his wisdom, his wisdom will endure; but anyone whose wisdom takes precedence over his fear of sin, his wisdom will not endure."

Accordingly, there is no one who will deny the great, absolute necessity of Mussar study in our times, when financial need pressures us and Divine service is diminished as a result of our agitation. The only course to follow, the only way to repair the breach in Heavenly fear, is to engage in the proper study of Mussar, which purifies all diseases of the soul.

A MAGNIFICENT GIFT

You are therefore fortunate that this great mitzvah came to your hands! It is a magnificent gift from the Almighty. Accept it with love and perform it with enthusiasm, strength, and vigor. You will then receive reward in equal measure to all those you influence, both in this world and the Next — as both you and your beloved friend, who seeks your good, desires.

Yisrael

TRANSLATOR'S SUMMARY OF LETTER ELEVEN

1. Letters of approbation from the *gedolei hador* will inspire Mussar study among the public.

2. Raising public awareness of the awesome war waged by the *yetzer hara* is vitally important.

3. Man cannot triumph in the conflict with his *yetzer hara* without proper Mussar study.

4. The mitzvah to strengthen others in Mussar is a great gift and precious merit from Hashem.

LETTER TWELVE

LISTEN TO HER VOICE

When a sensitive man is moved to enter the beis hamussar — to bring a "pure Minchah offering" and to pour forth his soul to Hashem — then I shall know that a seed of righteousness took root.

EAT AND LIVE FOREVER

MY PURPOSE IN THIS LETTER is to elaborate upon the topic that we discussed before I left on my trip, and to inspire you concerning the strengthening of the *beis hamidrash* as a means for spreading Torah — an undertaking more worthy than any other in the world. Of course, this is also true regarding the pursuit of *yiras Shamayim* and Mussar study, which must precede Torah — as is discussed in the works of our Sages. If we do not establish facilities devoted to this study, then those who seek Mussar will vanish. I know you are toiling to strengthen the "tree of life" [Torah — see *Mishlei* 3:18] by founding a place for theoretical and practical Torah study, and may you therefore "eat and live forever" (cf. *Bereishis* 3:22).[1] Therefore, I beg you, lend a hand to support its neglected younger sister [the *beis hamussar*] as well. From her fallen place in the dust she cries out, "Support me, please! Maintain me even in a small and unpretentious place" (cf. *Yeshayahu* 29:4, *Bamidbar* 22:26).

A SEED OF RIGHTEOUSNESS

When a soft-hearted man is moved to enter the *beis hamussar* — to

---

1   That is, may you receive eternal reward for your efforts.

bring a "pure Minchah offering" and to pour forth his soul to Hashem in a bro-
ken-hearted manner that is not despised (cf. *Tehillim* 51:19) — then I shall
know that a seed of righteousness took root. And then his heart will be humbled to somewhat improve his path (cf. *Vayikra* 26:41) and make his actions
upright, I will know that my ways will have succeeded to produce a precious
fruit in praise of Hashem.

Please! Listen to her voice [i.e., Mussar's voice, to found a *beis
hamussar*], and Hashem will listen to you. He will grant you success in all
your endeavors. I adjure you, be flexible and not obstinate. Be easygoing in
the demands [you make of those who show interest], for they are few and
their commitment is irresolute. Press too hard and you will repulse them and
turn them away from Mussar. Strengthen faltering knees and empower weak
hands to fear Hashem and to go in His ways for eternal good (cf. *Yeshayahu*
35:3).

Your beloved friend, who blesses you with a good year,

and seeks your peace and honor

TRANSLATOR'S SUMMARY OF LETTER TWELVE

1. When building a *beis hamidrash* it is imperative to also include a *beis
hamussar*.

2. When a sensitive person enters the *beis hamussar* and "pours forth
his soul to Hashem" — it is certain that he will improve his conduct
and character.

3. Hashem will answer the prayers of one who builds a *beis hamussar*.

4. When speaking to others about the importance of a *beis hamussar*,
be flexible and easygoing.

LETTER THIRTEEN

THE BEIS HAMUSSAR: PRIVILEGE OR NECESSITY?

In this letter, Rav Yisrael is responding to the comments of a certain individual who offered his observations on the drive to establish battei mussar — places devoted solely to Mussar study — and those who go to study there.

MEMEL, 5620

I SAW HIS WORDS and I quote them:[1] "Many tried, but did not succeed (cf. *Berachos* 35b), and as a result, they caused a *chilul Hashem* (profanation of the Divine name). 'I feared to clothe myself in robes that are not befitting me' (cf. *Bava Metzia* 113b)."[2]

I agree with his initial assertion, but take exception to his concluding words. He fell into the mistake of those who are antagonistic towards Mussar — those who assume that its study in a specially dedicated place is solely for those on an advanced level, an expression of piety not fitting for the general public. When people with this attitude see someone entering the *beis*

---

1   Rav Yisrael quotes from a letter that he received. The writer has asserted that those who dare to enter a *beis hamussar* and do not achieve perfection do an enormous disservice to Mussar. Therefore, the writer maintains it is better for the average man not to enter the *beis hamussar*, so as not to risk causing a *chilul Hashem*.

2   The writer is asserting that if one does not have total purity of character and deed, it is a *chilul Hashem* to study in a *beis hamussar*. Therefore, the writer did not dare to enter the *beis hamussar*, for he feared causing a *chilul Hashem*.

hamussar they cynically roll their eyes, as if to say, "Who is this person who presumes in his heart to act so, and to consider himself on such an exalted level?" (cf. *Esther* 7:5). Similarly, they scrutinize his every action and exclaim derisively, "A man such as this conducts himself thusly?"

AN ABSOLUTE REQUIREMENT

My brother, it is not so. Studying in the *beis hamussar* is not a virtue and is not indicative of a high level. Rather, it is an absolute requirement — necessary for a sick man who is infected with iniquity and transgression, and who faces a bitter end. If such a one goes there to pour out his soul in Mussar study, perhaps he will save it from some small measure of pain. Perhaps he will somewhat subdue his *yetzer hara*, so that it will not cause him to mischievously follow after his heart's desires (cf. *Yeshayahu* 57:17).

In truth, there are no grounds to suspect *chilul Hashem*, for its place does not lie here! The way to guard against such profanation is to increase one's performance of Torah and mitzvos, not to reduce them.[3]

The source of the criticism [against the establishment of a *beis hamussar*] is based on the desire [for honor]. Since man does not want his peers to mock him [for taking a positive stance], the *yetzer hara* stretches forth its hoof to clad itself in piety (cf. Rashi on *Bereishis* 26:34) [and gives rise to self-righteous comments].

SEEK A REMEDY

If a person forgets the day of reckoning, if he does not seek out a remedy for his soul's disease, then what more is there to say? When it comes to providing for physical needs, or to curing a bodily illness, man searches with all his might for relief — to at least find some minimal respite from his woes. Why does he not do the same for his soul? The sick man is not embarrassed to undergo procedures that are beneath his dignity. Why, then, when it comes to the health of his soul, does he peer over his shoulder and consider the

---

3   Therefore, it is improbable that studying in the *beis hamussar*, which strengthens Torah observance, could be a *chilul Hashem*; rather, it is the refraining from going there that can cause problems.

opinions of others (cf. *Shir HaShirim* 2:9), who in truth know nothing about him or his personal struggles? The reason he ignores the state of his soul is simple: he puts the thought of satisfying his every physical need and desire above all else, and is completely absorbed in the pursuits of this world. As a result, his heart becomes hardened, and he does not consider his life's true and eternal purpose.

There is but one remedy, but one salvation for man — particularly for a person burdened and preoccupied with business concerns. He must make an immutable resolution to go to the *beis hamussar* and pour out his soul and spirit there. He must be unshakable and not let anything in the world move him from this commitment. If he does so, then he can truly be called alive, and not dead and unfeeling — and all those who are joined to life have hope (cf. *Koheles* 9:4).

TRANSLATOR'S SUMMARY OF LETTER THIRTEEN

1. Studying in the *beis hamussar* is not a privilege reserved for special *tzaddikim*.

2. Study of Mussar in the *beis hamussar* is a necessity for any person who has spiritual ills and who has committed transgressions (i.e., the average person).

3. Just as a physically sick man is not embarrassed to undergo procedures that are not befitting his dignity, so, too, one who is spiritually ill should not be embarrassed to visit the *beis hamussar*.

4. The only remedy is to go to the *beis hamussar* and to pour out his soul and spirit.

LETTER FOURTEEN

PREPARATION FOR THE DAYS OF AWE

In this letter, Rav Yisrael reveals the source of physical corruption and spiritual impurity. He then discusses the healing antidote — Mussar — which has the power to change human nature.

"See, I present before you today a blessing" (*Devarim* 11:26).

ELUL

IT IS WELL KNOWN THAT in earlier generations, when the holy month of Elul was announced, everyone was gripped by fear (cf. *Iyov* 21:6). This fear generated a positive effect by drawing people close to Divine service, each man according to his level. Common sense suggests that one who distances himself from Hashem's worship the entire year would be consumed with fear and worry concerning the Day of Judgment much more than one who was faithful in his observance. This is especially so in light of the fact that the only shield against punishment is Torah study and the performance of good deeds. However, just the opposite occurs. We see that those who embrace the holy path during the entire year make a significantly greater effort to improve their deeds than those who walked in darkness.

PHYSICAL CORRUPTION AND SPIRITUAL IMPURITY

This phenomenon stems from the combined effects of physical corruption and spiritual impurity. The physical corruption is due mainly to the force of habit, whereby a person conducts himself in a mechanical fashion, merely going through the motions in whatever he does; this is true of both good and bad deeds. The spiritual cause is obvious: when a person sins, the force of impurity is drawn upon him, befouling his spirit and confusing his intellect. Regarding this, Chazal assert (*Sotah* 3a), "A person does not commit a transgression unless a spirit of foolishness enters him" — in other words, his conduct violates his own sense of right and wrong.

A person who is engaged in Mussar study — even minimally — sees clearly that a spiritually impure force stands ready to sabotage his efforts. It hardens his heart, so that he conducts himself in a way that is against his better judgment and beliefs. Certainly, the [influence of] the ways of the world and its perversions similarly assist in clouding one's discretion and discernment. Thus, in addition to the force of habit, there is another cause that hinders repentance: the tendency for man to act like a monkey, to ape the actions and fashions of others.

[We might ask, isn't it possible to use the propensity towards imitation and mimicry for good? Theoretically, the answer is yes, but in reality, there is no one left for us to emulate.] The masters of *yiras Shamayim*, whose countenance reflected their awe over the fear of the judgment, have vanished and are no more. If they were alive, they would make an impact on the hearts of those who followed them — but if there is no root, from whence will come the leaves?

THE PRIMARY IMPEDIMENT

In truth, however, the primary impediment working against man is the spiritual one. Therefore, as we see, the fear associated with Elul is virtually extinguished, *Hashem yeracheim*.

Yet, if we were to remove our coarse and sullied garments for a moment, and don fine white ones in their stead (cf. *Yeshayahu* 59:3, *Zechariah* 3:4),[1] we would see clearly that now more than ever we should fear and tremble, each person according to his level. Indeed, our fear should be doubled, and then

---

1   If we were to temporarily discard habit, imitation, and hard-heartedness, and contemplate matters in an objective fashion.

doubled again from what it was in previous generations. What, then, is there for us to do? [The answer to this question is quite complex, for] there are many various paths, that may be applied, according to each individual's unique circumstances and character.

However, there is a recognized general principle, born out by experience: It is possible to serve Hashem on an exalted level without Mussar study;[2] however, to change one's nature from evil to good without Mussar (and this includes not only formal study, but contemplating and understanding the messages Heaven sends a person through heartache and affliction and changing for the better) is like trying to see without an eye and hear without an ear. Therefore, the sages of old issued a decree [for Elul]. For these Days of Awe are times of preparation to face the upcoming judgment of Rosh HaShanah, and even more so, to prepare for Yom Kippur. It is impossible to sufficiently emphasize the importance of preparation for these holy days. It is impossible to portray the dramatic advantage conferred by such preparation regarding salvation from the terrifying punishments of the Next World. The more one realizes the magnitude of Yom Kippur, the more the degree of his repentance will be elevated. Therefore, the sages ordained that in Elul each person must fix a time to study works on Mussar and *yiras Shamayim*.[3]

Yet, what can be done about the wall of iron that separates us from

---

2   This seems to contradict Letter Eleven: "When devoid of *yiras Shamayim*, all Torah study and Divine service is mere mechanical performance of mitzvos, with virtually no spiritual component. A person going through life in this manner can be blown off course by the slightest breeze, as stated by Chazal (*Avos* 3:11): 'Rabbi Chanina ben Dosa says: Anyone whose fear of sin takes precedence over his wisdom, his wisdom will endure; but anyone whose wisdom takes precedence over his fear of sin, his wisdom will not endure.' " Perhaps the resolution to these conflicting concepts are the two divisions of Divine service elucidated in Letter Thirty. There the Rav defines "*kivush hayetzer*" as controlling one's impulses through the dominion of the intellect, and "*tikun hayetzer*" as transforming one's nature to unadulterated goodness. Although, the master of *kivush hayetzer* performs the Divine service on an exalted level, this is only an external service. Since he has not rectified his *middos*, he is still susceptible to their negative influence. This influence subconsciously distracts him from the path of integrity and untainted Divine service. In contrast, the master of *tikun hayetzer* has attained purity and is beyond corruption. See Letter Thirty, where this concept is masterfully elaborated in a contrast between Avraham and Eliezer.

3   In order to spur people on to repentance.

Hashem? This obstacle is the spirit of impurity that smothers and befouls man's spirit, and it effectively prevents him from saving himself. He is, thus, devoid of Mussar study's benefits, which improve the ways of man and draw him close to Hashem's service.

A QUORUM OF TEN

There is one thing, though, that has proven highly effective. Namely, assembling a quorum of ten men, each pouring out his soul to Hashem — intending in their prayer that Hashem pierce a small hole in this iron barrier. This is a small, easy matter that bears abundant fruits.

Since at the present time I am not at home, I am unable to gather a quorum of ten for this purpose. Therefore, I wish to bestir and encourage you, my precious students, to assemble in a quorum of ten people, while the time is propitious and it is within your ability to do so (cf. *Shabbos* 151b). Perhaps, I also will be granted assistance in my solitary prayer concerning this issue, *bli neder*, for considering the circumstances under which I find myself, it is of vital importance to me. Never before in my life did I accustom myself to pray alone — but at the present time there is no other option open to me.

Your beloved friend, Yisrael
written after the conclusion of Shabbos

TRANSLATOR'S SUMMARY OF LETTER FOURTEEN

1. The advent of Rosh HaShanah awakens *teshuvah* more so in people who are wholly devoted to Hashem than in people who are lax.

2. There are two factors that impede *teshuvah*: physical corruption (i.e., serving Hashem by rote); and spiritual corruption (i.e., the spirit of impurity that results from transgression).

3. It is impossible to change one's nature from bad to good without Mussar study.

4. Praying to Hashem with a minyan is an extremely effective method to cleanse our souls of spiritual impurity.

LETTER FIFTEEN

THE RECTIFICATION OF THE EASY ASPECTS

This letter discusses the relationship between building a beis hamussar and receiving atonement for inadvertent theft.

WITH RESPECTFUL GREETINGS. May you be blessed for good and inscribed in the Book of Life!

BUILD A BEIS HAMUSSAR

Due to my health, I do not have the strength to speak properly, as I have told you, my honored students. Nevertheless, I rejoiced upon receiving your letter of agreement to build [a *beis hamussar*]. Because this matter is also relevant to me — albeit in a spiritual and not a physical way — my heart is moved to pen a few brief, yet appropriate, words (cf. *Mishlei* 15:23).

THE DAYS OF REPENTANCE

The foundation of the Days of Repentance is to make a resolution to abandon iniquity. This is the most difficult task of Yom Kippur, may it come upon us for good. Moreover, the most difficult sin to refrain from is theft, as it is taught in *Vayikra Rabbah* 33:3: "In a basket full of transgressions, which is the first to accuse? Theft!" It is obvious that man should attempt to repent for at least his most serious iniquities — reckoned both according to the subject and the object. The reckoning of "the subject" concerns how difficult it would have been for him to refrain from stealing [henceforth referred to as the "degree of difficulty"], and the reckoning of "the object" concerns the degree of damage that resulted from the theft [henceforth referred to as "the degree of damage"]. As to the degree of difficulty, the easier it is for a person to refrain from a transgression, the greater is the severity of his punishment. As Chazal state (*Menachos* 43b): "Rebbi Meir said, '[In the mitzvah of tzitzis,] the punishment for not wearing white threads is greater than for not wearing blue ones.' "[1] Concerning the degree of damage, stealing from a poor person is more severe than stealing from a rich one, for the damage is much graver.

Indeed, it is extremely difficult for man to find a way [to desist from stealing]. However, if a person does not rectify this sin, then "woe to that shame, woe to that humiliation" (*Bava Basra* 75a) that he will ultimately face. [How lamentable] that man does not at least attempt [to partially rectify this terrible sin] by firmly resolving henceforth not to steal in at least one area of his life.[2]

THE DEGREE OF DIFFICULTY AND DAMAGE[3]

How advantageous it is when the opportunity [to provide for the public arises], thus allowing us to rectify even our inadvertent stealing![4] [Building a *beis hamussar*] comprises both the elements we discussed above — the degree of difficulty [in this case, involving how hard the project is to undertake], and the degree of damage [that will result if the project is not undertaken]. It

---

1   See Letter Eight.

2   For example, a person might simultaneously be guilty of improper conduct in many areas of money matters, such as not paying his monthly bill at the grocery store, not repaying his loans on time, and not giving the proper amount of charity. Rav Yisrael is advising, let him focus on one and only one of these three areas, and make a firm-hearted commitment to improve his behavior in it.

3   Here, Rav Yisrael temporarily digresses from his main topic of theft in general, and addresses how building a *beis hamussar* will specifically help his students in this area.

4   According to the Talmud (*Beitzah* 29a), if a person is either concerned that he inadvertently stole from others, or if he stole from someone (accidentally or purposefully) but does not know their identity and wishes to repent, he should do something for the public welfare. Thus, by contributing to the establishment of a *beis hamussar*, from which the public will benefit, one receives exculpation for this sin. Rav Yisrael's disciples were surely not guilty of a gross transgression of theft, but the possibility always exists that even a pious person may do something inadvertently.

is not difficult to contribute the required funds for building a *beis hamussar*.[5]
The same is true regarding the degree of damage [done by not engaging is
this undertaking; it is extremely grave]. Perhaps someone will want to pour
out his soul, and if there were to be no *beis hamussar*, he would not be able to
reach the same level of perfection, *chas v'shalom*, as if there were one.[6]

UPHOLD A RESOLUTION[7]

Absolutely no person is exempt from the responsibility to abandon iniquity. Each person — according to his particular circumstances and standing
— is obligated to seek out ways to uphold a resolution to disconnect from the
terrible sin of theft. At the very least, one should strive to desist from the
more severe aspects of this sin, according to the degree of difficulty and the
degree of damage that we mentioned above.

RECTIFY ALL TRANSGRESSIONS

Likewise, one must attempt to rectify all other transgressions, such as
the neglect of Torah study, which is more grave than anything else (as is explained by the Sha'arei Teshuvah in the name of the Sifri — see *Sha'ar* 3:14).
In this cardinal transgression as well, punishment is reckoned according to
the "degree of difficulty" and the "degree of damage." The degree of difficulty
concerns how easy it would have been for the person to have studied. (Two
examples of times when Torah study is considered easy are Shabbos, when
one does not have to work, and any time when one is free of other obligations.)[8] The degree of damage factored in for punishment relates to one's
lack of knowledge of how to conduct oneself according to halachah. This applies both to his personal deficiency of knowledge and his lack of understanding of when it is necessary to consult with a halachic authority. The same

---

5   Therefore, if we do not support this project, our punishment for inadvertent theft will be
    quite severe, since the rectification for it comes quite easily.

6   As Rav Yisrael has mentioned elsewhere, the atmosphere of a *beis hamussar* is essential
    and particularly conducive to studying Mussar, more so than anywhere else. Therefore,
    because of the serious damage that would be caused if we did not build the *beis hamussar*,
    our punishment would be grave.

7   Here, Rav Yisrael returns to his initial theme.

8   Refer to Letter Eight, where Rav Yisrael discusses this at length.

holds true for the entire Torah and all of the mitzvos. Whether in a deed that should be performed or an action that should be avoided, he will be punished for transgressing. Therefore, the easier an injunction is for the man to fulfill, the greater will be his punishment for transgressing it.

SAFEGUARD THE EASY ASPECTS

Man must thoroughly examine his ways, in order to make firm resolutions in virtually every area of his affairs. At the very least, he should safeguard those aspects of Torah and mitzvos that are easy for him to fulfill. This will provide him with the means to fulfill the mitzvah of repenting for his transgressions — at least the majority of them. The reason for this is because the tally of one's transgressions is not reckoned according to number, but according to the quality of their content (see *Rambam, Hilchos Teshuvah* 3:14).[9] Therefore, if a given injunction in one area is easy for him to observe, a single transgression will be considered much more serious than several transgressions of an injunction that is difficult for him to observe. Likewise, in the transgression itself, a single aspect that is easy for him to uphold is judged stricter and subjected to greater punishment than many other aspects of it that are difficult to observe.

TORAH STUDY

Let us consider, for example, the mitzvah of Torah study. Even if a person has a weak memory, it is very easy for him to review his studies many times over in his native language. Let him proceed this way, at a slow pace, in the Talmud or any other subject. He should concentrate almost exclusively on just knowing the concepts, without worrying about the name of the Tanna or Amora [who taught a given dictum]. Let him contemplate this when he walks through the streets, obviously, where the area is clean;[10] or when he is traveling (as a passenger); or even when he is actually engaged in his business dealings, as I have mentioned elsewhere. This type of contemplation is actually easier for a merchant than a Torah scholar, who does not have the time to repeatedly review

---

9   Refer to the third paragraph in Letter Eight, where this *Rambam* is discussed.

10 And not if the surroundings are dirty in a way in which it is forbidden to think Torah thoughts there.

material until he knows it by heart, for this would result in a inordinate neglect of his essential study. On the other hand, if in his spare moments a merchant goes over the material he is studying, then virtually the entire day is available to him to mentally review it over and over again.

HE WILL SEE THAT HE KNOWS TORAH

The man who is busy with his affairs must strengthen himself in this great undertaking. It is something that is very easy in theory, and one should see to it that its practice is easy as well. Let him not be deceived by the foolish arguments of the *yetzer hara* that it is too difficult. Ever so slowly, he will come to see that he knows Torah by heart. Truly, [this is no small thing, even if it is not in Hebrew,] but in one's mother tongue. This is a very easy matter even for a person who has a weak memory, if he reviews in this manner — and especially for a hard-working person, who has the opportunity to mentally review things despite his hectic schedule.

It is good to study Mussar works that speak about the great sin of neglecting Torah study. It will reinforce within one the lesson that he should not go for a long period without Torah study, for Torah is the life of the man!

Your beloved friend, Yisrael

eve of 8 Tishrei

TRANSLATOR'S SUMMARY OF LETTER FIFTEEN

1. The foundation of the Days of Repentance is to make a resolution to abandon iniquity.

2. The severity of a sin is determined by: a) the degree of difficulty required to refrain from the sin; and b) the degree of damage that results from the sin.

3. Building and sponsoring a *beis hamussar* rectifies the sin of inadvertent theft.

4. One should review all of his ways, and at the very least, safeguard those aspects of Torah and mitzvos that are easy for him to fulfill.

LETTER SIXTEEN

THE TEN DAYS OF REPENTANCE

If a person will pour out his soul to Hashem through the study of Mussar during the Ten Days of Repentance, he will truly be alive.

PREPARATION FOR YOM KIPPUR

"REMEMBER YOUR CREATOR in the days of your youth, before the evil days come" (*Koheles* 12:1). Rashi explains that] "the evil days" refer to the time of old age. [Indeed, I am no longer a young man.] It is difficult for me to answer the momentous question of how it is possible to vanquish the evil inclination — the very task for which we were created. There is neither a predictable pattern in this war with the *yetzer hara*, nor is there any certainty that a given strategy will be successful. Immerse yourself in Mussar study when the time is most appropriate — the Ten Days of Repentance. This is the time to prepare for Yom Kippur, when a person's judgment will be sealed, whether for life or death. [Therefore, the sages of old exhorted us to devote these days to Mussar study.]

POUR OUT HIS SOUL

How shall the servant be pleasing to his master except through a broken heart, as the verse states, "A heart broken and humbled, O God, You will not despise" (*Tehillim* 51:19). It is known that the source of a broken heart stems from diligent study of works on Heavenly fear. A person should literally pour out his soul to the Almighty. If he will do this, then he will truly be alive. Then, even after the days of judgment pass, the impact of the Mussar he studied will resonate within his soul, and the obligation to continue studying it will burn passionately in his heart. It will inspire him to fulfill the verse, "Hold fast to Mussar, do not let go. Guard it, for it is your life" (*Mishlei* 4:13).

Your beloved friend, who blesses you for a good year!

AN INTERNAL AWAKENING

An element that is fiery by nature will ignite and burn brightly from a mere spark. My precious students! Although my condition does not allow me to write at length, I still hope that a few words will remind and awaken you concerning what I taught you previously, which I am sure inspired you and penetrated your hearts. It is vital to attend the *beis hamussar* and to study there with passion and fervor! This is especially true during the Ten Days of Repentance. It is also important to recall the Talmud's teaching that prayer is more efficacious when offered with a quorum of ten (*Ta'anis* 8a). Finally, never lose sight of the fact that an internal awakening will overpower all opposition from the *yetzer hara*.

TRANSLATOR'S SUMMARY OF LETTER SIXTEEN

1. There is no predictable pattern nor certain strategy in the war of the *yetzer hara*.

2. One should immerse himself in Mussar during the Ten Days of Judgment — the time when a person's judgment will be sealed for life or death.

3. A broken and humbled heart of a servant of Hashem is pleasing to Hashem.

4. The source of a broken heart is Mussar study.

LETTER SEVENTEEN

ACHIEVING SPIRITUAL VITALITY

If one performs the difficult injunctions, as well as the easy ones, then his soul is empowered with the strength to withstand the challenges of the yetzer hara.

THE DOMINION OF HIS INTELLECT

THE TORAH'S] DEFINITION OF MAN is a being whose paths and affairs are ordained by the uncorrupted intellect. In contrast, animals follow their nature and temperament. Man conquers the *yetzer hara* [by following the instructions of his intellect,] without allowing himself to be influenced by the evil tendencies of his nature, *chas v'shalom*. Through the dominion of his intellect, man is endowed with the power to master his limbs [i.e., external conduct], each man according to the dictates of his wisdom. This capability is the true power of man, as is taught by our Sages (*Avos* 4:1): "Who is strong? He who subdues his evil inclination."

TWO ASPECTS OF DOMINION

There are two aspects of dominion over the *yetzer hara*. The first is for one to overcome his nature so that he does not commit evil. The second is to change one's nature so that he performs good. The second aspect is more difficult than the first, for it is more difficult to transform one's nature than to overcome his nature. Therefore, man must develop stage by stage. Initially, he should strive to fulfill the precept "Turn from evil" (*Tehillim* 34:15); this is the first aspect of growth. Afterwards, he should strive to fulfill the imperative to "do good" (ibid.), which is the second and more advanced level.

REWARD AND PUNISHMENT

In this light, we can explain the *mishnah* in *Pirkei Avos* (2:1): "Calculate the loss [entailed in the performance] of a mitzvah against its reward [in the World to Come], and the reward of a sin against its loss [in the World to Come]." On the surface, this statement seems quite perplexing. We know that even for not performing a mitzvah, a person is punished — whether in this world or the Next. Concerning this world, we read in the Talmud (*Menachos* 41a): "He [Rav Kattina] asked [the angel who appeared to him], 'Do you punish a person who neglects to perform a positive precept?' The angel replied, 'In a time of wrath, we do.' " Concerning the Next World, we find in Scripture, "One who grows lax in his work is also a brother to the master of destruction" (*Mishlei* 18:9). Similarly, a person receives reward if he refrains from transgressing. This is stated in the Talmud (*Kiddushin* 39b): "One who sits and does not commit a transgression receives reward as if he performed a mitzvah."

This being the case, why does the *mishnah* compare the loss that performing a mitzvah will entail, to the reward one will receive for it? [Instead, it should have contrasted the loss engendered by a mitzvah's performance to the punishment incurred for neglecting it.] Likewise, instead of comparing the gain of committing a transgression to the loss it will cause, [the *mishnah* should have contrasted the gain acquired by committing it to the reward accrued for refraining from it].

GRADATIONS OF REWARD AND PUNISHMENT

However, according to the above stated idea [that it is easier to overcome one's nature than to change one's nature], we can say that the *mishnah* is relating to the weightier aspect in each situation. We know that the greater the difficulty of a mitzvah, the greater is its reward, as taught in *Pirkei Avos* (5:26): "The reward is in proportion to the exertion." Similarly, the more minimal the hardship involved in performing a mitzvah, the greater the punishment if it is not performed, as the Talmud states (*Menachos* 43b): "Rebbi Meir said: '[In the mitzvah of *tzitzis*] the punishment for not wearing white fringes is greater than [the punishment for] not wearing blue ones.'" For it is less difficult to obtain white fringes than the more expensive blue ones. This same idea is true with regard to transgression. The easier it is to refrain from committing a transgression, the greater is the punishment for its commission. Likewise, the greater the difficulty required to abstain from committing a transgression, the greater the reward if one conquers his evil inclination and doesn't befoul himself with his desire.

Concerning "turning from evil" (*Tehillim* 34:15), the first aspect, the punishment for committing a sin is greater than the punishment for the omission of "doing good," for it is easier to refrain from transgressing than it is to perform a mitzvah.[1] However, concerning reward, the opposite is the case: the reward for "doing good," the second aspect, is greater than that for "turning from evil," because the former is more difficult than the latter.[2] This, then, is why the *mishnah* made the comparisons that it did, for in each case, it espoused the weightiest aspect as regards punishment and reward: the reward for performing a mitzvah is greater than the punishment for refraining from one, and the punishment for committing a transgression is greater than the reward for refraining from doing so.[3] It thus emerges that there are two

---

1   Sins go against the grain of our conscience, whereas the neglect of mitzvos is perceived to be less severe. It is easier to refrain from stealing from the charity box than it is to give charity. In truth, both the commission of sin and the neglect of mitzvos are violations of the Divine will. Yet since it is easier to refrain from committing a transgression than it is to perform a mitzvah — the punishment for committing a sin is a higher level of punishment than that for not performing a mitzvah.

2   Likewise, since it is more difficult to perform a mitzvah than it is to refrain from committing a sin — the reward for the performance of a mitzvah is on a higher level than the reward for not committing the sin. All the aforementioned calculations are also subject to the axiom "The reward is in proportion to the exertion." For instance, if one refrains from a sin that is particularly difficult for him to refrain from, he receives a greater reward than for refraining from a sin that is easy to refrain from.

3   The performance of a mitzvah is an aspect of "doing good" which involves changing one's nature, and is therefore subject to a "high level" reward. Whereas, the neglect of a mitzvah is subject to a "low level" punishment, since the performance of mitzvos is an aspect of the difficult "doing good." Since the punishment for neglecting a mitzvah is a "low

levels of reward and two levels of punishment: [reward for refraining from transgression and reward for performing a mitzvah; and punishment for committing a transgression and punishment for abstaining from a mitzvah.]

AGAINST HIS HEART'S WILL

Now, we know that "man was born to labor" (*Iyov* 5:7) — to fight the war against the *yetzer hara* that the Almighty commanded him to engage in. He is obligated to fully exert himself in the Divine service. Therefore, it is not sufficient to merely observe that which complies with his natural proclivities and disregard that which he finds difficult. When a person's observance is limited only to that which he finds convenient, it is not service of Hashem; rather, it is merely nature following its course. This approach could cause one to ultimately cast off the Divine yoke, *chas v'chalilah*, because he did not put any labor into his *avodas Hashem*; rather, he observed only that which was not a burden for him.[4] Indeed, the foundation of man's service to his Creator is to observe and perform even that which his heart does not desire. If he does not thoroughly resolve to act against his heart's will, it is likely he will come to violate all of the Torah's prohibitions, Heaven forbid — even those for which it is ostensibly not his habit or his nature to transgress.

MAN'S SUBCONSCIOUS FORCES

This is possible because of secondary causes, which activate opposing forces that influence one's habits and nature. For example, consider a scholar who constantly studies Torah out of habitual practice and temperament, but who has a subconscious desire for money. Since, due to his life's circumstances, he is not involved in business activities, this drive goes unrecognized. Because he never dealt with financial matters in his life, there is no cat-

---

level" punishment, the motivation to do mitzvos is based on the "high level" reward. Likewise, the reward for refraining from a sin is a "low level" reward, which is the aspect of "turn from evil"; therefore, the motivation to refrain from sins is based on the "high level" punishment. This "turning from evil" involves the relatively easier task of overcoming one's nature.

4   Refer to Letter Thirty. In brief, when a person only does things that are easy, or because they are easy, then when he is confronted with a more demanding situation he will not have the strength to overcome it, and he will be overwhelmed.

alyst that might activate it. As long as there is no physical stimulus, man's subconscious forces will remain dormant. They will remain hidden deep within
his being and will be neither manifest externally nor even perceived on a conscious level.

A MINOR CAUSE CAN AWAKEN A STRONG DRIVE

However, when a cause arises that necessitates his involvement in monetary affairs, such as providing for his family's needs, this drive can burst
forth. It can even cause him to almost entirely neglect the Torah study [that
he formerly held so dear].[5] Yet nobody — himself included — would have believed that he could so thoroughly disregard his studies. The same holds true
of all the positive forces and qualities in man — they can all be annulled by
opposing forces. Moreover, even a minor cause can awaken a strong drive
that will annul all of one's spiritual accomplishments.

ROUTINE TRANSGRESSIONS

Let us now consider transgressions that a person commits on a routine
basis, which have become in his eyes as if they are permitted, Heaven forbid.
[It goes without saying that such sins] do not awaken one's soul to study
Heavenly fear. (Such study as will spur him on to remember the many days of
darkness in the Hereafter. At that time, he will be struck with harsh and bitter punishment, *Hashem yeracheim*, for each and every transgression he committed. As Chazal state [*Bava Kamma* 50a]: "Anyone who says that Hashem
is forgoing, will forgo his life"; and "Hashem waits compassionately [for a person to repent, but if he does not seek atonement] then Hashem will eventually collect His due" [*Bereishis Rabbah* 67:4]. Can anyone gauge the severity
of his punishment — punishment that he alone, and no one else, will bear?)
For [routine sins] have become in his eyes as if they are actually permitted.
These are iniquities that a person neither sees nor senses.

HIS SPIRIT WILL BE AWAKENED

[What hope, then, remains for such a person?] There is one insight that

---

5   Unchecked, his subconscious drives can take total control of him.

can serve to arouse him. Let him consider how the passage of time and changes in circumstances can, due to an insignificant catalyst, transform his nature and cause him to fall into the gravest of transgressions. When he will commit such cardinal sins, he will still retain an intense awareness that he has indeed transgressed, and the fear of them will yet be visible on his countenance.[6] [Contemplating] this insight will rouse him to provide a remedy for himself [before reaching this sorrowful stage], by inducing himself to study Heavenly fear and Mussar. Then, his spirit will be awakened so that he is able to act against his own will.[7]

TRANSLATOR'S SUMMARY OF LETTER SEVENTEEN

1. The Torah defines man as a being whose paths are ordained by the uncorrupted intellect.

2. There are two aspects of dominion over the *yetzer hara*: to restrain one's nature from committing evil, and to change one's nature from bad to good.

3. The foundation of Divine service is to thoroughly resolve to fight against his heart's will.

4. If one does not fight against his heart's will, it is likely he will come to violate all of the Torah's prohibitions.

---

6   It is true that at that time, he will be much more likely to repent and study Mussar — but at such a fearful cost!

7   That is, to serve the Almighty even when it is inconvenient and burdensome — against his very nature.

LETTER EIGHTEEN

THE CRITERION OF TRUE TORAH

Rav Yisrael redefines the terms and process of true Torah scholarship for our generation.

THE MASTERY OF TORAH SCHOLARSHIP

I WILL ADD TO WHAT WE DISCUSSED when *k'vod Torah'to* [a formal title used to honor a Torah scholar] visited me. [If you will recall, we spoke of] the idea that the actual performance of a mitzvah precedes the [actualization of purity of] thought concerning it, whereas the study [of Torah] precedes the performance of a mitzvah.[1] The mastery of *darchei halimud* (the methods of

---

1   The paths of Divine service are structured in an ascending order of priorities and prerequisites. The actual performance of the mitzvah precedes mastering the purity of thought. In "The Gates of Light," chapter 1, Rav Blazer explains that there are two divisions of Divine service: the actual performance of the mitzvah and the purity of thought — which is the manner in which the mitzvah is performed and encompasses many levels. He further explains that the foundation of Divine service is the actual execution of the mitzvos. The term *eved Hashem* refers to one who has fulfilled the entire Torah and observed all of its commandments. On the other hand, purity of thought is only required for the perfection of Divine service. See the text there. In conclusion, the passage in "The Gates of Light" concurs with the concept expressed here: the performance of the mitzvah is the very essence of Divine service, whereas purity of thought, even though it greatly enhances the mitzvah, is not an indispensable criterion to fulfill the Divine will. In contrast, the proper and accurate knowledge of the Torah precedes the performance of the mitzvah. The mastery of Torah scholarship is indeed an indispensable criterion of Divine worship. For the greater one's ability to fathom and clarify the truth of the Torah, the wiser he is in the scrupulous performance of the mitzvah. Rav Yisrael will now define Torah scholarship.

Torah scholarship) is the key to enter the paths of Divine service. Now, since the Talmud's final redaction, the way is shut for us to understand and to render halachic rulings from the Written Law using the thirteen exegetical principles transmitted from Mount Sinai. Instead, we draw Toras Hashem and knowledge of His ways exclusively from the Talmud. Even the greatest and most advanced Torah scholar can do no more than seek out and reveal its secrets; nothing can be added [to the Talmud] or subtracted from it.

OUR GENERATION'S TALMUD STUDY

Accordingly, our generation's study of the Talmud is like Chazal's study of the Written Torah. Similarly, our study of the Written Torah is like Chazal's study of the *alef-beis*. Just as they employed the *alef-beis* as a vehicle to study the Written Torah, so do we come to study the Talmud through the agency of the Written Torah. Likewise, the works of our great halachic authorities, the Rishonim and the Achronim, to our generation resemble the aspect of the Mishnah in the days of Chazal.[2] A fitting and competent

---

2   Moshe Rabbeinu received the Torah from Hashem at Har Sinai, which included both the *Torah Shebichsav* (Written Law) and the *Torah Shebe'al-peh* (Oral Law). So from the time of the giving of the Torah at Har Sinai, the Jewish people have always had the *Torah Shebe'al-peh* (see beginning of *Kellallei HaTalmud* of Rav Shmuel HaNaggid). This early form of *Torah Shebe'al-peh* is referred to as the "*mesorah*" and the elucidation of it by the term "*s'varah*." The Talmud (*Avodah Zarah* 19a) explains that the teaching of the *mesorah* (here, the Talmud calls it *gemorah*) was comprised of two aspects: the transmission of the expert, general knowledge of the *mesorah*, and the transmission of the deep understanding of it (*s'varah*). When we call the Taanaim "the Sages of the Mishnah," we do not mean that there was no *Torah Shebe'al-peh* before their time. Rather, we mean that the Tannaim preceded the codification of the Mishnah by Rabbeinu HaKadosh (Rebbe Yehudah HaNasi). From the time the Torah was given on Har Sinai, the *mesorah* was passed down orally from generation to generation — for nearly a thousand years. Beginning in the early Tanna'ic period, there was a gradual decline in their capacity to perfectly remember the entire *mesorah*. This decline continuously worsened — until the last generation of the Tannaim, when forgetting the *mesorah* became widespread. At that time, Rabbeinu HaKadosh, who lived in the last generation of the Tannaim, ruled that the main laws of the Torah *Shebe'al-peh* must be codified. In order to preserve the *mesorah*, the Mishnah was codified and fixed. The Amoraim, the Sages that lived in the generation after the Tannaim, learned the codified Mishnah of Rabbeinu HaKadosh. Still their *darchei halimud* (method of learning Torah) was the same as the Tannaim. However, the Amoraim recognized the enormous *yeridas hadoros*, saying (*Shabbos* 112b): "If the earlier

scholar utilizes them to disagree with and modify rulings according to the required conditions of logic, and to render rulings — provided that he has a recognized authority as a basis of support. Perhaps an exceptional and outstanding scholar can even disagree,[3] as Chazal characterized Rav, who was like a Tanna to argue with the earlier Sages.[4]

TORAS EMES

After attaining fluent and extensive expertise in the Talmud Bavli and Yerushalmi, as well as proficiency in the works of the leading halachic authorities, and most importantly, sound knowledge in the study of *Tosafos* — then a person will come to the aspect of Talmud (which resembles the aspect of the Talmud studied in the days of Chazal). This level encompasses a depth of scholarship that enables one to draw basic Talmudic principles, with their details, from wide-ranging and scattered sources and apply them to understand and rule appropriately on new cases. This is what is known as *Toras Emes* (True Torah). It is acquired through mastery of the *mikra* (expertise in the Talmud Bavli and Yerushalmi), Mishnah (proficiency in the works of the Rishonim and Achronim), as well as ministering to Torah scholars. Indeed, a person who studies but does not serve Torah scholars is classified as an ignoramus (*Berachos* 47b).[5]

Sages were angels, we are humans; if the earlier Sages were human, we are donkeys." The stature of *Am Yisrael* has continued to diminish through the generations, so that the level of the Sages is unthinkable to us. Nevertheless, the Rambam assures us in the thirteen *ikarei ha'emunah* that our Torah is exactly that which Hashem gave to Moshe Rabbeinu.

3   Without the support of a higher authority.

4   The Sages of the Talmud were called either Tannaim or Amoraim, with the former chronologically preceding the latter. The Tannaim were recognized as having a much greater level of scholarship than the Amoraim, to the point where it is a general principle that an Amora can only explain, but not disagree, with a Tanna — unless he has a Tanna supporting his opinion. Rav was a member of the transitional generation, and is regarded as both the last of the Tannaim and the first of the Amoraim. Because of this, the Talmud (*Eiruvin* 50b) states that Rav could disagree with a Tannaic statement.

5   Rashi explains that this "service of Torah scholars" refers to learning from them how to employ Talmudic logic to understand the reasoning of the Mishnah, and to differentiate between different cases.

THE FEAR OF HEAVEN

Above all, the intellect is honed by this kind of study. Additionally, the understanding of one's personality traits is enhanced so that he can overcome his subjective inclinations and know how to truly take his mind down the straight way. To facilitate all this, however, one must make "the fear of Heaven his treasure" (*Yeshayahu* 33:6), so that he accepts the yoke of responsible scholarship upon himself to assiduously study the Almighty's Torah. Similarly, when studying with one's colleagues or debating with one's students (cf. *Avos* 6:6), a person should be courteous and pleasant (cf. *Yeshayahu* 30:15).

"Now, you, O blessed of Hashem" (*Bereishis* 26:29), young man, may there be many like you in Israel. May you know and comprehend the configuration of your [proper] path. And may you know on which hinge turns the door of your thoughts and desires. May Hashem plant you as a "stately vine" (*Yechezkel* 17:8), as befits your goodly soul and as your heart seeks.

Your beloved friend,

Yisrael

TRANSLATOR'S SUMMARY OF LETTER EIGHTEEN

1. The performance of a mitzvah precedes the purity of thought concerning it, whereas the study of Torah precedes the performance of a mitzvah.

2. The mastery of the methods of Torah scholarship is the key to enter the paths of Divine service.

3. The intellect is honed and one's personality traits are rectified through proper Torah study.

4. *Yiras Shamayim* is the crown that facilitates responsible Torah scholarship.

LETTER NINETEEN

THE UNIQUENESS OF EACH SOUL

There are two bodies of wisdom — the theoretical and the practical.
Rav Yisrael explains why Mussar is considered practical wisdom.

YOUR PRECIOUS LETTER dated the eleventh of this month reached me today. Due to the great esteem in which I hold you, I feel it imperative to respond immediately — for I did not respond to your previous letters. I have seen your great yearning to meet with me, and your judgment is correct, as the verse states, "In the aged there is wisdom" (*Iyov* 12:12).

THE TWO BRANCHES OF WISDOM

Allow me to explain what I meant in quoting the above verse. The various bodies of wisdom and branches of science can be divided into two general categories: that which is a product of in-depth study (henceforth referred to as "the theoretical") and that which is a function of practical training and experience (henceforth referred to as "the practical"). Those bodies of wisdom that are based on the study of paradigms and proofs belong in the theoretical category. On the other hand, those that are based on [the wisdom of] accurate approximation [i.e., application] fall under the rubric of the practical. Theoretical wisdom is not dependent upon age, for, as Chazal tell us (*Avos* 4:26), "There is a new jug with old wine." Indeed, we see that a sharp-minded youth has much more cognitive ability than an elderly person whose knowledge and understanding is feeble. Practical knowledge, however, is acquired with the passage of time and is established with old age. Now, "understanding" (an aspect of wisdom) is a function of accurate approximation [i.e., application of what is known in the practical sphere].[1] Therefore, the verse states, "In the aged there is wisdom, and [in] length of days understanding."

TORAH AND MUSSAR

The foundation of Torah study is the theoretical. This includes sharpness of intellect and comprehensive expertise. It also encompasses piercing, straightforward analysis, using logical demonstrations and proofs in order to clarify all aspects of a subject — all within rigorous Torah parameters as taught us by the Rishonim and Achronim, *zt"l*. Yet the study of Mussar and the improvement of character traits are founded on the practical. Regarding this, you, my honored correspondent, asked me a valid question to which I was lax in responding: What is the explanation for this being practical wisdom, and why is it so?

CUSTOM DESIGNED COURSE

In response, let me first reiterate and emphasize that yes, it is indeed as I said. The foundation of Mussar study and the improvement of character traits comes under the heading of practical wisdom. (Through life experience each person gains insights into the nature of his character. For a great man, and may there be many great people in Israel, there is no clearly demarcated path to follow for achievement in Mussar.) Indeed, the pursuit of such an illusory course may well be detrimental, *chas v'chalilah*.[2] Every person, and particularly a great man, is a world unto himself, and his path must be specifically designed according to his strengths and weaknesses. These include the powers of his soul and intellect, his temperament and emotions, and his unique circumstances in life.[3]

---

1   This wisdom is based on experience.
2   Since each man is unique, the wrong treatment could be harmful — just as taking the wrong medicine endangers a sick person.
3   The procedure of character development is unique for each person, for Hashem created each individual as a unique entity. Therefore, there is no universal method of character

CHARACTER PERFECTION

We know that concerning the healing of the body, there is an abundance of practical wisdom. Through application of the wonders of the theoretical wisdom that he learns — the comprehensive knowledge of theoretical medicine — the physician develops a broad-ranging sagacity of experience. Concerning the healing of our souls, however, there is no practical approximation that can be made [from the experience] of one man and his fellow.[4] A man's personal experience in character development cannot be applied to his fellow. Where is wisdom to be found (cf. *Iyov* 28:12) for one who seeks the correct answer to this question?[5] May you, esteemed Torah scholar, dwell tranquilly in your place, with peace of mind. It is my intention that we meet one day, God willing. At that time, we will, God willing, with deep sincerity, direct our thoughts more fully to your path in life and to your aspirations. In addition, we will analyze exactly what areas of Mussar and character perfection you need to focus on. We will do so in light of your particular situation, with an eye on making the optimal use of the time available — according to the most exact approximation that we can determine. May the Almighty come to our aid "for good and to do good."

Your beloved friend, who seeks your peace,

Yisrael

---

development. Rather, each man must apply the practical knowledge that he acquired by working on himself and formulate a customized plan for his rectification. His past observations of his intellectual and emotional tendencies, and the wisdom of Mussar, comprise the foundation upon which he designs his program.

4   Generally speaking, once practical wisdom is achieved, it can be applied to other subjects. For example, a surgeon who has attained proficiency in a particular operation can masterfully perform this operation on other patients. However, this is not true of character perfection. Even if a person forges his own path and successfully perfects his character, this knowledge is not necessarily applicable or transferable to anyone else.

5   The question of how to heal our souls in light of the fact that there is no practical application that can be drawn from others.

TRANSLATOR'S SUMMARY OF LETTER NINETEEN

1. The various bodies of wisdom can be divided into two general categories: theoretical and practical.

2. Torah study is theoretical, whereas Mussar and the improvement of character traits are founded on the practical.

3. There is no universal path of Mussar — each person must have a custom Mussar path designed according to his strengths and weaknesses.

4. Concerning the healing of our souls, there is no practical application that can be made from one person to another.

LETTER TWENTY

GUIDELINES FOR GREATNESS

In this letter, Rav Yisrael offers sage advice and warm encouragement to a budding Torah scholar.

MUSSAR IS PRACTICAL WISDOM

YOUR PRECIOUS LETTER, *k'vod Torah'to* [a formal title used to honor a Torah scholar], dated 22 Shevat reached me safely, and I consider it of paramount importance to respond to you. I already wrote that the process of Mussar development has its foundation in the realm of the practical. And there are no exact boundaries in the paths of Mussar, unlike business proceedings.[1] This is particularly so concerning a great man — may there be many in Israel. It is extremely difficult (and perhaps close to detrimental, *chas v'chalilah*) to convey in writing the hidden thoughts (cf. *Tehillim* 73) that penetrate a man's heart.

PATIENCE AND INTENSITY

In general, when addressing the diverse spiritual forces within man, [they are so intricate and complex that] advice concerning one area cannot be applied to another.[2] There are some ideas that will be easy for one to as-

---

1   Which are well delineated and defined.

2   In the previous letter, Rav Yisrael explained that the path of perfection is unique for each man and cannot be applied to another. Here, he is saying that even concerning a given individual, a successful technique in one area of character refinement cannot be

similate, while others will be very difficult for him to grasp. Difficult areas of growth require a gentle approach, with the awareness that it will take him a long time to achieve his goal. At the same time, he must have an intense desire for rapid success. Of course, these are two opposing forces, but a person must be sure to engage both of them. [The reason for this is quite simple:] if the desire diminishes, then the effort will weaken. On the other hand, if the intensity to succeed quickly is too strong, then the work will all but cease [from exhaustion] and will not bear any fruit, *chas v'chalilah*. A person with a good heart, who contemplates himself, will understand in general how to balance these two opposing forces and realize that there is not a fixed boundary between them.

UNDERSTANDING HUMAN CONDUCT

Active character development is an imperative task, and one that requires time (for one whose nature is not so predisposed). Practical experience shows us that the study of *middos* is almost entirely dependent on understanding general human conduct,[3] which is the antithesis of self-restraint and denial.[4] (Perhaps this investigation of character traits is what caused you to become somewhat lax in your obligation [to study Torah], as you mention in your letter.)[5]

Although it is difficult for me to fully express my thoughts to you, as I mentioned at the beginning of my letter, still I will attempt to do so — albeit concisely. As I mentioned when you were here, the foundation of Torah study is to seek out its central principle, by acquiring a comprehensive and fluent overview of the Gemara, so that one can clarify all the logical postu-

---

applied to another area.

3   See Letter Four.

4   Self-restraint is the limitation of the physical desires, whereas the natural impulse of man is the gratification of the physical. By observing his fellowman, he will come to recognize how man's nature pulls him to follow the whims of desire. He will then recognize similar folly within his own conduct and strive to correct his ways by acting with self-restraint.

5   Perhaps the intent is that since the student engaged in the study of general human conduct, it consequently took time away from his Torah studies. If this was the case, he is not at fault — because, as Rav Yisrael instructed, the study of human conduct is necessary for character perfection.

lates from Chazal and the foremost halachic authorities with clear thinking. Also in this,[6] there is no clearly demarcated foundation and boundary. It is also important to guard one's health (without excessive preoccupation; rather, to simply make sure to eat and sleep properly). Furthermore, one must be sure to not abandon his responsibility to his fellow humans — for example, the common courtesy of responding to one's correspondence. (Of course, in all of these matters, he should proceed with the appropriate in-depth study of the halachah required for one to follow the paths of Hashem, may He be blessed.)

In addition to this, it is also beneficial to spend some time contemplating the two opposing forces I mentioned previously: 1) self-restraint and abstinence, and 2) human character traits in the way of worldly affairs. There is no standard for the precedence that one should assign to the study of either of these areas over the other; rather, the experience that is garnered with the passage of time will enable you to judge this matter sensibly. Eventually, you will learn to view people's character traits and ways with a positive eye. Of course, the focus of this exercise is to help you examine your behavior and conduct. Eventually, you will perceive where to concentrate your main efforts in the pursuit of character development, according to what is necessary for both "your own good and for you to do good to others." Therefore, you should be sure to devote some time to this area of study.

HUMAN RELATIONS

And in general, a person should direct a small measure of his studies to the art of human relations. By doing so, he will learn how to purify his ways so that he can influence others. [Specifically, he must strive to understand what are] the factors that can help him attain this level [i.e., to influence others], and what are the factors that might prevent him from doing so. Of course, he must always keep in mind that Torah study must be his primary concern [for it is the foundation of all success.] A young man whose talents exceed those of his peers is thus charged with a great responsibility. On the one hand, he

---

6   In the Vilna edition of *Ohr Yisrael*, there is a note that interprets the text as: "Also in this fear." Meaning, a student must fear that he has not sufficiently clarified the concept of the Talmud or the *poskim* that he is trying to elucidate.

must consider himself a leader amongst leaders, so that he will find his heart ready to influence and help others. On the other hand, it is even more crucial that he considers himself a pliable youth, and trains himself to be prepared to help the public when the time is appropriate.[7] The essential thing is to not be strict and overbearing with others. Similarly, he should minimize the times that he insists that his opinion is correct and must be followed. Rather, he should conduct himself gently and pleasantly. If he does so, then his efforts will bear fruit over the course of time, with the help of Heaven.

Your friend who seeks your peace,

Yisrael

TRANSLATOR'S SUMMARY OF LETTER TWENTY

1. The techniques that are successful in one area of character refinement cannot be applied to another area of character (even in the same person).

2. Difficult areas of growth require a gentle, patient approach — and at the same time, one must have an intense desire for rapid success.

3. The study of character rectification is almost entirely dependent on understanding general human conduct.

4. A small amount of studies should be directed to the art of human relations.

---

7   If he sees himself as a leader and a great scholar, he will no longer grow. Therefore, he must always see himself as one who still is growing and has much to learn.

LETTER TWENTY-ONE

THE IMPORTANCE OF KNOWING PRACTICAL HALACHAH

In order to save ourselves from committing transgressions, it is crucial for us to learn practical halachah.

MY BELOVED FRIEND! I am quite surprised at the absence of your [return] letter, and that you have not informed me of how things are going with the system of study we discussed — teaching Gemara to lay people and businessmen, with an eye to showing them how the halachic conclusions are relevant to their lives. After all, this is a subject on which I invested much effort with you, and you know that I set great stock in its implementation — practical study, undertaken with a spirit of *yiras Shamayim.* Previously, I asked my beloved friend, R.G., to inform me concerning these matters, but I have heard not a word from him. [Under the circumstances, it is not inappropriate to say,] "Now, you have acted foolishly." I, therefore, will lay out my request before you yet again — send a response by mail with a clear explanation of the situation.

I wish now to stress to you the importance of knowing [practical halachah. By way of illustration,] let us consider the mitzvah of returning lost objects, which [requires for its full exposition] certain laws that appear in *Yoreh De'ah.*[1] Herein, I will present one example....[2]

---

1   Even though the primary source for this subject is found in *Choshen Mishpat.*
2   Apparently, the rest of this paragraph is not extant in the original letter. It would seem that Rav Yisrael proceeds to briefly discuss a halachah in this area, showing its

THE INITIAL OBLIGATION IN DIVINE WORSHIP

We have spoken previously about why such practical knowledge is important. The initial obligation in Divine worship is to "turn from evil" (*Tehillim* 34:15).[3] Therefore, a person needs to acquire as much halachic knowledge as possible, so that he can know what is permissible and what is forbidden before he acts. Then, when presented with a test, he will not be at a loss as to how to conduct himself. This is something that we pray for every single day. How, then, can we have the audacity to ask for Hashem's assistance that we not stumble and be ensnared, if we ourselves do not make a minimal effort to remove obstructions from our path by studying the halachah? Surely it behooves us to study and teach practical knowledge of the Torah's laws. This is the primary reason that study is greater than deed. As taught in the Talmud (*Kiddushin* 40b): "Study is greater than the deed, for study engenders the deed!" It is fitting to elaborate more on this topic, but I will wait to receive a prompt response from you. Read my letter carefully and correct any errors you find in it, and may Hashem be with you! Just as your souls desire perfection, so does the soul of your friend desire it for you.

Awaiting your reply,

Yisrael, the son of our master, HaRav Ze'ev Wolf, *neiro ya'ir*

Translator's Summary of Letter Twenty-one

1. It is important to know and teach practical *halachah*.

2. In order to fulfill one's obligation in Divine service, one must know as much halachah as possible.

3. If we know halachah, then, when presented with a test, we will know how to act.

4. Study is greater than deed, for study engenders deed.

---

relevance to everyday life.

3   That is, to refrain from transgressing prohibitions, as opposed to "doing good," i.e., performing positive commandments.

LETTER TWENTY-TWO

THE IMPERATIVE OF JOY IN DIVINE SERVICE

As a cholera epidemic rages throughout Europe, Rav Yisrael comforts a friend who has suffered loss and uplifts his spirit with words of kindness.

YOUR LETTER OF THIS MONTH has arrived, and as you have requested, I am assigning top priority to respond immediately.

CONTROLLING ONE'S EMOTIONS

"Man's whole duty" (*Koheles* 12:13) is to be a "master of his passions" (*Mishlei* 16:32), to bend his desires according to his will, depending on the requirements of any situation he finds himself in. A person should be capable of controlling his emotions — for example, to feel sad when someone dies, *chas v'shalom*. He should feel bitter because the deceased can no longer serve Hashem, for the dead are unable to perform mitzvos. On the other hand, if the deceased was righteous, one should also be capable of feeling solace and serenity, for the departed soul has left for its place in the World to Come — and this is the hope of every person on the face of the earth. Indeed, it is the purpose of our existence and the fruit of our labors, and "sweet is the sleep of the laborer..." (*Koheles* 5:11).

OUR SAGES INSTRUCT US TO MOURN

Of course, the reality is that if not for the forceful directives of our

Sages, which we must all strive to validate and uphold, cold logic would dictate that we not even think to be saddened at the loss of a righteous man —
and this is so even though the desire of man's physical side is for a long and
tranquil life in this world. After all, the deceased has gone on to claim his
rightful inheritance — a share in the World to Come! Moreover, who knows
if, had he remained alive, he would have continued to be victorious in his
battle against the *yetzer hara?* Nevertheless, our duty is to follow the authoritative words of our Sages, who instruct us to mourn. They teach us when and
how it is appropriate to arouse feelings of concern and sorrow in the heart,
and not to simply allow them free reign whenever one thinks them appropriate.

AT THIS TIME, TORAH OBSERVANCE IS ALTERED

Despite what we said above, nevertheless, there is a time for everything
(cf. *Koheles* 3:1). At the present time, there is a [cholera] epidemic raging
throughout the world, may Hashem have mercy, and it has reached this
country as well. At a time such as this, our duty is clear: we must not fear it —
for what value is the life of man when we consider the overwhelming potential for spiritual failure? Who knows if a person will succeed in his path (cf.
Koheles 11:6)?[1] Of course, this does not mean that we should fatalistically resign ourselves to dying and do nothing to protect ourselves. Rather, we must
follow the regimen that the learned physicians have prescribed, to insure
that we maintain our health. It is a Torah directive for us to proceed according to the light of their words, for our duty is to establish life in this world —
for the benefit of ourselves, as well as others. From prior experience, we know
that when this disease spreads, God forbid, those who intelligently undertake
to follow the doctors' orders concerning eating, etc., will emerge unscathed.

---

1   There are two perspectives of death: 1)The natural reaction of the human intellect,
    which views death as a refuge from the spiritual challenges of this world. 2)The Torah's
    understanding, which instructs us to mourn when the soul is taken from this world, for
    the deceased can no longer perform mitzvos. Although *klal Yisrael* must always conduct
    themselves in compliance with the Torah, at the time of the epidemic, Rav Yisrael instructed the community to alter their perspective and view death through the eyes of the
    intellect. They should not be overly concerned with dying, because in these dark times,
    the fear of dying will lead to despair and compromise their Divine service.

In light of this, we must clearly understand that all Torah observance is altered according to the dictates of the situation. The Tanach teaches that there should be no untoward bitterness during the Days of Awe; rather, it is the time to serve Hashem with uncompromising delight — for the joy of Hashem is your strength (cf. *Nechemiah* 8:10). In the same vein, if the epidemic claims a person's life, one should not lament the loss, for the deceased's sorrow has ended, and he has departed to the place of his desire — may his soul be bound up in the bond of life (cf. *I Shmuel* 25:29).[2] May the Almighty comfort you, my distinguished correspondent, and may you be blessed with good fortune and a year of life and peace.

TRANSLATOR'S SUMMARY OF LETTER TWENTY-TWO

1. Our Sages rule that if a member of *klal Yisrael* passes to the Next World, then mourning is the appropriate response.

2. During the time of a terrible epidemic, Rav Yisrael ruled that the community should not be overly concerned with death.

3. Moreover, Rav Yisrael ruled that during the time of the epidemic, when many people died, mourning should be less intense than under normal conditions.

4. The reason for Rav Yisrael's halachic modifications was that too much sadness could weaken the resistance of the living, as well as impede Divine service (of which happiness is an essential component).

---

2   Even though the Torah exhorts us to mourn for the departed, mourning is not appropriate during the epidemic. Since mourning weakens resistance to disease, we must refrain from mourning in order not to jeopardize our own health. This is consistent with the Torah axiom: "When life is endangered, the entire Torah is abrogated."

LETTER TWENTY-THREE

THE DESIRE FOR LIFE
AND THE DIVINE WILL

There are two motivations for man to desire life: one stems from his desire for earthly pleasure, and the other from his spiritual and intellectual understanding of the Divine will.

CHANUKAH

THE TALMUD (*Shabbos* 21b) STATES: "What is the reason for [the festival of] Chanukah? The Rabbis taught: 'On the twenty-fifth of Kislev, the days of Chanukah commence.... When the Greeks intruded into the Beis HaMikdash, they defiled all the oil designated for the menorah. And when the Chashmonaim prevailed against them, they searched and found a single cruse of oil with the *kohen gadol*'s seal on it. Yet, though it only contained enough for one day's lighting, a miracle occurred and the menorah remained lit with it for eight days. The following year, they established a festival for the recitation of Hallel and *hoda'ah* [special prayers of praise and thanksgiving to the Almighty].' "

NO FESTIVE MEAL

A question that presents itself is why do we not also make a festive meal on Chanukah, as we do on Purim? After all, didn't a miracle also occur on Chanukah that is relevant to the body?[1] Indeed, the Chanukah addition to

---

1   Typically, we understand that the reason Chazal instituted a festive meal on Purim was because we were saved from physical annihilation. On Chanukah, however, it was primarily our souls that were at stake, since the Greeks were principally interested in

the prayer service itself alludes to the physical aspect: "You delivered the strong into the hands of the weak, the many into the hands of the few" — implying that we were saved from physical annihilation.

MOURNING FOR A WORTHY MAN

In order to explain this, let us first turn to a statement in the Talmud (Mo'ed Katan 25a): "Why do a man's children die when they are young? Because he did not weep and mourn over the death of a worthy person [i.e., an upright person who was careful not to sin]." The justice of this punishment can be understood according to the principle of *middah keneged middah* (measure for measure).

TORAH IS A CHOK

To understand how [this punishment is *middah keneged middah*], we must turn to a passage in the Midrash (*Yalkut Shemoni, Tehillim* 710): "When the *HaKadosh Baruch Hu* gave the Torah to Israel, His voice traversed from one end of the world to the other. Upon hearing it, the kings of all the nations were gripped with fear. They all gathered around Bilaam and asked, 'What is this thunderous noise that we heard?' He answered, 'The Almighty has a precious treasure in His repository, and He is giving it to His people, as it says, "Hashem will give might to His nation" (*Tehillim* 29:11).' They responded together, chanting: 'Hashem will give His people strength, Hashem will bless His people with peace.' " To explain this passage, let us refer to a verse from the Torah regarding the festival of Shavuos: "You shall observe and perform these *chukim* [Torah statutes for which Hashem did not reveal the underlying reason]" (*Devarim* 16:12). We see from this that the Torah specifically defines Shavuos as a *chok*. However, regarding Pesach and Sukkos there is no such reference.

---

uprooting our faith. Rav Yisrael is asking: that may well be so, but once there was a war, our lives were also put in danger. That being the case, why don't we celebrate our physical salvation as well, in the same way that we celebrate it on Purim?

THE CREATION OF MAN

We can explain the reason for this in light of a debate in the Talmud (*Eruvin* 13b) between Beis Shammai and Beis Hillel over whether it would be better for man to have been created or better not to have been created, in which the latter view prevailed. The parameters of the debate are as follows: On the one hand, if he acts righteously, creation confers a profound advantage upon man — eternal reward in Gan Eden. On the other hand, it is very probable that creation will cause him great harm, for as we see, the majority of people stumble and transgress. Therefore, from the human perspective, it is better for man not to have been created.

AGREEMENT TO ACCEPT THE TORAH

The two sides of this debate were also relevant to the giving of the Torah, which effectively created a new reality in the world. The question lay in whether to fulfill the *taryag* (613) mitzvos, whose reward is incalculable, or to refuse the Torah and avoid the probable harm of punishment for violating them. The idolaters of the world declined to accept the Torah, for they did not want to risk the danger it entailed. Only the Jewish nation "walked in wholesome perfection" (*Shabbos* 88b) and accepted it. They reasoned that just as the Almighty created the world, even though it was not a good thing from the human perspective, so, too, they would agree to the Divine will, even though this acceptance [of the Torah] entailed risks that defied human logic.

Indeed, the punishments for transgressing the Torah are administered both in the Eternal World and in this one. However, regarding the punishments of this world, there is a rule stated in the Talmud (*Pesachim*; see also *Yalkut Shemoni Hoshea* 4:520): "Great is peace, for even if people serve idols, Hashem will not punish them if peace reigns amongst them." Now, the main fear of the idolaters that caused them to reject the Torah was the punishments that they would face in this world, for the concept of the afterlife is generally not so concrete and immediate. Thus, when the nations heard that the Jewish people had accepted the Torah, they all responded: "Hashem will bless His people with peace" — praying that the Jews would live peacefully together and be saved from the punishments of this world.

Therefore, from the human perspective, there is no place for rejoicing over the acceptance of the Torah on Shavuos. Rather, our acceptance of To-rah is a *chok* [as we rely on the superior wisdom and goodness of Hashem], and the Torah thus writes about Shavuos: "And you shall observe and per-form these *chukim*." On the other hand, the festivals of Pesach and Sukkos, which mark times of miracles and redemption, do not contradict our logic, and our intellect instructs us to rejoice in the miracles.

THE WILL TO LIVE

It emerges from the above that man's will to live springs exclusively from the desire of the body, for the intellect concludes, "It would be better had man not been created." Carrying this conclusion one step further, we can even say that death is preferable to life, *chas v'shalom*, because a person will thereby incur no further culpability from transgression. Nevertheless, we can still say that there is one rationale in favor of continued life: the rectification of one's past sins — for this is something that can only be accomplished while a person is alive.

MEASURE FOR MEASURE

[We are now in a position to understand how the death of one's children is a *middah keneged middah* punishment for not mourning the passing of a worthy person. As we have just noted, the only rationale for continued life is so that one can rectify his past sins.] This, however, does not apply to worthy people and young children: the former are careful not to sin, and the latter have not yet had the opportunity to do so. Accordingly, human logic dictates that it is actually good for them to die, *chas v'shalom*, so as to avoid the possi-bility of future sin. The Almighty, however, wants life — despite the conclu-sion [of the human intellect] that "It would be better had man not been cre-ated." We are therefore commanded to mourn the loss of a worthy individ-ual.[2] If a person chooses to ignore the Divine will, and instead reasons that it is illogical to mourn the passing of such a person, then *chas v'chalilah*, he will be punished measure for measure. He thought it was preferable for the worthy man to die and thereby not come to transgress. Therefore, the Almighty will apply the same reasoning to his own children, and for their own "benefit" [they will die before having the opportunity to sin].

Similarly, the intellect dictates that at a certain point, affliction is not advantageous. This is because man is obligated to observe the mitzvos even when he is afflicted. This is a difficult test.[3]

THE MOST OPPRESSIVE AFFLICTION IS CAPTIVITY

We find that the most oppressive affliction is captivity and subjugation. The Talmud states (*Bava Basra* 8b), "It is written: 'Whoever is destined for death [by natural causes], to death; whoever for the sword, to the sword; whoever for famine, to famine; and whoever for captivity, to captivity' (*Yirmeyahu* 15:2). Rebbi Yochanan said, 'Each punishment in this verse is more severe than the one preceding it. The sword is worse than death, because the sword maims and death does not maim. Famine is worse than the sword, because famine causes prolonged suffering and the other one [the sword] does not. Captivity is the most severe, because it includes the suffering of all of them.' "[4]

---

2   The Saba M'Kelm (*Ohr Rashaz*, article 149) cites the Ramban (introduction to *Toras Ha'adam*) who discusses the death of Socrates. As recorded by historians, Socrates was sentenced to death. When his friends asked him to beg forgiveness of the king, so that his life might be spared, Socrates refused. He viewed death as a happy occasion, like going to a dance. In contradistinction, Moshe Rabbeinu, *lehavdil*, pleaded for life, as did Chizkiyahu. Moreover, the Sages tell us to fear death because of the awesome judgments that take place. The philosophers followed the human intellect, which views death as an advantage, as Rav Yisrael explained. They are disgusted by the lowly body and its cravings, and welcome their demise. We, on the other hand, follow and accept the Divine will of He Who desires life. Life is precious to us because it grants us the opportunity to serve Hashem with the material elements. Therefore, we desire life and mourn when someone dies.

3   Just as the intellect concludes that it is better had man not been created — in order that he won't come to sin — so, too, it concludes that affliction is detrimental because it leads to transgression.

4   We see from this that performing mitzvos in a situation of captivity is very trying. Indeed, we might say that captivity can be so oppressive as to even preclude the possibility of following the commandments.

TWO PERSPECTIVES OF PURIM

[Rav Yisrael now returns to the question at hand: since we experienced a physical, as well as a spiritual, redemption on Chanukah, why isn't there a mitzvah to have a celebratory meal in the same way there is on Purim?] Now, the miracle on Purim can be viewed from two perspectives — spiritual and physical. A spiritual person, who directs his intellect to follow the Divine will, desires life for himself in the same way that the Almighty does.[5] Therefore, when Hashem saves his body, he perceives this as a miracle. On the other hand, a physically oriented person who is immersed in earthly passions is also filled with a desire to live, so that he can fulfill his bodily desires. Therefore he is also greatly pleased when Hashem saves his body, and perceives this as a miracle. [In truth, there is a third type of person as well,] one who is neither spiritually motivated nor physically impassioned. Such a person will not consider the saving of his body to be such a significant miracle, because he has no great desire to live. The existence of such individuals is deduced from a verse in *Megillas Esther* (4:3): "Sackcloth and ashes were spread out for the many." We see from this that not everybody endeavored to perform *teshuvah* in order to save their lives — many, but not all. The mitzvos of Purim are twofold, in order to reflect the first two perspectives: reading the *Megillah* corresponds to the spiritual aspect of the miracle, while making a festive meal corresponds to the physical aspect.

ONE PERSPECTIVE OF CHANUKAH

In contrast, Chanukah is commemorated only with the spiritual actions of Hallel and *hoda'ah*, and not with the physical commemoration of feasting, because the Greeks had conquered and enslaved the Jews.[6]

---

5   Up to this point we have said that the human intellect does not fathom the rational of why man should be created. However, as we saw from our willingness to accept the Torah, we defer to the infinite wisdom of Hashem. Hence, even though the logic is beyond human comprehension, we trust in the wisdom of Hashem — and choose to accept His will — that life is advantageous. This acceptance of the Divine begets the spiritual and intellectual desire of man for life.

6   Under normal conditions (like Purim, when there was no threat to their spiritual life), those whose desire for life stemmed from their earthly passions celebrate the miracle of being saved with a festive meal — because that best expresses the reason why they are

TRANSLATOR'S SUMMARY OF LETTER TWENTY-THREE

1. According to the human intellect, it is illogical to accept the awesome responsibility of the Torah.

2. The acceptance of the Torah is a *chok* (a mitzvah that is beyond the grasp of human comprehension).

3. The miracle of Purim occurred in a period when *klal Yisrael* were not in captivity — therefore, it is celebrated both on the physical and spiritual levels.

4. The miracle of Chanukah occurred during a period when the Greeks had enslaved the Jews — therefore, it is celebrated only spiritually but not physically (because there was no natural desire to live).

---

grateful to be alive. However, at the time of Chanukah, the Greeks had the Jewish people completely under their subjugation — they were effectively captives. As we mentioned, it is very trying to observe mitzvos when suffering this most extreme affliction. Therefore, at this time of captivity, even those whose desire to live stemmed from their earthly passions had no desire to live. The fear of violating the entire Torah because of the oppression crushed their physical desire for life. Therefore, during the period of Chanukah, the only desire that the Jews had to live emanated from the spiritual and intellectual understanding of Divine will.

LETTER TWENTY-FOUR

IMMUTABLE FAITH

The next two letters (24 and 25) were written by our master's teacher, the humble genius and pious servant of Hashem, Rav Yosef Zundel of Salant, zt"l. He wrote these letters from the holy city of Yerushalayim — may it be built soon, in our days — to his only son, who was performing the mitzvos of bikur cholim and pikuach nefesh (visiting the sick and saving a life) for his sister, who was detained in the city of Vienna.

The Creator constantly and continually oversees each individual aspect of every person's life. Moreover, to the degree that a man turns his heart to Hashem, so does Hashem direct His Providence towards him.

TRUST IN HASHEM

24 Kislev, 5618 [1857]

SHALOM, MY BELOVED SON!
I sent you recommendations, as you requested. However, do not place your faith in them, for they are only a vehicle so that your success needn't result from an open miracle. As Shlomo HaMelech tells us, the essential factor is to "trust in Hashem with all your heart, and do not rely on your own understanding" (*Mishlei* 3:5). Similarly, do not make excessive efforts, so that you should not think that "my strength and the might of my hand were the source of my salvation" (cf. *Devarim* 8:17). As Scripture states: "Do not rely on nobles, nor on a human being, for he holds no salvation.... Praiseworthy is

the one whose help is in Yaakov's God, whose hope is in Hashem, his God" (*Tehillim* 146:3, 5). I hope unto Hashem that He will provide you with more than sufficient funds to cover both your expenditures there and the cost of your return journey. The Almighty has many means and messengers at His disposal — whether through the principle "Hashem provides a worthy person with the opportunity to perform a meritorious deed," as we see with Rebbi Meir's dictum in *Bava Basra* (10a),[1] or by numerous other means.

RECITE VERSES OF FAITH

You should continually recite verses that speak of Divine providence, faith, and deliverance. For example, "Hope to Hashem; strengthen yourself, and He will give you courage, and hope to Hashem" (*Tehillim* 27:14). As well as, "Be strong and courageous, do not be afraid and do not be broken before them, for Hashem, your God — it is He Who goes before you, He will not release you nor will He forsake you" (*Devarim* 31:6). Also, "My eyes are constantly turned toward Hashem, for He will remove my feet from the snare" (*Tehillim* 25:15), and other similar verses. Divine assistance is found abundantly in times of troubles. By following this path, you will proceed with confidence, knowing that "the deliverance of Hashem comes in the blink of an eye" (*Shirei Rav Yehudah HaLevi*).

DIVINE PROVIDENCE

As we know, the Creator constantly and continually oversees each individual aspect of every person's life. Moreover, to the degree that a man turns his heart to Hashem, so does Hashem direct His providence towards him. As the verse states, "Hashem is your Guardian; Hashem is your protective shade at your right hand" (*Tehillim* 121:5) — meaning that the more a person turns to Hashem, the more Hashem will guard over him. As the Midrash states,

---

1   The Talmud (*Bava Basra* 10a) teaches: "Rebbi Meir used to say: The heretic may argue, 'If your God loves the poor, why does He not support them?' To this you can reply, 'So that through them we may be saved from the punishment of Gehinnom.' " Rashi explains that in the merit of giving charity, one will be saved from Gehinnom. Rav Zundel's intent is that perhaps his son's merit will itself cause another person to do a meritorious deed in turn — giving his son money and thereby accruing merit himself.

"Just as a single finger casts the shadow of a single finger, and a whole hand casts the shadow of a whole hand; similarly, to the extent that one endeavors to see Hashem, so will He will be seen by him." (See *Nefesh HaChaim* 1:7 for further elucidation.)

AFFLICTION AND ATONEMENT[2]

When a man is beset by punishment and he does not know the reason for it, [he should make a personal accounting]. Along these lines, the Talmud (*Yoma* 38b) tells us: "One who forgets any part of his Torah knowledge causes his children to go into exile, as Scripture states: 'As you have forgotten the Torah of your God, I, too, will forget your children' (*Hoshea* 4:6)." Moreover, who can claim that his heart is pure and he is free of sin (cf. *Mishlei* 20:9)? Indeed, transgression engulfs us, and our guilt extends to the very Heavens; therefore, we are embarrassed and ashamed to lift up our faces to God (cf. *Ezra* 9:6)! The neglect of Torah study is a particularly severe sin, as the Sifri teaches: "Just as Torah study is the most important [mitzvah], so, too, is neglect of Torah study the worst of all transgressions." Moreover, our Sages tell us (*Sanhedrin* 37b), "Exile atones for transgression." This is particularly true concerning an exile of penury, in which one is forced to endure the shame and degradation of asking others for charity. Consider this well in your heart: the more shame you suffer, the more atonement you will receive for your transgressions.

ACCEPT SUFFERING WITH LOVE

In light of this, you should accept your suffering with love, and rejoice over it more than if you had received all the wealth in the world! As it says in the Talmud (*Berachos* 5a), "Rabbah said in the name of Rav Secharah, who said in the name of Rav Huna: Whomever the Almighty desires, He crushes with afflictions, as it says, 'And the one whom Hashem desired, He crushed with illness' (*Yeshayahu* 53:10). One might think that this applies even if he

---

2   Up to this point in the letter, Rav Zundel encourages his son and instructs him to strengthen his faith in Hashem. Next he explains that the purpose of affliction is to bring about atonement. Therefore, the tribulations that his son endures should not sadden him; rather, they should gladden him, because they cleanse his soul.

does not accept them with love. Therefore, the verse continues, 'if his soul acknowledges guilt' — just as a guilt offering must be brought with consent, so, too, must a person endure his sufferings with consent. And if he does accept them, what is his reward? 'He will see children and live long days' (ibid.). Moreover, his Torah knowledge will endure within him, as the verse concludes, 'And the desire of Hashem will be successful in his hand.'" This teaching is particularly applicable to you, for you are pursuing the mitzvos of *bikur cholim* and *gemillus chasadim*, and there is no one else who could possibly perform them in your stead. Accordingly, it is considered as if you are actually fulfilling the injunction to devote all your energies to study Torah. As the Talmud teaches (Mo'ed Katan 9b) and the *Shulchan Aruch* codifies into law (Yoreh De'ah 246:18), the performance of a mitzvah that cannot be done by another is equivalent to fulfilling the mitzvah to "contemplate the Torah day and night" (Yehoshua 1:8).

Therefore, do not be saddened, but only rejoice! And when you inform me that you are neither distressed nor worried, rather only happy — then I will also be happy. "All there is for us is to rely on our Father in Heaven" (Sotah 49b). If He brings sorrow upon us, He will yet have compassion, in accord with His abundant kindness — for Hashem will not reject us forever. Hashem is good to them who hope in Him (cf. Eichah 3:32, 31, 25).

Your father,
Zundel of Salant

TRANSLATOR'S SUMMARY OF LETTER TWENTY-FOUR

1. In order to strengthen one's faith, a person should repeat aloud verses that speak of faith and deliverance.

2. The more a person looks to see Divine providence in his life, the more Hashem will direct Divine providence towards him.

3. Exile atones for transgressions.

4. One who accepts suffering with love will be blessed with children, live a long life, and will acquire Torah.

LETTER TWENTY-FIVE

THE BLESSING OF AFFLICTION

For a servant of Hashem, misfortune is considered a joy and perceived as an advantage. Since he lovingly accepts whatever Hashem decrees upon him, his acceptance of the bad is his Divine service, which is his only joy.

NEVER REGRET A MITZVAH

24 Nissan

MY BELOVED SON,
[I adjure you:] take care, lest your heart comes to regret the performance of this mitzvah, which forces upon you an ever-lengthening exile and the disgrace [of asking for charity]. As the Talmud states (*Berachos* 6b): "Rebbi Yochanan and Rebbi Eliezer both said: 'When a person needs the support of his fellowman, his countenance changes hue like a multicolored bird [i.e., he is subject to intense shame, which colors his face].' " Therefore, all the more so, you should make sure not to give verbal expression to any discontent, such as saying: "Had I known how difficult it would be, I would not have performed this mitzvah." As our Sages teach (Talmud Yerushalmi, *Pe'ah, perek* 1): "When a person regrets the performance of a mitzvah, he loses his reward." Similarly, the Talmud states (*Kiddushin* 40b): "If a righteous person rebels [against Hashem] at the end of his life, then he will forfeit his earlier good deeds.... [Asks the Gemara,] but why? Let him be accredited as

half sinful and half righteous [i.e., why isn't he punished for his sins and yet still rewarded for his mitzvos?]. Reish Lakish said, '[The case here is one in which] he regrets the good deeds that he performed earlier.' "

Let the following three ideas be your solace:

KINDNESS SUPERSEDES TORAH STUDY

1) You are performing the mitzvos of visiting the sick and of bestowing lovingkindness, and there is no one else able to do so in this case. Concerning this, Chazal rule (Mo'ed Katan 9b; see Rashi, ad loc., under the heading "cheftzi," and Tosafos under the heading "kan") that one should even abandon his Torah study in order to perform the mitzvah, and that it is actually more preferable than the Torah study. Therefore, at a time when you do not have the opportunity to study Torah, the deed you are performing is considered to be an even greater mitzvah!

YOUR REWARD IS GUARANTEED

2) Many people travel to far-off locations for business and do not concern themselves with the hardships of the journey. Neither rain, snow, cold, nor heat deters them — and this is so even when they are uncertain that they will be able to successfully conclude a deal. On the other hand, your reward for this mitzvah is absolutely guaranteed. As Chazal teach (Berachos 5a): "Rabbah said in the name of Rav Secharah, who said in the name of Rav Huna: Whomever the Almighty desires, He crushes with afflictions, as it says, 'And the one whom Hashem desired, He crushed with illness' (Yeshayahu 53:10): One might think that this applies even if he does not accept them with love. Therefore, the verse continues, 'if his soul acknowledges guilt' — just as a guilt offering must be brought with consent, so, too, must a person endure his sufferings with consent. And if he does accept them, what is his reward? 'He will see children and live long days' (ibid.). Moreover, his Torah knowledge will endure within him, as the verse concludes: 'And the desire of Hashem will be successful in his hand.' "

TORAH UPHOLDS THE WORLD

I heard the following directly from our holy master and teacher, Rav Chaim Volozhiner: "If, *chas v'shalom*, one principle of the Talmud were to be annulled, then the whole world would be destroyed."[1] The longer the exile and the more disgrace one endures — and the more he accepts his suffering with love, forbearance, and joy — the greater his reward will be. [He will be blessed with] numerous offspring, lengthy days, and the endurance of his Torah knowledge.

ABUNDANT REWARD

These are things that every single person hopes to merit, for they are the greatest acquisitions man can attain, both in this world and the Next. In general, however, a person is not worthy of them unless he invests tireless effort and enormous financial expenditure. Yet if "Hashem loves a person and castigates him with misfortune" (*Mishlei* 3:12) — whether through exile or degradation — and he accepts his suffering with love, then he merits these three things in but a brief time! Therefore, when you despair over the extended duration of your exile, and when the burden of distress and disgrace weighs heavily on your heart — remind yourself that your reward is exceedingly abundant.

ACCEPT THE DECREES OF HASHEM

3) When one accepts these tribulations with love and happiness, he is serving the Almighty. As the *Shulchan Aruch* rules (*Orach Chaim* 222:3): "A person is obligated to bless the bad with total conviction and acceptance, just as he joyfully blesses the good." This is because for a servant of Hashem, misfortune is [considered] a joy and [perceived as] an advantage. Since he lovingly accepts whatever Hashem decrees upon him, his acceptance of the bad is his Divine service, which is his [only] joy."

---

1   The "principles of the Talmud" are the very principles of reality that Hashem established when He created the world. Therefore, the annulment of a Talmudic axiom would mean the annulment of reality, i.e., the destruction of the world. Rav Zundel's intent is that, accordingly, the principle he notes in the previous paragraph — that one who accepts his sufferings with love will receive great reward — is immutable.

Never forget that salvation is in the Almighty's hands. When you go someplace and are in need of assistance, seek out the help of only two people, and do not exert more effort than this. As the Chovos HaLevavos writes (*Sha'ar HaBitachon* 3:3), "If a person trusts both in Hashem and in another, then his faith is not complete." And it says, "Commit your way to Hashem, rely on Him (exclusively on Him, and nothing else), and He (and He alone) will act" (*Tehillim* 37:5). Also it is written, "There is no other god besides Me; there is no righteous god besides Me and no savior other than Me" (*Yeshayahu* 45:21).

THE KINDNESS OF HASHEM

The recognition of the kindness that Hashem constantly bestows upon a person is greater in one who is humbled than in one who is exalted. How abundant is the kindness that Hashem has performed in each step that you take — for me, for my daughter there with you, and for you. He does not treat us according to what we deserve for our sins; rather, in the merit of our patriarchs and Yerushalayim, His kindness overwhelms us. "Until now, His mercy has helped us, and His kindness has not abandoned us" (*Nishmas* prayer of the Shabbos morning service). Many people have found themselves in your situation, and the least among them was more honorable than us (cf. *I Melachim* 12:10). They were superior to us and better than us according to every criteria; yet, they did not receive the warm and cheerful welcome that you did. Indeed, many esteemed men and rabbinic figures have written to me that it was a privilege for them to see you. I rejoiced in this, as it indicates that you have some measure of humility and modesty. As the verse states, "But to the humble He will find favor" (*Mishlei* 3:34). Similarly, "And humility precedes honor" (ibid., 15:33). Therefore, when your heart feels anguished and humiliated, and you feel yourself bowing under the weariness of your exile, take comfort in this letter, and be joyful and happy. "Hope to Hashem" (*Tehillim* 27:14), and He will deliver you in all your affairs. "Cast upon Hashem your burden and He will sustain you; He will never allow the faltering of the righteous" (ibid. 55:23). Always remember that "the deliverance of Hashem comes in the blink of an eye" (*Shirei Rav Yehudah HaLevi*), as the verse says, "Hashem desires those who await His kindness" (*Tehillim* 147:11).

Your father,
Zundel of Salant

TRANSLATOR'S SUMMARY OF LETTER TWENTY-FIVE

1. If one regrets a mitzvah that he has performed, he loses his reward.

2. One should stop studying Torah in order to perform a mitzvah that "comes to his hand" — and that mitzvah is even more important than Torah study.

3. The more one accepts his tribulations with love, the more reward he will receive.

4. Every principle of the Talmud is absolute and immutable.

LETTER TWENTY-SIX

HUMILITY

The next three "letters" are actually lectures given by Rav Yisrael, as recorded by Rav Blazer.

Since it was Rosh HaShanah Eve, the chassid wanted to repent on that very night and swiftly perfect the attribute of humility in his soul, before arising to face the next day's awesome judgment.

THE CHASSID

THE TALMUD (*Berachos* 18b) CITES the following incident: "On the eve of Rosh HaShanah in a year of drought, there was a certain chassid (pious man) who gave a coin to a pauper. [Since it was a time of scarce provisions and the chassid himself was not a man of means,] his wife vexed him (*v'hiknitahu*). [As a result, he left his house and] went to sleep in a cemetery. [While he was there,] he heard two spirits conversing...."

This account is astonishing! Of all places, why did this pious man choose to sleep in such an impure place as a cemetery? In his *Chiddushei Aggadata* (in *Sefer Ein Yaakov*), the Maharsha asks this same question, and the unusual nature of the event compels him to answer in a way that departs from the straightforward explanation. In brief, he writes that the correct interpretation is that given by the Ritva, who opines that the entire incident took place in a dream. However, based on a Mussar perspective, our holy master and teacher, Rav Yisrael, *zt"l*, gives a truly amazing explanation, asserting that the incident actually did take place and wasn't just a vision or dream.

He notes that the phrase "and his wife vexed him" clearly indicates that this chassid experienced an emotional response in reaction to his wife's scolding. In his heart, he felt anguish and affront, and even a trace of anger. As proof that "*v'hiknitahu*" refers to such emotions, he adduces the following passage from the Talmud (*Shabbos* 30b).

THE HUMILITY OF HILLEL

"Our Rabbis taught that a man should always be humble like Hillel and not stern like Shammai. It once happened that two people made a wager with one another, saying, 'Whomever goes and vexes (*yaknitu*) Hillel will win 400 *zuz*.' One of them said, 'I will vex him.' That day was Shabbos Eve, and Hillel was washing his hair. The man went, stood on his [Hillel's] doorway, and yelled out [disrespectfully], 'Is there one named Hillel here, is there one named Hillel here?' Hillel put his robe on, went out to him, and said, 'My son, what do you seek?' 'I have a question to ask,' he said. 'Ask, my son,' he [Hillel] replied. He [the man] then queried, 'Why are the heads of the Babylonians misshapen?' 'My son, you have asked a profound question,' he replied. 'It is because they do not have skillful midwives.' He [the man] departed, waited for an hour, and returned, yelling out, 'Is there one named Hillel here, is there one named Hillel here?' Hillel put his robe on, went out to him, and said, 'My son, what do you seek?' 'I have a question to ask,' he said. 'Ask, my son,' he replied. He then queried, 'Why are the eyes of the Tarmudians slitted?' 'My son, you have asked a profound question,' he replied. 'It is because they live in sandy places.' He departed, waited for an hour, and returned, yelling out, 'Is there one named Hillel here, is there one named Hillel here?' Hillel put his robe on, went out to him, and said, 'My son, what do you seek?' I have a question to ask,' he said. 'Ask, my son,' he replied. He then queried, 'Why are the feet of the Africans wide?' 'My son, you have asked a profound question,' he replied. 'It is because they live in marshy areas.' The man then said, 'I have many questions to ask, but I fear that you might become angry.' He [Hillel] donned his robe, sat before him, and said,

'Ask all the questions that you wish.' He then asked him, 'Are you Hillel, who is called Prince of Israel?' 'Yes,' he replied. 'If you are he,' he said, 'may there not be many like you in Israel!' 'Why, my son?' he asked. 'Because I lost 400 *zuz* on account of you!' He said to him, 'Be careful of your attitude; it is worth it for you to lose twice that amount, and that Hillel not be strict.' ' "

We thus see the connotation of *yaknitu* is to vex someone to the point of affront and anger. However, the man did not succeed in irritating Hillel with his quarrelsomeness and derision, for in his great humility, the Sage was unaffected. He did not feel angry nor come to any indignation whatsoever.

HUMILITY IS TO FEEL NO ANGER WHATSOEVER

On the other hand, in the incident with the chassid, the text states, "*v'hiknitahu* — and his wife vexed him." We see clearly, then, that the chassid was affected by his wife's provocation to the point where he felt indignant, and perhaps even angry. Hence the chassid faltered spiritually through a weakening in the trait of humility. Feelings of irritation and anger are foreign to chassidim, who are humble and lowly in their minds. The mark of true humility is to not feel any effrontery or indignation whatsoever, and to not let "the rod of indignity rest upon the lot of humility" (cf. *Tehillim* 125:3), no matter what the situation. The Talmud illustrates how Hillel, in his great humility, did not become piqued when the bettor tried to instigate him. Similarly, the Talmud records (*Sotah* 40a), "Rebbi Avahu said, 'Initially, I considered myself humble. However, when I saw Rebbi Abba of Acco offer one explanation and his spokesman offer another, yet he (Rebbi Abba) did not take umbrage, I realized that I was not humble.' " We see, then, that the foundation of humility is to never take affront, no matter what happens.

REPENTANCE FOR FAULTY CHARACTER

When the chassid sensed that he had been affected by his wife's provocation, becoming indignant and stumbling in the virtue of humility, he desired to repent and perfect the blemish he had discovered within himself. Now, we know that the foundation of repentance lies in: 1) abandoning the sin, and 2) resolving not to sin in the future. However, *teshuvah* for faulty character traits is more difficult than for other transgressions. A person can easily accept upon himself to exercise care in mitzvah observance or to refrain from transgressions. The roots of character traits, however, are anchored in the depths of the heart. Therefore, the rectification and elimination of negative traits requires great effort and understanding. Indeed, our Sages teach the way of acquiring the virtue of humility (*Avos* 4:4): "Rav Levitas of Yavneh says: 'Be exceedingly humble in spirit, for the anticipated end of mortal man is worms.'" In his commentary on this *mishnah*, the Rambam writes, "This means that you must force yourself to abandon arrogance by reflecting on the final end of the body — it returns [to the earth] to [be consumed by] maggots." Thus, humility is acquired by contemplating the ignoble end that man faces — maggots and worms. The Ramchal writes similarly in his *Mesillas Yesharim* (ch. 23): "When man contemplates the lowliness of his physicality...and when he likewise considers that after all of his greatness he will return to the earth as food for the worms, it is certain that his haughtiness will be humbled and his pride forgotten — for what is his goodness and what is his greatness, when his ultimate end is ignominy and humiliation?"

Therefore, it was incumbent upon the chassid to contemplate the ways of Mussar, to reflect on the worthlessness and lowliness of man and the fact that his hope is maggots. Under normal circumstances, it would be possible to engage in the aforementioned contemplation over a period of time. However, since it was Rosh HaShanah Eve, the chassid wanted to repent on that very night and swiftly perfect the attribute of humility in his soul before arising to face the next day's awesome judgment. Therefore, he saw fit to employ the most extreme means to intensify his contemplation of man's lowliness and worthlessness, in a way that would make an immediate impression and powerful impact on his heart.

THE END OF MAN

It is for this reason that he went and slept in a cemetery — the final destination for all the living and the end of every man. This location is the most conducive to insure a swift and profound arousal for the contemplation in which he needed to engage — that man's hope is maggots and his end, shame and humiliation. In this way, he could quickly acquire the very essence of humility and lowliness.

In light of this, the chassid's action was not astonishing at all, for when the righteous consider something to be crucial to their Divine service — and especially something concerning repentance — they do not reject any tactic or strategy in the world.

TRANSLATOR'S SUMMARY OF LETTER TWENTY-SIX

1. The mark of true humility is not to feel any effrontery whatsoever.

2. Repentance for character flaws is more difficult than repentance for other transgressions.

3. Humility is acquired by contemplating the ignoble end that faces man.

4. When the righteous consider something to be crucial to their Divine service — especially something relevant to repentance — they do not reject any tactic or strategy in the world.

LETTER TWENTY-SEVEN

TORAH AND YIRAH

*The more one increases his knowledge and wisdom, the better he will
be able to fulfill the mitzvos in the most optimal fashion.*

THE DAY OF JUDGMENT

THE TALMUD (*Shabbos* 31a) STATES: "Rava said: When a man is
brought to face judgment, they ask him: 'Did you conduct yourself with
honesty? Did you establish fixed times for daily Torah study? Did you engage
in procreation? Did you hope for deliverance? Did you engage in the dialectics of wisdom? Did you extrapolate from one concept in order to understand
another?' Yet even so, if '*yiras Shamayim*' is his treasure (cf. *Yeshayahu* 33:6),
then all is well, but if not, not. This may be likened to a man who says to his
worker, 'Bring a bushel of wheat up to the attic for me.' He went and brought
it up. He then asked him, 'Did you mix in a measure of preservative (*chumtin*)
with it?' (Rashi explains that *chumtin* is salty earth mixed in with produce
that preserves it from insect infestation.) 'No,' he replied. He said to him,
'Then it would have been better had you not brought it up.' "

Let us examine the conclusion of the parable: "Then it would have been
better had you not brought it up." The implication of the case at hand is that
if a person did not make *yiras Shamayim* his treasure, then it would have been
better had he not studied Torah at all! This is an astonishing concept, one
that is not mentioned anywhere else in the entire Talmud. It is true that the
Gemara states (*Berachos* 17a), "If one does not [study Torah] for the sake of
Heaven, it would be better had he not been created." However, Tosafos explains that refers only to an individual whose sole intention is to provoke

others and not to arrive at the truth. Moreover, even this statement — "it would be better had he not been created" — is only theoretical. However, once he has, in fact, been created, he is not at liberty to neglect any mitzvah — and *chalilah v'chas* to say that if one is devoid of *yiras Shamayim*, it would be better that he not study at all!

LIMUD HATORAH

In order to understand this, we must first digress into a discussion about the mitzvah of *talmud Torah*. This mitzvah is comprised of two parts: *limud haTorah* (the actual study of Torah itself) and *yedi'as haTorah* (the mastery of Torah knowledge). The mitzvah of *limud haTorah* is based on the verse, "And you shall contemplate it (the Torah) day and night" (*Yehoshua* 1:8). The Rambam (*Hilchos Talmud Torah* 1:8, and codified into law by the *Tur* and *Shulchan Aruch*) states, "Every Jewish male is obligated to study Torah, as it says, 'And you shall contemplate it day and night.'" This aspect of the mitzvah is fulfilled by studying any area of Torah, including Tanach, Mishnah, Gemara, Halachah, and Aggadah — for all of them were given to Moshe at Sinai. The Nefesh HaChaim (4:6) elaborates on this. Despite the fact that a halachic ruling cannot be established from a verse or a *mishnah*, and certainly not from Aggadah, nevertheless, the study of these things is a fulfillment of the mitzvah.

YEDI'AS HATORAH

On the other hand, the second aspect in the mitzvah of *talmud Torah* — *yedi'as haTorah* — is to master Torah knowledge and concepts. We find this discussed in the Talmud (*Kiddushin* 30a, b): "Our Sages taught: 'And you shall teach them diligently'[1] (*Devarim* 6:7). This means that the words of Torah should be sharp in your mouth, so that if anyone asks you a question, do not reply hesitatingly, but rather answer him immediately. As it says, 'Say to wisdom: You are my sister' (*Mishlei* 7:4), 'Bind them on your fingers, inscribe them on the tablet of your heart' (ibid. 7:3), 'Like arrows in the hand of a warrior, so are the children of youth' (*Tehillim* 127:4), 'Sharp arrows of the

---

1   "*V'shinantam*," which means "to teach," but is also related to the root *shinun*, which means "sharp."

mighty' (ibid. 120:4), and 'Your arrows are sharp, nations fall beneath you' (ibid. 45:6)." Commenting on the Gemara's statement that "the words of Torah should be sharp in your mouth," Rashi writes, "Review them and fathom their depths, so that if someone inquires of you, you will not need to hesitate; rather, you will be able to answer immediately." On the verse "Say to wisdom: You are my sister," he comments, "You should be an expert in it [Torah knowledge] in the same way that [you know] your sister is forbidden to you."

FLUENCY AND SAGACITY

The foundation of this mitzvah [i.e., yedi'as haTorah] encompasses two aspects. The first is to acquire a fluency in all areas of the Torah, to the point where one's knowledge comes easily to mind and flows effortlessly from the mouth. The second is the ability to cultivate intellectual sagacity through Torah study, to sharpen and hone the intellect and make it straight and true. One will thereby be endowed with the capability to engage in exegetical Torah discussion and debate — the "war of Torah" — and to "uproot mountains" with his brilliance. These two aspects are referred to by Chazal as "Sinai" and "oker harim" respectively. They are expressed in the aforementioned passage in Kiddushin: "Inscribe them on the tablet of your heart" refers to fluent and comprehensive Torah knowledge, while "Your arrows are sharp" refers to intellectual acuity and acumen. Mastery of Torah knowledge and concepts can only be acquired through studying Gemara and the works of the halachic authorities. Additionally, one must make sure to structure the order in which he studies the various Talmudic tractates so that he achieves the desired result, for not all areas of study are of equal weight. Chazal themselves allude to this at the end of tractate Bava Basra (175b): "Rebbi Yishmael stated, 'One who desires to be wise should engage in the study of monetary law.' "

The objective of yedi'as haTorah is to know, with absolute clarity, all of the laws and judgments of the Torah — in other words, to know how to observe and fulfill the entire Torah and all of the mitzvos. Concerning this, the Rambam (Hilchos Talmud Torah 1:11, and codified into law by the Tur and

Shulchan Aruch) writes, "A person is obligated to divide his study time into thirds: a third devoted to the study of the Written Law; a third to the Oral Law; and a third devoted to understanding and comprehending a logical conclusion from a premise, extrapolating an unknown concept from a known one, comparing one concept to another, and understanding the exegetical principles through which the Torah is expounded. All this is until the point where he knows what the central principles are, and how to derive what is forbidden and what is permitted, as well as similar methods that originate from Sinaitic tradition. This [latter third] is what is referred to as 'Gemara.'"

HARA'AH

The more one endeavors to enhance his wisdom and become adept in these skills — fluency in Torah knowledge and mastery of intellectual acuity — the more he will comprehend the knowledge of Torah judgment that is necessary to determine practical halachah. Moreover, he will be able to employ his incisive logic to innovate new laws and reconcile conflicting opinions. The ultimate goal is to attain a high level of proficiency in *hara'ah* (making halachic rulings), so that one is qualified to render decisions — both for himself and others, as we saw above: "So that if anyone asks you a question, do not reply hesitantly, but rather answer him immediately."

KNOWLEDGE AND MITZVOS

Now, there are some *yirei Shamayim* who believe that scholarly excellence is essentially necessary only for one who wishes to render halachic rulings for the public. They assume that anyone else can serve Hashem and fulfill the mitzvos even without being a great Torah scholar. This attitude, however, is a gross error. In fact, any person — even a private individual — who wishes to go in the Almighty's ways and live a Torah lifestyle is subject to the following axiom: the more one increases his knowledge and wisdom, the better he will be able to fulfill the mitzvos in the most optimal fashion. Therefore, a person must have expertise in all areas of Torah knowledge. It is vital that he have a perceptive heart and penetrating mind so that he can observe and fulfill the Torah's precepts according to their true parameters. Further-more, this is true even concerning the laws in *Choshen Mishpat* and *Even HaEzer*[2] — a person must acquire a fluent knowledge of their practical application.[3]

Delving into the matter, we find that there are certain processes con-nected to the mitzvah of *yedi'as haTorah* that are unacceptable in the quest to fulfill the mitzvah of *limud haTorah*. Indeed, if utilized in connection with the latter, these same procedures are considered *bitul Torah* (a waste of precious study time)! For example, in order to fulfill the mitzvah of *yedi'as haTorah*, which concerns mental acuity, it is permitted to take the time to travel from city to city — even to far-off locations — to seek an outstanding mentor. This is because hearing the living Torah that flows from his lips, and learning his method of scholarship and analysis, are indispensable components in the cultivation of intellectual acumen. Likewise, according to the demands of his nature, a student can take time to rest and sleep, so that he can engage in in-depth thinking with a clear and lucid mind. As is self-evident, these steps are not relevant to the mitzvah of *limud haTorah*.

Likewise, the utilization of mental exercises and mind-sharpening tech-niques is only applicable regarding the intellectual ability of *yedi'as haTorah*. Interestingly, we find that Chazal permit a teacher to occasionally say an un-truth in class in order to sharpen his students' minds and prompt discussion amongst them. The Talmud gives an example of this (*Niddah* 45a): "Rebbi Akiva only said it in order to sharpen his students' minds." Obviously, this is not appropriate for the mitzvah of *limud haTorah* in and of itself.

Just as mitzvos in general have no specific relevance to *yiras Shamayim*, so, too, with the essential mitzvah of *limud haTorah*. Every minute one spends studying, he is fulfilling the positive commandment of "and you shall con-template it day and night," regardless of whether he has *yiras Shamayim* or not. In this respect, it is equal to all the other mitzvos, for example, shofar,

---

2   The sections of the *Shulchan Aruch* dealing with monetary law and marital and divorce law. There is a tendency for people to assume that only the *poskim* are required to achieve proficiency in these laws. Rav Yisrael stressed that this was a mistaken assumption, and that everyone needs to become proficient in them.

3   Rav Blazer notes that at this point that the Rav gave several examples to punctuate his point, but he did not record them.

sukkah, and *lulav*, the fulfillment of which is not dependent on *yiras Shamayim*.

YEDI'AS HATORAH REQUIRES YIRAS SHAMAYIM

On the other hand, *yedi'as haTorah* is quite different. The fulfillment of this mitzvah involves understanding, comprehending, and perfecting oneself in Torah wisdom. The foundation of this achievement is to know the laws of the Torah and to attain the level of expertise required to render halachic rulings, both in ritual and monetary law. It is vital that this scholarship be permeated with *yiras Shamayim*, for without this critical factor, one's wisdom can be a source of corruption and serve as a stumbling block for sin. Indeed, regarding one's own observance and the importance of *yiras Shamayim*, Chazal exhort us (*Shabbos* 31b): "Any person who has acquired Torah yet does not fear Heaven is like a treasurer who has been entrusted with the keys to the inner vault, but who does not possess the keys to the exterior door. How, then, shall he enter?" Rashi explains this in the following manner: "If a person fears Heaven, he will zealously observe and perform the commandments. However, if he has no fear, he will disregard his Torah knowledge." In light of this, if one does not make *yiras Shamayim* his "treasure," then his care in mitzvah observance will not be commensurate with his Torah knowledge, and his punishment will be exceedingly severe.

Moreover, *yiras Shamayim* is indispensable in rendering halachic decisions for the public, insuring that one toils to attain a proper understanding of any given halachah. Indeed, concerning a person who is devoid of *yiras Shamayim*, we read (*Avodah Zarah* 19a): "The verse states, 'For she has felled many victims' (*Mishlei* 7:26). This refers to a student who makes halachic rulings even though he has not reached a level of proficiency to do so." The Talmud similarly states that a halachic arbiter must genuinely fear giving legal rulings (*Sanhedrin* 7a): "A judge should always imagine that a sword rests between his thighs and that Gehinnom gapes below him." We thus see that a halachic authority must set the fear of Hashem before his eyes.

Likewise, the status of being a Rabbinic judge demands that one be crowned with sterling character traits and exalted virtues, so that he is free of any personal prejudice or bias. In the introduction to his work *Sefer Tevunah*, where at one point he discusses the search for truth, Rav Yisrael writes concerning this: "This is termed 'scientific determination' by secular scholars. The sages of Mussar refer to it as 'shedding of the physical,' meaning detachment of the intellectual facilities from the other forces within man. Without this, the inclination of the other powers within the soul will obstruct his recognition of the truth...and this inclination distorts, leading one on a crooked path."

MISTAKEN RULINGS

Even more than this, if a person has *yiras Shamayim*, it makes no difference to him whether he has already given a ruling or not [since his sole concern is to arrive at the truth]. As every person is bound to make an occasional mistake [a God-fearing person] should have no self-serving motivation to want to stand behind his [erroneous] ruling, and will have no compunction in retracting it, even if he has already issued it. Indeed, we find that our Sages were not embarrassed to recant their words and to publicly declare, "The ruling I made was mistaken" (*Shabbos* 63b).

As our master, Rav Yisrael, has said: "Who is more eminent amongst us than the pious genius, HaRav Zvi Hirsch Brodie, *zt"l*, the former head of the Salant Beis Din (Rabbinical Court)? On occasion, he would rule on the kashrus of a chicken, and the questioner would return home. Subsequently, he would pose a certain doubt about the ruling he made, and he would request that the chicken be brought back to him for a second look."

Without *yiras Shamayim* and a sterling character, a person may become gripped by numerous perversions and face stumbling blocks, for vested interest and personal prejudice can corrupt the intellect and cause one to stray down a distorted path. If he occasionally errs in a ruling, he will be too ashamed to retract it. Instead, he will stubbornly hold onto his conclusion and forcefully insist on its propriety. This is true not only of his official legal rulings, but even of his informal opinions — he will be unable to admit the truth.

The above-mentioned conduct constitutes a grievous sin, for the Torah is not man's that he can do with it as he pleases; it belongs entirely to the Almighty. All the effort a person exerts to render a particular decision or to comprehend a certain halachah is solely to know and fathom the Divine intent according to the Torah. It is vital to always remember that the Torah is an expression of His wisdom and His will. However, if one is mislead by personal bias, if he is inclined by an ulterior motive to rule or explain a particular halachah according to his own will, which he knows in his heart is false, then he is guilty of fabricating a "new Torah" from his own intellect. In doing so, he destroys the Torah's very foundations, God forbid. Similarly, if he does not have *yiras Shamayim* and a sterling character, he will be too embarrassed to consult with others concerning a particular ruling — even if they are greater than he is. He will also fail to be deliberate in passing judgment, and will not sufficiently exert himself until a matter is clear to him.

In summation, in order to fulfill the intended purpose of *yedi'as haTorah* — to know halachah with clarity, in order to rule for oneself and for others — it is absolutely essential that a person have *yiras Shamayim*. Without it, he could conceivably come to numerous perversions and countless blunders, and in so doing, destroy an entire world.

Let us also take note of the following distinction between *limud haTorah* and *yedi'as haTorah*. The mitzvah of *limud HaTorah*, which is the fulfillment of the verse "You shall contemplate it day and night," is accomplished as soon as one begins perusing a *sefer*. Every hour and every second that a person studies, he fulfills this positive commandment. However, such is not the case with the mitzvah of *yedi'as haTorah*. The fulfillment of the mitzvah "the words of Torah should be sharp in your mouth" is to perfect oneself in Torah wisdom. This requires both the acquisition of knowledge and the sharpening of the intellect, so that a person can competently engage in Talmudic discourse and debate, with wisdom, an understanding heart, and keen analytical ability. This goal is not attained in an hour or even in a few days. Rather, it requires consistent and unwavering effort over an extended period of time, and the desired goal is only achieved after many years of diligent toil. Therefore, the focus of study and effort in *yedi'as haTorah* is on the future. This is similar to a person who stores grain in a silo, intending to keep it there for an extended time. When the market price goes up, he will then sell it and realize a handsome profit. Likewise, one who toils in *yedi'as haTorah* gathers wisdom and stores knowledge. He continuously deposits his "grains of wisdom" in the storehouse of his mind, "until the end," when he obtains his goal (cf. *Daniel* 11:34).

We have already explained that there are many things that are permitted regarding the mitzvah of *yedi'as haTorah* which are inappropriate for *limud haTorah*, such as employing mental exercises and "wasting" significant amounts of time traveling from city to city. If a person makes *yiras Shamayim* his "treasure," then he will master his intended goal with perfection. For such a person, the above-mentioned steps and procedures are entirely appropriate. He will, therefore, rejoice over his efforts to fulfill the mitzvah of *yedi'as haTorah* and will declare, "Wisdom is my sister," ruling according to what the halachah truly is. However, if one does not have *yiras Shamayim*, then even if he knows how to engage in Talmudic debate and give halachic rulings, nevertheless, he has not attained the desired goal. His wisdom is likely to be a source of corruption and a stumbling block for sin, as we mentioned previously. If so, it was not appropriate for him to engage in mind-sharpening techniques and wasting travel time so that he might train himself to "uproot mountains" with his mental prowess. Not that he shouldn't have studied Torah altogether — would that he had spent all of his time immersed in Torah study! Rather, it would have been far preferable had he engaged solely in fulfilling the mitzvah of *limud haTorah*.

This, then, is the intention of Chazal's statement: "When a man is brought to face judgment, they ask him: 'Did you conduct yourself with honesty? Did you establish fixed times for daily Torah study? Did you engage in procreation? Did you hope for deliverance? Did you engage in the dialectics of wisdom? Did you extrapolate from one concept in order to understand another?' Yet even so, if 'yiras Shamayim is his treasure,' then all is well, but if not, not." They are not referring to the mitzvah of *limud haTorah* — "You shall contemplate it day and night" — for this mitzvah has no specific relevancy to *yiras Shamayim* in the same way that mitzvos in general have no specific relevancy to it. Rather, the questions "Did you engage in the dialects of wisdom? Did you extrapolate from one concept in order to understand another?" are connected to the mitzvah of *yedi'as haTorah*. Concerning this,

Rava concludes, "Yet even so, if *yiras Shamayim* is his treasure, then all is well, but if not, not." If *yiras Shamayim* is not a person's treasure, then he did not attain his goal; instead, his wisdom is a stumbling block for sin. Therefore, it would have been better had he not engaged in the pursuit of this aspect of *talmud Torah* at all.

With this in mind, we can understand that the parable we initially quoted is eminently proper for the point under consideration: "This may be likened to a man who says to his worker, 'Bring a bushel of wheat up to the attic for me.' He went and brought it up. He then asked him, 'Did you mix in a measure of preservative with it?' 'No,' he replied. He said to him, 'Then it would have been better had you not brought it up.' " When the man had wheat brought up to his attic, it was self-evident that he intended to store it there for a long time — either until the price rose, or for whatever other purpose he had in mind. However, when he discovered that it might become infested because there was no preservative, he said, "Then it would have been better had you not brought it up." It would have been preferable to eat it or sell it immediately than to let it spoil. The same is true concerning the mitzvah of *yedi'as haTorah*. Engaging in Talmudic exegesis and learning how to extrapolate one concept from another is comparable to storing grain for the future. However, if *yiras Hashem* is not one's treasure, then wisdom can be a source of corruption and a stumbling block for sin. Therefore, it would have been preferable had he not engaged in these pursuits, and not wasted any time "storing the grain in the silo." Rather, he should have just studied Torah continually on its most basic level, in order to fulfill the mitzvah of "You shall contemplate it day and night" — the purpose of which is attained immediately, as mentioned above.

Therefore, the questions put to a person on the Day of Judgment are ordered in a precise fashion. "Did you establish fixed times for Torah study?" — this refers to the mitzvah of *limud haTorah*. "Did you engage in the dialects of wisdom? Did you extrapolate from one concept in order to understand another?" — this refers to the mitzvah of *yedi'as haTorah*. Concerning these latter questions, Rava notes: "Yet even so, if *yiras Shamayim* is his treasure, then all is well, but if not, not."

TRANSLATOR'S SUMMARY OF LETTER TWENTY-SEVEN

1. The mitzvah of *talmud Torah* is comprised of two components: 1) *limud haTorah* (Torah study), and 2) *yedi'as haTorah* (mastery of Torah knowledge and scholarship).

2. In order to fulfill the mitzvah of *yedi'as haTorah* — to know halachah with clarity and how to rule on halachah — it is absolutely necessary that a person have *yiras Shamayim*.

3. *Yedi'as haTorah* requires consistent and unwavering effort over an extended period of time (i.e., many years).

4. If someone does not have *yiras Shamayim*, he should only learn *limud haTorah* and refrain from pursuing *yedi'as haTorah*.

LETTER TWENTY-EIGHT

HILLEL AND SHAMMAI

The spiritual level of Hillel was no greater than that of Shammai, and in the World of Truth, they sit side by side and enjoy together the radiance of the Shechinah.

TRANSCENDING ONE'S NATURAL CHARACTER

THE TALMUD (*Ta'anis* 25b) RELATES: "[Rebbi Eliezer once] descended before the ark [to lead the communal prayer service] and recited [the Amidah of] twenty-four blessings [enacted for fasts in times of drought] — but he was not answered. Rebbi Akiva then descended after him and exclaimed: 'Our Father, our King, we have no King but You! Our Father, our King, for Your sake, have mercy on us!' — and rain fell. [Upon seeing this,] the Rabbis then began whispering [about how Rebbi Akiva seemed to be greater than Rebbi Eliezer, for the former's prayer was answered, while the latter's was not]. A Heavenly voice then went forth and proclaimed: 'Not because this one [Rebbi Akiva] is greater than this one [Rebbi Eliezer] [was the former's prayer answered,] but because this one [Rebbi Akiva] transcends his natural character [by always forgiving other people's offences], whereas this one [Rebbi Eliezer] does not transcend his natural character.' "

This passage is absolutely astonishing! Isn't the virtue of "transcending one's natural character" sufficient in its own right to deem Rebbi Akiva greater than Rebbi Eliezer? The inestimable value of this precious virtue is well known, as Chazal teach in the following passage (*Rosh HaShanah* 17a): "Whoever transcends his natural character [by forgiving other people's offences] will have his transgressions overlooked, as it says, He pardons iniquity and overlooks transgression" (*Michah* 7:18). This being the case, how can we understand the Heavenly proclamation as not testifying that Rebbi Akiva was greater than Rebbi Eliezer?

OUR SAGES WERE ANGELS

We heard an answer from our holy teacher, the Admor, the "holy one of Israel." Chazal tell us (*Shabbos* 30b): "A person should always be humble like Hillel, and not stern like Shammai." The Talmud then recounts several incidents portraying Hillel's humility and Shammai's severity. Now, most people think Hillel's spiritual level was greater than Shammai's, for the virtues of humility and the defects of severity are well known, as is taught in many places throughout the Talmud. Therefore, people feel certain that Hillel's level is greater than that of Shammai. In reality, however, this is a flagrant error! It is true that the reason underlying Shammai's sternness seems difficult to understand. After all, we know that our outstanding Sages — both those of latter times and, all the more so, those of earlier generations — are literally likened to ministering angels. They fulfilled the entire Torah and perfected themselves in every virtuous character trait. If so, what impelled Shammai to act in a severe manner? Was it that he was stern by nature? Could it be that he lacked the ability to conquer his natural character traits and bend them to his will, to perfect the quality of humility within himself?

CORRECT PATH OF DIVINE SERVICE

The answer is that this issue of severity springs from a disagreement between Shammai and Hillel over the correct way to serve Hashem. Just as Shammai and Hillel disputed throughout the Torah over various halachic principles, so, too, they disagreed over the correct path of Divine service. Should one conduct himself in a humble fashion, or is it necessary to conduct oneself in a stern manner for the honor of the Torah? Shammai felt that the latter way was proper, while Hillel felt that the former one was, and each conducted himself according to his own view. However, had Shammai thought as Hillel did — that according to the Torah, it is necessary to conduct oneself with the trait of humility — then he would have been as humble as Hillel; and vice versa. Thus, their difference in conduct was due to an external factor — their respective opinions regarding the proper path of Divine worship — and not the result of an internal character flaw. Shammai ruled that for the honor of the Torah, a person must conduct himself sternly. On the other hand, Hillel ruled that one must conduct himself with humility. Each of them conducted himself according to his respective view, as we mentioned above.

YIBUM

In *Yevamos* (13a), the Talmud records a debate between Beis Shammai and Beis Hillel over whether it is permissible to perform *yibum* with a *tzaras ervah*.[1] Beis Shammai permits it whereas Beis Hillel forbids it. The Talmud states, "Shmuel said, 'Beis Shammai conducted themselves according to their own ruling.' " This means they allowed the *yavum* to perform *yibum* with a *tzaras ervah*. However, we rule that the law is in accordance with Beis Hillel. This means that if one performs *yibum* with a *tzaras ervah*, he violates the prohibition against marrying one's brother's wife, which incurs *kareis*

---

1   According to the Torah, when a man dies childless, his widow must marry one of his brothers in order to perpetuate the deceased's family line. This marriage is called *yibum*, or Leverite marriage. The prospective groom is referred to as a *yavum*, and the bride is called a *yevamah*. Either party can refuse to go through with the marriage, in which case a special ceremony called *chalitzah* — "release" — is performed. There are certain circumstances under which *yibum* cannot be performed, for example, if the widow and brother are forbidden to marry due to the prohibition against incest. In Torah law, polygamy is permissible, and it was not uncommon during Talmudic times. When a man had two wives, each was called in relation to the other a *tzarah* — a co-wife. Generally, the deceased's brother could perform *yibum* or *chalitzah* with either wife he chose (but not both), exempting the other from any further obligation. The case under consideration is when one of the deceased's (Reuven) co-wives (Sarah) is forbidden to marry Reuven's brother (Shimon) because of incest (*ervah*) — for example, if Shimon was already married to Sarah's sister, Rachel. On the one hand, the second co-wife (Rivkah) is permissible to Shimon in and of herself — that is, if Rivkah had been Reuven's only wife, it would have been permissible for Shimon to perform *yibum* with her. The question is whether or not the fact that Sarah is Rivkah's co-wife makes it forbidden for Shimon to perform *yibum* with Rivkah because of her status as a *tzaras ervah* — a co-wife of someone prohibited because of incest.

(spiritual excision), and makes the children *mamzeirim*. Of course, it is self-evident that when the disciples of Beis Shammai followed their own ruling and performed *yibum* with a *tzaras ervah*, they were not committing any transgression whatsoever. This is true to the point that they were not even viewed as having unintentionally transgressed a prohibition against incest.[2] The fact that Chazal ultimately ruled in accordance with Beis Hillel did not retroactively have a bearing on every member of Beis Shammai until that time, who had maintained that the halachah was in accordance with their opinion. Indeed, before Chazal issued their definitive ruling, the disciples of Beis Shammai were actually required by the Torah to conduct themselves according to their own view. As a result, not only did they not incur any liability whatsoever, but even more dramatically, they were even rewarded for their performance of *yibum* with a *tzaras ervah*! However, once Chazal ruled that the halachah is in accord with Beis Hillel in all cases, then whoever performs *yibum* in such a fashion will incur *kareis* — including the disciples of Beis Shammai.

HILLEL WAS NO GREATER THAN SHAMMAI

This idea also applies to the disagreement between Hillel and Shammai over the correct path of Divine service — whether to conduct oneself with severity, for the sake of the Torah's honor, or to conduct oneself with humility. Here as well, each one conducted himself according to his understanding of what the halachah was. That being the case, Shammai was rewarded for his severity just as Hillel was for his humility, because both of them were performing the Almighty's will. The spiritual level of Hillel was, thus, no greater than that of Shammai, and in the World of Truth, they sit side by side and enjoy together the radiance of the *Shechinah* — each in reward for his own conduct, according to his halachic view. Yet once Chazal ultimately ruled in accordance with Hillel and said, "Let a man always be humble as Hillel and not

---

2   There is a halachic concept that if one commits an act because he believes that it is permissible, while in fact it is not, he is considered to be an unintentional transgressor. While there is still a level of culpability in such a case, it is not as severe as that of a purposeful transgressor. Rav Yisrael is telling us here that Beis Shammai is not even considered as having transgressed on this lower level.

severe like Shammai," then whoever subsequently conducts himself in a severe fashion commits a great transgression.[3]

REBBI AKIVA WAS NOT GREATER THAN REBBI ELIEZER

With this idea, we can also understand why the Heavenly proclamation was not testimony that Rebbi Akiva was greater than Rebbi Eliezer. Can we realistically entertain the notion that Rebbi Eliezer was unable to transcend his natural character and bend it to his will? Obviously not! Rather, Rebbi Eliezer conducted himself as he did because, as is well known, he was a *Shamosi* (a student of Beis Shammai). Therefore, he ruled in accordance with Beis Shammai — that for the honor of the Torah, one needs to conduct himself with the trait of severity. Because of this, he did not transcend his natural characteristics. Rebbi Akiva, on the other hand, was a disciple of Beis Hillel. Accordingly he ruled according to that school's understanding — that a man needs to conduct himself with the trait of humility — and as a result, he transcended his natural characteristics. Thus, in reality, Rebbi Akiva was not greater than Rebbi Eliezer. Rather, each one conducted himself according to his own understanding of the halachah.

MEASURE FOR MEASURE

We are now left with one final point to explain. If Rebbi Akiva was in fact not greater than Rebbi Eliezer, then why was his prayer the one that was answered? What is the relevance of the fact that he transcended his character traits while Rebbi Eliezer did not? The explanation of this is as follows:

---

3   We have concluded that Shammai ruled that a rabbi should conduct himself with severity for the sake of the Torah's honor. This being so, we would expect that Shammai would relate to people in a formal and strict manner. However, the Mishnah (*Avos* 1:15) teaches: "Shammai says...receive everyone with a cheerful face." This warmth and friendliness contradicts our image of Shammai. Therefore, we must conclude that only when the honor of Torah was degraded did he act with strictness — for the sake of the Torah's honor. Hence, in general, when the honor of Torah was not at stake, he conducted himself with humility and warmth, exactly as Hillel. Their dispute, therefore, was only in situations where the honor of Torah was at stake. But in all of his other human interactions, Shammai "received everyone with a cheerful face."

We know that Hashem relates to us in a fashion that is *middah keneged middah* (measure for measure). As Chazal tell us (*Shabbos* 151b): "Anyone who shows mercy to others — Heaven will treat him mercifully." And similarly (*Rosh HaShanah* 17a): "Whoever transcends his natural character [by forgiving other people's offences] will have his transgressions overlooked." Now, to pray for the public's welfare, to entreat the Almighty to mercifully overlook people's transgressions and answer them, requires special merit. The best-qualified person for this task is one who himself transcends his nature and is forgiving of others. Measure for measure, his prayer will be received favorably, as we mentioned above.

THE WORTHY PRAYER

In this light, it was Rebbi Akiva, who followed Hillel's path and transcended his nature, whose prayer was answered — measure for measure. Yes, Rebbi Eliezer, who acted severely in the way of Shammai, would receive great reward for performing the Divine will according to his outlook. However, as a result of his halachic view, his prayer could not induce Heaven to overlook the people's transgressions. Therefore, he was not answered. This is what the Heavenly voice meant by its proclamation, "Not because this one is greater than this one; rather, because this one transcends his natural characteristics." Therefore, *middah keneged middah*, Rebbi Akiva was answered.

TRANSLATOR'S SUMMARY OF LETTER TWENTY-EIGHT

1. Hillel's level of spirituality and character is not greater than Shammai's.

2. Hillel and Shammai debated over the correct path of Divine service — whether to conduct oneself with strictness for the sake of the Torah's honor, or to conduct oneself with humility under all circumstances.

3. The source of Shammai's strictness was not a character flaw, but rather a chosen path of *hashkafah*.

4. The prayers for forgiveness of one who practices "forgive and forget" will be received favorably by Hashem — "measure for measure."

LETTER TWENTY-NINE

THE PARAMETER OF A MITZVAH

This letter is an excerpt from the introduction to the work Sefer Tevunah (a Torah journal published by Rav Yisrael), excluding the material that is specifically relevant to Sefer Tevunah.

WE READ IN *PIRKEI AVOS* (2:2): "All who exert themselves for the community should exert themselves for the sake of Heaven." [It is interesting that] the *mishnah* did not state: "All who exert themselves for the community should make their intentions for the sake of Heaven."

THE PURPOSE OF WISDOM

This [underlying difference between these two phraseologies] sheds light on a question raised by Tosafos on two seemingly contradictory passages in the Talmud. In *Berachos* (17a) we read: "The purpose of wisdom is [to engender] repentance and good deeds...as it says, 'The beginning of wisdom is the fear of Hashem, good understanding to all their [the mitzvos'] performers. His praise is everlasting' (*Tehillim* 111:10). It does not state 'to all performers,' rather 'to all their performers' — [implying] those who perform them for their [i.e., the mitzvos'] sake, and not for those who perform them for ulterior motives. If one performs them for ulterior motives, it would have been better had he not been created." On the other hand, in tractate *Pesachim* (50b) it states: "A man should always occupy himself with Torah and mitzvos even if his motives are not for the sake of Heaven, for through [performing mitzvos] for ulterior motives, he will come to [do them] for the sake of Heaven."[1]

EACH MITZVAH HAS PRECISE PARAMETERS

I would like to suggest an answer to their question. Each mitzvah has precise parameters that define the way it must be performed, as specified by the Talmud and the halachic authorities. If a mitzvah is performed in a manner that is not consistent with these parameters, then by definition, it is not a mitzvah.[2] As Chazal tell us (Yerushalmi, *Challah* 1:5 and cited by the Rosh in *Pesachim*, sec. 18): "The verse states, 'These are the mitzvos...' (*Vayikra* 27:34). This means that if they are done as commanded, it is a mitzvah; if not, it is not a mitzvah."

CORRUPTION OF A MITZVAH

Occasionally, the thrust of the [individual's] core proclivity[3] is so out of concert with the mitzvah's parameters that an intense conflict is created. If the force of the proclivity prevails and the mitzvah is performed according to it [i.e., the core proclivity] then it is not a mitzvah. For example, could it possibly enter one's mind to perform the mitzvah of the four species by using a stolen *lulav*, no matter how exceptional its beauty and quality? There is no doubt that such a person's punishment would be extraordinary, for he would thereby be annulling a positive commandment.

ACCURACY OF MITZVOS

This idea is somewhat implicit in the language of the aforementioned passage from the Talmud: " 'The beginning of wisdom is the fear of Hashem, good understanding to all their [the mitzvos'] performers. His praise is ever-

---

1   Tosafos offer their own resolution to this contradiction (*Berachos* 17a, under the heading *Ha'oseh*).

2   This must be qualified somewhat. In addition to their optimal fashion — "*lechatchilah*" — mitzvos can be performed in an ex post facto, inferior manner — "*bedi'eved*." The extent to which a mitzvah's execution deviates from its optimal performance determines whether it is *bedi'eved* or not even considered a mitzvah at all.

3   That is, an individual's personality bent and subjective interests.

lasting.' It does not state 'to all performers,' rather 'to all their performers' "
— in other words, a mitzvah must be executed according to its true and
proper parameters. "Those who perform them for their [i.e., the mitzvos']
sake" — this means that they perform the mitzvah within the same parameters as one whose intentions are for the sake of Heaven.[4] The central concern of a person who acts this way is to make sure that his mitzvah performance accurately reflects the mitzvah's parameters as specified by halachah.
The passage continues: "...and not for those who perform them for ulterior
motives" — meaning that the influence of his personal, opposing proclivities
causes him to distort the mitzvah. The more that a person compromises the
mitzvah by subjecting its performance to his own deviation, the further he is
removed from the aspect of *lishmah* (doing it for the sake of Heaven).

THE DISCIPLINE OF HALACHAH

However, when a person makes an ironclad rule, disciplining himself to
act according to the dictates of the laws, then all the winds in the world will
not budge him from his place. Even if his intention is not *l'shem Shamayim*, if
he steadily seeks to improve his actions and fortify his behavior, then the
force of his personal inclinations will be weakened. Since he prevails upon
himself to perform the mitzvah correctly even though its requirements are at
odds with his subjective desires and goals, he will eventually overcome his
proclivities. At that point, he will have reached the level of *lishmah*. This is
implied in the above quoted passage from *Maseches Pesachim*: "A man should
always occupy himself with Torah and mitzvos even if his motives are not for
the sake of Heaven, for through [performing mitzvos] for ulterior motives, he
will come to [do them] for the sake of Heaven."[5]

The same concept applies in dedicating oneself for the betterment of
the community — "All those who toil for the community should toil for the

---

4   [The verse only mentions performing and nothing about intentions. How, then, does the
    Talmud interpret the verse to mean that they do the mitzvos with the correct intentions?
    Chazal are teaching us that the mitzvah should be performed according to the same speci-
    fications as one who performs it for its own sake; in deed, not in thought. Therefore, the
    text is really saying: "They do the mitzvos according to the same specifications as one
    whose intentions are for the sake of Heaven."

5   Note that the emphasis in this passage is on the action, and not the intention.

sake of Heaven." Perhaps we can say that the *mishnah* is not burdening us with a requirement that our intentions be strictly *l'shem Shamayim*. Rather, it is telling us that our actions should be in keeping with those of one who toils for the sake of Heaven — without being influenced by our subjective interests. That is, our efforts on behalf of the community should be undertaken solely in accord with the dictates of Torah and halachah.

THE PARAMATERS OF TRUTH

Of greater concern to me is the quest to know the parameters of truth [whether in Torah study, character perfection, or toiling on behalf of the community]. When I am tending to my physical needs, thoughts flit through my mind like dreams. My mind wanders in a conscious stream of random ideas that have been gnawing on my thoughts. [In this dissertation,] I rely on the reader's critical review to purge my words of all falsehood, for if I have erred, critique will set me straight.

THE FOUNDATION OF TRUTH

On what foundation is the truth to be built [specifically, as regards the resolution of a Talmudic passage]? It is not established solely on the *pashtus* (straightforward meaning of a phrase's wording), for this constitutes merely one type of proof. Indeed, in most cases it is refuted by difficult questions that spring from initial working premises. [These assumptions] stand quite strongly bound together (and they cannot be easily disassembled. If the premise is so firmly based that it is irrefutable, then no proof can be brought against it — as the Ramban writes in the introduction to his work *Sefer Milchamos Hashem*), and stand poised to dispute the *pashtus* and repudiate it. We see this clearly in the words of the Talmud in the *okimtos* (presumptions) it offers to explain a particular passage,[6] as well as in the brilliant observations of the Ba'alei Tosafos.[7]

---

6   An *okimtah* is a way of explaining a case that does not deal with the words of the text, but rather reveals presumptions and stipulations that render it understandable. The text is understood in its basic meaning; however, the explanation qualifies it by clarifying an unstated assumption.

7   They employ incisive questions to prove that the text must be understood in a particular

Likewise, the truth is not supported by concise and innovative explanations that do not stray too far from the *pashtus*. Such ideas are built on premises that do not necessarily hold up to analysis, to the point that they do not contain even a scent of the truth. On the other hand, a more elaborate hypothesis might be based on a series of solid steps that logically link together, so that it homes in on the truth. Nevertheless, it requires extensive examination and inspection, since it is constructed from so many steps. In such a case, if even one step is disproved, then the whole structure might be placed in danger of collapsing.

Similarly, man's desire to search for the parameters of truth is not sufficient to build it; the reasoning of man's intellect does not necessarily gain access to its chambers. We see this clearly from a verse in *Mishlei* (2:4, 5): "If you seek it [as if it were] silver, if you search for it [as if it were] hidden treasures, then you will understand the fear of Hashem." (The *Yalkut Shemoni* explains that this verse is referring to the Torah, as is the beginning of the passage [ibid. 2:1]: "My son, if you take my words...") Consider the pursuit of wealth: the mere desire for it is not sufficient to guarantee a person's success; rather, he must engage in the preparations that are relevant to this pursuit. The same is true regarding the quest for Torah — and even more so. Concerning financial success, Divine assistance is the essential factor. On the other hand, in Torah study it is a person's preparation (whether on one's own, or with help from others) that constitutes the prime factor for success — only by laying the proper groundwork will the Divine splendor shine upon him.

We read that the Torah is "not in Heaven" (*Devarim* 30:12); rather, Hashem entrusted it to man's hands. Nevertheless, this does not mean that it is man's captive, to do with it as he wishes. Instead, he must approach it with intellectual honesty, employing the proper tools[8] that will help him achieve his goal — knowing the truth.

NATURAL ABILITY AND PURITY OF THOUGHT

In general, there are two axiomatic principles that pertain to the pursuit

---

way, one that differs from the *pashtus*.

8   As will be explained shortly.

of truth: natural ability and purity of thought. "Natural ability" refers to comprehensive knowledge of all the details relevant to a hypothesis formulation, as well as an extra dimension of sharp and true understanding, to erect a sturdy structure — like a mirror formed of cast metal (cf. *Iyov* 37:18) — then clarifying the truth after in-depth consideration of each and every side. "Purity of thought" is what secular scholars refer to as "scientific determination." The sages of Mussar refer to it as "shedding of the physical," meaning detachment of the intellectual facilities from the other forces that comprise a person's makeup. Without this, the inclination of the other powers within the soul will obstruct his recognition of the truth. Moreover, the capability of rendering a straight value judgment is impaired, and this inclination will lead one on a distorted path.

"Natural ability" springs from [a willingness to be influenced] by the incomprehensibly great understanding of our sages and wise men [i.e., to learn from the wisdom of those who have preceded us], as has been done in the days of Chazal and our ancient Sages of blessed memory. "Purity of thought" is manifest when one's [opposing] emotional forces are balanced equally on both sides of the scale, so that the intellect stands free from all bias.[9] After the requisite preparation is accomplished, then Hashem, the benevolent One, does not withhold any goodness from those who walk in purity (cf. *Divrei HaYamim* 30:18 and *Tehillim* 84:12), and He will fill their eyes with the light of the Torah.

Perhaps the following passage in the Talmud alludes to this (*Sotah* 22a): "The verse states, 'Fear Hashem, my child, and the king; do not mix with inconsistent people (*shonim*)' (*Mishlei* 24:21). Rebbi Yitzchak said, 'This refers to people who study (*shonei*) halachah.' "[10] Let us attempt to understand this. The Torah commands us to observe the statutes of an earthly king, even if we have never seen him and don't know who he is. As Chazal state (*Gittin* 10b), "The law of the government is tantamount to Torah law."[11] The reason for

---

9   One who has attained purity of thought balances his desire for victory with a sense of humility. Hence, he balances out his emotions in order to pursue pure truth.

10 Rashi explains that although they study halachah, they do not learn from *talmidei chachamim*. Therefore, they are not trained to develop their Torah thoughts based on the axiomatic principles of the Mishnah.

11 Meaning that we are bound to live by the laws of whatever country we find ourselves in,

this is because the tools the king has to arrive at the unadulterated truth —
natural ability [the talents of his staff and advisors] and purity of thought [his
devotion to his people] — are in the king's hands. As a result, he merits having Divine assistance. As the verse says, "The heart of the king is in the hand
of Hashem" (*Mishlei* 21:1). The same applies to *yiras Hashem*, which is a reference to the honest pursuit of Torah. (We see this from a passage in the Talmud, *Bava Basra* 16a, which quotes a verse from *Iyov* (15:4): "So, too, you
have undermined awe [*yirah*].")[12] The foundation of true and honest Torah
is ability and purity, and when a person has these, then the Almighty will
grant him Divine assistance. However, "with *shonim*" — those who study
halachah without Talmud[13] — "do not mix."

PILPUL

Just as halachah without Talmud is deficient, the *chachmei Mussar* similarly
felt that Torah students should be strongly discouraged from engaging in *pilpul*
[penetrating analysis of a halachic principles based on extremely fine logical dis-
tinctions], precisely because they opined that it deviates from the truth. In my
opinion, however, the exact opposite is the case! *Pilpul* is the great and mighty
foundation of the quest for truth, and without it, truth will almost certainly not
be established. This assertion is based on two rationales. First, the development
of a piercing and honest intellect is the main prerequisite (after establishing the
essential foundation of *bekius* — fluent and comprehensive Torah knowledge) in
advancing towards the truth. It is a crucial obligation to expand, sharpen, and
objectify the intellect — each person according to his ability. This is nearly impossible to accomplish by engaging in an aspect of truth — the *pashtus* — that is
constrained on every side.[14] On the other hand, by engaging in *pilpulistic*

---

as long as they do not conflict with the Torah.

12   The context of the verse is as follows: Iyov claimed that whether a person will be righ-
     teous or wicked is predetermined, and therefore the concepts of reward and punishment
     are irrelevant. His friends rebutted his assertion by telling him that *yiras Shamayim* em-
     powers man with the ability to change himself. On this, the Talmud comments: "The Al-
     mighty created the *yetzer hara*, and He created the Torah as an antidote for it," meaning
     that Torah study imparts fear, and it has tremendous ability to combat the *yetzer hara*.

13   That is, they have not developed intellectual ability based on apprenticeship to a knowl-
     edgeable and sagacious scholar.

contemplation, and by freeing one's mind of strictures, a person will embark on a pleasurable and beautiful journey that will illuminate his eyes and hone his intellect so that it will be sharp and true. Then, if this exercise is united with the expertise of *bekius*, it will be within his power (each person according to his ability) to discover the truth.

The second reason is based on a strong realization that was impressed upon me by the experiences of my youth, when I dedicated myself to study Mussar and learn its statutes.

> FOOTNOTE OF RAV YISRAEL: I was privileged to study under the tutelage of my teacher, HaRav Yosepf Zundel, who currently resides in Yerushalayim, may it speedily be rebuilt. To this very day, I do not even reach up to his ankles. On the one hand, he was a "ladder set earthward" (*Bereishis* 28:12) — occupied with thoughts of business in order to provide for himself, just as an ordinary layman is burdened by his pursuit of his livelihood. On the other hand, his head "reached heavenward" (ibid.) — thoroughly engrossed in providing for the needs of his soul. His central focus was the in-depth study needed for practical Torah observance. He studied the Talmud and its commentaries, the *Beis Yosef* [a commentary by Rav Yosef Karo on the *Tur*, a halachic compendium compiled by Rav Yaakov ben Asher; Rav Karo's authoritative work, the *Shulchan Aruch*, is based on the *Beis Yosef*], and the works of the major Achronim. His main emphasis was on the Vilna Gaon's *Bi'urei HaGra*. When studying a section of the *Shulchan Aruch* or a particular topic with the relevant commentaries, he envisioned it as if there was an actual case before him on which he needed to rule. He would ponder it deeply with a penetrating analysis, until it stood before him in complete clarity. Then he would review it numerous times, until he had a firm and solid grasp on it — as if it were neatly packaged

---

14 Because, as Rav Yisrael notes earlier, the *pashtus* is limited to the straightforward meaning of the words.

in a container (cf. *Yoma* 75). The foundation of all his study — of Tanach, Gemara, Midrash, and the *Zohar* — was the search for knowledge of practical application. Above all else was the intense effort he exerted to rectify and perfect his character traits and to fulfill the "duties of the heart." With these words, I have recounted just a small amount of this great man's virtues — in my estimation, he illuminates the entire world (cf. *Yeshayahu* 60:19). May Hashem lengthen his days and years, so that we all might take note of his words and follow in his ways.

At one point, I made a decision to force my *yetzer hara* (which urged me to show off my intellectual acumen to my peers) to totally abandon *pilpul*. I decided that I would look only to the truth (I was young, and did not know that the place of truth was as far from me as East is from West), according to where I imagined it to be: the *pashtus*, elegant brevity, and the desire to seek it out. While proceeding in this method, I engaged in a critical self-evaluation, and realized that the desire to demonstrate my mental capabilities had caused me to breach the boundary of the truth. I saw that my intellect had strayed, bending the truth to my desire — and that the "truth" was founded on my desire to demonstrate the power of my intellect![15] I, then, said to myself, it would be far better for me to permit myself to utilize *pilpul* without any doubts or fears (just as Chazal permitted it to help sharpen one's mental acuity), so that my mind would be free from captivity by the *yetzer hara*. This idea is so clear that it is difficult for me to believe that a person could otherwise maintain his intellectual integrity (with the exception of a few special individuals). Unless he grants himself unrestricted freedom to engage in *pilpul*, it is inconceivable that the desire to show off one's brilliance will not deceive him into believing that it [i.e., an untrue assertion] is a function of his pure intellect.

---

15 With striking honesty, Rav Yisrael admits that when he limited himself to learn according to the *pashtus*, he was still motivated to demonstrate his cleverness — and this caused him to "deviate from the truth." He concluded from this that man should allow himself to learn with *pilpul*, for that is a legitimate framework to innovate theories and arrange proofs. By allowing himself the opportunity to express his need to demonstrate his wisdom, his thinking process will be pure and straight.

THE SEARCH FOR TRUTH

In regards to this, even if the path to seeking the truth is not found, it is still incumbent upon every person to engage in Torah study. Moreover, permission is also granted to make halachic rulings even if one has not reached this exalted level [and does not have the "ability" and "purity" that bring Divine assistance]. Nevertheless, there is an unquestioning obligation on every Torah student — including a lay person who fixes set times for Torah study — to search for the truth as he would search for a buried treasure. And where is truth found (cf. *Iyov* 28:12)? [To seek it out,] must a person carry a sack of flour on his shoulder[16] and go to a great sage who has all of the attributes that are needed[17] to find the truth?

TRUTH AND CHARACTER RECTIFICATION

Now I will discuss one additional topic concerning truth as it relates to the development of character traits and their subdivisions. Here, objective truth is exceedingly difficult to find, for truth [as it relates to character traits] is based on commonly held ethical values, and differs greatly from that of pure intellectual thought. Purely intellectual concepts are defined by all in terms of true and false, free of emotional influences. [In contrast,] commonly held ethical values are defined in terms of good or evil, repulsive or pleasing — and even though the foundation of this understanding is also determined by the unencumbered intellect, with no interference from prejudices, nevertheless, the emotions still wield influence. [Therefore, when considering issues of *middos* development, the unencumbered intellect] must carefully restrain them [the emotions] so that they don't trespass the boundary of their worth [and assume undue prominence]. However, it is very likely that the influence of the emotions will cause the intellect to stray from its true course.

[Since *middos* relate to commonly held ethical values,] it is usual for a person to sway the truth towards an acquired desire [or value, which he absorbed from the surrounding culture. Unlike a purely intellectual subject,

---

16 That is, entirely renounce life in this world, forsaking every physical comfort and agreeing to live in penury.

17 "Ability" and "purity" that bring Divine aid.

one engaged in the analysis of ethical values is not instilled with] the natural desire which is planted in the heart of every upright man (one whose character traits are uncorrupted in his straightforward circumstances, whereby there is no issue of, nor is he supplanted or corrupted by, any outside influence.) [These natural desires of the upright man] are the primary foundations upon which the intellect builds syllogisms that are accurately configured.[18]

MIDDOS AND RHETORIC

Additionally, the language in matters of *middos* is different than the language of scholarship. In the intellectual realm, flowery speech and rhetoric is unacceptable.[19] However, the opposite is true concerning character traits; it is essentially impossible to present or explain them without expressing a rhetorical conceptualization — for the purpose of such language is to awaken emotional forces, which are dependent on *middos*. [Of course, there is a danger in this as well,] for the more a man is able to employ rhetorical language to correctly explain a concept, the greater potential there is for him to err by cloaking falsehood with the mantle of rhetoric. An effective strategy against this is to present one's proposition [to a number of people who are unfamiliar with it.] By "exposing part of his essay to the light of day," the public will review his words with sharp critique, [and he will be able] to polish and refine its every measure[20] ([constructive criticism] being a vital foundation for success in both physical and spiritual endeavors). Then it will be a beacon of truth for all who wish to seek it.[21]

---

18 As explained at length in Letter Thirty, a person who has attained the level of *tikun hamiddos* has transformed his nature so that his only desire is for righteousness and goodness. Hence, when an upright man is engaged in the purely intellectual realm, his thinking is instilled with his pure character traits. His internal purity provides a basis for him to build sound, logical constructions. In contrast, when engaged in the realm of *middos*, one cannot but help being influenced by his subjective values and emotions.

19 Because they virtually insure that an idea will be cloudy and obscure.

20 So that it sparkles with truth from all angles.

21 And any who hear it will be motivated to make their own *middos* shine.

CONSTANT VIGILANCE

There is yet another precious concept that I feel is important to discuss (according to my estimation), one that results from the unification of the disparate elements that comprise the work [*Sefer Tevunah*]. [Namely, I wish to explain the proper approach of] *middos* rectification and habituation for a sharp-minded youth (who, in general, needs careful supervision in all matters pertaining to character development, so that the force of his intellect does not bend his *middos* to his subjective desires) while he is still fresh (cf. *Iyov* 8:12) and untouched by the vicissitudes of time and circumstance (whatever situation he happens to be in.) [When a person is older and preoccupied with the burdens of life,] it is difficult for him to assimilate new ideas; all the more so, to habituate himself [to constantly engage in the pursuit of self-perfection]. Only in the days of his youth can he grasp new concepts in their fullness and discipline himself to attain an exceptional level of *middos* perfection — before the passage of time (places him in a situation where his heart and mind are distracted and not fully able to contemplate and oversee them).

[If he does so, then even when he is older, the knowledge and discipline he acquired while still young] will have struck a root that will always bear the fruit of success; namely, to conduct himself with the appropriate upright virtues, in just the right measure according to his disposition and situation.

Consider the following: The careful and precise study of military strategy renders potent and impressive results — yet in a time of war, it is virtually impossible to pursue it. The same is true of learning the wisdom of the tactics to battle and conquer one's *middos*, to bend and accustom them to follow an upright path. They must be studied and diligently implemented with precision while a person is still young [and has not yet faced spiritual conflict]. Even though when he is later "immersed in the sea of life," his *middos* will not function without flaw,[22] nevertheless, he will find the successful path. What

---

22 One must realize that with the march of time, his success will be somewhat tempered, even if only marginally. Although a person has absorbed the lessons of character improvement and is operating with the discipline of habit, nevertheless, when spiritually challenged, it is impossible to maintain the level of commitment he had while actually studying them.

might be a proper milieu to help one study and practice upright *middos*? This very work [*Sefer Tevunah*] provides a synthesis. There are few other similar works available, and those that do exist are not of the highest quality.

TRANSLATOR'S SUMMARY OF LETTER TWENTY-NINE

1. Every mitzvah has precise parameters as specified by the Sages. If a mitzvah is not performed in a manner that is consistent with these parameters, then it is not a mitzvah.

2. If a person makes an ironclad rule to discipline himself to act according to halachah, he will eventually overcome all of his proclivities.

3. There are two axiomatic principles that pertain to the pursuit of truth: 1) Natural ability — comprehensive knowledge of all details relevant to a hypothesis formulation and in-depth clarification of the truth; and 2) purity of thought — detachment of the intellectual faculties from the emotions.

4. Since *middos* relate to universally categorized ethical judgments, it is common for a person to sway the truth towards an acquired value.

LETTER THIRTY

HISPAILUS AND WISDOM: THE POWER OF CHANGE

Man was created to attain the purity of the avos, and every person has the power within himself to rectify all of the forces that are joined to his physical being.

1) THE PURIFICATION OF HUMAN NATURE

GOD IS IN YOUR MIDST

WE READ IN THE TORAH: "And Yehoshua said to the Childen of Israel, 'Come here and hear the words of Hashem, your God.' [And] Yehoshua said, 'Through this you will know that the Living God is in your midst'" (*Yehoshua* 3:9, 10).

The Midrash (*Bereishis Rabbah* 5:7) explains Yehoshua's words: "Rav Huna said, 'He (Yehoshua) stood them (*b'nei Yisrael*) between the two staves of the ark.' Rav Acha bar Chanina said, 'He leaned them [according to the commentaries, he stood them at an angle, which allowed him to fit more people in] between the two staves of the ark.' The Sages said, 'He compressed them between the two staves of the ark.' Yehoshua said to them, 'Through the fact that the two staves of the ark can contain you, you will know that the Divine Presence is amongst you,' as it is written, 'Yehoshua said, "Through this you will know that the Living God is in your midst.'"

HUMAN TEMPERAMENT

Before we begin to breathe life into this midrash (even if they [i.e., Chazal] did not intend this understanding, perhaps [through our efforts the midrash] will take on an additional dimension), we must have a brief and general discussion on the variations of the human temperament.

We find that some individuals have an [inherently] good temperament and naturally pleasant character traits. On the other hand, other people are just the opposite [i.e., they have a negative temperament]. Likewise, even concerning the particular person himself, sometimes his emotional tendencies are at odds with each other. Some of these proclivities proceed on an upright path (with no prompting or guidance), while others stray off on a crooked course. These forces can burst forth in destruction if they are not restrained by the power the intellect.

A person should not say, "What the Almighty propagated cannot be altered! He implanted a negative propensity within me, and I have no hope of uprooting it." Such is not the case, for the forces in a man's soul can be mastered and transformed!

A PERSON CAN TRANSFORM HIS NATURE

We see this with animals. Man has immense control over them, and can bind them with the force of his will so that they will neither harm nor destroy (cf. *Yeshayahu* 11:9). He can even tame them — change their natures and uproot evil from their temperaments. In a similar way, he has the ability to gain mastery over his *yetzer hara* so that it has no influence over his deeds. Indeed, through study and the force of habit, a person can actually transform his nature [from evil] to good. (One example of a work that gives guidelines in this area is *Cheshbon HaNefesh*.)

In reference to this, our Sages teach (*Avos* 4:1): "Who is strong? He who subdues his personal inclination, as it is said: 'He who is slow to anger is better than a strong man, and a master of his passions is better than a conqueror of a city' (*Mishlei* 16:32)." "Strength" is defined by the capability to vigorously stand up against one's opponent and forcefully prevail over him. "Conquering a city" means that the inhabitants of the city willingly and lov-

ingly submit themselves to the conqueror's rule; they do not find it difficult
to fulfill his commands, and they observe his directives with happiness and
joy.

PURIFICATION OF CHARACTER

In a similar vein, a person who subdues his *yetzer hara* is naught but the
gibor — one who galvanizes himself to restrain his desires. Doing so establishes him in the category of being "slow to anger" — when someone has a
fierce temper but restrains and suppresses it. Starting from this point, a person will eventually reach the level of being a "ruler over his spirit." Then, the
passion of his desire will be channeled to the jurisdiction of the objective intellect, so that he will love righteousness and not crave its opposite. The entire purpose of man's existence is to purge every negative trait and character
attribute from his heart. As long as he is not cleansed of their taint, then even
if he overcomes his *yetzer hara* in numerous instances, he will eventually fall
into their net (see *Sha'arei Kedushah* 1:3).[1]

THE SPIRITUALITY OF AVRAHAM

Purity was the special quality of Avraham Avinu, *a"h* — he rectified all
the internal forces that are part and parcel of the body. As the midrash states
(*Bereishis Rabbah* 46:3): "HaKadosh Baruch Hu said to Avraham, 'There is no
impurity within you save for the foreskin (*orlah*), remove it and eliminate
your blemish — "Walk before Me and be perfect" (*Bereishis* 17:1).' " Similarly, we read (*Bereishis Rabbah* 11:6), "Everything that came into being during the six days of Creation requires improvement — for example, the mustard seed needs to be sweetened...even man needs rectification."

> FOOTNOTE OF RAV YISRAEL: This idea clarifies the midrash
> (*Bereishis Rabbah* 30:10): "The verse states, 'Noach walked with
> God' (*Bereishis* 6:9). Rav Yehudah said: This may be likened to a

---

1   Even though here the sequence of change starts with *kivush* and then advances to *tikun*,
    this is not necessarily the preferred order of procedure. We will see in section 2 of this let-
    ter, Rav Yisrael teaches that the time of youth is the appropriate time for *tikun* and not
    kivush, whereas the older years is the appropriate time for *kivush*.

king who had two sons — one an adult and the other a child. To the child he said, 'Walk with me,' but to the adult he said, 'Come and walk before me.' Similarly, to Avraham, whose strength was great, [He said,] 'Walk before Me and be perfect' (*Bereishis* 17:1). However, to Noach, whose strength was weak, [the Torah says,] 'Noach walked with God.' "

Since Noach (according to his level) was not commanded concerning *bris milah*, he did not have the ability to achieve true rectification. Rather, the level he reached, with the help of Heaven, was that of subduing his evil inclination. As Chazal state (*Sukkah* 52b): "A person's [evil] inclination intensifies itself over him every day, and if not for the help of *HaKadosh Baruch Hu*, man would not be able to overcome it" (see the text). This is the meaning of the verse: "Noach walked with God." On the other hand, after Avraham removed his blemish (his foreskin), all the forces of his personality were rectified. Therefore, he was able to proceed on his own, to observe the way of Hashem "with heartfelt gladness, like one who walks with a flute" (*Yeshayahu* 30:29). This is the meaning of the verse, "Walk before Me."

Moreover, we read in *Tanna D'Bei Eliyahu* (25): "Therefore, I say that every member of the Jewish people is obligated to say, 'When will my deeds reach the level of those of my forefathers, Avraham, Yitzchak, and Yaakov?' "

These passages shed light on the following midrash (*Bereishis Rabbah* 46:1): "[The verse states (*Hoshea* 9:10),] 'I found Israel like grapes in the desert; like a ripe fruit on a fig tree in its beginning did I view your fathers.' Rebbi Yudan said: Just as the fig has no inedible portions save for its stem, and even this defect is neutralized with its removal, so did Hashem say to Avraham, 'There is no impurity within you save the *orlah*; remove it and eliminate your blemish.' "

We read further in the midrash (*Bereishis Rabbah* 1:4): "Six things preceded the creation of the world. Some of them were actually created, while others entered into [Hashem's] thoughts to be created.... The forefathers... entered into [Hashem's] thoughts. From where do we know this? As it says, 'I found Israel like grapes in the desert; like a ripe fruit on a fig tree in its beginning did I view your fathers'" (*Hoshea* 9:10). The explanation of this is as follows: It is known that concerning the performance of a deed, the cause precedes the effect. The effect (which is the purpose) develops from the causes that preceded it. On the other hand, the opposite is true concerning the mechanics of a thought — here, the effect precedes the cause. After the desired result is contemplated, the appropriate preparatory steps [i.e., causes] are taken to engender it.[2]

THE ADAM HASHALEIM

Now, we know that the underlying purpose of the world's creation is the *adam hashaleim* (the completed man), who fears Hashem and observes His commandments. As the Talmud states (*Shabbos* 30b), "What is the meaning of the verse 'Fear God and keep His commandments, for that is man's whole duty' (*Koheles* 12:13)? Rebbi Eliezer said, '*HaKadosh Baruch Hu* said: The entire universe was only created for the sake of this [type] of man.'" According to the passage we quoted above from the *Tanna D'Bei Eliyahu*, it is clear that the central purpose of the creation is for the exalted man who fulfills his obligation to rise to the level of the *avos*.

This is the intention of the midrash's statement: "The forefathers entered into [Hashem's] thoughts to be created." The purpose of the world's creation, as conceived in Hashem's thoughts (which preceded the cause, which was creation) is the level of completion reached by the *avos*.

This is also the meaning of the midrash: "I found Israel like grapes in the desert; like a ripe fruit on a fig tree in its beginning did I view your fathers." Said the midrash, "Rebbi Yudan said: Just as the fig has no inedible portions

---

2 For instance, concerning a deed: the planting of wheat is the cause that engenders the effect — the sprouting of the wheat. Sequentially, the cause precedes the result. However, concerning envisioning an idea, the result precedes the cause. For instance, an architect conceptualizes a palace, i.e., the result, and then implements the required steps to actualize his vision, i.e., the causes.

save for its stem, and even this defect is neutralized with its removal, so did Hashem say to Avraham, 'There is no impurity within you save the *orlah*; remove it and eliminate your blemish.' " Man was created for this purpose, and every person has the power within himself to rectify all of the forces that are joined to his physical being, except for the part of the body that Avraham was commanded to cut off.

However, in the process of rectification, one should not desist from subduing the *yetzer hara*, for even though he has uprooted the evil that was within him, a sullied spring still lurks within his subconscious, waiting to issue its waters (cf. *Mishlei* 25:26 and *Yirmiyahu* 6:7). All it needs is a single powerful stimulus to arouse it and cause it to burst forth from its hiding place and wreak destruction.[3] For example, consider one who has habituated himself to act patiently, so that when something is done against his will or to his detriment, he doesn't lose his temper in even the slightest degree. Nevertheless, if he does not delve down to the very foundations of forbearance, he cannot rest assured that he will maintain his equilibrium when confronted with a serious challenge. Being thrown into such a conflict will weigh upon him like a load of wet sand, and he will require an extra measure of fortitude to triumph over his desire — but he will be unaccustomed to the struggle.[4]

---

3   Above, Rav Yisrael mentioned two different stages of character perfection: being "slow to anger" — controlling one's urges through the dominion of the intellect — and "ruling over one's spirit" — actually transforming and sublimating them. He equates this level of purity with reaching the level of the *avos*. This person requires minimal effort to maintain spiritual harmony, because he has neutralized the inner conflict between his body and soul. Here the Rav cautions that even after one reaches this stage, he must still be on his guard. This is because even though the "ruler over his spirit" has achieved a more exalted level than one who is "slow to anger," the latter, nevertheless, maintains an advantage over him. Since his inner conflict between body and soul still rages within him, the one who is "slow to anger" requires enormous fortitude to restrain his *yetzer hara*. Therefore, he is accustomed to waging battle against his opponent. On the other hand, the "ruler over his spirit" has all but forgotten this conflict. As a result, if he is suddenly confronted with a test that requires great strength, he will very likely find himself helplessly weak. The Rav therefore cautions the "ruler over his spirit" to "keep in shape," in the event that he will be confronted with an unexpected trial.

4   True, he had once made conquering his anger a part of his nature. However, since considerable time has elapsed since he engaged in this struggle, his earlier habitude in this area has evanesced.

Who knows if it was not for just such a time as this that he attained the trait of valor [conqueror of the *yetzer hara*], which, without habitualization, is exceedingly difficult to acquire?

MASTERY OF MIDDOS

Accordingly, how virtuous it is for a man of upright character traits to elevate them to a sublime level of mastery, to accustom himself to forcefully transform his base traits, and to light a guiding candle for the "evil days" (*Koheles* 12:1) — so that when a trial materializes, the strong and virtuous pillars he labored to erect will not collapse, *chas v'shalom!*[5] On the other hand, it is undeniable that to constantly engage the trait of valor to conquer one's nature and to bear continual suffering and burden is overwhelming. Therefore, a person should seek out counsel and strategy on how to rectify his *middos* and emotions — whether a little or a lot — so that at the very least, [the possibility] of their corruption will be quite remote. Once he merits to rectify his *middos*, he will only need to invoke the trait of valorous opposition on an intermittent basis, at the time he is faced with an actual test — each person according to his circumstances and the condition of his soul.

BETWEEN MAN AND HIS FELLOW

This idea is the basis underlying a statement made in *Pirkei Avos* (4:2): "Flee from the sin."[6] This refers to the fact that every individual has different character traits. Therefore, each person must be extremely careful to determine which of his *middos* is most likely to ruin him. He must work methodically to rectify this negative trait, until its ways are foreign to him. The fundamental basis of rectification lies in the realm of matters that are between man and his fellow [and not matters between man and Hashem] — an area of

---

5   Rav Yisrael's intent here is that once a person has triumphed in rectifying a certain trait, he should not become complacent. Rather, he should continuously envision situations that he knows might test him in this area, and ponder how to overcome them. Then, when he is confronted with an actual test, he will not have lost his "edge" and will not risk seeing the edifice that he so carefully and painstakingly constructed collapse around him.

6   Instead of cautioning us to flee from sin in general, the *mishnah* speaks specifically: "the sin." What is "the sin" that is being referred to?

transgression which Yom Kippur does not atone for (see *Yoma* 85b). This concept is expressed in the verse "Let us fall into the hand of Hashem, for His mercies are abundant; but let me not fall into human hands" (*Shmuel II* 24:14).

"RULING OVER ONE'S SPIRIT" AND "PIETY"

The Rambam writes (*Shemonah Perakim* 6):

"Concerning the 'ruler over his spirit,'[7] the philosophers said that even though he performs good and noble deeds — [at the same time that] he does them he desires and is drawn to committing evil deeds. He conquers his *yetzer hara*...and performs the good acts, yet he is anguished and pained while performing them. The 'pious one,' however, is drawn in his actions after that which arouses his passion and yearning. He performs good deeds, desires them, and is drawn to them. The philosophers agree that the 'pious one' is worthier and more complete than the 'ruler over his spirit.' Nevertheless, they said that in many respects the 'ruler over his spirit' is similar to the 'pious one'.... Shlomo HaMelech, *a"h*, already taught similarly [concerning this distinction between the 'ruler over his spirit' and the 'pious one'], 'The soul of the evildoer desires evil' (*Mishlei* 21:10).

"Whereas the 'pious one' rejoices in the good deed, one who is not righteous is pained by its performance. This is the meaning of the verse 'The performance of justice is joy to the righteous, but destruction to propagators of iniquity' (ibid. 21:15). It thus appears that the words of our prophets are in accord with the statements of the philosophers [that "piety" is a more exalted level than "rulership"].

---

7   The Rambam agrees that there are two classifications of *middos* development: the first being control and the second being transformation. However, whereas Rav Yisrael refers to the former as "slow to anger" and the latter as "ruling over one's spirit," the Rambam refers to them as "ruling over one's spirit" and "piety," respectively.

THE ADVANTAGE OF THE RULER OVER HIS SPIRIT

"However, when we examine the words of the [Talmudic] Sages in this matter, we find that they consider one who desires and yearns to commit transgressions more worthy and complete than one who does not desire to commit them and is not pained at refraining from them.... Moreover, they charge that a person should have a longing for transgressions, to the point where they enjoin us not to say, 'By nature, I have no desire for this sin — even if the Torah did not forbid it.' As Chazal state (*Toras Kohanim, Parashas Kedoshim*): 'Rabban Shimon ben Gamliel said: A person should not say, "I could not possibly eat a combination of meat and milk." Rather [he should say], "I would very much like to eat a combination of meat and milk, but what can I do — my Father in Heaven decreed that it is forbidden to me." '

UNIVERSAL EVIL

"On a simple level of understanding, these two points of view (of the Sages and the philosophers) are in conflict with each another. In reality, however, both of them are true, and there is no disagreement whatsoever. The evil, about which the philosophers asserted 'the one who has no desire for it is more exalted than one who does [desire it] but overcomes his inclination,' is referring to universally recognized acts of evil — for example, murder, theft, robbery, cheating, a person harming someone who did not do him evil, repaying good with evil, disgracing one's parents, etc. It is concerning these prohibitions that Chazal state (*Yoma* 67b), 'Even had they not been written [in the Torah], they would be fitting to be written....' There is no doubt that the person who desires and yearns [to commit these iniquities] is surely lacking, and the noble soul has no desire whatsoever for any of these evils and is not discomfited by refraining from them.

RITUAL LAWS

"However, the things about which our Sages said, 'the one who subdues his [evil] inclination is more noble and his reward is greater' are the ritual laws (in other words, the ritual mitzvos that we heard at Har Sinai. If Hashem had not taught them at Sinai, logic would not have obligated us in their performance). And in truth, if not for the Torah, these things would not be considered evil at all. Because of this they [the Sages] said that a person needs to allow a love of these transgressions to remain in his heart, and only refrain from [committing] them because of the Torah. Examine the Sages' wisdom and the focus of their allegory: they did not say, 'Let a man not say, "It is impossible for me to murder, it is impossible for me to steal, it is impossible for me to lie." Rather, he should say, "I would very much like to murder, or steal, or lie, but what can I do — my Father in Heaven decreed that it is forbidden for me." ' Rather, all of the sins that the Sages instructed us to have a penchant for infringing are ritual laws: the prohibition against eating milk and meat, of wearing *sha'atnez*, etc."

UPROOT EVIL TRAITS

The Rambam's ruling does not conflict with our assertion that man is required to rectify all of his bodily drives [i.e., even those that conflict with the observation of ritual laws, about which the Rambam says one should maintain his desire to transgress]. The solution to the apparent contradiction is that there are two types of rectification. The first is that a person should transform his emotional forces and character traits for the good, until the power of evil is entirely uprooted from within him. In this area, it does not suffice to correct one's will in a general manner, to make oneself desire good and hate evil. Rather, a person must seek out the way to correct each individual character trait and emotional force. This aspect of rectification refers to the rational mitzvos that are between man and his fellow, as the Rambam, *zt"l*, mentioned above.

THE LOVE OF MITZVOS

The second type of rectification is that of the will in general: to love and observe Hashem's utterances concerning His mitzvos, and to seek to minimize the power of desire in every detail.[8] The goal in this area is to reach a point where the difference between "I would very much like to eat a combination of meat and milk [but I cannot because Hashem forbids it]" and "I could not possibly eat a combination of meat and milk" is basically only one of form and not substance; of intellect and not emotion.[9]

2) THE RECTIFICATION OF CHARACTER TRAITS

The most difficult aspect of rectification concerns the correction of one's character traits. A major principle in this area is that most positive traits are only relevant to a person as regards himself. However, in his conduct with his fellow, he is obligated to employ the opposite of the virtue that he maintains for himself. For example, to flee from honor is a precious quality. As Chazal state (*Avos* 4:28): "The desire for honor removes a man from the world." However, the reverse is true concerning others, as the Sages said (ibid. 4:1): "Who is honored? He who honors others." Similarly, abstinence,

---

8   In other words, one's duty is not to uproot his desire for eating a milk and meat combination, which is bad not because the human intellect tells us that it is intrinsically evil, but because the Torah forbade it. Rather, one should see to it that his love for fulfilling the Almighty's will is so great that it overshadows his desire for eating such a combination. Regarding every transgression in this category, one should seek out ways to increase his desire to follow Hashem's commandments. Thus, concerning sins that the intellect tells us are intrinsically evil, such as murder and stealing, one must bring himself to actually hate them. However, regarding ritual law, one must reach a state where he says, "How is it possible to desire this thing, if the Almighty forbade it!"

9   That is, the difference between "A," who naturally dislikes eating milk and meat, and "B," who only hates it because the Almighty commanded him so, is only theoretical and not practical — for in reality, both hate it: the one because of his personal taste and the other because of his desire to perform his Creator's will. Accordingly, we can understand Rabban Shimon ben Gamliel's adjuration as follows: "A person should not say, 'It is impossible for me to eat a combination of meat and milk because I find such a mixture repulsive.' Rather, he should say, 'I would like to, but what can I do? My Father in Heaven promulgated a decree, and because of this, it is repulsive to me, i.e., it is repulsive for me to transgress the Almighty's will.' "

which is a sublime quality found in spiritually elevated people, is only applicable to a person as regards himself. However, concerning the benefit and pleasure of others, one's obligation is to employ the opposite of this trait. For this, one must be willing to go out to the marketplaces and streets of the city to seek benefit for one's fellow — and all the more, that of the public at large. As Chazal state (*Devarim Rabbah* 11): "What is [the meaning of the verse,] 'Moshe, the man of God' (*Devarim* 33:1)? From his waist down he was a man, and from his waist up he was like God." As far as his own affairs were concerned, Moshe Rabbeinu was a "man of God" — holy and removed from all worldly pleasures. Nevertheless, in his relationship to the Jewish people he functioned as a human being, relating with sensitivity to the people who depended upon him for leadership.

This formula applies to the majority of character traits. The virtue that is required for oneself is the diametric opposite of that which one is required to exercise in relationship to others. This is particularly true concerning humility, which is the sublimest of all traits. A person is required to exercise it to the utmost degree. As Chazal state (*Sotah* 5a), "Rav Acha Bar Yaakov said, 'A Torah scholar should not have any arrogance whatsoever. Not part of it and not even a trace of it.' " The Rambam (*Hilchos Dei'os* 2:3) writes similarly in explaining the *mishnah* in *Pirkei Avos* (4:4): "Be exceedingly humble in spirit." On the other hand, one should not treat one's fellow with this trait and degrade his status in the name of humility, *chas v'chalilah*.

We find that this concept is given expression in the *Tosefta* (*Berachos*, ch. 4):[10] "Shaul merited kingship only because of humility, as the verse states, 'Lest my father forget the donkeys and worry about us' (*Shmuel I* 9:5)." He thus equated his servant with himself. [Continues the *tosefta*,] "With Shmuel, however, such was not the case, as it says, 'Your father has forgotten

---

10 "This *tosefta* (the *Tosefta* in general being a collection of statements by the Talmudic Sages which loosely parallels the Mishnah, and which is found at the back of every Talmudic *masechta*) is based on the following episode: Shortly before Shaul HaMelech was appointed king, he and a servant were searching for a lost herd of donkeys that belonged to Shaul's father. They searched for three days, but without success. Knowing that his father would be concerned at such a long absence, Shaul made a comment to the servant. At one point, they consulted with the prophet Shmuel, who appointed Shaul king, and then told him not to worry, that, in fact, the missing animals had been found.

about the donkeys and has begun to worry about you, saying, "What shall I do about my son?" ' (ibid. 10:2)." Concerning himself, Shaul employed the trait of humility, equating his servant to himself. Shmuel, however, was dealing with someone other than himself, and in regard to how one treats others, there is no room for humility whatsoever — could he compare Shaul to a servant? Therefore, Shmuel said that the central concern of Shaul's father was for his son, who was much more precious than a servant.

THE TRAIT AND ITS OPPOSITE

It is imperative that a person strive to attain this goal. Man must endeavor to acquire within his soul each character trait and its opposite. Even more, he must train himself so that at the time he needs to exercise a character trait relevant to himself, it will be awakened within him and its opposite forgotten. On the other hand, at a time when its opposite is required to be employed on behalf of his fellow, this opposing one should be awakened, and the foundation of the trait should be momentarily forgotten.

Let a person's heart not despair at the prospect of this concept, and let him not be astonished at it. Within the human temperament, we constantly see the manifestation of both a trait and its opposite. Man regularly employs both these opposing forces as a matter of course (with neither external stimulation nor prodding), and activates the trait most appropriate for the circumstances under which he finds himself — for example, regarding remembering and forgetting, and other similarly conflicting forces.

So, too, man has the capacity to expand the powers of his character traits and to naturally activate a given virtue or its opposite. As Chazal teach (Bereishis Rabbah 14:3): "Rav Tifdai said in the name of Rav Acha, 'Hashem reasoned: If I create him [man] from the celestial elements, he will live forever and not die; while if I create him from the terrestrial elements, he will die and not live [for eternity]. Therefore, I will create him from both elements; if he sins he will die, and if he does not sin, he will live [for eternity].' " Man was, thus, created with a makeup that allows him to rectify the forces within his soul. As far as he himself is concerned, he is crowned with all the character traits and virtues of the celestial beings, and he has the capability to separate himself from all worldly delights. As far as his relations with others, he is endowed with properties similar to the terrestrial forces. He senses and is aware of every worldly delight. He can, therefore, work on behalf of the public and interact with them in a way to which they can relate. As Chazal teach (*Kesubos* 17a): "The disposition of man should always be pleasant with people."

TIKUN HAMIDDOS IN TIME OF YOUTH

In general, when a person is young and has not yet faced life's tribulations, it is difficult for him to engage in subduing his negative character traits. In contrast, it is relatively easy for him to rectify them. This is alluded to in the *mishnah* (*Avos* 4:25): "One who studies [Torah] while [he is still] a child, to what can he be likened? — to ink written on fresh [clean] paper."[11] On the other hand, when one is older and more set in his ways, rectifying his *middos* is an onerous task. As the *mishnah* continues, "And one who studies [Torah] as an old man, to what can he be likened? — to ink written on smudged paper." Because of the vicissitudes of age, he is more set in his ways and his negative traits are more firmly embedded in his heart. Subduing his traits, however, is not so burdensome to him, since he is accustomed to the burden of pursuing a livelihood and fulfilling his needs and desires.

SUBDUE HIS MIDDOS IN HIS ELDERLY YEARS

This being so, the appropriate focus of Divine service varies according to one's stage in life. While in his youth, a person should concentrate on rectifying his *middos*, so that he can serve Hashem with ardor and happiness. As he grows older, his Divine service should focus on subduing them, which doesn't require such great fervor and desire. When a person becomes habituated to *middos* rectification during his youth, it prepares a path to help him subdue his *middos* when he becomes old (a time when there are numerous causes for provoking bad character traits, as we mentioned above).

This is the meaning of the verse "Train the youth according to his way"

---

11 The ink is easily absorbed but hard to remove. This portrays both the ease of character rectification and the difficulty of subduing the *yetzer hara* during one's youth.

(*Mishlei* 22:6). (Youth is an opportune time to eliminate the evil from within a person, as the verse states: "Foolishness is bound in the heart of a youth, but the rod of discipline will drive it far from him" [ibid. 22:15]. By dealing with it when one is young, the evil will not be a barrier that deters a person from achieving character rectification.) Then, even when he grows elderly, (although his ability to rectify his traits will not be as effective as when he was young, nevertheless,) the influence of his youth will not abandon him.[12] This idea is alluded to in *Koheles* (12:1): "So remember your Creator in the days of your youth, before the days of evil come." Chazal explain (*Shabbos* 151b) that the "days of evil" refer to the time of old age, the time about which a person will say, "I have no desire for them." Perhaps we can relate this concept to the following passage in the Talmud (*Shabbos* 63b): "Rav Huna said: What is the meaning of the verse, 'Rejoice, young man, in your childhood, let your heart cheer you in the days of your youth; follow the path of your heart and the sight of your eyes — but know that for all these things, God will call you to account' (*Koheles* 11:9)? [The first part of the verse,] up until [the words] 'but know that for all these things,' are the words of the *yetzer hara*; from then onwards are the words of the *yetzer tov*." As Chazal state elsewhere (*Berachos* 54a), "[You shall love Hashem, your God] with all your heart" (*Devarim* 6:5) — with both of your inclinations, the *yetzer tov* and the *yetzer hara*.[13]

THE INTELLECT IS THE YETZER TOV

We can explain this as follows: The Sages referred to the intellect as the *yetzer tov* and the other forces within a person's soul as the *yetzer hara* [see

---

12 For example, let us assume that during his youth a person was successfully able to remove anger from his heart. However, the vagaries of age provided a powerful stimulus that triggered a new dimension of rage and frustration within him. Since he has already rectified this trait, he still has the capability and moral sense to control his emotions, even though the control will now spring primarily from subduing the trait and not rectifying it. Thus, the training of his youth, in concert with the strength to subdue that comes with age, will enable him to overpower his anger, and he will not depart from the upright path.

13 Rav Yisrael is applying and equating the aspects of the *yetzer hara* and the *yetzer tov* as expressed in the verse from *Koheles*, to the concept in *Berachos* 54 of serving Hashem with both inclinations. His equation also includes the variation in method for a "young man" in contrast to an older person, in relationship to *middos* development. He will elaborate these concepts in the ensuing paragraphs.

Chovos HaLevavos, Sha'ar Avodas Elokim, in the debate between the intellect and the spirit]. The intellect is termed the "*yetzer tov*" because its modus operandi is to investigate the final result [of an act]. It does not set its eye on the short-term view, even though it might be a "delight to the eyes" (cf. *Bereishis* 3:6). Nor does it allow itself to be caught up in passions that are "sweet to the palate" (cf. *Shir HaShirim Rabbah* 2:12). Rather, it gazes off into the distance, to the ultimate consequence. If the final result is upright, then the intellect decides to embrace it from the outset. In contrast, the other forces within a person — "this is their way; folly is theirs," (*Tehillim* 49:14) — look only to short-term results and the immediate pleasures and gratification of a thing, even though its end will be bitter. Since "the Almighty brings all of a person's actions to judgment, whether good or evil" (cf. *Koheles* 12:14), the objective intellect determines to observe each of the Almighty's utterances. This clarity of thought is the *yetzer tov*. Conversely, man's bodily forces draw the sweetness of the moment into their net, even if this entails rebelling against Hashem. This shortsighted force is the *yetzer hara*.

When a person is in the state of subjugating his base traits and the desires of his spirit — which is accomplished by employing the overpowering force of the intellect — he is called "one who serves Hashem with his *yetzer tov*," i.e., with his intellect. When he is in the state of rectifying his character traits and the desires of his spirit, to the point where he wishes solely to fulfill the Divine will, he is called "one who serves Hashem with his *yetzer hara*," i.e., the forces of his soul that are essentially attuned to evil. This person, however, rectifies them, sweetening their bitterness and transforming them to good.[14] This, then, is the meaning of "to serve Hashem with both inclinations — the *yetzer hatov* and the *yetzer hara*." Divine service by employing the *yetzer hatov* is the subduing of one's

---

14 Passion for material pleasures is a natural human instinct. However, the person who rectifies his *yetzer hara* effectively purifies his *yetzer hara* so that it no longer desires material gratification. Yet the innate passion remains alive, albeit converted into a positive force. In the rectified soul, the passion and will is redirected to intensely desire and pursue good. The drive to do good and the actual doing of good fills the soul with joy and contentment. A man so elevated experiences exalted dimensions of spiritual excitement and happiness that extend infinitely beyond the physical pleasures. This, then, is the meaning of the first section of the verse — "Rejoice, young man" — which relates to serving Hashem with the *yetzer hara*.

middos, while employing the *yetzer hara* is the rectification of one's *middos*.

PASSION FOR GOOD

During his youth, the foundation of a person's development is the quest to fulfill the imperative of character rectification, so that the forces of his soul are attracted only to righteousness and integrity. When he achieves this, he will be truly happy, as the verses states, "Rejoice, young man, in your childhood ... follow the path of your heart and the sight of your eyes" (*Koheles* 11:9). This means utilizing the power of passion, which, by nature, seeks immediate gratification. This is the meaning of Chazal's explanation that the first half of the aforementioned verse [which enjoins us to rejoice and follow our heart's desire] is the *yetzer hara* speaking. In other words, this is a reference to a person's state when he is young — namely, to see to it that his *middos* are rectified and his deeds [mitzvos] are performed through his passions, which are called the *yetzer hara*.[15] From this point onward, as he be-

---

15 We learned above that one who follows his *yetzer hara* views the world through a short-term view that pursues immediate gratification, without consideration of the consequences of his act. We might have assumed that such a pleasure orientation perspective is corrupt and shallow, and therefore invalid. However, this is a false assumption. For Rav Yisrael teaches us here that even after a person ascends to the high level of character rectification, his sense of passion is just as intense as it was prior to the *tikun*. What has switched is the source of stimulation. Before his *tikun*, he was attracted to the bodily delights, whereas afterwards it is the spiritual delights that appeal to him. Hence the short-term view, the pursuit of "immediate gratification," is now activated for the spiritual pleasures. His purification has reached such an exalted level — the aspect of the *avos* — that he instinctively desires and delights in doing good. In other words, he no longer has to filter his deeds through an intellectual analysis, i.e., the *yetzer tov*, to determine the ultimate consequence of the deed. He will not have to look off to the distant future of how this deed will be judged before Hashem. Rather, since his heart is purified of desire for the bodily pleasures, and is permeated with a desire for the spiritual pleasures of Torah and mitzvos, he can "follow his heart." This is not to say that he does not need to analyze his deeds. He still must determine if what he wants to do is truly a mitzvah, and what priority it has over other mitzvos. Once he determines that it is a mitzvah, and now is its time, he will be filled with a passion to fulfill it and will quickly and joyously perform it, without having to motivate himself by reflecting on the ultimate reward and punishment. Apparently, when the Torah commands us not to "follow your heart," this is referring only to one who is sensually motivated. This distinction is supported by Rav Yisrael's explanation of the Chazal quoted above, which exhorts us to serve Hashem with both the

comes more set in his ways, his primary direction is to progress according to
the spirit of his intellect, which gazes to the distance. Through this, he will
subjugate his passions and know that "the Almighty will bring all these deeds
to judgment." These are the words of the *yetzer tov*, which is the province of
the intellect.

Of course, there are also exalted individuals who, even in their elderly
years, devote most of their energies to rectifying their *middos* and the
make-up of their spirits. They persist in this task until it even becomes easy
for them to bear the yoke of old age (which is extremely trying in most cases
due to the lack of rectification of *middos* and spiritual make-up) with regard
to both body and soul. However, if they are occasionally forced to resort to
middos suppression, it will be difficult for them. The difficulty is a consequence of not engaging in this aspect of *middos* control for a long period of
time (as we mentioned previously). [Therefore, even these sublime individuals should practice *middos* subjugation from time to time, so that it will be
available to serve them when they need it.]

THE BLESSING OF AVRAHAM

With this in mind, we are now in a position to understand the following
passage found in Chazal (*Bereishis Rabbah* 59:7): "[The verse says,] 'And
Hashem blessed Avraham with everything' (*Bereishis* 24:1). This means that
He granted him mastery over his *yetzer hara*." The Midrash states further
(*Bereishis Rabbah* 59:8): "[The verse says,] 'And Avraham said to his servant...
who controlled all that was his' (*Bereishis* 24:2). This means that he [his servant Eliezer] ruled over his *yetzer hara* just as he [Avraham] did." This is astonishing! How could Eliezer have attained the same level of perfection on
his own that came to Avraham by way of a blessing? According to what we
have said above, however, we can explain that Eliezer's mastery was in the

---

good and bad inclination, i.e., both hearts. Therefore, the definition of rectifying the
yetzer hara is 1) purification from the desire to follow the sensual drives, and 2) developing
the desire to serve Hashem. Rav Yisrael taught these two stages of rectification above,
when he explained the difference between rational mitzvos and ritual mitzvos in *tikun
hamiddos*. As far as rational mitzvos are concerned, the rectification involves the purging
the heart from all negative drives; whereas the rectification concerning the ritual mitzvos
involves the developing of the general will — to love to serve Hashem.

realm of *middos* subjugation [whereas Avraham mastered *middos* rectifica-
tion]. We see this from the continuation of the midrash (59:9): "[The verse
states,] 'The servant said to him, "Perhaps the woman shall not wish to follow me to this land; should I take your son [Yitzchak] back to the land from
which you departed?" ' (*Bereishis* 24:5). Concerning this, it is written, 'Canaan, the scales of deceit are in his hand, who loves to cheat' (*Hoshea* 12:8).
[Says the midrash,] 'Canaan,' this was Eliezer. 'The scales of deceit are in his
hand,' for he sat and weighed [considered] whether his daughter was fitting
or not fitting [as a wife for Yitzchak]. 'To cheat the beloved one' (ibid.)
[means] to cheat the most beloved one in the world, namely Yitzchak. He
said, 'Perhaps the maiden will not want...and I will give him my daughter.' "
One who has merited the virtue of *middos* rectification has nothing to do
with the *yetzer hara* and corrupt character traits, and he has no affinity for
them. However, someone who has only attained the level of *middos* subjugation is still subject to the desires of his *yetzer hara*, and he loves them — but,
nevertheless, resists them.

Moreover, even if one who has not attained *middos* rectification evaluates his path — in keeping with the verse: "Weigh the course of your foot,
and all your ways will be established" (*Mishlei* 4:26) — nevertheless, his every step is entangled with misjudgment. The reason for this is because the
forces of desire inject their poison into his intellectual faculties, blinding the
eyes of the wise (cf. *Shemos* 23:8 and *Devarim* 16:19).

THE SUPERIORITY OF MIDDOS RECTIFICTION

This is the meaning of the statement in the midrash, " 'The scales of deceit are in his hand,' for he sat and weighed whether his daughter was fitting
or not fitting." There is no doubt that Eliezer ruled over his *yetzer hara* and
would not allow himself to indiscriminately say something before "sitting
down and weighing" whether or not it was proper. Nevertheless, his "scales"
were "scales of deceit." Since he merely ruled over his *yetzer hara*, falsehood
— i.e., "deceit" — crowned him against his will (cf. *Tehillim* 8:6), and truth
still stood at a great distance from him (cf. *Yeshayahu* 59:14). Accordingly,
even though Eliezer had the same quantitative mastery of his *yetzer hara* as

did Avraham, qualitatively, Avraham's mastery was far superior. Avraham attained the level of *middos* rectification — and *middos* subjugation, i.e., the power of control, was quite accessible to him as well, having come to him in the form of a blessing.[16]

3) THE SECRET BLESSING OF HISPAILUS

TWO CATEGORIES OF RECTIFICATION

Indeed, there are two categories of rectifying the *yetzer hara*. The first is the rectification of one's emotional forces so that they desire only to do good, as dictated by the objective intellect (which is not corrupted nor bound by the forces of his body, which, for the most part are inclined towards evil). The second is the elevation of these forces to an exalted level, above and beyond the comprehension of human intelligence.[17] Virtually the entire foundation of the trait of humility (which, according to Rebbi Yehoshua Ben Levi, is the greatest of all virtues, as stated in *Avodah Zarah* 20b) is based on the aspect of rectification that transcends the human intellect.

---

16 "Avraham's level was such that even when facing the most intimidating test — a test which even a rectified trait would not be able to withstand — he was still able to subdue his *yetzer hara*. Such was not the case with Eliezer, however, who had not reached this stage of rectification. Apparently, the midrash teaches that Hashem blessed Avraham with mastery over the *yetzer hara*. Later in this letter, the Rav reveals the secret of how one can merit an aspect of this blessing — studying Mussar with *hispailus* brings a Divine blessing that transforms our nature. Apparently, this enhances and inculcates both rectification and subjugation.

17 In the first level, the rectified *middos* passionately follow the moral bidding of the human intellect. In the second one, they actually overpower the intellect, ascending to a higher state and achieving a level of righteousness that transcends the moral sense of the human intellect. Perhaps we can say that the Akeidah is an example of this. Hashem's command to Avraham to offer Yitzchak as a sacrifice contradicted the very essence of the Torah. Nevertheless, Avraham's devotion to Hashem transcended the capacity of his intellect to understand His ways. Avraham wholeheartedly trusted in Hashem, the source of all good, and totally submitted himself to performing the Divine will, even though his own, human intellect could not fathom its rationality. This concept is explained in Letter Twenty-three. Rav Yisrael now illustrates how humility is an example of this exalted level.

FOOTNOTE OF RAV YISRAEL: Refer to tractate *Derech Eretz Zuta*, chapter 2, where it states, "If you have done a lot of good, let it be in your eyes as if it were a little...and if others do a little good for you, consider it a lot. Do not say, 'Because of my good deeds'...and if you did a little bad, let it be in your eyes as if it were lot...and if others did a lot of bad to you, consider it as a little..." (see the text). Refer further to *Chovos HaLevavos* (*Sha'ar HaK'niah* 10): "One of the Sages was asked, 'How did you come to be accepted as the leader of the entire generation?' He replied, 'I never met a person in whom I did not perceive a virtue in which he was superior to me. If he was wiser than I was, I would say, "Because of his superior wisdom, he must revere Hashem more than I do." If he was inferior to me in wisdom, I would say, "On the day of judgment, he will be held less accountable than I, for my transgressions were committed with knowledge and intent, while his were committed unwittingly." If he was older than I was, I would say, "His merits must exceed mine, since he came into the world before me." If he was younger than me, I would say, "His iniquities are fewer than mine are." If he was equal to me in age and wisdom, I would say, "Perhaps his heart is more devoted to Hashem than mine, for I know of my own failings, but I do not know of his." If he was wealthier than I, I would say, "On account of his wealth, he is able to serve the Creator, perform acts of charity, and give to the poor in a greater measure than I." If he was less advantaged, I would say, "On account of his poverty, he is more humble and lowly in spirit than I am, and a better person than me." In this way, I always respected everybody and was humble towards them' " (see the text). This perspective does not comply with the dictates of the objective intellect, which looks towards every side of an issue and defines everything according to the sum total of its powers. Unlike the method taught here, the intellect does not focus on individual details, to either elevate or devalue a subject. These are ideas that are

exalted beyond human comprehension. Nevertheless, we are obligated to acquire the sublime virtue of humility.

THE HUMILITY OF MOSHE

For example,[18] the Torah (*Bamidbar* 12:3) attests that Moshe Rabbeinu
was, on one hand, "the humblest of all men" (this refers to humility toward
one's fellow, as the verse suggests). On the other hand, he was greater and
more exalted than any of his contemporaries.[19]

Moshe's humility is in accord with Talmudic principle (*Niddah* 30b):
"Even if the whole world calls you a *tzaddik*, you should view yourself as if you
are wicked." In truth, this concept is beyond human understanding. This being
the case, we might ask, what engendered Moshe's humility? Isn't man's ability
to grow spiritually dependent on his intellect (which distinguishes him from
the animals, which cannot rise above the imprint of their creation)? If so,
how can man transcend his intellect?[20]

INTELLECTUAL AND EMOTIONAL THOUGHT

In answer to this, let us say as follows: As is known, there are two modes
of speech and thought — intellectual and emotional.[21] Whereas the standards of intelligent thought are universal, the emotional responses of each
person are unique. Even two people in the same situation and of the same
character will react differently due to their distinct natures. (This variation
of temperament may be inherited from birth, or acquired through association

---

18 Here, we return to the discussion of humility.
19 The reader might well ask, if Moshe was the greatest person in his generation, how could
    he view himself with such profound humility? The answer is that this phenomenon was
    engendered by the level of rectification that transcends the intellect. Logic would say that
    his awareness of his unique level of spirituality should have given him cause to feel supe-
    rior to his peers — for, in fact, he was. Nevertheless, his *middos* rectification elevated him
    to a level of righteousness that transcended the scope of human understanding. As a re-
    sult, despite his awareness of his eminence, he had the deepest humility.
20 Since he knew, factually, that he was the greatest man, how could his logical mind agree
    to assess his worth as the least of all men?
21 For example, intellectual speech or thought is related to the study of mathematics, while
    emotional speech or thought is related to poetic expression.

with others, or by training and studying how to rectify one's character traits.) Moreover, even a single individual will be inconsistent in his emotional responses due to variations in his mood.[22]

FLUCTUATIONS IN EMOTIONAL RESPONSE

In fact, however, all the fluctuations in one's reactions are only illusory changes in his emotional response. (The responses are not valid truths in themselves; rather, the cause of fluctuation is a valid truth.)[23] All the more so, variant reactions are illusory when one's temperament is the same on two occasions, but the stimuli are different.[24]

---

22 This is an invaluable insight into mastering human relations. We naturally tend to view others' emotions and perceptions through our own eyes. Meaning, in general, we assume that other people feel and react the same as we do to the various events and situations of life. Rav Yisrael enlightens us that each person experiences every detail of existence in his unique way; and there is a wide spectrum of feelings and reactions that fluctuate amongst people. Moreover, feelings vary, even int he same person in the same circumstances. This knowledge significantly enhances our relations with others in the following way. By giving each person his "right to feel" his own set of emotions, we are in a better position to understand and relate to him. We realize that instead of imposing our feelings on others, we must first determine what they are feeling and experiencing. This communication — asking of others to disclose how they are feeling about the relevant issue — is the foundation of good relations. (We can also train ourselves to be more intuitive of others' feelings.) Only after we have shown them that we care to learn how they are feeling, can we begin to share with and relate to them. This sensitivity will enhance all of our relationships and broaden our capacity to understand ourselves.

23 We are defining truth as something that is constant under all circumstances. Therefore, emotional responses cannot be considered true because they are always in flux and subject to change when the same stimulus occurs under different conditions. In other words, in two distinct incidents, when the stimulus is the same but the mood is different, the reaction will vary. This is true whether we are considering two different people or even one person. For example, in the morning when a mother is rested, she responds happily to her crying baby's needs. However, in the evening, when she is exhausted from her exertions over the course of the day, she responds with frustration. Neither her happiness nor her frustration is true according to the definition offered above — something that is constant under all circumstances. Since there is no universal emotional response, we cannot define them as true. What is true is the cause behind the change in mood, but not the change in mood in and of itself.

THE UNVARYING TRUTH

On the other hand, the intellect remains constant at all times and is not dependent on variation of temperament or subject matter. Accordingly, if two people do not come to the same conclusion regarding a matter of logic (even though in the majority of cases, the dispute is generated from differences in temperament or outlook), we say that one of them is mistaken. Such is not the case, however, with the emotions. When two people experience different feelings about the same subject, both of their reactions are correct and valid, with the variance being due to the connection of the effect to its cause. (This is because the application of truth in the emotional realm is manifest in the relationship between cause and effect.)[25]

These criterion for truth apply to the individual [in the same way they apply to two people]. If, at two different times, a person's intellect is inconsistent regarding the same subject, we say definitively that he erred on one occasion (which is obvious upon comparing the contradictions and alterations between the two times). Such is not the case, however, regarding emotions. Here, differing responses to the same stimulus do not present an essential

---

24 In this case, in two different incidents when the mood is the same but the stimulus is different, the reaction will also vary. For example, if a man is in a good mood when Shabbos arrives, it will awaken him to greater happiness. However, when Tisha B'Av ensues, then even if he was in a good mood beforehand, the spirit of the day will awaken sorrow within him. Therefore, since his emotions are in concert with the circumstances under which he finds himself, they only appear to be either happy or sad. In reality, since the next stimulus will change his emotional state, his current one is only transitory and, therefore, not "true."

25 The initial stimulus evokes a subsequent feeling, which is true because it is the natural consequence of its provoking cause. For example, if someone enters a dangerous situation, he will be afraid. Since danger evokes fear, fear is the true, natural reaction to the circumstances. However, other people of a more courageous nature, when confronting the same danger, may experience no fear whatsoever. Both emotional reactions are valid emotional responses. However, in the intellectual realm, the truth must be proven. The thought processes that the mind goes through to reach a conclusion are fraught with error. Take, for example, a principle in physics. People originally thought that heavier objects fall faster than light ones, but when this commonly held "truth" was tested, it was found to be mistaken. Even though the initial assumption was engendered by a natural thought process, it was nevertheless false, for an intellectual truth must be true in reality as well. Emotional truth, however, derives solely from the true relationship between cause (the stimulant) and effect (the resultant emotion).

contradiction, for they are both true (the differences occurring only in the aspect of their causes. These can be either in temperament or in stimulus).

According to this, the intellectual, which is not subject to change or alteration, comes under the rubric of the permanent. In a case where one finds evidence or proof (each branch of wisdom according to its tenets of investigation) that alters an established intellectual principle, we term the mistaken notion illusory, and not intellectual, for the incorrect version is null and void.[26] Such is not the case with emotional response, which is transitory, according to the circumstances of the moment.

Perhaps this understanding is alluded to in the Talmud (*Shabbos* 10a): "Rava saw that Rav Hamnuna was extending the duration of his prayers. He [Rava] said to him: 'You are setting aside eternal life (Torah study) and involving yourself in temporal concerns!' " The truth of Torah is founded on pure logic, stripped of all desire and emotion (as was explained in the introduction to *Sefer Tevunah*, which I published in 5622 [see Letter Twenty-nine]). In contrast, prayer is based on the emotional arousal of the moment. As Chazal state (*Ta'anis* 2a): "[The verse says,] 'And serve Him with all your heart' (*Devarim* 11:13). What is the service of the heart? This refers to prayer." Hence, prayer is temporal, while Torah study is eternal and everlasting.

[Here we refer you to the Addendum to Letter Thirty, "Further Remarks by Rav Yisrael," p. 352. In the Hebrew edition of *Ohr Yisrael*, the addendum is located here in the text. However, although it relates to Letter Thirty, the section is somewhat tangential — in addition to being quite thorough and including a brilliant analysis of the debate between Beis Hillel and Beis Shammai and the utterance of the *bas kol*. We believe that by relocating these remarks at the end of the chapter, it will make it easier for the reader to grasp the structure of Letter Thirty, which is quite long, as well as highlight the outstanding scholarship of the remarks.]

---

26 Since the intellectual is constant, it must be that one of the two hypotheses is mistaken. Therefore, the incorrect one is not properly termed "intellectual." Rather, the correct one is given this term, while the mistaken one is called "illusory."

4) HISPAILUS AND TRANSFORMATION

THE INTELLECT AND THE EMOTIONS

The intellect functions to uncover the hidden-most secrets of wisdom. It stimulates man's knowledge and council (cf. *Mishlei* 1:4) to seek and inquire, and to clarify matters that are in doubt. The emotions serve to open the sealed chambers of the heart and to pour waters of understanding upon it; he begins to understand that which he already knows intellectually, but has not entered into the inner sanctum of his heart. Consequently, the study of improving one's character and purifying one's negative traits is different then that of all other areas of Torah study and wisdom. Concerning Torah study, knowledge and the knowledgeable person are two separate entities. Man's mere mastery of Torah knowledge suffices for him to acquire perfection and to conduct himself according to his clear and accessible Torah knowledge.[27] However, such is not the case with character rectification and the purification of negative emotional forces. The mere acquisition of knowledge does not help a person to conduct himself in an upright fashion. Rather, the principles he has learned must be inculcated within his heart — bound and joined to him so that they and he are united as one.

HISPAILUS

The special method of implanting the wisdom of Mussar within his heart is called *hispailus* [i.e., the conscious awakening of the heart through fervent recital of Mussar concepts]. The power of *hispailus* bequeaths a blessing to [change the nature of] man. Even after he ceases from actively employing this exercise, the blessing is neither diminished nor lost; rather, it leaves behind a subtle imprint that continues to inspire his spirit. By profuse engagement in *hispailus* (particularly at properly organized times, each person according to his situation and circumstances), the fruits of his efforts will increase and be intensified, and ultimately his temperament will be transformed for the better.

---

27 In other words, once a person has clear knowledge of halachic precepts, it is relatively simple for him to conduct himself according to his knowledge.

In light of this, we can explain the verse, "My child: If you accept My words and conceal My commandments within you" (*Mishlei* 2:1). It is known that the Torah is divided into two general categories. The first is the legal aspect — the commandments, statutes, and laws of Hashem. The second is the remainder of the Torah. The function of the latter is to draw the wisdom of character perfection and emotional purification from the hidden depths of the heart [see the beginning of *Iggeres HaMussar*], to the point where one's sole desire is to perform good — in the eyes of both Hashem and man.

The phrase "If you accept my words" corresponds to this second realm. Man pursues the study of these Mussar concepts as though procuring an acquisition, so that he and the wisdom are united as one. On the other hand, the words "and conceal My commandments within you" refers to the first realm. It is sufficient for man to merely know them — to hide them within himself (as we explained above).

THE INTENSITY OF THE HISPAILUS

[Like a river] that overflows its banks, the power and virtue of the intellect is that it surges expansively to explore and examine every facet of an issue. In contrast, the technique of *hispailus* is to focus all of one's energy on the particular emotion that the *hispailus* comes to address, until all other feelings are temporarily forgotten and extinguished. The magnitude of this response corresponds to the intensity of the *hispailus*.

The same is true concerning the subconscious mind and its hidden recesses in which the emotional forces are rooted. These are the sturdy hinges upon which revolve all a person's deeds and desires (as we explained above [see Letter Six]). The power of *hispailus* also affects the subconscious (even if the impression is virtually imperceptible), to reinforce a particular emotional force until all the other forces are pushed aside and nearly extinguished. (These forces will remain latent until such time that a spirit of arousal awakens them to emerge. They then become seen and known to him).

In light of this, we should not be surprised by someone who esteems himself better than his peers, despite the greatness of his flaws and the paucity of his character. The praise he received, for example, from his family members, served as an *hispailus* to magnify his sense of self-importance. As a result, the shame of his deficiencies was deflected and totally extinguished from his awareness.

ANALYSIS OF ARROGANCE

The innate desire to be better than one's fellow engenders a similarly corrupt effect. It serves as *hispailus* to see others in a negative light, and it intensifies one's proclivity to ignore the virtues of others. Consequently, he feels only admiration for himself and contempt for everyone else. In due course, conceit fills every chamber of his soul, without him realizing it.

In the same vein, man has a remarkable capacity to employ the force of *hispailus* to sense his own flaws, to the point where he can banish self-esteem from his heart and purge self-aggrandizement from his soul. The more he increases his *hispailus* to focus on his insufficiencies, the more he will disregard the sense of his own worthiness. This is the law of the process to acquire humility, and this is its general constitution (cf. *Vayikra* 11:41).

HISPAILUS AND HUMILITY

In light of this, we can explain the passage in the Talmud (*Berachos* 32b): "[The verse states:] 'Can a woman forget her baby (*ulah*)?' (*Yeshayahu* 49:15). [The meaning of this is as follows:] *HaKadosh Baruch Hu* said [to Israel], 'Can I possibly forget the sacrifices [*olos* — from the singular *oleh*, similar to *ulah*] of rams and the firstborn animals that you offered to Me in the wilderness?' She [Israel] responded, 'Master of the Universe, since there is no forgetfulness before the Throne of Your Glory, perhaps You will not forget the sin of the [golden] calf?' He replied, 'These also will be forgotten.' "

We know that Hashem conducts Himself with the attribute of *middah keneged middah*. (Although it may not appear to be so on a superficial level, intellectually, we know this to be true.) Thus, when a person embraces the path of righteousness, examining his conduct and working on himself to disregard his virtues, then Hashem too, as it were, acts with lovingkindness and "forgets" his shortcomings. Moreover, the righteousness of [the person's] good deeds are recalled before Him, since the person remembers his lowliness.

This is the intention of Chazal's interpretation of the verse, "Can a woman forget her baby?" When the Jewish people forget the sacrifices of the rams that they offered in the wilderness (their forgetting resulting from the *hispailus* that they employ to remember the sin of the golden calf), then "These also will be forgotten." In other words, Hashem, as it were, forgets the sin of the golden calf and remembers the sacrifices.[28] It was in reference to this that Hashem said: "Can I possibly forget the sacrifices of the rams and the firstborn animals that you offered to Me in the wilderness?"

THE SANCTIFICATION OF CHARACTER TRAITS

This idea applies to the rectification of every character trait. If a person utilizes the procedure of studying Mussar with *hispailus*, it will bequeath a lasting blessing within his spirit (as mentioned above). Eventually (through abundant study and by methodically conducting himself according to the principles he has learned), the inspiration of the *hispailus* will be implanted within the inner recesses of his heart, and its effect will be intensified. In due course, the Mussar will become a part of his very being; by continually conducting himself according to the principles he has learned, it will be steadfastly established within him — like a stake set firmly in the earth (as the Rambam explains in *Hilchos Dei'os* 1:7). At that point, there will be no bounds to the sanctification of his character traits, and they will be elevated to a level above and beyond the comprehension of human intelligence. This is analogous to the other natural components within a person's temperament that are not encompassed by the intellect. With this, a person's spirit will ascend to exalted heights.

Likewise, it may plunge downward, *chas v'shalom*, until he does not realize his own evil. This occurs when a person engages in frequent *hispailus* of physical gratification, which implants a root of corruption in his soul. In light of this, when man reflects on his desire to live (a life of the intellect, because all living creatures feel),[29] let him study and repeatedly review Talmudic dic-

---

28 The Jewish people deliberately engaged in *hispailus* in order to remember the disgrace of the sin of the golden calf. As a result, they forgot their meritorious deeds. In response, Hashem, in His lovingkindness, reciprocates by forgetting their sin and remembering their merits.

29 A man who is truly alive feels his lackings and is aware of his transgressions.

tums that speak about character perfection and eternal life, so that his heart might be awakened [to realize his shortcomings].

A BLESSING WITHIN HIS SPIRIT

When a person engages in *hispailus* and feels that it has left no imprint on his heart, let him not fall into despair. Rather, he should know with certainty that his efforts have not been in vain. Although he may not sense it, a blessing was implanted within his spirit. With abundant *hispailus*, it will strike a root that will ultimately bring forth righteous fruit. This may be likened to water dripping on a stone for days and years on end. Eventually, the stone will be worn away — even though the first drop had no perceptible effect. So it is with "pouring" Chazal's words upon a heart of stone: if a person delves intensively into them, they will eventually penetrate his heart.

Perhaps this concept is alluded to in Chazal's statement (*Avos D'Rebbi Nosson*, ch. 6): "How did Rebbi Akiva begin [in his Torah studies]? It is told that at the age of forty, he had learned no Torah whatsoever. Once, while standing next to a well, he queried: 'Who chiseled this stone?' They responded to him: 'The water that continuously falls on it every day.' They said to him [further]: 'Akiva, aren't you aware of the verse, "Stones are worn away by water"? (*Iyov* 14:19).' Immediately, Rebbi Akiva applied a *kal v'chomer* [an exegetical method wherein a conclusion is inferred from a weaker situation to a stronger one] to himself: 'If that which is soft wears away that which is hard, then all the more so, the words of Torah, which are as hard as iron, will penetrate my heart, which is flesh and blood!' Immediately, he returned to study Torah...."

In his initial period of study, Rebbi Akiva did not experience any spiritual stirring within his soul. This struck at his heart, and he said in despair, "My labor is in vain (for, as it says in *Pirkei Avos* 3:17: "If there is no fear of Hashem, there is no wisdom"), and I am foolishly expending my energies (*chas v'chalilah!*)." However, when he saw that water has the power to carve stone, even though its effect is not immediately apparent, his soul was invigorated and he was gripped with determination — for "The end of a matter is better than its beginning" (*Koheles* 7:8).

5) SENSITIVITY

MAN'S HEART SHOULD TREMBLE

How man's heart should tremble, and how he should be overwhelmed with fear, when he considers that perhaps, *chas v'shalom*, he is out of touch with his heart's innermost thoughts and that his feelings have become desensitized! This is true even if there is just a single area in which he has not done *teshuvah*, for it is known in Heaven that he is in the category of "one who does not repent." In such a case, he would be liable for death, *chas v'shalom*. As Chazal teach (*Yalkut Yechezkel* 18): "They asked Prophecy, 'What is a sinner's punishment?' She replied to them, 'The one who sins shall die' … They asked *HaKadosh Baruch Hu*, 'What is a sinner's punishment?' He replied to them, 'Let him repent, and he will be granted atonement.' " Similarly, we find in the Talmud (*Niddah* 70b): "One verse states, 'For I do not desire the death of one who should die' (*Yechezkel* 18:32), while another verse states, 'For Hashem desired to kill them' (*Shmuel I* 2:25). [What is the resolution?] Here [the first verse] they are repenting, whereas there [the second verse], they are not repenting."

A VIRTUOUS LIFE

Those who have endured the vicissitudes of time and are preoccupied [with the burden of pursuing a livelihood] are especially prone to unknowingly commit grave transgressions. This is particularly true concerning transgressions between man and his fellow, such as jealousy, hatred, *lashon hara*, embarrassing others, and, worst of all, engaging in deceitful business practices. Therefore, if a person hopes to merit a virtuous life, he must act in a fair and upright fashion, and amass mitzvos and good deeds in order to counterbalance his many transgressions.

THE BOOK OF LIFE

Yet, what can a person do when he must face life's vagaries each and every day? It requires just a simple skill. It requires neither clarity of mind nor a lengthy commitment of time. Let him repeat the Mussar teachings of Chazal several times, until the *hispailus* is momentarily awakened in his soul. And even if it does not initially stir him to improve his ways, he is still considered as being inscribed in the Book of Life! Since he is alive with feeling [the desire to change], he fulfills the verse "For he who is attached to all the living has hope" (*Koheles* 9:4), and he is numbered amongst those who repent.

HASHEM DESIRES REPENTANCE

This idea sheds light on the following verses (*Yechezkel* 33:8–11): "When I say [to the prophet to tell] to the wicked, 'O wicked man, you shall surely die,' and you [the prophet] do not speak to warn the wicked man concerning his path, he is wicked: he shall die in his iniquity — but his blood I will demand of your hand. And you, if you warn the wicked one concerning his path to turn from it, but he does not turn from his way — he shall die of his iniquity, and you will have saved your soul. Therefore, O son of man, say to the House of Israel: Thus you have spoken, saying, 'Our sins and iniquities are upon us, and we are wasting away because of them; how can we live?' Say to them: 'As I live, says the Lord God, I do not desire the death of the wicked, but that the wicked one return from his path and live. Repent, repent from your evil ways, for why should you die, O House of Israel?' "

TWO FACTORS OF PUNISHMENT

We find that punishment for sin hinges on two factors. The first is termed: "His measure is full," as Chazal teach (*Sotah* 9a): "*HaKadosh Baruch Hu* does not exact punishment from a man until his measure is full."[30] At that point, he is considered a wicked man before Hashem. As the Ran comments (*Rosh HaShanah* 16b) on the statement "Three books are opened...the wicked...," "wicked" refers to one's liability in one particular judgment (see the text).[31] The second factor regards one who has committed a transgression such that the Heavenly court has deemed him "one who does not repent." This determination is made according to the faculty of human intel-

---

30 When the measure of his sins exceeds a certain quantity or quality, he is punished.

31 According to the Ran, if he is liable in one particular sin beyond a certain measure — this constitutes "his measure is full" and he is punished.

lect, according to a cause and effect relationship.[32]

NATURAL FORCES AND UNNATURAL FORCES

This is so because everything that occurs in this world falls under two general categories. The first is the realm of natural forces, which are apprehensible to the human intellect. Here, each effect is generated by its cause, and that cause itself is the effect of a previous one, etc., until the entity emerges. The second category is the effect that comes without previous cause. (It exists solely because of the Almighty's decree. This is also true of miracles, which are beyond human comprehension.)

ABSOLUTE KNOWLEDGE AND HUMAN INTELLIGENCE

In a similar vein, there are two types of knowledge. The first is absolute knowledge, which is subject to neither change nor alteration. The second is knowledge that is the product of human intelligence and deductive reasoning. Such knowledge is achieved by following a sequence of precipitants and results[33] until one arrives at the final result. This knowledge is subject to alteration, because sometimes a result is generated without a precipitant or even from a precipitant that is counter-intuitive and in opposition to the result (something we refer to as an aspect of the miraculous). The first category — that of absolute knowledge — is beyond the bounds of human comprehension (unless through the agency of prophecy). Additionally, man falls short in his ability to arrive at a result even in the second category, due to his lack of knowledge of the myriad causes that will contribute to its consummation. Accordingly, we see that human understanding is too feeble to achieve perfect knowledge of something.[34]

---

32 This judgment is not based on Hashem's knowledge of the future. Rather, He judges a person based on the perspective of the human intellect, taking into consideration his spiritual condition and determining that there is no cause that will stir him to repent.

33 Suppose, for instance, you see a rich man talking to a poor man. You think to yourself: If a poor man is speaking to a rich man, it must be that he is asking to borrow money. When the rich man takes money from his wallet and gives it to the poor man, you see that as a proof for your theory that a loan is being negotiated.

34 Revisiting our story with the rich man and the poor man, let's look at the real facts. The rich man sits next to the poor man in shul. One morning, the rich man forgot his wallet

FREE WILL

Free will — man's quandary over whether to pursue good or evil — is also comprised of two categories. The first is the free choice of the intellect, wherein a person considers the effect that will result from any given cause. In a situation where he is drawn to evil — for example, if he is tempted with lust — he considers the consequence of his action. Similarly, if he is drawn to good — to conduct himself according to the ways of the Torah and the wisdom of Mussar — he looks to the consequence of his deeds. The second [category of free will] is that of man's simple and intuitive sense of good and evil, wherein a person makes an impulsive decision without calculation or consideration. In this realm, even one who has sunken to the depths of evil can choose to do good, or an outstandingly righteous person can choose to perpetrate evil, *chas v'shalom* — something that is unlikely when a person views things through the lens of the intellect. At all times and at every moment he retains his ability to choose, with nothing to restrain him.

THE FOREKNOWLEDGE OF HASHEM

Additionally, the Almighty's foreknowledge of what a person will choose is divided into two types. The first is absolute knowledge,[35] something that is beyond man's ability to fathom why it does not contradict the notion of free will (as the Rambam explains in *Hilchos Teshuvah* 5:5). The second is His extrapolative knowledge of what a man will choose based on an evaluation of the man's conduct, nature, and affairs. This is an intellectual extrapolation — albeit Divinely precise — of whether a person will be good or evil in the future, based on his actions in the present. It is with this latter type of knowledge that Hashem rules His world in order to bestow good. (That is, specifically to bestow good and not to render punishment, for the Almighty only judges a person according to his current status, as explained in the Talmud [Yerushalmi, *Rosh HaShanah* 1:3]. If he is good now, then Hashem will

---

and wanted to give some charity. The poor man sitting next to him realized his plight and lent him five dollars. The interaction that you witnessed today was not the poor man borrowing money; rather, it was the rich man returning that debt to the poor man.

35 Hashem knows with complete certainty everything that a person will do and what the outcome will be.

extend His blessing "on credit," even if He knows that the person will turn to evil in the future. Chazal discuss this idea in *Yalkut Iyov* 41, where it states, "[The Almighty said to Iyov,] 'Who preceded Me that I should reward him?' " (*Iyov* 41:3). [The meaning of this is as follows:] Can one perform *bris milah* before My having given him a son?[36] Can a person tie *tzitzis* before My having given him a garment?...)

THE BLESSING AND THE CURSE

This understanding sheds light on the following verses (*Devarim* 11:26–27): "Behold, I set before you today a blessing and a curse...." Concerning the blessing, it states (ibid.): "The blessing, so that you obey the commandments of Hashem..." — the blessing is extended on credit, so that you will listen and do good with My blessing. On the other hand, regarding the curse, it states: "If you do not listen to My commandments..." — punishment is only given after a transgression is committed.[37]

Similarly, it clarifies Chazal's statement (*Pesachim* 118a): "Rav Chisda said, 'What is meant by the verse: "Give thanks to Hashem, for He is good"? Give thanks to Hashem, Who collects man's debts by means of His goodness: the wealthy man through his ox, and the poor man through his sheep....' "[38]

THE BLESSING OF REWARD AND THE BLESSING OF GOOD FAITH

[This passage is based on the principle that] there are two types of blessings which Hashem bestows upon man. The first is the reward that He bestows upon a person for the good he has performed. This blessing does not

---

36 In other words, although a person may not be deserving of a child, and what would grant him the merit to have one would be his performance of the mitzvah of *bris milah*, nevertheless, Hashem grants him a son as an "advance." Moreover, this is true even if He knows that ultimately, the father will not do the mitzvah, for He does not punish transgressions that a person will commit in the future.

37 "If" implies a stipulation: if you sin, you will be cursed. On the other hand, "if" does not appear in the verse of blessing. This intimates that Hashem will grant blessing without stipulation, even before one accrues merit.

38 When a person sins, Hashem punishes him by detracting from the blessing that He has already bestowed upon him.

fall under the category of "Give thanks to Hashem for He is good" (in an imprecise sense),[39] because the individual earned the reward — like a hired worker who awaits payment for his work. What is the kind of good that is unqualified and revealed? This refers to the second type: the blessing that Hashem extends on good faith that man will utilize it to perform good.

If a person is deserving of financial punishment, it would be fair and proper for Hashem to exact it from money that he acquired as payment for his toils. What is the true kindness that Hashem bestows? The fact that He collects the person's debt from "His goodness" — from the money He granted him in good faith that he would act fairly and justly. However, the person disregarded the Almighty's intention and misused the funds. The dictates of justice would demand that Hashem take His money back, for this was not why He gave it to him. Furthermore, this taking should not be considered as being sufficient payment for the person's sin.[40] It is incumbent upon us to thank Hashem for this kindness: He considers His taking back of the money He gave in good faith to be sufficient payment for the debt.

EXTRAPOLATIVE KNOWLEDGE

On what basis does Hashem determine to whom it is fitting to extend a blessing, if not from the perspective of His extrapolative knowledge? Can any person be sure that he is fitting to have received the blessing extended him?[41] (Even if man [will misuse the blessing; nevertheless, he always retains the unimpeded free will to] sometimes change his ways [from bad to good. If so, it would seem fitting to extend blessing on credit to everyone, for a person can

---

39 "Imprecise" meaning for the intent and purpose of this discussion. Relatively speaking, the good bestowed upon a person in reward for his actions is something he deserves. Ultimately, however, the Creator has performed myriad kindnesses for us, and in return, we are obligated to comply with His bidding. Compared to what He has done for us, anything we do in return is but a drop in the ocean.

40 Rather, He could insist on collecting the debt from the money that the person earned himself, i.e., his reward. The revoking of the funds extended in good faith should not be considered a punishment. Since they were misused, it is only proper that they be withdrawn. In addition to this, the actual punishment should still have to be rendered from the person's "own" money.

41 In other words, perhaps Hashem knows through His extrapolative knowledge that a person is destined to misuse the blessing Hashem extends him.

always change from evil to good.] However, since the Almighty does not conduct the world from the perspective of absolute knowledge [to know that an evil person will ultimately choose good] — something that would render free will meaningless — He refrains from ruling the world from the perspective of absolute knowledge.)

THREE LEDGERS

With this, we can understand the following passage in the Talmud (Yerushalmi, *Rosh HaShanah* 1:3): "There are three ledgers.... The ledger of the *beinonim* (those of indeterminate status) — they have already been granted the Ten Days of Repentance between Rosh HaShanah and Yom Kippur. If they repent, they are inscribed with the righteous; if they do not, they are inscribed with the wicked.... Rebbi Chananya, Chavron D'Rabbanon, inquired, 'Doesn't *HaKadosh Baruch Hu* see the future?'[42] [However,] he [Rebbi Chananya] was unaware of the statement made by Rebbi Shimon in the name of Rebbi Yehoshua ben Levi: '*HaKadosh Baruch Hu* only judges a person according to his present status' " (as we mentioned above).

This is astounding! The Talmud is asking about the paradox of man having free will even though Hashem knows the future, a topic that is beyond human comprehension, as noted above in the name of the Rambam. The subject is discussed in relation to a particular case. However, it is actually addressing a much wider point — the whole issue of the extrapolative knowledge through which Hashem conducts His world.

The matter of whether or not one repents is also related to Hashem's extrapolative knowledge. If, from this perspective, a person is apt to repent, then Hashem waits patiently for him to do so and grants him life. On the other hand, if it seems unlikely that he will repent (not withstanding the fact that he always retains the ability to do so), then, *chas v'chalilah*, Hashem desires to take his life. In this case, the person's only hope is that he has the merit of a special deed to tip the scales of judgment to the side of life.

---

42 Meaning, since Hashem knows the future, He already knows whether or not a person will repent. If so, why does He not judge the *beinoni* immediately?

THE KEY ELEMENT

What is the key element indicating that a man is prepared to repent? The fact that he can sense his shortcomings — for this shows that he is truly alive and feeling.[43] If he has this sensitivity, then there is hope that he will arouse himself to repent. However, if he is blind to his deficiencies, from whence will repentance spring? Of course, it is important to understand that this is only the case if his soul is so numbed that he does not respond to rebuke or admonishment. Such apathy shows that he is effectively unable to repent, for even the exhortations of others are unable to awaken him from the slumber of his wickedness.

This understanding sheds light on the resolution, alluded to in the verse, that is offered for the contradiction in the above quoted Talmudic passage (*Niddah* 70b): "Here, they are repenting." The verse states, "For I do not desire the death of one who should die...repent (in other words, such people are prepared to repent, therefore,) and live! (for there is no repentance after death)" (*Yechezkel* 18:32). Whereas concerning the Talmud's statement (ibid.), "Here, they are not repenting," the verse reads, "But they did not listen to the voice of their father, for Hashem desired to kill them" (*Shmuel II* 2:25). This is because they were not aroused by the rebuke of their father, Eli, who was the *gadol hador* (leading sage of the generation). This showed that they were effectively unable to repent — for if they would not listen to the *gadol hador*, then who would they listen to?

SENSE ONE'S SHORTCOMINGS

We can now comprehend the meaning of the verse: "When I say [to the prophet to tell] to the wicked: 'O wicked man, you shall surely die!' and you [the prophet] do not speak to warn the wicked man concerning his path" (*Yechezkel* 33:8). (Here, the sinner is still reasonably capable of repenting, for perhaps he would have been aroused by the prophet's rebuke.) The Almighty does not put a person to death until his "measure is

---

43 Above, Rav Yisrael mentioned that a person is deserving of life only if he is apt to do *teshuvah*. Therefore, as far as man is concerned, the awareness of his flaws motivates him to repent, which in turn grants him the merit to continue living. See Letter Ten.

full." At that point, "He is wicked; he shall die in his iniquity." The passage continues (verse 9), "And you, if you warn the wicked one concerning his path to turn from it, but he does not turn from his way (in other words, he is not moved by rebuke; for if it did move him and he sensed his shortcomings, he would be considered as one who is capable of repenting but was previously unaware of his wickedness. However, since he did not respond to rebuke, he is classified as being unable to repent. Then,) he shall die of his iniquity" — even if his measure is not full. In this instance, although he is not classified as being wicked (rather, this is the general judgment for someone who is iniquitous and is not in the category of "one who repents"), he will still die because of his iniquity. Since he is not aroused by rebuke, the Almighty's extrapolative analysis shows that he will not come to repent. What is his remedy? To awaken within himself a sense of his deficiency. By arousing feelings of anguish and sorrow, he will thereby enter the company of "those who repent," and he will live.

This idea continues with the next verse (33:10): "Therefore, O son of man, say to the House of Israel (by way of cause and effect): Thus you have spoken, saying, 'Our sins and iniquities are upon us, and we are wasting away because of them, how can we live?'" This statement indicates that they are numbered amongst "those who repent," since they sense their shortcoming and worry. Accordingly, this precipitates the result of Hashem commanding the prophet in verse 11: "Say to them, 'As I live, says the Lord God, [I swear that] I do not desire the death of the wicked, but that the wicked one return from his path and live.'" Even if this is only the first stirrings of repentance, they are still classified amongst "those who repent," since by dint of their feelings they are prepared and will gradually enter the category of those who properly repent. The verse, thus, concludes: "Repent, repent from your evil ways, for why should you die, O House of Israel?"

6) THE SPIRITUAL PROTECTION OF TORAH

THREE LEVELS OF DIVINE SERVICE

From the above, we derive that there are three levels of Divine service. The first one — the gateway and the beginning — is sensitivity [to one's flaws and one's need to repent]. This is engendered by studying Chazal's dictums and our Sage's Mussar teachings. A person must repeat them over and over until he is finally moved and senses a lacking in his soul. He then advances to the second level: the conquering of the evil inclination. He then ascends the third level: the rectification of the evil inclination, so that he will rejoice and delight in his Divine service.

The elixir against the *yetzer hara*, to insure that it will not undermine these three levels, is the Torah. As Chazal state (*Kiddushin* 30b): "I created the evil inclination, and I created the Torah as its elixir."

THE THREE ELEMENTS OF TORAH

In light of this, perhaps we can say that the Torah is comprised of three elements. The first is that of "wall." ([As it says in the Talmud] (*Bava Basra* 7b), "[The verse states: 'I am a wall...' (*Shir HaShirim* 8:10).] 'Wall' — this is Torah.") This refers to the *adam hashaleim* [the perfected man] who is exalted in his level of *yetzer* rectification. The Torah is a protective wall that surrounds him, shielding him from powerful external forces so that they cannot harm nor spoil his pure soul.

The second is that of "medicine." ([As it says in the Talmud] (*Kiddushin* 30b), "[The verse states: 'You shall place these words of Mine (*v'samtem*) upon your heart' (*Devarim* 11:18).] '*V'samtem*' — i.e., *sam tam* (perfect medicine).... This may be likened to a man who struck his son with a serious blow and placed a bandage on the wound.... So, too, the Almighty said to the Jewish people, 'I created the evil inclination for you, and I created the Torah as an elixir for it....' " This refers to one who is on the level of conquering the evil inclination. Because the *yetzer hara* battles within him, he is gravely ill. The Torah helps him to withstand its attacks.

The third element is that of "life." ([As the Talmud states] (*Avodah Zarah* 3b), "[Just as when fish come out of the water they immediately die,] so, too, when human beings separate from Torah, they immediately die.") This refers to one who is on the level of true sensitivity. The Torah guards him, so that he does not lose his sensitivity, in order that he will not, *chas v'shalom*, be like one who is dead and unfeeling.

THE MANNA

This concept is reflected in the Midrash (*Yoma* 76a) that we presented in our opening words,[44] concerning the time of Israel's sojourn in the wilderness: "Rebbi Shimon ben Yochi's disciples asked him, 'Why didn't the manna fall just one time a year?' He replied, 'I will answer you by way of a parable: There was a king who had a son. Initially, the king decided to give the boy a yearly allowance for his food. As a result, however, the king only saw him one time a year. Therefore, the king decided to provide for his needs on a daily basis, and he then saw the boy every day. So, too, with Israel. A person who had four or five children would worry and say, "Perhaps the manna will not descend tomorrow, and they will all die of starvation!" As a result, all of the Jewish people would direct their hearts to their Father in Heaven' " (see the text). In the wilderness, the Jewish nation constituted a very interdependent and insular unit, with every faction of the community relying on each other and setting the tone and attitude for the entire people. The fact that the manna fell every day provided strong impetus for those individuals on the level of "sensitivity" to retain their faith in the Almighty — for if the manna were to stop falling, how could they survive? In turn, this influenced those people on the levels of "conquering" and "rectification" to remain steadfast as well. However, when the manna stopped falling and they entered the Land [of Israel], everyone dispersed to their respective heritage and turned to the earth and to farming for sustenance.[45] As a result, the very real threat arose that the *yetzer hara* might "dance amongst them" and interfere with their Divine service, causing them to gradually lose their sensitivity.

---

44 This letter began with the midrash where Yehoshua brought the entire Jewish people between the two staves of the ark. This took place prior to entering the Land of Israel. Rav Yisrael is explaining that, at that time, the people were apprehensive about maintaining their spiritual level because once they entered the Land they would live a natural existence. The passage from *Yoma*, now cited in the text, portrays how the manna kept them spiritually fit.

45 The manna was no longer their source of sustenance, and because the intensity of their communal bond was somewhat diluted, they were no longer in a position to influence each other's faith in such an effective manner.

THE TORAH PROTECTION

In response to this concern, the Almighty showed them that the ark provides protection for all three of the spiritual levels. Let us now explain the midrash we quoted above in conjunction with Yehoshua's remark: "Yehoshua said to the Children of Israel, 'Come here and hear the words of Hashem, your God.' Yehoshua said, 'Through this you will know that the Living God is in your midst' " (*Yehoshua* 3:9–10). Comments the Midrash (*Bereishis Rabbah* 5:7): "Rav Huna said, 'He [Yehoshua] stood them [the *b'nei Yisrael*] between the two staves of the ark' " — meaning that the ark served as a wall for them. This refers to the level of "rectification." "Rav Acha Bar Chanina said, 'He leaned them [according to the commentaries, he stood them at an angle, which allowed him to fit more people in] between the two staves of the ark' " — meaning that the ark supported them. This refers to the level of "conquering," so that they would not fall beneath it. "The Sages said, 'He compressed them between the two staves of the ark' " — meaning that the ark provided support for those on the level of "sensitivity," so that they would not lose their awareness and thereby cease performing the Divine service. Indeed, if there is no sensitivity (the gateway and the beginning), *chas v'shalom*, from whence will inspiration spring?

TWO CATEGORIES OF DIVINE SERVICE

There are two categories of Divine service. The first is to serve Hashem without critical analysis and contemplation, but instead with simple faith and wholeheartedness — to observe His word and go in His ways, by improving one's character traits and performing deeds of lovingkindness. On this level, there is no way to safeguard the status of a person's Divine service, for a mild breeze can abruptly dispel all the good of his ways, *chas v'chalilah*, and there is naught to guard them. The second — and essential — category involves the critical analysis and contemplation of the ways of Divine service and the state of one's character. Pursuit of this path implants a secure stake to firmly anchor a person's Divine service (cf. *Yeshayahu* 22:23), so that all the winds of the world cannot dislodge it from its place. Yet who can know if a person has fully utilized his intellect to maintain his spiritual level, so that his

Divine service is steadfastly secured? Only the Almighty possesses this knowledge.[46]

THE NATURALISTIC CAUSE

Similarly, there are two ways in which the Almighty conducts the course of affairs in the world. The first is through the naturalistic, wherein events seem to be engendered by a cause-effect relationship. In this framework, a person is likely to believe that he is fully responsible for the success of his endeavors. Of course, this is patently wrong — it is the Almighty alone "Who gives man the power to triumph" (cf. *Devarim* 8:17) and provides the cause that produces a successful result.

THE MIRACULOUS CAUSE

The second is through the miraculous, wherein there is no discernable cause for a given effect. In this framework, man sees with his own eyes that the hand of Hashem brought it about (cf. *Tehillim* 118:23). This aspect is referred to as "*Shechinah ba'aretz*" — "the Divine Presence is on the earth." (See the *Rambam, Moreh Nevuchim* 1:5, concerning the root "*shachan.*")

From the perspective of the sensorial cause [the naturalistic course of events in the world is more comprehendible than the miraculous].

> FOOTNOTE OF RAV YISRAEL: Every action that is brought to fruition is engendered by two causes: the sensorial [the physical-mechanical activity that actualizes a deed] and the intellectual [the motivation behind the deed's performance] (whether it is for a particular purpose, or for reward or punishment). For example, when the earth brings forth produce, the sensorial cause is the plowing and sowing undertaken by a farmer. The intellectual

---

46 Hashem does not judge the quality of a person's analysis and understanding of Divine service by looking to the future to see whether he will be a *tzaddik* or *rasha*. Rather, He looks to the current degree of his effort and understanding. If logic dictates that the present quality of his understanding will lead him to righteousness, then Hashem will help him, as explained in the next paragraph.

cause is the motivation behind his course of action — i.e., to enjoy the benefit of the harvest, or to make a financial profit. The
true intellectual cause is Divine providence, which decreed that a
given outcome should come to fruition, with man being the agent
that effects the deed. It thus transpires that man's actions are an
aspect of the "true cause."

With this understanding, we can explain the verses: "Whose
decree was ever fulfilled unless the Lord ordained it? Is it not from
the mouth of the Most High that evil and good emanate? Of what
should a living man complain? A man for [the punishment of] his
sins; let us search and examine our ways, and return to Hashem.
Let us lift up our hearts with our hands to God in Heaven" (*Eichah*
3:37–41). At first impression, man mistakenly thinks that he himself directs his affairs, whether for good or evil. In truth, however,
he does not, for everything comes from Heaven. (See Tosafos'
comment on the passage [*Kesubos* 30a]: "Everything is from
Heaven except for [sickness induced by] cold and heat.") This is
the explanation of the verse, "Whose decree was ever fulfilled unless the Lord ordained it?" Nevertheless, what is the hinge on
which the door of Divine providence revolves? The deeds of man.
Man's actions provide the way through which Divine providence is
manifest, and he is the first cause that engenders the actualization
of his enterprises. This is the meaning of the verse, "Is it not from
the mouth of the Most High that evil and good emanate?" Therefore, a person should not complain over any evil occurrence or mishap. He should not lament that his physical conduct resulted in
the evil that overtook him (for at first glance, he mistakenly thinks
that this is the reason). Neither should he blame the Almighty.
Rather, he should attribute it to his spiritual conduct (the foundation of the first cause [Divine providence, which was aroused
against him]). This is the meaning of the verse, "Of what should a
living man complain? A man for [the punishment of] his sins."

Accordingly, if a person wishes to change his fortune for the better, it will not avail him to merely improve his physical situation. Neither is it proper for him to petition the Almighty in prayer and supplication. His only hope is to rectify the ultimate cause; to improve his spiritual side and the ways of his soul. As Chazal tell us (*Berachos* 5a): "If a person sees that afflictions have come upon him, let him examine his deeds, as it says, 'Let us search and examine our ways, and return to Hashem' (*Eichah* 2:41). Once he does that, then, "Let us lift up our hearts with our hands to God in Heaven."

THE INTELLECTUAL CAUSE

However, the opposite is true concerning the intellectual cause. The precipitating factor for the performance of a miracle must be inordinately greater than the need for things to continue operating in a naturalistic fashion. Why should Hashem alter His method of conducting the world without a great and overriding motivation? Only when provided with an exceptional cause to do so will He elevate a person beyond the strictures of nature — and this is in accord with the Divine attribute of *middah keneged middah*. It is obvious that the reason a person merits to have a miracle performed for him is because he perfected his intellect in the service of the Almighty and conducts his affairs with logic and reason. As a result, the Almighty responds in kind and elevates him above nature, a response that is founded upon the intellectual cause.[47]

This was the virtue enjoyed by Avraham Avinu, *a"h*, whose Divine service did not emanate exclusively from his own intellect[48] (for there was no other cause, neither from his parents nor from his environment). Hence, the Almighty elevated him "beyond the realm of the heavens" (*Bereishis Rabbah* 44), i.e., beyond the confines of natural law.[49]

---

47 It is incumbent upon man to direct the full power of his intellect to understand and act in accord with the Divine will. Moreover, character rectification is the purpose of creation. Therefore, if a person pursues this to the utmost degree, in return he will receive a blessing of wisdom that is beyond the bounds of nature.

48 Rather, Hashem granted him additional dimensions of understanding.

49 Avraham deeply contemplated existence and Hashem. He engaged his whole soul in this

THE SHECHINAH RESTS AMONGST YOU

Let us now apply this concept to the midrash's description of the ark embracing the Jewish people in various manners. It is important for us to understand that each individual member of that lofty generation was perfect in his respective capacity of intellectual groundedness.[50] Yehoshua, thus, said to them, "From the phenomenon of the two staves of the ark embracing you, you know that the *Shechinah* rests amongst you in order to lead you in a miraculous fashion." This miracle was the result of an intellectual cause; namely, that you employ your intellect in your pursuit of Divine service, as mentioned above.

TRANSLATOR'S SUMMARY OF LETTER THIRTY

1. Every person can change every part of his character traits and emotions.

2. There are two levels of change: 1) *kivush hamidos* (controlling one's natural drives), and 2) *tikun hamiddos* (transformation of nature from bad to good).

3. The primary method of change is *hispailus* (emotional arousal that renders subconscious imprints).

4. The Torah safeguards three ascending levels of Divine service: 1) sensitivity to recognize one's shortcomings, 2) *kivush hamiddos*, and 3) *tikun hamiddos*.

---

reflection, until he reached the boundary of human comprehension. At that point, Hashem appeared to him and revealed the entire Torah.

50 That is, in the three different levels of Divine service — sensitivity, conquering, and rectification.

ADDENDUM TO LETTER THIRTY

FURTHER REMARKS BY RAV YISRAEL

THE ABILITY OF MAN TO RENDER PURE JUDGMENTS

DESPITE ALL THIS [that the truth of Torah is founded on pure logic], man will always remain human. Therefore, even if he has the capability to strip his intellect of the influence of his emotions, to the point where they lie quiescent (without awakening, so that they do not interfere with the intellect and cause it to stray)... [This remark continues on page 358 — "still, he is a human being...."]

> FOOTNOTE OF RAV YISRAEL: When man analyzes a character trait, it is virtually impossible for him to purify his intellect and strip it of all emotional influence — because the very study and thought of his emotions precipitates their arousal! Accordingly, even when one considers a middah that relates to a universally accepted value, his intellectual sense of good and evil is somewhat influenced by his emotions.[1] In contrast, the malachim (Heavenly agents or angels), who embody pure intellect, are not subject to emotional influence. Consequently, their perception of good and evil enters the realm of truth and falsehood.[2] (Perhaps this

---

1   See Letter Twenty-nine.
2   Perception of good and evil is open to subjectivity, whereas the realm of truth and falsehood is objective and absolute. This is because good and evil are relative, while truth and

concept addresses a question raised by the Akeidas Yitzchak in *sha'ar* 10 of his commentary on the Torah.) The following verse in Tanach alludes to this (*Shmuel II* 14:17): "For like an angel of God, so is my lord the king, listening to the good and bad..."[3] (also cited in *Akeidas Yitzchak*). Similarly, Chazal comment (*Shabbos* 10a): "Every judge who renders a truthful legal decision according to its [or His] truth (*l'amito*)... it is as if he becomes a partner with Hashem in the act of Creation."[4]

By way of explanation, the pursuit of truth follows after the paths of wisdom and the various methods of rational analysis — as is known. For example, certain aspects of wisdom are captured through the use of clear proofs built by logical syllogisms; other truths and are revealed through proofs and verifications apprehended through deduction; while others are only established through the careful application of commonsense deliberation. Often, man glorifies himself only through the latter, exulting, "I am the seer, and the secrets of wisdom are revealed to me" (cf. *Shmuel I* 9:19). However, such pride [in one's subjective abilities and scorn at more objective tools] is unfounded. The man to whom Hashem grants the knowledge and intelligence to discover syllogisms and the ability to offer proofs (without making improper comparisons) — he is the one whose commonsense evaluations will be upright, and many people will be drawn after his light. The Talmud (*Bechoros* 8b) alludes to this, in an interchange

---

falsehood are unequivocal. For example, whereas most people condemn murder as evil, to the cannibal, it is good. On the other hand, it is universally agreed that black is black and white is white. To say otherwise would not be evil, it would be false. From this perspective — that of the angels — it is clear that murder is false.

3 We thus see that angels have a qualitatively different ability to discern good and evil than man, for the verse praises the king's ability specifically as that of an angel, and not of a man.

4 Just as the king in the above mentioned verse was praised as having an objective perspective, so, too, a judge who renders truthful decisions operates from an unbiased perspective and is unencumbered by emotional subjectivity. We, thus, see from here as well that there are two different levels of discerning the truth.

between Rebbi Yehoshua ben Chanina and the Athenian sages:
"[They asked him,] 'Where is the center of the world?' He raised
his fingers and said to them, 'Here.' They responded, 'Who can
prove this?' He said to them, 'Bring ropes and take measure.' "

Now, the Rambam writes in the beginning of *Hilchos Dei'os*
that a person must conduct himself according to the middle path.
Yet, is there anyone who can fathom this, and is there a seer who
can declare, "Here is the mid-point"? This matter cannot be
proven by syllogism, nor even by deductive reasoning. Rather, it
can only be determined by a wise man using his faculty of common sense, each according to his place and time. The Athenian
sages asked, "Where is the center of the world?" meaning, "What
is the way to determine the middle path?" Rebbi Yehoshua replied, "Here," meaning, "According to the judgment of your intellect." (Based on what? [What intellectual proficiency empowers them to determine approximations?] On your ability to clarify
issues that are dependent on syllogisms or proofs. Therefore, in
these matters [matters which cannot be proven by logical proofs]
as well, you have the free will to determine the center.) They responded to him, "Who can prove this?" meaning, "This is beyond
us, since we do not have the ability to bring a proof for our judgments and assessments." He said to them, "Bring ropes and take
measure," meaning, "The logic to clarify a given matter is like a
precision measuring instrument, which does not err. However,
since the 'mid-point' cannot be determined through logical deduction, a person can rely only on the commonsense judgments
of the Sages, and one should conduct himself according to the
wisdom of their words."

Perhaps a similar idea is found in the Mishnah's teaching
that faith in the Sages is one of the forty-eight qualities through
which Torah is acquired (*Avos* 6:6). The obvious question is
since Torah understanding is dependent on intellectual tools,

such as the use of logical proofs, what place is there for faith? The truth is arrived at through proofs! The answer is that there is a great axiom in arriving at halachic decisions: follow the ruling of an eminent Sage who is a master in the area of proofs and analysis, and submit to his opinion, even if his words are only based on common sense evaluation. This idea is encapsulated in the following passage (Yerushalmi, *Berachos* 1): "To what may a prophet and a sage be likened? To a king who sends two of his emissaries to a country. Concerning one of them he wrote, 'If he does not show you my seal, do not believe him.' Concerning the other, he wrote, 'Even if he does not show you my seal, believe him.' So, too, the Torah writes concerning a prophet: 'And he will produce to you a sign or a wonder' (*Devarim* 13:2). Here, however [i.e., concerning a sage], it states: 'According to the teaching that they will teach you' (ibid. 17:11)."

The explanation of this is as follows: A sign refers to a proof that is open to dispute. On the other hand, a wonder (in the majority of cases) indicates a decisive proof. The Rambam writes (*Hilchos Yesodei HaTorah* 8): "The Jewish people did not base their belief in Moshe Rabbeinu on the signs he performed, for one who believes based on signs has a flaw in his heart — because it is possible that the signs were accomplished through sorcery...." (On what was their faith based? The revelation at Har Sinai — for it was our eyes that saw and our ears that heard, and not those of others [see the text]. Nevertheless, a sign falls in the category of "proof" — but only to those who understand how to interpret it; the majority of people need to see a wonder, which is an everlasting proof. This is the meaning of "And he gives you a sign," or even "It will be a wonder in your eyes" — still, do not listen to the prophet to worship idols. However, listen to him concerning other mitzvos, even by virtue of a sign, as the Rambam wrote in the above quoted passage. Here, however [concerning a sage], "According to the law which they shall teach you," i.e., you should heed his directives even if they are only according to the evaluation of his common sense. The Talmud teaches this (*Sanhedrin* 88a): "Even if he [the rebellious sage] says, 'I base my ruling on tradition,' and they [the Sages] say, 'It appears thusly in our eyes [i.e., commonsense evaluation],' he is executed, so that strife should not proliferate in Israel."

The boundaries of truth are established by pursuing the rigorous study of wisdom. Let man not always ascend the path of "wonders" in his pursuit of the truth. Rather, let him utilize his God-given abilities of investigation and analysis — for this is the zenith of truth. This is called truth; this is its name and this is its remembrance (cf. *Shemos* 3:15). Similarly, it is difficult to establish the truth in legal judgments because of the mind's inclination to love and hate, as well as other subjective considerations — which blind the eyes of the wise. Even if a person carefully guards himself from any suspicion of vested personal interest (see *Kesubos* 105b), nevertheless, who will extend him a "level and plumb line" (cf. *Kings II* 21:13) to detect any deviation? Man makes decisions by "tying string to string and hair-strand to hair-strand" (*Bereishis Rabbah* 93:4), by joining many thoughts and strands together. By the time he reaches a conclusion, he cannot fully identify the sequence that lead to it. Perhaps this is the reason the Talmud issues a warning to judges (*Sanhedrin* 7a, specifically referring to civil and monetary matters): "A judge should always imagine that a sword rests between his thighs and that Gehinnom gapes below him," because judgments are extremely vulnerable to corrupt influences. They did not mention this [warning] regarding a question of *treifos* [that was brought before Rav Ashi (ibid.)] because deviation from the truth is much more common in civil and monetary judgments than in ritual matters.

Nevertheless, if a person devotes his heart and soul to purifying his thoughts to the best of his knowledge, then he has fulfilled the Divine injunction to pursue righteousness. This is the connotation of the expression (*Shabbos* 10a, quoted above): "Every judge who renders a truthful legal decision according to His truth (*l'amito*)," meaning that the judgment has reached the standard of truth demanded by the Torah [i.e., the judge has made every effort to remove all prejudices from his thinking so that he can make a correct ruling according to the best of his ability]. Perhaps the Talmud alludes to this in the following passage (Yerushalmi, *Sanhedrin* 6b): "Two men came to Rebbi Yosi bar Chalafta to be judged by him [in a monetary dispute]. They said to him, '[We will submit to your judgment] on condition that you judge us with a Torah judgment.' He responded, 'I do not know what a Torah judgment is.' " The explanation of his response is that the authentic standard of Torah is rendered by pure intellect, unadulterated by any personal inclinations whatsoever (as mentioned above). In actuality, it is quite unlikely that such absolute purity of thought will be found in legal thinking — for who can fathom one's own hidden, ulterior motives? The remedy for this is to cultivate a powerful level of *yiras Shamayim*. This will ensure that a person constantly suspects that perhaps he has not fulfilled his obligation to be intellectually honest.

Perhaps Chazal refer to this (*Sanhedrin* 6b): "Perhaps the judge will say, 'Why should I bring trouble upon myself?' [i.e., "If I make a mistake, I will be punished. If so, I am better off not serving as a judge" — Rashi]. The Torah, therefore, says, 'With you in the matter of judgment' (*Divrei HaYamim II* 19:6) — [This teaches that] a judge is only expected to judge on the basis of what his eyes see." No matter how much effort a judge makes to purify his thoughts, he can never be sure that he is not being influenced by his subconscious. Therefore, providing that he made

an honest attempt to reach the correct verdict, he will not be
punished, because this is considered as "what his eyes see" and
justice is with him. This is true even though his decision is influenced by his particular emotional makeup and not based on pure
intellect, the nature of which is unvarying.

In contrast to all the above, the judgments of a king, who is
elevated over all his people, are in the realm of true judgments.[5]
His judgments are clear as wonders, absolute truth. This is in
keeping with the verse "For like an angel of God, so is my lord
the king listening to the good and bad" (*Shmuel II* 14:17).
Whereas the judgment of the "commoner" merely falls within the
category of being "good," the judgment of the king comes under
the classification of "truth," similar to the angels, as mentioned
above.

THE TORAH WAS GIVEN TO MAN TO MAKE JUDGMENTS

...still, he is a human being. He thus remains saddled with emotional
forces and does not have the ability to detach his intellect from them. Therefore, man does not have the capacity to apprehend true wisdom, absolutely
purified and divorced from human emotion. The Torah, however, was given
to man to make judgments according to the human intellect (with the greatest purity possible, as the Talmud states [*Bechoros* 17b], "The Almighty says,
'Do it, and in whatever manner you are able to do so, it will be satisfac-
tory' "). Matters are clarified by accumulating proofs and evaluating them.
Whichever side of the proofs is stronger — according to either greater quantity or quality of reason — will determine the decision and thus establish the
matter.

All men are equally fit in their intelligence to determine which side has
the greater quantity of proofs, providing that the heart accurately understands them. However, concerning the evaluation of the quality of proofs,
each person's spirit differs from the next. These are the value judgments we

---

5   See Letter Twenty-nine for the reason why this is so.

have been discussing, and there is a vast difference in people's analytical abilities.[6]

THE EVALUATION OF PROOFS

The dispute between Beis Shammai and Beis Hillel was based on the evaluation of proofs. Each side clearly knew the required proofs that were relevant to a given debate. Their general dispute was sparked by the debate associated with the evaluation of proofs — whether to follow quantity or quality.[7] This is indicated by the following passage in the Talmud (*Eruvin* 13b): "Rav Abba said in the name of Shmuel: Beis Shammai and Beis Hillel debated for three years. They [Beis Shammai] said, 'The law is as we said,' and they [Beis Hillel] said, 'The law is as we said.' " Beis Shammai reasoned that rulings should be made according to the quality: they possessed superior analytic abilities and, therefore, said, "The law follows our opinion." On the other hand, Beis Hillel reasoned that the rulings should be made according to the quantity: they had greater numbers and, therefore, said, "The law follows our opinion."

The three-year debate was not fought in order for one school to impose their opinion on the other. Rather, it was for the sake of justice and truth, with purity of thought and no personal motivation. The disagreement was not an egotistic battle of conviction; rather, it hinged on an incidental factor, each side feeling that their position was the superior and decisive one.[8]

Ultimately, a *bas kol* (Heavenly voice) proclaimed that the law is in accordance with Beis Hillel. Therefore, in the pursuit of truth, quantity is preferable to quality. Hence, the authoritative halachic arbiters ruled that "num-

---

6   The proofs on one side might be more numerous. However, an accomplished scholar might determine that the quality of proofs points to the side of the lesser quantity.

7   This does not refer to the quality-quantity division that Rav Yisrael mentioned above. Rather, their argument was completely within the category of quality. As we shall see, their dispute was over what are the criteria to determine the superiority of the given proofs — sharpness of scholarship or greater number of students.

8   In other words, it was not that Beis Shammai held they were right simply because they were the superior scholars. Rather, it was coincidental that the members of Beis Shammai were both superior scholars and held that this was the decisive factor; they would have maintained their position even if Beis Hillel's scholarship had been superior.

bers are greater than wisdom" (see the *Shach, Yoreh De'ah*, ch. 242, in the procedure for deciding matters of *issur v'heter*).

THE BAS KOL

Perhaps this is why the *bas kol* announced, "These and those are the words of the Living God." It did not come to inform us of a new idea (that even the rejected view is included within the Torah). That concept was well known — deriving from the verse "Torah is not in Heaven" (*Devarim* 30:12) — and there is no doubt that Beis Shammai's view was handed to Moshe on Sinai with the rest of the Torah and was not forgotten. Rather, the *bas kol* conveyed that people should not suspect that perhaps, *chas v'shalom*, Beis Shammai deviated in some slight measure from having purity of thought and were tainted by a modicum of self-interest. People might have assumed that this was why Hashem did not choose to transmit His Torah to Beis Shammai. Moreover, they might have mistakenly assumed that the rejected view of Beis Shammai is not part of *Toras Hashem*. Therefore, the *bas kol* came to inform us that their thoughts were favorable to Hashem, and that the debate centered on an incidental factor. Each school of thought clung tenaciously to its opinion, for each held that their respective view was the correct one. The *bas kol* thus proclaimed that the rejected words of Beis Shammai are also words of the Living God, and that one who contemplates them, contemplates Hashem's Torah.

This announcement ["These and those..."] had a very specific function: to reveal that the intentions of both schools were pure. This did not interfere with the axiom "Torah is not in Heaven," which only applies to the overarching principle involved in rendering a halachic decision [in other words, a halachah used on a constant basis, as opposed to a specific insight] — for example, the halachah concerning "the sin offering whose owners have died," which is mentioned in the Talmud (*Temurah* 16a).[9]

---

9   This is one of the halachos that were forgotten due to the grief and mourning the people went through upon Moshe's death. They asked Pinchas (the *kohen gadol*) to inquire of Hashem (through the *urim v'tumim*) for a clarification of the ruling. Pinchas replied, "The Torah is not in Heaven."

THE MESSAGE OF THE BAS KOL

Perhaps this message of the *bas kol* — that the rejected view of Beis Shammai is pure and part of the Torah — is reflected in a statement made by Chazal (*Midrash Koheles* 1:4): "The Sages wanted to hide the book of *Koheles*, because they found in it concepts that might be construed as heretical. They said, 'All the wisdom of Shlomo, who came to say, "What benefit is there for man in all his labors," could be interpreted as meaning that laboring in Torah study is futile.' Other Sages responded and said, 'He did not say "in all labor"; rather, "in all his labor," i.e., in his labor [to fulfill earthly pursuits] there is no benefit, but there is benefit in the labor of Torah study.'" Likewise, in the Talmud we read (*Shabbos* 30b) [commenting on the same verse: "What benefit is there for man in all his labors under the sun"]: "Rebbi Yudan said, ' "Under the sun" [i.e., regarding earthly pursuits] he has no benefit; [however] above the sun [i.e., regarding spiritual concerns] he has benefit.' " Moreover, Chazal tell us (*Pesachim* 50b): "Rava noted a contradiction between two verses: It is written, 'For Your kindness is great unto the Heavens' (*Tehillim* 57:11), and it is written, 'For Your kindness extends beyond the Heavens' (ibid. 108:5). What is the reconciliation? Here [in the latter verse] it concerns those who act [i.e., who study Torah and perform mitzvos] for the sake of Heaven; and there [in the former verse, it is written concerning] those who do not act for the sake of Heaven. And as Rav Yehudah said in the name of Rav, 'A man should always be involved in Torah and mitzvos, even if it is not for the sake of Heaven, because through [doing them] not for the sake of Heaven, he will come to [do them] for the sake of Heaven.' "

A NEW TORAH PRINCIPLE

According to the above, involvement for the sake of Heaven is classified as being "above the sun," while involvement not for the sake of Heaven as "under the sun." When a person discovers a Torah concept that is accepted as halachah, it is not his creation; rather, it is the unearthing of an idea that was previously concealed. On the other hand, if it is not accepted as halachah, it is, nevertheless, *Toras Hashem*, and one who contemplates and considers it receives reward. The rejected view belongs to its promulgator, for he labored to generate a new Torah concept that did not previously exist.[10]

However, all this is on condition that his effort was with purity of thought and no personal motive. Such purity is the foundation of Divine service that is "for the sake of Heaven." This is the meaning of, "What is the (eternal) benefit of all his labor ("his" implies that the concept was not accepted as halachah) that he labored under the sun (not for the sake of Heaven)." Yet if a person's labor is "above the sun" (for the sake of Heaven), it provides an eternal benefit, for he engendered a new Torah concept.

Perhaps this concept is alluded to in the verse "There is nothing new beneath the sun" (*Koheles* 1:9 — see Rashi's explanation). Any principle discovered by man that is not within the compass of *Toras Hashem* is not an intellectual innovation, but a visceral one, for this is only the revelation of the hidden through the synthesis of previously known concepts.[11] The same is true concerning *Toras Hashem*: a concept that is accepted as halachah is the Torah itself, and the one who uncovers it is merely revealing a concept that was already in existence. What is considered true (intellectual) innovation? A Torah thought that is not accepted as halachah. Through a person's discovering of it, it becomes a part of the Torah. This is the explanation of "There is nothing new beneath the sun." (Meaning, something that is not for the sake of Heaven — for even Torah that is accepted as halachah, although it has an advantage over that which is not accepted as halachah, it is still not called new. The same is true of a concept that is not accepted as halachah, for if the study is not for the sake of Heaven, it is not called Torah.) However, if something is "above the sun" (i.e., it is for the sake of Heaven), then not only is it part of the Torah, it is also a new creation. These are the concepts that were not originally within the parameters of Torah, but through man's toiling

---

10 When a person discovers a concept that is applicable as practical halachah, he did not invent something new and it is not "his"; rather, he uncovered a latent Torah principle that belongs to the entire Jewish people. Conversely, when one engenders an idea that is ultimately rejected, not only does its rejection not mean that it isn't Torah, but the one who proposed it is actually considered as having created it, and it belongs to him.

11 In this context, "visceral" means something apprehensible to the senses that was previously unknown. For example, the discovery of electricity was not a creation. Rather, it revealed a natural force that always existed and proved the relationship between a conductor and electricity, which was a natural law that already existed.

over them in purity of thought, they came into the chambers of the Torah.

TORAS HASHEM

This is the meaning of the verse, "But his desire is in the Torah of Hashem, and in his Torah he meditates day and night" (*Tehillim* 1:2) — for man's desire and the focus of his energies is to purify his intellect; to separate it from emotional influences and attain an aspect of true intellect. This is *Toras Hashem* [i.e., concepts that are accepted as halachah]. Despite all this, he is human, "and on his Torah (his personal Torah), he meditates day and night (on his ideas which, although for the sake of Heaven, are not accepted as halachah). (Generally, the second half of this verse is understood as referring to Hashem's Torah [with the "h" of "His" being capitalized]. Here, however, it is taken as a reference to the "man" spoken of in the first verse — "Fortunate is the man who does not walk in the counsel of the wicked...in his Torah he meditates day and night.")

In keeping with this idea, the Talmud teaches (*Berachos* 5a), "The character of human beings is such that when a person sells a [precious] article to his fellow, the seller is sad and the buyer is happy. However, *HaKadosh Baruch Hu* is different. He gave the Torah to Israel and rejoiced, as it says 'For I have given you a good teaching; do not forsake My Torah' (*Mishlei* 4:2)." In this sense, giving is a subcategory of selling: the article is basically separated from its owner. Now, the Almighty gave man the Torah to make judgments with, according to his intellect, and it is not the same in man's hands as when it was in Hashem's trust.

> FOOTNOTE OF RAV YISRAEL: This is because the secrets of the Torah are not revealed to man from Heaven. Rather, he discovers them himself by employing logical proofs to ascertain the truth. This intellectual process itself is *Toras Hashem*. (See *Temurah* 16a: "Three thousand laws were forgotten during the days of mourning for Moshe Rabbeinu. They said to Yehoshua, 'Inquire [of Heaven].' He replied, 'It [Torah] is not in Heaven.' ...It was taught: One thousand and seven hundred *kal v'chomers*, *gezeiros shavos*, and *dikdukei sofrim* were forgotten during the

period of mourning for Moshe. Rav Avahu said, 'Nevertheless, Osaniel ben Kenaz restored them through his intellectual acuity' " — see the text.)

The question of whether Heaven has the authority to decide a halachic dispute is dependent on a comment made by Tosafos in *Maseches Yevamos* (14a). The Talmud's discussion there centers on whether or not Beis Shammai complied with the ruling of the *bas kol* to follow Beis Hillel. In the course of the discussion, the Gemara asserts: "The opinion that states, 'They acted [in accord with their own rulings]' is like Rebbi Yehoshua, who says that we do not heed a *bas kol*." [On a somewhat tangential note,] Tosafos point out that in *Bava Metzia* (59b), the Gemara rules we do not heed the *bas kol* that supported Rebbi Eliezer's view; instead, we say in every place that he was a Shammusi [under the ban], and the halachah is not in accord with his opinion. However, concerning the *bas kol* that supported Beis Hillel, we do, in fact, heed it and rule in accord with their opinion. Query Tosafos, what is the difference between these two cases?[12]

Tosafos offer two answers in response. The first is that in Rebbi Eliezer's case, the only purpose of the *bas kol* was to honor him.[13] Second, it might be that the *bas kol* concerning Rebbi Eliezer was disputing the opinion of the Rabbis, who were the majority. Therefore, the halachah does not follow Rebbi Eliezer, because we rule according to the majority. On the other hand, we follow the *bas kol* of Beis Hillel because that school was the majority

---

12 In other words, in the case of Rebbi Eliezer, who was excommunicated for arguing against the majority positon of the Sages, we rule that we do not follow a *bas kol*. We might, therefore, make a general presumption that the halachah is never in accord with a *bas kol*. The question then arises: Why do we rule in accord with the *bas kol* that the halachah is like Beis Hillel?

13 In other words, Rebbi Eliezer's case was unique, and therefore we cannot learn from it a general presumption that we never heed a *bas kol*'s proclamation. In actuality, a *bas kol*'s intention usually is to issue a halachic ruling, and that is why we heed its ruling in regard to Beis Hillel.

opinion, not withstanding the fact that the Beis Shammai's scholarship was more proficient.

According to the first answer of Tosafos, it turns out that "the Torah is in Heaven" [i.e., the Torah may be decided by Divine fiat]. However, this only applies if a given view is represented in the world — even if it is only that of a lone individual in conflict with the majority opinion.[14] However, according to the second answer, Torah is, in fact, "not in Heaven." Rather, the *bas kol* only has the authority to give deference to one of the views when the two opposing sides are basically equal — for example, the case at hand, where one side had a greater number of students and the other side had sharper scholarship. In such a situation, the *bas kol* adds force to one side in order to "weigh down the scale" and determine the decision. Of course, all of this is only in accord with the opinion that we give credence to a *bas kol*.

In contrast, according to Rebbi Yehoshua, who maintained that Beis Shammai followed their own opinion even after the *bas kol*, the Torah "is not in Heaven" in any way whatsoever — not even to give added weight to one of the sides. Moreover, according to what we have discussed concerning the intellect and the emotions, it seems clear that this is Rebbi Yehoshua's position.[15] This is the way of the intellect — to be on guard against all emotional influences. The more a person debates against another in an intellectual matter, the more he must distance himself from

---

14 We do not rule like Rebbi Eliezer because he specifically invoked the *bas kol* as proof of his position, and it issued forth solely in his honor. However, if the *bas kol* had issued its proclamation unbidden, then the halachah would have been established in accord with it. Thus, the halachah follows a *bas kol* even if it opposes the majority view. Therefore, in the dispute of Beis Shammai and Beis Hillel, wherein the latter formed the majority, the halachah certainly follows the *bas kol*'s pronouncement.

15 This addresses the second question raised by Tosafos in *Yevamos*: Perhaps Rebbi Yehoshua's ruling that we do not heed a *bas kol* was made specifically concerning the debate with Rebbi Eliezer, but generally he does concede that we take the *bas kol* into account.

the emotional forces that are likely to result from man's love of victory, which can extinguish the light of the intellect. An indication that one is successful in his effort to proceed with purity of thought is if he can keep his emotions in check when engaged in debate. This is manifest when he listens to and supports the arguments of his opponent; even if these proofs are not fully compelling, he still remains completely calm and collected. If he needs to arouse his emotions in order to counter his opponent's passionate expressions, he abandons them when they are no longer necessary to ensure that his intellect remains unaffected and in control.

In keeping with this, we see that Rebbi Yehoshua used emotion to parry emotion in his dispute with Rebbi Eliezer. At the end of the stormy and awe-inspiring debate, Rebbi Yehoshua stood up (an act with dramatic effect) and proclaimed, "We pay no heed to a *bas kol*."[16] We understand from this that according to Rebbi Yehoshua, Torah is "not in Heaven" in any way whatsoever — not even to add weight to someone's opinion. Indeed, it is not even a semblance of a proof. For this reason, Rebbi Yehoshua employed emotion in order to neutralize the astonishment of the students to the *bas kol*. They were young, and the

---

16 We view the value of his standing up as an emotive act in the following way: When Rebbi Eliezer called upon the carob tree as proof, and it uprooted itself and moved, Rebbi Yehoshua did not respond dramatically. Rather, he merely observed, "We do not bring proofs from a carob tree." When Rebbi Eliezer called upon the water to back his case and it flowed backwards, Rebbi Yehoshua again did not respond with an action, and repeated, "We do not bring proof from water." Similarly, when Rebbi Eliezer called upon the walls of the *beis midrash* to collapse if he was right, Rebbi Yehoshua rebuked them and told them not to mix into an argument that wasn't theirs, but took no action. It was only at the end, when Rebbi Eliezer invoked the *bas kol*, a stunning ploy which dwarfed all that had preceded it, that Rebbi Yehoshua resorted to dramatic action himself and stood up. From this we see that, according to Rebbi Yehoshua, Torah is not in Heaven in any way at all — because he did not stand up for anything else! Therefore, the proof that Rebbi Yehoshua maintained that "Torah is not in Heaven" does not derive from the fact that he uttered these words, as Tosafos understands, but from the fact that he stood up.

light of pure truth had not yet shone upon them; therefore, they were likely to be overwhelmed by something as striking as a Heavenly voice.[17] According to Rebbi Yehoshua, however, its awesome nature did not make it any different from any other emotion-based argument. Torah, he maintained, is not in Heaven at all. Therefore, a *bas kol* cannot stand against the intellect, and cannot even add weight to a given opinion.

> (See *Drashos HaRan, drush* 7, under the heading, "M'an Nokach Nokach Rabbah bar Nachmani," *Bava Metzia* 86a)

THE CAUSE OF THE DEBATE

In this light, we can explain the debate between Beis Shammai and Beis Hillel: How did it come about, and what was its cause? Why did all the members of each school agree to their respective opinions, and what bearing does an individual school of thought have on this matter?

THE DIFFERENCE IN TEMPERAMENT

The cause of their debate was the difference in temperament of the two schools. It is impossible for man to divorce his intellect from the influence of his emotions (as mentioned above). One who delves into the Torah can "only see what his eyes see" (*Bava Basra* 131a). This means that he searches for the truth according to the proficiency of his scholarship, guarding the integrity of his logical propositions so that they remain within the bounds of classic Torah discourse and, in as much as is humanly possible, striving for purity of thought. In the majority of cases, the members of a particular school of thought are subject to common emotional influences,[18] for they all share the same basic outlook, and it is for this reason that they grouped together. This is the meaning of the expression, "These and those are the words of the Living God" — for there was no contradiction in the fact that the two

---

17 Such an astonishing occurrence was likely to cloud the students' judgment. Therefore, Rebbi Yehoshua felt it proper to stand up and announce, "We do not heed a *bas kol*" in order to counter the emotional impact of Rebbi Eliezer's argument.

18 Those tendencies that are beyond their ability to divorce from the intellect.

schools had differing opinions, with both being valid Torah thoughts.[19] While it may be true that man's emotions are in constant flux,[20] nevertheless, they do not alter the integrity of judgment (of one who purifies his intellect in an upright way).[21] [On the other hand, the emotions that can be detached from the intellect] are subject to change if acted on by external stimuli; [this, however, has no bearing on the emotional forces that cannot be divorced from the intellect].

"This is the Torah of man" (cf. *Shmuel II* 7:19), this is his obligation: to strive with all his might to ensure that his emotions are calm and quiet when he contemplates an intellectual matter. When the individual [members of a school of thought] are in the same mode of emotional tranquility, they share the same outlook. This is particularly true for the *adam hashaleim* [the person who has perfected his character], who guards himself against the effects of powerful external stimuli, which can implant forces in his spirit that are subject to constant alteration.

With this, we can understand the following Talmudic passage (*Eruvin* 7a): "[When ruling in two parallel cases] we may not follow the [respective] stringent ruling of two [authorities who differ from each other in both of the rulings at hand] in cases when their views are mutually contradictory,[22] for example, regarding the spine and the skull[23]...but when the views are not

---

19 In other words, the members of both schools had purified themselves of all extraneous emotional influences, and all that remained were those emotional forces that are impossible for a person to separate from the intellect. Therefore, they were not tainted by any personal motivations or considerations. All that was left was the essential makeup of the individual, which influenced his thought processes, and the result was two valid Torah opinions.

20 That is, even those which are impossible for a person to entirely eradicate.

21 This is because those emotions that a person cannot entirely uproot are not influenced by external considerations. Accordingly, the conclusions of such a person's intellect do not change because of external stimulai.

22 For instance, in debates between Beis Hillel and Beis Shammai, if we adopt the strict view of Beis Hillel in one case, we cannot adopt the strict view of Beis Shammai in a parallel case.

23 Regarding the laws of ritual impurity, Beis Shammai rules that a human spine in an enclosed space still causes impurity if it is missing a single vertebra, but not two. Similarly, a ritually slaughtered animal is still considered kosher if it is missing one vertebra, but not two. On the other hand, Beis Hillel rules that even if a human spine is missing only one

mutally contradictory we may adopt [the two different rulings]. We may even adopt the lenient opinions of both authorities [in the two different cases, as long as they are not mutually contradictory]. But this [permission to rule according to two different authorities in two different cases] only applies to a scholar of sufficient stature who is able to synthesize his thinking to rule according to both authorities.[24]

But if he does not [have this expertise] it is completely contradictory to rule sometimes like Beis Shammai and other times like Beis Hillel, for the foundation of their debates stems from a single cause.[25]

Indeed, even when the Talmud states (*Eruvin* 6b): "One who wishes to act in accord with the rulings of Beis Shammai may do so; [and one who wishes to act] in accord with the rulings of Beis Hillel may do so," it refers specifically to one who has the expertise to make halchic rulings (as explained in *Choshen Mishpat* 25:2, gloss): "Let not a person say, 'I will rule according to whom I desire in a matter where there is a debate.' " How awesome is this vision (cf. Bereishis 28:17): to engage in profound analysis of the words of our Rabbis, the halachic authorities, *zt"l*; to penetrate and explore the reason for their disagreements[26] and that which results from their differences in basic temperament.[27] Then to join them together into an inseparable covenant and observe the leniencies of both authories. [Moreover, even if the two views are mutually contradictory, the scholar may rule like both authorities] if a resolution or a third reconciling view can be found.

---

vertebra, it no longer causes impurity, and if an animal is missing only one vertebra, it is not kosher. If a person rules like Beis Shammai concerning the spine's ability to ritually defile and like Beis Hillel regarding an animal's kosher status, he is considered to be a fool, for he is emplying contradictory facts.

24 So that in one case he rules according to the strict opinion of Beis Hillel and in another case according to the strict opinion of Beis Shammai; and similarly he rules with leniency in one case according to Beis Hillel and in another case according to the lenient opinion of Beis Shammai.

25 The core emotions that cannot be divorced from the intellect.

26 That is, to recognize the significant differences in their respective core personality attributes.

27 The actual rulings and debates.

LETTER THIRTY-ONE

THE THREE ASPECTS OF TORAH STUDY

The key to mastering middos is chok: the unequivocal acceptance of the Torah's injunction against negative character traits, and the realization of their gravity and the severity of their punishment — as Chazal have underscored in numerous places.

BEN SORER U'MOREH

THE TALMUD (*Sanhedrin* 71a) STATES, "There never was a *ben sorer u'moreh*, nor will there ever be one. If so, why was it [the topic] written [in the Torah]? So that one should study it and receive reward." This is absolutely astonishing! Even if a person were to live for a thousand years, there is enough content in the remaining sections of the Torah for him to occupy himself with their study and receive reward!

THE GOLDEN CALF

In order to understand this, let us first turn to another enigmatic passage, this one in the Midrash (*Yalkut Shemoni, Shimini* 521).[1] "[Chazal query,] And what did the people of Israel discern [that motivated them] to bring more [sacrifices] than Aharon?[2] Rather, He [Hashem] said to them, 'You

---

1   In discussing the repercussions of the incident with the golden calf, the midrash relates that Aharon was commanded to bring a calf-offering as an atonement for his involvement in that sin. The rest of the people, however, were commanded not only to bring a calf-offering, but a goat-offering as well.

2   In truth, the language of this midrash is somewhat perplexing, as it was not that the

have [a transgression] in your hand from the beginning' [of the Jewish people's formation, as it says (*Bereishis* 37:31),] 'And they slaughtered a young
goat' [referring to the brothers selling Yosef]; 'and you have one in your hand
in the end' [i.e., they themselves, who sinned with the golden calf, as it says
(*Shemos* 32:8),] 'Make for them....'' "

   This text is also astounding! Didn't Aharon also have a transgression
"in the beginning" [for Levi, his ancestor, also participated in the sale of
Yosef], as well as the end, as the verse states (*Devarim* 9:20), "Hashem became exceedingly angry with Aharon..." [for his error in the sin of the
Golden Calf]? [Why, then, did he not require expiation for both the sale of
Yosef and the sin of the golden calf, in the same way as the rest of the people?]

MISHPAT AND CHOK

   Perhaps we can answer this question as follows: The Talmud states
(*Sanhedrin* 27b), "It is written, '[Hashem] visits the transgression of the father upon the children...' (*Shemos* 20:5). This applies when [the sons] embrace the sinful deeds of their fathers...." It seems logical that this is only
when the negative quality of the son's deeds are equal in severity to those of
the father, and not when the transgressions of the father were greater in severity than those of the son. In yet another Talmudic passage, we read (*Yoma*
67b): "The verse states (*Vayikra* 18:4), 'Perform My laws (*mishpatim*) [refer-
ring to laws that would be dictated by logic even if they were not written in
the Torah]' — concepts that even if they were not written, it would be proper
to write them. For example, idolatry, immorality, robbery, etc. 'And safeguard
My statutes (*chukim*) [referring to decrees of the Torah that defy reason]' —
concepts that the *satan* ridicules. For example, the prohibition against eating
unclean animals, wearing *sha'atnez*, etc." (The *satan* ridicules them because
their rationale does not enter the realm of human logic. Rather, we observe

---

Jewish people discerned anything; it was that the Almighty commanded them! This is not
the place to analyze why Chazal phrased the midrash in the way that they did. However,
we can say that they meant to ask as follows: "What was the reason the Almighty had the
Jewish people bring a goat-offering and a calf-offering, while He only required Aharon to
bring a calf-offering?"

them because, as the passage concludes: 'I am Hashem' — I, Hashem, promulgated them [chakaktim], and you do not have permission to question
them.) Logic dictates that it is far more severe to transgress a mishpat than to
transgress a chok.[3]

We read further in the Talmud (Yoma 85b): "The Torah declares: 'Pro-
fane one Shabbos so that you may observe many Shabboses' "[4] We derive
from this that even though the prohibition against idolatry is a mishpat (as
per the aforementioned Talmudic passage), the injunction to give up our
lives rather than worship idols is a chok.[5]

AHARON VIOLATED A CHOK

With this in mind, we are now in a position to answer the question of
why Aharon was not held culpable for the sin of selling Yosef as the rest of
the people were. The Talmud teaches (Sanhedrin 7a), "The verse states,
[regarding the sin of the Golden Calf]: 'And Aharon saw' (Shemos 32:5).
What did Aharon see? That Chur was murdered [for chastising the people
over the deed they wished to commit. Subsequently, they approached
Aharon to enlist his support.] He [Aharon] said: 'If I do not listen to them,
they will do to me as they did to Chur, and the verse "Could a priest or
prophet be murdered in the Sanctuary of Hashem?" (Eichah 2:20) will be
fulfilled through me.' " It thus transpires that Aharon violated a chok [the
injunction to give up his life rather than submit to idol worship]. Therefore,
the Torah does not consider him as one who "embraced the sinful deeds of
his fathers" (and he was not held culpable for the brothers' transgression of

---

3   This is because the breach of a mishpat goes against the grain of our conscience, and we
    are aware of the deed's inherent corruption. However, since the underlying meaning of a
    chok is incomprehensible to the human mind, we do not grasp its significance. Therefore,
    the culpability for transgressing a mishpat is greater than that for transgressing a chok.

4   For example, a critically ill person is permitted to violate Shabbos in order to be cured, so
    that he can observe future ones. This ruling is consistent with human logic. Hence, the
    injunction to abrogate a Torah law in order to save our lives so that we can observe future
    mitzvos is a mishpat.

5   We have already concluded that it is logical to violate a commandment in order to save a
    life. Therefore, when the Torah commands us to submit to death rather than engage in
    idolatry, this is perforce a chok. As we explained, a chok is a commandment that does not
    conform with the tenets of the human intellect.

selling of Yosef) — "and they slaughtered a young goat" — which constituted the breach of a *mishpat*.[6]

SAFEGUARD AND PERFORM

Let us now turn to the verse in *Vayikra* (18:4): "Perform My *mishpatim* and safeguard My *chukim*." It is important to note that there is a variation of language in this verse. First, it exhorts us to perform the *mishpatim* — which implies the fulfillment of a positive commandment. Then it cautions us to safeguard the *chukim*, which implies the avoidance of transgressing a negative one.[7] There is also a variation between this verse (18:4), and the following one (18:5): "You shall safeguard My *chukim* and *mishpatim*." In the former, *mishpat* precedes *chok*, whereas in the latter, *chok* precedes *mishpat*. Moreover, in the first verse, "performance" is employed in relation to *mishpat*, while in the second verse, "safeguarding" is used.

MERITS AND TRANSGRESSIONS

The reason for this difference is as follows: The Rambam writes (*Hilchos Teshuvah* 3:1–2), "Each and every human being has merits and transgressions. One whose merits exceed his transgressions is a *tzaddik*, while one

---

6   When the brothers sold Yosef, they violated a commonly accepted ethical principle — a *mishpat*. On the other hand, Aharon's decision to participate in the sin of the golden calf rather than submit to death was the violation of a *chok*. Since Aharon merely violated a *chok*, his sin was considered as being less severe than that of his ancestors, who transgressed a *mishpat*. Therefore, his involvement with the golden calf did not render him accountable for his ancestors' sin. The rest of the Jewish people, however, violated a *mishpat* when they worshipped the golden calf, and as a result, they were rendered accountable for their forebears' sin.

In light of this, whereas Aharon was only required to bring one offering — to atone for violating the *chok* — the people were required to bring two offerings: one to atone for violating the *mishpat* that prohibits idol worship, and another to atone for the sin of their ancestors' selling of Yosef. Their violation of the *mishpat* prohibiting idolatry was comparable to their ancestor's violation of a *mishpat* in selling Yosef. Therefore, they, the sons, were held culpable for the sin of their fathers. Rav Yisrael is revealing a frightening principle: if the descendants repeat the same sin of their ancestor, they reawaken the accountability of the misdeed. If that happens, they are obligated to make atonement both for their own sin, as well as the sin of their father.

7   See *Menachos* 36b for the source of this definition of "perform" and "safeguard."

whose transgressions exceed his merits is a *rasha*. [One who has] half [transgressions] and half [merits] is a *beinoni*.... This determination is not made according to the relative number of merits and transgressions, but rather according to their respective magnitude. There are individual meritorious acts that outweigh several transgressions, as it says, 'Something good…has been found in him' (*Melachim I* 14:13), and there are single transgressions that outweigh several meritorious acts, as it says, 'But a single rogue can ruin a great deal of good' (*Koheles* 9:18). These assessments are made only in the mind of the One Who Knows All, and He knows how to evaluate the merits against the transgressions."

ASSUMING IGNORANCE

Now, there are numerous factors that contribute to the heightened significance assigned to a particular meritorious act or transgression. Here, however, we will only focus on one of them. We read in Tanach: "Many designs are in a man's heart, but the counsel of Hashem, only it will prevail" (*Mishlei* 19:21). Consider a person who sets his heart to examine his ways and discerns that there is a certain transgression that he frequently commits (and he imagines that he is unable to abstain from it). Moreover, he does not familiarize himself with Chazal's discussions about this transgression, assuming that his general ignorance will render him an unintentional sinner and not a purposeful one, which reduces his level of culpability. Indeed, this idea is discussed by Chazal (*Devarim Rabbah, Parashas Ki Savo*): "One who studies Torah but does not fulfill it, is punished more severely than one who never studied at all." This attitude, however, does not reflect a Torah perspective, and such a person can be considered as enwrapping his wickedness in a mantle of righteousness. As Chazal comment (Talmud Yerushalmi, *Chagigah* 2:1), "The verse states, 'You push man to the crushing point, and You say, "Repent, O sons of man" ' (*Tehillim* 90:3). [This means] to the point where his life is leaving him."[8]

---

8   The Talmud there records an exchange between Rebbi Meir and his teacher Elisha ben Avuya, who had become a heretic long before. Elisha was near death, and Rebbi Meir was telling him that it is never too late to repent. As proof for his assertion, Rebbi Meir adduced the above quoted verse, which states that Hashem cries for a person to repent even

THE DEED AND THE INDIVIDUAL

How can we help a person to "chop off branches with an ax" (*Yeshayahu* 10:33) — how can we help him to uproot this notion,[9] and what is the instrument for him to utilize in this task?[10] Let him consider the following: The Almighty analyzes a person's every act according to two criteria: the essential deed itself and who the individual is. As regards the deed, each positive act yields reward in relation to the results engendered in its wake — the more "fruits" that the act generates, the more the perpetrator is blessed; the more the fruits multiply (even though they are now detached from their original foundation and exist independently), the more is his reward increased. Chazal discuss this concept in the Talmud (*Kiddushin* 40a): "A meritorious act has a principle and a dividend...whereas a transgression has a principle, but no dividend.[11] This being the case, how do I interpret the verse: 'They [the wicked] will eat the fruit of their way, and will be sated with their own schemes' (*Mishlei* 1:31)?[12] The answer is that a transgression which 'bears fruit' [i.e., which influences others to adapt negative behavior], has fruit [i.e., is punished both for the act and the negative effect], whereas a transgression which does not bear fruit [i.e., which does not negatively influence others], has no fruit [i.e., is not punished more than the inherent wickedness of the act]." Accordingly, the Almighty's desire to bestow good (which far exceeds His imperative to mete out punishment) guarantees that when a person performs a mitzvah yielding "fruits" [i.e., that positively influences others], he will in turn be rewarded with copious and abundant dividends.

---

when his life is leaving him. Rav Yisrael's point is, if so, how can a person possibly refrain from repenting by claiming that it is better to remain an ignorant and inadvertent sinner than to become a purposeful one?

9   The notion that he will be considered an unintentional sinner if he deliberately withholds himself from learning the halachah.

10 The task of teaching him that he cannot hide behind ignorance.

11 In his commentary to the Gemara, Rashi explains this as meaning that a meritorious act is granted reward in excess of its inherent level of goodness, while a transgression is not punished in excess of its inherent level of wickedness.

12 Rashi explains that they will eat the fruit (i.e., dividend) of their misdeeds in this world, while the principle remains intact for punishment in the World to Come.

FOOTNOTE OF RAV YISRAEL: With this idea in mind, we can answer a question posed by Tosafos on the following passage in the Talmud (*Shabbos* 55a): "The Almighty said to Gavriel, 'Go and mark a *taf* [a Hebrew letter] of ink upon the foreheads of the righteous so that the destroying angels will not have power over them, and a *taf* of blood upon the foreheads of the wicked so that the destroying angels may have power over them.' Rav said: '*Taf* stands for "you shall live" (*tichyeh*); *taf* stands for "you shall die" (*tamus*).' Shmuel said: 'It denotes that the merit of the *avos* [patriarchs] will "be exhausted" (*tamah*).' " Further on, Rebbi Yehoshua ben Levi and Rebbi Yochanon [and others] offer their opinions of exactly when the merit of the *avos* was exhausted. Tosafos queries, "We constantly invoke the merit of the patriarchs in our prayers. To what purpose do we do so, if it has been exhausted?"

According to what we said above, we can say that there are two aspects relating to this matter. The first is the merit of the *avos* that was engendered by the awesome deeds that they themselves performed; even though these ended when they passed away, the light they generated would continue to shine on their descendants — if not forever, then at least for a fixed amount of time that would only come to an end after many generations. In the Gemara, the Amora'im debate over when this fixed time was.

The second aspect is the merit that the patriarchs gain through the deeds of their children, for the patriarchs are the foundation and true source of every good deed performed by their progeny. The merit of their offspring creates continuous dividends, without boundary or limit. It is impossible for this aspect of the patriarchs' merit to be exhausted, because "Israel is not widowed" (*Yirmeyahu* 51:5), and righteous people are to be found in every generation. Moreover, "Even the transgressors of Israel are full of mitzvos like a pomegranate [has seeds]" (*Eruvin* 19), and the actions of later generations — which derive from the power of the patriarchs — help to increase the patriarchs' own merits. [This merit is, therefore, always available to protect their children.]

We find a similar idea reflected in the following Talmudic passage (*Arachin* 16a): "*Nega'im* [a skin disease] come on account of seven sins: for *lashon hara*.... Can this be so? But Rebbi Anani bar Sasson said, 'Why is the [Torah] section concerning the priestly garments placed next to the section concerning sacrifices? To tell you that just as sacrifices procure atonement, so do the priestly garments procure atonement ... the robe procures atonement for *lashon hara*....' There is no contradiction: This one results when his actions were effective [i.e., when the *lashon hara* which he spoke resulted in strife], the other when they were not effective. If his actions were effective, *nega'im* come upon him; if his actions were not effective, the robe procures atonement." Although the speaking of *lashon hara* is equal in both cases, nevertheless there is a great distinction between them: namely, the resultant consequences. When the act is effective, thereby increasing the *lashon hara*'s power, it requires additional atonement. The same holds true concerning a positive deed. If a person's action is effective and bears fruitful produce, then the merit of the act's source [the *avos*] will be increased. It is for this reason that we continually invoke the patriarchs' merit, which is forever aroused through the acts of their descendants.

Likewise, every evil act incurs punishment in relation to the results that follow in its wake. The more "bitter fruits" that the act produces, the more its evil will be magnified, and the greater will be the intensity of the perpetrator's punishment.

KEEPING THE AWARENESS

Often, a person can still guard his path even if he does not have a naturally strong propensity to overcome his desires[13] — if he sees clearly that his deed will burst forth in destruction [by adversely affecting others] like an arrow, which cannot be retrieved after being shot. The key is to insure that the obligation to be vigilant with oneself — which is engendered by detailed examination of our Sages' dictums — is not extinguished from the soul. This being the case, how can a person propagate the delusion of this falsehood within his soul — that his transgression will be considered unintentional (when in truth, this is only so in his imagination, for the Talmud tells us [Bava Metzia 33b] that when a person makes a mistake based on faulty Torah study, it is accounted as intentional) — in such an inferior manner,[14] when he can distance himself from it in such a lofty and exalted fashion?[15]

THE DIFFICULTY OF RESTRAINT

Let us now turn from the deed itself to the second aspect: who the individual is. A good deed is accorded reward in relation to the quality of its undertaking, as measured by how difficult it is for the act to be performed. As Chazal state (Avos 5:26): "The reward is in proportion to the exertion." Likewise, an evil act is punished according to how hard it is to refrain from committing it. The more this difficulty is increased, the more a transgression's severity is diminished. As Chazal tell us (Menachos 43b), "Rebbi Meir said: [In the mitzvah of tzitzis,] the punishment for not wearing white threads is greater than for not wearing blue ones.[16] To what may this be likened? To a king who spoke to two of his two servants, saying to one, 'Bring me a seal of clay,' and to the other, 'Bring me a seal of gold.' Both were negligent and did not bring it. Which received a more severe punishment? We must say, the one he told, 'Bring me a seal of clay,' but did not bring it."

---

13 See last paragraph of Letter Seventeen.

14 Inferior, because even assuming this claim (that he thought ignorance is considered unintentional) has any validity whatsoever, it still wouldn't count for much, because after all is said and done, the person had the ability to study Chazal's admonitions and thereby prevent himself from sinning in the first place.

15 Again, by studying the Sages' words, and thereby distancing himself from sin even if he doesn't have a naturally strong propensity to do so.

16 This is due to the fact that the white threads are readily available, whereas the blue ones are made from a rare dye.

NEVER DESPAIR

This being the case, it is incumbent upon man to keep watch on all of his ways, without falling into the clutches of despair. As long as he is sensitive to the possibility of evil within himself, he can rest assured that [at least] when temptation is not pressing hard upon him, he will guard himself. As a result, he will be saved from a significant measure of sin and punishment.[17] Is there a fool who could be so enamored of folly as to bless himself in his heart (cf. *Devarim* 29:18) and say, "It's good for me to close the eyes of my understanding"? Such a one believes he can minimize the severity of his transgression through dubious classification as an inadvertent sinner, blithely abandoning the more exalted level of observance of distancing oneself from sin.

SUBCONSCIOUS ROOTS

This idea is consistent with the aforementioned assertion of the Rambam, that man is not endowed with the ability to know the consequences of his deeds, to clarify the value of mitzvos or transgressions according to what they will bring in their wakes. Likewise, he is unable to calculate the value of any difficulty involved in fulfilling and observing the mitzvos. The reason for this is because man's emotional forces progress from the antecedent to the resultant; from the innermost depths of the heart, to the revealed. There are abundant external stimulants that can amplify and expose a given latent force, which, if not awakened, is comparatively weak in relation to the other proclivities in one's subconscious.[18] In light of this, when a person attempts to trace the antecedent back from the resultant, he will

---

17 If a person is careful not to transgress in areas where his desire is not stimulated, then when he does sin, *chas v'shalom*, it will only be in an area in which it is difficult for him to refrain. Therefore, his punishment will be less severe.

18 For example, a person might live under circumstances that stimulate his anger, and as a result, this trait will be revealed and grow stronger within him. On the other hand, he may have a much stronger proclivity for gluttony, but the setting in which he lives does not give this trait cause for expression. Based on his conduct, he will automatically conclude that he has a much greater problem with anger than with gluttony, when in truth, the exact opposite is the case. It turns out that anger comprises a relatively insignificant component of his makeup, but external factors conspire to draw the majority of his attention to it.

make ponderous errors in trying to determine the subconscious roots that engender pain in transgression avoidance or pleasure in mitzvah observance. As long as an emotional force is hidden in its root, it will remain concealed from man's understanding. Moreover, it will continue to influence his actions, for he is not even aware of its existence.[19] Therefore, it is not within man's grasp to accurately define and evaluate the level of difficulty in fulfilling and observing the Almighty's Torah. Only He knows the true measure of these hardships, as Chazal teach (*Avos* 4:29): "He is the One Who understands."

TWO LEVELS OF REWARD AND PUNISHMENT

In general, there are two levels of reward and punishment relating to the performance of positive precepts and abstinence from negative acts. Under circumstances that make it difficult to fulfill a mitzvah or refrain from a transgression, a person will be richly rewarded for success but not unduly punished for failure. On the other hand, if circumstances make it easy for a person to perform a mitzvah or avoid a sin, then the respective reward will be milder and the punishment more severe. Therefore, the performance of a *mishpat* (specifically, one that is a positive commandment) and the observance of a *chok* (referring to one that is a negative precept) are equivalent.[20]

Theoretically, *mishpatim* [which are apprehensible to the intellect] are

---

19 For example, financial duress may awaken stinginess within a person. Due to the stimulus that provokes it, this negative force is easy for him to detect. On the other hand, there is another subconscious force at work that influences him to neglect his health. Since this force influences him with no external stimulation, it is not detectable. However, its hidden influence is as negative as stinginess and even more dangerous, because it is unconscious.

20 With this, Rav Yisrael answers the question he raised above, about why the Torah mentioned *mishpat* in connection with positive precepts and *chok* in connection with negative ones. He answers that the Torah is thereby showing that they share a commonality. Namely, the performance of a *chok* is more difficult than that of a *mishpat*. Therefore, the reward for performing the former is greater than that for the latter. Conversely, the violation of a *mishpat* is more severe than violation of a *chok*. Hence, the punishment for the former is more severe than that for the latter. This is why the Torah exhorts us both to perform the *mishpat* and to not to violate the *chok*, showing that the reward for performing a *mishpat* is proportional to the punishment for violating a *chok*.

easier for us to observe than *chukim* [which transcend logic]. The Torah's phraseology reflects this two-staged dichotomy, as it states, "You shall perform My *mishpatim* and you shall observe My *chukim*" (*Vayikra* 18:4). The fact that *mishpatim* are mentioned first indicates that they are the first tier of our approach. In practical observance, however, almost the exact opposite is the case, for there are numerous factors that can actually make *mishpatim* more difficult to observe than *chukim*.[21] As a result, *chukim* quite often serve as the rungs upon which one ascends to the tier of *mishpatim*. This is particularly true concerning *middos*, which, despite being *mishpatim*, cannot be properly rectified and perfected no matter how much toil and energy a person invests in them on this level.[22] His only resort is to get in tune with the intellectual side of his makeup, which has a natural love of uprightness and abhorrence of distortion (even without the Torah's admonitions). This is accomplished through profound contemplation of this aspect of his nature. Otherwise, the traits that are stamped into his very being are likely to control him, despite all his efforts to improve them, for human beings are intrinsically inclined to follow their emotions.

PLUMB THE DEPTHS OF HIS HEART

Let us take the example of a person who is predisposed to excessive irritability and is easily aroused by the mildest of provocations. Suppose he repeatedly recites the statement of Chazal (*Nedarim* 22a), "A person who gets angry is afflicted by all types of Gehinnom," until it is burned into his consciousness and always before his eyes. Unfortunately, however, as soon as he is given cause for anger, his heart is not with him and he is transformed into a different person. All of the beautiful images that he worked so diligently to

---

21 For example, the injunction to not eat blood is a *chok*, while the injunction not to hurt others is a *mishpat*. Theoretically, it should be easier not to do the latter than the former. However, when a person is overwhelmed with fury at another, at that moment it is easier for him not to eat blood than to not injure the subject of his grievance.

22 Meaning, on the level of *mishpat*. Even though proper conduct and virtuous character traits are founded on ethical principles that are consistent with logical tenets, nevertheless, it is often difficult to act in accordance with them. For example, even though we recognize how reprehensible the trait of anger is, we may find it difficult to restrain our temper when we are irritated.

acquire are immediately forgotten, and they vanish into thin air. Such a one has no remedy unless he sets his mind to plumb the depths of his heart and its roots. He must seek comprehension of the general forces that drive him, which are liable to be aroused by the slightest external stimulation.[23] He will then be able to "pour waters of understanding" (cf. *Tzefanyah* 3:8) upon them and somewhat dampen them, so that they won't be so hastily and fiercely aroused. Eventually, he will have the power to completely master his spirit.

MIDDOS ARE CHUKIM

Arousing the resolve to subdue unchecked desire by rectifying one's *middos* is a formidable task. From where can man draw the understanding that will enable him to carry out this difficult undertaking? The primary vehicle is the acknowledgement of *chok* — specifically, the acceptance of the Torah's injunction against anger, and the realization of the gravity of this transgression. As the Talmud relates (*Nedarim* 22a), "A person who gets angry is afflicted by all types of Gehinnom."[24] Concern over the dire punishment for anger has the power (in direct proportion to the strength of one's anxiety) to sharpen one's intellect (each person according to his abilities) so that he now can fathom that which he was initially unable to contemplate.[25]

---

23 In other words, even though the result of the stimulation is anger, he must probe deeper to see if the anger itself stems from a more fundamental subconscious force, such as arrogance.

24 With these words, Rav Yisrael is expanding on the assertion he made two paragraphs earlier, that although *middos* are *mishpatim*, *chukim* serve as the rungs by which a person ascends to them. In other words, even though *middos* are ultimately *mishpat* (because logic recognizes the virtue of refined character traits), they also contain an element of *chok*. Regarding anger, the specific trait discussed here, the explanation of this is as follows: Even though we realize that anger is a reprehensible trait, we nevertheless find it difficult to believe that we are accountable for feelings of the heart — for how can a person control his emotions? This concept of punishment for negative character traits does not comply with the human intellect. Therefore, the injunction to believe that negative traits are punished is classified as a *chok*.

25 The reason for this is as follows: The new awareness that he cultivates will grant him such profound clarity that it will touch even his heart, and bring his feelings into consonance with the ethical understanding of his mind.

For one example of the effectiveness of this principle, let us consider the positive effect that worry and necessity have on man as regards his business affairs. Concern keeps a person on edge and constantly exercises his intellect so that his mental prowess is heightened to a greater extent than he originally thought possible. This idea holds true with virtually all *middos*: the key to mastering them is *chok*. This involves the unequivocal acceptance of the Torah's injunction against negative character traits, and the realization of their gravity and the severity of their punishment — as Chazal have underscored in numerous places. On the other hand, the cultivation of a virtuous character trait is a sublime mitzvah — as Chazal have similarly elaborated on. Therefore, by persistently contemplating the *chok*-like aspect of *middos* and truly grasping the harsh punishment and rich reward they engender, a person will be able to ingrain virtuous traits into his character. At that point, he will be able to relate to them on their true level — as *mishpatim*. This is the reason that *chukim* are mentioned before *mishpatim* in Vayikra 18:5.[26]

GOVERNMENTAL STATUTES

This same idea applies to the observance of governmental statutes. On one hand, they fall into the category of *mishpatim*, for man's intellect directs him to fully and carefully comply with them, even without anyone monitoring his conduct. Nevertheless, they also contain an aspect of *chok*, for both the Written and Oral Law unequivocally exhort us to observe all governmental legislation.[27] This grants a person the fortitude to

---

26 With this, Rav Yisrael resolves the anomaly he noted above, that the order of these two terms is reversed in *Vayikra*, ch. 18, verses 4 and 5. In his typically brief fashion, he is telling us that verse 5 is not referring to classic *chukim*, such as not eating unclean animals, etc. Rather, the Torah is alluding to the idea we have discussed above, that in order to truly observe even a *mishpat* as a *mishpat*, one must first approach it as a *chok*. By doing so, a person will be able to instill within his nature a love of virtue and a hatred of distortion, which is the only way to rectify those matters which we typically understand as being *mishpatim*. We thus read, "And you shall safeguard My *chukim* [i.e., you should initially understand *mishpatim* as being *chukim*] and My *mishpatim* [i.e., you will then be able to truly relate to them as a *mishpatim*]."

27 The Talmud (*Gittin* 10b and numerous other places) explicitly states this *chok*: "The law of the government is tantamount to Torah Law."

ignore the provocations of desire, so that he can clearly perceive matters in their true light, and unreservedly commit his allegiance to the rule of his host country's law.[28]

OUR ORIGINAL QUESTION

Let us now return to our original question: Since the Torah contains enough practical law to occupy a person for several lifetimes, why does it contain such an arcane topic as the *ben sorer u'moreh*? In order to answer this, we must first determine whether the mitzvah to study Torah is a *chok* or *mishpat*. Logic dictates that even the study of the laws concerning a *chok* is considered a *mishpat*.[29] The Talmud itself alludes to this idea (*Bava Kama* 17a): "[The verse states,] 'And they honored him at his death' (*Divrei HaYamim II* 32:33). This refers to Chizkiyahu, the king of Yehudah...upon whose bier they placed a Torah scroll and declared, 'This one fulfilled that which is written in this.' [The Gemara asks,] nowadays, we do the same thing [so what is so special about this? The answer is]...We place [a Torah scroll on the bier], and even declare, 'He fulfilled [the Torah],' but we do not say, 'He taught [it].' [The implication being that by Chizkiyahu, it was stated not only that he fulfilled it, but that he taught it as well.] But did not Mar [lit. "the Master"] say, 'Great is Torah study, for study engenders deed'?" In explaining the Gemara's question, Tosafos, quoting Rabbeinu Tam, comment as follows: "Once we say that a person 'fulfilled,' this automatically includes the fact that he studied, for if he did not study, how can he fulfill, since 'study engenders deed'?"[30] We, thus, see that even though a given mitzvah may be a *chok*,

---

28 Even though a person may acknowledge the wisdom of obeying the law, his *yetzer hara* might influence him to disregard it by arguing that the Torah does not obligate him in this matter. The Almighty counters this strategy by making it a *chok* to obey the *mishpat* of submitting to governmental authority.

29 Because it is obvious that in order to implement a *chok*, it is necessary to study the laws pertaining to it.

30 The Gemara's question (tangential to Rav Yisrael's main point) is thus: What is said nowadays — that a person fulfilled the Torah — is in effect also saying that he studied it (with no distinction being drawn between studying and teaching). Therefore, there was nothing exceptional said about Chizkiyahu that is not said about any other scholar! The Gemara answers by saying that, in fact, there is a difference between studying and teaching — and teaching is a much greater praise. Therefore, by Chizkiyahu, who is considered

the study that is required in order to fulfill it is a *mishpat* — for "if one does not study, how can he fulfill?"

THE DIMENSION OF CHOK IN TORAH

On the other hand, Torah study — even as regards the laws concerning *mishpatim* — is not entirely removed from the dimension of *chok*. This is because Torah study is a mitzvah in and of itself, even if it does not lead to performance. Consider the mitzvah to learn about the *ben sorer u'moreh* (according to the view quoted above that there never has been and never will be an actual case [there is another opinion that this phenomenon can and has happened]). The human intellect rebels against the obligation to study something that has no practical application. Therefore, we learn it only because "I, Hashem, promulgated it" (*Yoma* 67b). The same holds true concerning every section of the Torah — the imperative to study, in and of itself, and distinct from the intention to observe — involves an aspect of *chok*. The only difference [between the essential study of *mishpatim* and *chukim* that have practical application and of *chukim* that are purely theoretical] is a mental distinction.

Perhaps Chazal were alluding to this idea in the phraseology of the *mishnah* (*Avos* 4:5), saying: "And the one who studies on condition to do," instead of "And the one who studies in order to do."[31] This is because it is appropriate to regard the study itself as a *chok* — an intrinsic mitzvah, even if a deed does not result from it — and not just as practical instruction. This is a more exalted level than "*mishpat*-style" study, wherein one studies solely in order to do. Of course, this "*chok*-style" study should be undertaken on condition that it will consummate with the execution of a deed. Therefore, it must proceed in a fashion that facilitates practical application.[32] Namely, one must strive to have a fluent and penetrating grasp of the material, with the highest level of

---

to be the teacher par excellence, it is stated that he taught Torah, but by other scholars it is only said that they studied it.

31 The implication of the latter being that the study only has value as a vehicle to enable performance. On the other hand, the former implies that the study has its own inherent value (for study is a mitzvah even if it is not acted upon), and that it is being undertaken on condition that it will result in action.

32 This is so even if one's goal is not to perform a deed, or if performance is impossible, such as with the topic of *ben sorer u'moreh*.

proficiency and precision (each person according to his ability). In other words, one must have a frame of mind that is in keeping with the required condition — the desire to perform the deed.

THEY DID NOT MAKE A BLESSING ON THE TORAH

These words shed light on the following passage in the Talmud (*Nedarim* 81a). The Gemara is discussing why Torah scholars cannot assume it as a given that their children will follow in their scholarly footsteps: [We read in Tanach,] "But Hashem has said: Because of their forsaking My Torah that I put before them: moreover, they did not heed My voice nor follow it" (*Yirmeyahu* 9:12). [Queries the Gemara:] "Is not, 'They did not heed My voice,' the same as, 'nor follow it'? Rav Yehudah said in the name of Rav: 'They did not make a blessing on the Torah beforehand.' " Rashi explains this as follows: "When they awoke in the morning, they did not recite the blessings over the Torah before studying." This illogical attitude stuns all who contemplate it: they weren't too idle to pursue Torah study, which diminishes a man's strength, yet they would not make a blessing over it beforehand? (The Ran writes in the name of Rabbeinu Yonah, *zt"l*: "They were constantly involved in Torah study, but would not recite the blessing over the Torah beforehand. In other words, they did not consider the Torah important enough to make a blessing over it. This is because they did not study it purely for Heaven's sake, and therefore, they made light of the blessing." This is absolutely incredible! Because their intentions were not pure, they made light of the Scriptural imperative to make a blessing over the Torah — something that has no negative desire to interfere with it!)

"MISHPAT-STYLE" TORAH STUDY

However, according to what we stated above, we can explain as follows. The Talmud states (*Menachos* 42b), "Any mitzvah whose performance constitutes the completion of the mitzvah — such as *bris milah* — requires a blessing. And any mitzvah whose performance does not constitute the completion of the mitzvah — such as the making of tefillin (for the mitzvah is not consummated when they are completed, but when one dons them) — does not require a blessing." According to this, there is no requirement to make a blessing over *mishpat*-style Torah study, for the mitzvah is not consummated with the study itself, but with the fulfillment of what one learned. This is because the purpose of this mitzvah to study Torah is so that one will know how to perform the act. Hence, the foundation of the blessings over the Torah rests on the mitzvah of *chok*-style study, wherein the study itself constitutes a mitzvah. Based on this, we might say that the reason the people did not recite the blessings over the Torah was because they were overpowered by the desire to only engage in *mishpat*-style study. As we have noted, human logic justifies the necessity of such study because it enables mitzvah performance. However, the intellect rebels against *chok*-style study, because it doesn't seem to serve any practical purpose. The *yetzer hara* reinforced this idea within their minds, and convinced them that Torah study purely for its own sake is repugnant. Thus, even though they studied Torah, their intention was solely for *mishpat*-style study. Therefore, they did not regard their study as a complete and independent mitzvah unto itself, and accordingly, did not recite a blessing over it.

It transpires that the reward for Torah study is not confined to the combination of *mishpat*-style study with *chok*-style study [i.e., when a person studies both for the mitzvah of Torah study itself and to acquire practical knowledge for performance]. Rather, the greatest level of reward is reserved for pure *chok*-style study. This is the intention underlying the passage with which we began: "There never was a *ben sorer u'moreh*, nor will there ever be one. If so, why was it [the topic] written [in the Torah]? So that one should study it and receive reward." Chazal are referring here to the reward for study that is rooted solely in *chok*, a level that is more sublime than other areas of Torah study, which are founded on *mishpat*. (Of course, the preeminence of "*chok*-style" study only for itself is limited to this one aspect, for since it does not ultimately lead to a deed, its value is diminished in other respects. As the Talmud teaches [*Kiddushin* 40b]: "The Sages unanimously concurred that Torah study is greater than the deed, for study engenders the deed.")[33]

---

33 That is, since other areas of Torah study lead to practical application, their study is on a higher level than that of *ben sorer u'moreh*. On the other hand, in one aspect the study of

---

TRANSLATOR'S SUMMARY OF LETTER THIRTY-ONE

1. If the descendants repeat the same sin of their ancestor, they are obligated to make atonement both for their own sin, as well as the sin of their father.

2. The Almighty analyzes every person's deed according to two criteria: 1) the essential deed itself — i.e., the result of the act; and 2) who the individual is — i.e., the level of difficulty.

3. The primary vehicle to facilitate *middos* rectification is the acknowledgment that it is a *chok*.

4. There are two types of mitzvos: 1) possible to fulfill, and 2) impossible to fulfill; and three types of study: 1) *mishpat* study, 2) *chok* study, and 3) combined *chok-mishpat* study.

---

the latter is more sublime, because since it is entirely theoretical, with no supposition of fulfillment, the intellect rebels against engaging in its study.

In summation, there are two different types of mitzvos (relevant to Rav Yisrael's points in this letter), and three different levels of study. The two types of mitzvos are those that are possible to fulfill, such as the four species, and those that are impossible to fulfill, such as *ben sorer u'moreh*. The three types of study are pure *mishpat*-style study, wherein one studies solely for utilitarian purposes; pure *chok*-style study, wherein one studies for the sake of study itself; and combined *chok-mishpat*-style study, wherein one studies to be able to fulfill mitzvos, but also regards the study as an end unto itself. Since the ultimate purpose of study is to be able to perform the mitzvah, combined *chok-mishpat*-style study is on a very elevated level. On the other hand, the study of a mitzvah that is impossible to fulfill is also exalted in its own unique way, for the intellect rebels against such study.

אגרת המוסר

IGGERES
HAMUSSAR

THE MUSSAR TREATISE

Rav Yisrael Salanter

THE MUSSAR TREATISE

IGGERES HAMUSSAR

*Man is [created to be] free in his imagination and bound by his intel-
lect.[1] His unbridled imagination draws him mischievously in the way
of his heart's desire, without fear of the certain future — the time
when Hashem will examine all of his affairs. He will be subjected to
severe judgment [for any transgressions that he committed]. There is
no one else to take his place.[2] He alone will bear the fruit of his sin;[3]
the transgressor and the punished are one and the same.[4] It is very*

---

1   The imagination is not subject to the constraints of truth, whereas the pure intellect operates within the realm of truth. If utilized for the good, the imagination is one of the most
vital spiritual powers we have; however, if it is misused it is one of the most dangerous.
Rav Yisrael reveals that the primary strategy of the *yetzer hara* is to subvert man is through
the power of his own imagination. Despite the fact that we know intellectually that
Hashem will judge all of our deeds at the time of our demise, our imagination simply overwhelms this awareness. Even though intellectually we have no doubt that we face judgment at the end of our lives, the *yetzer hara* manipulates the free imagination to fantasize
that there is no judgment. When the imagination imposes this notion, man is stricken
with spiritual blindness: he falsely assumes that he can pursue his heart's desires with no
accountability.

2   Even when a person knowingly transgresses the Torah, he instinctually blames others for
his misdeed. Indeed, in the first episode of sin in the Torah, Adam HaRishon blames
Hashem for giving him Chava, who tempted him to eat of the forbidden fruit. Hence, it is
necessary for a person to realize that no one but the perpetrator — i.e., he himself — will
be held responsible for his misdeed.

3   Since the entire blame is his, the entire punishment devolves upon him alone.

4   After one's demise, his spirit — his thoughts, feelings, and his complete personality — remains exactly as it was when he was still alive. In other words, death is a bodily death, but
his inner being continues to live. Hence, let him entertain no delusions that the entity
that will ultimately receive the punishment in the Next World will be different than him

bitter. Let no man say: This is my illness that I can bear.[5]

The calamities of this world are very small compared to the pun-
ishments of sin [in the Next World]. The soul of man will be ex-
tremely anguished. One day will seem like a year. Woe to us for the
imagination, this evil enemy! It is within our hands, within our power,
to repel him by giving an attentive ear to the intellect, to grasp the
truth and measure the reward [i.e., gratification] of sin against its loss
[i.e., punishment]. Yet what can we do? The imagination is an over-
flowing river, and the intellect will drown unless we place it on a ship.
[The ship is] the awakening [of fear of Hashem] in the soul and the
great dread [of His punishments] in our spirit.[6]

THE GENERAL AND THE PARTICULAR

In all matters and things there is the general and the particular. If we do
not study the general then we cannot understand the particular. For the particular must have the qualities of the general, yet there can be a general with-

---

— the deceased — himself. Hence, "the transgressor and the punished are one and the
same." (See Letter Six.)

5   Let one not assume that he will be able to endure the punishments like one endures the
suffering of an illness in this world. The anguish of most illnesses is tolerable, whereas the
punishments for transgressions in the Next World are intolerable.

6   The awakening of *yiras Shamayim* is achieved through *hispailus*, i.e., emotional arousal
(see Letters Six and Thirty). In its natural state, the heart — which is the emotional core
— is sealed, i.e., the knowledge attained by the mind does not penetrate the heart's barrier. However, the technique of *hispailus* transfers the knowledge of the mind to the inner
chambers of the heart. The process of *hispailus* is initiated by consciously stimulating a
particular emotion through verbal expression.

For instance, let's assume that a person chooses to instill the wisdom of *yiras*
Shamayim within his heart. By fervently reciting Torah concepts that evoke the fear of
Heaven, a subconscious imprint is created. If this stimulation is regularly applied — over
time — the impact of the subconscious imprints will aggregate, intensify, and ignite into a
live, passionate feeling of *yiras Shamayim*. Once the heart is awakened and electrified — it
bolsters, stabilizes, and anchors the intellectual concepts (in this case *yiras Shamayim*)
against the false images of the imagination.

Hence, *hispailus* serves to create the boat that protects the intellect from the raging
flood waters of the imagination.

out the specific qualities of the particular. Hence, the beginning of every-thing is the general, and the particulars emanate from this.[7]

Now, let us consider our obligatory service to our Creator, may He be blessed. Should we not consider what is the general, from which the particu-lars emanate?[8]

THE ALMIGHTY IS THE JUDGE

Without knowledge or contemplation, we can recognize that we are aware of the belief that the Almighty is the Judge, rendering to each man ac-cording to his actions. (If a man's ways are bitter and evil, he will be afflicted with severe punishments, either in this world or the Next World, the eternal world — no one can estimate the quality and quantity of this severity. And if his ways are pure and his conduct is straight, he will be blessed with sublime delights in this world and more in the Next World — with wondrous plea-sures far beyond our ability to understand and experience.) This [awareness of the awesome Divine judgment and the subsequent reward and punish-ment] is the beginning step in our service of Hashem, may He be blessed.

This concept is mentioned in the Talmud (*Makkos* 24a): "Chavakuk came and unified the entire Torah into one principle: the *tzaddik* (the righ-teous man) lives by his faith.[9] Also Chazal state (*Bava Basra* 78b): "Therefore the rulers say, 'Come let us make an accounting: the loss of a mitzvah versus its reward, and the reward of a transgression versus its loss.' "

MUSSAR AWAKENS HEAVENLY FEAR

Yet, most unfortunately, this general awareness of faith [that Hashem will judge all of our deeds] remains hidden within us, concealed in the depths

---

7   For instance, in the classification of living things, the term "mammal" refers to animals that nourish their young with milk produced by mammary glands. If not for this definition it would be impossible to identify the particular animals that are in the mammal category. However, once we know the general rule, it is easy to determine which particular crea-tures are mammals.

8   For if we do not grasp the general principle of the Torah, we will have no understanding of Torah whatsoever — neither the general rule nor its particulars.

9   If he has faith that Hashem will judge all of his deeds, he will fulfill the Torah and thus merit a share in the World to Come.

of our hearts. We are devoid of conscious awareness [of the fear of judg-ment], unless we devote ourselves to till the soil of our hearts through the ex-pansive thoughts of Mussar. Without making this effort, our general faith [in the coming judgment] does not send its tendrils over the bodily passions, to bind them with the constraint of fear. The particulars of our conduct do not emanate from the general principles of faith, safeguarding us from the most obvious transgressions.[10] We constantly succumb to principal transgressions that reach to the Heavens — endless transgressions of speech, countless un-ethical business practices, and worst of all, the neglect of Torah study. In short, there is no soundness in any part of our body.

This is especially true in light of the statement of our Sages (*Sukkah* 52a): "The greater the person, the greater the *yetzer hara*." Thus, we perpe-trate grave and consequential transgressions. Yet, because of the darkness in our hearts, we are as the blind — we do not see their enormity. Only if we view them through a magnifying lens — the healthy intellect looking through the lens of the faithful Torah — only then, do we perceive the great overwhelming seriousness of our transgressions. (For instance, even though the size of a star far exceeds the size of the earth, nevertheless it appears to us as a small point of light. Yet when viewed through a telescope, the star ap-pears a bit larger than when viewed with the naked eye. However, in truth, we cannot conceive the true enormity of the star, and so it is [with our transgressions].)

THE SINS THAT CAUSED THE DESTRUCTION OF THE TEMPLE

Our Sages, of blessed memory, allude to this (*Yoma* 9b): "Why was the First Temple destroyed? Because of the following three sins that occurred there: idol worship, immorality, and murder. Yet in the period of the Second

---

10 Since we lack mastery of the general principle of the Torah — the conscious awareness of the Divine judgment — we cannot possibly fulfill the particulars of the Torah, i.e., the in-dividual mitzvos. Every mitzvah requires conduct that transcends human nature, and without the fear of judgment, it is impossible for a person to perform the mitzvos. For in-stance, we know that *lashon hara* is a most terrible sin. Yet our natural penchant to speak *lashon hara* urges us to speak *lashon hara* with a drive that can only be extinguished with *yiras Shamayim*.

Temple, they were involved in Torah study, mitzvos, and acts of kindness — so why was it destroyed? As a result of the baseless hatred that was there. Rebbi Yochanan and Rebbi Eliezer both said, 'Since concerning the First Temple, their transgressions were revealed — their time of redemption was revealed. In the Second Temple, where their sins were not revealed — their time of redemption was not revealed.' "

(The concept that the sins of the First Temple period were revealed means that the transgressions were severe and apparent to the eye of the observer. Whereas in the period of the Second Temple, these transgressions could only be detected by an exacting contemplation of their immense severity, and of their ceaseless branching out into more and more transgressions [in every aspect of their lives]).

THE GREATER THE MAN, THE GREATER THE EVIL

The passage (*Yoma* 9b) continues: "The Rabbis asked which was better, the First or Second Temple period? They answered: Look with your own eyes — the First Temple was restored after seventy years, whereas the Second Temple has not yet been rebuilt." This is an application of the principle that we mentioned above: the greater the person, the greater the *yetzer hara*. Thus, during the Second Temple period, when [the Jewish people] were involved in Torah study, mitzvos, and acts of kindness, their *yetzer hara* was enormous. It caused them to fall into potent transgressions. Those who contemplate the truth know the awful evil of these sins [the root of which was baseless hatred].

THE ALMIGHTY EVALUATES EVERY ACT THAT THE INDIVIDUAL HAS DONE

Now, in every situation in which a man finds himself, what is he to do?[11] The day of death is hidden from everybody. It comes suddenly, and the Al-

---

11 Whether engaged in Torah and mitzvos, or immersed in transgressions, man is spiritually blind if he does not learn Mussar. Without Mussar, he does not recognize his transgressions. If so, how can he prepare himself for the eventual, inescapable judgment?

mighty evaluates every act that the individual has done, as it was recorded in the ledger. Hashem evaluates the days of one's life; not one day is missing. More bitter than death will be his end, with no refuge and no escape. As it says in *Koheles* 9:4, "For he who is attached to all the living has hope, a live dog being better than a dead lion." For as long as a man is alive, he has security and hope that he may direct his heart to repentance, but when he dies, his hope is lost [for he can no longer repent].

A GREAT OBSTACLE BLOCKS THE PATH TO TESHUVAH

This being so, as long as our souls remain within us, we should quickly correct our course to the good. Yet, there is a great obstacle which blocks our path: we do not fear the day of death, even if we mention it with our own mouths. This is stated in Chazal (*Shabbos* 31b): "Perhaps you will say death has been forgotten?" Also, if we see with our eyes the death of people like ourselves, it does not move our souls to repent with our full hearts to our Creator. Yet, ultimately, we will come before Him for judgment, and he will rebuke us for all the evil we have committed. This most common reaction [i.e., indifference and apathy to what will take place after our demise] is just the opposite of what it says in *Koheles* 7:2: "It is better to go to the house of mourning than to go to a house of feasting — for that is the end of all men, and the living will take it to heart." Our numbness [to the fear of judgment and the necessity to repent before our demise] is due to the multitude of sins that have dulled our hearts — they have become as hard as a stone.

Thus, it is stated in the Talmud (*Yoma* 39a): " 'Do not defile yourselves with them or become defiled through them' (*Vayikra* 11:43). [The Talmud extrapolates:] Do not follow the primary meaning of defiled, rather follow the secondary meaning — dulled." Therefore, our transgressions are also hidden from us,[12] and we do not readily recognize them. As Chazal state (*Kiddushin* 40a): "When a person transgresses and repeats the transgression, it becomes as if it were permitted to him" — these sins will surround him on

---

12 Not only are we undaunted by the ultimate judgment awaiting us, but we are also blind to our multitude of transgressions.

the Day of Judgment. Our Rabbis, of blessed memory, mention this (*Avodah Zarah* 18a): "The sins that a person casts under his heels surround him on the Day of Judgment." Alas! Have we lost our hope, God forbid? Is there no remedy for us, Heaven forbid?

THE SOLUTION

Only one thing have we found; it is wisdom and not an art. Let us discuss it a little, and it will benefit us greatly.

THE TWO TYPES OF TRANSGRESSIONS

Let us contemplate with our hearts the nature of transgressions. We will see that there are two categories. One stems from unbridled desire, to love the momentary pleasure without considering the result, even though it will ultimately be bitter. We find an example of this in worldly affairs. The foolish man, and particularly the sick person whose intellect is weakened, loves to gulp down food which is sweet to his palate, and he forgets that this will bring him to a greater deterioration of his health. Therefore our Rabbis, of blessed memory, said in the Talmud (*Tamid* 32a), "Who is the wise man? The one who foresees the future."

It also says in the Talmud (*Sotah* 3a): "A man does not transgress unless a spirit of foolishness enters within him." This is the sum total of all his work in his service to the Blessed One — to contemplate the fear of Heaven contained within the fear of punishment. This is accomplished by means of Mussar books and the Aggadic literature of our wise teachers, of blessed memory. These teachings should be internalized to the extent that a person will hear with his ears and almost see before his eyes the great punishments, both quantitative and qualitative. As our Rabbis, of blessed memory, state (*Sanhedrin* 7a): "A judge should always picture a sword between his thighs and Gehinnom open beneath him." (This visualization assists the judge to be intellectually straight; it also applies to everyone else, to guard oneself from the evil mishap of severe transgressions.) If he will do this and his heart will understand — he will repent, and it will heal him.

THE SPIRIT OF IMPURITY

How great is the evil of man upon the earth! There are none who seek righteousness and none who contemplate the fear of Hashem. No one sets fixed and organized times to toil in understanding the fear of Hashem; to draw up the waters of understanding from the belief [that Hashem will judge all of our deeds] that is hidden and concealed in the inner recesses of his heart; [and still further,] to broaden and fortify this belief; to give it strength and power; and to place the burden on his shoulder to rule over the limbs of his body [i.e., his external conduct] by acting according to the Torah, without overstepping any forbidden boundaries.

This is the second category of transgression,[13] and there is no example found amongst worldly affairs. On the contrary, in worldly affairs there is no one whose troubles hover over him who does not take the time to consider how to save himself. Desire is not the cause of this type of transgression. For [the cause of] this transgression is a wonder, as it is wondrous that a person does not apply his heart to contemplate the fear of Hashem and the teachings about His punishments. These types of transgressions cannot be from the first category, because desire is not strong enough to cause them. Rather, they are generated from the spirit of impurity that induces man to sin. This is especially true about the transgressions of speech, for what benefit does the speaker derive from doing them?[14]

THE DEFINITION OF THE YETZER TOV AND THE YETZER HARA

We can apply these two categories of sin in order to find a compromise between two schools of thought, concerning the definition of the *yetzer hara* and the *yetzer tov*. The first, more common view asserts that the *yetzer hara* is

---

13 Hence, the first category of transgression stems from pursuing unbridled desire, without considering the bitter consequence of one's deeds. The second category of transgression stems from the spirit of impurity (as will soon be explained), which causes man to avoid active contemplation of *yiras Shamayim* and prevents him from engaging in daily Mussar study.

14 While the transgressions that stem from desire have a "rational" motivation, i.e., self-gratification, the transgressions that stem from the spirit of impurity influence us to engage in conduct and character traits that violate our own values.

the force of impurity in man that induces him to transgress. Whereas the good inclination is the force of holiness in man that inspires him to perform good deeds. The second school of thought asserts that the *yetzer hara* is the force of desire that looks to [get pleasure from] every sweet thing in its time. The power of that passion "brings him within her house and he clings to her in love."[15] Whereas, the *yetzer tov* is the straight intellect that looks and gazes towards the [inevitable] consequence of our deeds — namely, the trepidation of the fear of Hashem and His exceedingly terrible judgments. And he chooses the advantageous way, to conquer his desire, so that he will be sated with delight and with wondrous pleasure in the World to Come. The glory of this pleasure is beyond description.

EACH PERSON CLINGS TO DIFFERENT TRANSGRESSIONS

We see that the affairs of man constantly vary, each person clinging to different transgressions. There are those whose transgressions are more inclined towards neglect of Torah study than unfaithful business practices and not giving charity, and there are those who are more inclined towards unfaithful business practices and not giving charity than neglect of Torah study. No person is like another when it comes to transgression.

Yet, if the *yetzer hara* were only the force of impurity and not desire, why is everybody not corrupted equally and in the same way,[16] if we do not take into account their supernal roots?[17] However, if we assume that the *yetzer*

---

15 Rav Yisrael likens a person who succumbs to the temptation of bodily gratification to one who is drawn into the house of a harlot and is unable to remove himself from her enticement.

16 If the *yetzer hara* is the spirit of impurity, it will affect everybody with the same spiritual ailments, just as a disease affects each person with the same disorders and symptoms.

17 Rav Yisrael here brings proofs that support both schools of thought concerning what is the *yezer hara* — i.e., the spirit of impurity or the power of desire. First, he proposes that since each person is drawn after different sins, the *yetzer hara* must be the power of desire. This proof is based on the following process of elimination: The spirit of impurity is manifest the same within each person. Therefore, the fact that each person is drawn after a different sin indicates that the *yetzer hara* is the power of desire and not the spirit of impurity.

However, this is only true if we do not consider the effects of the supernal roots — the innate personality drives. In other words, even though the spirit of impurity on its *hara* is also the power of desire, then we can explain the vast range of human behavior. Since the desires of man are dependent upon his temperament (his birthplace, constitution, time, and affairs), each person's transgressions vary according the unique elements of his life.

Yet even this vast range of temperaments and desires cannot explain the phenomena of human conduct. Don't we see with our own eyes people committing transgressions that actually oppose their natural desire? For example, everybody acknowledges that self-aggrandizement is repulsive, yet a person will abuse his own value system in the pursuit of self-aggrandizement. This conflict in personality is caused by the impurity of spirit [and not by desire].

We now understand that the *yetzer hara* is both the power of desire as well as the impurity of spirit. Likewise, the good inclination is the healthy intellect that sees the results of a person's deeds, as well as the holiness of spirit within man.

THE PRESERVATION OF THE SOUL WITHIN THE BODY

Behold! The two aspects of man, the physical and the spiritual, are in accordance with the two components of man's creation — his body and soul. The bodily aspects are apparent to the physical eye, whereas the aspects of the soul are known only from the functioning of the body.[18] The strategies and designs to maintain the soul within the body are focused exclusively on the body. This is accomplished through a wholesome diet and protection

---

own is manifest in consistent, universal symptoms — the combination of the spirit of impurity plus the supernal roots could engender variations in the effects of the spirit of impurity. However, Rav Yisrael is isolating the two definitions of the *yetzer hara* and is not considering the effects of the supernal roots.

Subsequently, Rav Yisrael brings a different proof that the spirit of impurity does affect human conduct, for people often behave in ways that violate their own value systems. Such behavior is an indication of the influence of the spirit of impurity. Therefore, Rav Yisrael concludes that the *yetzer hara* is both the spirit of impurity, as well as the powers of desire.

18 Since the soul is composed of a spiritual element, it cannot be seen by the physical eye. However, evidence of the soul can be perceived by the functions of the body, i.e., the movement of the limbs, the perception of the senses, the cognitive ability of the mind, the emotions of the heart, the countenance of the face, etc.

from danger. In this way [through addressing the needs of the body] the soul is preserved within the body. On the other hand, the preservation of the soul within the body is not naturally accomplished by procedures that nurture the soul; for the soul is neither seen nor experienced independently of the body. (However, on the spiritual plane, in truth, the essential preservation of the soul within the body is dependent exclusively on the soul — according to the level of one's Divine service.)

THE PRIMARY SPIRITUAL DEVICE

Likewise, in the service of the Eternal, may His name be blessed, the primary spiritual device — to empower the *yetzer tov* with both the force of holiness and the clarity of intellect, and to repel the *yetzer hara* and diminish its forces of impurity and desire — is dependent upon the corporeal aspects. That is to say, this is also accomplished by nourishing the body with "good foods": the contemplation of fear of Hashem and Mussar, which emanate from the pure Torah.

IYOV

This concept is taught by our Rabbis, of blessed memory (*Bava Basra* 16a): "Iyov endeavored to exempt all of mankind from judgment. He spoke before the Eternal: 'Master of the Universe! You created the ox with cloven hoof, and You created the donkey with uncloven hoof. You created Gan Eden, and You created Gehinnom. You created righteous people, and You created evil people. Who can overcome Your power?' Iyov's friends answered him, 'You have denied fear of the Eternal One and you have diminished the power of prayer.' " *HaKadosh Baruch Hu* created the *yetzer hara* as well as its remedy, the Torah.

THE PHYSICAL REMEDY OF THE TORAH

Based on this encounter, our Sages, of blessed memory, taught us that the remedy of the Torah is the fear that emanates from it. This is derived from the words, "You have denied fear of the Eternal...." This refers to the physical aspect of fear, which is viscerally perceptible. Thus, the healing remedy for all the ills of the soul is for man to focus his heart and soul on the fear of punishment that is taught in the Torah. Whether in general: to know and understand from the Torah that corresponding to each transgression there is a devastating and awesome punishment, and corresponding to each mitzvah there is a reward of unimaginable elevation. Or in particular — and this is the prime factor — to study the laws of Torah that pertain to each transgression. For instance, for arrogance [one should study] the sections of the Torah germane to arrogance; for unethical business practices, the sections of the Torah that treat the ethics of business affairs; and so, too, for each mitzvah and each transgression, [one should study] its appropriate Torah teachings.

THE HEALING POWER OF HALACHAH STUDY

The handle and prime element in the utilization of the healing powers of the Torah to cure the disease of the *yetzer hara* is the intense, concentrated, and deep study of the laws of the particular transgression.[19] Man naturally refrains from many transgressions, and he will not submit to them even under pressure or duress. On the other hand, there are more stringent transgressions which one will easily commit. For instance, a great portion of our brethren, the Children of Israel, will not eat bread without washing their hands even at a time of great hunger and distress. However, concerning the more serious sin of slander, they will easily transgress — even without the strong drive of desire normally associated with transgression.

THE PREREQUISITE TO TRANSFORM ONE'S NATURE

We see [from the above example] that it is essential, in order to guard oneself from transgression, to persist in good conduct until this good conduct becomes second nature. Therefore, even if one sincerely strives to walk on the paths of Mussar, to dedicate himself with all his feelings and thoughts to

---

19 Although in general, the study of *yiras Shamayim* and Mussar is the cure for spiritual illness, Rav Yisrael reveals here that the primary transformative technique is centered on focused study of the particular attribute at hand. Therefore, change in human nature is rendered by the deep and concentrated study of the trait that needs to be corrected or strengthened.

refrain from speaking slander — even so, he is likely to fail. As long as he has not transformed his nature and his habits of conduct to the extent that he has no natural tendency to speak slanderously, he will still succumb more easily to slander than to eating without washing of the hands. This is the pattern in all types of transgression, each one in accordance with the individual, his time, and his place. Each place varies according to its situation. Every district has certain transgressions which the community easily refrains from and naturally avoids.

We know that the transformation of nature is generated by study and consistency of habit. Therefore, the main principal and the strong pillar to prepare oneself to guard against transgression and to perform mitzvos is the study of the law germane to that transgression or mitzvah. This study must be pursued in great depth and detail. This method of study affects a strong acquisition within the soul; one's character will gradually change so that the transgression is naturally distant from him.

THE PROCLIVITY TO OBSERVE KASHRUS

For an illustration, in our district, praise to the Almighty, the injunction to abstain from non-kosher meat is naturally implanted within the souls of Israel. So strong is this proclivity that no one has to force his nature and desire to abstain from non-kosher meat — it is foreign to him. There is no kosher butcher who would not consult a competent, halachic authority concerning the status of any questionable meat. Even if his inquiry would cause him a significant loss, the fear of Hashem is within him — in his nature and in his ways. This generates the attitude: "God forbid that I should do evil and deceive my fellow Jews."

THE MULTITUDE OF SINFUL BUSINESS DEALINGS

However, in the multitude of our sinful business dealings, we find just the opposite. Most people do not seek advice concerning a suspicion of stealing from their fellow. Oftentimes they oppress victims, even before legal claims are fairly evaluated. Some people, even after legal decisions are made, execute deceptive or strong-arm tactics. Doesn't the Torah view all these things equally? All of them are classified as transgressions, according to the Torah and its judgments. Thus, whether concerning [the Torah injunctions pertaining to non-kosher meat] like: "You shall not eat of the flesh of an animal torn in the field" (*Shemos* 22:30) and "You shall not eat any carcass" (*Devarim* 14:21), or [the Torah injunctions pertaining to monetary rulings] like: "You shall not oppress your fellow and you shall not steal" (*Vayikra* 19:13) — all of these are equally transgressions of the Torah [and must be stringently observed].

It is naturally ingrained in the soul of Israel that all non-kosher meat is forbidden to him; whatever meat is declared non-kosher by a halachic authority — he will distance himself from it and conduct himself only according to the Torah. So, too, in money matters — whatever the Torah classifies as belonging to one's fellow, if someone else besides the owner has it, this is stealing, and he transgresses "you shall not steal." We see, in the multitude of our transgressions, that even the scholars, as well as nearly the God-fearing people, are not careful to refrain from this sin. And, yet, so serious is this transgression that Yom Kippur, and even death, do not grant atonement.

Yet, if a man will direct his heart and soul to learn in-depth the laws germane to business matters from the Talmud and the halachic authorities — each person according to his ability — a character transformation will take place. If the focus of his study is to internalize the knowledge of the forbidden and the permitted, then his study will be particularly effective to guard him from stealing. Even if at first he is unable to desist from all infringements of stealing, he should not despair — for this is due to the strong desire to steal, as well as the prevalent practices of society. He should know with certainty how great is the power of Mussar, that slowly a vast acquisition of knowledge and new habits will take root in his soul. Eventually, questions concerning kashrus and questions concerning stealing will be equally important in his eyes.

TESHUVAH FOR TRANSGRESSIONS NOT GENERALLY COMMITTED

Even if a man has fallen to transgressions that are not generally committed, like adultery and the like — as the Talmud (*Bava Basra* 165a) says: "The majority of people fall to the sin of stealing, the minority fall to the sin of adultery, and all of them fall to the sin of slander" — appropriate study will change him. If the *yetzer hara* has so overcome him that he considered the sin permitted, may Hashem have mercy — the essential remedy (besides the contemplation of the fear of Heaven and Mussar from the *aggados*, the mid-rashim of Chazal, and the Mussar books that are relevant [to the particular transgression at hand]) is the deep study of the relevant laws, with intention to fulfill them. This will slowly bear fruits to empower his soul to be on guard against descending to Gehinnom; or at least, he will not brazenly commit the sin.

> FOOTNOTE OF RAV YISRAEL: At first, let him fulfill the as-pect of the precept that is not in conflict with his *yetzer hara*. The Talmud (*Chullin* 4a) refers to this incremental approach in the case of *mumar lete'avon* (an apostate who violates Torah injunc-tions, not out of rebellion, but in order to satisfy his appetite): "The leavened bread of transgressors (those who kept leavened bread in their domain during Pesach) is permitted [to be eaten] immediately after Pesach, because they exchange it [after Pesach for non-Jewish bread]." Rashi explains that we assume he ex-changed the forbidden bread with permitted bread in order to lighten the sin. And we relay on this [assumption], that he defi-nitely [exchanged the forbidden bread with permitted bread].[20]
>
> When we contrast the religious level of the early generations with our generation — how can we not be embarrassed and mor-tified? In the times of the Talmud, it was second nature for a *mumar* who kept bread in his house during Pesach to lessen the

---

20 According to halachah, all leaven must be destroyed before Pesach. Any leaven that is al-lowed to remain in the domain of a Jew is forbidden to eat even after Pesach. However, all leaven found in the house of a *mumar lete'avon* is permitted after Pesach. Even though he violated the precept to remove all leaven from his house before Pesach, this sin stemmed from desire, not from rebellion. Therefore, we can assume that after Pesach he will ex-change the forbidden bread for permitted non-Jewish bread in order to limit his sin. For we assume that when the precept is not in conflict with his *yetzer hara*, he will certainly comply with the Divine will.

culpability of his sin by complying with the aspects of halachah that did not conflict with his cravings. Whereas, our generation, in the multitude of our sins, fall into the status of *mumar lehachis* [an apostate who violates the Torah out of defiance and rebellion]. For we make no attempt to lessen the degree of culpability concerning the sins that we commit on a habitual basis. Hence, our corruption is tantamount to *mumar lehachis*, may Hashem show us mercy.

We see that the halachic ruling is different in our day than in the time of the Talmud. The *Shulchan Aruch* (*Yoreh De'ah* 2:2) rules: "A *mumar* who lustfully eats non-kosher meat yet knows the laws of *shechitah* (ritual slaughter of animals) [is allowed to *shecht* an animal *only* if his knife was checked beforehand for proper halachic sharpness]."[21] Moreover, it appears that in our day, we are not permitted to partake of *any* food from a person who we suspect lustfully eats non-kosher meat. We must suspect that in all cases he has subverted the holiness of the food. (Meaning, that he is suspect of violating halachah even in matters where he is *not* lustful. Whereas, in the earlier generations, only food that he lustfully ate in violation of the Torah was forbidden to others.) How much more so is it now forbidden to give him a pre-checked kosher knife with which to *shecht*, and eat of his *shechitah* (although this was permitted in the time of the Talmud). One who does this is considered a *mumar* of the entire Torah.

Ultimately, he will gain strength and resolve through much study of the relevant laws associated with the accustomed transgression. Eventually this will help him acquire a different nature, and the notion to transgress will not arise in his heart, even if the situation is difficult.

---

21 In other words, even though he could perform a kosher *shechitah* with a kosher knife — without conflict with his desire — we do not trust him. Since we are not allowed to rely on his word that the knife was kosher, the halachah requires that we check the knife ourselves.

THE SPIRITUAL REMEDY OF THE TORAH

Amongst the Torah's remedies for the *yetzer hara*, there is also a spiritual aspect of healing. As it says in Chazal (*Sotah* 21a): "All the time that a person studies Torah, the Torah saves him." It makes no difference which subject he is learning. If he is studying the laws of property damage — it will save him from speaking slander. Even if the Torah topic he is perusing does not pertain to the transgression, the spirituality of the Torah will protect him.

THE CENTRAL STRATEGY FOR THE CURE FOR THE YETZER HARA

If we look with a penetrating eye, we see that the central strategy for the cure for the *yetzer hara* lies within the physical aspect — the contemplation of the fear of Hashem and the study of the appropriate laws. The other remedy, the spiritual aspect, comes in only subsequently; it is, therefore, classified as a secondary cure. The mitzvah to study Torah is separate and independent of our current discussion, and the parameters of obligation in this mitzvah are delineated in the laws of Torah study. The degree to which the *yetzer hara* is overwhelming does not change how much Torah a person is obligated to learn. Rather, one needs to fulfill his obligation of Torah study, regardless of the condition of the *yetzer hara*. Furthermore, it may not be within his power to learn more than his requirement. Hence, when he properly fulfills his mitzvah of Torah study, at least the spiritual remedy for the *yetzer hara* will accordingly be extended to him.

THE CURE IS BASED ON THE SEVERITY OF THE ILLNESS

However, the physical aspect — the contemplation of the fear of Hashem and the study of the relevant laws — is a primary remedy. A person needs to conduct himself with regard to this primary remedy in the same manner as he does with the healing of bodily disease. That is to say, the severity of the illness is proportionate to the strength of the remedy — in quality and quantity. Likewise, in disease of the soul, the cure is based on the severity of the illness. As long as this *yetzer hara* is attacking him, so is there a demand

to increase contemplation of the fear of Hashem and the study of the appropriate laws. If man does not use this physical remedy, then also the spiritual
remedy, the study of Torah, will not render much influence over the illness of
the *yetzer hara*. This is comparable to the health of man, in that the spiritual
function — the soul — is sustained by the corporeal functions.

A HEART OF STONE

The enemy that ambushes man is the *yetzer hara*. It works on him to
turn his heart to stone. Man is rendered so blind that he does not sense his
awful transgressions, nor his shortcomings. Hence, he does not endeavor to
save himself. He does not contemplate the fear of Hashem to seek an effective remedy — the physical aspect of healing.

A MAN SHOULD INFLUENCE OTHERS TO STUDY MUSSAR

In order to heal himself, then, a man should direct his heart to bring
merit to the public by arousing them to contemplate the fear of Hashem and
Mussar.[22] It is human nature to observe other people's shortcomings and recognize that they need much Mussar. Thus, he should strengthen himself with
all of his power to inspire the public study of Mussar. When many people will
be helped and the fear of Hashem will be increased, then the merit of many
will be dependent on him. Consequently, ever so slowly, the study of Mussar
will guide him on the path of righteousness. Thus, his public teaching of
Mussar will be a physical, as well as a spiritual, healing to him. As taught by
Chazal (*Yoma* 87a), "Everyone who brings merit to the public — no sin will
come to his hand."

---

22 Although Rav Yisrael has eloquently proven that Mussar study is crucial and indispens-
     able for our spiritual success and welfare, nevertheless, he also realizes that the *yetzer hara*
     will not allow us to devote ourselves to Mussar with our full hearts. By dampening the re-
     quired intensity of Mussar pursuit, the *yetzer hara* impedes *yiras Shamayim* from awaken-
     ing within our hearts. Therefore, in order to counter the machinations of the *yetzer hara*,
     Rav Yisrael devised a brilliant strategy. Essentially, his plan calls for all those committed
     to Mussar and *yiras Shamayim* to dedicate themselves to strengthen others in Mussar and
     yiras Shamayim. See Letters One and Two for further elaboration.

NO GREATER MERCY

How exceedingly great should this mitzvah be in the eyes of man! He should dedicate his heart and soul to guide people to study Mussar — to save their souls from Gehinnom. It says in the Talmud (*Shabbos* 151b), "All who have mercy on the creations, Heaven will have mercy on them." There is no greater mercy than to remind and inspire people to study the fear of Hashem. Then, their eyes will see, and their ears will hear, and their heart will understand the great stumbling block before them. They will sigh about the time of judgment. Then they will return to Hashem, may He be blessed, so that they will "depart from evil and do good."

The man that is inspired to do this will share a goodly portion in everything that is generated from his efforts. He will delight in the eternal delights — which no physical eye has ever seen. It is beyond human understanding to fathom and perceive the quantity and quality of the reward of this mitzvah. The effort is relatively small and the reward is great — beyond all our ability to value and measure. Every man should put his eye and the power of his intellect to this great thing — if he is a *ba'al nefesh* [a master of his soul]!

נתיבות אור

PATHS OF LIGHT

Rav Yitzchak Blazer

A BRIEF PROFILE
OF THE ADMOR,
HAGAON HECHASSID RAV
YISRAEL SALANTER, ZT"L

PATHS OF LIGHT

MY PURPOSE IS NOT TO RELATE the life story of the Rav, *zt"l*. Rather, my primary goal is to publish, with the help of the Almighty, a collection of his holy letters that discuss Heavenly fear and Mussar study. Additionally, however, my heart yearns to provide others with a glimpse of his incomprehensibly great Torah wisdom, *yiras Shamayim*, piety, and the sanctified path he tread. This endeavor will also bring to light a few of his brilliant and holy thoughts and words, so that future generations can appreciate that his soul emanated from a sublime place.

The Admor, one of the mighty shepherds of Israel, was unparalleled in his genius, righteousness, and humility. His ways were exalted, and his penetrating thoughts raised him to the vertex of Divine service. Therefore, his lofty deeds and actions will serve as a guide to all who seek to fulfill the Divine will. May those who fear Heaven learn from his example and walk in his footsteps, and may the entire House of Israel follow after him, following the upright path of his goodly Mussar. May we apprehend even an inkling of his deeds, manner, and character virtues.

THE EARLY YEARS

We mentioned previously that when the Admor was still a youth in Salant, his mind touched the clouds. His towering intellect, mighty wisdom, and powerful understanding were without peer. Even then, he was renowned as a mighty *gaon* who embodied the splendor of Israel. In those times, the method of Torah study was different from the current approach. Then, the custom was to focus solely on incisive and syllogistic Talmudic study, with singular reliance on the commentaries of Tosafos and the Maharsha. The works of the great Ashkenazic scholars, which have opened the gates of light for us in the paths of Torah study, were not yet available in our lands. And when the "Light of Israel" [a word play based on *Yeshayahu* 10:17, referring to Rav Yisrael] shone forth like the sunrise, a new luminary illuminated the paths of Torah and the in-depth study of halachah. Indeed, he began to relate novel Torah concepts and logical constructs, compounding the whole of *Shas* and *Tosafos* like fine incense, by means of his razor-sharp intellect. His brilliance was a wonder to behold and amazed the great men of the generation.

For several years, his wife involved herself in business concerns in order to provide for the family. Because of her endeavors, Rav Yisrael was able to devote himself wholeheartedly to Torah study and Divine service. At one point, however, while the Admor was still a relatively young man, various events conspired to bring his wife's business undertakings to an end. At that time, the distinguished leaders of the Jewish community in Vilna requested that he move to that illustrious city and assume the position of *rosh hayeshivah*. The providence in this request was twofold: not only did it come at an auspicious moment, it also allowed him to avoid taking up the yoke of the rabbinate, which he had always hoped to avoid. Therefore, he acquiesced to their petition and accepted the appointment. During this period, he presented daily classes in the yeshivah that were extraordinary in their sharpness and profundity and which left the listeners amazed at his genius.

However, after a brief time, he relocated to Zaretza, a small and unassuming town that, nevertheless, boasted a *beis midrash* full of accomplished Torah scholars. This group of *talmidei chachamim* was comprised of both native residents and those who had traveled from other locales. Under Rav Yisrael's tenure, even more outstanding scholars streamed there to study under his tutelage. Most of them subsequently took up positions of authority in numerous and varied Jewish communities and were recognized as the preeminent leaders of the generation. As in Vilna, the Admor gave classes on a daily basis. There, he opened his treasure chest of Torah knowledge, displaying his might and mastery in all areas of Torah study — whether in employing dialectic casuistry and sharp analysis to elucidate a passage's simple meaning or to plumb the depths of halachic investigation. Likewise, he taught his disciples how to derive practical rulings concerning a given topic of study, simultaneously revealing a wondrous ability to divulge new pearls of Torah law.

The most esteemed sages of the city would occasionally come to drink of his profound wisdom, and they trembled in awe over the splendor of his brilliance. Moreover, his teachings were discussed in the various *batei midrash* of the city, with the conceptualizations he innovated on a daily basis being a favorite topic of debate and discourse. I heard from a reliable source that when the incomparable genius, our master and teacher Rav Dovid Luria, *zt"l*, from Bichav, visited Vilna, he would sporadically attend the Torah lectures that the Admor presented to the public. Rav Luria lavished great praise on our master's keen and recondite intellect, which I elected not to commit to writing.

In truth, however, I do not know any adjectives that come close to depicting his greatness, or that can convey the full magnitude of his righteousness and piety, for his level of spirituality was so exalted as to be above all praise. Here I can only hope to provide the barest glimpse of his majesty. Suffice it to say that just as he was a *gaon olam* in his wisdom and Torah knowledge, so, too, he lit up the entire the world with his righteousness and piety.

RAV YOSEF ZUNDEL

We already mentioned above that when the Admor was still a tender youth, he drew near to the pious and holy *gaon*, our master Rav Yosef Zundel, *zt"l*, renowned and known to all as Rav Zundel Salanter. This virtuous and humble scholar spread his spirit and the nobility of his righteousness over his young disciple and profoundly influenced him with the holiness of his ways. It was he who inflamed Rav Yisrael's heart to study Mussar and the fear of Heaven. When the youth began directing his footsteps in the path of his pious teacher — to seek wisdom, *yiras Shamayim*, and righteous humility — his heart was set afire and his soul was inspired to attain this precious attribute. He continued to grow in this way until his entire being was infused with Heavenly fear that was sublime in every dimension and aspect. The fear of judgment and the dread of punishment were continually in his conscious-ness. In his *Iggeres HaMussar*, the Admor wrote, "Chazal's statement (*Sanhedrin* 7a), 'A judge should always be fearful and imagine that a sword rests between his thighs and that Gehinnom gapes below him,' does not pertain exclusively to judges. Rather, it applies to every man, in order to protect against the evil occurrence of grievous sin. Judges were specified only because they are apt to stumble in applying the law." The powerful *yirah* that the Rav acquired through studying Mussar was a lamp to light his path. It cleared the way before him to serve the Almighty, and facilitated his acquisition of all the virtues and positive character traits in the world.

THE BEGINNING OF RAV YISRAEL'S DIVINE SERVICE

When the Admor first uplifted his heart to seek the Almighty's will, he set his attention to deeply fathom the wisdom of *yirah*, so that he might comprehend the ways of Divine service. He endeavored to determine the straight and sure path that he should choose at every juncture. The beginning of his holy service was to delve into the concept of studying Torah *lishmah* in its most exalted aspect. In his wisdom, he discerned that in the wake of the desire to study *lishmah*, a judge could render a distorted ruling. The pursuit of this ideal can weaken the desire to develop an enhanced proficiency in one's study and to sharpen the intellect to the heights of acuity and wisdom. Likewise, it alters the order of Torah study in a way that does not necessarily suit the requirements of each individual, so that a person's talents may not be developed to the fullest. These two flaws can combine to cause immense damage to the perfection of one's wisdom. Therefore, the Admor elaborated extensively on this topic to his closest disciples, to alert them against inhibiting their growth. He demonstrated that proficiency of learning — acquiring a wise and understanding heart, sharpening and straightening the intellect, and attaining a comprehensive expertise of Torah knowledge — is a crucial component in every person's Divine service.[1] The more one's wisdom and knowledge is increased, the more one is able to perfect his *avodas Hashem*.

---

1   See Letter Twenty-seven.

PILPUL

Likewise, Rav Yisrael was drawn after the exercise of *pilpul* as a means to sharpen the mind in Torah study. This was true despite the fact that many *gaonim* and pious men of previous generations strongly exhorted against this method of study, and instead advocated the development of straightforward conceptual innovations firmly grounded in *Toras emes*. The Admor labored and toiled extensively to seek an exact parameter for the definition of *Toras emes*.[2] Ultimately, he decided that there is no problem with employing this method of analysis [i.e., *pilpul*], as he writes in the introduction to *Sefer Tevunah* — see there, where he presents his initial elaboration concerning the concepts of wisdom that are pertinent to defining *Toras emes*.[3] After this discussion, he wrote: "The *chachmei Mussar* similarly felt that Torah students should be strongly discouraged from engaging in *pilpul*.... In my opinion, however, the exact opposite is the case...based on a strong realization that was impressed upon me by the experiences of my youth, when I dedicated myself to study Mussar and learn its statutes. At one point, I made a decision to force my *yetzer hara*...to totally abandon *pilpul*. I decided that I would look only to the truth.... While proceeding in this method, I engaged in a critical self-evaluation and realized that the desire to demonstrate my mental capabilities had caused me to breach the boundary of the truth. I saw that my intellect had strayed, bending the truth to my desire — and that the 'truth' was founded on my desire to demonstrate the power of my intellect! I then said to myself, it would be far better for me to permit myself to utilize *pilpul* without any doubts or fears, just as Chazal permitted it to help sharpen one's mental acuity...."[4]

SETTING HIS COURSE

When yet tender of years, Rav Yisrael consecrated his heart to pursue the paths of Hashem and the power of his righteousness was like the majesty of thunder. At this time, he thought to embrace the course of abstinence — to be as one "hidden amongst the vessels" — a *nistar* [a *tzaddik* who modestly conceals his splendor]. His intention was not to detach himself from the

---

2   See Letter Twenty-nine.
3   Ibid.
4   See Letter Thirty.

world and human interaction. Rather, he sought to conceal his wisdom, deeds, and conduct from the eyes of every person. He did not want people to apprehend his eminence, nor to detect his essence whatsoever. Therefore, he planned to search for a place to live where he could reach this goal, and he began making preparations to pursue this objective. Indeed, those that know of Divine mercy, know that this wondrous course of abstinence brings those who seek to fulfill the Divine will very close to acquiring great perfection in *avodas Hashem*. It also has the power to elevate one to lofty and exalted heights in the paths of spirituality. This is particularly so in a man like Rav Yisrael — with the power of his wisdom, genius, and his great *yiras Shamayim*.

Nevertheless, this course of abstinence has a disadvantage. It impedes man from performing valiant deeds on behalf of Hashem and His Torah. Namely, it precludes from him the opportunity to assist others in their spiritual development, and to bring merit upon the public. Therefore, he reflected deeply on this until he determined that abstinence is not the path that Hashem desires. Should a man who shines with wisdom, whose strength is *yiras Hashem*, and who has the strength of spirit to perform mightily for the Torah of Hashem and for the fear of Heaven — sit securely and concern himself only with bringing merit to himself? Moreover, upon considering the plight of the generation, one who comprehends *yiras Hashem* may not be silent at this time! Focusing exclusively on one's own spiritual growth is as reprehensible as one who engages in worldly pursuits only to feed his own mouth, God forbid. Rather, let him consider the verse from *Tehillim* (89:3), "The world is built on kindness." Therefore, let him devote his goodness also to help others and consider those less fortunate than him. This idea is conveyed in the introduction to the book *Nefesh HaChaim*, in the name of the pious *gaon* Rav Chaim Volozhiner. There it states that Rav Chaim always reiterated the concept that man was not created to benefit himself. Rather, man was created to help his fellowman — with all of his strength (see the text). Likewise, in his pursuit for eternal life in *olam haba*, one should not seek, gather, and hoard all the spirituality only for himself, saying, "Peace upon you my soul!" Rather, his intention should be to increase the honor of Heaven, as well as to have compassion and mercy on people; to direct their hearts to *yiras Shamayim* and to walk in His ways. Therefore, Rav Yisrael regretted — and retracted — his original thinking. He began to perform activities for Torah and *yiras Shamayim* and bring merit upon the masses.

He was strong and unrelenting in his opinion. When living in Vilna an incident occurred revealing his unwavering view of this conviction. The residents were in awe of one man who seemed to be a *nistar*. He worked in a sawmill. Many people sensed uniqueness about him because he wore *tefillin* all day and his lips continually uttered words in silence. Many people in the community desired to unmask the secrets of this man and to unveil the source of his goodness. They approached the Admor and requested that he reveal the inner essence of this man. The Admor responded to them with the following answer, "Behold, a man who is on the highest level of wisdom and *yiras chet* (fear of sin), I don't believe, during times like this, would conceal himself and 'hide amongst the vessels' — sitting alone and silent, without worrying whatsoever about the generation. However, perhaps this man here in Vilna is a *talmid chacham* and *tzaddik*. At this time, nobody is able to recognize his devotion and modesty in Divine service. He has no conflicts with any man. Hence, he is very fortunate because his service is concealed in the celestial heights. Therefore, it is easy for him to serve Hashem with pure *avodah lishmah* and to study Torah *lishmah*. If so, why should we scrutinize and examine his affairs, and divulge his essence to the public? For if we so disturb him, we will remove from him this precious virtue of *avodah* and learning Torah *lishmah*."[5]

HALACHIC ARBITER

For private reasons, never in his lifetime did Rav Yisrael accept a rabbinical position. However, he did not advocate this path for his students. Indeed, in general, he opined that in our generation, proficiency in rendering halachic ruling is the strength of the foundation of Torah observance. Like-

---

5   This man conducted himself as a *nistar*. However, Rav Yisrael held that in light of the spiritual downfall of the generation, a *tzaddik* should not hide himself. Rather, he should reveal His light to others. Therefore, although the man conducts himself as a *nistar*, he is not a true *nistar*. For anyone who achieved the true level of *nistar* would reveal himself for the sake of helping *klal Yisrael*. Yet, surely, he is on a high level — so, better not to disturb him.

wise, he wrote in one of his letters, "Something which stands in the heights of the World of Truth is to give one's heart to strengthen the status of halachic ruling amongst the people of Israel — for upon it rests the foundation of religion. Namely, to show to the nation which deed should be done and the path of Torah upon which they should walk." Consequently, in particular, he directed the greatest of his students to incorporate the study of rendering halachic rulings within their learning curriculum so that they would be prepared to make a halachic ruling when time required.

Some of his greatest students imagined that they would be able to be spared from undertaking a public position. In this way, wouldn't they be able to sanctify their days, "Holy to Hashem" (*Shemos* 28:36), without accepting upon themselves the yoke of the rabbinate? Therefore, they asked him for his counsel [whether they should train to render halachic rulings]: "Is it possible that Torah study in preparation for the rabbinate be within the framework of Torah *lishmah*?"

The Admor answered them with the sweetness of his words: "There is no *lishmah* greater than this! Your imagination deceived you. Do not mislead yourself with the notion that you will be able to withstand the test. Indeed, when financial pressure forces you to take a rabbinical position to sustain your family — then all your devises will vanish. Then, necessity will compel you to accept upon yourself the yoke of halachic arbiter. It is worse than this, for even if you are not accomplished and competent to fulfill all the requirements of an arbiter, nevertheless, you will not restrain yourself from accepting the yoke of arbiter. Necessity rules over everything, and as a matter of course, this will ultimately come about. Therefore, the goal of Torah learning is not for the sake of the 'Torah of the rabbinate.' Rather, it is vital to prepare oneself for the eventuality when it will be necessary for one to make halachic decisions — [which he will have to do] whether or not he is competent. Furthermore, learning the method of how to make halachic rulings is *lishmah*, as long as his intention is to prepare for the time that necessity forces him to take a rabbinical position, so that he will not mislead the public. On the other hand, if he issues erroneous rulings he will be demoted to the group that Chazal warned about (*Avodah Zarah* 19b): 'For many dead were cast down' (*Mishlei* 7:26); says Chazal, 'This refers to a student who has not reached the level of halachic arbiter and, nevertheless, decides.' Therefore, there is no *lishmah* greater than this preparation for the inevitable future."

BETWEEN MAN AND HASHEM

The path of Rav Yisrael's *avodas hakodesh*, in the aspect of Torah that deals with the relationship between man and Hashem, was one of great watchfulness and zeal. He devoted himself to fulfill all the words of the Torah — both in "turning away from evil" (*Tehillim* 34:15), as well as in "performance of good deeds" (ibid.). He would often quote the verse, "If you seek it like silver and search for it like buried treasure, then you will understand *yiras Shamayim*" (*Mishlei* 2:4). He would say that the general rule is that the service of Hashem is parallel to the methods of business. He gave many examples of how the ways of business apply to watchfulness and zeal in *avodas Hashem*. One time he sent a telegraph from the city of Memel to Vilna to his son-in-law, the *gaon*, *zt"l*, on the thirteenth of Nissan, concerning the matter of checking his room for *chametz*.[6]

The extreme caution he exercised to prepare the *kezayis* matzo, in order to fulfill the mitzvah of eating matzo on the first night of Pesach, would seem to us unnecessary. One man would cut a few stalks [of wheat] by hand, while intending, as he cut, "for the sake of the mitzvah." Then Rav Yisrael would dry and thresh them, and after the threshing he would place them in a small container and keep it in his house in a hidden place. Then he would grind them before Pesach with a hand mill and make a bit of flour, in order to fulfill the mitzvah with it on the first night of Pesach. How much effort he put into this and sometimes at such great expense! I saw one letter that was written when he was abroad to one of his relatives concerning careful preparation for the obligatory matzos. Here is a quote of his pure language: "I request from you, whom I deeply respect, and forgive me for asking: Perform a little preparation for Pesach night on my behalf. Do not spare any expense whatsoever that this may require, because this mitzvah is as precious to me as the *esrog*, where there is no sparing of expense." And in a letter from a different year he wrote in his pure words, "Do not spare any expense, even many rubels. The

---

6 Classically, a telegraph is sent to convey an urgent message. Rav Yisrael considered the fulfillment of a halachah a matter of utmost urgency, worthy of a telegraph.

mitzvah of matzo is not less than the mitzvah of the four species."

He also guarded his mouth and tongue with extreme caution from uttering forbidden words, such as *lashon hara*. Although he conducted himself with great pleasantness with people, nevertheless, he was careful not to engage in idle conversation. On one occasion, he admonished a member of his family concerning an issue of improper speech. He said to him as follows: "Regarding *lashon hara* you cannot say to me, 'Remove the beam' (*Bava Basra* 15b).[7] Apparently, he was of the same opinion concerning idle conversation. If the Admor, despite his humility, held such a position for others concerning forbidden speech, undoubtedly he was very cautious about his own speech.

Once the Admor spoke with one of his relatives about worldly matters in a jovial manner. One God-fearing student heard the tone of the conversation, and it seemed to him that the Rav was engaging in unnecessary speech. On one occasion, the student spoke with the Admor concerning the boundaries of idle conversation. He nerved himself to ask the Admor on what basis did he allow himself to speak in that manner with that man. The Admor, in his humility, did not take offense at his question. He answered, "This man was deeply aggrieved in spirit. Therefore, it was a great mitzvah of kindness to brighten his melancholy soul and to relieve his mind of worry and sadness. Now, what was I to do to revive his spirit — mention ideas of *yirah* and Mussar? Rather, [his heart needed joy of] sweet conversation concerning worldly events." We can surmise from here how precisely he weighed his words on the scale of *yiras Shamayim*.

I also remember once, when I was in my youth, I walked with the Admor to pray in a field behind the city. I was filled with an awesome reverence for him. Therefore, because of this great fear, I never spoke with him in the same manner that I spoke with others. My conversations with him never touched on worldly affairs. Rather, I always pricked up my ears to capture his sweet words and teachings. However, once I had a reason to convey to him an incident concerning worldly events. When I finished speaking, he asked me whether or not I had a purpose in what I related to him. When I began to ex-

---

7   The Talmud teaches that since people can no longer accept reproof, therefore reproof should not be offered. However, Rav Yisrael held that, nevertheless, we are still required to admonish one who speaks *lashon hara*.

plain my purpose, he stopped me and did not want to listen. He told me, "You do not have to answer, for it makes no difference to me. I just want to caution you concerning unnecessary speech."

Indeed, we merited to see his splendor and to always observe his paths, his activities, and his movements. Therefore, according to our estimation, he did not walk four steps without thinking about Torah and *yiras Shamayim*.

From the days of his youth, he labored and toiled to rectify his *middos*. He pursued this with the power of the wisdom of Mussar and Torah, as well as the implementation of proper habit. Ultimately, he ascended to a sublime spiritual level and perfected all of his emotions, thoughts, and character traits. He persisted until he mastered all of the good and desirable virtues of character and internalized them as his permanent nature.

ATTITUDE TOWARDS MONEY

Most people are driven by the desire for money and the desire for honor. However, Rav Yisrael had no such proclivities — in fact, those desires practically repulsed him. Since he never accepted a rabbinical position, he was always subject to hardship and poverty. Yet he was never disheartened for the lack of anything material. In fact, no one ever heard him say that he was lacking something. Indeed, he never mentioned anything about his physical situation.

When his dignified presence resided in the city of Vilna, he presented Torah lectures for which he received payment. Subsequently, for reasons known only to his family, he left the city and moved to the city of Kovno. The Jewish dignitaries there appointed him to administrate the Torah affairs of the city, and he received a stipend for this. In the middle of his term, he resigned from the post. Then, left with no income, he needed to benefit from others. One of his special students, from among the greatest of them, granted the necessary funds. This matter troubled the *tzaddik* all the days of his life. He held the view of the Rambam (*Avos* 4:5) that a *talmid chacham* should not benefit from the honor of his Torah. Even more, he feared for his life, frightened that the world would accuse him of benefiting from stolen money. He anguished and suffered constantly over this.

Once a great Rav, a close confidant, was lodging in Rav Yisrael's house.

Before the meal, the Admor said to him, "Perhaps my distinguished guest might partake of a bit of food. You can eat, because it is kosher." The Rav asked him to explain the "riddle." The Admor answered with the brilliance of his words: "It is conceivable that my food is not kosher, for it is stolen money in my hand.[8] However, I already acquired it through changing it by its preparation. Therefore, as far as my honored guest is concerned, it is kosher food."[9]

Throughout the duration of his wife's life, his modest income came through her efforts. He knew nothing about the details of the monies, and he practically never looked at the shape of a coin. When he was old, his wife passed away and left an extremely small sum of money. Since he received assistance from others, he did not touch even one cent of this money. Neither did he give any of it to his descendents. Rather, he distributed it to charity.

Before he grew old, the Admor never accepted a gift from any man. Afterwards, in his later years, it was necessary for him to benefit from others. However, besides the meager stipend that he received from one of his special students, as we mentioned above, he did not accept any gifts. I know of several instances in which people wanted to endow him with special grants, yet he would not accept under any circumstances. This was so even after his wife died and he was left alone. If he had wanted to use his prestige to take advantage of the situation, he would have been able to live and support himself with great honor. However, he was frugal and spent as little as possible on food and clothing. He accepted the bare minimum so that he should not overly benefit from others.

A trustworthy man from Konigsberg related to me the following inci-

---

8   At this period of his life, Rav Yisrael was sustained by a stipend that he received from one of his students. Rav Yisrael felt that his benefactor granted the funds based on the assumption that he was a *tzaddik*. Yet Rav Yisrael, in his great humility, did not consider himself to be a *tzaddik*. Therefore, since the funds were given under "false pretenses" — they were considered as "stolen money" in his hand.

9   Something stolen and then, subsequently, changed by the thief is exempt from the obligation to return stolen property. However, the thief is required to make alternative restitution. Even though Rav Yisrael worried that his funds were "stolen," nevertheless, changing the food through preparation renders the food exempt from the obligation to return the stolen object.

dent. The Admor spent the last winter of his life in the city of Konigsberg. A
wealthy man from a remote part of Germany, who had great *yiras Shamayim*,
happened to be there in Konigsberg. He visited the honorable Admor in his
house. Upon viewing his spartan living quarters and constrained financial ar-
rangements, he offered to provide for him with great generosity. The Admor
refused to hear of it and would not accept under any conditions. Subsequently, when this wealthy man prayed in the *beis midrash*, he noticed that
the Admor was wearing an extremely old tallis. He asked the friends and
family of the Admor, "Speak to his heart — let him at least accept this small
gift," for he wanted to buy for him a new, fine tallis. The man who related this
story to me would frequently visit the house of the Admor. He was charged
with the mitzvah of discussing the matter of the tallis with Admor. He spoke
to him at length, explaining that it was a mitzvah to have a beautiful tallis.
During the conversation, the man said, "I also have an old tallis. If Hashem
sent me money, the first thing I would buy is a nice tallis." The Admor answered him with a smile, "If Hashem granted me a certain sum of money, I
would also buy a beautiful tallis." The end of the story is that he would not
accept under any condition.

At the time of his death, he applied to himself the verse "And they shall
leave their substance to others" (*Tehillim* 49:11), just as the Talmud (*Gittin*
47a) relates concerning Resh Lakish, "At the time of his death he left a *kav* of
saffron, and he applied to himself the verse, 'And they shall leave their substance to others.' " The Talmud (ibid. 12a) explains that this is a very small
measure of saffron. However, the Admor did not leave to his sons even a *kav*
of saffron, not even a book. The reason for this is because he did not want to
use "other people's money" to buy books for himself. Therefore, all of his
books were borrowed. The only possessions that he left were a very old tallis
and his tefillin.

ATTITUDE TOWARDS HONOR

Concerning his rectification of the natural inclination to seek honor, he
all but reached the level of equating praise with disgrace, as mentioned by
the pious author of *Chovos HaLevavos*. He once said about himself that con-

cerning the trait of honor, he adopted an intellectual approach.[10] Therefore, the path of seeking honor was utterly disgusting to him. Indeed, he fled from honor as much as he possibly could. In the early years, when the bestowing of titles was not so widespread, he would be distressed when he received a letter with flatulent titles. He would hide the letters and be adverse to even look at them. Only afterwards, when the use of titles became widely popularized, did he not take issue with titles.

When a great man came to the city, the Admor wanted to visit this guest. He did not stand on the usual ceremony of courtesy, that the guest should first visit the resident. Rather, he quickly and immediately went to the lodging of the guest, in order to show proper respect. Likewise, when a particular situation so demanded, he did not hold himself back from going to anyone's house.

I saw with my own eyes, when the Admor was in one place for a duration of time, another great, highly distinguished man happened upon the city. The Admor needed to discuss a certain spiritual matter and went to his house several times. Not only did this great man not receive the Admor at first, even worse, he did not conduct himself with the courtesy to pay a return visit to the Admor in his home. A few distinguished members of the community were incensed over this, for they saw it as a slight of honor. One of them asked the Admor why he went to visit first and why he went back several times even though the great man did not reciprocate. Afterwards, the Admor spoke with me privately about these events and about social protocol. He expressed his words with great emotion and said to me, "Under no circumstances can I understand this matter of 'who should go first to visit' and 'will he reciprocate to visit me or not.' In my eyes, this is like games of children, especially because I needed something from him." He elaborated in this manner with wisdom and with great and powerful emotion, until I was amazed at the sight of his passion.

HUMILITY

Suffice it to say that Rav Yisrael's extraordinary excellence was counter-

---

10 He did not follow the natural emotions, which desire honor. Rather, he ruled over his emotions with the power of his intellect to be repulsed by honor.

balanced by his humility. It is impossible to record on paper, nor can there ever be accurately portrayed, how all of his ways, words, and movements were infused with *yiras Hashem* and the humility of righteousness. He did not consider himself worthy in the aspects of *avodas Hashem*, may His Name be blessed. During his lessons that he gave privately to his students, it was his practice to speak with emotion to awaken and arouse their hearts. Indeed, streams of water would flow from his eyes as he lamented his spiritual condition.

Also, concerning his external conduct in dress, he did not follow the accustomed manner of distinguished men who elegantly garbed themselves. He wore the same clothing that all the multitudes of the House of Israel wore, as if he was one of the common people, in order to avoid *ayin hara*. Therefore, when he was either traveling or in a foreign place, no one recognized him, since he did not reveal who he was. It was not apparent from his clothing that he was a dignitary. People could not sense who he was — except for the fact of the light of his pure countenance, which he was unable to hide. His wisdom and Heavenly fear illuminated his countenance with the splendor of the countenance of the Living King.

In his elderly years, he would refer to himself as "the poor old man." He would speak rhetorically, saying, "What sense is there for a poor old man to ask for worldly pleasures?" A trustworthy man from the city of Koeningsberg told me [about the time when] the Admor suffered the final illness before his demise there [in Koeningsberg]. When his illness intensified, many people from amongst the distinguished and honorable members of the community regularly came to visit. They realized that a large clock, which beat very loudly, stood in the room where he was laying. They decided to remove the clock from this room and place it in another location. The Admor made out the words of their whispering. He exclaimed to them, "What do you want to do? I am a poor sick old man. So what if a clock beats in my ears? Will you say next to pave the street with hay and straw?"

FORGIVENESS

We know that the basis of humility is the abilty to be forgiving and to suppress any inclination to short-temperedness. This is revealed by our Sages, zt"l (*Shabbos* 30b, 31a), "Our Rabbis taught: A man should always be humble like Hillel and not stern like Shammai." Similarly, it is related in the Talmud (*Sotah* 40a), "Rav Abbahu also said: At first, I used to think that I was humble, but when I saw Rav Abba of Acco offer one explanation and his own translator offer another without his taking exception, I said, 'I am not humble.'" Indeed, a foundational element of humility is not to show any harshness whatsoever.

Therefore, coupled with his great humility, the Admor also excelled in the traits of forgiveness and suppressing short-temperedness, in extremely wondrous ways. We know this from many astonishing incidents that occurred with people who harmed him — and his way of conducting himself with them. Even more, it was his holy way that if somebody sinned by committing an evil deed against him, or caused him pain — immediately he would search for an opportunity to bestow kindness upon that person. Perhaps he could perform a particular good deed, to pay him back good for evil. He would say that this conduct is a mitzvah from the Torah of adhering to the attributes of Hashem. As our Sages, of blessed memory, said in *Sotah* (14a), "Rav Chama the son of Rav Chanina further said: What is the meaning of the verse, 'You shall walk after the Lord, your God'? Is it possible for a human to walk with the *Shechinah*? For it has been taught, 'For the Lord your God is a devouring fire.'" Rather, [the meaning] is to emulate the attributes of *HaKadosh Baruch Hu*. Let us contemplate the ways of the attributes of Hashem. Indeed, when man transgresses, rebelling against the will of Hashem — at that exact moment *HaKadosh Baruch Hu* bestows good upon him and grants him life. It is impossible to live even for one second without His benevolence. Likewise, man needs to conduct himself in a similar way in his attitude towards one that provokes or pains him. The Admor actively conducted himself with this attribute — may the straight people learn his way.

Once the Admor revealed to his students a judicious strategy to uproot the trait of sternness and to accustom oneself to extend forgiveness beyond the scope of one's natural proclivity. Moreover, this method enables one to purge animosity, hatred, and harshness from his heart — towards anyone

who adversely affects him. He himself used this advice in the days of his
youth.

The idea is based on a concept found in several places throughout *Shas*
— "He can only have *tarumos* (resentment) [and not monetary claims
against the one who damaged him]." For instance, in *Bava Metzia* (75b), in
the beginning of the chapter *Hasocher es Ha'umanin*, it states, "And they deceived each other." Says the Gemara, "They can only have resentment
against each other." [This is also mentioned on pages 78a and 52a; see the
text there.] This seems strange, for why is it necessary to mention the idea of
resentment at all? The text should have just said that he does not have any
monetary claims against him — for the feeling of resentment will come instinctively.

However, the answer to this question is as follows: Resentment is sternness and hatred in the heart. If a man sins against his fellow, even if he angers
him with words alone, he must pacify and appease the victim, as explained in
the Talmud (*Yoma* 87a). As long as the perpetrator does not appease his fellow, the halachah permits the offended one to have feelings of resentment
and irritation. Yet, if the perpetrator does appease him, then the offended
one should not cruelly withhold his forgiveness. This is parallel to a case
where someone sins against his friend, thereby causing an indirect monetary
loss. Even though the one who caused the indirect loss to his friend is legally
exempt, and the plaintiff cannot raise any monetary claims against him, the
plaintiff is, nevertheless, permitted to have feelings of resentment. However,
if a person harbors baseless resentment and irritation towards his fellow, then
he is committing a very great sin. Now, in a case when a person is obligated to
pay — then the plaintiff has the halachic right to make a monetary claim.
Likewise, in a case where one is permitted to have feelings of resentment —
then the offended one has the halachic right to feel resentment. This is what
our Sages, of blessed memory, have said, "They can only have resentment
against each other." This means that although one has no monetary claim
against the other, nevertheless, he does have permission to have feelings of
resentment towards him. As they said in *Bava Metzia* (76a), "If the homeowner said four, they [the workers] can have resentment, what else can he
do?" (see the text there). Hence, in that case, where the house owner said

four, the [workers] are only permitted to have resentment.

Consider a monetary case in which a person is obligated to pay money to his fellow. Suppose the plaintiff pardons the defendant (and a pardon is valid even without a formal act of acquisition), then, subsequently, the plaintiff regrets his agreement and demands payment for the debt. This is considered unadulterated stealing because he already pardoned the debt. Likewise, suppose a man has a claim against his fellow for a particular sin which this fellow committed against him. According to halachah, the man has permission to feel resentment and irritation towards him. However, if the defendant appeases him and the plaintiff pardons him, and he continues to harbor the feelings he has of sternness and hatred in his heart against him — this constitutes a cardinal sin. He is claiming something from his fellow, even though he has already forgiven him.

Therefore, based on this, Rav Yisrael suggested the following advice to remedy the trait of sternness. If someone sins against his fellow, either in speech or action, let the victim immediately verbally express his forgiveness. If, afterwards, there is still some negativity in his heart against him — let him consider with his soul that this is a sin of great magnitude. Just like the case where one demands payment for a debt that he already forgave, and it is obvious to everyone that this is unadulterated theft — so, too, if one is irritated with his friend for a certain sin which he already forgave, [it is an obvious sin].

HIDDEN ATTRIBUTES OF HASHEM

The Admor, *zt"l*, in the splendor of his brilliance, searched and found hidden treasures concerning the attributes of *HaKadosh Baruch Hu*. He adhered to these attributes in order to emulate them. For instance, I will recount a phenomenal incident. On one occasion, a great rabbi, who was one of his acquaintances, happened to be in his house. They conferred for some time and then completed their discussion. The aforementioned rabbi requested permission to be excused and take his leave. The Admor also prepared to leave his house. The rabbi noticed and discerned that the Admor was carrying a certain sum of money. "What is that [money] in your hand?"

asked the rabbi. The Admor answered him, "This money belongs to a certain rabbi, and I am going to deliver the money to him personally." The rabbi, quite puzzled, asked him, "Why do you have to trouble yourself? Can't the money be sent by a courier?" The Admor answered him, "In my opinion, a law of the Talmud obligates me to do this." The rabbi continued to express bewilderment, saying to the Admor with a smile, "If there is a particular law in the Talmud concerning this issue, then I would know about it." Admor answered him whimsically, "Perhaps it is not written in your version of the Talmud, but it is written in my version of the Talmud." The rabbi insisted that he explain this riddle.

The Admor answered him as follows: "The Talmud (*Yevamos* 78b) elucidates the verse, 'And there was a famine in the days of David for three years.... And David asked Hashem [the reason for the famine]. And Hashem said, "It is for Shaul and his bloody house...."' 'For Shaul,' because he was not mourned for in a proper manner; 'and his bloody house,' because he put to death the Gibeonites. Then the Talmud asks, 'Justice is demanded for Shaul because he was not mourned for in a proper manner, and justice is demanded because he [Shaul] put to death the Gibeonites?' Yes, for Resh Lakish stated, 'What is meant by the verse, "Seek Hashem, all you humble of the earth, that have performed His judgments"? Where there is His judgment, there is also [mentioned] the performance of his good deeds.' Rashi explains, 'Where there is His judgment: At a time when man is judged, then, at that very moment, the righteous deeds that he has performed are mentioned.' "

[Continued Rav Yisrael,] "We see from this passage a wondrous attribute of Hashem: at the very time when man's transgression is judged, at that very moment, Hashem remembers the righteous deeds that he has performed. Behold, from the death of Shaul — which is the beginning of David HaMelech's reign — until the end of David's days, *HaKadosh Baruch Hu* did not judge Israel for not adequately eulogizing Shaul. Only at the time when the Divine will arose to exact retribution on account of Shaul's sin of killing the Gibeonites, did He mention Shaul's righteous deeds and punish *klal Yisrael* for not eulogizing him according to halachic requirements.

"This is the reason why I am personally obligated to deliver the money. I have a claim to lodge against this particular sage (mentioned above): in my

opinion, he did something that was not correct. Now, it is a mitzvah to adhere to the attributes of Hashem, may His Name be blessed. Since I am lodging a claim against his transgression, therefore, I am obligated to also mention his Torah scholarship. Hence, I must bestow upon him this excess
honor, even though at other times I would not act in this manner. Yet presently I find myself obligated to do this, because the time of judgment is the
time to mention his righteous deeds."

Let us now reflect: How elevated were his paths! How deep were his
thoughts in *yiras Hashem* — to inspire him to find this precious attribute of
Hashem, may He be blessed, and afterwards, to make himself adhere to this
attribute and conduct his deeds accordingly! We see the conduct of the
world is quite the opposite. When someone harbors resentment against his
fellow, whether it is a personal issue or a spiritual matter — the claimant will
no longer make any mention of his rival's Torah or righteousness.

Allow me to say rhetorically that there are those who reverse this attribute so that it becomes, "In the time when his righteousness is mentioned, at
that very moment, the accusation against him is also remembered." For instance, let us assume that a person harbors resentment against his fellow for a
certain sin or transgression. When the person is asked to perform a favor for
this fellow, which would require him to remember the fellow's praiseworthy
virtues, he instead levels accusations against him. Either in this way, or by ne-
gating his good points, he withholds from him each and every favor — for at
the time when his righteousness is mentioned, at that very moment, the accusation against him is also remembered.

BETWEEN MAN AND HIS FELLOW

His ways and his conduct in the sector of Torah concerning the laws between man and his fellow were upheld with the ultimate sensitivity and zeal.
The wonderful beauty of his conduct is unfathomable to us. This praise applies to his fulfillment of both aspects of the verse "Turn from evil and do
good" (*Tehillim* 34:15). He would be just as exacting with *Choshen Mishpat*
(civil law) — precisely analyzing each question upon the scale of justice — as
he was with *Orach Chaim* and *Yoreh De'ah* (ritual law). He revealed many

wondrous examples of how, according to Torah law, a person could falter in the sin of stealing and in issues of damage. These examples are well known.

Behold, from time to time, the Admor would write a recommendation for a certain impoverished individual. Afterwards, people would come to him and speak disparagingly about the poor man. They would charge that this man was not worthy of receiving a letter, because he acted improperly. The custom in the world, in an incident such as this, is to immediately seek counsel to rescind the letter. The Admor was neither afraid nor alarmed. He would say, "Did I not give him the letter as a gift? It is his. If revoked, it would be an unadulterated theft."

Once he was in a particular town with his students. It was said that certain *tzaddikim* in that city had the power to affect *Shamayim* with their words. Whatever they said to a person would be decreed in Heaven and enacted on earth. Occasionally, when someone would damage or pain them, they would strike back at them with words. The curse would cause damage, for whatever they said — without exception — would come to pass.

The Admor spoke about this with eloquence: "A person who is on such a high level that his words take effect must exercise extreme caution. He must guard his tongue and lips from emitting any negative word, for he could easily become classified as an '*adam hamazek*' (a man who is accountable for damages). Is there a difference whether he damages him with his hands or with the lash of his tongue — to strike his fellow secretly, with the power of a Divine decree?"

These words give us an insight into the essence of the Admor's spirit — his conviction and his perspective on the paths of conduct relevant to man and his fellow. We know from experience that sometimes even the great *yirei Shamayim* are ensnared and provoked into acting with anger towards people who cause them pain and harm. They lash their tongues against them, wishing to severely punish them through Divine powers. We should not be amazed at this, for anger resides within the nature of man. For instance, let us consider a man who is a *yirei Shamayim*, yet is stingy by nature. He doesn't touch his money, not wanting to show pity and mercy to the poor. However, he does not refrain from bestowing spiritual treasures. On the contrary, he showers endless blessings upon his fellow. Similarly, as far as cursing others, there is a type of man who is a *yirei Shamayim* who becomes angry with some-one who distressed him. Yet he will not [physically] harm even the little fin-ger of his hand. However, as far as employing spiritual powers, he will hurl upon him burning coals and sulfur. Nevertheless, this is not the path that Hashem advocates, because causing punishment is not a good thing for *tzaddikim*. (See *Tosafos* in *Berachos* 7a, "*Hahu tzeduki...*")[11]

How remarkable and beautiful are the essential principles of the Admor, *zt"l*, who classified one who harms his fellow — even through Divine power — as a destructive person. Clearly, we never saw the Admor display an exam-ple of this negative behavior. His exquisite language was as refined as pure gold. He was extremely careful not to utter any negative word from his mouth, even against someone who injured or aggrieved him. Rather, the ex-ample we saw from him was that he endeavored immediately to bestow kind-ness toward whoever harmed or distressed him. He adhered to the attributes of Hashem, may He be blessed, as we mentioned above.

KINDNESS

Likewise, concerning issues relevant to conduct between man and his fellow, he bestowed benefit and kindness to his fellow with the ultimate zeal and diligence. Sometimes he would annul a pious virtue in order to pursue the path of lovingkindness. When a person who suffered difficulties would come to him for advice, he would put his heart deeply into the matter with great deliberation, in order to correct the problem with good advice. Once I saw an impoverished man, who suffered and lacked money, come to him for help. He poured out his bitter words and the sadness of his heart. The man said his only option for making a living was to visit the surrounding cities and

---

11 Rav Yisrael is pointing out that one's *yiras Shamayim* or Torah scholarship does not pre-clude the possibility that he may have negative traits, such as anger. Externally, he con-ducts himself righteously, holding his peace, i.e., he doesn't hit out when he is angered. However, he spews curses against the one who distressed him. His curses are particularly potent because the merit of Torah is upon him. However, Rav Yisrael justly rules that damage is damage — whether caused by hand or by mouth. In addition, we understand from here that a *yirei Shamayim* can have serious character flaws, and these flaws are capa-ble of destruction. Hence, the importance of *mussar* and *tikun hamiddos* for both layman and *tzaddik* is clearly demonstrated.

give a sermon to the congregations. However, this was not possible because he was not skilled in the art of public speaking and could not please his audience. Therefore, he requested that the Admor kindly teach him a sermon. The Admor granted that which he requested and taught him a certain sermon. He even helped him practice it two or three times.

Rav Yisrael was not reluctant to go to the house of one of his acquaintances to perform a certain favor or act of kindness. Even rain and snow did not prevent him or interfere with his path. The Admor spoke of this in *Sefer Tevunah*: "However, concerning the benefit and pleasure of others, one's obligation is to employ the opposite of abstinence. For this, one must be willing to go out to the marketplaces and streets of the city to seek benefit for one's fellow — and all the more so, that of the public at large." He would literally tremble with fear when in the presence of a bitter, distressed man or an impoverished soul who made the rounds from door to door. The reason for his fear was because the person was afflicted and crushed in spirit.[12]

It is known that amongst the ways of bestowing goodness and kindness is to greet everyone with a cheerful countenance and to speak gently. This is especially true for a person under duress. Says the Reishis Chochmah (*Sha'ar HaYirah*, ch. 12), "Rabbi Yosi said: At the moment a person expires from the world, not only is he frightened by the angel of death...but they also ask him, 'You did not involve yourself in Torah study? Nor did you perform acts of kindness, nor did you proclaim morning and evening that your Creator is King? Nor did you crown your friend as a king, treat him with pleasantness?' " This aspect of Divine service — to crown your friend as a king, treat him with pleasantness, and greet him with a cheerful countenance — is much more difficult to fulfill when the friend is immersed in worry and fear, his face downcast, and his heart closed.

The Admor cautioned that sometimes worry and fear over spiritual shortcomings provoke a perversion of character. For instance, during the *yamim noraim*, when a person is overwhelmed with *yiras Shamayim* and is full of trembling and fear of judgment — this could cause laxity of care in relating to his friend. He must crown his friend and treat him with pleasantness, but

---

12 Because of Rav Yisrael's love and sensitivity for all people, he could not bear to see others suffering.

sometimes [at this time of anxiety] he falters into anger or the like. Yet in truth, at this time he must follow the straight path of character traits. Even more, he must be pleasant and helpful to his friend. The reason for this flaw is because man is not accustomed to give his heart over to concepts relative to *yirah* and Mussar. Rather, he is accustomed to follow his natural inclinations.

The Admor told us that when he was in his youth, the study of Mussar captured his heart and inspired him to contemplate the paths of *yiras Hashem*. Once, on *erev Yom Kippur*, he was going to the *beis hamidrash* to pray the evening service. He met a man who was one of the great *yirei Shamayim* — trembling and fear of judgment were etched upon his countenance, and tears were on his cheeks. Rav Yisrael asked him about a certain pressing matter. Yet this man who had *yiras Shamayim* did not answer him whatsoever, because of his great despondence and trembling. The Admor commented as follows: "After I passed this man I thought in my heart, 'Why am I at fault and guilty because you have *yiras Shamayim*, and you are afraid and tremble from *yom hadin*? Why is that relevant to me? Aren't you obligated to pleasantly answer my question, because this is the proper conduct according to the paths of goodness and kindness?' "

CHILDREN

Rav Yisrael's conduct with his children and descendants was indeed phenomenal. The passionate nature of a father's love for his offspring has caused the downfall of many. For the love of a father blinds the eyes of the wise, corrupts the path of discipline, and prejudices the father's opinion of his children. The Admor conquered his nature to the extent that he did not differentiate between his offspring and the children of others — whether in material things or spiritual matters. The only exceptions were his halachic obligations and responsibilities, as is well known.

One of his sons was a distinguished merchant. Rav Yisrael almost never asked him about the nature of his business or his financial situation. However, when the son would come to visit his father to see if he was well, Rav Yisrael would ask him if he fixed daily times for Torah study. Also, there was a period when Rav Yisrael did not see one of his sons for a few years. When this son came to visit, the Admor received him quite calmly. He greeted him as if he had seen him recently. When one of his sons was in tight straits, he did not use his powers of influence on his behalf, just as he did not use his powers of influence for his own benefit.

HONORING OTHERS

Even more remarkable was that as far as he himself was concerned, Rav Yisrael withdrew from all worldly pleasures — desire, greed, and honor seeking. Yet as far as the pleasures of other people were concerned, he would perceive and be sensitive to all of their longings and provide them with delights from around the world. The Admor wrote the following quote about this in *Sefer Tevunah*: "The most difficult aspect of rectification concerns the correction of one's character traits. A major principle in this area is that most positive traits are only relevant to a person as regards himself. However, in his conduct with his fellow, he is obligated to employ the opposite of the virtue that he maintains for himself. For example, to flee from honor is a precious quality. As Chazal state (*Avos* 4:28), 'Glory removes a man from this world.' However, the reverse is true concerning others, as the Sages said (ibid. 4:1): 'Who is honored? He who honors others.' Similarly, abstinence, which is a sublime quality found in spiritually elevated people, is only applicable to a person as regards himself. However, concerning the benefit and pleasure of others, one's obligation is to employ the opposite of this trait. For this, one must be willing to go out to the marketplaces and streets of the city to seek benefit for one's fellow — and all the more, that of the public at large."

How pleasant are his holy words; how beautiful are his teachings! Just as exquisite was his fulfillment of these ideals: his masterful ability to oscillate between the *middos* that where relevant to himself and the *middos* that were relevant to his fellow. As we mentioned above, he was devoid of the trait of honor-seeking to the extreme. Nevertheless, he was extremely careful to honor people with the accustomed courtesies of honor. When he would pass through a city, he would visit the home of the rabbi of the city in order to honor him. We already mentioned above that he was not adverse to go to the house of his acquaintances to perform a particular favor or kindness to his fellow.

Faith is an extremely precious and important virtue. Chazal have already said (*Sotah* 48a): "Rebbi Eliezer the Great said, 'Anyone who has bread
in his basket and says, "What will I eat tomorrow?" — is surely one who is
small in faith.' " However, this only applies to the man himself. As far as that
which is relevant to his fellow, God forbid that he should think to employ this
virtue against him. On the contrary, as far as his friend is concerned, he is obligated to worry for him — "What will he eat tomorrow, and also in the more
distant future?" Likewise, he must make every effort to help his friend grow
spiritually — and not rely on the virtue of faith.

I know of a wondrous thing. There was something that the Admor was
involved with and, subsequently, realized that in the future it would generate
weakness in a certain Divine matter. He immediately began to worry about
correcting this flaw. He toiled and labored to rectify this matter for many
years. There was no end to his efforts. Everything was done secretly; only a
few special people knew of this. Hashem knows all hidden things and rewards
bountifully those who fear Him. All of the Admor's exertion and efforts are
revealed before Hashem.

HOLINESS

His path was like that of one who traverses many waters yet his footsteps
are unknown. He was a hidden craftsman. He effectively concealed the excellence of his Torah knowledge and righteousness. However, he was unable
to conceal the breadth of his intellect and the sharpness of his mind when
the times required him to assist *klal Yisrael*. This was especially so when he
disseminated Torah to his students and when he taught public classes. When
he would mingle with the great men of Torah, he would "hide amongst the
vessels" (*Shmuel I* 10:22) and hide his wisdom as much as possible. Therefore, it was impossible to know the true measure of his expertise in Torah. If
he would mention a certain concept from *Tosafos* during one of his Torah lectures, he would invariably say, "By coincidence, I recently saw the words of
Tosafos...."

Let me share with you something remarkable that I heard with my own
ears. Once I took lodging with him in a place on *Shabbos Kodesh*. It was win-

tertime, during the month of Teves. The Admor was sleeping in his room, and I was reposing in the room next door. Something caused the candle in his room to be extinguished. There was only the light of a gas streetlamp opposite his window. The Admor awoke at midnight and sat on a chair near the window. He began to learn by memory the Talmud (*Bava Basra* 79a, the topic "*Moalin b'hen u'bameh shebetochan*"). He learned sequentially the words of the Talmud and reviewed all the words of *Tosafos*. He sat down in one place and reviewed in a very sweet and pleasing voice — practically until the morning light.

Apparently, he also knew a vast amount of the hidden wisdom of the Torah, for he had *sifrei Kabbalah*, and sometimes he would search by candlelight for a certain *sefer Kabbalah*. However, as was his usual path in holiness, he never spoke a word of this to any person. Therefore, as far as this is concerned, we do not know the path of his footsteps.

Once, a great rav, one of the great *gaonim* of the generation, came to Rav Yisrael's town with a new book that he printed. They did not know each other. The Admor went first to visit the highly esteemed *gaon* in his place of lodging to see if all was well with him. The aforementioned *gaon* presented his book to the Admor and requested that he examine it. The Admor responded to him, "Pardon me sir, but I do not easily grasp ideas, and it is difficult for me to examine the book." The aforementioned *gaon* was not satisfied with this answer. Yet the *gaon* tarried there a few weeks, and during that time they met together a few times. The *gaon* had the opportunity to recognize, a little bit, the essential spirit and holy path of Admor.

Prior to the departure of this *gaon*, many distinguished members of the city came to receive his farewell blessing. The *gaon* said these words about Rav Yisrael before the assembled group, "Concerning the *gaon*, the Light of Israel, allow me to quote the midrash about Shaul HaMelech, may peace be upon him: '*HaKadosh Baruch Hu* said to the ministering angels, "See this creation that I created in My world. The accustomed way of conduct in the world...." ' Likewise, I say, see this creation that *HaKadosh Baruch Hu* created in His world. Behold, all men endeavor and toil to make known their special nature and greatness to the world. Moreover, they worry and fear lest, God forbid, the world may lack any knowledge of the essence of their worth.

Whereas, the *gaon*, the Light of Israel, labors with phenomenal diligence to conceal from people his greatness and wondrous powers."

The Admor would lament and deeply regret the immorality of the generation and the dramatic decline of the majesty of Torah and *yiras Shamayim*. Once, on Simchas Torah, they noticed that the light of his countenance diminished. His students asked why was he not joyful: "Isn't today Simchas Torah? Doesn't one need to rejoice on Simchas Torah?" He answered them with the sweetness of his words: "Imagine a person experiences a happy event and a sad event at the same time — two unrelated matters. Isn't it necessarily so that the happiness with which he rejoices in his heart from one side will buffer his worry and pain from the other side? However, this is not so when the happiness and pain are from the same source. For instance, if a man has an only son, he is far more precious than all the sublime delights. The father's soul is bound to the soul of his son, and he greatly rejoices in him. If it so happens that this beloved son becomes critically ill, may Hashem have mercy — is it possible that the father's joy in his son will neutralize his worry and sadness over his son's illness? Isn't it just the opposite: the more he thinks of his beloved, precious son, the more his pain and sadness will multiply.

"This is analogous to our situation today. On one hand, we should rejoice in our holy Torah. However, in the wake of our joy, opposing feelings of distress are awakened — because in the multitude of our transgressions the Torah is perishing, may Hashem have mercy. Her students and those who fulfill her injunctions diminish from day to day. Therefore, the more a person intensifies joy in his heart for our holy Torah, the more feelings of pain and sadness are aroused due to the frightful situation — because the Torah has fallen down most dramatically." Nevertheless, he eloquently explained with sweet and pleasing words that despite all this, still there is reason to rejoice.

APPEARANCE

He was a fulfillment of the verse, "Then all the peoples of the earth will see that the Name of Hashem...and they will revere you" (*Devarim* 28:10). His appearance was exalted, as was the splendor of his countenance. Moreover, Hashem granted him a gift of grace and beauty, for he was exceedingly handsome. Together with this, his wisdom and *yiras Shamayim* illuminated his pure face with the light of the Living King. When he reflected on a particular topic, either in Torah or *yiras Shamayim*, his soul would practically disengage from his physicality. His pure face would be radiant like a flame of fire, his appearance like an angel of Hashem. This image was so intense that the assemblage feared to approach him. Someone who did not see this splendor with his own eyes cannot possibly imagine it. The spirit of Hashem was spread over his face, and he was like the sun rising in its strength. He never permitted an artist to draw his image on a paper, for he did not desire this under any circumstance.

More significant than his brilliance and piety were his phenomenal merit and the extraordinary merit that he bestowed upon his people. He restored the honor of Torah and *yiras Shamayim* throughout the Jewish world, and especially in our district. In particular, in every place where he dwelt his sanctity had a powerful effect on his acquaintances and their families. Each person who came in contact with him was spiritually uplifted according to his level. One source of his influence was his sermons, which he presented to the public from the days of his youth. His words were hewn to inflame the hearts of his listeners with the fire of *yiras Shamayim*. Words of honey poured from his lips — sweet, pleasant, and healing to the soul. And pearls of wisdom flowed from his mouth. He was the fulfillment of the verse, "Then all the people of the earth will see..." (ibid.). For whoever contemplated his paths, his deeds, and his virtues of character would be awestruck — and *yiras Shamayim* would be imprinted in his heart.

INFLUENCE

A trustworthy individual told me the following story: When this individual was visiting a certain town, he met by chance an elderly man who was wealthy, distinguished, and a well-known *yirei Shamayim*. Eventually, they began to discuss the Admor, *zt"l*. Suddenly, the elderly man seized him by his beard and said, "Believe me, all that remains within me, the little bit of *yiras Shamayim*, may His Name be blessed, is from the 'Holy One of Israel.' For in the days of his youth, I merited to come close to him."

In particular, he influenced his students with his majestic spirit. They gathered together under his protective shadow and took shelter in the shade of his branches. From the days of his youth, many great men of Torah placed themselves under his guidance. They heard his words of wisdom, his profound sagacity and *yiras Shamayim*, and they observed his exalted paths of Divine service. He devoted himself even more to his great students who he knew were proper and fitting vessels to receive his influence. He would speak with them privately and teach them the ways of Hashem and the wisdom of pleasing virtues. He revealed to them knowledge and understanding of Torah and pure *yiras Shamayim*.

Besides the public sermons that he presented before congregations, he would also give private sermons to his students. These sessions were not focused on the extrapolation of verses or midrashim. Rather, these classes were based on his brilliant, innovative concepts — deep investigations into the paths of Divine worship, as well as secrets about reward and punishment and the attainment of good virtues. He would speak for a few hours. Sometimes, he would present a certain concept, employing the rhetoric of a verse or a certain statement of Chazal; the power of his speech was awesome indeed. The concept of reward and punishment was a constant theme of his. Hence, he resuscitated and revived the souls of many.

When mentioning the sermons that he arranged before his students, there is another aspect that should be noted. There were many times when he would detain himself the entire week with abstinence and isolation in the nearby city of Aleksat, which was on the other side of the Neeman River. Only on *Shabbos Kodesh* would he come to his house here in the city of Kovno. His closest students would go once a week to his place of solitude — a full minyan of ten souls. After they prayed Minchah, Rav Yisrael would wrap himself in a tallis and begin to speak about *yiras Shamayim*, as was his holy way. Sometimes he would speak for a few hours. In the middle of his sermon he would begin to say fiery and inspiring words of spiritual matters. He would continue with great fervor until our hearts melted. He would weep profusely and awaken and stir us to beseech mercy for spiritual growth from Hashem. In the middle of these fiery talks, he would start to repeat a certain verse that depicted the praise of Hashem. Afterwards, he would say verses that expressed supplication for Divine mercy, for instance, "Return us, Hashem, to You, and we shall be returned." "Elokim, create for me a pure heart, and renew a good spirit within me." We would pray together as a *tzibbur* against the *yetzer hara*, beseeching Hashem to soften our hearts of stone and purify our hearts to serve Him in truth.

The Admor advocated the recitation of this prayer [of supplication before Hashem while in a minyan] to facilitate spiritual elevation. He based this on the words of Chazal (*Rosh HaShanah* 18a and *Yevamos* 49a): "Because it says, 'For Hashem our God is near whenever we call upon him' (*Devarim* 4:7). But it is written, 'Seek Hashem when He can be found' (*Yeshayahu* 55:6). This [second] verse speaks of an individual, the other [verse] of a community [minyan of ten men]. When can an individual [find Hashem]? Rabbah Bar Abbuha said: 'These are the ten days between Rosh HaShanah and Yom Kippur.' " We understand from here that the power of the prayer of the community throughout the entire year is equivalent to the time of the Ten Days of Repentance — of which the prophet said, "Seek Hashem when He can be found." Therefore, the prayer of a minyan, who pray together against the *yetzer hara*, is a very exalted matter and begets great spiritual benefit.

Once, Rav Yisrael was in another country during the Ten Days of Repentance. He wrote a letter to his students and relatives to awaken their hearts to prepare for Rosh HaShanah, at which time they would stand in judgment before the throne of the Righteous Judge. Here is a quote of his holy language (Letter Fourteen): "Yet, what can be done about the wall of iron that separates us from Hashem? This obstacle is the spirit of impurity that smothers and befouls man's spirit, and it effectively prevents him from saving himself. He is thus devoid of Mussar study's benefits, which improve the ways of man and draw him close to Hashem's service.

"There is one thing, though, that has proven highly effective [to help a person break through the barrier]. Namely, assembling a quorum of ten men and pouring out one's soul to Hashem [to help him] — intending in their prayer that Hashem pierce a small hole in this iron barrier. This is a small, easy matter that bears abundant fruit.

"Since at the present time I am not at home, I am unable to gather a quorum of ten for this purpose. Therefore, I wish to bestir and encourage you, my precious students, to assemble in a quorum of ten people, while the time is propitious and it is within your ability to do so (cf. *Shabbos* 151b)."

THE DISSEMINATION OF MUSSAR

Rav Yisrael's crowning attribute above all of his achievements was his phenomenal merit and the extraordinary merit that he bestowed upon his people through the study of *yirah* and Mussar. Many *gaonim* and men of piety wrote books of *yirah* and Mussar so that people might study and contemplate Heavenly fear. Likewise, many *gaonim* and men of piety exhorted us to study the books of *yirah* and Mussar. Nevertheless, the study of Mussar did not take root. It was practically forgotten, until Rav Yisrael illuminated the darkness like the dawn. He restored the crown of Heavenly fear to its ancient glory. He publicized the obligation to study *yiras Shamayim* and Mussar throughout the world. Hashem bestowed upon Rav Yisrael the privilege to convey merit to the Jewish people — to render redemption in the midst of the earth to resuscitate souls. We explained this at length in the Introduction and in "The Gates of Light."

Indeed, nothing could hold the Admor back from performing whatever he considered to be the will of Hashem, may His Name be blessed. No obstacle could deter him from his path, especially to bring merit to the public. It is known that in his elderly years, he troubled himself to travel to the city of Paris. His intention was to institute activities which he thought would bring merit to the public. He existed there under great hardship, difficulty, and oppression because he would not receive a gift from anyone, except for the meager stipend that was sent to him from our country. Due to the high costs of housing and basic necessities, he lived in one, narrow room. One could not believe that a human being was capable of living there. He also lacked other basic necessities of life. He suffered all of this in order to fulfill the will of Hashem, may His Name be blessed.

I heard from Rav Yisrael the following incident that occurred when he was in Paris. One time he slipped and fell down two flights of stairs. When they lifted him from the ground he was almost without life. But Hashem, may

His Name be blessed, performed a miracle for him, and after a few days — his health was restored. When he told me about this incident he said to me, "My heart did not despair, nor did I fear. For my presence in Paris was not for any personal reason. It was only to fulfill the Divine will. Therefore, Paris could not damage me."

These are a few highlights of his holy paths — for who can recount his glory and all of his righteous deeds? May the *yirei Hashem* learn his path and follow in his footsteps, and may they glimpse an inkling of his wondrous deeds and good virtues.

> Signed by the author, his student, who trembles and fears to mention
> his holy name — Yitzchak, the son of *Moreinu haRav* Shlomo Blazer

My beloved friend and companion, Rav Naftalie Amsterdam, who was born here in Salant, wrote the following passage for me. He was one of the great students of Rav Yisrael. His words concern the teacher of Rav Yisrael — the pious and holy *gaon*, our honorable teacher, Rav Yosef Zundel of Salant, *zt"l*. The following is a quote from the aforementioned *gaon*, Rav Naftalie Amsterdam:

> Let us examine what Rav Yisrael wrote in the introduction to *Sefer Tevunah* (in the footnotes): "I poured water on the hands of my master, Rav Yosef Zundel, who lives in Jerusalem, may it be rebuilt soon within our days." (See the text there, from the words "I did not reach up to his ankles..." until the words "...so that the *baalei batim* would listen and go in his footsteps.") There the Admor also praised his master, Rav Yosef Zundel, *zt"l*: "I have recounted just a small amount of this great man's virtues...." Even though these few words of Rav Yisrael capture much of the exalted attributes and righteousness of Rav Zundel — this is only a general perspective. However, in regards to the particular, Rav Yisrael would describe in detail astonishing accounts of Rav Zundel — his deeds, righteousness, and piety. His righteous deeds were wondrous, and all of us who heard Rav Yisrael speak of Rav Zundel would be amazed.

Rav Zundel resided in our city of Salant. One time we found him at nighttime making a path of stone with his hands in street that was soiled with mud and mire. His purpose was to honor his mother, who always passed by this route on her way to the *beis hamidrash*. Likewise, we once found him standing next to the small door that was in his courtyard. There was a hammer and nails in his hand, and he was banging nails with zeal. The reason for his action became known afterwards. Due to a broken lock, the door would lock by itself. Thus, the poor people, who went door to door, were not able to open the door. This is in violation of the Talmudic dictum (*Bava Basra* 7b): "This is to say that a gatehouse is an improvement?... This refers to one that has an opening...."[13]

Rav Yisrael told many similar stories of Rav Zundel's piety, which was indeed wondrous. Just as the great power of his righteousness, abstinence, and the love and fear of Hashem burned in his heart, so, too, he made great efforts to proceed with modesty so that externally his true worthiness could not be recognized. He labored on this to the extent that people who did not know him perceived him as a simple man.

He did not benefit from Torah to receive compensation from the world as was the custom. Rather, he made a living from the labor of his hands and lived in poverty. He did not have a steady income. He would sometimes teach a student. Once he dealt in certain

---

13 The *mishnah* in *Bava Basra* 7b state: "He [a resident of a courtyard] may be compelled [by the other residents of the courtyard] to [contribute to] the building of a gatehouse and a door for the courtyard." The Talmud, discussing this passage of the *mishnah*, asks, "This would seem to show that a gatehouse is an improvement: yet how can this be, seeing that there was a certain pious man with whom Eliyahu used to converse, until the man made a gatehouse, after which he did not converse with him anymore." Rashi explains that the gatehouse, which sealed the entrance to the courtyard, prevented the cries of poor men being heard in the courtyard. Therefore, Eliyahu, who was concerned for the poor, refused to converse with the man who built the gatehouse. If so, why does the *mishnah* advocate the building of a gatehouse? The Talmud resolves this contradiction by making the following distinction: in the case of the *mishnah* there was an outer door which granted access to poor people; whereas in the case of the pious man, there was no door — thus the cries of the poor could not be heard.

merchandise in the city of Memel in nearby Prussia. Intermittently, he would leave town in order to study under conditions of abstinence for the duration of a year. At one time, he traveled to study in the city of Mir, staying there and studying Torah for a complete year. At those times of exile he studied Torah under deprivation, spending only two *zahuvim* per week.

Rav Yisrael also told us of Rav Zundel's great humility — so much so, that it would inspire wonder and overwhelm all of his listeners. When he made his return journey from the city of Mir to his home in the city of Salant, he happened to travel together in a wagon with merchants who were going to Memel on business. They did not recognize him and considered him to be a simple, poor peasant. The merchants were devoid of *yiras Shamayim*. During the whole ride they mocked him and made him the object of many jokes and derision. When taking shelter on the road, the chassid, Rav Zundel, laid down to sleep on a bench, as was the way of the lowly paupers. The merchants, who were in good spirits, whispered together, "That worthless, poor man is sleeping. Let us draw the flame of a candle to his beard to burn some hairs." And so they did. When the chassid sensed this in his sleep, they suddenly heard him uttering from his mouth, "A little more." Indeed, this great disgrace that he was receiving from them awakened happiness within him. Momentarily, they were afraid and alarmed at his reaction. Notwithstanding, they did not take it to heart, and they laughed and mocked him unceasingly for the entire journey. The merchants arrived in the city of Memel and tarried there to conduct business.

The chassid, Rav Zundel, returned to his city and began to deal in merchandise. After some days, he had occasion to travel to the city of Memel. Once, those same merchants met the chassid in the market. Behold, he was speaking and exchanging secrets with a great, very distinguished man. The merchants were amazed amongst themselves. When they investigated the matter, it became known to them that he was the highly esteemed, pious *gaon* Rav Yosef Zundel. They came and bowed down before him and begged him to forgive them for what they did to him on their journey. He granted their request and forgave them on the condition that they accept upon themselves never to mock or make fun of any person all the days of their lives. Rav Zundel always conducted himself to flee from honor in the extreme. There are other stories that depict his virtue of humility but the written page cannot contain them.

Likewise, Rav Zundel labored and toiled to perfect the attribute of faith. He accomplished and attained things that were even beyond nature. Rav Yisrael told awesome, remarkable accounts of Rav Zundel's attribute of faith, stories that portrayed his greatness, the wonders of his carefulness, and his profound piety. These narratives would astonish all listeners. Likewise, the Admor would describe many incidents that depicted the masterful precision in mitzvah performance and devout piety of Rav Zundel. For instance, once Rav Zundel was speaking with people during the days of Chanukah. In the midst of the conversation they mentioned something sad. He said to them, "Please, be quiet! One should not mention something sad during these days, as our Sages forbade eulogies during the days of Chanukah." Likewise, he fulfilled each and every nuance of halachah, as the Mesillas Yesharim teaches that this is the essence of piety that was depicted by our Sages, zt"l: "Give pleasure to his Creator — to understand a concept from a known concept to perform the will of his Creator."

Once, Rav Zundel walked by a place of Jewish gardens and fields. When he passed in front of the fields and gardens, his students noticed that he placed his finger against the side of his nose and squeezed it tightly. They were perplexed over this conduct. Afterwards, the reason for this was made known to them. It was his way to search in everything that he learned in the Torah for the knowledge of how to apply it to a real situation. Behold, Chazal said in the beginning of Bava Basra (2b): "It is forbidden for a man to stand in the field of his fellow at the time when his produce is there." Rashi explains, "So that he should not damage it with *ayin hara*." However, sometimes it is impossible to guard oneself from looking momentarily. Behold, in *Berachos* (55b) it says: "If a man entering into a town is afraid of the evil eye...if he is afraid of his own evil eye, he should look at the side of his left nostril." Therefore, just in case that he might cause an *ayin hara*, he followed the advice of the Torah.

Also, he never rested from fulfilling the precept (*Avos* 1:6), "Appoint a teacher for yourself; acquire a friend for yourself." As we know, Rav Zundel was the primary student of the pious *gaon*, the leader of all the children of the exile, our master, Rav Chaim Volozhiner, *zt"l*. He would regularly travel to the Rav to receive his holy teachings. After the pious *gaon*, Rav Chaim Volozhiner, *zt"l*, departed to the Heavenly abode, the leadership of the entire Jewish exile passed to the pious *gaon*, our master, Rav Akiva Eiger, *zt"l*. Rav Zundel [then] journeyed to the city of Posen to contemplate the paths of righteousness and piety of the *gaon* Rav Akiva Eiger and resided in Posen for a short time.

I elaborated on the story of the chassid Rav Zundel for two reasons. First, as was written in *Sefer Tevunah*: "In order that the world should hear the deeds of this man who was in our generation and follow in his footsteps." Second, so that the world will recognize the exalted quality of Mussar study — its power and wondrous capabilities. Behold, it is clear that the profound righteousness, sanctity, and piety of Rav Zundel was expressly engendered by the study of Mussar. For he would employ and labor in the wisdom of Mussar — repeating many, many times a certain verse or statement of *aggadah* from Chazal, with great depth of understanding, as Rav Yisrael told us.

I, the author, remember something from the days of my youth in the city of Salant. After the chassid Rav Zundel traveled to the holy city of Yerushalayim, I viewed a few pages written in his pure handwriting. They were answers to questions that he asked his master, Rav Chaim Volozhiner. There also were wonderful stories about Rav Chaim. I saw there that, at the time Rav Zundel departed from Volozhin, he asked

Rav Chaim which Mussar books are good to study. He answered him with these words: "Every Mussar book is good to study. However, the book *Mesillas Yesharim* should be your guide."

Now, let us return to the honorable holiness of Rav Yisrael. Indeed, when he was still in his youth and had already achieved great brilliance, he began to pour water on the hands of his rabbi, Rav Yosef Zundel. From him alone did he receive this great wisdom — the study of Mussar — to study and repeat many statements of Chazal and Mussar books with deep understanding. Rav Yisrael served him and accepted him as his primary rabbi. He would say that Rav Zundel placed him on the path of Divine service and sanctity. When Rav Zundel traveled to the holy city, the Admor traveled to escort him three *parsa'os*, in observance of the law for one's primary rabbi.

Rav Yisrael told us that when he heard the voice of Rav Zundel instruct him to study Mussar — it penetrated into the chambers of his heart like a burning fire, and he began to immerse himself in this study. It is incumbent upon us to consider how fruitful was the study of Mussar for the pious Rav Yisrael. He illuminated the world and attained universal prestige. All of us saw with our eyes the intense power of his righteousness and piety, the purity of his heart and his holiness. We saw it in his awesome deeds, how he never detached his mind from the Divine service, even during the time that he was speaking with people. And we witnessed his excellent virtues of character, which were almost beyond the scope of human nature, like his revulsion to monetary gain and honor, as well as his attribute of kindness and bestowing goodness upon others. He also possessed all the good virtues: humility, patience, etc. The study of Mussar was the genesis for all of his righteousness and powerful achievements in deed and in *middos*. May the glorious example of Rav Yisrael inspire the people of our generation to embrace this wisdom — the study of Mussar. [Here end the words of Rav Naftalie Amsterdam.]

In respect of what Rav Naftalie Amsterdam wrote, that the exalted level of Rav Zundel was not externally perceptible, [I would like to add the following account]. In my youth I heard from the renowned rabbi, Rav Gershon Amsterdam, zt"l, of Vilna, that he had never met Rav Zundel until one time Rav Zundel happened to be in Vilna and brought a letter from someone in Salant to Rav Gershon Amsterdam. Rav Zundel stood at the door and handed him the letter. Rav Gershon Amsterdam thought him to be a simple man, like a wagon driver, and wanted to show him appreciation for his trouble. He served him a glass of sharp wine and asked him to drink. It was obvious that the chassid would not refuse any request because of the dictum (*Pesachim* 86b): "Everything the host asks of you, you must do," so he drank a little of the sharp wine. Afterwards, Rav Gershon Amsterdam asked him, "Aren't you from the city of Salant? How is the chassid, Rav Zundel?" He responded with the appropriate courtesy. Rav Gershon Amsterdam continued to inquire about Rav Zundel. Rav Zundel began to stammer in his answer, intending to diminish his own stature. Upon hearing these words, Rav Gershon thought to himself, "Perhaps this is the chassid, because it is said that he is undetectable." Rav Gershon said to him, "Tell me the truth, what is your name?" He said to him, "My name is Zunda." Rav Gershon said to him, " 'Hashem does the will of those who fear Him' (*Tehillim* 149:19) — they can totally conceal themselves."[14]

---

14   When Rav Zundel said his name was Zunda, Rav Gershon realized that his hunch was correct, and the man was, in fact, Rav Yosef Zundel.

כוכבי אור

STARS OF LIGHT

Rav Yitzchak Blazer

SELECTIONS CONCERNING

HEAVENLY FEAR

AND REPENTANCE

ARTICLE ONE

THE REWARD OF MITZVOS

"Behold, *yiras Hashem* is wisdom."

(*Iyov* 28:28)

REBBI YOCHANAN BEN ZAKKAI

THE TALMUD (*Berachos* 28b) TEACHES: When Rebbi Yochanan ben Zakkai took ill, his students went in to visit him. When he saw them he began to weep. His students said to him, "Lamp of Israel…why are you weeping?"

He said, "Even if I were being taken before an earthly king…if he became angry with me…I would certainly weep. And now that I am being taken before the Supreme King of kings, *HaKadosh Baruch Hu*, Who lives and endures forever, if He becomes angry with me, His anger is everlasting…. And moreover, when there are two paths before me, one leading to Gan Eden and the other to Gehinnom, and I do not know on which path I will be led, shall I not weep?"

Rebbi Yochanan's words "And moreover…" require further analysis. Why did he mention the additional fear of not entering the path to Gan Eden? [Had he not already mentioned that the fear of Hashem's anger was sufficient cause for him to weep?]

OBLIGATORY AND NON-OBLIGATORY DEEDS

The implementation of true judgment is axiomatic to all upright people and societies. We believe that a person's deeds will be rewarded: perpetrators of iniquity will be punished and performers of good will be rewarded. Also, every nation has laws and rules. Fitting punishments protect every statute and ethical principle, while rewards are designated for virtuous and noble deeds. However, it is self-evident that an obligatory deed should not be subject to both reward and punishment. One who neglects an obligation deserves punishment, but reward is only relevant when a non-obligatory deed is performed. Logically, one should not expect a reward for merely fulfilling an obligation, nor for refraining from committing a violation. Likewise, there should be no punishment for one who does not perform a non-obligatory good deed.

THE JUSTICE OF HASHEM

However, the method of the justice of Hashem, Who deals fairly with all of His creations, is different. The ways of justice of Elokim, the Judge, are based on punishment and reward, according to the deeds of each person. Hashem discharges fearful punishments to those who transgress His will and abundantly rewards those who fulfill His will.

TRIAL BEFORE AN EARTHLY KING

There is a difference between the trial before an earthly king to determine the faithfulness of a servant, and the trial of each person who ultimately will stand before the King of kings, *HaKadosh Baruch Hu*, to be judged on all deeds. The purpose of the judgment of an earthly king is specifically to determine whether or not the accused should be punished. An innocent verdict exempts the accused from punishment, while a guilty verdict makes punishment inevitable. However, there is no concept of losing a reward that would have been received had there not been a conviction. Even a verdict of innocence does not entitle one to a reward. The only consequence of a verdict of innocence is exemption from punishment.

THE FUTURE JUDGMENT

However, this is not the case in the future judgment, when one will stand before the King of kings, *HaKadosh Baruch Hu*, for an accounting of all deeds. In that judgment, the difference between innocence and guilt will be the difference between awesome punishment and exalted reward. A righteous individual will delight in the pleasantness of Hashem together with the righteous in Gan Eden, while one found guilty will be led to Gehinnom along with the perpetrators of iniquity. Consequently, besides the bitter punishment received by the guilty, the great reward that a meritorious judgment would have achieved is also lost.

THE LOSS OF GAN EDEN

Rebbi Yochanan ben Zakkai was referring to this additional loss when he added, "And moreover, when there are two paths before me, one leading to Gan Eden and the other to Gehinnom, and I do not know on which path I will be led, shall I not weep?" Before an earthly king there is only one path for someone being judged — either punishment or annulment of punishment — but no anticipation of reward. However, before the Supreme King of kings, *HaKadosh Baruch Hu* there are two paths — one to Gan Eden and one to Gehinnom. Someone found guilty not only suffers in Gehinnom, but also does not delight in the pleasantness of Hashem in Gan Eden. Hence, the punishment is multiplied.

WHY DID REBBI YOCHANAN FEAR?

We will soon see a further incredible insight into Rebbi Yochanan's statement, "And I do not know on which path I will be led." Why did the wholly righteous Rebbi Yochanan fear so greatly? If he had committed a sin, the gates of repentance are never locked and nothing prevented him repenting and receiving forgiveness. Besides, it is known that all our holy Sages fulfilled the entire Torah and no sin ever came to their hands. Our Sages even praised the elevated level of Rebbi Yochanan in *Bava Basra* (134a), saying, "He did not neglect any *pasuk* or *mishnah*" (see the text). Therefore, we must say that Rebbi Yochanan did not sense any sin whatsoever in his soul.

Rebbi Yochanan's great fear was due to his contemplation of the exceptional depth of Divine judgment. Our Sages taught in the Talmud (*Pesachim* 54b): "Seven things are concealed from a man, and these are: the depth of judgment...." Rashi (in his second comment) explains that this refers to "the depth of judgment of the future." The depth of this judgment is concealed from us because our intellect and comprehension cannot fathom the magnitude of the truth of the final judgment and reckoning that each one of us will face for our deeds. This depth of understanding belongs only to the Almighty. Chazal (*Avos* 4:29) allude to this: "He is the Discerner...." The depth of judgment frightened Rebbi Yochanan ben Zakkai. Even if he were righteous in his own eyes and could not perceive a single sin or iniquity in his soul, nonetheless, when exposed to the secret depths of Hashem's judgment, he did not know if he would meet the criteria of the multitude of reckonings demanded by Divine judgment. That is why even the righteous Rebbi Yochanan said, "And moreover, when there are two paths before me...and I do not know on which path I will be led...."

THE FUTURE PATH IS UNCERTAIN

If a person understood how to calculate his final reckoning and verdict, he could already predict his future direction and final location — either the path that ascends to Gan Eden or the frightening path that leads to the depths of Gehinnom. With this foreknowledge, he would be less worried. A person with pure deeds could well rejoice with the goodly portion to come. Whereas one with perverted ways would be able to return to Hashem, Who is abundantly merciful.

However, since one cannot calculate the final reckoning and verdict of Hashem, the future path is uncertain. A person may think that he is completely righteous and heading for Gan Eden, whereas really, according to the depth of the Divine judgment and reckoning, he did not fulfill his required Divine service and is really heading for Gehinnom. One who thinks like this will also fail to repent.

THE FEAR OF GEHINNOM

This story teaches a profound Mussar lesson concerning the fear of punishment and reward. We see how holy men feared and trembled at the spiritual punishment of Gehinnom, and how deeply they worried about losing their reward. Despite all the trepidation of Rebbi Yochanan ben Zakkai, it is still hard to imagine that he feared a punishment of a twelve-month stay in Gehinnom, which is the sentence of the totally wicked. Rather, it appears that he feared and wept at the possibility of being judged for Gehinnom for even a brief moment. The Talmud (*Bava Metzia* 85a) alludes to this concept: "Rabbi Zeira observed one hundred fasts when he went to the Land of Israel.... And he observed another hundred fasts so that the fire of Gehinnom should not dominate him..." (see the text). It appears that Rabbi Zeira was worried about even a minimal exposure to the fires of Gehinnom; he did not want the fires to touch him at all. So, too, Rebbi Yochanan feared because he did not want to see the edge of Gehinnom for even the briefest moment. It was over the possibility of this brief moment that he feared greatly and wept, even though it was only a doubt in his mind. As he said, "And I do not know on which path I will be led...."

SPIRITUAL PUNISHMENT AND REWARD ARE BOTH VERY GREAT AND AWESOME

The fundamental principle taught in this story is that spiritual punishment and reward are both very great and awesome. The Ramban wrote about spiritual punishment (*Toras HaAdam, Sha'ar HaGemul*): "The general rule explained by our Sages is that Gehinnom is a place to administer the judgment. There, the soul of the sinner is afflicted with tribulations and pain. There is no equivalent pain in this world, as the sufferings of this world are in the lowly body, dense of feeling. On the other hand, punishment in Gehinnom is ministered to the soul, which is the clear and pure.... The capacity of the soul to feel its pain is infinitely greater than the capacity of the body...." This is attributed to the soul's extreme sensitivity and purity. Our Sages (*Avos* 4:22) taught: "Better one hour of spiritual bliss in the World to Come than the entire life in this world." Similarly, one hour of punishment in Gehinnom is more severe than all the punishments of this world. The loss of even a single hour of reward in the World to Come is a very great loss indeed.

Not only do we have a weak capacity to sense spiritual punishments, but our capacity to sense spiritual reward is even weaker. Since punishment is closer to the senses than is reward, we are better able to imagine punishment than reward. Our Sages teach that the punishment of Gehinnom is burning fire. This provides us with a frame of reference, for we can easily picture a physical fire that consumes both body and soul. In contrast, it is very difficult to imagine the spiritual reward of the World to Come where we delight in the pleasantness of Hashem and rejoice in the splendor of the *Shechinah*. Without a comparable earthly pleasure, we cannot imagine this. Therefore, we would easily choose to forfeit much of our reward for mitzvos in the World to Come in order to reduce our punishment there and be saved from the burning fire.

THE REWARD OF A MITZVAH

In truth, however, the reward for a mitzvah is much more valuable than being spared the punishment for a transgression. As it mentions in the Talmud (*Tosefta Sotah* 4:1): "The attribute of the goodness of Hashem is five hundred times greater than His attribute of justice." If a certain mitzvah was equivalent in quality to one transgression, then this mitzvah would really be worth much more. As the Rambam mentions in *Hilchos Teshuvah* (3:5): "And if the reward of the mitzvah and the punishment of the transgression are put on the scale, then the reward will weigh much more than the punishment."

ACHER

We can offer a good example to grasp the superiority of spiritual reward in contrast to punishment: Every person would be willing to forfeit much reward to avoid suffering a small amount of pain. Accordingly, to accept upon oneself to suffer a certain pain, one would have to be offered a very great reward. Yet when we consider the pleasures and delights of this world, there is no goodness in existence that one would not willingly exchange to gain relief from pain and suffering. A person would not accept any payment whatsoever to experience difficult and bitter sufferings. Rather, all the delights and pleasures of this world would be utterly rebuffed.

Indeed, our Sages told about Acher ["Acher" is the title used to refer to

Elisha Ben Abuyah, a Tannah who strayed from the path of Torah] who abandoned Torah to live an evil existence (*Chagigah* 15b): "When Acher expired they said [i.e., in Heaven], 'Let him not be punished, nor enter the World to Come.' 'Let him not be punished' because he studied much Torah. 'Nor enter the World to Come' because he sinned. Rebbi Meir said, 'It is preferable for him to be punished so that he will enter the World to Come. When I die, I shall cause smoke to ascend from his grave.' When Rebbi Meir expired, smoke ascended from the grave of Acher. Rebbi Yochanan said, 'What an heroic act, to burn his master. There was one of us who went astray, yet we cannot save him. If I would take him by the hand, who would take him from me? When I die, I will extinguish the smoke from his grave.' When Rebbi Yochanan died, the smoke ceased from the grave of Acher."[1]

Now, from the day of Rebbi Meir's death until the time of Rebbi Yochanan's death, approximately 150 years elapsed. Therefore, the smoke ascended from the grave of Acher for the lengthy period of about 150 years. Thus, Acher was punished in the fire of Gehinnom until the merit of Rebbi Yochanan saved him.

The calculation is as follows: Rebbi Meir was one of the oldest students of Rabbeinu HaKadosh ("Rebbi"), for Rebbi Meir was one of the students of Rebbi Akiva (*Yevamos* 62b). On the day that Rebbi Akiva died, Rebbi was born (*Kiddushin* 72b). Rebbi lived an exceptionally long life of one hundred years. Therefore, at the time Rebbi died, a few decades had passed from the time of Rebbi Meir's passing. Now, Rebbi Yochanan's life extended more than ninety years after the death of Rebbi. For after the death of Rebbi, Rebbi Afas took over the leadership for two and a half years, and after him Rebbi Chanina ben Chama led for ten years, and then Rebbi Yochanan led for eighty years. All of this is recorded in the tradition of the Ra'avad and in *Sefer Yuchsin* (see the text).

It was worthwhile for Acher to be purged in the burning fire of Gehinnom, like the smelting of silver, for about 150 years. All this suffering was worthwhile in order to merit afterwards the delight of the pleasant good-

---

1   According to the simple *peshat* Rebbi Yochanon was praising Rebbi Meir for "getting" Acher into Gehinnom. And Rebbi Yochanon finished the mission — he got him into Gan Eden.

ness of the World to Come. If Rebbi Yochanan had not saved Acher, who knows how much longer he would have been punished. Moreover, all of this was only a kindness of the Creator, may His Name be blessed, in the merit of Rebbi Meir who had beseeched mercy so that Acher might be punished and enter the World to Come.

From this incident we can understand the value of the great pleasure of the World to Come as a reward for Torah and mitzvos. It is worthwhile to suffer difficult and bitter tribulations in the depths of Gehinnom — to be burnt in a raging, frightful fire for the duration of many years — in order to afterwards merit the delight of the precious pleasantness and eternal splendor of the World to Come.

A WISE MAN

The Talmud states (*Tamid* 32a), "Alexander Makedon asked the Sages of the South ten things.... He said to them, 'How do you define a man of wisdom?' They said to him, 'Who is a wise man? One who sees the future....' " The commentators explain "One who sees the future" as one whose heart understands what the future will bring and exercises caution accordingly. Their statement, "Who is a wise man? One who sees the future," includes all matters of the world. But even if a person sees the outcome of all of his ways and affairs, yet does not open his eyes to see what will happen at the end of his days — an act that would cause him to worry and ultimately enable him to save himself from Gehinnom and inherent eternal life — then all this foresight is not that of a wise person, but rather that of a fool.

It is known that the foundation of *yiras Hashem* extends only from the power of seeing the future. As our Sages said (*Avos* 2:1): "Calculate the cost of a mitzvah against its reward, and the reward of a sin against its cost." In addition, they said in the third chapter of *Avos* (3:1): "Consider three things and you will not come into the grip of sin. Know whence you came, whither you go, and before Whom you will give justification and reckoning...." After the premise stated by the Sages of the South, "Who is a wise man? One who sees the future," the purpose of wisdom is only to fear God. Therefore, the one who fears God and departs from evil is the wise person who sees the future outcome. Likewise, Shlomo HaMelech, may peace be upon him, said in *Mishlei* (14:16): "A wise man fears and turns away from evil." This is also what the verse says (*Iyov* 28:28): "Behold, *yiras Hashem* is wisdom" — for there is no wise man like one who fears God.

ARTICLE TWO

IRREVOCABLE REWARD

"The wise will shine like the radiance of the firmament, and
those who teach righteousness to the multitudes [will shine]
like the stars, forever and ever."

(Daniel 12:3)

THE FEAR OF LOSING GAN EDEN

BEHOLD, THE REWARD OF MITZVOS supercedes everything in the
spiritual world, for one hour of pleasure in the World to Come is worth
more than all the pleasures of this world. However, wouldn't it be wonderful
if every man was guaranteed that the reward for his mitzvos, whether a little
or a lot, would be preserved for him in Gan Eden? If this were so, even though
"there is no righteous man on the earth who does not sin," nevertheless, every man would be filled with hope. For after one would receive the punishment for all of his transgressions, he would ultimately receive his reward in
Gan Eden. The very fruit of his deeds — "his inheritance" — is the reward
for his mitzvos. Therefore, truthfully, just as he should fear the punishment
for his transgressions, to save his soul from Gehinnom, so, too, he must worry
that he has not lost the reward of mitzvos in Gan Eden. For sometimes a man
receives his reward in this world [instead of the World to Come].

The Talmud (*Shabbos* 32a) teaches that even the patriarchs feared this:
"A man should never stand in a dangerous place…if Hashem must perform a
miracle to save him — then it is subtracted from his merits. Rebbi Chanina
said, 'What is the meaning of the verse [wherein Yaakov expressed his fear],

"I have been diminished by all the kindness..." (*Bereishis* 32:11)?' " Rashi explains, " 'I have been diminished' — My merits diminished and lessened because of the kindness which You did...." (See the text.)

"FEAR NOT, AVRAM"

Also, the *Midrash Rabbah* (*Parashas Lech Lecha* 44:3) extrapolates the verse in *Bereishis* (15:1): " 'Fear not, Avram' — Avraham Avinu was afraid and said, 'I descended into the fiery furnace and was saved, I went down to fight the war of the kings and was saved. You [Hashem] will say that I received my reward in this world, and I have no portion left for the World to Come.' *HaKadosh Baruch Hu* said to him, 'Fear not, Avram. I am your shield. Everything I did for you in this world was gratis, but your reward is fixed for the future to come' " (see the text of the *Midrash Rabbah*).

REWARD IN THIS WORLD

We should be amazed and perplexed by the statement of Avraham Avinu, may peace be upon him, "I descended into the fiery furnace and was saved." He went into the fiery furnace to give up his life in order to sanctify the Name of Hashem! Common sense tells us that when *HaKadosh Baruch Hu* performed a miracle and saved him, this miracle did not detract from the reward for offering his life for the sanctification of the Divine Name, nor from the reward for other mitzvos. On the contrary, the fact that *HaKadosh Baruch Hu* performed this great miracle of saving him from the fiery furnace was a sign and a proof of His great power, and of how beloved and cherished Avraham was to Hashem. If so, his great reward should have been preserved for the World to Come. Nevertheless, we see that Avraham Avinu was afraid that perhaps he received the reward for his mitzvos in exchange for the miracle. He was also afraid that because he was saved from the war of the kings (*Bereishis* 13), perhaps he received his complete reward and had nothing at all left for the World to Come.

Likewise, we must comprehend the answer of *HaKadosh Baruch Hu*, "Everything I did for you in this world was gratis." We can, therefore, infer that if one does not merit "free" kindness, then even if he is willing to give his life to sanctify Hashem — and *HaKadosh Baruch Hu* performs a miracle for him and saves him in some way — his merits will be subtracted.

REBBI ELIEZER

Indeed, also our Sages (*Sanhedrin* 101a) feared receiving their reward of the World to Come in this world: "Rabbah bar bar Channah said: When Rebbi Eliezer fell ill, his students went to visit him.... They began to cry, and Rebbi Akiva began to laugh. They said to him, 'Why are you laughing?'... He responded, 'I am laughing because whenever I saw that the wine of Rebbi did not turn to vinegar nor was his flax smitten...I said, "Perhaps, Heaven forbid, Rebbi has received his World" [Rashi explains, 'Rebbi has received his World' — all his reward]. But now that I see Rebbi suffering — I am happy.' He [Rebbi Eliezer] said to him, 'Akiva, there was not one part of the Torah which I did not fulfill.' He [Rebbi Akiva] responded to him: 'Our Sages taught us: There is no righteous man on the earth who does not sin.' "

From this remarkable story we should understand and comprehend that these matters are as stated. Even the greatest of the *tzaddikim* are sometimes in doubt about whether "perhaps he has received his World." For behold, if Rebbi Eliezer the Great said about himself that he feared that perhaps he received his World to Come in this world — it would have been possible to think that this fear was an exaggeration as a result of his piety and humility. However, because it was Rebbi Akiva who feared that perhaps, God forbid, Rebbi Eliezer already received his portion of the World to Come — now it is revealed and clear that the things are just as they are written.

THE DEPTH OF JUDGMENT

It is astonishing! Would we think that Rebbi Eliezer the Great, a rabbi who resembled an angel of Hashem and one of the Heavenly hosts, would receive his portion of the World to Come in this world? Is this Torah and its reward? And even Avraham Avinu, may peace be upon him, was afraid that perhaps he received his reward in this world. However, sometimes one sin causes the punishment whereby he is paid the reward for his mitzvos in this world. How much more so, when we consider the depth of judgment and the

Divine reckoning, which are hidden from man and amongst the secrets of Hashem, our God.

In this respect, Rebbi Eliezer said, "Akiva, there was not one part of the Torah which I did not fulfill." At first glance how does this relate to Rebbi Akiva's answer? Also here, the explanation is based on the understanding that one sin can cause a person to receive his [portion of the] World to Come in this world. Therefore, he said, "There was not one part of the Torah which I did not fulfill." Rebbi Akiva responded, "Our Sages taught us: There is no righteous man on the earth who does not sin."

"I TOILED FOR NAUGHT"

With this understanding, we can well understand the words of the *Midrash Rabbah* (*Parashas Chayei Sarah* 62:2), "When Rebbi Avahu was stricken, they showed him thirteen rivers of Afarsamon. He said to them, 'Whose are they?' They said to him, 'They are yours.' And I [Rebbi Avahu] said, 'I toiled for naught, I expended my strength for emptiness; yet surely my right is with the Lord, and my recompense is with my God' (*Yeshayahu* 49:4)." The suspicion of Rebbi Avahu, that he "toiled for naught" and expended his strength for nothing, seems quite amazing. Didn't Chazal (*Avos* 2:21) say, "Your employer can be relied upon to pay you the wage of your labor"? However, the axiom here is that all the pleasures and goodness of this world are worthlessness and total emptiness. Therefore, if someone receives his World to Come — the reward for his Torah and mitzvos — in this world, then all his toil and effort was to receive an inferior reward of total emptiness and worthlessness.

Behold, it appears that *HaKadosh Baruch Hu* granted benefit to Rebbi Avahu even from the good of this world. The Talmud (*Chagigah* 14a) tells us that he received favor and was honored by the Caesar. The Talmud (*Kesubos* 17a) also recounts that he was afforded great honor in the royal palace: "When Rebbi Avahu came from the yeshivah to the court of the Caesar, handmaids from the royal house went out towards him and sang before him, 'Prince of his people, leader of his nation, shining light, blessed be your coming in peace.'" Therefore, Rebbi Avahu constantly feared lest Hashem subtract from his merits with the exchange of the nothingness and emptiness of this illusionary honor. Thus, "When Rebbi Avahu was stricken, they showed him thirteen rivers of Afarsamon. He said to them, 'Whose are they?' They said to him, 'They are yours.' And I said, 'I toiled for naught, I expended my strength for emptiness.' " This is based on what we just mentioned — that he thought he had received the reward of his toil and effort in exchange for the nothingness and emptiness of the worldly pleasures.

OUR HEARTS SHOULD TREMBLE

Now that we know this concept, our hearts should tremble with fear when we evaluate our situation. Each person's transgressions tower over his head, every person according to his own stature. Who knows how much he will endure and suffer in the World of Truth for his load of transgressions? Let's assume that one person was purged like the smelting of silver, and all of his transgressions were cleansed. Now the time arrives to receive the reward for his mitzvos. Indeed, notwithstanding, all of his righteous deeds are like a soiled garment that is small in size, poor and sparse in quality. For the perfection of the mitzvah is based on two aspects. The first is the accuracy of the deed — each mitzvah should be performed according to the statutes of the Torah and the parameters of its judgments. The second is the purity of thought — that it should be performed with pleasing intention, only for the sake of Hashem. Who can say, "I fulfilled the entire Torah, and I purified my heart?" After all this, who can know how much Hashem subtracted from his impoverished merits in exchange for rewards of this world, whether a little or a lot? Or perhaps, Heaven forbid, he received the entire portion of his World to Come in this world — something even our avos feared, as we mentioned previously. For every man is constantly replenished with the kindness and goodness of the Creator, may His Name be blessed. This includes not only what we see with our own eyes, but also the hidden miracles, as the verse says, "He does great miracles privately" (Tehillim 72:18).

TO BRING MERIT TO THE PUBLIC

We have found one solution. There is one mitzvah which is exalted and elevated in worth above all other mitzvos. Besides the great reward earned for the peformance of this mitzvah, even more importantly, man is guaranteed that the righteousness of this deed will stand forever. Therefore, he will receive the reward of this mitzvah in the World of Bestowal, the World to Come, and Hashem will not deduct its reward from the pleasures of this world. This mitzvah is to bring merit to the public — to be numbered amongst those who turn the many to righteousness. We will now explain why this mitzvah cannot be paid back in this world, with the help of Hashem.

FOUR DIVISIONS OF ATONEMENT

Behold, the Talmud (*Yoma* 86a) classifies the four divisions of atonement that Rebbi Yishmael taught: "1) If a person transgresses a positive commandment and then repents — he is forgiven immediately. 2) If a person transgresses a negative commandment and then repents — his repentance suspends the punishment and Yom Kippur atones. 3) If a person violates a precept that incurs spiritual excision and the death penalty — Yom Kippur suspends the punishment and suffering cleanses. 4) But if he has committed a *chilul Hashem* — repentance does not have the power to suspend the punishment, nor does Yom Kippur atone, nor does suffering cleanse. Rather, in this case, all of these together suspend the punishment and death cleanses…" (see the text). There is an apparent question here: Why doesn't suffering have the power to cleanse a *chilul Hashem*? Doesn't death atone because of the sufferings incurred by death, may the Merciful One save us? If so, how come suffering while alive does not cleanse?

THE SUFFERINGS OF THIS WORLD CLEANSE A MAN'S TRANSGRESSIONS

[The explanation is as follows:] the axiom is that sometimes a man receives his World to Come, the reward for his mitzvos, in this world. On the other hand, sometimes the sufferings of this world cleanse a man's transgressions. This is explained in the Talmud (*Kiddushin* 40a): "Rebbi Eliezer ben Rebbi Tzadok said, 'To what are the righteous compared in this world? To a tree standing wholly in a place of purity, but its branch overhangs into a place of impurity; when the branch is cut off, it stands entirely in a place of cleanliness. Thus, *HaKadosh Baruch Hu* brings suffering upon the righteous in this world, in order that they may inherit the future world, as it says, "Then, though your beginning was insignificant, your end will flourish exceedingly" (*Iyov* 8:7). And to what are the wicked compared in this world? To a tree standing wholly in a place of impurity, but a branch overhangs into a place of purity, when the branch is cut off, it stands entirely in a place of impurity. Thus, *HaKadosh Baruch Hu* showers goodness upon the wicked in this world, in order to destroy and consign them to the lowest rung, for it is said, "There is a way which seems right to man, but at its end are the ways of death" (*Mishlei* 14:12).' " Doesn't this seem amazing? The reward and punishment which come to a man in the Next World from the fruit of his deeds are both so awesome that it is far beyond our ability to even imagine. The reward is wondrous delight — "Better is one hour of spiritual bliss in the World to Come than the entire life of this world" (*Avos* 4:22). And the punishment is terrible and bitter — one hour is worse than all the difficult suffering of this world. Now that we established this, then, there is a mystery. How is it possible to bestow reward for a mitzvah in this world in a way which is commensurate with the vast reward in the spiritual world? Furthermore, how is it possible to cleanse transgressions in this world with suffering commensurate with the ominous punishment of the spiritual world?

THE WORLD TO COME

Hashem, may He be blessed, decreed in His wisdom that the standard measure of true compensation is only in the spiritual world [the World to Come]. There is the appropriate place to bestow the great reward for those who perform the Divine will, and for the awesome punishments for the perpetrators of sin. However, if *HaKadosh Baruch Hu* pays man his reward or his punishment in this world, then the degree of both the punishment and the reward will be exponentially smaller in magnitude many thousands upon thousands of levels. This is a very minute fraction in contrast to the reward and punishment in the spiritual world. Therefore, it is possible in reality to cleanse iniquity through suffering in this world — even though there is no comparison to the great punishments in the spiritual world. Likewise, there is an actuality to subtract the reward of a mitzvah through the enjoyment of pleasures in this world, even though there is no comparison to the great reward of the World to Come. The greatest evil to befall man is for him to receive the reward for his mitzvos in this world, in exchange for insignificant, base pleasures. Whereas the greatest good is for man to be cleansed of his sins through the sufferings of this world.

Behold, this is certainly a just calculation: exchanging fractional amounts of punishment and reward of this world for the punishment and the reward of the Next World. Just as the punishment of sin in the Next World is proportional to the severity of the sin — so that the greater the sin, the greater the punishment — so, too, the cleansing of the sin through suffering in this world is proportional to the severity of the sin. The greater the sin, the greater the punishment required in the World to Come; likewise, the greater the suffering that he will need to endure in order to cleanse the sin in this world. The amount of punishment he must endure in this world is proportional to the magnitude of punishment required in the Next World — sometimes more [for greater sins] and sometimes less [for lesser sins]. Likewise, the reward that one receives in this world in exchange for the reward of the World to Come correlates to the quality of the mitzvah and the greatness of the reward in the World to Come.

A CHILUL HASHEM

With this principle we can explain the statement of Rebbi Yishmael, "But if he has committed a *chilul Hashem* — repentance does not have the power to suspend the punishment...nor does suffering cleanse. Rather, all of these together suspend the punishment and death cleanses." The reason for this is because *chilul Hashem* is a very great sin — worse than all other transgressions, as the Talmud explains in the passage we quoted from *Yoma*. Therefore, the punishment for the sin of *chilul Hashem* that he receives in the World to Come is extremely terrible and fearful — and far exceeds punishments for all other transgressions. Therefore, it is impossible for punishments in this world to cleanse this transgression of *chilul Hashem*. The punishments of this world are a fractional amount of the severity of the great punishment in the World to Come. Therefore, in reality there is no suffering in this world which would have the power to eradicate this transgression. For all the suffering which exists in the realm of nature that man could bear and remain alive, does not correlate to even a fraction of the amount required of the great punishment that he receives in the World to Come. Therefore, only death eradicates the sin of *chilul Hashem*. The reason that death is an atonement is because the sufferings of death, may the Merciful One save us, which is the separation of the soul from the body, are excessively horrible. The nature of this pain is hidden from the eyes of all living men. There is no comparable suffering that is found when the man is alive. Therefore, only the sufferings of death, may the Merciful One save us, eradicate the transgression of *chilul Hashem*. For the severity of the suffering of death correlates in magnitude to a semblance of the punishment of the World to Come.

Behold, the Talmud (*Yoma* 86a) states, "What is an example of *chilul Hashem*? Rav said, 'For example, if I buy meat from the butcher, and do not immediately pay the money.'" Rashi explains: "When I delay payment, he says about me that I am a thief, and he learns from me to rationalize stealing." The Talmud states further, "Rebbi Yochanan said, 'For instance, in my case [it is a profanation] if I walk four cubits without words of Torah or wearing tefillin.'" Rashi explains: "'For instance, in my case' — not everyone realizes [that the reason for my conduct is] that I became weakened from my learning, and they learn from me to refrain from learning Torah." The parameter of *chilul Hashem* is one who causes another to learn from him to denigrate a particular mitzvah. Consequently, it is understood — how much more so if one performs a negative act to turn back the hearts of people, so that they denigrate one of the mitzvos of Hashem; his deeds, or words will have a definite effect. This is the worst *chilul Hashem*.[2]

---

2   The examples cited in the Talmud did not involve any violation of halachah. Rather, the Rabbis explained that if they were lax in immediately fulfilling a mitzvah, like paying immediately for goods received, it is considered a *chilul Hashem*. Although they surely intended to fulfill their obligations, their apparent delay might be interpreted as "stealing." Hence, since they are the role models for the community, people may incorrectly deduce from their actions that it is permissible to steal, *chas v'shalom*. Therefore, on their level, even if they cause people to make an incorrect inference, it is a *chilul Hashem*. However, if

KIDDUSH HASHEM

Since an act is defined as a *chilul Hashem* if it causes others to denigrate a mitzvah, then correspondingly, it is self-evident that a *kiddush Hashem* is an act that causes others to learn to value and love a mitzvah. How much more so is this true of someone who strives to bring merit upon the public, to draw their hearts to the service of Hashem, may His Name be blessed, to observe and fulfill the Torah and mitzvos; to "depart from evil and do good" (*Tehillim* 34:15). This is an absolute *kiddush Hashem*, the opposite of the transgression of *chilul Hashem*. Rabbeinu Yonah (*Sha'arei Teshuvah*) confirms this concept: "Even though this disease has no cure...if Hashem will help him to publicly make a *kiddush Hashem*...then his sin will be erased by means of the great significance of his deed. For it is the opposite of the foolish deed which he previously committed."

Indeed, just as a *chilul Hashem* is the worst of all sins, correspondingly, a *kiddush Hashem*, as we wrote above, is the greatest of all mitzvos. Likewise, just as the punishment for a *chilul Hashem* exceeds all other punishments, correspondingly, the reward for the mitzvah of *kiddush Hashem* exceeds the reward for all other mitzvos. We explained above that the reward for a mitzvah exceeds in magnitude the punishment for a sin, if they are placed together on the scale [for the positive value of a good deed is greater than the detrimental value of a corresponding sin]. Therefore, the reward for a *kiddush Hashem* exceeds the punishment for a *chilul Hashem*. Now, we learned from Chazal that the sin of *chilul Hashem* couldn't be purged through suffering. We explained that because of the severity of the sin, there is no suffering that exists in this world that has the power to purge this sin. For all the sufferings of this world do not add up to even a fraction of the severity of punishment in the Next World for this sin. Therefore, all the more so, there can be no reward for the mitzvah of *kiddush Hashem* that exists in all the goodness and delights of this empty world that could detract from the reward. For all the goodness of this world is not sufficient to equal a fraction of the magnitude of the great reward of this mitzvah in the World to Come.

---

someone was to actually violate the halachah, and, for example, to really steal — for sure this is a *chilul Hashem*. For if causing an incorrect inference is a *chilul Hashem*, surely an actual negative deed is a *chilul Hashem*.

HIS REWARD IS IMMUTABLY SAFEGUARDED

This is the meaning of the verse, "Those who teach righteousness to the multitudes [will shine] like the stars, forever and ever" (*Daniel* 12:3). The meaning of the phrase "forever and ever" appears to be unclear. If the verse is teaching us that the reward is eternal, then clarification is required, for isn't the reward of every mitzvah eternal? Rather, the explanation is as follows: There is no guarantee concerning the reward of all other mitzvos. There is no assurance that one's reward is safeguarded for him to enjoy in the World to Come. Perhaps he will receive his reward in this world through the worthless temporal pleasures. However, this is not the case with one who "teaches righteousness to the multitudes." His reward is immutably safeguarded for him in the World to Come, which is eternal. Just as suffering in this world does not have the power to purge a *chilul Hashem*, as we wrote above, likewise, there is no magnitude of good in this world to exchange for the reward of the *kiddush Hashem*, of turning the many to righteousness. His reward is immutably safeguarded for him in the World to Come, and this is the meaning of "Those who teach righteousness to the multitudes [will shine] like the stars, forever and ever."

ARTICLE THREE

THE FOUNDATION OF REPENTANCE

"Therefore, you son of man, say unto the House of Israel: You spoke in this manner, saying: Our transgressions and our sins are upon us, and we waste in them: how can we live? Say unto them: As I live, says Hashem, our God, I have no desire for the death of the wicked, rather that the wicked turn from his way and live."

(*Yechezkel* 33:10)

RASHI COMMENTS ON THE WORDS "Our transgressions and our sins are upon us, and we waste in them: how can we live?" and says, "You have no desire to repent because you don't believe *teshuvah* will help you."

A STRANGE ATTITUDE

Shouldn't we be amazed at the attitude of this generation [that lived at the time of Yechezkel]? They amassed transgressions against Hashem and acted amorally in His presence. Therefore, Hashem sent His servants, the prophets, to speak to them day by day, both morning and evening. However, they did not want to accept the words of the prophets, who urged them to do *teshuvah*. Their resistance was effected by the *yetzer hara*, as the Torah teaches, "The imagery of man's heart is evil from his youth" (*Bereishis* 8:21) and "Sin rests at the door" (ibid. 4:7). Yet their conduct is perplexing. The verse [in *Yechezkel*] implies that they already regretted the evil of their ways and that their hearts were inclined to do *teshuvah*. The only deterrent [preventing their repentance] was their lack of belief that their *teshuvah* would be accepted. This attitude thwarted their will to return to Hashem. This is astounding! What did they see and how did they reach a conclusion that led them to insult and reject the prophets, who were living angels? This is especially strange in light of the fact that from ancient days the prophets urged the people, in the Name of Hashem, to do *teshuvah*. They assured *b'nei Yisrael* that if they would repent from their evil ways — all of their sins would be forgiven, and their transgressions would no longer be remembered.

OUR GENERATION

When we think about this a little more deeply, we will be even more astounded [when we consider a glaring contrast between that generation and our generation]. Let us contemplate the difference between the faith of that generation and the faith of our generation. Isn't it apparent that, in general, our faith is very fragile? Even in our earthly affairs, we are sorely lacking in recognition of Divine providence and in trust of Hashem. [For example,] the Talmud (*Bava Basra* 10) teaches that the sustenance of man for the entire year is set on Rosh HaShanah [yet who really amongst us conducts themselves in accordance with this teaching?] Moreover, Chazal tell us that no one can touch a hairbreadth of the share that was apportioned for his fellow. There are many other statements in the Torah that instruct us to place our faith in Hashem for our sustenance. However, our faith in this area is deficient and feeble.

FAITH IN REPENTANCE

It is amazing that despite this, the faith of our generation is very strong regarding the path of *teshuvah*. We also believe with complete faith that *HaKadosh Baruch Hu* pardons and forgives all those who repent from their transgressions. We also believe the dramatic teaching of the Talmud (*Kiddushin* 40b): "Even a person who was absolutely evil his entire life, then at the end of his life does *teshuvah* — Hashem will not remind him of his evil deeds." We also accept Chazal's interpretation of the verse, "You reduce man unto pulp" (*Tehillim* 90:3), meaning, until his spirit is humbled. Indeed, we believe in the power of *teshuvah* — even beyond its true parameters. That is, we believe that with even a little repentance — if one would just return to Hashem and confess his transgressions — then all of his sins will be forgotten. The same is true of Yom Kippur. As long as he afflicts himself with fasting, confesses his sins, and sequesters himself all day in shul, reciting prayers and supplications, he believes with perfect faith that Hashem will grant his atonement, purify him from all sin, and that all of his transgressions will vanish like a cloud.

CONTRAST BETWEEN GENERATIONS

How strange is this contrast between generations! The generation of Yechezkel attained the level of regretting the evil of their ways. They deeply desired to return to Hashem. Nevertheless, they lacked the faith that *teshuvah* would be beneficial to them. Therefore, they did not have the motivation to do *teshuvah*. While we, who are shallow and weak of faith, and devoid of regret over our ways, nevertheless possess unwavering faith in repentance. We are confident that with a minimal effort on our part, *teshuvah* will render forgiveness for all of our sins. Is there anyone in our generation who professes to return to Hashem, but is deterred because his heart is too feeble to believe in *teshuvah*?

THOSE OF LITTLE FAITH

Indeed, the Talmud (*Pesachim* 118b) states, "Rav Huna said: 'The people of Israel of that generation [of the Exodus from Egypt] were of little faith,' and as Rabbah bar Mari expounded: 'What is taught by the verse, "But they were rebellious at the sea, even at the Red Sea"? This teaches us that at that very moment, the people of Israel rebelled and said, "Just as we ascend on one side of the sea, so, too, are the Egyptians ascending on the other side." [They did not believe that Hashem drowned the Egyptians.] Then *HaKadosh Baruch Hu* ordered the ministering angel presiding over the Sea, "Spit them [the Egyptians] out on the dry land"...And Israel came and saw them, as it says, "And Israel saw the Egyptians dead on the seashore" (*Shemos* 14:30).' " Behold, Rav Huna is not asserting that the Israelites of that generation were totally devoid of faith. Rather, they were of little faith, meaning that they did not have total faith. We must clarify, then, what is the definition of "little faith," and also, why did Israel rebel at the sea, saying, "The Egyptians are ascending on the other side"?

THE ULTIMATE LEVEL OF TOTAL FAITH

Now, it appears that the ultimate level of total faith is to believe in Hashem and even in things that conflict with the normative logic of the intellect. The defining quality of the giants of faith is that their belief in Hashem and His Prophets extends even above and beyond the intellectual powers of man. However, the defining quality of "little faith" is when they believe only in that which coincides with the ways of logic. However, if the belief disputes the logic of the human intellect, then the power of their faith collapses. [In our generation, the opposite is true. We believe in the counterintuitive concept of *teshuvah*, but not in the rational understanding that our livelihood comes from Hashem.] This is alluded to in the Tanach (*Malachim II* 7:1). When the man of God [Elisha] spoke to the king, saying, " 'At this time tomorrow, a *se'ah* of fine flour [will be bought] for one shekel and two *se'ahs* of barley for one shekel at the gateway of Shomron.' The king's captain...answered the man of God and said, 'Even if Hashem were to make windows in the heavens, can this thing happen?' [Elisha] replied, 'You will see it with your own eyes, but you will not eat from it!' " And so it happened to him, etc.

Now, when the Jewish people said, "Just as we ascend on one side of the sea, so, too, are the Egyptians ascending on the other side," their faith in the power of Hashem was never in question. It was not illogical for them to think [that Hashem would save them from the Egyptians]. They believed that Hashem would perform anything that He so desires to do, and no one can be saved if Hashem decides to destroy them. Their assumption [that the Egyptians were escaping unharmed] was based on the fact that *b'nei Yisrael* were on a very low level in Egypt. Chazal (*Yalkut Reuveni, Parashas Beshalach*) states this: "They [the Egyptians] worshiped idols and they [the Jewish people] worshiped idols." Therefore, they considered it illogical that *HaKadosh Baruch Hu* would destroy a complete nation for their sake. They could not conceive that Hashem would abolish the Egyptians and drown them all in the sea. Although Moshe Rabbeinu said, "For as you have seen Egypt today, you shall not see them ever again" (*Shemos* 14:13), nevertheless, their belief in this promise was weak. Their faith was too small to firmly believe in a promise that they considered illogical. This is the reason that they said, "Just as we ascend on one side of the sea, so, too, are the Egyptians ascending on the other side."

FAITH BEYOND LOGIC

The Torah alludes to the Jewish people's deficiency of faith: "Hashem saved Israel...and Israel saw the Egyptians dead on the seashore...and they had faith in Hashem and in Moshe, His servant" (*Shemos* 14:30). Let us ask the following question: Why were they deemed to have faith now at the sea, more so than by all the other signs and wonders which Hashem performed before their eyes in Egypt? Indeed, the answer is that the Jews of that generation were of small faith. In other words, their faith was too weak to believe in a Divine assurance that countered human logic. Since Hashem performed signs and wonders in Egypt, they therefore did not consider the omnipotence of Hashem illogical. However, when they came to the sea, and Moshe Rabbeinu said to them: "For as you have seen Egypt today, you shall not see them ever again" — it was illogical to them that Hashem would drown all of the Egyptians in the sea. Therefore, they responded, "Just as we ascend on one side of the sea, so, too, are the Egyptians ascending on the other side." However, afterwards, when they saw the Egyptians dead on the seashore, and all of Moshe Rabbeinu's words were fulfilled — then their minds opened up to understand and comprehend that man cannot fathom the sublime compassion of Hashem. Nor can the human intellect ascend to the heights to grasp the realm of the Lord. At that point, the faith to believe in Hashem and His servant, Moshe, even in matters that are above and beyond human comprehension, was deeply implanted in their hearts. This is what the Torah is teaching: "And Israel saw the Egyptians dead on the seashore…and they had faith…." At first they were of small faith, and said, "Just as we ascend . . .the Egyptians are ascending…." However, when they saw the Egyptians dead on the seashore, then they believed in Hashem and His servant Moshe.

REPENTANCE IS COUNTERINTUITIVE

The foundation of repentance — that Hashem accepts penitents and pardons and forgives their iniquities — is also a contradiction to human logic. It is illogical for Hashem to pardon and forgive even one transgression; how much more untenable is the statement of Chazal that we quoted previously: "Even a man who is totally evil all the days of his life, and performs repentance at the end — Hashem will not remind him of his past." This is, understandably, a very strange concept for the human mind to fathom.

Indeed, just how far the concept of *teshuvah* is beyond human comprehension is dependant on the quality of man's recognition and examination of the sin; on his contemplation of how great is the blemish of the sin, which, in fact, is literally a rebellion against the Divine will. If one does not feel, examine, or consider the serious nature of the sin and transgression and the immense accountability of the perpetrator, then the fundamental principle of repentance will not seem irrational to the human mind. Since he does not view the actual sin as a great culpability, and he believes that Hashem is merciful and gracious — why will He not pardon and forgive those who do *teshuvah* for their iniquity and sin?

However, the more one strives to recognize and examine the dire gravity of transgression, as well as to understand and comprehend the terrible corruption and the vast culpability of sin and transgression — a rebellion against the Divine will, may His Name be blessed, the Supreme King of kings, *HaKadosh Baruch Hu* — to that extent the principle foundation of repentance will be more illogical.

THE ACCOUNTABILITY OF SIN

Man will not truly recognize the degree of accountability of sin until he knows the exalted majesty and great honor of Hashem, may His Name be blessed. This is written in the book *Mesillas Yesharim* (ch. 24): "Concerning the fear of sin, in the category of the fear of His exalted majesty, a man should distance himself from the sins, and he should refrain from committing sins in deference of His great honor, may His Name be blessed. How can he take sin lightly? And how can man, who is flesh and blood, lowly and disgusting, do something against the Divine will of the Creator, may His Name be blessed and exalted? But behold, it is not so easy to grasp this type of *yiras Shamayim*. It is attained only through the knowledge and comprehension that facilitates understanding of the exalted majesty of Hashem, may His Name be blessed, and reflection on the lowliness of man."

KNOWING THE EXALTED MAJESTY OF HASHEM

Therefore, when man reaches this level of knowing the exalted majesty of Hashem, may His Name be blessed, then he will comprehend and understand the terrible corruption and vast accountability of sin. [He will then be overwhelmed by the shame of] his flesh and blood, that will now seem lowly and disgusting, and [he will admit] that by nature his heart desires to rebel against the will of the Divine, may His Name be blessed, the Supreme King of kings, *HaKadosh Baruch Hu*. And when he recognizes the true seriousness of his sin, then the foundation of repentance will seem quite strange to the paths of the intellect, as we mentioned above.

GREAT IN FAITH

Nevertheless, if he is amongst those who are great in faith, then his heart wholly believes, with absolute steadfast faith, even those ideas that are contrary to human rational. Indeed, "The righteous man shall live through his faith" (*Chavakuk* 2:4). Hence, *HaKadosh Baruch Hu* promised us through his servants, the prophets: "Let the wicked one forsake his way...let him return to Hashem and He will show him mercy" (*Yeshayahu* 55:7). However, it is just the opposite concerning one whose attitude towards *teshuvah* is one of small faith; that is, his belief dissipates in the face of principles that defy human logic. Conceivably, his heart will be weak in accepting the foundation of *teshuvah* — Hashem pardons and forgives penitents. Likewise, someone who does not recognize and detect the accountability of sin and transgression will believe in the foundation of *teshuvah*, even if he is of small faith. It will not seem contrary to logic.

In the light of this understanding, we can explain why in the generation of Yechezkel HaNavi, the Jewish people said, "Our transgressions and our sins are upon us, and we waste in them: how can we live?" It seems perplexing — why did they have a lack of belief in repentance, and why did they think that repentance would be of no avail to them? Also, why is there an antithesis between them and us — why do we have complete, absolute faith in repentance? The answer is that the generation of Yechezkel lived in the period when the Temple still existed. They saw the holiness, the Sanctuary, and the honor of Hashem that dwelt within the Temple. Therefore, they beheld His exalted majesty, the splendor of His honor, may His Name be blessed. An illustration of the intensity of their perception of the exalted majesty of Hashem, may His Name be blessed, is taught by our Sages (*Tanna D'bei Eliyahu*): "Yechezkel HaNavi said to the Elders of Israel, 'Perform repentance.' They responded, 'We are embarrassed....' " How sublime is the feeling of being embarrassed in the presence of Hashem, may His Name be blessed. [They were so embarrassed] by the seriousness of their sin that the notion that they would be forgiven [was overwhelming for them] and, thus, they could not fathom beseeching from Him pardon and forgiveness. Indeed, this embarrassment is a most worthy attribute in the paths of *yiras haromemus* (the fear of Divine majesty), as we know.

THE GENERATION OF YECHEZKEL

In any case, the generation of Yechezkel felt the great majesty of Hashem, may His Name be blessed. Therefore, even though they did not have the power to stand against the *yetzer hara*, still, they clearly recognized the vast, awesome accountability of sin and iniquity. Since they perceived the seriousness of the sin, the principle of repentance was irrational to their intellect. Coupled with this, they were "of little faith," for their belief was weak concerning concepts that were contrary to logic. In the wake of this, they also did not believe that repentance would avail them forgiveness for all of their transgressions, nor did they believe that if they repented they would be granted life.

INSENSATE TO YIRAS SHAMAYIM

However, we do not have the same sensitivity that they had, as the enormous number of our sins has rendered us insensate to *yiras ha'onesh* (the fear of punishment), even though the concept of bodily punishment is something that, theoretically, we should be able to understand. How much more so are we lacking all sensitivity to *yiras haromemus*. We do not recognize the magnitude of culpability of sin and iniquity, nor do we fathom how serious and awesome it is — the sin itself is very light in our eyes. Therefore, the concept of repentance is not illogical to us whatsoever; it is not perplexing to us at all. Even those of us who really are of little faith, whose belief is weak concerning a concept which is beyond our common sense, nevertheless believe with perfect faith in the paths of repentance. We are certain that *HaKadosh Baruch Hu* pardons and forgives those who repent from sin. This is not contrary to our reasoning at all.

THE DEGREE OF PUNISHMENT

We are far away from feeling *yiras haromemus*, which would enable us to examine the great culpability of sin and iniquity. Nevertheless, there is a method that can help us make a true estimation of the seriousness of sin, with the help of Hashem, based on the punishments of the transgressions and the rebuke. The degree of punishment sheds light on what is the culpability of sin — what it means to rebel against the Divine will of the King of kings, *HaKadosh Baruch Hu*. Chazal (*Eruvin* 19a) taught, "Rebbi Yehoshua ben Levi said: What is the meaning of the verse, 'Those who pass through the valley of weeping make it into a wellspring; also the rain clothes it with blessings' (*Tehillim* 84:7)? 'Those who pass through' — these are the people who transgress the Divine will of *HaKadosh Baruch Hu*. 'Valley' — meaning that Hashem deepens Gehinnom for them. 'Weeping' — meaning that they weep and shed tears like the spring of Sheeten. 'Also the rain clothes it with blessings' — they concede the justice of their punishment, and say before Him, 'You have judged beautifully; you have acquitted beautifully; you have convicted beautifully; you have prepared Gehinnom for the wicked beautifully...' " (see the text). This seems amazing, indeed. Why is it remarkable that in the World of Truth, where the evil inclination does not corrupt man, the wicked concede the justice of their punishment and praise the righteousness of Hashem?[3]

A GOD WITHOUT INIQUITY

In *Parashas Ha'azinu* the verse says: "The Rock! — perfect is His work, for all His paths are justice; a God of faith without iniquity, righteous and fair is He" (*Devarim* 32:4). It seems strange that the Torah praises Hashem for being without iniquity. For isn't iniquity a deficiency? The accolade that he is "without iniquity" is a fitting praise for man, as the verse says, "The remnant of Israel shall not commit iniquity..." (*Tzefanyah* 3:13). However, Hashem, may His Name be blessed, is the source of perfection. How can we ascribe to him the accolade of "without iniquity"? Shall the Judge of the earth judge unfairly?

[The praise of Hashem in this verse pertains to the just application of punishment.] All the inhabitants of the world agree upon the indispensability of the penal system, and we try to sentence all perpetrators of crime with a punishment concordant with the evilness of their crime. [But they cannot be exact and perfect like Hashem.] In fact, all the governments have statutes and corresponding penalties — divisions of punishments corresponding to every infraction of law and ethics. However, even though the world agrees to the principle of punishment, nevertheless, the severity and quantity of punishment for each sin is a matter of compromise and approximation. But really there is no scale that can configure the transgression with the punishment — to weigh the severity of the punishment against the intent of the sin. Therefore, the severity of the punishment is only an approximation, and the ordi-

---

3   What new concept does the Talmud teach us here? Surely in Gehinnom, where the truth is revealed, the perpetrators recognize the justice of their punishment. If so, why does the text point out that the souls that are punished in Gehinnom admit and praise Hashem for the perfect punishment that they receive there?

nances of punishments are not identical amongst the various governments. Every government sets down statutes, judgments, and punishments for all sin and iniquity — according to their best efforts of approximation. Sometimes, the punishment of the sin will follow the whim of the ruler according to his will at the time — to punish with either severe or light punishment.

PERVERSION OF JUDGMENT

In any case, there is neither level nor scale to compute the punishment of the sin. It is beyond the power of the human intellect to gauge the precise dosage of punishment that corresponds to the magnitude of the sin. Therefore, in the process of justice, there could sometimes be a distortion and perversion of judgment in the prescription of the punishment. The human intellect is not able to assess the severity of the punishment that corresponds in a reciprocal fashion to the sin. For instance, if an individual is penalized for his transgression with some punishment for a set duration of time, is there any scale or weight to compute the accurate time of punishment? Or does the human intellect possess the power to fix the time of punishment so that it corresponds precisely to the severity of the sin — not a day less or more? If so, by definition, there could be a perversion of justice. However, even though man is deficient in this power of computation, he has no alternative but to punish criminals. Thus, the judge can only adjudicate according to what makes sense to his intellect.

PERFECTION OF JUDGMENT

Let us now turn from this idea and contemplate the judgments of Hashem, may His Name be blessed. He administers punishment to the wicked according to the evil of his deeds, particularly in the World of Bestowal [of reward and punishment]. The myriad of terrible, awesome punishments are precisely befitting the sinners. They will be smelted in fire, like the smelting of silver. Shall we also ask, where are the scale and weights to calculate the degree of punishment that corresponds to the intention of the transgression? Shall we also say, God forbid, that the punishment is only an approximation and a practical compromise; that Hashem randomly decides how much to punish each sinner and transgressor? If so, a perversion of justice is also plausible, as we mentioned above. God forbid, this never occurs with the Judge of the entire world! Even though this is unattainable for man — can there be anything too wondrous for Hashem? He can make a scale that computes the severity of the sin and the appropriate punishment, without deviation. The weights and scales of justice are in the hand of Hashem. Thus, He places the transgression on one side and the punishment on the other side. The scales equally balance so that the quality of punishment corresponds in weight to the quality of the sin, to the exactness of a hairsbreadth.

THE WISDOM OF KEL DEI'OS

The Rambam (*Hilchos Teshuvah* 3:1, 2) states, "Each and every person has merits and transgressions. If his merits exceed his transgressions, he is a righteous man. And if his transgressions exceed his merits he is an evil man.... This computation is not calculated according to the quantity of the merits, rather, according to the quality of them. There are merits which outweigh many transgressions.... And there are transgressions which outweigh many merits.... This computation can only be calculated by the wisdom of *Kel Dei'os* (Hashem, Who knows all wisdom). And He knows how to balance the merits against the transgressions" (see the text). Is it within the power of the human intellect to imagine the actual scale that weighs the quality of merits and the transgressions, to the extent that he can ascertain that one merit outweighs the sum of many transgressions? Likewise, that one transgression outweighs many merits? However, *HaKadosh Baruch Hu* is omnipotent, and there is no wonder which He cannot perform. Thus, this computation of the severity of punishment corresponding to the transgression is within the wisdom of *Kel Dei'os*. He is the One who knows how to arrange the punishment corresponding to the sin on the scales, so that the scales are equally balanced.

JUDGE OF THE WHOLE WORLD

This is what is written in the Torah, "The Rock! — perfect is His work, for all His paths are justice; a God of faith, without iniquity" (*Devarim* 32:4). The purpose of this verse is not to suggest that *HaKadosh Baruch Hu*, the Judge of the whole world, judges unfairly. If the remnant of Israel does not judge unfairly, how much more is this true concerning the Supreme King of kings, *HaKadosh Baruch Hu*. Rather, the intention of the verse is that as far as man is concerned in the process of justice, there are no actual weights and scales to compute the punishment appropriate for the transgression. Therefore, even though the judges strive to be straight in rendering judgment, nevertheless, there could be a flaw in their judgment, as we mentioned above. Therefore, the verse says, "The Rock...a God of faith, without iniquity," teaching us that He is omnipotent, and in His hand are the weights and scales of justice, to compute the sin with the appropriate punishment. He is the One who knows to arrange the magnitude of the punishment that corresponds with the magnitude of the sin, so that their scales are balanced to the exactness of a hairsbreadth.

VALLEY OF TEARS

With this concept, let us comprehend the passage in the Talmud (*Eruvin* 19a) that we cited above: " 'Also the rain clothes it with blessings' — they concede the justice of their punishment, and say before Him, 'Master of the universe, You have judged beautifully....' " In this world, man does not recognize the great seriousness of sin. Thus, imagine that man could see with his eyes the awesome punishments in the Valley of Tears, and the great, awesome fire that burns in the depths of Gehinnom, which consumes both soul and body for every sin. His mind could not comprehend that this was precisely computed by weights and a scale and that the awesome punishment corresponds to the culpability of the sin. Rather, he would assume the punishment is a matter of policy. That is, the will of Hashem, may His Name be blessed, is to punish each sin and iniquity with a punishment that is exceedingly great and awesome. Man would think that the punishment is seven times worse than the sin.

THE EXACTNESS OF DIVINE PUNISHMENT

However, in the World of Bestowal [of reward and punishment], the wicked people know and recognize the frightening seriousness of sin, which constitutes rebellion against the will of the Supreme King of kings, *HaKadosh Baruch Hu*. They know how exceedingly weighty and awesome is the matter of sin. There, in the World of Truth, they know and understand that the bitter punishment is not arbitrary, but is exactly equal to the level of sin. The weights and the scales of justice are in the hand of Hashem, may His Name be blessed. The scales balance the iniquity and the punishment equally. The great, awesome punishment counterbalances the accountability of the sin, to the exactness of a hairsbreadth. This is what they say, "Master of the Universe, You have judged beautifully...You have prepared Gehinnom for the wicked beautifully and Gan Eden for the righteous."

Now that we understand the exactness of punishments in the Spiritual World, we can accept the apparent severity of punishment. Since He is "The Rock a God of faith, without iniquity," the punishment is administered with exactness that corresponds to the sin, as we mentioned above. Also, we believe the teaching of Chazal, that the punishment in the Spiritual World for transgressions is exceedingly terrible and beyond any of the sufferings of this world, as the Ramban wrote in *Sha'ar HaGemul*. Thus, by awakening to the great and exceedingly awesome punishment which man deserves for sin, we can fathom the great and exceedingly awesome magnitude of culpability of sin. How awesome is this concept to one who contemplates it.

CULPABILITY

Indeed the, Talmud (*Nazir* 23a) states, "Our Rabbis taught: [In the verse (*Bamidbar* 30:13),] 'Her husband has made them void, and Hashem will forgive her.' (The Gemara is speaking of a woman whose husband has declared her [vow] void without her knowledge, implying that she requires atonement and forgiveness [i.e., even though she was a *nazirah* she thought to drink wine which was forbidden to her. However, her husband, unbeknownst to her, released her *nazirus*. Nevertheless, she requires atonement and forgiveness].) When Rebbi Akiva reached this verse he wept: 'For if one who intended to take swine's flesh and, by chance, takes lamb flesh stands in need of atonement and forgiveness, how much more does one who intended to take swine's flesh and actually took it stand in need of atonement and forgiveness?' " Indeed, this is Mussar reproof. We should know and recognize the magnitude of culpability of an intentional transgression, from the magnitude of culpability of an unintentional transgression. However, even when a person doesn't realize his culpability, he bears the responsibility.

THE KORBANOS

To further elaborate on this concept, let us contemplate and understand the words of the Ramban, *zt"l*, in his commentary on the Torah in *Parashas Vayikra*, in which he explains the reason behind the *korbanos*: "For an act of man is composed of thought, speech, and deed. Therefore, Hashem, may His Name be blessed, commanded that when man sins and he will bring a *korban*, he should place his hands on it — corresponding to the deed. He should confess with his mouth — corresponding to the speech. He should then burn with fire the stomach and the kidneys, which correspond to the faculties of thought and desire, and then burn the legs — corresponding to the hands and legs of man, which perform all his deeds. He should sprinkle the blood on the altar — corresponding to his lifeblood. All these acts are required so that when he performs them, he should think that he sinned against his Lord with his body and with his soul, and it is fitting that his blood should be spilled and his body should be burnt — if not for the kindness of the Creator who accepts from him a substitute and the atonement of this *korban*, its blood in place of his blood, and its soul in place of his soul, and its major limbs in place of his limbs..." (see the text there).

How awesome is this matter! We see again that when a person sins unintentionally, it would be fitting to punish him with the spilling of his blood and the burning of his body. It is only the Creator's kindness towards him that when he performs repentance and brings his *korban* as his substitute — that its blood is in place of his blood and its soul is in place of his soul, and he is forgiven. Yet, without repentance, this punishment remains for him. If this is the proper punishment for an unintentional sin — namely, that his blood should be spilled and his body should be burnt — then how much more frightening is the proper punishment for an intentional transgression, for one who sins with awareness and volition. There certainly is neither likeness nor comparison between the severity for culpability of an unintentional sin, and the severity of culpability for an intentional sin.

MAN IS DEFICIENT

Behold, how deficient man is in recognizing the level of magnitude of culpability and the severity of punishment for an unintentional sin, and even more so for an intentional sin. Therefore, when a man unknowingly [violates the Torah,] he does not consider nor view this as such a significant matter that he should put it upon his heart and worry about it. Yet, when we contemplate the spirit of the people in the days of the generation of Chazal, even those from the general populace of the House of Israel, we see how they viewed the severity of sin, even an unintentional transgression.

THE EMBARRASSMENT OF SIN

The Mishnah (*Chullin* 41b) says: "If a man slaughtered [an unconsecrated animal outside the Temple court] declaring it to be a burnt offering...the slaughtering is invalid. If a man slaughtered [an unconsecrated animal outside the Temple court] declaring it to be a sin offering...the slaughtering is valid." The Gemara explains: " 'If a man slaughtered, declaring it to be a sin offering, it is valid.' Rebbi Yochanan said: 'This *mishnah* refers only to the case when he [the slaughterer] was not obligated to bring a sin offering. [If, however,] he was obligated to bring a sin offering, it would have been assumed that he was slaughtering the animal as his sin offering.' " Rashi explains that when the slaughterer was not obligated to bring a sin offering, "People would not say, 'It was at this moment that he consecrated it,' because a sin-offering is not consecrated with a vow, and, therefore [they would correctly assume that he meant to say] it was a free-will offering. Behold, the Rabbis were not concerned that perhaps those who saw him would think that he was obligated to bring a sin offering. It is public knowledge that someone has committed an unintentional transgression. Moreover, he does not hide it, for in this way he will be embarrassed, and the embarrassment will serve as an atonement."

It's apparent from here that the Rabbis made a simple assumption: that everyone who committed even an unintentional sin was wrought with worry about receiving an atonement for his transgression. Therefore, he did not hide this transgression; [on the contrary] he wanted the public to know about it. In this way he would be embarrassed, and that would be an atonement for him. Now let us contemplate this. How fantastic is the difference between them and us! First, in their time, even the general populous of the House of Israel, even if they committed an unintentional transgression, would worry about attaining atonement for their soul. Second, a person who committed an unintentional transgression in the time of Chazal would be embarrassed and mortified if it became public knowledge. A person committing an unintentional transgression, then, underwent great shame and embarrassment, such that if his unintentional sin became public knowledge, the sinner would be exceedingly embarrassed. His extreme embarrassment and shame would be considered an atonement for this transgression.

WE HAVE NO SENSE OF SHAME

Now, let us contemplate our perception of the severity of an unintentional transgression. If someone in our times commits an unintentional transgression, does his heart seek to attain atonement? Would it be that when he commits intentional transgressions he is awakened to seek atonement! Second, who amongst us is embarrassed by an unintentional transgression? If someone unintentionally violates one of the forbidden acts of Shabbos — for instance, the prohibition of separating — would he be embarrassed to mention this to anybody? He would not be at all embarrassed, nor would he know any shame, for an unintentional transgression is not considered an embarrassment or shame whatsoever. Nowadays, committing an unintentional transgression does not decrease a person's stature whatsoever!

ARTICLE FOUR

ROSH HASHANAH, THE DAY OF JUDGMENT

THE MISHNAH (*Rosh HaShanah* 16a) STATES: "At four periods [of the year] judgment is passed on the world.... On Rosh HaShanah all creatures pass before Him, like *b'nei Maron*, as it says, 'He formed the heart of all of them; He perceives all of their deeds' (*Tehillim* 33:15)." The Talmud (*Rosh HaShanah* 18a) asks: "What is *b'nei Maron*? Here [in Babylon] it was translated, 'like a flock of sheep.' Reish Lakish said, 'Like the ascent of Beis Meron.' Rav Yehudah said in the name of Shmuel, 'Like the troops of the house of David.' "

A FLOCK OF SHEEP

Rashi explains: " 'Like a flock of sheep' — Like sheep that are counted for tithes. They pass one by one through a small opening, and they cannot pass through together [as one]. 'Like the ascent of Beis Meron' — A narrow pass where two people cannot go side by side, for the gully is deep on both sides. 'Like the troops of the house of David' — They counted them one after the other when they went out to war."

Behold, it appears from Rashi's explanation that all the Amora'im were consistent in defining "What is *b'nei Maron*?" Namely, that the Tanna's intention in this parable is only to say that all the inhabitants of the world do not pass together as an entire group before *Hashem Yisbarach*. Rather, they pass one by one, like *b'nei Maron* — either as a flock of sheep, or as the ascent of Beis Meron, or as the troops of the house of David.

This seems quite curious: Why does the Tanna need a parable to explain such a simple concept? Why are all the inhabitants of the world, passing before *Hashem Yisbarach* one by one, likened to *b'nei Maron*? Who would not understand this, the idea of "one by one"? The Tanna should have simply stated: "On Rosh HaShanah all the inhabitants of the world pass one by one before Hashem." Moreover, why did the Tanna emphasize in the parable a place where they must pass in single file? This is true, whether *b'nei Maron* refers to counting flocks of sheep, where the opening is so small that they cannot exit together; or whether it refers to the ascent of Beis Meron, in which the path was so narrow that two people could not walk side by side.

Indeed, there is an axiom contained in the concept of, "All the inhabitants of the world pass before *Hashem Yisbarach* one by one like *b'nei Maron*." We must endeavor to understand and comprehend the reason for this: What is the ultimate purpose and goal of this individual passing before Hashem? Is it too wondrous for Hashem to bring before Him all the inhabitants of the world together?

DIVINE KINDNESS

However, it appears there a very deep intention for this. All of this emanates from the wisdom of *Hashem Yisbarach* and the boundless mercy and kindness He bestows upon those who find grace in His eyes. He opens a path before them, to create a future and good hope for them on the awesome Day of Judgment. It is an axiom of judgment and law: whether they will find punishment or kindness depends to a large degree on the order in which they pass before *Hashem Yisbarach* — one by one, to be exact. With the help of Hashem, the subsequent paragraphs will explain this.

A KING AND A COMMUNITY

It says in the Talmud (*Rosh HaShanah* 8b): "Rav Chisda said, 'When a king and a community appear together [for trial], the king is brought up for judgment first, as it says: "The judgment of His servant [Shlomo HaMelech] and the judgment of His people." What is the reason [that the king is tried first]? The king is tried before the Divine wrath becomes really fierce.'"

Rashi explains: "His anger is inflamed because of the transgressions of the community." Behold, isn't everything revealed and known to *Hashem Yisbarach* — all the thoughts and motivations of man, as well as the wandering of his footsteps? Even before the community comes for judgment, Hashem knows everyone's deeds!

PROCEDURES OF JUDGMENT

Hashem, may His Name be blessed, in His wisdom, established all procedures of judgment and justice according to the structure of earthly kingdoms. Therefore, he set a special day on which He sits on the Throne of Judgment to judge the nations. And every act of man, which is recorded in the Ledger of Remembrance, is brought before Him. The *paytan* (author) established the procedure of the Day of Judgment in the *Nesaneh Tokef* prayer: "He writes, seals, counts, and numbers. The Ledger of Remembrance is opened and He reads from it." And likewise there are numerous accusers and defenders. Even though *Hashem Yisbarach* knows all that is hidden and nothing is concealed from His eyes — He is the one who understands, He is the witness, He is the judge — nevertheless, Hashem deliberately conducts the procedure of judgment and justice according to the ways of the earthly kingdom.

Certainly, even before the community is brought before Him for judgment He already knows everyone's deeds. Nevertheless, *Hashem Yisbarach* does not allow His comprehensive knowledge of everyone's deeds to make an impression on Him. Thus, "burning wrath" does not dominate until He sits on the Throne of Judgment and "understands" all of their deeds in judgment. Then, because of the transgression of the community, the burning wrath of Hashem is inflamed, God forbid.

STATUTE OF REMEMBRANCE

Likewise, Rosh HaShanah is the awesome Day of Judgment; it is a statute of remembrance for Hashem to examine every spirit and soul. The creations are evaluated on this day — to be remembered either for life or death. The remembrance of every deed comes before *Hashem Yisbarach*, and He requires every action to be judged. Therefore, if all the inhabitants of the world would pass together before Him, "He formed the heart of all of them," and He would certainly know all of their deeds. If the transgressions of the community were exceedingly great, and if their sins were very severe, than the wrath of Hashem would burn because of the iniquity of the public. Indeed, who can stand before His anger, and who can exist before His burning wrath? Both the righteous and the wicked would be enmeshed in the net of the wrath of Hashem, which would rage without any healing, God forbid.

HIS ABUNDANT MERCY

Therefore, in the wisdom of *Hashem Yisbarach* and His abundant mercy and His great kindness, all the inhabitants of the world pass before Him one by one, one after the other. Now, we already mentioned that Hashem, may His Name be blessed, does not allow His knowledge of man's deed to ignite His wrath as long as he has not passed before Him in judgment. Therefore, the burning wrath of *Hashem Yisbarach* over the transgressions of the general populace of the world neither includes nor encompasses everybody. Rather, the matter depends on who will pass first before *Hashem Yisbarach*, until the last one who passes at the end. Indeed, whoever passes first before *Hashem Yisbarach* is fortunate. His path is more advantageous than the one who passes after him. Each soul bears "only" the burning wrath of *Hashem Yisbarach* from the iniquities of all those who already proceeded him, but it does not bear the wickedness and transgressions of those who pass after him, as we mentioned above.

ONE SIN HAS THE POWER TO MAKE AN IMPRESSION

Behold, even one sin has the power to make an impression, as it is written, "A single rogue can ruin a great deal of good" (*Koheles* 9:18); how much more so, all the sins of one man. Therefore, each successive individual inhabitant of the world who passes before *Hashem Yisbarach* on the Day of Judgment is in a less favorable position than those who preceded him. Likewise, he is more fortunate than those who pass after him. Thus, each one of his iniquities is added to the total of sins of those who passed before him. It is capable of making an impression that will ignite burning wrath, also felt by those who will follow him, as we mentioned.

THE SEQUENCE OF HOW THEY PASS

Indeed, the verdict of the judgment and the justice of whether he will be punished or blessed is quite dependant on the sequence of how they pass before Hashem, may His Name be blessed. The path of all those who pass first before *Hashem Yisbarach* is favorable, for they are more sheltered from the burning wrath of the Divine Judgment. Now, what determines the order of position in this line, where all the inhabitants of the world pass before Hashem? Who merits to pass first, and who will go at the very end? — for it is Hashem who imposes the order.

This is exactly what the *mishnah* in *Rosh HaShanah* is teaching us, "All the inhabitants of the world pass before Him like *b'nei Maron*...." The *mishnah* is not coming to explain allegorically how they pass in single file, like *b'nei Maron*, for this is quite simple. That concept can be easily conveyed without allegory or rhetoric. Rather, the purpose of the *mishnah* is to reveal the order of all the inhabitants of the world as they pass individually before Hashem. Who will merit to pass first before Hashem, and who will be at the end? In reference to this, the *mishnah* teaches that the single file order of all the inhabitants of the world as they pass one by one will be comparable to *b'nei Maron*.

THREE ASPECTS

In general, the order is self-evident. The one who is good and has found grace in the eyes of Hashem will have a more advanced position. This will shield him from the burning wrath so that he will have a good hope to be written in the Book of Life. However, in particular, who are the ones that find grace in the eyes of Hashem to be meritorious in judgment? When we contemplate the primary factors of a meritorious judgment, we see that there are three categories. 1) They merit according to justice. 2) They merit mercy because of good deeds. 3) They merit for a hidden reason — only because it is the Divine will to have mercy on them even though they are undeserving.

Indeed, the Talmud (*Rosh HaShanah* 16b) teaches, "Rebbi Kruspedai said in the name of Rebbi Yochanan, 'Three books are opened on Rosh HaShanah…the totally righteous are immediately written and sealed for life, the totally wicked are immediately written and sealed for death, and the judgment of the intermediate is suspended from Rosh HaShanah until Yom Kippur. If they merit, they are sealed in the Book of Life, if they do not merit they are sealed in the book of death.' " The Ran explains that the term "intermediate" implies that the term "righteous," as it is used here, conveys those whose merits are greater than their sins. Whereas the term "wicked" conveys those whose sins are greater than their merits. Yet if this is true, then a deep question arises. We see that many "righteous" are, in fact, written for death, and many "wicked" are written for life! However, we can answer this question according to the view of the Ri HaZaken Mitrani, who wrote that this *mishnah* is referring to those who are classified in judgment as righteous or wicked. In other words, our *mishnah* defines "totally righteous" as those who merit in judgment because of a certain good deed [see category 2, above]. They are "totally righteous" in this judgment, even though they have more sins than merits. Likewise, "totally wicked" are those who are convicted in judgment because of a certain [minor] sin. They are "totally wicked" in this judgment, even though they have more merits than sins. "Intermediate" refers to those people whose judgment is balanced. Their fate is suspended until they tip the scale to either merit or conviction.

PRIMARY JUDGMENT

However, even though occasionally the totally righteous are liable in judgment because of a small [minor] sin, and totally wicked are meritorious in judgment because of a small favor [minor merit] — these are the exceptions. Yes, there are instances of the righteous being lost despite his righteousness, because of a small sin, and the wicked continuing despite his evil, because of a small merit. However, we must believe, in general, that primary judgment on Rosh HaShanah is based on the majority of his deeds. The Talmud (*Kiddushin* 40b) confirms this: "Rebbi Elazar ben Rebbi Shimon said,

'Since the world is judged by the majority of its deeds, and an individual is judged by his majority, if he performs one good deed, happy is he for inclining the scale — both for him and for the whole world — to the side of merit. If he commits one transgression, woe to him for inclining himself and the whole world to the side of culpability.' " Rashi explains that a person should view himself as balanced; if he does one mitzvah he tips the scales, his merits decide, and he is righteous, as the verse says, "A single rogue can ruin a great deal of good" (*Koheles* 9:18) — on the account of the single sin which this man commits, he and the whole world lose much good.

The Rambam (*Hilchos Teshuvah* 3:1, 2) also wrote, "Each and every person has merits and sins. One whose merits outweigh his sins is a *tzaddik*, and he whose sins outweigh his merits is a *rasha*.... Just as they weigh the merits of man and his sins at the time of his death, so, too, each year they weigh the sins of all the inhabitants of the world and their merits on the *yom tov* of Rosh HaShanah. He who is found to be a *tzaddik* is sealed for life, and he who is found to be a *rasha* is sealed for death. And the fate of the *beinoni* is suspended until Yom Kippur…" (see the *Kesef Mishnah*).

WEIGHING SINS AGAINST MERITS

Indeed, in general, the foundation of judgment, whether a man is a *tzaddik* or *rasha*, is based on weighing the sins against the merits. If his merits outweigh his sins, he is righteous in his deeds, and he merits in judgment. While if his sins outweigh his merits, he is evil in his deeds, and he is liable in judgment. There are many verses that teach that a *tzaddik* merits life by virtue of his good deeds, whereas the *rasha* is sentenced to death due to his sin, and if he repents he will live. There are exceptions, as sometimes the *tzaddik* is lost despite his righteousness, when he is liable in judgment because of a small [minor] sin, and sometimes the *rasha* merits in judgment because of a small [minor] deed that he has performed, as the Ran explained.

TWO CATEGORIES OF THOSE WHO MERIT IN JUDGMENT

In conclusion, there are two categories of those who merit in judgment.

The first is one whose merits outweigh his sins. Hashem considers him a *tzaddik*. All the more so does a total *tzaddik*, who is clean from sin and transgression, merit life through his righteousness. The second category consists of someone whose sins outweigh his merits. He is a *rasha* before Hashem; all the more contemptible is a total *rasha* [who has an overwhelming majority of sins over merits]. Nevertheless, he merits in judgment because of Hashem's mercy or account of some good deed that he has performed.

The first category is comprised of the *tzaddikim* and the *chassidim*. As a rule, Hashem guards those that love Him, and He watches over those that fear Him in order to save them from calamity. Likewise, on the awesome Day of Judgment, when all the inhabitants of the world pass individually before Hashem — Hashem draws the *tzaddikim* and the *chassidim* close to Him so that they will be amongst the first to pass before Him. He does so to shield them from His Divine wrath. The more righteous a person's deeds, the earlier he will pass before Hashem.

LIKE B'NEI MARON

This is the meaning of Chazal's statement in the *mishnah*, " 'Like *b'nei Maron*,' that is, like *b'nei Imrana* [Aramaic for a flock of sheep]." Rashi explains, "Like sheep that are counted for tithes. They pass one by one through a small opening, and they cannot pass through together [as one]." The nature of animals corralled in a pen is to rush for the gate when it is opened. If the opening is narrow, so that they can exit only one at a time, they push each other closer to the gate in order to get out. However, it is self-evident that the ones that get out first are the healthier, stronger sheep, who are able to exploit their power. They will turn to the right and to the left, and they will strengthen themselves to get out first. Whereas the weaker sheep, who are meek, will be the last ones out.

It is exactly the same on the Day of Judgment, when all the inhabitants of the world pass individually before Hashem. Each one wants an advanced position in the line so that he can be amongst those who pass first before Hashem. This is analogous to the tithing of sheep. The *tzaddikim* and *chassidim* are the strong ones of the world, as the Talmud states (*Berachos*

17b), " 'Listen to me, you strong-hearted people, who are far from charity'
(*Yeshayahu* 46:12). The whole world is sustained by [Hashem's] charity, and
they [the righteous] are sustained by their own power." Rashi explains the
phrase "by their own power" to mean by virtue of their own merit. In contrast, the sinners and transgressors are the weak ones of the world. Rashi alludes to this in the verse, "All the weaklings who were behind" (*Devarim*
25:18), meaning, the members of *klal Yisrael* who were weak because of their
sins and were expelled from the clouds. The same is true of the Day of Judgment. The *tzaddikim* and *chassidim* come with their strength — the power of
their good deeds (Tosafos on *Berachos* 17b). This is the theme of the poet in
the *Zichronos* prayer, "*Ani Efchad*," recited on the second day of Rosh
HaShanah: "They come with the power of their deeds." Therefore, *tzaddikim*
and *chassidim*, who have a "powerful arm" by virtue of their good deeds, are
empowered to pass first. The early position of each one to pass first depends
on the "power" of his deeds. Whereas, the weaklings, who are enfeebled because of their sins, pass at the end. This, then, explains the analogy *b'nei
Maron*, according to the view that they pass like sheep at the tithing.

PREPARATION

Let us now discuss the second category of finding favor in judgment.
This refers to those people whose sins outweigh their merits; nevertheless,
they merit mercy from Hashem because of a certain good deed that they performed. Indeed, the human intellect is not capable of fathoming Hashem's
examination of this deed. We can neither understand nor comprehend the
substance of the merit that stands for him on the Day of Judgment, to incline
his judgment towards kindness and revival. However, ultimately, the man
merits by virtue of Hashem's compassion. Therefore, logic dictates that in
the final analysis, man is worthy of mercy. His preparation, his worry, and his
fear of the Day of Judgment generate this merit. Just as he awakened himself,
so, too, the attribute of mercy was awakened on his behalf.

Preparation is the primary factor that awakens the grace of Hashem.
While the time was still ripe, he initiated preparations for Rosh HaShanah.
We see that this is normative behavior for someone who faces a court case.

For instance, let us consider someone who is enmeshed in a monetary dispute or even in a capital case. Depending on his level of fear and trepidation, the litigant will begin to worry many days in advance about a plan for escape from the entrapment — so that he will be found innocent in judgment. All the more so should a person begin to worry well before the fearful Day of Judgment, at which time he will stand in front of the throne of the Righteous Judge. The earlier generations relied on the teaching of *Pirkei D'Rebbi Eliezer* that instructs us to begin sounding the shofar on Rosh Chodesh Elul. There are also those who begin to recite many chapters of *Tehillim* and supplications on Rosh Chodesh Elul, as stated by the Tur (*Orach Chaim* 581). Therefore, how crucial it is for man to begin preparation — from Rosh Chodesh Elul — upon hearing the sound of the shofar. Let us realize that in the wake of our many sins our hearts are dull and as hard as rock and flint. Therefore, one should fix set times to read and contemplate the books of Mussar and *yiras Shamayim*. This should be done with fervor of the soul, so that the fear of the Day of Judgment softens one's heart and breaks his spirit. Each person should strive to upgrade his deeds and improve his conduct, according to his level. Additionally, he should offer prayers and supplications requesting mercy.

Let us assume that someone spurs himself to activate this early preparation. He begins to worry about the Day of Judgment many days in advance — so that his heart should melt and his spirit should be humbled, allowing fear and trembling of the judgment to enter his soul. Moreover, it makes an impression in his heart — so that he strives to improve his deeds and pray for mercy. Even if his efforts are not sufficient to incline the scale of merits over sins, so that according to the letter of the law he is not meritorious — nevertheless, he has the power to awaken mercy, from the Source of mercy, and to incline his judgment towards kindness and revival. On the other hand, let us assume the man forgets his spiritual impoverishment and ignores the significance of [the entire month] of Elul. He is neither concerned nor worried whatsoever about the approaching Day of Judgment, which is a statute of remembrance when each spirit and soul is inspected. If so, there is no place for mercy, *chalilah*.

Chazal express this category of finding favor in judgment, when they interpret *b'nei Maron* [as "a narrow pass where two people cannot go side by side, for the gully is deep on both sides"]. Imagine the conventional conduct in places where masses of people gather to fulfill a particular purpose. For instance, in a train terminal where many people come to purchase tickets. Each traveler wants to be the first one to obtain his objective. In response to this situation, there is an established protocol. Whoever comes first will attain his goal first. Therefore, all the travelers line up in single file, so that order is maintained. In this way, whoever comes to the station first will be closer to the counter, and he can purchase his ticket first.

A MORE FAVORABLE POSITION

It is just the same on the awesome Day of Judgment, when all the inhabitants of the world pass individually before Hashem. Whoever has the merit to pass first is in a more favorable position, as written above. Now, everyone does not come at the same moment to stand in judgment before the Throne of the Righteous Judge. There are those who come early. As soon as they hear the sound of the shofar on Rosh Chodesh Elul, they begin to worry and prepare themselves to stand before the throne of judgment. They are involved in preparation the entire month. On the other hand, there are those who delay their coming to judgment. Many days of the month pass, yet they don't take it to heart at all. They only wake up a few days before the Day of Judgment. Even worse are those who are neglectful until the very last day before the Day of Judgment. Only then do they allow it to enter their heart.

THE IMPORTANCE OF EARLY PREPARATION

Let us assume the deeds of those who come early to prepare are equal in value to the deeds of those who come late to prepare. Nevertheless, at the time when all the creations pass before Hashem, the principle of [Beis Meron lining up at the terminal] influences the judgment. There are people who "came early" and prepared themselves weeks in advance. They are awaiting and anticipating standing in judgment. These people pass first before Hashem. The attribute of mercy clears the way for them to pass first. This conforms to a standard rule in worldly affairs: whoever comes first will achieve his desired goal first. Therefore, each person's advance position in line before the throne of judgment depends upon how early he began his preparation, each person appearing before Hashem in his proper place in line.

THE RIGHT OF WAY

This is the meaning of Chazal's interpretation of *b'nei Maron*, "Like the ascent of Beis Meron — a narrow pass where two people cannot go side by side, for the gully is deep on both sides and they have no choice but to proceed individually." Now, who has the right of way on this narrow path? Isn't it obvious that whoever arrives first has the right of way? The later one comes, the closer he will find himself to the end of the line. Precisely the same system dictates the order of passing on the Day of Judgment. All the creations pass before Hashem in compliance with this placement. Whoever is first, will pass first. One's position in judgment depends on how early he prepared to stand before the throne. This is the application of the analogy *b'nei Maron* — like the narrow paths of Beis Meron.

DIVINE COMPASSION

The third category of finding favor in judgment pertains to those who find Divine compassion without a known merit. Their deliverance stems solely from the Divine will. Hashem desires to extend mercy to them, even though they are undeserving. The Talmud (*Berachos* 7a) teaches, "Rebbi Yochanan said in the name of Rebbi Yose, 'Moshe asked three things of *HaKadosh Baruch Hu*, and they were granted to him.... He requested that He show him the ways of *HaKadosh Baruch Hu*, and it was granted to him....' This [statement of Rebbi Yochanan] is in dispute with the statement of Rebbi Meir. For Rebbi Meir said, 'Only two requests were granted to him, and one was not granted to him. For it is written, "I shall show favor when I choose to show favor" (*Shemos* 33:19), even though he is not worthy, "And I shall show mercy when I choose to show mercy" (ibid.), even though he is not worthy.' " Rashi explains that Moshe asked Hashem to "show him [Moshe] the ways of Hashem," to reveal to Moshe the workings of Divine justice. For instance, why is it that some righteous men prosper and others are in adversity, some wicked men prosper and others are in adversity? The phrase "even though he is not worthy" teaches that there are cases where a person will receive favor even though he is totally devoid of merit. This assertion is based on the premise that if the person were worthy, then Hashem, Who is merciful, would not have to proclaim His determination to show him compassion. Hence, there are hidden and concealed aspects in the attribute of Divine judgment. These secrets were not even divulged to the master of all prophets. Hashem did not reveal to Moshe why His mercy is temporarily aroused upon a person who is neither worthy nor deserving.

This same principle functions on the Day of Judgment. Some people find favor only because it is the Divine will to be gracious and merciful to them, even though they are undeserving. This attribute influences the placement of all the creations when they pass individually before Hashem. Those undeserving people to whom Hashem shows mercy will pass first.

THE WILL OF THE COMMANDER

This is the third interpretation of the phrase in the *mishnah*, "*b'nei Maron* — like the troops of the house of David [HaMelech]." Rashi comments, "For this is the way they counted them, one after the other [they marched in formation] when they went out to war." Clearly, the military commander assigned the respective position of each soldier. However, the decision to place a particular soldier in the front ranks and a different one in the rear — depended on the will of the commander at that moment.

Similarly, Hashem determines the placement of the creations when they pass before Him on the Day of Judgment. Moreover, one of the ranking procedures defies logic and order. If the Divine will desires to favor and show mercy to someone who is undeserving, then he will be amongst the first to pass in front of Hashem. This is the intent of the analogy for *b'nei Maron* — "Like the troops of the house of David."

AWAKEN YIRAS SHAMAYIM

The second category of Divine favor, "*b'nei Maron* — like the narrow paths of Beis Meron," is most relevant to our situation. As we explained, the earlier one "brings himself" to the Day of Judgment — that is, to prepare for the trial and judgment — the earlier he will pass before Hashem.

The foundation of this preparation is to arouse and awaken one's heart with fear and trepidation [of the judgment and law]. For this fear does not quickly enter his heart. It requires exertion and effort. We mentioned this in "The Gates of Light" (ch. 2): "The fear of Hashem and His punishment is in an entirely different category from other natural fears, which a man will feel with his senses without exertion or effort. [This fear is not found innately within man's nature.]"

THE DESIRE TO LIVE

The desire to live is the strongest force within man. When a person's physical life is at risk, he will give everything that he has in order to save himself. This is so, regardless of how slight the chance of mortal danger. However, when a person's spiritual life is at risk, he is not affected. Indeed, man believes that Rosh HaShanah is the Day of Judgment. It is the day when every being is examined to decide whether he shall live or die. Nevertheless, he does not sense the fear of this danger.

WHO WANTS LIFE?

The Talmud (*Avodah Zarah* 19b) alludes to this, "Rebbi Alexandri once called out, 'Who wants life? Who wants life?' All the people came and gathered around him. They said to him, 'Give us life!' He then quoted the verses, 'Who is the man who desires life, who loves days of seeing good? Guard your tongue from evil and your lips from speaking deceit. Turn from evil and do good, seek peace and pursue it' (*Tehillim* 34:13–15), and exclaimed, 'The only good is Torah.' " A similar passage is found in the Midrash (*Vayikra Rabbah* 16:2), "There was an incident with a peddler who visited the various cities around Tzipori. He would call out, 'Who wants to buy the elixir of life?' They would gather around him, and he would show them the verses, 'Who is the man who desires life, who loves days of seeing good? Guard your tongue from evil and your lips from speaking deceit. Turn from evil and do good, seek peace and pursue it.' "

This is quite amazing! What was the objective of Rebbi Alexandri when he called out, "Who wants life?" and for what purpose did the peddler call out, "Who wants to buy the elixir of life?" Moreover, what was the significance of reciting the verses from *Tehillim*? Doesn't everybody know these verses? What message were they imparting to the listeners? Furthermore, everybody gathered around saying, "Give us life!" The response they recieved was, "Guard your tongue from evil." Didn't the public view this as a joke?

However, in truth they acted with profound counsel in order to teach the people wisdom and an ethical lesson. The verse states, "Who is the man who desires life...?" Hence, since man has a powerful desire to live, shouldn't he fulfill every word of the verse — in order to ensure life and goodness? If we would see with our eyes that everyone who does not speak *lashon hara* would live a long life, and that everyone who does speak *lashon hara* would quickly perish — then everyone would fulfill this verse, because they desire to live. However, since this does not appear to be an absolute rule, people tend to lose faith. Sometimes a *tzaddik* dies even though he is righteous, and sometimes a *rasha* lives despite his evil. Therefore, people do not uphold this verse. However, this rationalization is unfounded. Unquestionably, the promise of the verse is true. However, sometimes there are exceptions to the rule. Nonetheless, this axiom is relevant because "Life [is] in the power of the tongue" (*Mishlei* 18:21), and the Torah is a "tree of life" (*Mishlei* 3:18). A physically ill person will not refrain from taking medicine, even if the effects are very doubtful. He will even consider treatment that is illogical.

THE TREE OF LIFE

This is the Mussar lesson that Rebbi Alexandri demonstrated to the crowd. When he called out, "Who wants life?" everyone gathered around him and said, "Give us life." Evidently, they thought he had a physical remedy in hand that imparts life and longevity. This notion is terrible foolishness. Is there any physical substance that grants life? Only the Tree of Life in Gan

Eden gives life. Likewise, the peddler who called out, "Who wants to buy the elixir of life?" — is there a medicine [drug] that bestows life?

LIFE IS MANIFEST IN SPIRITUALITY

However, since the passion for life is so powerful, a person will believe even in deceptive foolishness. It was a tactic when Rebbi Alexandri called out, "Who wants life?" because no man can offer life. Nevertheless, the crowd gathered around him and said, "Give us life." He responded to their request with the verse, "Who is the man who desires life...?" His message was, "As long as you imagine that I have a physical substance that can impart life, then you believe in a worthless deception." This is born out by their request, "Give us life." "Indeed," he explained to them, "isn't life manifest in spirituality? As the verse says, 'Who is the man who desires life?...guard your tongue from evil.' This is easily attainable. Why do you refuse to accept this axiom as a method to grasp onto the life you so desire?" It is the same concept with the peddler, when they came to buy the elixir of life from him. "This is ridiculous," he reasoned. Therefore, he said to them, "Who is the man who desires life?...guard your tongue from evil."

MUSSAR

Indeed, it is not easy for a person to sense *yiras Hashem* and the fear of punishment. However, a person can achieve it and imprint it within his soul with effort and perseverance. This will enable him to experience the fear of Hashem the same way that he inherently fears worldly danger. We mentioned this in "The Gates of Light." The same idea applies to the fear and trepidation of Rosh HaShanah, the Day of Judgment. Therefore, when a person devotes himself to toil in order to attain fear, his effort will enable him to instill it within his heart. This trepidation is a powerful force to impel him to draw close to the Divine service and to improve his deeds. The primary factor is to learn Mussar with fervor and imagery. The power of imagery greatly enhances Mussar study.

ARTICLE FIVE

THE TEN DAYS OF REPENTANCE

"Seek Hashem when He can be found, call upon Him when He is near."

(Yeshayahu 55:6)

MERITS AND SINS

THE RAMBAM WRITES (*Hilchos Teshuvah* 3:1–3), "Each and every person has merits and sins. If his merits exceed his sins he is a *tzaddik*. If his sins exceed his merits he is a *rasha*. If his merits and sins are equal he is designated as a *beinoni* (of intermediate status).... A man whose sins exceed his merits dies immediately in his wickedness, as the verse says, 'because of the multitude of your sins...' (*Hoshea* 9:7). And just as the merits and sins of man are weighed at the time of his death, so, too, each and every year on the *yom tov* of Rosh HaShanah, Hashem weighs the sins and merits of all the inhabitants of the world. He who is found to be a *tzaddik* is inscribed for life. And he who is found to be a *rasha* is inscribed for death. And the fate of the *beinoni* is suspended until Yom Kippur. If he does *teshuvah* he is inscribed for life, and if he does not do *teshuvah* he is inscribed for death."

THREE BOOKS ARE OPENED ON ROSH HASHANAH

Indeed, the Rambam derives this teaching from the Talmud (*Rosh HaShanah* 16b), "Rav Kruspedai said in the name of Rebbi Yochanan, 'Three books are opened [in Heaven] on Rosh HaShanah: one for the thoroughly wicked, one for the thoroughly righteous, and one for the individual of intermediate status. The thoroughly righteous are written and sealed immediately for life; the thoroughly wicked are written and sealed immediately for death; the fate of the intermediate is suspended from Rosh HaShanah to Yom Kippur...." The Ran explains that the term "intermediate" implies that the term "righteous" in this context refers to those whose merits outweigh their sins. Whereas the term "wicked" conveys those whose sins outweigh their merits. Yet if this is true, then a deep question arises. Many "righteous" are written for death, and many "wicked" are written for life. However, we can answer this question according to the view of Ri HaZaken Mitrani, who wrote that this *mishnah* is referring to those who are classified as righteous or wicked. In other words, our *mishnah* defines "totally righteous" as those who merit in judgment because of a certain good deed. They are "totally righteous" in this judgment, even though they have more sins then merits. Likewise, "totally wicked" are those who are convicted in judgment because of a certain sin. They are "totally wicked" in this judgment, even though they have more merits then sins. "Intermediates" are those people whose judgment is balanced. Their fate is suspended until they tip the scale to either merit or conviction.

However, it is clear that Rambam explains the Talmud according to the classic reading [and not according to the Ran]. Thus [according to Rambam], *tzaddikim* are those people whose merits exceed their sins, and *rasha'im* are those people whose sins exceed their merits. Similarly, the Rambam states, "If his merits exceed his sins he is a *tzaddik*. If his sins exceed his merits he is a *rasha*. If his merits and sins are equal he is a *beinoni*...so, too, each and every year on *yom tov* of Rosh HaShanah, Hashem weighs the sins and merits of all the inhabitants of the world. He who is found to be a *tzaddik* is inscribed for life. He who is found to be a *rasha* is inscribed for death. The fate of the *beinoni* is suspended until Yom Kippur." This verifies that the Rambam's definition of a *tzaddik* is one whose merits exceed his sins, and a *rasha* is one whose sins exceed his merits. The Ra'avad and the Kesef Mishnah also agree that this is the understanding of the Rambam.

TESHUVAH AND THE BEINONI

However, a question arises on what the Rambam wrote concerning the judgment of the *beinoni*: "The fate of the *beinoni* is suspended until Yom Kippur. If he does *teshuvah* he is inscribed for life, and if he does not do *teshuvah*, he is inscribed for death." Why is his fate dependent on *teshuvah*? A *beinoni* has an equal number of merits and sins. Therefore, he is only lacking one mitzvah to incline the scales to the side of merit. If so, even if he did not do *teshuvah*, he could easily find merit. The performance of one mitzvah would tip the scales to the side of merit. Then he would be deemed a *tzaddik* and inscribed in the Book of Life. The Talmud (*Kiddushin* 40a) teaches this concept, "Our rabbis taught, 'A person should always see himself as if he is half liable and half innocent. If he does one mitzvah, he is fortunate, because he inclines his judgment to merit.' " Rashi explains that this man should see himself as if his deeds are balanced, half good and half bad. If he does one mitzvah, his merits tip the scale and he will be found to be a *tzaddik*.

THE MERIT OF A MITZVAH

The Talmud clearly states that the fate of the *beinoni* is suspended from Rosh HaShanah to Yom Kippur. If he merits he is then inscribed for life. It is possible to interpret the words of Chazal "If he merits" as referring to only one mitzvah. In other words, if he performs any one mitzvah, he will incline his judgment to a meritorious status and be found righteous. Therefore, the Rambam's assertion, "if he does *teshuvah*, he will be inscribed for life," is quite perplexing. Even if he did not do *teshuvah*, he can be found meritorious in judgment by virtue of adding one mitzvah before Yom Kippur. He will incline the scale of judgment to merit, which will classify him as a *tzaddik*, and he will be sealed for life. He will be equal to one whose merits exceeded his sins on Rosh HaShanah — even without *teshuvah* he is classified as a *tzaddik* and sealed for life.

DELAY OF TESHUVAH

Indeed, it is also known that besides the judgment and accounting of man for his transgressions, there are also claims brought against him if he did not do *teshuvah*. For his heart did not consider thoughts of *teshuvah* — to re-turn to Hashem from all of his sins. Rabbeinu Yonah teaches this in his book *Sha'arei Teshuvah* (1:10): "Know that if the sinner delays repenting from his sins, his punishment will worsen everyday. For he knows the Divine anger is burning against him, and he has a refuge in which to flee — the refuge is *teshuvah*. Yet he remains in his rebellion and persists in his wickedness, even though he has the opportunity to extricate himself from the destruction. He does not fear the Divine wrath, therefore his evil is great."

Likewise, the Reisheis Chochmah (*Sha'ar Teshuvah*) wrote, "Since *teshuvah* is so exalted that it can atone for all of man's sins…therefore, it is not appropriate for man to be lax in performing repentance. For His right hand is extended to accept penitents, and the gate is forever open. There-fore, if he does not repent, he will be severely punished in the World to Come. Chazal (*Midrash Koheles* 7:32) composed a befitting parable for repen-tance based on the verse, 'And the eyes of the wicked shall be darkened, and the refuge shall be lost to them' (*Iyov* 11:20). The midrash likened this to a band of thieves who rebelled against the king. They were captured and placed in prison. What did they do? They dug a hole and escaped. However, one stayed behind and the king found him in the morning. He said to him, 'Fool, the escape route was open before you and you did not flee.' So, too, *HaKadosh Baruch Hu* says to the wicked, '*Teshuvah* is before you and yet you do not repent.' This is the meaning of the verse, '…and the refuge shall be lost to them.' "

PROSELYTES

Let us reflect on a passage in the Talmud (*Yevamos* 48b) that teaches about the punishment meted out for delaying repentance. Asks the Gemara, "Why are proselytes at the present time oppressed and visited with afflic-tions? Because they delayed their entry under the wings of the *Shechinah*. Rebbi Abbahu [or it might be said Rav Chanina] asked: What is the scrip-tural proof? 'Hashem will reward your work, and your reward will be com-plete from the Lord, the God of Israel, under Whose wings you have come to take refuge' (*Rus* 2:12)." This passage teaches us how quickly man is required to return to do *teshuvah*. Indeed, a *ben Noach* has no obligation to bring himself under the liability and yoke of Torah and mitzvos. Nevertheless, the Talmud says the proselytes were punished because they did not bring themselves beneath the wings of the *Shechinah* sooner. How much more so does this apply to *klal Yisrael*, who already accepted the Torah and mitzvos. How terribly severe is the punishment for any member of *klal Yisrael* who turns away from Torah and mitzvos. He distances himself from Hashem if he delays in doing *teshuvah*. Moreover, he delays bringing himself beneath the *Shechinah* and drawing himself close to Hashem.

THE URGENCY OF REPENTANCE

There is a constant obligation upon man to perform *teshuvah*. The severity of the punishment intensifies exponentially with each day the sinner delays repenting from his sin (*Sha'arei Teshuvah* 1:2). However, the obligation to repent is far greater during the period between Rosh HaShanah and Yom Kippur. The urgency of repentance during the days between Rosh Hashanah and Yom Kippur is far more imperative than the obligation during the rest of the year. We will now explain the reasons for this.

THE MITZVAH TO REPENT

1) We understand the obligation of *teshuvah*, as the Midrash depicted, "*HaKadosh Baruch Hu* says to the wicked, '*Teshuvah* is before you and yet you do not repent.' " Nevertheless, there is no specific positive commandment to repent during the rest of the year [though, certainly if he does repent, he has fulfilled a great mitzvah]. However, on Yom Kippur there is a positive commandment in the Torah to do *teshuvah*. Rabbeinu Yonah, in the *Sha'arei Teshuvah* (sha'ar 2, path 4), writes, "There is a positive commandment from the Torah for a person to arouse his soul to do *teshuvah* on Yom Kippur, as the verse says, 'Before Hashem you shall be cleansed from all of your sins' (*Vayikra* 16:30). Therefore, the verse exhorts us to purify ourselves in front of Hashem by virtue of our repentance. And He will grant atonement to us on this day to purify us." Likewise, the Rambam (*Hilchos Teshuvah* 2:7) wrote: "Yom Kippur is a time of *teshuvah* for every individual and community. It is a

time of pardon and forgiveness for Israel. Therefore, everyone is obligated to do *teshuvah* and confess their sins on Yom Kippur."

Indeed, we know that the various mitzvos are not of equivalent value. Thus, it is self-evident that this primary, positive commandment of *teshuvah* is extremely precious. Conversely, the neglect of this mitzvah is a calamitous sin. Any way we look at it, anyone who does not do *teshuvah*, especially on Yom Kippur, is liable for twofold and threefold punishment. He has also ignored the great positive commandment, "Before Hashem you shall be cleansed from all of your sins."

THE REWARD IS COMMENSURATE WITH THE DIFFICULTY

2) Let us consider the well-known axiom that the reward of a mitzvah is commensurate with the difficulty required for its performance. Our Sages (*Avos* 5:26) teach this: "The reward is in proportion to the exertion." Conversely, the punishment of neglecting the mitzvah is proportional to the effort required to perform the mitzvah. The easier the fulfillment of a mitzvah, the greater is the sin of its neglect. The Talmud (*Menachos* 43b) teaches this principle: "Rebbi Meir said, 'Greater is the punishment for the [non-observance of the] white fringes than for the [non-observance of the] blue fringes. This may be illustrated by a parable. A king of flesh and blood gave orders to two servants. To one he said, 'Bring me a seal of clay,' and to the other one he said, 'Bring me a seal of gold.' And they both failed in their duty and did not bring them. Now, who deserves the greater punishment? Surely it is the one to whom the king said, 'Bring me a seal of clay,' but did not do so." Therefore, since the mitzvah of the white fringes is easier to fulfill than the mitzvah of the blue fringes, the punishment is greater for not having white fringes. Likewise, our Sages illustrated the nature of punishment meted out for those who delay in repenting. As we mentioned, the Midrash likened this to "a band of thieves who rebelled against the king. They were captured and placed in prison. What did they do? They bore a tunnel and escaped. However, one prisoner stayed behind and the king found him in the morning. He said to him, 'Fool, the escape route is open before you and you

did not escape.' " It is self-evident that the level of punishment depends on the level of difficulty required to perform a complete repentance deemed acceptable by Hashem.

WHEN HASHEM IS NEAR

The Talmud (*Rosh HaShanah* 18a and *Yevamos* 49b) points out two contradictory verses: "One verse says, 'For which is a great nation that has a God Who is close to it, as is Hashem, our God, whenever we call to Him?' (*Devarim* 4:7). Yet it is also written, 'Seek Hashem when He can be found' (*Yeshayahu* 55:6)." Rashi explains that the second verse implies that there are times when Hashem is not found. The Talmud resolves this question: Whenever one prays with a minyan, Hashem is always present, whereas when an individual prays alone, Hashem makes Himself present only at particular times. "When is this time [that Hashem is present for the individual (Rashi)]? Rav Nachman answered in the name of Rabbah bar Avuha, 'The ten days between Rosh HaShanah and Yom Kippur.' "

In addition, the Rambam (*Hilchos Teshuvah* 2:6) writes, "Even though repentance and prayer are always beneficial, during the ten days between Rosh HaShanah and Yom Kippur, [repentance] is even more beneficial. [*Teshuvah*] is accepted immediately, as it says, 'Seek Hashem when He can be found, call upon Him when He is near' (*Yeshayahu* 55:6)."

Indeed, the most auspicious time for man to repent is during the days between Rosh HaShanah and Yom Kippur; this is the time when Hashem is found and near. Since *teshuvah* and prayer are more effective and readily accepted at this time, it is easier for man to proceed upon the paths of repentance, as born out by the verse, "Seek Hashem when He can be found, call upon Him when he is near." Whereas, during the other periods of the year, it is difficult for man to perform the Divine service of *teshuvah* with the same quality as during the Ten Days of Repentance, when his *teshuvah* is readily accepted before the Divine throne. During the rest of the year, *HaKadosh Baruch Hu* is neither found nor close to man — therefore, one must exert himself more. Thus, anyone who does not perform *teshuvah* during the days when Hashem is found and near, and repentance is readily accepted, is subject to even greater punishment, as his sin is more severe. This is even more so on Yom Kippur, which is a day especially devoted to repentance.

THE TEN DAYS OF REPENTANCE

(3) Let us contemplate deeply the awesome obligation of *teshuvah* — to regret one's sins and to beseech Hashem to grant forgiveness — during the ten days between Rosh HaShanah and Yom Kippur. Consider the incident recorded in the Talmud (*Yoma* 87a): "When Rebbi Zeira had a complaint against any man, he would repeatedly pass before him [in order to make it easier for the offender to ask forgiveness], showing himself to him so that the man could come forward to appease him. Rav once had a complaint about a certain butcher, and when on the eve of Yom Kippur he [the butcher] still did not come to him, he said, 'I will go to pacify him.' Rav Huna met him [Rav] and asked, 'Where is the master going?' Rav replied, 'To pacify him [the butcher].' He [Rav Huna] thought, 'Abba [the real name of Rav] is about to cause the butcher's death.' [He knew the butcher was a stubborn man and would not accept Rav's offer of reconciliation.] He [Rav] went there and remained standing before him [the butcher], as he was sitting and chopping the bones from the head [of an animal]. He raised his eyes, saw him [Rav], and said, 'You are Abba, go away, I will have nothing to do with you.' While he was chopping the bones of the head, a chip flew off, struck his throat, and killed him."

RAV AND REBBI ZEIRA

Let us understand the source of the pious conduct of Rav and Rebbi Zeira. According to halachah, if someone afflicts his fellow — even with words alone — he must appease him. If the offended party does not, at first, grant forgiveness, then the offender must return to him a second and third time. However, the offended party should not cruelly deny forgiveness. These laws are explained in the *Shulchan Aruch* (*Orach Chaim* 606 — see the text there). Now, let us consider the conduct that Rav and Rebbi Zeira employed when someone sinned against them and did not come in order to appease them and ask forgiveness. They would make themselves available to the offender. Perhaps, when the offender sees them — and does not have to make the effort to go to them — he will consider asking them for forgiveness. How phenomenal was their exalted behavior. What is the source and root of this virtuous conduct? Moreover, wasn't Rav's going to the butcher a slight to the honor of Rav's Torah knowledge?

It appears that the foundation of their pious ways was based on the exalted attributes of *HaKadosh Baruch Hu*. This is the way that Hashem conducts himself with the Jewish people, and it is a mitzvah to cleave to Divine attributes. Therefore, Rav and Rebbi Zeira conducted themselves with this attribute.

WHEN TESHUVAH IS ACCEPTED IMMEDIATELY

Indeed, I cited above the words of the Rambam (*Hilchos Teshuvah* 2:6): "Even though repentance and prayer are always beneficial, during the ten days between Rosh HaShanah and Yom Kippur, [repentance] is even more beneficial. [*Teshuvah*] is accepted immediately, as it says, 'Seek Hashem when He can be found, call upon Him when He is near.' " If repentance and prayer are always beneficial — for the gates of *teshuvah* are never locked, and nothing can stand in front of *teshuvah* — what, then, is the reason why Hashem is revealed and close, more so during these ten days than the rest of the year? Could the reason for the closeness during these ten days be to lighten the effort required to do *teshuvah*? — for when Hashem is close, *teshuvah* and prayer are accepted immediately. However, since the sinner abandoned the Torah and mitzvos of Hashem, and rebelled against the Divine will, why should we be concerned if he has to toil and work hard? Let him toil and work in the paths of *teshuvah* — then he will receive his reward in the presence of Hashem!

Rather, this closeness emanates from the mercy and kindness of Hashem. When Hashem is not close, it is very difficult for man to perform *teshuvah* that will be accepted before the Divine Throne. Hashem knows the constant battle of man's negative impulse and that consequently man is quite lazy in performing *teshuvah*. Therefore, when the offender is distant from Hashem, it is likely that he does not want to toil in repentance. Therefore, he may retreat and prevent himself from doing *teshuvah* before Hashem and from supplicating Him for forgiveness. However, Hashem takes pity on the soul of the sinner so that his stubbornness should not bring about his destruction. The days between Rosh HaShanah and Yom Kippur precede the day when the performance of *teshuvah* is an absolute necessity for man — namely, Yom Kippur, which is the time of repentance for everyone and the period of Divine forgiveness for the Jewish people. Therefore, during the Ten Days of Repentance, Hashem acts with kindness and draws close to man. Since He is present and close, *teshuvah* is immediately accepted. Therefore, the offender sincerely performs a complete *teshuvah* in the presence of Hashem and prays for forgiveness.

CLOSENESS TO THE OFFENDER

Let us, once again, examine the righteous conduct of Rebbi Zeira and Rav. They brought themselves in close proximity to anyone who sinned against them. Their closeness to the offender was in order to motivate him to request forgiveness and pardon. This is the very attribute of Hashem, Who conducts Himself with this righteousness when dealing with the sinner. Imagine man sins when Hashem is not close. He is, nevertheless, obligated to do proliferate *teshuvah* until Hashem accepts his repentance, even though He is far away from man. However, the sinner may not want to make such a great effort, and he might, therefore, withhold himself from *teshuvah*. Therefore, Hashem draws His Presence close to the sinners, so that they will find it in their heart to repent and pray for forgiveness. Therefore, Rav and Rebbi Zeira put themselves in the presence of one who sins against them — in order to cleave to the attribute of Hashem.

The tragic fate of the butcher and his severe punishment enlightens us with wisdom and Mussar concerning the significance of doing *teshuvah* during the Ten Days, and especially on Yom Kippur itself. If Rav had not visited the butcher, then even if the butcher had refused to visit Rav to ask forgiveness, or even if he met Rav by chance and did not seek appeasement, in either case the butcher definitely would not have received such a severe punishment. However, the kindness and humility of Rav's gesture to visit the butcher unintentionally caused the downfall of the butcher. This was the premonition of Rav Huna, who thought, "Abba is about to cause [the butcher's] death." On the other hand, Rav's reasoning was sound. A normal person upon seeing Rav would be embarrassed and fall at his feet to ask forgiveness. However, the butcher reacted with a stubbornness that Rav did not anticipate, and defiantly refused to plead for forgiveness. Therefore, the butcher was punished severely and died.

The Maharsha also writes that the butcher was punished because he sinned against Rav, being that he was obligated to appease him. However, the Maharsha's contention that the butcher degraded Rav by referring to him as "Abba" is not correct. For Rav Huna himself said, "Abba is about to cause...." How could Rav Huna know that the butcher would call Rav by his name? Moreover, the Tosafos Yashanim writes that "Abba" was a respectful title, like "Avi Avi Rechev Yisrael." If this is not so, then how could Rav Huna, his student, call his Rebbi by his name?

Therefore, we must say that the main reason why the butcher was punished was because Rav went to him, and, nevertheless, he hardened his heart, stood in his rebellion, and did not appease Rav. Thus, Rav Huna said, "Abba is about to cause [the butcher's] death," for he thought that it was likely that the butcher would stand in his rebellion and not ask for forgiveness from Rav.

HASHEM DRAWS CLOSE TO MAN

Now, we have already explained that the pious conduct of Rav and Rebbi Zeira — making themselves readily available to one who sinned against them — is modeled after the virtuous way of *HaKadosh Baruch Hu*. Hashem conducts himself with this same attribute during the Days of Repentance. Namely, He draws close to man — so that thoughts of *teshuvah* will awaken in his heart. Then he will regret his transgressions and request pardon and forgiveness, as we mentioned above.

THE DANGER OF A HARD HEART

Therefore, despite all that we have explained, if man will still harden his heart and spirit, and withhold himself from repenting even on Yom Kippur — which is the time of pardon and forgiveness for the people of Israel — he is conducting himself like the butcher who said to Rav, "Go away, I will have nothing to do with you," Heaven forbid. If the sin of the butcher against Rav was so severe, then how much more severe it is if a human being sins in this way against the Supreme King of kings, *HaKadosh Baruch Hu*. How enormous is his sin, how terrible his accountability, and how awful his punishment will be. How frightening is this concept to one who thinks about it deeply.

SEEK HASHEM WHEN HE CAN BE FOUND

In reference to this, the prophet said, "Seek Hashem when He can be found, call upon Him when He is near. Let the wicked man depart from his path...and let him return to Hashem..." (*Yeshayahu* 55:6–7). Chazal explain, "These are the ten days that are between Rosh HaShanah and Yom Kippur." The intention of this statement is not to show that during these days *HaKadosh Baruch Hu* is found and close and so these days are more appropriate for repentance and prayer, thereby making them a good and beautiful time to seek Hashem and for the wicked man to depart from his path. Rather, the intention is to elucidate that during these days when He is found and close, man's obligation to seek Hashem is increased, as is the wicked man's obligation to depart from his path. The reason is as follows: since the attribute of mercy and kindness of *HaKadosh Baruch Hu* is near to man during these days, it could possibly cause a calamity and be a stumbling block for a severe sin to occur — if man withholds himself from performing repentance. It would then be comparable to the incident of the butcher with Rav, as we mentioned. In reference to this, the verse says, "Seek Hashem when He can be found, call upon Him when He is near" — for the obligation is upon them to seek Hashem when He is found and when He is close, as we mentioned.

This principle enables us to comprehend the words of the Rambam, *zt"l*: "The fate of the *beinoni* is suspended until Yom Kippur. If he performs repentance, he is inscribed for life, and if he does not...." The words "if he performs repentance" seem quite strange. Since a *beinoni* is one whose deeds are equally balanced, he can therefore attain a favorable judgment even if he does not perform repentance. If he would add but one mitzvah in order to tip the scales to the side of merits, then he would be deemed a righteous man and sealed for life. He would be equivalent to someone who was found to be righteous on Rosh HaShanah because his merits exceeded his transgressions. Even without his performing repentance for his transgression, he is sealed for life.

THE BEINONI IS SUSPENDED

However, according to what we have said above, we can well understand the words of the Rambam. The distinction between the righteous man and the intermediate is in the respective time of their judgment and sentencing. The righteous man merits in judgment on Rosh HaShanah, whereas, the fate of the intermediate is suspended, so that his final judgment is on the Day of Atonement. The foundation of Rosh HaShanah is only judgment and verdict; the obligation to repent is no different than the rest of the year. Even though the day is sanctified, and *HaKadosh Baruch Hu* is found and near, still, isn't there time remaining to repent until the Day of Atonement? Therefore, one who is classified as a righteous man on Rosh HaShanah, for his merits exceed his transgressions, merits in judgment and is sealed for life. This is so even if he did not repent afterwards, even on the Day of Atonement — still, he already merited in judgment on Rosh HaShanah.

However, someone whose status is *beinoni* on Rosh HaShanah, as his deeds are equally balanced and he is not able at that time to merit in judgment — his fate is suspended and his final judgment is decided on the Day of Atonement. At that time, there is an obligation of repentance — the positive commandment of "Before Hashem you shall be cleansed" (*Vayikra* 16:30). Woe to a man who does not perform repentance on this day! The Day of Atonement is the time of repentance for everyone, of forgiveness for Israel, and the time that *HaKadosh Baruch Hu* is near to man, as we mentioned. Therefore, the mere withholding of repentance on this holy day is a severe, very awesome transgression, which is added to all of his other sins. The Rambam already wrote in the third chapter of *Hilchos Teshuvah* (halachah 2),

"The weighing of the merits against the transgressions is not according to quantity, rather quality.... There is a transgression that outweighs several merits, as it says, 'One sin destroys much goodness' (*Koheles* 9:18)."

It is in reference to this that the Rambam ruled that those of intermediate status, whose final judgment is on the Day of Atonement, can only be saved by the performance of *teshuvah*. If he does not do *teshuvah*, then the performance of one additional mitzvah will not incline the scale to the side of a meritorious judgment. The flagrant transgression of withholding oneself from performing repentance on Yom Kippur will incline the scale of judgment to a guilty verdict. Who can estimate how many countless mitzvos are outweighed by this appalling transgression? As the Rambam wrote, "Those of intermediate status are suspended until the Day of Atonement. If he performs repentance, he is inscribed for life, and if he does not...." Since his final judgment is on the Day of Atonement, there is neither wisdom nor advice that would advocate achieving a meritorious judgment by the means of performing one or even many mitzvos. On this day there is only one mitzvah that is effective to tip the scale of judgment to his favor — the performance of *teshuvah*. If he performs repentance, he is sealed in the Book of Life.

Behold, the Ran wrote, "The terminology of Chazal, 'righteous, wicked, and intermediate,' refers to righteous and wicked in status of judgment. In other words, those people who merit in judgment due to a particular meritorious deed are classified here as totally righteous — even though their transgressions exceed their merits. Likewise, the righteous...since they are liable in judgment even because of a small transgression which they committed — regarding this judgment they are classified as wicked. Of intermediate status are those people whose judgment is equally balanced from Rosh HaShanah. They are suspended and stand until they incline themselves either to merit or liability, from Rosh HaShanah until the Day of Atonement." Behold, the phrase "until they incline themselves either to merit or liability" means, due to a particular merit that is added to their judgment from Rosh HaShanah until the Day of Atonement. Hence, the wicked may be found meritorious in judgment on Rosh HaShanah by virtue of one worthy act. Likewise, those of intermediate status, whose judgment is indeterminate on Rosh HaShanah and whose fate is suspended until the Day of Atonement — they are able to merit in judgment from Rosh HaShanah until the Day of Atonement by performing one worthy act.

A WORTHY ACT ON YOM KIPPUR

However, according to what we mentioned above, it appears that there is a great distinction between the criteria of a worthy act on Rosh HaShanah and the criteria of a worthy act on Yom Kippur. For the aspect of merit that would suffice for man to be judged favorably on the day of Rosh HaShanah will not suffice for the *beinoni* to find favor in judgment on the Day of Atonement. For on Rosh HaShanah, the obligation of repentance is not incumbent on man any more than it is the remainder of the year. However, one who is classified as a *beinoni* on the day of Rosh HaShanah, because his judgment is equally balanced and his fate is suspended, then on the Day of Atonement, the obligation of repentance already is incumbent upon him. If he will refrain from repentance on this day of Yom Kippur, then this evil will also be joined to his sin. Nevertheless, there is a possibility to merit in judgment because of a particular meritorious deed; still, who can estimate the substance of the merit that is then required to incline the scales to a favorable judgment?

After comprehending these true words, one must reflect on two thoughts. First, how crucial it is for man to worry for his life, while still in the period of Elul before Rosh HaShanah. Then, to endeavor to perfect his deeds — to improve his paths and conduct, and to devote himself to a full measure of Torah and mitzvos — so that he will be able to merit in judgment, as we mentioned.

Second, man cannot comprehend the depth of Divine judgment and punishment. Hence, let him consider that perhaps he is classified as a *beinoni* so that his judgment will not be final on Rosh HaShanah, and his fate will be suspended until the Day of Atonement. Therefore, it is crucial for him to be involved in the paths of repentance as much as he possibly can. How awesome is this concept of the Rambam, "And the fate of the *beinoni* is suspended until Yom Kippur. If he performs repentance, he is inscribed for life." Behold, one who is classified as righteous on Rosh HaShanah — that is to say, his merits exceed his transgressions — merits a favorable judgment and is sealed for life, even without performing repentance. Nevertheless, as far as one of intermediate status is concerned, his final judgment is not dependent on his being found righteous on the Day of Atonement. "Righteous," that is, by virtue of adding one mitzvah to tip the scale of judgment to the side of merits. Rather, the Rambam wrote, "If he performs repentance, he is inscribed for life." The final judgment of those of intermediate status is on the Day of Atonement, which is the time of repentance for everyone and a time of forgiveness for Israel — and the period when *HaKadosh Baruch Hu* is found and near. Therefore, if he withholds himself from performing repentance, he is acting like the butcher who hardened his heart in the incident with Rav, as we mentioned above. Therefore, it is difficult to replace the lack of repentance with the performance of mitzvos. There is no counsel other than performing repentance.

ARTICLE SIX

DIVINE ASSISTANCE IN TESHUVAH

"For this commandment, that I command you today — it is not hidden from you.... Rather, the matter is very near to you, in your mouth and in your heart to perform it."

(Devarim 30:11, 14)

IN YOUR MOUTH AND IN YOUR HEART

THE RAMBAN, *zt"l*, IN HIS COMMENTARY on the Torah, wrote, " 'For this commandment' refers to repentance, as it states in the *parashah*, 'Then you will take it to your heart...and you will return to Hashem your God' *(Devarim 30:1, 2)*. For this thing is neither hidden nor far from you; rather, it is very close to do at every moment and at all times. Hence, the reason why the verse says 'in your mouth and in your heart, to perform it' is to indicate that they should verbally confess their sins and the sins of their fathers; they should return in their hearts to Hashem and accept upon themselves the Torah for generations." The Reishis Chochmah (first chapter in the *Sha'ar HaTeshuvah*) quotes the words of the Ramban that we just mentioned: " 'For this commandment' refers to repentance." He says as follows: "In my opinion, when the verse states, 'Rather, the matter is very near to you, in your mouth and in your heart to perform it' — 'in your mouth' is referring to the verbal confession that one needs to declare, and 'in your heart' is referring to the acceptance of repentance in his heart and departing from the sin."

THE ESSENTIAL COMPONENTS OF REPENTANCE

Now, we know that the essential components of repentance are: 1) departing from the sin, 2) the resolution for the future, and 3) the remorse over the past. According to this, we understand that remorse is included in the general category of the confessional statement that is written in the verse "in your mouth," for anyone who makes a confessional statement definitely feels remorse. Moreover, departing from the sin is included in that which is written "and in your heart," which is the resolution of the heart not to sin in the future. However, an explanation is still required as to why the verse specified the confessional statement ["in your mouth"] and the resolution of the heart for the future ["and in your heart"], but not the two essential components of repentance — remorse and departing from the sin.

Likewise, the literal meaning of the verse, "Rather, the matter is very near to you, in your mouth and in your heart to perform it," implies that repentance is quite simple to perform — for it is right "in your mouth and in your heart." However, don't we recognize the difficulty involved in traversing the paths of repentance? [For it entails the fulfillment of the verse:] "For the wicked man should depart from his path and the man of iniquity should [depart] from his thoughts, and regret his sin" (*Yeshayahu* 55:7). Moreover, it is especially difficult for someone who sinned exceedingly to conquer his evil inclination and to depart from his evil path.

THE EASY MATTER

However, it seems that the verse, "Rather, the matter is very near to you, in your mouth and in your heart to perform it," in truth is referring only to the aspects of repentance relevant to the confessional statement and the resolution in the heart for the future. The verse does not mention whatsoever the essential concepts of departing from the sin and remorse. Therefore, in truth, repentance appears to be a very easy matter [as expressed by the verse, which does not include the difficult aspects in the formula for *teshuvah*]!

The Talmud (*Pesachim* 54a) reveals the primary effect of repentance. In this Talmudic passage, Chazal teach that repentance is one of the seven things that were created before the creation of the world. The essential purpose of repentance is to facilitate forgiveness for transgressors. In the beginning of *Sha'arei Teshuvah*, Rabbeinu Yonah also writes about this: "Amongst the goodness that Hashem, may He be blessed, bestows upon His creations is that He prepares the path for them to ascend from the debasement of their deeds, and [grants the opportunity] to flee from the snare of their transgressions — to rescue their soul from destruction, to turn His wrath away from them, and to teach them and caution them to return to Him — for they have sinned against him. [Hashem, may He be blessed, does all this for them] due to His abundant goodness and straightforwardness, for He knows the [power of the] evil inclination. This is mentioned in the verse, 'Good and straight is Hashem, therefore, He teaches sinners the path.' Furthermore, [even] if man grievously sins, rebels, and betrays [Hashem], the doors of repentance are, nevertheless, not closed to him...."

FORGIVENESS

In truth, the goodness and the kindness of the attribute of repentance, to pardon and forgive those who repent from iniquity, is the most precious thing in the world. For if *teshuvah* did not exist — then the sin of anyone who transgressed would leave an eternal, indelible stain. Indeed, as we know, the punishment for a sin is frightfully terrible and awesome, as the Ramban wrote in *Sha'ar HaGemul* (see the text). Therefore, since "there is no righteous man on earth who does good and does not sin" (*Koheles* 7:20), then [without the opportunity to do *teshuvah*] surely everyone would be sent to Gehinnom. It would have been necessary for every soul to endure and suffer terrible, excruciating punishments; to be smelted like silver in the infernos of Gehinnom. However, through the attribute of repentance, everyone is granted the opportunity to be cleansed of all of his transgressions.

Now what does *HaKadosh Baruch Hu* require from man, in exchange for the great favor of pardoning iniquity, and what is the quality of repentance that will engender abundant pardon and forgiveness? Let us contemplate the words of the Rambam (*Hilchos Teshuvah* 2:2), remembering that all of his statements concerning repentance are halachic rulings: "And what is repentance? That the sinner should depart from this sin and remove it from his thoughts. In addition, he must decide in his heart that he will never commit it again, as it says, 'The wicked man should depart from his sin, and the man of iniquity should [depart] from his thoughts.' Likewise, he should regret his past [sins], as it says, 'For after I returned, I regretted.' [Hashem,] who knows the hidden things, will, in turn, testify that he will never revert to this sin.... And he must confess with his lips and verbalize these matters that he resolved in his heart."

Indeed, the Rambam considers four things here. One is the departure from sin; two is to resolve in his heart that he will never repeat [the sin] again; three is that he regrets the past; and four is that he must confess with his lips.

THE RESOLUTION

In truth, these are two elements that are really four. The resolution for the future that he will never repeat the sin is associated with the essential element of departing from the sin. For even if the sinner abandons his sin, nevertheless [his *teshuvah* is not complete without a resolution for the future.] For as long as he does not accept upon himself the resolution that he will never repeat the transgression, and as long as Hashem, Who knows all secrets, has not testified that he [the sinner] will never revert to this transgression — then this is not repentance! Indeed, his transgression will not be forgiven, even if he never again reverts to this transgression.

Likewise, the confessional statement is associated with the essential element of remorse. Hence, in conjunction with the essential remorse, a verbal confessional statement is also needed. Moreover, other declarations [besides the confession] are included in the confessional statement, as the Rambam wrote in *Hilchos Teshuvah*. Nevertheless, the confessional statement is relevant to the remorse. Hence, Chazal taught in *Yoma* (87b) that the declaration "But we sinned" is the essential confessional statement (see the text there). Likewise, Rabbeinu Yonah comments in *Sha'arei Teshuvah* on the verse, "One that admits and departs [from his sin] will be shown mercy" — that remorse is included in the general meaning of "one that admits" [which teaches the obligation to verbally confess] — for one who confesses also has remorse.

THE TWO ESSENTIAL COMPONENTS OF REPENTANCE

Now, the two essential components of repentance — which are remorse and, especially, departing from sin — are [usually] not easily attained. The conquering of the evil inclination, to depart from one's evil path and to observe the entire Torah and mitzvos, [seems to be] a very difficult task. However, the two particulars that are associated with them, namely, the confessional statement and the resolution for the future to never sin again, are easy matters. The reason they are easy is because once a person leaves his sin and regrets his transgression, it is clearly easy for him to resolve not to repeat the sin in the future and to verbally confess.

However, when we reflect deeply on the nature of *teshuvah*, we will recognize that [even though *teshuvah* seems very diffiuclt to perform, in reality] repentance is a very easy matter. [We will come to realize that] even the two essential components of repentance — departure from the sin and remorse — are not considered the least bit difficult. In fact, these essential components are not included at all within the formula of repentance, the process that engenders forgiveness for sinners. Indeed, departure from the sin does not stem exclusively from the attribute of *teshuvah* and forgiveness that *HaKadosh Baruch Hu* created in the world. For even if the attribute of *teshuvah* and forgiveness did not exist in the world, nevertheless, the sinner would be forced to abandon his sin and to observe and fulfill the entire Torah and mitzvos.

LET THE WICKED ONE FORSAKE HIS WAYS

The truth of the matter is found in what the prophet said, "Let the wicked one forsake his way and the iniquitous man his thoughts; let him return to Hashem and He will show him mercy; to our God, for He is abundantly forgiving" (*Yeshayahu* 55:7). However, does the wicked man leave his path only because Hashem is gracious enough to forgive? If *HaKadosh Baruch*

Hu would not pardon and forgive, would, then, the wicked man not leave his path? Does he have permission to commit evil, to add sin upon iniquity, and to go forever after the whims of his heart? Isn't it known that for each sin and transgression, man is punished with a very terrible and bitter punishment that transcends all worldly sufferings? Even if man's life will extend as long as the life span of a tree — moreover, even if the man will live for a thousand years, sinning in all of them — Hashem will bring every one of his deeds to judgment. Every act will be accounted for, and *HaKadosh Baruch Hu* will not overlook a fitting punishment even for a light transgression. Therefore, even if the attribute of *teshuvah* that leads to forgiveness of sins did not exist, still the sinner would be forced to leave his path — so that he should not be destroyed through his evil. Would a person abandon his soul to Gehinnom for future sins, just because there is no rectification for the past? Yet even though the sinner is forced to depart from his path, as we just mentioned, nevertheless, *HaKadosh Baruch Hu* shows mercy. When man departs from sin, Hashem accepts him and forgives the transgressions which he already committed. Once we understand this, we can no longer maintain that departure from the sin is a difficult aspect of repentance. Indeed, departure from sin is a task that man must always perform, even without the principle of repentance!

REMORSE

The same is true as far as the principle of remorse is concerned — it is not a concept that stems exclusively from the power of repentance. This is so because the importance of remorse is understood through the logical thought process. Rabbeinu Yonah writes about this in *Sha'arei Teshuvah*: "The first essential principle is remorse, namely, that one understands that leaving Hashem is evil and bitter. He should also consider that there is punishment, reprisal, and retribution for the sin. In addition, he should say in his heart, 'What did I do? I did not fear the rebuke of the afflictions of sin, or the terrible punishments....' " Let us assume that *teshuvah* — the attribute to pardon and forgive penitents — did not exist in the world. Would it not be clearly sensible to man to regret his wicked deeds? Would he not say in his heart, "What did I do? How could it be that I did not fear the rebuke of the afflictions of sin and the terrible punishments?" In fact, there would be an even greater intensity of regret over his transgressions, when he considers that what he corrupted cannot be rectified. Indeed, he would despair of any hope of being saved from Gehinnom. Since departure from sin is a necessity for man, consequently, when he does depart from his sin, thereby fulfilling the verse "Turn from evil and do good" (Tehillim 34:15) — then he will definitely regret the past.

TWO ASSOCIATED ASPECTS OF REPENTANCE

Hence, the two other aspects of repentance — the resolution for the future and the verbal confession — are merely associated with remorse and the departure from sin. These associative aspects are additional tasks delegated to the one who repents. These tasks extend from the principle aspects of repentance, as commanded by Hashem.

DEPARTURE FROM SIN

Let us now discuss the resolution not to sin in the future. The essential departure from the sin would still be necessary even if there was no attribute of teshuvah and forgiveness, as we mentioned above. However, without the mitzvah of repentance, there would be no demand to make a resolution not to sin; rather, it would suffice to be careful at every moment to simply avoid all sin. However, it is quite different concerning the attribute of teshuvah and forgiveness that Hashem has prepared for the sinner. For one of the stipulations of repentance is that more is required than the sinner stopping himself from ever again committing the sin. Namely, he is obligated to sincerely resolve for the future not to ever commit the sin again. Then, Hashem, Who knows all hidden things [including the inner feelings of man], will testify that he will never again revert to this sin.

THE ASPECT OF REMORSE

This is also true concerning the aspect of remorse. As far as the essence of the remorse is concerned, even if the attribute of teshuvah did not exist, nevertheless one would regret his evil deeds — how wicked and bitter he has been to forsake Hashem. However, he would not verbally confess his transgressions. *HaKadosh Baruch Hu*, however, commanded that when the sinner repents from his sin, he is required to verbally confess his sin, this being the fulfillment of a positive commandment. The Rambam (*Hilchos Teshuvah* 1:1) also writes about this: "All commandments in the Torah, whether positive or negative injunctions, if man transgresses one of them.... When he will perform repentance and abandon his sin, he is obligated to verbally confess.... As the verse states, 'Man or woman when they do...and they should confess their sin which they committed' (*Bamidbar* 5: 6–7). This is a verbal confession, and this confession is a positive commandment, etc."

THE EASE OF REPENTANCE

What we have just explained leads us to the conclusion that repentance is a very easy matter. Notwithstanding, [before we become aware of the aforementioned explanation,] the two essential components of repentance — leaving the sin and remorse — seem, in fact, difficult tasks that require the conquering of the *yetzer hara*. However, leaving the sin and remorse are not exclusive to the process of repentance. Even if the attribute of repentance and forgiveness did not exist, nevertheless, the departure from sin would be absolutely crucial for man so that he should not be destroyed in his evil. If so, it is inconceivable to say that repentance is a difficult matter, for his very survival depends on his departure from the sin! Similarly, remorse has no exclusivity to the process of repentance and forgiveness. Even if there was no concept of repentance, still, one would regret his transgressions. For his heart would understand that there is punishment, redress, and retribution for his transgression. Moreover, he would have even more remorse, since he will suffer inevitable punishment.

The two associated aspects of the mitzvah of *teshuvah*, namely, verbal confession and the resolution never to sin again — which are relevant to remorse and departure from the sin — are truly easy. Indeed, the sinner, [for his own extrication from punishment,] must depart from and regret his sin. Hence, once that is accomplished, it is an easy matter to make a resolution for the future that he will never repeat the sin again and to verbally confess his transgression.

The verse with which we began this essay refers to the easy nature of *teshuvah*. States the verse, "For this commandment that I command you today — it is not hidden from you and it is not distant.... Rather, the matter is very near to you — in your mouth and in your heart to perform it." We explained above that the phrase "in your mouth" teaches the mitzvah of verbal confession, and the phrase "in your heart" teaches the mitzvah of making the resolution never to repeat the sin. Indeed, the verse speaks about the Divine formula of repentance [resolution and confession,] which renders the pardoning of the sin. Whereas, departure from and remorse for the sin are not limited to the realm of repentance. Even without the institution of repentance and forgiveness, still, departure from sin and remorse are instinctual human reactions [upon realizing the ruination of his deed].

CLOSE TO YOUR HEART

However, *HaKadosh Baruch Hu* commands the sinner only to perform the Divine process of repentance: the verbal confession and the resolution. Indeed, it is a very easy matter, as we mentioned. The verse implies this ease when it states, "Rather, the matter is very near to you." The prescribed course of repentance, which renders forgiveness, "is very near to you." It is easy for you to do, for it is "in your mouth and in your heart to perform it," that is, the verbal confession and the resolution for the future, as we mentioned.

THIS CONCLUSION SHOULD AWAKEN US TO RETURN TO HASHEM

The significance of this conclusion should awaken us to return to Hashem, may His Name be blessed. Even when man reflects on the awesome magnitude of reward and punishment, the human intellect lacks the capacity to fully comprehend. At that point, [when he acknowledges his inadequacy to grasp the true dimension of reward and punishment,] let him supplement his understanding by reflecting on this principle that we outlined above.

Namely, that the departure from transgression has no relevance to the Divine process of repentance and forgiveness. The course correction the sinner must make is unrelated to whether *HaKadosh Baruch Hu* will compassionately forgive him, or whether He will not forgive, God forbid. [In any case] he must depart from his path and return to observe the entire Torah and mitzvos. Even if there would be no rectification for past misdeeds, nevertheless, it would be necessary for him to avoid transgressions in the future, so that he is not destroyed and obliterated through his evil.

THROUGH TESHUVAH HE FINDS A PRICELESS TREASURE

However, ultimately [through the Divine process of *teshuvah*], with departure from the transgression, he is even able to receive pardon and forgiveness for his transgressions. That is, to cleanse himself from all his transgressions and to expunge them, so that they vanish like a passing cloud. Hence, through *teshuvah* he finds a priceless treasure. This is especially true because in granting forgiveness, Hashem does not require from the sinner any additional task other than to depart from his crooked path and to observe the Torah and the mitzvos. Yet Torah observance is obligatory, even if *HaKadosh Baruch Hu* did not ever grant forgiveness. Therefore, the forgiveness of the transgression is a gift of kindness, [because once the sinner corrects his behavior to comply with Torah law, Hashem forgives his past transgressions without requiring him to make amends.]

SINS WHICH HINDER REPENTANCE

The Rambam (*Hilchos Teshuvah* 4:1) wrote the following: "There are twenty-four sins which hinder repentance. Four of them are heinous sins, and if a person commits any one of them, *HaKadosh Baruch Hu* does not afford him the means to perform repentance because of the severity of his sin. These are the [four sins]: One who causes the public to sin, etc.; one who corrupts his fellow [to desist] from the good path [and] to [take the] evil path, etc.; one who sees his son displaying evil conduct and does not protest, etc.; and one who says, 'I will sin and then repent.' " (See the text there, in which he enumerates all of the twenty-four sins.) He gives a natural reason for all of them [as to why they hinder repentance], except for the first four [one who causes the public to sin; one who corrupts his fellow; one who sees his son displaying evil conduct and does not protest; and one who says 'I will sin and then repent']. [These four are different] because there is a spiritual factor that hinders repentance.[4] Namely, because of the severity of these four sins, Hashem does not help him perform repentance. This concept is also found in the Talmud (*Yoma* 87a): "One who says, 'I will sin and then I will repent,' or one who causes the public to sin, will not be afforded the means [*ein maspikin b'yado*] to perform repentance."

HEAVEN DOES NOT PREVENT REPENTANCE

At the end of this section, the Rambam (*Hilchos Teshuvah* 4:6) writes, "All of these sins and things similar to these, even though they [Heaven] hinder repentance, they [Heaven] do not prevent it. Rather, if man repents from these [twenty-four sins], he is deemed a *ba'al teshuvah*, and he has a share in the World to Come." Indeed, the simple understanding of what Chazal said, that these sins do not afford him the means to perform repentance, seems to suggest that Heaven prompts causes that hinder and restrain him from performing repentance. According to this, [that Hashem hinders and restrains,] we must understand the words of the Rambam, "Four of them…and if a person commits any one of them, *HaKadosh Baruch Hu* does not afford him the means to perform repentance." Yet he wrote, "All of these sins and things similar to these, even though they hinder repentance, they do not prevent it." [On the one hand, the Rambam stated that if someone committed one of the first four sins that he enumerated, Hashem does not afford him the means to repent. On the other hand, the Rambam concludes that Hashem does not prevent repentance in any of these twenty-four sins.]

---

4   Repentance is hindered in the other twenty sins not because of a spiritual factor, but because of natural consequence — it is simply hard to physically correct these other twenty sins.

THE LETTER HEI

Perhaps there is an alternative interpretation to what the Rambam wrote [concerning the four heinous sins]: "*HaKadosh Baruch Hu* does not afford him the means to perform repentance." Indeed, Chazal state (*Menachos* 29b), "Why was this world created with the letter *hei*? Because it is similar in structure to a portico [closed on three sides and open on the fourth], and whoever wishes to go astray may do so. What is the reason the [left] leg [of the *hei*] is suspended? To indicate that whoever repents is permitted to re-enter [through the small opening where the leg is divided from the roof]. And why should he not re-enter by that same [big hole that he originally came out of]? That would not help him, as Resh Lakish taught, 'What is the meaning of the verse, "If [one is drawn] to the scoffers, he will scoff; but [if one is drawn] to the humble, He will find favor" (*Mishlei* 3:34)? If a man comes to purify himself, they [Heaven] assist him, but if he comes to defile himself, they open the door for him.' " Rashi explains the words "That would not help him" as follows: "The repentant sinner requires encouragement and support, so that an additional entrance is made only for him." He then explains the words "They assist him": "Therefore, [this implies that] he needs assistance."

ASSISTANCE FROM HEAVEN

In any case, it is clear that anyone who comes to purify himself and to perform repentance receives assistance from Heaven to repent. Indeed, the term "*sipuk*" [written in the form "*maspikin*" in the passage of the Rambam quoted above] means to help and assist, as explained in several places throughout *Shas*. Hence, everybody that returns to Hashem is granted help and assistance from Heaven to repent. Likewise, the concept of *sipuk* is mentioned in *Avos* 4:6: "One who studies [Torah] in order to teach is given the means [*maspikin*] to study and to teach...." This means that he will certainly be helped and assisted from Heaven in order to be able to study and teach. In any case, if he repents from any transgression, he is granted help from Heaven to perform repentance, as we mentioned.

However, if someone commits one of the four heinous transgressions that we mentioned, then *HaKadosh Baruch Hu* does not grant him help to perform repentance. This means that Heaven does not afford the sinner the means to perform repentance. Therefore, even if he comes to purify himself and to perform repentance — since he is not helped from Heaven he is far away from repentance. This follows what Rashi explained, that the one who comes to purify himself needs help because of the fierce war of the evil inclination, as we discussed.

THE WILL TO REPENT

Yet each of these four sins is a very severe transgression. If anyone commits any one of these, Hashem will not help him to perform repentance, as we mentioned in the name of the Rambam. This means that Heaven does not afford him the means to repent. Nevertheless, man should not say to himself, "I despair of performing repentance." Yes, it is difficult to perform repentance, to succeed against the evil inclination without assistance from Heaven. Still, *HaKadosh Baruch Hu* gives strength and power to man, so that when he wants to gird himself with strength and power, he will be able to defeat his evil inclination. Then he can perform repentance — even without any assistance or help from Heaven whatsoever.

AN IRON WILL TO REPENT

The Rambam that we quoted was referring to this concept [of *teshuvah* without assistance], "All these sins and things similar to these, even though they hinder repentance, they do not prevent it...." *HaKadosh Baruch Hu* does not help him to repent from these transgressions. Therefore, these [twenty-four sins] are different than other transgressions. For concerning other transgressions, Chazal say, "The one who comes to purify himself [to perform repentance] — they assist him." However, concerning these [four heinous sins], even though Hashem does not help him to repent, nevertheless, He does not prevent him. This means that Heaven does not place obstacles to forcefully prevent him from performing repentance, God forbid. Rather, He just does not assist him to repent. Yet, if he wants to steel himself with inner strength, to defeat his evil inclination and the desire of his heart

— the ability to repent lies within his hand. He can perform repentance, even without any assistance from Heaven, as we mentioned.

ELISHA

This concept is implicit in the words of Chazal (*Sanhedrin* 107b): " 'And Elisha came to Damascus' (*Melachim II* 8:7): Where did he go? Rebbi Yochanan said: He went to bring Gechazi back to repentance, but he would not repent. He said, 'Repent.' He replied, 'I have learned from you: He who sins and causes the public to sin is not afforded the means to repent.' " This appears rather perplexing! The prophet told him — "Repent!" Yet Gechazi replied, "He who sins...is not afforded the means to repent." This only means that Hashem will not furnish him with assistance to repent; however, Hashem does not prevent him from repenting. If he wants to steel himself with inner strength, he is then able to perform repentance even without help from Hashem. Therefore, Elisha the Prophet told him to repent. Yet Gechazi replied to him, "I learned from you: He who sins...is not afforded the means to repent." That is, since *HaKadosh Baruch Hu* did not want to help Gechazi repent, he therefore despaired and did not want to repent.

ACHER

This is what Chazal explain in *Chagigah* (15a), "A *bas kol* proclaimed, 'Return mischievous children — except for Acher'...Acher pursued a path of great evil...Acher said to him [Rebbi Meir], 'Rebbi Akiva, your master, said...a scholar, though he has sinned, has a remedy.' Then he [Rebbi Meir] said to him, 'Then you also repent!' He replied, 'I have already heard from behind the veil, "Return mischievous children — except for Acher." ' Our Rabbis taught: Once Acher was riding on a horse on Shabbos. Rebbi Meir was walking behind him in order to learn Torah from him. He said to him, 'Meir, go back [so you do not violate the Shabbos by walking too far].' He replied to him, 'Also you should go back [repent].' He replied, 'Have I not already told you that I have heard from behind the veil, "Return mischievous children — except for Acher" ' " (see the text).

"RETURN MISCHIEVOUS CHILDREN — EXCEPT FOR ACHER"

Apparently, Acher was able to return in repentance. Even after Rebbi Meir told him to repent, he replied, "I have heard from behind the veil, 'Return mischievous children — except for Acher.' " Nevertheless, Rebbi Meir said to Acher a second time, "Also you should go back [repent]." See the *Tosafos* (*Chagigah* 15a), who cite a passage from the Talmud Yerushalmi, which teaches that in the end of his life, Acher took ill. Says the Yerushalmi, "Rebbi Meir went to visit him. He said to him, 'Repent.' Acher cried and expired. Rebbi Meir said, 'It appears he died in the midst of repentance' " (see the text there). According to this text, Acher did, in fact, do *teshuvah*. If so, what is the meaning of the declaration of the *bas kol*, "Return mischievous children — except for Acher"?

HASHEM DESIRES REPENTANCE

We can answer this according to what we mentioned above. Hashem, in His goodness and kindness, created the compassionate attributes of repentance and forgiveness. Even more, Hashem expanded His kindness so that He desires that the sinner return to Him. Imagine a case in human relations where one man sins against his fellow, or a son sins grievously against his father. When the sinner comes to appease and to request forgiveness, the injured party will forgive him. Notwithstanding, sometimes in his heart, the person who was wounded would rather that the perpetrator not come forward to ask forgiveness. However, *HaKadosh Baruch Hu* desires that the wicked return in repentance before Him. As we say in the Neilah prayer, "And you want the wicked to repent…" Also, we say every day in the Shemoneh Esrei prayer, "Blessed are You, Hashem, Who desires repentance."

HASHEM REQUESTS REPENTANCE

An even more wondrous aspect of His kindness is that Hashem requests from the sinner that he performs repentance. This is written in the verse, "The word of Hashem, which I sent to them with My servants the prophets, arising early and sending [them]..." (*Yirmeyahu* 29:19). Likewise, all of the prophets would come to the people of Israel, conveying a message in the Name of Hashem, that the people should repent from their ways. For instance, it is written, "Return mischievous children" (ibid. 3:14).

TWO RULES OF REPENTANCE

Indeed, we have already written that there are two rules of repentance. One is that whoever is in the category of "one who comes to purify himself" merits further Divine assistance. Two is that under certain conditions, Hashem does not assist a person to perform repentance. That means, that Hashem does not afford the sinner the means to perform repentance. However, nevertheless, Hashem does not prevent him from doing so. Furthermore, the desire of Hashem for the sinner to repent only applies to the first category, "The one who comes to purify himself — they help him." However, this is not the case concerning the second category of "They do not assist him to perform repentance." Those sinners merit neither the assistance nor desire of Hashem to repent. Rather, if they come to repent of their own accord — they are not prevented from repentance. Moreover, the verse which says, "Return mischievous children," revealing that *HaKadosh Baruch Hu* requests from them to repent, refers only to those who are on the level of "The one who comes to purify himself — they help him." However, it does not apply to those who are in the category, "They do not assist him to perform repentance."

THE WITHDRAWAL OF DIVINE ASSISTANCE

Indeed, after he sinks to the category of "They do not assist him to perform repentance," Heaven no longer affords him the means to repent. This is what the *bas kol* said, "Return, mischievous children — except for Acher." Hashem did not request that Acher repent. However, it was disconcerting to Acher that Hashem demoted him to a worse level of evil than all other sinners. Therefore, even though he had the ability to repent, "For they do not prevent him from repenting," nevertheless, he did not want to return to Hashem. He was aghast that Hashem singled him out as more evil than all

other sinners and did not request from him to perform repentance. Therefore, Rebbi Meir pleaded several times with Acher to repent. However,
Acher was of a different opinion: "I have heard from behind the veil, 'Return, mischievous children — except for Acher.' " Therefore, he did not
want to return to Hashem, May His Name be blessed.

PREVENTED FROM REPENTANCE

Yet, there are transgressions even more severe than those mentioned by
the Rambam, for which Hashem does not assist him to repent, yet does not
prevent *teshuvah*. However, [there are other transgressions] for which
Hashem does prevent him from repenting. Indeed, the Rambam wrote
(*Hilchos Teshuvah* 6:3), "It is possible that a man will commit a severe transgression or a myriad of transgressions, until judgment demands — before the
True Judge — that the punishment for the sins, which the sinner willfully
and knowledgeably committed, will be that he be prevented from repentance. They shall not grant him permission to repent from his wickedness, so
that he will die and be destroyed in his evil.... In reference to this, the verse
says, 'And they insult the angels of Elokim and disgrace His words...until the
anger of Hashem is spent on His people, until there is no cure" (*Divrei
HaYamim II* 36:16). This means that they willfully sinned and multiplied
transgressions until they [the Heavenly host] were obligated to withhold
from them the opportunity of repentance, which is the cure..." (see the text).

THREE LEVELS OF REPENTANCE

In summation, there are three levels in the path of repentance. The first
one is the category of "The one who comes to purify himself — they help him."
If he wants to perform repentance, he will receive further help and assistance
from Heaven. The second concerns those who are not assisted to perform repentance because of the severity of their transgression. This means that they
do not afford him the means from Heaven to repent; however, they do not prevent him from repentance. Therefore, if he will steel himself with inner
strength, he will have the capability to return with repentance, even without
assistance from Heaven. The third category refers to one who is held account-

able for his transgressions, so much so that he is prevented from repentance. They do not grant him permission to repent from his wickedness, so that he will die and be destroyed in his sin, as we mentioned.

THE MOST SEVERE PUNISHMENT

This concept enlightens us with a profound Mussar lesson. Indeed, the most severe punishment in this world is when the sinner's transgressions are so serious, God forbid, that Heaven fights against him — denying him permission to repent from his wickedness. Clearly, there is no difference between one who does not repent because he was denied permission to repent, and one who is still in the category of "The one who comes to purify himself — they help him," but nevertheless, since he is lazy, he does not want to repent. Ultimately, he remains without repentance. Indeed, it is the same thing whether the reason he does not perform *teshuvah* is because Heaven punishes him and denies him the opportunity, or whether he decides and wills himself not to repent.

Consequently, when a person withholds himself from *teshuvah*, he consciously and willfully brings upon himself the worst punishment. The prevention of repentance is the punishment that Hashem administers to the worst transgressors. Therefore, one who withholds himself from *teshuvah* punishes himself with the most severe punishment. Let us consider a person who is in the category "They do not assist him to perform repentance." Since they do not prevent him from doing *teshuvah* — if he does not repent, he brings the ultimate punishment upon himself. Moreover, if he is in the category of "The one who comes to purify himself — they help him," and yet does not repent — he also punishes himself with the most severe punishment, namely, the very punishment that Hashem administers to the worst sinners, who are prevented from repenting. The more we reflect on this, the more awesome is this concept.

THE SEVERITY OF ONE SIN

The Rambam wrote, "It is possible that a man will commit a severe transgression or a myriad of transgressions, until judgment demands, before the True Judge, that the punishment for the sins…will be that he be prevented from repentance." We see from the Rambam that sometimes the severity of the sin is the cause for the sinner to be prevented from performing *teshuvah*, as the verse says, "One sin destroys an abundance of good" (*Koheles* 9:18). On the other hand, sometimes the quantity of sin causes the prevention of *teshuvah*, for the sins multiply on themselves. The Talmud (*Shabbos* 10b) alludes to this: "Let man always dwell in a recently populated city, for since the city is new, the sins are few. As the verse says, 'Behold now, this city is near (*kerovah*) to flee to, and it is a little one' (*Bereishis* 19:20). What is meant by *kerovah*? Since it is recently populated its sins are few." This teaches that quantities of sins, which are compounded, cause much culpability.

This is, indeed, awesome. Chazal tell us that the city of Sodom was built one year before the city Zoar. Sodom was fifty-two years old, whereas Zoar was fifty-one years old. The severity of the sins of Zoar was definitely equivalent to the severity of the sins of Sodom and Amora. However, the sins of Sodom and Amora exceeded in quantity, by one year, the sins of Zoar. Therefore, Hashem destroyed Sodom and Amora with sulfur and salt, whereas Zoar was spared because it was one year younger.

WE FALL EVERY MOMENT TO ENORMOUS SINS

Indeed, every man is apt to fall to sins that are severe in quality and exceedingly great in quantity. The quantity factor increases on a daily basis. The Admor referred to this in the *Iggeres HaMussar*, "We fall every moment to enormous sins which reach the heavens. Namely, with sins of speech — with no one able to stop us — a host of unethical business practices, and, worst of all, *bitul Torah*. In general, there is no soundness in any of our limbs. If you contemplate well this matter...." Therefore, through a multitude of sins, man can sink to the lowest level. He will be sentenced by the True Judge to be prevented from *teshuvah*.

Therefore, it is extremely crucial for man to do *teshuvah* before his sins tower over his head, and while he is still in the category of "The one that comes to purify himself — they help him." Then it will be easy for him to do *teshuvah*, for Hashem "will dispatch him help from the Sanctuary" (cf. *Tehillim* 20:3).

ARTICLE SEVEN

THE PROCESS OF TESHUVAH

FOUR STEPS OF TESHUVAH

THE RAMBAM WRITES (*Hilchos Teshuvah* 2:2), "What is *teshuvah*? *Teshuvah* takes place when the following occurs: 1) The sinner ceases committing the sin and removes all thoughts of it from his mind. 2) He then resolves in his heart never to repeat [the sin]. These first two steps are based on the verse, 'Let the wicked one forsake his way and the iniquitous man his thoughts' (*Yeshayahu* 55:7). 3) Next, he should regret his past misdeed, as the verse says, 'After I returned, I regretted' (*Yirmeyahu* 31:19). 4) [Finally, his repentance should be such that] the One Who knows all secrets will testify that this man will never revert to this transgression...."

The formula of the Rambam seems to be slightly out of order. He mentions here the two primary foundations of repentance: 1) resolution for the future and 2) regret for the past. It would appear that the fourth step, "The One Who knows all secrets will testify that this man will never revert to this transgression," pertains to the second step, his resolution for the future. Why, then, did the Rambam place the procedure of regret between resolution and the testimony of Hashem? Would it not have been more accurate for the Rambam to teach: What is *teshuvah*? 1) Ceasing from the sin, 2) resolution never to repeat the sin, 3) the testimony of Hashem that the penitent will never repeat the sin, and 4) regret?

RESOLUTION AND REGRET

Indeed, the two primary foundations of *teshuvah* are resolution for the future and regret for the past. It would appear that these two procedures are of one theme and complementary to each other. That is, one who resolves to forsake his evil path certainly regrets his past misdeed, and vice versa. Therefore, we would expect that the magnitude of one's determination and resolution not to repeat any misdeed in the future, would be commensurate with the intensity of his remorse for the past. We would tend to think that the sense of remorse has an advantage over the resolve to make a resolution. In other words, is it not easier to regret the sins that we committed in the past than to accept a resolution not to repeat the sin in the future? The durability of the resolution for the future is limited by the fierce war of the *yetzer hara*. Whereas it is just the opposite concerning sins that have already been committed and for which the passion has been extinguished. In this case, [it would seem that] his heart would easily be moved to feel remorse for his past sins. The ancient dictum alludes to this, "The wicked are full of regrets," for after they perpetrate their schemes, they regret their misdeeds. Likewise, it would seem that if someone resolved to improve his deeds in the future, he certainly would regret the past even more.

A COMMENSURATE SENSE OF REGRET

To our astonishment, we see in reality that just the opposite occurs. It is more difficult for man to regret the past than to resolve to improve the future. Many God-fearing people, who seek to fulfill the Divine will, endeavor to improve their deeds and to accept resolutions to abstain from several transgressions that they had given into. They also try to be more zealous to fulfill mitzvos that they were lax in. Nevertheless, they know in their heart that they will not feel a commensurate sense of regret for the past, or perhaps, they will not feel any regret whatsoever. However, in a parallel situation, regret is an automatic response. For instance, let us consider normative behavior. Imagine that someone feels remorse over something he unwittingly did [like accidentally injuring somebody], that caused a great deal of harm. As soon as he feels regret, the remorse will be apparent on his face and in all of his movements, for he will not be able to remove worry and sadness from his heart. He will be downcast and will not be able to sleep even when he lies down. How much more so should a person experience remorse for a sin. However, man knows in his heart that he does not feel worry and anguish for the sins that he committed. His peace of mind is not disturbed — even if he does accept upon himself to observe and fulfill this injunction in the future.

ELUL

The Admor wrote [in Letter Fourteen], "It is well known that in earlier generations, when the holy month of Elul was announced, everyone was gripped by fear. This fear generated a positive effect by drawing people close to Divine service, each man according to his level. Common sense suggests that one who distances himself from Hashem's worship the entire year would be filled with fear and worry concerning the Day of Judgment, much more than one who was faithful in his observance. This is especially so in light of the fact that the only shield against punishment is Torah study and the performance of good deeds. However, just the opposite occurs. We see that those who embrace the holy path the entire year make a significantly greater effort to improve their deeds than those who walked in darkness."

As we mentioned, the multitude of our sins has diminished our ability to recognize the enormous culpability of sin, and we do not realize that to commit a transgression is to rebel against the Divine will of the King of kings. Man's unawareness of the great, exalted honor of Hashem causes him to misconceive the accountability of sin as a very insignificant matter indeed. He also does not perceive the base emptiness of man, nor does he have any sense of *yiras ha'onesh*.

THE CAUSE OF UNDERESTIMATING THE SEVERITY OF SIN

Indeed, the main reason that man underestimates the severity of sin is explained in the Talmud (*Kiddushin* 20a and *Arachin* 30b): "Rav Yose beRebbi Chanina said, 'Come see how hard are the results of [violating the laws] of the seventh year. A man who trades in seventh year produce must eventually sell his movables, as it says, "In this jubilee year, you shall return each man to his ancestral heritage" (*Vayikra* 25:13), and in juxtaposition it says, "When you make a sale to your fellow or make a purchase from the hand of your fellow" (ibid. 25:14). ["From the hand of your fellow" implies] moveable items [that he was forced to sell as a punishment for transgressing the laws of the jubilee]. If he disregards this [i.e., does not perceive this as a punishment], he eventually sells his estate, as it says, "If your brother becomes impoverished and sells part of his ancestral heritage" (ibid. 25:25). He has no opportunity [for repentance] until he sells his house, as the verse says, "If a man shall sell a residence house in a walled city" (ibid. 25:29). Why state there [pertaining to the first punishment], "If he disregards this," whereas here [the second punishment], "He has no opportunity [for repentance]"?' This is in accordance with Rav Huna. For Rav Huna said, 'Once a man has committed a transgression and repeated it, it is permitted to him.' [Asks the Gemara,] 'Permitted to him' — can you think so? Rather, say it seems to him as if it were permitted."

THE REPETITION OF SIN

Rashi explains the words "If he disregards" as follows: "He does not perceive the punishments that come upon him as a warning to repent from the sin he has committed." And in *Arachin*, Rashi explains the phrase "It seems to him as if it were permitted": "Therefore, the first time, when he had transgressed but once, it states, 'If he disregards.' This implies that he knew and realized that he was transgressing, nevertheless he did not withdraw from the sin. Rather, he committed the sin. The second time he commits the sin, the text says, 'He has no opportunity for repentance,' as he did not even realize that it was a sin."

HE WILL PERCEIVE THE SIN AS PERMITTED

How awesome is this matter! Chazal take for granted that the repetition of the same sin twice will make an impression in man's soul. He will perceive the sin as permitted and will adopt this forbidden deed into his natural conduct. He will not consider thoughts of doing *teshuvah*. Even worse, the punishments that come upon him, one after the other, will not motivate him to repent, for the sin has already become as permitted in his eyes.

DUPLICATION OF SIN

Chazal teach us that if a person sins and repeats it even one time, the sin becomes as permitted in his eyes. Nevertheless, this does not mean to say that the effect only occurs between the first and second times. On the contrary, each time he repeats the sin, commensurately, his soul will become more insensitive to the sin. The sin will become increasingly more permissible in his eyes — for there is no limit to how insignificant the sin can become to him. The duplication of transgression is the main reason that he disregards sin. The constant repeating and endless multiplying of the sin renders the transgression so permissible in his eyes, that eventually he does not sense the sin whatsoever.

PERMITTED IN HIS EYES

Chazal teach that Hashem will punish someone who does commerce with produce of the seventh year. If he does not direct his heart to retract from the sin, he will bring increasingly worse punishments upon himself. Even though in the eyes of man, the more he sins, the lighter the sin appears to him, nevertheless his culpability in the eyes of Hashem increases incrementally. The very fact that he disregards the sin causes the sin and punishment to be more and more severe. Rabbeinu Yonah teaches this in *Sha'arei Teshuvah* (1:5), "*Teshuvah* is very difficult for one who repeats the sin, because the transgression has become permitted in his eyes. Therefore, his sin is much more serious. As the prophet wrote, 'Behold, you spoke and carried out evil deeds, as much as you could [*vetuchal*]' (*Yirmeyahu* 3:5). The explanation of 'as much as you could' is as follows: the evil has become as something permitted, something you are capable of and within your allowance (*be'reshusecha*) to perform. As the verse says, 'In your [outlying] cities, you may not (*lo tuchal*) eat' (*Devarim* 12:17). The Targum learns, '*Leis lach reshu*' — 'you are not allowed [to eat].' "[5] Therefore, the more he repeats

---

5   *Reshu* stems from the same root as *be'reshusecha*, implying that as long as a sin is not performed, it remains unallowed in the mind of the individual. However, once the individual can bring himself to transgress — in other words, he is able to overrule his conscience and perform the sin — it eventually begins to appear to him as allowed.

the sin, the deeper is the impression that it is permissible. Consequently, the more he repeats the sin, the more severe it is, and this severity continually increases. Hence, when he deals commercially in produce of the seventh year, his sin continually increases. Correspondingly, Hashem brings increasingly more severe punishments, each one worse than the one preceding it.

GEHINNOM IS DEEPENED

In light of this, we can understand the words of the Talmud (*Eruvin* 19a), "Rav Yehoshua ben Levi said: What [is the meaning of] what is written, 'Passing through the valley of Bacha, they make it a place of springs; yes, the early rain clothes it with blessing' (*Tehillim* 84:7)? 'Passing' is an allusion to men who transgress the will of *HaKadosh Baruch Hu.* 'Valley' is [an allusion to the men] for whom Gehinnom is made deep. 'Of Bacha' [signifies] that they weep and shed tears. 'They make it a place of springs,' like the constant flow of the altar drains [i.e., where the blood drains off the altar]. ['Yes, the early rain clothes it with blessing': they acknowledge the justice of their punishment and declare before Him, 'Lord of the universe, You have judged well, You have condemned well, and rightly provided Gehinnom for the wicked and Gan Eden for the righteous.']"

This text is puzzling. The phrase "for whom Gehinnom is made deep" seems to pertain to a particularly enormous sin, which bears a severe punishment. In other words, "for whom Gehinnom is made deep," suggests a more severe and bitter punishment. Whereas less severe sins will be punished in a part of Gehinnom that is not so deep. However, the text also says that "passing" is an allusion to men who transgress the will of *HaKadosh Baruch Hu* — and in reference to them, Gehinnom is deepened. If Gehinnom is deepened even for these general sinners, who have not committed a particularly severe sin, then for which people is it not deepened? Moreover, the phrase "for whom Gehinnom is made deep" is itself incomprehensible.

CONTINUOUS TRANSGRESSION

However, these questions can be answered according to the concept that we mentioned above. Each successive time that he repeats the sin, the

culpability increases over the previous time. Consequently, each time that
he repeats the sin, his punishment is increased ad infinitum. "Men who
transgress the will of *HaKadosh Baruch Hu*" does not connote those who occasionally sin, but rather those who continuously transgress the Divine will.
Consequently, they constantly duplicate their sins, the gravity of the sins increase, and the punishment exponentially intensifies. This is the meaning of
the passage, " 'Valley' is [an allusion to those men] for whom Gehinnom is
made deep" — Gehinnom is continuously deepened for them. Each time
they repeat the sin, Gehinnom is continuously increased. Moreover, from
the first time they commit the sin to the last time they commit it, Gehinnom
is deepened incrementally.

SURGING WATERS

Let us now explain the passage, " 'Of Bacha' [signifies] that they weep
and shed tears. 'They make it a place of springs,' like the constant flow of the
altar drains." A spring begins as a trickle of water. As it flows it gradually wid-
ens, and eventually it fills its banks. So, too, as Gehinnom deepens, their
punishment intensifies. Just as Gehinnom is continuously deepened in order
to intensify and exacerbate their punishment, commensurately, they cry
more deeply and shed copious tears. Moreover, just as there is no comparison
between the first trickle of a spring and the later surging waters, so, too, there
is no comparison between the punishment for the first sin and the
ever-increasing punishment for the multiplicity of sins. Likewise, the intensity of their crying will also increase and their eyes will stream with tears, like
a flowing spring. The power of their sorrow will increase, until their weeping
will be without end.

THE PARADOX OF ELUL

In light of this, we can explain the paradox that we see each Elul. The
man who follows the holy path throughout the year is struck with more fear
and worry than the man who walks in darkness the entire year. Is this not ab-
surd, as the Admor pointed out [in Letter Fourteen]? We can explain this by
the axiom of Chazal, "When a person commits a sin and then repeats it, it be-

comes as if permitted to him." Moreover, the more he persists in the sin, the more it becomes permitted to him. Therefore, the person who strays from the path will always be confused, and he will repeat the sin numerous times. His heart will neither faint from nor fear the dread of judgment, because all the sins become permitted. Therefore, why should he fear?

WHAT WILL AWAKEN REMORSE?

Based on this we can understand the distinction between two principles of *teshuvah*: resolution for the future and regret for the past. Experience shows us that the resolution is easier than the regret. Even if one accepts upon himself to improve his deeds in the future, nevertheless, he is still quite far from feeling total remorse deep in his heart. This seems to be counterintuitive. However, the explanation is as follows: Each person, according to his level, has committed sins — and repeated them many times over. This has formed an impression in his heart that the sin is permitted. Obviously, it is quite difficult to uproot this impression from his heart. Therefore, even if he accepts upon himself to abandon the sin from now and in the future, nevertheless he is like someone who abstains from something permitted. Therefore, since the sin is permitted in his eyes, what will awaken the remorse?

For instance, let us assume someone decides to adopt a particular pious attribute, an attribute of which he was not previously watchful. Even though he accepts upon himself to be heedful of this in the future, still, is it likely that he will have total regret for the past? After all, this is something totally permissible that he now decides to observe with a higher level of observance. This situation is comparable to someone who has repeated a sin so many times that it has become permitted in his eyes. Therefore, he considers the avoidance of this sin as an uncommon level of piety. As long as he perceives that the sin is permissible, it is impossible that he will experience any regret or worry over the sin. Moreover, even if one accepts upon himself to abstain from the sin in the future, nevertheless he is like someone who accepts upon himself to abstain from something permitted.

RESENSITIZE HIS HEART

Therefore, man does not easily feel total remorse. Rather, only after his divorce from the sin extends over many days and much time passes will his watchfulness be steadfast. Then he will not transgress the sins that he had previously violated. He will toil exceedingly to acquire *yirah*, wisdom, and Mussar; *yiras ha'onesh* and *yiras haromemus*. He will also make accountings of his soul. Ultimately, he will sensitize himself to the severity of the sin. Little by little, the sense of permissibility will diminish, and sensitivity to the severity of the sin will be restored. He will consider the culpability of the sin with the same sorrow as one who had never sinned in his life. Then he will feel the remorse, realize his foolishness, and the sin will make a powerful impact in his heart. The more he understands and comprehends the immense culpability of sin, and how terrible it is to rebel against the will of the King of kings, *HaKadosh Baruch Hu* — the more he will be anguished by his remorse and worry.

Now we can explain the passage of the Rambam that we cited above, "And the One Who knows all secrets will testify that this man will never revert to this transgression." This is a shocking statement. The Rambam implies that if the man ever commits this sin again — then he has not done *teshuvah*. This is perplexing, because Chazal teach us that if someone does complete *teshuvah*, then all of his sins are forgiven. If afterwards he happens to revert to the sin, he is considered as one who sinned for the first time, and the first sins that were already forgiven are no longer remembered. If so, the fact that *HaKadosh Baruch Hu* is aware that in the future he will revert to this sin does not ruin the holy status of total *teshuvah*.

TWO CATEGORIES OF KNOWLEDGE

However, let us consider the words of the Admor in *Sefer Tevunah* [Letter Thirty], "Likewise, there are two categories of knowledge. The first is absolute knowledge, which is subject to neither change nor substitution [an "eternal truth"]. The second is deduced knowledge [truth determined by the process of logical thought], which is established according to the arrangement of logical steps — from cause to another result. In this procedure, the concept develops until it comes to the final result. This knowledge is subject to substitution, because sometimes a concept is generated without a cause, even if the cause logically opposes its result [the conclusion is counterintuitive, otherwise known as "the aspect of miraculous"]. The first category, absolute knowledge, is not found within human parameters [unless through the aspect of prophecy]. Moreover, even in the second category, deduced knowledge, man falls short in his ability to apprehend the result because of the insufficiency of his knowledge of the myriad causes relevant to the conceptualization of the future concept. In respect to this, human understanding is too feeble to formulate a concept which is logically perfect."

TWO CATEGORIES OF THE FOREKNOWLEDGE OF HASHEM

[Letter Thirty continues,] "The knowledge of what man will choose [even before he chooses] is also divided into two divisions. The first is absolute knowledge. [Hashem knows whether a particular man will be a *tzaddik* or a *rasha*.] It is beyond human understanding why this is not a refutation of free choice [as the Rambam explains in *Hilchos Teshuvah* 5:5]. The second division is deduced knowledge — the knowledge of what a man will choose based on an evaluation of the conduct of man, his nature, and his affairs. The intellect considers these factors and calculates whether he will be a *tzaddik* or a *rasha* in the future. It is with this knowledge [intellectual computation] that *HaKadosh Baruch Hu* rules His world according to the current good of man, and does not consider the future, even in a case when Hashem knows that man will ultimately corrupt himself."

TWO CATEGORIES OF KNOWING IF HE WILL REVERT TO THE SIN

According to this concept of the Admor, we can assume that in reference to doing *teshuvah*, there are also two aspects of knowing whether or not a person will revert to the sin. The first aspect is *yediah sichlis*, or deduced knowledge. Indeed, the foundation of *teshuvah* is to depart from one's path and not to do any more evil in the eyes of Hashem. This requires an absolute resolution in a man's heart never to revert to the sin again. The magnitude of his repentance must be evaluated [by Hashem]. Is his resolution never to sin again strong and enduring, or is his *teshuvah* not so absolute, he being likely to revert to his sin? In this analysis, man is also unable to grasp the ultimate truth. For the magnitude of *teshuvah* is dependent on the spirit of man, his properties, character traits, nature, and temperament. Based on the inner dynamics of his *teshuvah*, He knows according to *yediah sichlis* whether the level of *teshuvah* suffices to influence him so that he will not revert to the sin. A man cannot know himself as well as Hashem, Who created him from nothing. Hashem examines the heart of man, and knows according to *yediah sichlis*, according to his level of repentance and the inner dynamics of his *teshuvah*, whether he is likely to revert to the sin or will never again revert to it.

The second aspect is *yediah muchletes* — absolute knowing without estimating cause and effect. For even if, according to the analysis of the *yediah sichlis*, he is unlikely to ever revert to this sin, nevertheless, doesn't man have free choice? Therefore, he might return to his folly. Hashem knows what man will do in the future, yet man's conduct is still dependent on the free choice.

HASHEM WILL TESTIFY

In light of this, we can explain the words of the Rambam, "And the one Who knows all secrets will testify that this man will never revert to this transgression." This knowing is based only on *yediah sichlis*. In other words, is the power of his repentance — his resolution not to sin — sufficient that Hashem, Who knows the secrets of the heart, will testify on his behalf that according to a logical analysis, the power of his repentance is so strong that he will never revert to the sin? If the *teshuvah* is with his full heart, then Hashem, Who knows all secrets, will testify that he will never revert to the sin. Even if Hashem knows according to *yediah muchletes* that in the future he will revert to the sin, nevertheless, this will not harm the holy status, nor will it destroy his previous *teshuvah*.

THE PROCESS OF LOGICAL THOUGHT

In light of this, we can understand the sequence of the Rambam's steps of *teshuvah*. Let us reflect on the knowledge of the magnitude of *teshuvah*. The process of logical thought is employed to determine whether his resolution not to sin will or will not endure. Indeed, the resolution alone does not prove anything — for he may easily be inspired to improve his ways. Therefore, even if he resolves with a pure heart and a willing soul to abstain from all sin, nevertheless, as long as he does not feel total remorse, he does not recognize the magnitude of the sin. Even worse, the sin appears to him as permitted. Ostensibly, his resolution may not endure, because he may easily be tricked by the *yetzer hara* and return to his folly. Since the actual sin is light in his eyes, he does not recoil nor fear the sin.

MAGNITUDE OF TESHUVAH

Rather, the magnitude of *teshuvah* that is measured in order to project his future standing can only be determined by the level of his remorse. When he reaches the level of recognizing the degree of culpability that he caused to his soul, he will fully regret his evil deeds. His kidneys will be afflicted and he will groan in the bitterness of his heart, as Rabbeinu Yonah wrote in *Sha'arei Teshuvah* regarding genuine remorse. Whether the magnitude of his repentance and his resolve never to sin again will endure is determined by the level of great bitterness and the degree of worry and anguish, as well as by how much he recoils from and fears committing the sin.

In this light, let us reexamine the Rambam: "What is *teshuvah*? *Teshuvah* takes place when the sinner ceases committing the sin and removes all thoughts of it from his mind. He then resolves in his heart never to repeat [the sin].... Next, he should regret his past misdeed.... And the One Who knows all secrets will testify that this man will never revert to this transgression." The phrase "And the One Who knows all secrets will testify that this man will never revert to this transgression" is actually part of his resolution, as the Rambam states, "He then resolves in his heart never to repeat [the sin]." Nevertheless, the Rambam wrote, "Next, he should regret his past misdeed," before, "And the One Who knows all secrets will testify that this man will never revert to this transgression." The Rambam chose this sequence because a mere resolution that he will never sin again, even if his resolution is sincere, is still insufficient. As long as he does not feel profound remorse in his heart over the past, Hashem will not testify on his behalf that he will never repeat the sin. However, only after he totally regrets the past does he reach the level of "And the One Who knows all secrets will testify that this man will never revert to this transgression." When Hashem knows and perceives the bitterness of his heart and his anguish — that he has become so aware of the enormity of the sin that he recoils from it and fears committing it — then Hashem testifies on his behalf that, according to *yediah sichlis*, he will never commit the sin again.

ARTICLE EIGHT

INCOMPARABLE REWARD

REBBI SHIMON BEN CHALAFTA

THE MIDRASH (*Midrash Rabbah, Parashas Pekudei*) TELLS US: "Once, Rebbi Shimon ben Chalafta had no food on the eve of Shabbos. He went to the outskirts of the city and prayed to Hashem. He [Hashem] gave him a precious gem from Heaven. He sold the gem and bought food for Shabbos. His wife asked him, 'Where did you get this food?' He responded, 'From the sustenance of Hashem.' She insisted, 'If you don't tell me the source of the food, I will not partake.' He began to explain to her, 'I prayed to Hashem and He gave me [a gem] from Heaven.' She said, 'I will not eat anything until you assure me that you will return it on the conclusion of Shabbos.' He asked her, 'Why?' She answered, 'Do you want that [in the World to Come] your table will be lacking, whereas the table of your friend will be full?' Rav Shimon went and told the story to Rebbi, who said to him, 'Go back and tell your wife that if anything will be lacking from your table, I will replenish it from mine.' When he told this to his wife, she responded, 'Take me to he who has taught you Torah.' When she came to him she said, 'Master, does one man see another in the World to Come? Does not every man have a world for himself? For does it not say, "So man goes to his eternal home, while the mourners go about the streets" (*Koheles* 12:5)? It does not say, "...home," rather, "his...home." ' When [Rebbi Shimon ben Chalafta] heard this, he immediately returned the [remaining value of the] precious stone to Heaven."

THE ENIGMATIC RESPONSE

Indeed, the enigmatic response of Rebbi Shimon's wife, which countered the proposal of Rabbeinu HaKadosh, is quite astonishing. What is the meaning of her words, "Master, does one man see another in the World to Come? Does not every man have a world for himself?" Will it be necessary in the World of Truth to search amongst all the righteous and pious people in order to locate Rebbi? Is it possible that they will be unable to find Rebbi, in order for him to fulfill his assurance, or that they will be denied access to him? Is it possible that Rebbi will give his word and not uphold it, or that he will not fulfill his promise, God forbid?

THE CONVENTIONAL PAYMENT SCALE

We learned in the Mishnah (*Avos* 5:26), "Ben Hei Hei says: The reward is in proportion to the exertion." Let us consider the conventional payment scale for wages paid to a hired worker. They are not paid very much for the effort and toil of their labor [their wages are fixed on a per-day basis, regardless of the degree of difficulty of the work]. The manual laborers, like the bricklayers and hewers of stone, who toil by the sweat of their brow, receive minimal wages for their day's work. The backbreaking work that they endure is not factored into their wages. What's more, there is no consideration of whether the worker is a man of great strength and the work is easy for him, or whether he is feeble and the work is a fierce struggle for him. Neither is the state of the worker's health — whether sound or infirm — reflected in his wages.

THE REWARD IS IN PROPORTION TO THE EXERTION

However, this is not the calculation that Hashem employs when He configures the reward for those who perform the Divine service. Indeed, besides the reward for the mitzvah — the actual observance of the injunction — there is compensation based on the difficulty of service, as Chazal state, "The reward is in proportion to the exertion." Hashem measures the distress endured by soul and body in the performance of the Divine service. There is a vast difference in reward whether he learned Torah in comfort or whether he learned under duress; if he was of sound or feeble health. Likewise, there is no comparison between one who performed the mitzvah with ease and one who struggled against the *yetzer hara*, needing to overcome his physical desire and conquer his *yetzer*. According to the effort and exertion of Divine service, the reward is increased exponentially, ad infinitum, for "The reward is in proportion to the exertion."

Chazal (*Avos D'Rebbi Nosson*) extolled the advantage of *avodah* performed under duress, over *avodah* performed in comfort: "If you learned Torah in times of ease, it does not compare to [Torah] in times of duress. For one thing, [a mitzvah performed] with difficulty is worth more than a hundred mitzvos performed with ease." Likewise, it is written in *Sefer Chassidim*, "A mitzvah that necessitated the conquering of the *yetzer* is one hundred times greater than a mitzvah that does not require the conquering of the *yetzer*."

The Talmud (*Bava Basra* 78b) teaches, "What is the meaning of the verse, 'Therefore *hamoshelim* would say: Come to Cheshbon...'? '*Hamoshelim*' means those who rule over their evil inclination. 'Come to Cheshbon' means the following: Come let us consider the account of the world — the loss incurred by the fulfillment of a mitzvah against the reward for its observance, and the gain of the transgression against its loss."

This passage requires an explanation. Who does not know the concept of the reward of mitzvos and the punishment of transgressions, that *HaKadosh Baruch Hu* bestows abundant reward upon those who do His will and fitting judgments against those who commit transgressions? The point is that it is easy for a person to proceed on the straight, paved path of Divine service — when it is not burdensome for him. However, if he encounters any deterrent on the path of his *avodas Hashem* or any challenge that necessitates the conquering of his *yetzer hara* — his service will weaken. Therefore, if any trial, whether corporal or monetary, comes upon man in the performance of a mitzvah, let him reflect on the concept that we explained. Don't the deterrents and difficulties of Divine service increase the reward a hundredfold? If he withstands the trial and conquers his *yetzer hara*, won't his reward for fulfilling this one mitzvah be more abundant than the fulfillment of a hundred other mitzvos performed with neither difficulty nor impediment of the *yetzer*?

THE ACCOUNT OF THE WORLD

This is what the rulers over their *yetzer hara* say, "Come let us consider the account of the world: the loss incurred by the fulfillment of a mitzvah against the reward for its observance." They are teaching us that besides the reward for the actual mitzvah, there is another calculation of reward based on the difficulty of performing the mitzvah, for "The reward is in proportion to the exertion." This is the meaning of "the loss incurred by the fulfillment of a mitzvah" — the calculation of the loss [difficulty] of the mitzvah, in contrast to the reward for the difficulty of performing the mitzvah. The difficulty endured in the performance of the mitzvah is the factor that dramatically increases the reward.

Likewise, the second statement of the rulers over their *yetzer hara*, "[and calculate] the gain of a transgression against its loss," requires an explanation. At first glance this seems to be obvious, for it is elementary that sinners are justly punished. However, we can also explain this as we did the first clause. The Admor, *zt"l*, wrote in Letter Thirty-one , "A good deed is accorded reward in relation to the quality of its undertaking, as measured by how difficult it is for the act to be performed. As Chazal state (*Avos* 5:26), 'The reward is in proportion to the exertion.' Likewise, an evil act is punished according to how hard it is to refrain from committing it. The more this difficulty is decreased, the more a transgression's severity is increased. As Chazal tell us (*Menachos* 43b), 'Rebbi Meir said: [Regarding the mitzvah of *tzitzis*,] the punishment for not wearing white threads is greater than for not wearing blue ones.' " He also referred to this concept in *Sefer Tevunah*. The axiom is as follows: The punishment of a sin is proportional to the level of difficulty required to refrain from committing it. If this is so, then a question arises concerning the punishment accorded to the sins of stealing and promiscuity. The Talmud (*Makkos* 23b) states that a man has a natural desire to commit these sins. Therefore, the level of difficulty required to restrain oneself from stealing and adultery is immense, because the desire is inflamed and the *yetzer* incites him. If so, these severe sins of stealing and adultery should receive a lesser level punishment, which is counterintuitive.

PUNISHMENT FOR THE PLEASURE OF THE SIN

However, it appears that there is yet another determinant. We mentioned in relation to mitzvos the principle, "The reward is in proportion to the exertion." Besides the reward for the actual mitzvah, there is another calculation based on the difficulty he endured in carrying out the Divine will. Likewise, regarding a sin, besides the punishment for the actual sin, there is another calculation of punishment for the pleasure that he enjoyed in violation of the Divine will. Just as for mitzvos the rule is "The reward is in proportion to the exertion," so, too, for *aveiros*, the rule is that the punishment is in proportion to the pleasure. Indeed, the Vilna Gaon wrote in his commentary to *Mishlei* that all the pleasures a man enjoys in this world will become bitter for him in the grave. The flesh that desires [gratification] will be punished in the *chibut hakever* [the severe afflictions that the body suffers in the grave]. There [in the grave], each body part that took pleasure in this world, not in the context of a mitzvah, will be burnt with [a fire that will inflict pain] like the poison of a snake. Whereas, for the *tzaddik*, who intends [when partaking of this world] for the sake of Heaven, it is just the opposite. The pleasure is considered a mitzvah, and his eating is like a *korban*.

Therefore, according to the Vilna Gaon, man will be severely punished for all the pleasures that he enjoys in this world — this even includes something permissible — if he did not intend it to be for a mitzvah. Each body part that took pleasure will be burnt as if with the venom of a snake. Based on this, we can calculate the onerous punishment that will be administered for partaking of a worldly pleasure that is forbidden by the Torah; he, then, delights in something which is a rebellion against the Divine will — and the punishment for the pleasure of a sin is infinitely greater than the punishment for something permissible. How awesome is this idea! Therefore, when his *yetzer hara* incites him to commit an *aveirah*, or even to partake of something forbidden,[6] let him consider the following: besides the punishment for the actual sin, he will be chastised many more times for the indulgence.

In light of this, we can answer the question that we raised concerning stealing and illicit relations. On one hand, man naturally desires to steal and

---

6   Since people derive great pleasure from food, the punishment will be severe.

engage in illicit relations. Therefore, the punishment for the actual sin is diminished because of the difficulty required to restrain himself. On the other hand, the gratification of these sins is quite intense. Therefore, the calculation of his enjoyment for rebelling against the Divine will serves to substantially amplify the punishment.

This is what the rulers over their *yetzer hara* say: "Come let us consider the account of the world: the loss incurred by the fulfillment of a mitzvah against the reward for its observance; and the gain of a transgression against its loss." We understand from this text that besides the punishment for the actual sin, there is an additional calculation: the punishment for the gain of the sin, i.e., the pleasure which one enjoyed from the sin. This is the meaning of weighing the gain of the transgression against its loss, i.e., the calculation of the pleasure received. Meaning, the punishment will increase exponentially for the pleasure he received from the sin.

TRIALS IN DIVINE SERVICE

Indeed, the level of difficulty in performing the mitzvah substantially amplifies the reward, in accordance with the principle, "The reward is in proportion to the exertion." Let us consider someone who is challenged with trials in the pursuit of his Divine service. If he merits to withstand the test, overcoming his troubles and the obstacles — how goodly is his portion — for his reward is inconceivably vast. However, there is a critical danger intertwined with these trials. They might so overwhelm him that he will be powerless to withstand them; then he will stray from the good, straight path. Therefore, we pray every day, "Do not bring me into a test" (Morning Blessings).

NO RISK

However, we have found one aspect of difficulty in Divine service that will significantly amplify the reward without any risk. Despite this difficulty, man is assured that this challenge will neither detract nor deter him from the holy path. It will not be a trial for him nor will it subvert him to corruption.

The Talmud (*Kiddushin* 31a) relates an incident that occurred in

Ashkelon between an idol worshipper and his father: "The Sages sought jewels for the *ephod* [from Dama ben Nesinah] at a price of 600,000 [gold dinar]. But since the key was lying under his father's pillow, he did not disturb him. The following year *HaKadosh Baruch Hu* gave him his reward: a red heifer was born to him in his herd.... Rebbi Chanina made the following observation: 'If one who is not commanded, yet does so, is so [rewarded], how much more so one who is commanded and does so!' As Rebbi Chanina said, 'He who is commanded and fulfills [the command] is greater than he who fulfills it even though he is not commanded.' Rav Yosef [who was blind] said, 'Originally, I thought that if anyone would tell me that the halachah agrees with Rebbi Yehudah, that a blind person is exempt from mitzvos, I would make a banquet for the Rabbis, seeing that I am not obligated, yet fulfill them. However, now that I have heard Rebbi Chanina's ruling — that he who is commanded and fulfills [the command] is greater than he who fulfills it even though he is not commanded — on the contrary, if anyone should tell me that the halachah does not agree with Rebbi Yehudah, I would make a banquet for the Rabbis.' "

Tosafos, commenting on this Talmudic passage, explain the preeminence of one who is commanded and fulfills, over one who is not commanded and fulfills: "Apparently, the reason that one who is commanded is superior, is because his worry and anguish that he may transgress [exceeds that of one who is not commanded]."

THE REWARD OF WORRY OVER A MITZVAH

It is clearly revealed from this passage that the worry and anguish that a person endures in the fulfillment of a mitzvah — the fear that he might transgress — is equivalent to the element of difficulty that amplifies the reward of mitzvos. The distress generated on account of his *yiras Shamayim* is the reason why "He who is commanded and fulfills [the command] is greater than he who fulfills it even though he is not commanded." This distress that results from his *yiras Shamayim* is also included in the axiom, "The reward is in proportion to the exertion" (*Avos* 5:26). Moreover, it is self-evident that even in the category of "one who is commanded and fulfills," not everyone is equal in the amount of worry and anguish experienced in the fulfillment of the mitzvah. The intensity of disquiet is commensurate with the level of *yiras Shamayim* that the man has acquired. The magnitude of worry and disquiet in the fulfillment of mitzvos is determined by the quality of *yiras Shamayim*.

Likewise, the more *yiras Shamayim* one possesses — the more worry and disquiet he will feel, lest he transgress and not fulfill one of the Divine commandments or not perform the mitzvah according to specification. In proportion to the degree of *yirah*, worry, and disquiet that he feels in regards to fulfilling the Divine will — to that degree, his reward will be dramatically elevated and exalted, for "the reward is in proportion to the exertion."

On the contrary, if his spiritual status is low, he will be subject to the converse of this axiom. If he is devoid of *yiras Shamayim*, then ostensibly he will only receive reward for the mitzvos that he performs as one "who fulfills even though he is not commanded." As we mentioned, the preeminence of "one who is commanded and fulfills" over "one who fulfills even though he is not commanded" is solely his worry and disquiet that he may come to transgress. However, one who does not have *yiras Shamayim* within his heart, does not worry or feel anguish at the thought that he might transgress. Consequently, even the mitzvos that he performs will only be rewarded according to the status of "one who fulfills even though he is not commanded." After all, of what quality is his mitzvah, if he does not worry and anguish over fulfilling the Divine will?

GREATER IF COMMANDED

In light of this, we can explain the words of the Talmud (*Avodah Zarah* 2b): "Rav Yosef taught [the verse], ' "He stands and shakes the earth, He sees and releases the nations." What did he see? He saw that the nations did not observe the seven mitzvos that the *b'nei Noach* had accepted. Since they did not fulfill them, He [Hashem] stood and released them from their obligations.' [Asks the Gemara:] If Hashem released them from their obligations, then they benefited by the violation of the commandments — according to this, a sinner will be benefiting! [Mar bar Ravina answers], 'The release from these commandments means only that even if they observed them, they would not be rewarded.' What is meant [by Mar bar Ravina] is that they are rewarded not as greatly as one who is commanded, but as one who is not commanded and fulfills. For Rebbi Chanina said, 'He who is commanded and fulfills [the command] is greater than he who fulfills it even though he is not commanded.' "

Now, we understand that they are deserving of punishment for not upholding the seven mitzvos allotted to the b'nei Noach. However, why should they receive the double punishment of having their reward diminished, since they will only receive the reward accorded to "one who fulfills even though he is not commanded"?

We can answer this question according to the concept that we presented above. The worry and anguish engender the superior reward of "one who is commanded and fulfills," because of the thought that he may come to transgress. Now, Hashem saw that the nations did not uphold their seven mitzvos. Therefore, it was clear that they had no desire to bear the yoke of the Divine will. Consequently, they did not worry nor feel any anguish whatsoever over fulfilling the commandments of Hashem. Therefore, even if they would fulfill a particular mitzvah, their reward would only be in accordance with those who fulfill even though they are not commanded.

THE REWARD OF AVRAHAM

In light of this, we can understand the following words of Chazal (Bava Metzia 86b): "Rav Yehudah said in the name of Rav: Everything that Avraham personally did for the ministering angels, HaKadosh Baruch Hu personally did for his descendents. And whatever Avraham did through a messenger, HaKadosh Baruch Hu did for his descendents through a messenger. [Therefore, we see in the Chumash,] 'And Avraham ran to the herd' — 'And a wind went forth from Hashem.' 'And he took butter and milk' — 'Behold, I will rain bread from heaven for you.' 'And he stood by them under the tree' — 'Behold, I will stand before you there upon the rock.' 'And Avraham went with them to bring them on the way' — 'And Hashem went before them by day.' 'Let a little water, I pray, be brought' — 'And you shall smite the rock, and water shall come out of it, that the people may drink.' "

The phenomenal reward that Avraham received for one act of hospitality is amazing. This deed of kindness brought about all the miracles and wonders that Hashem did for our ancestors in the desert: He caused the manna to descend for them; He sent them the quail; He sent forth water from the rock; He went before them in the pillar of cloud by day. All of these miracles were bestowed in the merit of this mitzvah that Avraham performed. How awesome is this reward! Is every man who performs a good deed but once entitled to such reward?

As we mentioned, according to Tosafos, worry and anguish over fulfilling a mitzvah compound the reward, as expressed by the axiom, "He who is commanded and fulfills [the command] is greater than he who fulfills it even though he is not commanded." This worry and anguish emanates from the power of *yiras Shamayim*; the intensity of his worry and anguish that he might transgress is proportional to the magnitude of his *yiras Shamayim*. It is known that *yiras Hashem* has neither measure, nor boundary, nor end, nor limit. Chazal (*Niddah* 13a) tell us that even the Amora'im had a profound level of fear, for they said, "The fear of Hashem was upon him [Rav Yehudah]. For Shmuel said regarding him [Rav Yehudah], 'This man is not born from a women.' " In other words, because of the great fear that Rav Yehudah had of the Divine majesty, Shmuel praised him by comparing him to an angel of Hashem, as he stated, "This man is not born from a women." Rav Yehudah was likened to the angels, who are separate from all physicality and without corporal substance. Therefore, it is easy for them to comprehend the exalted holiness of Hashem. Consequently, they fear and shake with the ultimate magnitude of *yiras Shamayim*.

If this was the level of *yirah* of the Amora'im, we can only imagine the level of fear of our holy *avos*, who were exalted many levels above the Amora'im. We can estimate the difference between the Amora'im and the earlier generation of the Tanna'im; between the Tann'aim and the Nevi'im; and finally all the way back to the *avos*. How awesome was their fear! It was equivalent to the fear of the *serafim*, *ofanim*, and holy *chayos*. Chazal (*Tanna D'Bei Eliyahu*) explain the verse, "Do not fear, Avraham" — " 'Do not fear' is only said to someone who truly has *yiras Shamayim*."

Now we are no longer astonished at the phenomenal reward of our holy *avos*; namely, for the one mitzvah that Avraham performed, Hashem bestowed unlimited bounty, goodness, deliverance, and blessing upon his descendents. Just as we cannot envision the impassioned *yirah* of the angels, so, too, we cannot fathom the impassioned *yirah* of Avraham. The depth of his worry and anguish over the fulfillment of mitzvos is commensurate with the magnitude of his fear. Therefore, the reward of his mitzvos is infinitely increased, as "the reward is in proportion to the exertion."[7]

THE TREASURE OF YIRAS SHAMAYIM

We now are enlightened to understand the inestimable treasure that is hidden within *yiras Shamayim* — for a man who is permeated with this fear. The first advantage of *yiras Shamayim* is that it is the cause of observance and fulfillment of all the Torah and mitzvos. Moreover, a mitzvah that is performed with *yiras Shamayim* — where one fears and trembles at the notion that he might transgress — is accorded substantially amplified reward. This worry and anguish that he might sin is equivalent to other types of difficulty that challenge a man in his Divine service. It is included within the principal, "The reward is in proportion to the exertion." Each man is judged according to his level, because he does not assign the same value to each mitzvah. Some mitzvos are very important in his eyes, and he will not transgress them, regardless of circumstance. Whereas, other mitzvos are minor in his eyes. It is self-evident that the mitzvos about which he fears and trembles more, lest he sin, will be accorded abundant reward.

THE NEGLECT OF TORAH STUDY

We should carefully consider the mitzvah of Torah study, which is accorded the greatest reward of all mitzvos. However, there is something that can destructively diminish the reward of this great mitzvah. Chazal teach in the *Sifri*, "Just as the reward of Torah study is the greatest reward of all mitzvos, so, too, neglect of Torah study is the greatest sin of all the sins." Nev-

---

7   Since he had the ultimate level of *yiras Shamayim*, he had the highest level of worry concerning the fulfillment of mitzvos. This worry is equivalent to the difficulty in performing the mitzvos, the factor that amplifies the reward. Therefore, his unbounded reward reflects his unbounded level of *yiras Shamayim*.

ertheless, we see in the world that the neglect of Torah study is perceived as the least severe of all the sins. If a person happens to neglect a mitzvah — davening, for instance, or neglecting to put on tefillin — he will be profoundly distressed. Whereas, if he neglects Torah study for a period of time, even if there is no reason for his laxity, he will be neither concerned nor worried whatsoever. Only certain, special people, who Hashem has blessed, will consider the neglect of Torah study as severe as other sins. The reason for this leniency is because permission is given to neglect Torah study, for example, if one has to make a living or to perform a mitzvah that is impossible for anyone else to do. Nevertheless, to some people, this mitzvah is in the category of "one who fulfills it even though he is not commanded." He thinks he has the mitzvah "in the basket": if he wants, he will learn, and if he doesn't want, he won't learn, as Tosafos explained in *Kiddushin*. Therefore, since his worry over the fulfillment of this mitzvah is neutralized, the reward is diminished. Therefore, how significant is the effort to upgrade the mitzvah of Torah study to be equivalent, at least, to the seriousness of other mitzvos, as well as viewing the neglect of Torah study as as grave a sin as the neglect of other mitzvos. The advice to accomplish this awareness is to learn *sifrei Mussar* which elaborate on the severity of *bitul Torah*. The in-depth study of the laws of Torah study is also beneficial to instill within oneself the importance of Torah study. The Admor, *zt"l*, wrote about this in the *Iggeres HaMussar*.

THE VALUE OF TORAH UNDER DURESS

Now, let us return to the midrash that we mentioned at the beginning of this essay. The wife of Rebbi Shimon ben Chalafta refused to accept the gem that Hashem gave to her husband. She insisted that her husband return the gem to Heaven so that his table should not be lacking in the World to Come. However, she feared not only that the benefit of the miracle would be subtracted from his merits, but that even more would be lost, as Rebbi Chalafta was extremely poor, and he learned Torah under duress. The worth of such learning is explained in *Avos D'Rebbi Nosson*: "If you learned Torah in times of comfort, do not abandon it in times of pressure. For man receives more reward for one mitzvah done with difficulty, than a hundred mitzvos done with ease." Now, once Heaven gave him the gemstone, he was able to learn Torah with ease. His pious wife was concerned that he would lose the sublime reward of learning Torah under duress. Therefore, she shook with this extraordinary fear and exhorted her husband to return the gem to Heaven. She elected to live in poverty and distress in order that her husband would continue to have the merit of learning Torah under duress.

UNIQUE REWARD

Let us explain her cryptic response to Rebbi, "Does one man see another in the World to Come? Does not every man have a world for himself?" Apparently, the delight and pleasure of the World to Come is not limited to the same pleasure for each mitzvah. Just as there is a diverse assortment of pleasures in this world, so, too, there is an expansive variation of spiritual delights granted for each mitzvah. Likewise, the magnitude of reward for each mitzvah varies according to the difficulty of the mitzvah — "The reward is in proportion to the exertion." The level of difficulty also generates a different type of spiritual pleasure and delight. In each tzaddik's world of reward there are various spiritual pleasures and delights in accordance with the mitzvos he did in his lifetime. The difficulty of the mitzvah also affects the magnitude and kind of reward. The tzaddik delights in his world with various spiritual pleasures according to the number of mitzvos he has performed, the reward of each mitzvah being more pleasurable than all the combined pleasure of all the delights of this world.

INDEPENDENT WORLDS

This is what the wife of Rebbi Shimon ben Chalafta meant when she said, "Does not every man have a world for himself?" A unique spiritual delight and pleasure is designated for each mitzvah. It is clearly understood that the reward of each tzaddik will be customized for him alone. Even if a man is a lesser tzaddik than another is, his reward may be greater. For instance, if the quality of one of his mitzvos is greater in and of itself or greater because of the difficult circumstances under which it was performed, his reward for that mitzvah will be greater than the bigger *tzaddik*'s. Therefore, it is necessary for each *tzaddik* to have his own independent world. He is not permitted to enter the domain of another *tzaddik*, even into the realm of a *tzaddik* that is smaller than him. He cannot experience the pleasure and delight of a mitzvah that his friend performed, because he could not possibly perform the mitzvah in the same way as his friend. This is the rhetoric of the pious woman, "Does one man see another in the World to Come?" In other words, each *tzaddik* has his own world — and no other *tzaddik* is granted permission to enter the domain of his friend.

Rabbeinu HaKadosh was undoubtedly on a higher level than Rebbi Shimon ben Chalafta. However, Rebbi Shimon excelled in one mitzvah, more than Rabbeinu HaKadosh; namely, he learned Torah under duress. Rebbi Shimon ben Chalafta was so impoverished that he did not have food for Shabbos, whereas Rabbeinu HaKadosh was extraordinarily wealthy, as taught in the Talmud (*Bava Metzia* 85a), "Rebbi's house steward was wealthier than King Shappur." Therefore, since he did not worry about sustenance whatsoever, he did not learn Torah under duress. We explained that the reason why the wife of Rebbi Shimon ben Chalafta refused to accept the gem that was given to her husband from Heaven was because she valued the exalted reward of learning Torah under duress; she elected to live in poverty. Therefore, when Rabbeinu HaKadosh said to Rebbi Shimon ben Chalafta, "Go back and tell your wife, that if anything will be lacking from your table, I will replenish it from mine," a question arises. There is a unique reward of pleasure and delight for each mitzvah, as well as the reward variation engendered by the factor of difficulty. If so, how could Rabbeinu HaKadosh replace the reward for learning Torah under duress with his reward? Since he was a man of great wealth, he never performed the mitzvah of learning Torah under duress!

This was the response of the wife of Rebbi Shimon ben Chalafta to Rabbeinu HaKadosh. Her mouth spoke with wisdom, "Master, does one man see another in the World to Come? Does not every man have a world for himself?" [She was making the following point:] Why does every *tzaddik* have his own world? Is it not because the reward for each mitzvah is a unique pleasure and delight? Likewise, the level of difficulty engenders a unique reward.

Therefore, each *tzaddik* cannot enter to see the world of reward of his friend. Since Rabbeinu HaKadosh was extraordinarily wealthy, and he learned Torah in comfort, how could he replace the lack of reward for Torah learned under duress with his reward of Torah learned in comfort?

Article Nine

RELIANCE ON HASHEM

THE HELP OF HASHEM

THE TALMUD (*Sukkah* 52b) TEACHES, "Rav Shimon ben Lakish said: The *yetzer hara* of a man grows in strength from day to day and seeks to kill him, as it is written, 'The wicked watches for the righteous and seeks to slay him.' And were it not that *HaKadosh Baruch Hu* is his help, he would not be able to withstand it [the *yetzer hara*], as it is said, 'Hashem will not leave him in his hand, nor will He condemn him when he is judged.' "

MAN CANNOT DEFEAT THE YETZER HARA WITHOUT DIVINE ASSISTANCE

A deep question arises from this passage in the Talmud: Why did Hashem create man in such a way that he does not have the power to defeat his *yetzer hara* without the help of Hashem? Why did Hashem grant such power and strength to the *yetzer hara*, that man cannot defeat him without His assistance? What is the advantage of pitting man against such an overwhelming challenge? The Admor, *zt"l*, touched on this topic in *Etz Pri* [a publication that included an article of Rav Yisrael on strengthening the study of Torah].

The verse says, "You shall love Hashem, your God, with all your heart..." (*Devarim* 6:5). The Talmud (*Berachos* 54a) explains this verse, " 'You shall love Hashem, your God, with all your heart' — with both of your inclinations, with the good inclination and the evil inclination." We know the two pillars of Divine service that uphold the entire Torah and its mitzvos are *yiras Shamayim* and *ahavas Hashem*. The Rambam writes (*Hilchos Yesodei HaTorah* 2:1) that both *yiras Shamayim* and *ahavas Hashem* are positive commandments: "It is a mitzvah to love and fear Hashem, the most honored and the most revered, as it says, 'You shall love Hashem, your God,' and it says, 'You shall fear the Lord your God.'"

TWO ASPECTS OF YIRAS SHAMAYIM

Indeed, *yiras Shamayim* is comprised of two aspects, which the Sages, well versed in *yiras Shamayim*, defined as *yiras ha'onesh* (fear of Divine retribution) and *yiras haromemus* (awe of the Divine Majesty). Also, the *Chovos HaLevavos* (*Sha'ar Ahavah* 6) writes, "There are two kinds of *yirah*. One of these is fear of His punishments and trials. The second [kind of fear of Hashem] is awe, inspired by His magnitude, sanctity, and awesome power." Likewise the *Mesillas Yesharim* (ch. 24) writes, "There is *yiras haromemus* and *yiras ha'onesh*. *Yiras ha'onesh* is self-evident: man fears transgressing the commandments of Hashem, his God, because of the punishments to both body and soul. Whereas, *yiras haromemus* is when man distances himself [from sin] and will not commit sins because of the awesome majesty of Hashem."

TWO ASPECTS OF AHAVAS HASHEM

Just as there are two aspects of *yiras Hashem*, so, too, there are two aspects of *ahavas Hashem* (love of Hashem): *ahavas hatov* (love of the Divine good), and *ahavas haromemus* (love of the Divine majesty). *Ahavas hatov* is the love of the Creator that is inspired by the good favors and kindness that He continuously bestows upon man, whereas *ahavas haromemus* is to love Hashem because of His exalted honor and majesty. The *Chovos HaLevavos* (*Sha'ar Ahavah* 2) writes, "How many kinds of love of God are there? A servant's love for his master will be one of three kinds.... Analogously, we may love Hashem on account of His abounding kindness and constant goodness towards us; our soul may be bound to Him with love because of the hope of reward; or we may love Him on account of His very essence, to magnify Him and exalt Him. This is the pure love of Hashem."

AHAVAS HATOV

Now, just as *yiras ha'onesh* is the fear of punishments to both body and soul, so, too, *ahavas hatov* is the love of the Creator engendered by His goodness and kindness to the body with pleasures of this world, as well as the goodness and kindness to the soul in the World to Come. The reward of the World to Come is the unbounded recompense that is stored away for those who observe the Divine will. These are the two aspects of love referred to in the passage of *Chovos HaLevavos* that we mentioned: "We may love Hashem on account of His abounding kindness and constant goodness towards us." These are the physical pleasures. He then writes, "Our soul may be bound to Him with love because of the hope of reward." This is the good that Hashem bestows upon the souls, the goodly reward that He grants to those who fear Him.

DIFFERENCE BETWEEN YIRAS HA'ONESH AND AHAVAS HATOV

However, there is a significant difference between *yiras ha'onesh* and *ahavas hatov*. When reflecting upon *yiras ha'onesh*, it becomes clear that man fears punishment to his soul more than punishment to his body. This is because he believes that sinners receive Divine retribution in the Next World, where there is no hope to flee or escape. However, when considering bodily punishments for transgressions in this world, his response is less intense. The reason for this weaker reaction is due to the fact that the ways of Hashem are concealed in this world. It seems, sometimes, that wicked individuals and men of leisure attain success, whereas the soul of the righteous suffers from tribulations. The wicked continue to live in their wickedness, whereas the righteous expire despite their goodness. Yirmeyahu the Prophet lamented over this, "Why do the ways of the wicked succeed?"

However, when man reflects upon *ahavas hatov*, the love he feels for the Creator because of all the good He bestows upon him, man rejoices more over the physical pleasures than the spiritual reward. The reason is because he constantly experiences these tangible pleasures. With but minimal contemplation, regardless of his situation, everyone will perceive and discern that every second of his life he is the recipient of unbounded goodness from his Creator.

Let man not say that all the goodness of this world is "futility of futilities," and that all the physical pleasures and delights are worthless and base. Neither should he think that to be blessed with wealth, possessions, and honor is emptiness and futility. Again, let him not profess: Is it proper to base one's love for Hashem on the material gifts, which are nothing more than deceptive worthlessness? Is this not like a small child who appreciates and loves someone who gives him a simple toy? Should man love Hashem in this way? Does the Divine King benefit from this type of love?

REMEMBER THE KINDNESS OF HASHEM

On the contrary, Hashem wants man to continuously recognize and contemplate the unbounded goodness and kindness that He bestows upon him — for the more man is aware of these favors, the more he is inspired to appreciate and love Hashem. As it states in *Sha'arei Teshuvah* (3:17), "It is a virtue to remember the kindnesses of Hashem and to contemplate them, as the verse says, 'And you shall remember all the way...' (*Devarim* 8:2). And David HaMelech said, 'Your kindness is before my eyes' (*Tehillim* 26:3)."

Chazal (*Berachos* 54a) refer to this concept, " 'You shall love Hashem, your God, with all your heart' — with both of your inclinations, with the good inclination and the evil inclination." This passage reveals that the two inclinations engender the two kinds of love that we mentioned: namely, *ahavas hatov*, which is to love Hashem for the goodness and kindness that He bestows upon man, and *ahavas haromemus*, which is to love Hashem because of His exalted honor and majesty. The force of the *yetzer tov* establishes *ahavas haromemus*. For *ahavas haromemus* is awakened exclusively by the power of wisdom and understanding that fathoms and apprehends the exalted majesty of Hashem. [See Letter Thirty, where the *yetzer tov* is defined as the intellect.]

The Rambam (*Hilchos Yesodei HaTorah* 2:2) teaches this, "What is the path to the love and fear of Hashem? When man contemplates His wondrous and magnificent deeds and creations, and is awestruck by His infinite wisdom...immediately he loves and praises Hashem." This is the force of the *yetzer hatov*, the intellectual powers, which give rise to the love of Hashem with the *yetzer hatov* [through appreciation of the exalted majesty of Hashem].

AWAKENING AHAVAS HASHEM

However, the love of Hashem that is awakened from the ample kindness and constant goodness of bestowing material favors upon man has two components. The first is the love of Hashem for the spiritual aspects of the physical, and the second is the love of Hashem awakened by the gratification of the *yetzer hara* and bodily desire. Moreover, the more the heart of man loves and desires the benefits and pleasures of this world, the more he will love Hashem for bestowing favors of this world upon him, satisfying his desire. Therefore, this love of Hashem that is awakened by the granting of material gifts is called "love with the *yetzer hara*." Chazal refer to this in the passage we mentioned, "You shall love Hashem, your God, with all your heart — with both of your inclinations, with the good inclination and the evil inclination." This teaches that you have to love Hashem with the two aspects of love. Love of Hashem is based both on the *ahavas haromemus*, which is with the *yetzer hatov*, as well as the *ahavas hatov*, which is with the *yetzer hara* — the love of Hashem that is inspired by His bestowal of the physical favors.

The same principal applies to praise, blessing, and prayer to Hashem for the granting of all the earthly needs of this world. It is the Divine will that man endeavors to recognize, contemplate, and thank Hashem for His bountiful goodness and kindness; to bless Hashem for each particular pleasure that he enjoys in this world. The Talmud (*Berachos* 35a) speaks about this, "It is forbidden for man to benefit from this world without making a blessing." Even though all the pleasures of this world are worthless and hollow in and of themselves, nevertheless, Hashem desires that we bless Him for these pleasures. Hashem also desires that we constantly beseech mercy from Him that He fulfills our needs, desires, and requests of our heart. Call out and Hashem will answer.

TRUST IN HASHEM

This concept is taught in the Midrash (*Eichah* 3:9): "The Lord is good to all those who trust in Him, to the soul that seeks Him" (*Eichah* 3:25). Says the midrash, "Could it be that Hashem is good to all? [Rather, the Torah teaches that Hashem is good] to the soul that seeks Him." This is faith in Hashem, as expressed in many verses; namely, that man should not rely on his fellow, rather his trust should be only in Hashem: "Blessed is the man who trusts in Hashem..." (*Yirmeyahu* 17:7). Let's imagine that a benefactor promises to provide the needs of a poor man, and he fulfills his commitment by constantly supplying these necessities. Would it be proper for the poor man to plead every day with his benefactor not to terminate his kindness, and not to leave him without bread? Surely, this would be improper conduct and a breach of *derech eretz*. Therefore, since Hashem commands man to place his trust in Him, and Hashem constantly satisfies the desire of every living thing — therefore, one might think it is also unnecessary to always beseech mercy from Hashem.

THE PREREQUISITE OF PRAYER

However, this is a fallacy, because faith alone is not sufficient. Rather, the Divine will decrees that together with faith, man must pray and continually petition for mercy from Hashem to provide his needs. If he follows this path, his eyes will be turned to Hashem — to find favor before Him — so that He fulfills the requests of his heart for good. For this reason, the *avos hakadoshim* instituted prayer three times a day. This is the meaning of the midrash, "The Lord is good to all those who trust in Him; to the soul that seeks Him." The midrash had asked, "Could it be that Hashem is good to all?" meaning, even to a person who does not pray to Hashem at all? Is it conceivable that man only needs to hope and trust in Hashem, with prayer not being necessary? Therefore, the Torah teaches, "to the soul that seeks Him," meaning, together with faith it is also necessary to constantly seek and pray to Him. If you seek Him, you will find Him.

REMEMBER HASHEM

The reason Hashem obligates man to actively strengthen his faith and persist in prayer is solely for the benefit of man. Hashem, Who is exalted beyond all blessing and praise — and everything is revealed before Him — does not need the praise of man. Yet we know that the purpose of man's creation in this world is only to enable him to receive benefit in the Next World, to grant him the inheritance of eternal life and everlasting joy. There in the World of Recompense, he will receive the fruits of his efforts and exertions for Torah and mitzvos. This concept is taught in *Mesillas Yesharim* (ch. 24). Clearly, the mitzvah to "Watch yourself, lest you forget the Lord, your God" (*Devarim* 6:12) serves the same purpose as prayer, as Rabbeinu Yonah wrote in *Sha'arei Teshuvah*, "Through this mitzvah, we are exhorted to always remember Hashem." This means that when man continuously reflects on Hashem, he will proceed in the straight paths of Hashem — observing Torah and mitzvos. This is the first halachah in the *Shulchan Aruch*, " 'I place Hashem ever before me' — this is a primary axiom of the Torah, and [fulfilled in] the exalted level of the *tzaddikim*."

MAN IS DISTRACTED

However, since the soul of man is imprisoned within the body, and "man's heart is evil from his youth" (*Bereishis* 8:21), and his heart is attracted to earthly passions — man is apt to forget Hashem and to stray from the path of Torah and mitzvos. Therefore, Hashem wisely opened a path for man through which his interaction with the physical actually serves to constantly remind him of Hashem. It is for this reason that Hashem commands man to always pray to Him and to plead for mercy that Hashem provide his needs. Likewise, man must always remember the constant lovingkindness and unbounded goodness of Hashem, thank Him for the kindness that He bestows, and bless Hashem for each pleasure that he enjoys in this world.

THE MANNA

The Talmud (*Yoma* 76a) refers to this concept: "Rebbi Shimon ben Yochai's disciples asked him, 'Why didn't the manna fall just one time a year?' He replied, 'I will answer you by way of a parable: There was a king who had a son. Initially, the king decided to give the boy a yearly allowance for his food. As a result, however, the king saw him only one time a year. Therefore, the king decided to provide for his needs on a daily basis, and he then saw the boy every day. So, too, with Israel. A person who had four or five children would worry and say, "Perhaps the manna will not descend tomorrow, and they will all die of starvation!" As a result, all [of the Jewish people] would direct their hearts to their Father in Heaven.' "

This text is astonishing: the generation that was redeemed from Egypt saw and experienced the exalted, awesome honor of Hashem. Assuredly, their Divine service was on the highest level of *yiras haromemus*. Why was it necessary to scare and alarm them even more with the lower level of *yiras ha'onesh* — that perhaps they will die through starvation?

Yet Hashem's intention was not to scare them through *yiras ha'onesh*, the threat of starvation, in order to force them to perform *avodas Hashem*. Rather, for every man, according to his level of *yirah*, it is required that *yiras Hashem* be ever apparent on his countenance, so that he does not forget Hashem even for a brief moment, as the verse says, "Guard yourself, lest you forget the Lord, your God." However, man is likely to forget. Therefore, Hashem places man in a position to always need the kindness of Hashem in order to attain his material needs, and He commands that we pray and plead for mercy. This dependency on Hashem then becomes the cause that man does not forget Him. Consequently, man will perform his Divine worship, according to his appropriate level of *yiras Shamayim*. This is the meaning of the passage, " 'Perhaps the manna will not descend tomorrow, and they will all die of starvation!' As a result, all [of the Jewish people] would direct their hearts to their Father in Heaven." The fear that perhaps the manna will not descend tomorrow was the just the impetus to remember Hashem, in order that they "would direct their hearts to their Father in Heaven" every day. They would pray to Him, plead for mercy from Him, and always thank Him for His unbounded kindness. As a result, their Divine worship was in accordance with their exalted levels of *yiras haromemus* and *ahavas Hashem*.

DEPENDENCE ON HASHEM

Now we can understand the words of Chazal (*Sukkah* 52b), "The *yetzer hara* of a man grows in strength from day to day and seeks to kill him, as it is written, 'The wicked watches for the righteous and seeks to slay him.' And were it not that *HaKadosh Baruch Hu* is his help, he would not be able to withstand it [the *yetzer hara*]." It is astonishing that Hashem gave so much more power and strength to the *yetzer hara* than He gave to man, that man cannot defeat the *yetzer hara* without Divine assistance. The answer to this mystery is as follows: Indeed, Hashem provides all the material needs of man. Therefore, man is always dependent on the kindness and goodness of Hashem, and he must constantly plead for mercy. This dependency on Hashem causes him to constantly remember Hashem and to proceed on the proper path — the observance of Torah and mitzvos. However, regarding spiritual matters of Divine service, there was nothing to serve as an impetus to remind him of Hashem. Since man has free choice, he had no real dependence on Hashem.

Therefore, Hashem, in His wisdom, saw that it would be advantageous to bind the hand of man, so that in spiritual matters he also cannot progress without the help of Hashem. Therefore, Hashem gave sufficient strength and power to the *yetzer hara* to subdue man, unless Hashem grants assistance. Now that man needs the help of Hashem, he must continuously pray and beseech Hashem for mercy so that Hashem does not abandon him to his *yetzer hara*. How many supplications David HaMelech offered over spiritual matters! Likewise, we pray every day, "Let not the evil inclination dominate us...." Indeed, man has free choice, therefore, this concept is based on the aforementioned idea, "...and were it not that *HaKadosh Baruch Hu* is his help, he would not be able to withstand it." Nevertheless, this does not refute free choice whatsoever, for when man does as much as he can to defeat the *yetzer hara*, even if the *yetzer* has the superior power, nonetheless, Hashem will help and not abandon him to the *yetzer hara*.

Since man is dependent on Divine assistance for every aspect of his life, he must continuously pray and beseech Hashem for mercy, both for his physical and spiritual needs. Consequently, both his physical and spiritual needs serve to help him always look to Hashem, and not to forget Him, even for a brief moment.

Article Ten

PLIMO

SATAN VISITS

THE FOLLOWING PASSAGE IS FOUND in the Talmud (*Kiddushin* 81a, b): "Plimo was accustomed to say everyday, 'Arrows in the eyes of Satan.' One day, on the eve of Yom Kippur, he [the *satan*] disguised himself as a poor man and went and called out at his [Plimo's] door. Bread was taken out to him. 'On a day such as this, when everybody is inside, shall I be left outside?' he asked. Therefore, he was brought inside the house, and bread was offered to him. He then said, 'On a day like this, when everyone sits at the table, shall I sit alone?' He was ushered [to the dining room] and sat down at the table. As he sat, his body became covered with festering boils, and he was behaving repulsively. 'Sit properly,' he [Plimo] rebuked him. He said, 'Give me a drink,' and was given one. He coughed and regurgitated into it [the cup]. He [Plimo] yelled at him, and he [the *satan*] fell and died. They then heard people calling out, 'Plimo has killed a man! Plimo has killed a man!' He [Plimo] fled and hid in a bathroom. He [the *satan*] followed him [and appeared to him in the bathroom.] When he [Plimo, saw the *satan*, Plimo] fell [in shock] before him. Seeing he was distressed, he [the *satan*] disclosed his identity and asked him, 'Why do you always speak those words ['Arrows in the eyes of Satan']?' [So Plimo asked,] 'Rather, what should I say?' [Responded the *satan*,] 'You should say, "Merciful One, rebuke Satan." ' "

Rashi comments: "Sit properly" — sit properly and do not act repulsively. "He coughed and regurgitated into it" — mucus that comes up from the lungs. "He yelled at him" — he rebuked him. "He fell" — he feigned death. "They heard people calling out, 'Plimo has killed a man!' " — he made a voice be heard coming from the outside, that the people of the house [should hear]. "Plimo fled" — he thought the officers of the king would come to kill him. "He hid in a bathroom" — outside the city. "He" — the *satan* saw that Plimo was distressed. "Why do you always speak those words ["Arrows in the eyes of Satan"]?" — why are you accustomed to curse me? "Rather, what should I say?" — to drive you away from me that you should not cause me to sin. It appears from Rashi's commentary that Plimo's habit of saying every day, "Arrows in the eyes of Satan," was intended to drive the *satan* away, so that he should not cause him to sin.

A CRYPTIC RIDDLE

This entire episode is a wondrous occurrence — an enigmatic, cryptic riddle. [We must ask the following questions about this incident:] 1) Why did Plimo curse the *satan* on a daily basis? Is this a required practice to be victorious in the war against the *yetzer hara*? 2) The *satan* is an angelic spirit. Is he subject to anger and wrath? Does he descend to earth and assume a physical form, and walk about like a regular man? Moreover, does he perform wonders and frightful tactics in order to take revenge — in this case against Plimo — by scaring him with murder charges and the fear of death? Does the *satan* take revenge? Is he prone to hostility? Isn't anger relegated exclusively to physical beings, who are formed of the earth? 3) Furthermore, how do we understand the repulsive behavior of the *satan*? For instance, after Plimo asked him to sit properly, the *satan* requested a drink and then regurgitated into the cup. This disgusting act did not serve his purpose of reprisal. Nor was there any retaliation accomplished when he feigned death and caused a voice to declare, "Plimo has killed a man." It seems like these antics were little more than foolish pranks. Is the *satan* a jester, who took pleasure by ridiculing Plimo? 4) Why did he choose to bring all this about on *erev* Yom Kippur, in lieu of any other festival? 5) What is the meaning of Plimo's statement to the *satan* at the end of the story, "Rather, what should I say?" Is there no other way to defeat the *satan* than by cursing him? We also need to explain many other strange events in this incident.

Let us now address all of the difficulties that we thus far pointed out. First, we will explain why Plimo was in the practice of declaring every day, "Arrows in the eyes of Satan." It is important to realize that Plimo did not express this as a curse, for the wisest of men, Shlomo HaMelech, portrayed the relationship between the *yetzer hara* and the bodily forces as war between two enemies. In light of this, it says in *Koheles* (9:114): "There was a small city, and few men within it, and there came a great king against it, and surrounded it...." As Chazal taught in *Maseches Sukkah* (52a), "The evil inclination has seven names.... Shlomo called him 'enemy,' as the verse says, 'If your enemy is hungry....' " In *Chovos HaLevavos* it is written, "Man, it is fitting for you to know that the greatest enemy that you have in the world is your evil inclination.... He shoots his deadly arrows at you to uproot you from the land of the living..." (see the text).

REVENGE AND VICTORY

Indeed, we know from our nature how intense are the powers of revenge and the drive for victory within the heart of man. For instance, how consuming is his desire to seek revenge and to defeat his hated enemy who seeks to kill him. What's more, at the time of attack, when he sees his enemy face to face in the battlefield, the vehemence of revenge and victory is ignited within him. A spirit of courage awakens within his breast, and he girds himself with strength and tenacity to fight even until death. In this way, he is empowered to sometimes defeat a stronger foe.

Hence, it is a striking paradox: the evil inclination hates man with the epitome of animosity, and he plots evil against him the entire day, to ensnare him in a trap and to uproot him from the earth — yet man "walks with his evil inclination" in peace and serenity? Even if his physical eyes do not perceive the *yetzer hara*, nevertheless, the eyes of his intellect acknowledge him. Why doesn't man's heart burn with vengeance? Why is he not impassioned to conquer his evil inclination and to be victorious in the war, as would be the expected attitude towards any hated enemy? However, we should not be amazed at the indifference of man, for we are quite distant from sensing spiritual matters, and this war of the *yetzer hara* is not vividly imagined within our heart. Moreover, we have no concept of the true measure of spiritual reward and punishment.

THE WAR AGAINST THE EVIL INCLINATION

However, Plimo clearly envisioned this war with the evil inclination as an actual war between enemies. He girded himself in his war against the evil inclination with the power of revenge and the desire for victory. This was why he was accustomed to recite every day, "Arrows in the eyes of Satan." He would gloat before the evil inclination, threatening him that he would defeat him and shoot his arrows at him. In this way, he would gird himself with strength to conquer his evil inclination and be victorious in the war.

THE HELP OF HASHEM

Although it is essentially beneficial for man to desire, defeat, and take revenge against his evil inclination, Plimo went a bit beyond the acceptable parameters. For he boasted before the evil inclination — threatening to defeat him and to shoot arrows at him, declaring, "Arrows in the eyes of Satan." This is not consistent with the following statement of Chazal in *Maseches Sukkah* (52b): "The evil inclination of a man looks each day to kill him, and if not for the help of *HaKadosh Baruch Hu*, man would not be able to withstand it." Indeed, the strength and power of the evil inclination is, in truth, far superior to the strength of man. Man cannot really gloat in front of the evil inclination, for his own strength cannot save him. It is only within the power of the "right hand" of Hashem to conquer the *satan*. Only with the help of Hashem does man valiantly win this war. We have already written that all of these phenomena are intentionally initiated from the wisdom of Hashem, may His Name be blessed. He grants this potent strength and power to the evil inclination, so that man is unable to defeat him without help from Hashem, may He be blessed. Indeed, this mismatch is the impetus for man to direct his heart to his Father in Heaven; his eyes will always be lifted unto Him — for Hashem will not abandon him to the hand of his evil inclination. However, Plimo thought in truth that just as the *HaKadosh Baruch Hu* transferred the free choice to man, so, too, man has the inherent power and might to be able to defeat and conquer his evil inclination.

PEACE WITH HIS ENEMIES

Let us consider the statement of Chazal found in the *Midrash Rabbah* (ch. 54), "When Hashem is pleased with the ways of a man, even his enemies will be at peace with him." Says the midrash, "This refers to the evil inclination." It appears to me that this text does not mean that the evil inclination makes peace with man, withholding his hand from attacking him. Rather, the intention of the midrash is that even when the *yetzer hara* makes peace with man, nevertheless, he still hates the man with the epitome of detestation and wants to hurl burdens upon him, to uproot him from the land of the living.[8] Nevertheless, when Hashem is pleased with the ways of the man, then the evil inclination also makes peace with him. He becomes a friend to him and is happy to be defeated by man. Indeed, Plimo reached this level: Hashem was pleased with his ways, and the evil inclination made peace with him and became his friend.

THE TESTS OF PLIMO

The *satan* saw that Plimo erred in thinking that the power of his right hand alone was sufficient to defeat and subdue his evil inclination, without any assistance from Hashem, may His Name be blessed. Therefore, the *satan* arranged this entire episode, in my opinion, with the purpose of bringing Plimo to a great test in the paths of character traits. Specifically, to provoke him to anger, as we will now explain with the help of Hashem. He demonstrated to him that man does not have the inherent power to defeat the evil inclination. The power of the evil inclination is far superior to that of man. The *yetzer hara* has the capability to spread a net beneath the feet of the *yirei Shamayim* and all of Hashem's devoted servants, by means of horrifying tests, and to entrap them in his fortress. If Hashem does not guard the "small city,"

---

8 Even though the *yetzer hara* makes peace with a *tzaddik*, nevertheless, the *yetzer* does not have permission to abandon the purpose of his creation: to test man with severe trials. Therefore, on one hand, the *yetzer hara* attempts to destroy man, while on the other hand, he befriends the *tzaddik*, i.e., he helps him (like he helped Plimo), and he is happy to be defeated.

then immediately "the great king surrounds it" (cf. *Koheles* 9:14) — this is the evil inclination. The effort of man to guard himself from the onslaught of the *yetzer hara* is futile. Only Hashem, may His Name be blessed, can protect His devoted servants from being ensnared by the *satan*. He will not abandon them to the hand of their evil inclination. As Chazal stated, "The evil inclination of a man looks each day to destroy him, and if not for the help of *HaKadosh Baruch Hu*, man would not be able to withstand it."

THE REVELATION OF THE SATAN

Indeed, the *satan*'s revelation to Plimo was quite extensive. Since the *satan*, the evil inclination, made peace with Plimo and became his friend, he wanted to show him the ways in which he conducts himself with man. There was not one superfluous detail in this encounter. Concealed within this tale are riddles and parables that depict the tactics of the evil inclination. When the identity of this "poor man" was revealed to Plimo, he then comprehended and understood all the messages of the entire episode. Behold, I will now remove the veil that covers this tale and reveal the secret intentions, also presenting the riddles, parables, and their solutions. Indeed, I will sequentially review the story and clarify each point, with the help of Hashem.

WATCHFULNESS DURING THE TEN DAYS OF REPENTANCE

1) "One day, on the eve of Yom Kippur, he [the *satan*] disguised himself as a poor man…"

As we explained above, the *satan* drew Plimo to a test of his character traits, and specifically besieged him in the trait of anger. In reference to this, the *satan* deliberately chose the time of *erev* Yom Kippur, because during the Ten Days of Repentance man is obligated to straighten out his affairs and improve his deeds. Even concerning pious behavior, with which he does not usually conduct himself during the year, during the Ten Days of Repentance he must exercise caution. For instance, the first chapter of *Maseches Shabbos* (Yerushalmi) states, "Rav Chiya Rabbah instructed Rav, 'If you are able to eat the entire year in purity — eat in that state. If you are not able, then eat in purity seven days of the year.' " In *Rosh HaShanah*, the Rosh (end of note 14) cites the Ra'avyah who explains that these seven days are the seven days between Rosh HaShanah and Yom Kippur. Based on this, the Rosh wrote that there is a custom in Ashkenaz [the Jewish community in Germany] that even those people who do not refrain from eating gentile bread throughout the year, do refrain during the Ten Days of Repentance. Likewise, issues of character traits must be weighed with more seriousness during these days. How much more so is this true on the eve of this holy day! Therefore, the *satan* showed him that even on this day, he wields great strength and power to draw man to the grips of a test and to ensnare him in his fortress.

THE RESTRICTION OF THE SATAN

2) "He disguised himself as poor man and went and called out at his door…"

The Sages versed in the topic of *yirah* wrote an explanation of the following verse: "Surely, if you improve yourself, you will be forgiven. But if you do not improve yourself, sin rests at the door" (*Bereishis* 4:7). In this verse, Hashem informs Kayin of the confined power of the evil inclination. He is restricted in that he may not come "within the house" to tempt man to sin. He may only stand at the entrance to the house, like a poor man at the doorway. This is spoken about in the Talmud (*Sukkah* 52b), "First he [the *yetzer hara*] is called a 'passerby,' then he is called a 'guest,' then he is called a 'man' " (see the text there, with Rashi's commentary). This is the meaning of "sin rests at the door." When man hearkens a little bit to the voice of the evil inclination, so that he opens the door for him, the *yetzer hara* overpowers him to become a guest in his house. This is what the *satan* showed Plimo through parables and riddles. At first, he appeared to him as a poor man. He stood outside the door, and he called out for Plimo to open it, which we now understand.

THE SATAN ENSNARES WITH THE PHYSICAL ASPECT OF MITZVOS

3) "Bread was taken out to him. 'On a day such as this, when everybody is inside, shall I be left outside?' he asked. Therefore, he was brought inside the house, and bread was offered to him. He then said, 'On a day like this, when

everyone sits at the table, shall I sit alone?' He was ushered [to the dining room] and sat down at the table."

The pious Vilna Gaon, *zt"l*, wrote in his commentary on *Mishlei*, "It is not the way of the evil inclination to [immediately] force a person to sin; rather, at first he shows him love. When the evil inclination sees that he cannot overpower the person, he attempts to draw him into his net. Then he begins to tempt him to perform mitzvos that are relevant to bodily pleasures, for instance, mitzvos that involve eating and celebration. When he has become accustomed to enjoy the pleasures of the mitzvah, he then begins to draw him after the pleasures of this world."

Indeed, the evil inclination is tantamount to desire. The *satan* hinted to Plimo that he employs this tactic against man. For the evil inclination — in other words, "desire" — first called at the doorway and requested a piece of bread. Meaning that initially, desire requests mercy from man, as if to say that man should not totally neglect [his needs] in this world. When he opened the door for him and he brought him a piece of bread, he said to him, "On a day like this, when everyone sits at the table, shall I sit alone?" That is, on the eve of Yom Kippur it is a mitzvah to partake of a festive meal, as is explained in the Talmud and *poskim* (see the *Tosafos* in *Kesubos* 5a, beginning with the words, "Rather, they were accustomed to feast with chickens and fish"). This is what the *satan* said, "On a day like this...," meaning, "Isn't it a mitzvah to partake of a festive meal today?" He was conveying this message to Plimo by means of a parable and a riddle. We see the evil inclination — "desire" — initially only requested a piece of bread. Shortly afterwards, however, he began to draw him into the net of a mitzvah that has an element of bodily pleasure.

THE EVIL INCLINATION ONLY GOES TO A PLACE OF FILTH

4) "As he sat, his body became covered with festering boils."

Let us refer to the explanation of the Vilna Gaon on a passage from the Talmud (*Berachos* 61a). The Gaon asks why the Talmud compared the evil inclination to a fly, as the verse says, "Dead flies putrefy the perfumer's oil" (*Koheles* 10:1). The Vilna Gaon explains that a fly only rests on a foul place.

Likewise, the evil inclination only goes to a place of filth. This is what the *satan* hinted to Plimo when he clothed himself in a physical form. He was covered with festering boils, for he only dwells in a place of blemish.

THE YETZER HARA HAS NO FEAR OF MAN

5) "...He was behaving repulsively. 'Sit properly,' he [Plimo] rebuked him. He said, 'Give me a drink,' and was given one. He coughed and regurgitated into it [the cup]."

Let us explain the symbolism of the Talmud likening the *yetzer hara* to a fly. All animals and birds naturally fear man, as the verse says, "Your fear and dread will be over them." Therefore, conceivably when man drives the animals away, they will not be quick to return. The one exception to this rule is flies; they do not fear man. When man brushes flies away from his face, in but a moment they return and land on his face again. There is no method of driving them off, short of constantly waving them away. This is the intention of Chazal likening the *yetzer hara* to a fly: to impart to us that the *yetzer hara* has no fear of man. Even if man rebukes and drives away the *yetzer hara*, in practically the next second he will be upon him.

The only sure advice is not to lose sight of him for a second and to constantly drive him away. The Talmud (*Berachos* 10b) alludes to this, "And she said to her husband, 'Behold, now I know that he is a holy man of God.'" Ask Chazal, "How did she know this? Because she never saw a fly pass over his table [she knew, therefore, that the prophet, Elisha, was a holy man.]" The *yetzer hara* is analogous to a fly. The holy prophet was not influenced by the *yetzer hara*; therefore, she never saw a fly pass over his table.[9]

This is what the *satan* showed Plimo. He is like a fly and it is hard to drive him away. When he did repulsive things, Plimo said to him, "Sit properly." Yet he did not fear whatsoever. The very next instant he demanded a cup and regurgitated into it.

---

9   See the Talmud (*Berachos* 61a): "Rav said: The *yetzer hara* resembles a fly and dwells between the two entrances to the heart, as the verse says, 'Dead flies putrefy the perfumer's oil' (*Koheles* 10:1). Shmuel said: It is similar to a species of wheat [*chitah*], as it says, 'Sin [*chet*, which means 'sin,' closely resembles the word *chitah*, 'wheat'] rests at the door.' "

THE ENORMITY OF THE SATAN'S POWER

6) "He [Plimo] yelled at him."

According to the flow of the story, Plimo first spoke gently to the *satan*, telling him to "sit properly." Rashi explains this as follows: Plimo told the *satan* to sit properly and to stop acting repulsively. Afterwards, Plimo gave him a drink, and he regurgitated into the cup. At that point, "He yelled at him." Rashi comments that this implies that he raised his voice, and in reaction to this "he [the *satan*] fell and died." Rashi explains that he feigned death, meaning that he acted as if he was so terrified and stunned from Plimo's reprimand — that he suddenly died.

It appears that the main goal of the *satan* was to perturb and anger Plimo, to incite him until he verbally rebuked him. Indeed, he brought a formidable test upon Plimo: a destitute stranger is invited to join the family for a meal and displays the most offensive behavior. When Plimo requests that he act properly, this "guest" demands a drink and then regurgitates into the cup. He persists in this revolting conduct until he disgusts the diners.

However, we know that the path of true humility is not to become angry over any provocation whatsoever. The Talmud (*Shabbos* 30) tells us of the humility of Hillel. A certain individual attempted to anger him with outrageous, disrespectful behavior. However, he was unable to agitate and anger Hillel at all. Therefore, according to the path of true humility, Plimo should not have reacted with anger and rebuke. Moreover, it was *erev* Yom Kippur, a time that demands an even higher level of piety in respect to virtues of character. The goal of the *satan* in this tale was to display the enormity of his power and strength to Plimo. Furthermore, he conspired to bring a great trial upon him, and to cause him to stumble into anger. The purpose of the *satan* was to stop Plimo from boasting about his dominion over him, as he was accustomed to say, "Arrows in the eyes of Satan." Since our holy, pious Sages were as pure as the ministering angels, even a slight flaw in any character virtue is an unspeakable downfall.

THE PHENOMENAL STRENGTH OF THE HUMAN SPIRIT

7) "He fell and died."

Rashi explains that he feigned death. Here, the *satan* revealed the phenomenal strength of the human spirit. In fact, sometimes man is stronger and, in fact, overpowers the *satan*. For when Hashem cursed the serpent, He said, "I will put enmity between you and the woman, and between your offspring and her offspring. He will pound your head, and you will bite his heel." Despite all the strength and power of the *yetzer hara* and the frailty of man, nevertheless, there is one area where man's strength is superior to the *yetzer*; namely, that the *yetzer hara* is not able to subvert man in one thrust. The *yetzer hara* does not have the capability to engage a man of perfect faith, a guardian of Torah and mitzvos, and to incite him to instantaneously abandon the straight path and do all manner of abominations, let alone idol worship. Rather, he can only incrementally corrupt him, slowly and gradually luring him away from the good path, until eventually he is completely immersed in degradation. Chazal (*Shabbos* 105b) speak about this phase-by-phase method of the *yetzer hara*, "Today he says to him, 'Do this'; tomorrow he tells him, 'Do that'; until he urges him, 'Go and serve idols,' and he goes and serves [them]." Likewise, the Talmud (*Sukkah* 52b) says, "First it only causes them to err, but ultimately it enters inside them."

However, man is invested with a dynamic power that operates in the exact opposite manner of the gradual process of the *yetzer hara*. Even if man is already trapped in the snare and captured in the fortress of the *yetzer hara*, plummeting to the lowest level of abandoning Torah and mitzvos — nevertheless, he has the power to steel himself with strength and might. He is able to conquer and overthrow his *yetzer hara* in one effort, to return to Hashem and do *teshuvah*. The Talmud (*Avodah Zarah* 17a) relates, "It was said of Rebbi Elazer ben Dordaya that he came to every harlot in the world, without exception. Once, on hearing that there was a certain harlot in one of the towns by the sea who accepted a purse of gold for her hire, he took a purse of gold and crossed seven rivers for her sake. As he was in her company, she blew forth breath and said, 'As this breath that I blow will never return to its place, so, too, will Elazar ben Dordaya never be received in repentance.' He placed his head between his knees and wept aloud, until his soul departed. Then a *bas kol* was heard proclaiming, 'Rebbi Elazar ben Dordaya is destined for the life in the World to Come!' When Rebbi heard this, he wept and said, 'One may acquire eternal life only after many years, yet another — in an hour.' " There are many similar stories in Chazal.

This sharp contrast between man and the *yetzer hara* is expressed in the verse, "He will pound your head, and you will bite his heel" (*Bereishis* 3:15). [This verse is referring to the relationship that will exist between man and his descendants, and the snake (which enticed Chava to sin in Gan Eden) and its descendants.] It is known that the snake of Gan Eden was, in fact, the *satan*, who is none other than the *yetzer hara* himself. The verse informs us that man will be able to overpower the *yetzer hara* in a flash and pound on its head — enabling him to return to Hashem. Yet as far as the *yetzer hara* is concerned, says the verse, "and you will bite his heel"; you [*yetzer hara*] will be initially constrained to only bite his heel. As Chazal say, "Today he says to him, 'Do this'; tomorrow he tells him, 'Do that'; until he urges him, 'Go and serve idols,' and he goes and serves [them]."

The *satan* demonstrated this contrast of strength between man and the *yetzer hara* to Plimo. When Plimo rebuked him, the *satan* feigned death. This reveals that man has the power to instantly fortify himself with strength and rebuke the *yetzer hara*, grinding him into the ground until he falls vanquished at his feet. On the other hand, we already explained the symbolism of the *satan* disguising himself as a beggar and calling out at the door, afterwards saying, "On a day such as this, when everybody is inside, shall I be left outside?" and afterwards, "On a day like this, when everyone sits at the table, shall I sit alone?" He was hinting to Plimo that his method of attacking man is one step at a time, as the Talmud (*Sukkah* 52b) tells us, "First he is called a passerby, then he is called a guest." Therefore, afterwards, the *satan* divulged to Plimo the inherent power of man to conquer his *yetzer hara* and cast him down helpless at his feet.

THE SATAN NEVER RELINQUISHES HIS BATTLE

8) "He [Plimo] fled and hid in a bathroom. He [the *satan*] followed him....
When he [Plimo, saw the *satan*, Plimo] fell [in shock] before him."

The *satan* taught Plimo the proper attitude to take in the war of the
yetzer hara. He enlightened him with the understanding that even if a man
achieves mastery and subjugation over his *yetzer hara* — even if it appears
that he has defeated him — the *tzaddik* should not imagine that he has over-
thrown the *satan*. Man should not think that he is victorious, because the
satan never relinquishes his battle with man. In but a moment after his defeat, he will revive and endeavor to engage man in battle. The *Chovos
HaLevavos* (*Sha'ar Yichud Hama'aseh* 5) refers to this: "It is an amazing thing,
my brother. Any other enemy, when you defeat him once or twice, will leave
you alone and give up the idea of attacking you. Once aware of your superior
strength, he loses hope of ever defeating and overpowering you. The *yetzer
hara*, however, will not leave you alone after one or even one hundred defeats, regardless of whether it defeats you or you defeat it. For if it defeats you,
it will utterly destroy you; and if you defeat it once, it will lie in wait for you all
your life in order to subdue you, as Chazal (*Avos* 2:5) said, "Do not believe in
yourself until the day you die." The *satan* demonstrated this to Plimo by falling dead and arising the next moment and running after Plimo.

THE SATAN IS INTERNAL AND EXTERNAL

9) "He...hid in a bathroom."

Here the *satan* demonstrated his immense power and strength. Not only
does the *yetzer* set his ambush in the heart of man in order to draw him away
from the good path, but he also has the ability to oppress man in his external
surroundings in order to interfere with his Divine service. He disturbs his
peace of mind and confuses his thoughts. Indeed, it was *erev* Yom Kippur, a
time when a man should be calm in order to prepare himself for the holy day,
a day to return to Hashem. Nevertheless, the *satan* stirred up the fear of false
murder allegations and the danger of death to the point where Plimo was
forced to flee outside the city. Moreover, he hid in an outhouse, a filthy place
where it is forbidden to think *divrei Torah*.

MAN ALONE CANNOT DEFEAT SATAN

10) "Seeing he was distressed, he [the *satan*] disclosed his identity and asked him, 'Why do you always speak those words ['Arrows in the eyes of Satan']?' "

The *satan* was suggesting, "Do you really think that with your strength and power you can defeat the *yetzer hara*? Do you think you can take pride over me because you shoot arrows?"

REQUEST FOR ADVICE

11) "Rather, what should I say?"

Plimo said to the *satan*, "Considering that your power and strength is superior to man's, and you can conquer him, for he is unable to defeat you — if so, what should I say?" He meant, "What advice and strategy can you offer me that I should be able to defeat you?"

REVELATION OF THE SECRET

12) "[Responded the *satan*] You should say, 'Merciful One, rebuke Satan.' "

Herein, he revealed to Plimo the secret. For in truth, man cannot defeat the *yetzer*. Only Hashem has the power to save him from the attacks of the *yetzer* and conquer the *satan*. As the Talmud (*Sukkah 52b*) states, "The *yetzer hara* of a man grows in strength from day to day and seeks to kill him… and were it not that *HaKadosh Baruch Hu* is his help, he would not be able to withstand it [the *yetzer hara*]." Therefore, man should not glorify himself in the face of the *yetzer*; rather, he should beseech Hashem for mercy and continuously pray that He send him help from Heaven, and that He should not leave him in the hand of his *yetzer*. Hashem guards the footsteps of the pious so that they should not be ensnared, for His eye looks to those who fear Him and to those who await His kindness.

ARTICLE ELEVEN

THE WAY OF TORAH

" 'You save both man and beast, O Hashem' (*Tehillim* 36:7). [Says the Gemara,] Rav Yehudah said in the name of Rav, 'This refers to those who are wise in understanding and conduct themselves humbly like animals.' "

(Chullin 5b)

A LIFE OF DEPRIVATION

WE LEARNED IN *PIRKEI AVOS* (6:4), "This is the way of the Torah: Eat bread with salt, drink water in small measure, sleep on the ground, live a life of deprivation — but toil in the Torah! If you do this, 'You are praiseworthy and it is well with you' (*Tehillim* 128:2). 'You are praiseworthy' — in this world; 'and it is well with you' — in the World to Come." What is the meaning of the phrase "live a life of deprivation"? Does it not appear to be superfluous? If someone eats bread with salt, drinks water in small measure, and sleeps on the floor — is this not a life of deprivation?

THE MANNA DIRECTS MAN'S HEART TO HASHEM

The Talmud (*Yoma* 76a) teaches, "Rebbi Shimon ben Yochai's disciples asked him, 'Why didn't the manna fall just one time a year?' He replied, 'I will answer you by way of a parable: There was a king who had a son. Initially, the king decided to give the boy a yearly allowance for his food. As a result, however, the king only saw him one time a year. Therefore, the king decided to provide for his needs on a daily basis, and he then saw his son every day. So, too, with Israel. A person who had four or five children would worry and say, "Perhaps the manna will not descend tomorrow, and they will all die of starvation!" As a result, all [of the Jewish people] would direct their hearts to their Father in Heaven.' "

YOUR LIFE WILL HANG IN THE BALANCE

This passage seems astonishing in light of a different teaching in the Talmud (*Menachos* 103b): "Rav Chanin said, 'It is written (*Devarim* 28:66), "Your life will hang in the balance" — this refers to one who buys grains from year to year; "and you will be frightened night and day" — this refers to one who buys grains from week to week; "and you will not be sure of your livelihood" — this refers to one who has to rely upon the bread dealer.' " Rashi explains, "one who buys grains from year to year" refers to someone who does not own land to sow, thus his life "will hang in the balance," because he doesn't know if he will have money for the next year.

THE WORST OF ALL THE CURSES

Clearly, the verse is written in descending order, so that the later the category is mentioned in the verse, the worse is the correlating curse. Thus, there are three tiers going from least to most severe: 1) "Your life will hang in the balance" — this refers to one who buys grains from year to year; 2) "and you will be frightened night and day" — this refers to one who buys grains from week to week; 3) "and you will not be sure of your livelihood" — this refers to one who has to rely upon the bread dealer. In this last category, he does not buy grains whatsoever, and he does not know if he will have the funds to buy bread tomorrow, or perhaps the bread dealer will simply not bake. In any case, we derive from here that someone who is not even sure if he will have funds tomorrow to purchase food is subject to the worst of all the curses, for he will have no assurance of his life. In light of this, the passage "Why didn't the manna just fall one time a year.... A person who had four or five children would worry and say, 'Perhaps the manna will not descend tomorrow, and they will all die of starvation,' " is shocking, indeed. According to the passage in *Menachos*, the daily descending of the manna was a curse of rebuke from

Hashem. Can it be that *HaKadosh Baruch Hu* gave a curse of rebuke to the *dor hamidbar* (the generation that was redeemed from Egypt)?

A MAN OF GREAT FAITH DOES NOT WORRY

We can answer this question from a different statement in the Talmud (*Sotah* 48b): "It was taught: Rebbi Eliezer HaGadol said, 'Anyone who has bread in his basket and nevertheless says, "What shall I eat tomorrow?" belongs to them who are of little faith.' " Indeed, a man of great faith does not worry in the least about what he will eat tomorrow. He believes in Hashem, and he places his trust in Hashem, for He gives bread to all the living. On the other hand, someone who worries and says, "What shall I eat tomorrow?" has a sin in his hand, for he belongs to them who are of little faith. In contrast, consider someone who is of perfect faith. Even if Hashem places him in a situation where his sustenance only comes day by day, and he does not know whether or not he will have food tomorrow, nevertheless, he does not perceive this as a curse. Indeed, he does not worry in the least, because he trusts that Hashem will never let him be without sustenance — "For there is no deprivation for His reverent ones" (*Tehillim* 34:10). Moreover, this "curse" is transformed into a blessing for him and a source of spiritual benefit. His predicament, that he does not know whether or not he will have food tomorrow, causes him to subjugate his heart to Hashem.

A MAN OF LITTLE FAITH

However, let us consider someone of little faith, who worries about what he will eat tomorrow. Imagine if each day he earns his livelihood by seeking his daily bread, yet each day he is unsure if he will have food to eat tomorrow. Moreover, if he has children, he is worried that tomorrow they will ask him for bread — and he doesn't know if he will have any provisions to give them. All things considered, he is unable to remove worry from his heart. As far as he is concerned, his predicament is truly a curse of Divine rebuke — for "[his] life hangs in the balance," and "[he] will not be sure of [his] livelihood." Furthermore, since he is of little faith, his predicament does not help him turn his heart to Hashem. Even worse, his incessant worry befouls his spirit, confuses his mind, and afflicts his heart with bewilderment.

THE SPIRITUAL BENEFIT OF WORRY

Now we can answer the question that we asked concerning the manna. We know that the curses enumerated in *Parashas Tochachah* (*Bechukosai*) apply only if *b'nei Yisrael* do not follow the Divine will, which decrees that we observe and perform all of the mitzvos. As far as those people who stray from the path of Torah are concerned — whether they purchase grain in the market and are unsure if they have sufficient funds, or whether they must rely on the baker for their daily bread — this predicament is considered a curse. The verse that we cited refers to them, as "[their] lives will hang in the balance...and [they] will not be sure of [their] livelihood." Whereas, the *dor hamidbar* were on an exalted spiritual level. When they crossed the Yam Suf, perfect faith in Hashem was implanted within their hearts, as the verse says, "And the people revered Hashem, and they had faith in Hashem and in Moshe, His servant" (*Shemos* 14:31). Yet Hashem did not distribute the manna to them on a annual basis, rather, the manna descended each day — and they worried, "perhaps the manna will not descend tomorrow." Nevertheless, this predicament was not a curse for them; rather, it was a blessing. Their worry served to benefit them spiritually, because it motivated all of the people to turn their hearts to Hashem. Once they looked to Hashem for help, they no longer worried about tomorrow, for "they had faith in Hashem and in Moshe, His servant."

A NATURAL LIFESTYLE

In light of this, we can explain the statement of Chazal, "Torah was given specifically to the generation who received the manna." This is in accordance with the concept that in order for Torah to be on the highest level it is imperative that it be accompanied by *yiras Shamayim*. The Mishnah (*Avos* 3:21) refers to this: "Rabbi Eliezer ben Azariah says: '...If there is no wisdom, there is no fear of God; if there is no fear of God, there is no wisdom.' " At the time of the *dor hamidbar* the manna sustained the people of Israel; Hashem provided them each day with their daily portion of manna. This situation was the impetus for the entire Jewish people to direct their hearts to Hashem. Consequently, their *yiras Shamayim* ascended to an exalted plane, and Torah and *yirah* perfectly complemented each other like inseparable twins.

However, since those times, *klal Yisrael* have never had such days of glory. When they entered Eretz Yisrael, they endeavored to settle the land and live according to a natural agricultural existence. Thus, in the days of the harvest, they gathered their produce and filled their storehouses with grain. Hashem blessed the work of their hands, and with time, their miraculous existence was replaced by a new natural lifestyle. Thus, their livelihood no longer was an impetus to direct their hearts to Hashem. Not only did they no longer worry about tomorrow, their confidence extended into the distant future. Yet, as the motivation to turn their hearts to Hashem diminished, so, too, did their exalted level of *yiras Hashem* gradually decline. This is the meaning of the statement of Chazal, "Torah was given specifically to the generation who received the manna."

THE HIGHEST ASPECT OF FAITH

When we examine the proper relationship between Torah and *derech eretz* [in this context, making a living], we find on one hand that man has permission to engage in earning a livelihood either through labor or trade. However, on the other hand, the Mishnah (*Avos* 4:12) teaches: "Rabbi Meir says: 'Limit your business activities and engage in Torah study.' " It has also been stated (ibid. 1:15), "Shammai says: 'Make your Torah [study] a fixed practice.' " The essential point is that if a man aspires to earn a substantial income and establish savings in order to prepare for the future, as well as to leave an estate for his children — he will be forced to increase his time of work and reduce his Torah study. Yet, the highest aspect of faith is to engage each day in *derech eretz* to earn just enough to sustain himself for that day alone. This is in accordance with the ruling of the Rema in the *Shulchan Aruch* (*Yoreh De'ah, Hilchos Talmud Torah* 246:21), "Let him engage in work each day to sustain himself, if he does not have any food to eat, and the remainder of the day and night he should study Torah." The Talmud (*Yoma*

35b) alludes to this: "Hillel HaZaken worked every day to earn one *tropaik*, half of which he gave to the guard at the house of learning, the other half being spent for his food and for that of his family." When a person conducts himself in this manner, this predicament will stir up worry about what he will eat tomorrow. Nevertheless, if he is a man of great faith, this situation will ultimately enhance his soul. It will be an impetus to turn his heart to Hashem — and then [with his faith restored], he will not worry in the least. His faith will be continuously revitalized like the generation who ate the manna.

However, if one has not yet reached this level of complete faith and trust in Hashem [he should not despair,] because this is quite difficult to achieve, as the Mishnah (*Sotah* 48a) says, "When the [Second] Temple was destroyed, the men of faith disappeared from Israel." The Talmud there explains, "These are men who had faith in *HaKadosh Baruch Hu*. For it was taught: Rebbi Eliezer HaGadol declares, 'Anyone who has bread in his basket and nevertheless says, "What shall I eat tomorrow?" belongs to them who are of little faith.' " Even if one has not ascended to this level [of complete faith and trust in Hashem], and he cannot stop worrying obsessively about tomorrow, nevertheless, let him conduct himself in the path of Hillel. He must strengthen his faith as much as possible and endure a bit of discontentment.

THE PATH OF HISTAPKUS

This is the meaning of the *mishnah* that we mentioned above, "This is the way of the Torah: Eat bread with salt, drink water in small measure, sleep on the ground, live a life of deprivation — but toil in the Torah." This life of deprivation refers to a person who does not know if he will have food tomorrow, for this is one of Hashem's curses written in *Parashas Tochachah*. The Torah emphasizes the severity of this curse: "Your life will hang in the balance, and you will be frightened night and day, and you will not be sure of your livelihood." The Torah advocates the path of *histapkus* (being content with a little), that man should suffice himself with dry bread, salt, water by measure, and live a life of deprivation. The *mishnah* is teaching that man should not aspire to store bread, salt, and quantities of water for a long period of time; in fact, he should not gather provisions for more than one day at a time. Rather, he should live a life of deprivation, and each day he should work just enough to live; he should earn just enough to procure bread, salt, and a small quantity of water for that day only. The remainder of the day and night should be utilized for Torah study.

Man should follow the path of Hillel, as the Talmud relates, "Hillel HaZaken worked every day to earn one *tropaik*, half of which he gave to the guard at the house of learning, the other half being spent for his food and for that of his family." The Rambam (commenting on *Pirkei Avos* 4:7) wrote that Hillel HaZaken earned his daily sustenance by working as a hewer of trees. The Admor pointed out that a half *tropaik* was a very small amount of money. For that was the fee that he gave to the guard of the house of learning, and since everyone paid this fee, if it was of significant value then the guard would have become wealthy. Nevertheless, he made this tiny amount of half a *tropaik* suffice for both himself and his family. He did not even prepare this small amount for the next day. Rather, each day he would chop trees until he earned a *tropaik*, half of which sufficed for the provisions needed for that day alone. This is the true path of Torah.

THE BLESSING OF HASHEM

The Talmud (*Berachos* 35b) teaches, "Rabbah bar bar Channah said in the name of Rebbi Yochanan, the teaching of Rebbi Yehudah bar Illai, 'See what a difference there is between the earlier and the later generations. The earlier generations made the study of Torah their main concern and their work subsidiary to it, and both [endeavors] prospered in their hands. The later generations made their work their main concern and their study of Torah subsidiary, and neither prospered in their hands.' " The proper explanation of this passage divulges the commonality between bodily needs, such as one's livelihood and the like, and spiritual needs, such as Torah and *yiras Shamayim*. Even if man pursues either of these endeavors with diligence and enthusiasm, nevertheless, it is impossible to succeed without Divine assistance.

It is well known that all financial success is dependent on the Heavenly blessing. Even though the Torah permitted *derech eretz*, as the Talmud (*Berachos* 35b) states, "Our Rabbis taught, 'And you shall gather in your corn.' What is to be learned from these words? Since in [a different] verse it states, 'The Book of the Torah shall not depart from your mouth' (*Yehoshua* 1:8), I might think that this injunction is to be taken literally [meaning that man may only involve himself in Torah study and not work whatsoever]. Therefore it says, 'And you shall gather in your corn,' which implies that you are to combine the study of them [words of Torah] with a worldly occupation. This is the view of Rebbi Yishmael." Nevertheless, he needs Divine assistance in order that the blessing of Hashem will be in his house and field, as the Torah teaches in *Parashas Bechukosai* (*Vayikra* 26:3–13). Likewise, he is dependent on the blessing of Hashem in his spiritual endeavors, as taught in the Talmud (*Sukkah* 52b), "The *yetzer hara* of a man grows in strength from day to day and seeks to kill him…and were it not that *HaKadosh Baruch Hu* is his help, he would not be able to withstand it."

THE DIFFERENCE BETWEEN THE PHYSICAL AND SPIRITUAL DIMENSION

Despite this similitude, there is also a difference between the physical and spiritual dimension. As far as the physical proceedings are concerned the primary factor of success is Divine assistance, and only "Hashem's right hand does valiantly" (*Tehillim* 118:15). Man only needs to make a small effort so that there will be a place for the blessing of Hashem to manifest. There is no power that can prevent any aspect of Divine redemption. Therefore, the smaller the effort that man makes so that "he casts his burdens on Hashem," and the more he decreases his work so that he can study Torah, commensurately, the more the labor of his hand will be blessed with Divine assistance. Whereas, in the spiritual matters of Torah and *yiras Shamayim*, it is just the opposite: the primary factor is the effort of man. When man does everything possible within his power to devote his soul to Torah and *yiras Shamayim*, then Hashem will draw His spirit upon him and dispatch His "help from the Sanctuary" (*Tehillim* 20:2).

This is the intention of the passage we mentioned: "The earlier generations made the study of Torah their main concern and their work subsidiary to it, and both [endeavors] prospered in their hands." They succeeded in their Torah study because they made it their main concern, and they succeeded in their work because they made it subsidiary. Thus, the blessing of Hashem accompanied their efforts. Whereas, "The later generations made their work their main concern and their study of Torah subsidiary, and neither prospered in their hands." They did not succeed in their Torah study because they only made it subsidiary, and they did not succeed in their work because they made it their main concern. They relied on their own strength and power, and they did not trust in Hashem, Who gives man the power to perform valiantly.

This is also the meaning of the *mishnah* in *Avos* that we cited, "This is the way of the Torah: Eat bread with salt, drink water in small measure, sleep on the ground, live a life of deprivation — but toil in the Torah! If you do this, 'You are praiseworthy and it is well with you.' 'You are praiseworthy' — in this world; 'and it is well with you' — in the World to Come." Thus, he follows the path of Torah, which is to make the Torah his primary concern, and make himself content with bread, salt, and water in small measure, so that he can occupy himself with Torah. Hence, he makes his work subsidiary, for he lives a life of deprivation. He does not aspire to prepare even minimal provisions for tomorrow, but only concerns himself with his livelihood for that day alone, for he follows the path of Hillel HaZaken. Consequently, both endeavors will prosper in his hands. Therefore, he will be praiseworthy in this world because Hashem will grant him his "bread and water," and he will never lack sustenance. In addition, all will be well with him in the World to Come, because he will also flourish in Torah study.

FEAR AND CONTENTMENT

In light of this, we can now explain the passage that we cited at the beginning of this essay, "You save both man and beast, O Hashem" (*Tehillim* 36:7). Says the Gemara (*Chullin* 5b), "Rav Yehudah said in the name of Rav, 'This refers to those who are wise in understanding and conduct themselves humbly like animals.' " In order to clarify this, let us first turn to a teaching of the Talmud (*Tamid* 32a), "Who is the wise man? The one who sees the ultimate result." It is self-evident that the foundation of wisdom is to see the ultimate result in spiritual matters, to reflect on what will occur to him at the end of days and after many years [Divine judgment]. Then he will fear and turn away from evil, in order to save his soul from Gehinnom and to inherit eternal life and everlasting pleasure. Whereas, in physical matters, the opposite approach is employed. The proper conduct dictates that man should not worry at all, not even about tomorrow. Indeed, even an animal is only concerned about food at the moment the need arises; at the time it is hungry it cries out. Therefore, it has not a trace of fear whatsoever. Sometimes, it even discards the excess. Therefore, consider the man who only worries about being satisfied with a portion of bread at that moment and has no concern over "what [he will] eat tomorrow." From the physical perspective he is similar to the animals, whereas from the intellectual perspective he is a man of vast faith. Thus, "Anyone who has bread in his basket and nevertheless says, 'What shall I eat tomorrow?' belongs to them who are of little faith."

Let us consider the aforementioned statement of Chazal, "Rav Yehudah said in the name of Rav, 'This refers to those who are wise in understanding and conduct themselves humbly like animals.' " For in truth, they are wise enough in understanding to see the ultimate result: to worry about their souls for endless generations and to merit eternal life. On the other hand, they "conduct themselves humbly like animals." Thus, as far as their physical needs are concerned, they conduct themselves humbly like animals so that they will not worry whatsoever over the future — not even about tomorrow's sustenance. The last part of the verse says, "You [Hashem] save both man and beast," meaning that because of their fulfillment of both aspects, they merit Divine assistance. Concerning spiritual matters, the "right hand" of Hashem delivers them because they worry about their soul. Concerning physical matters, i.e., bodily needs, they merit Divine redemption and blessing because they make themselves like animals. In other words, they do not worry about the future; rather, they place their trust in Hashem and hope for His kindness.

HAPPINESS WITH ONE'S PORTION

The essential factor in fulfilling "This is the way of the Torah: Eat bread with salt, drink water in small measure..." is to have *histapkus*, to be happy with one's portion. The Talmud (*Ta'anis* 24b) states, "Rav Yehudah said in the name of Rav: Every day a *bas kol* is heard declaring, 'The whole world draws its sustenance because [of the merit] of Chanina, my son, and Chanina, my son, is satisfied with a *kav* of carobs from one Shabbos eve to another.' The text does not say, 'and Chanina, my son, has a *kav* of carobs,' rather, it says, 'and Chanina, my son, is satisfied with a *kav* of carobs from one Shabbos eve to another.' " The crucial element is that he is satisfied with what he has, for there is "no deprivation for his reverent ones."

Indeed, the Talmud (*Berachos* 34b) relates, "Rebbi Chanina ben Dosa went to study Torah with Rebbi Yochanan ben Zakkai. The son of Rebbi Yochanan ben Zakkai fell ill. He [Rebbi Yochanan ben Zakkai] said to him [Rebbi Chanina], 'Chanina, my son, pray for him that he might live.' He [Rebbi Chanina] put his head between his knees and prayed for him, and he lived. Said Rebbi Yochanan ben Zakkai, 'If Ben Zakkai had put his head between his knees for the entire day, no notice would have been taken of him.' His wife then asked him, 'Is Chanina greater than you are?' 'No,' he answered, 'but he is like a servant before the king, and I am like a minister before the king.' " It is incumbent upon us to understand — what is the difference between a servant and a minister?

A SERVANT AND A MINISTER

On one hand, both a king's servant and a king's minister are faithful, devoted attendants who love the king. Nevertheless, if they have a request to make of the king, the king may be more responsive to the servant than the minister. The difference, in the eyes of the king, between the servant and the minister is as follows: Although the minister serves the king out of his powerful love and devotion to him, nevertheless, he benefits from the king. For the minister receives reward from the king and lives like one of the nobles. However, the servant is a simple man of valor and does not receive any reward — he lives on bread alone. Nevertheless, if the servant devotes himself to the king out of his love for him, then if he has a certain request, the king will quickly grant it to him. For what else does he enjoy from the king in exchange for his faithfulness and devoted service? However, this is not the case with the minister, who receives great reward from the king, as we have mentioned; even if the king does not fulfill the request of the minister, he has no complaints.

This is the meaning of the passage in which Rebbi Yochanan ben Zakkai said, "Chanina is like a servant before the king." The difference between these two men is that Hashem bestowed benefit upon Rebbi Yochanan ben Zakkai from the goodness of this world; furthermore, he was the *nasi* of Israel and was elevated over his brethren. Whereas Hashem deprived Rebbi Chanina ben Dosa of all benefit from this world, as he did not have provisions except for a *kav* of carob from Shabbos eve to Shabbos eve. Therefore, when he pleaded for mercy from Hashem, his prayer was answered. For what else did he have from Hashem except for this? Rebbi Yochanon ben Zakkai, however, was like a minister before the king and was therefore not answered as readily by Hashem.